AFGHANISTAN

LOUIS DUPREE

Afghanistan

OXFORD
UNIVERSITY PRESS

OXFORD

UNIVERSITY PRESS

Great Clarendon Street, Oxford OX2 6DP

Oxford University Press is a department of the University of Oxford.
It furthers the University's objective of excellence in research, scholarship,
and education by publishing worldwide in

Oxford New York

Auckland Bangkok Buenos Aires Cape Town Chennai
Dar es Salaam Delhi Hong Kong Istanbul Karachi Kolkata
Kuala Lumpur Madrid Melbourne Mexico City Mumbai Nairobi
São Paulo Shanghai Singapore Taipei Tokyo Toronto
and an associated company in Berlin

Oxford is a registered trade mark of Oxford University Press
in the UK and in certain other countries

Printed in Pakistan by
Mas Printers, Karachi.
Published by
Ameena Saiyid, Oxford University Press
5-Bangalore Town, Sharae Faisal
PO Box 13033, Karachi-75350, Pakistan.

CONTENTS

Lists of Illustrations, Maps, Charts, and Diagrams   *vii*
Introduction   *xvii*
Acknowledgments   *xxi*

PART I. THE LAND   1

1. Geographic Zones   3
2. Water   33
3. Areas Drastically Affected by Man   43
4. Domesticated Animals   47
5. Fauna   51

PART II. THE PEOPLE   55

6. Ethnic Groups   57
7. Language   66
8. Religious Non-Literacy in a Literate Culture   95
9. Folklore and Folk Music   112
10. Settlement Patterns   132
11. Life Cycle   181
12. The Inward-Looking Society   248

PART III. THE PAST   253

13. The Prehistoric Sequence   255
14. East and West Meet and Mingle   272
15. Invasions and Commerce   296
16. Islam Spreads Its Banner   312
17. The Age of European Imperialism   343

PART IV. THE PRESENT   415

18. Amir Abdur Rahman Khan: 1880–1901   417
19. Habibullah: 1901–1919   430
20. King Amanullah: 1919–1929   441
21. King Mohammad Nadir Shah: 1929–1933   458
22. The Avuncular Period: 1933–1953   477

23. The Decade of Daoud: 1953–1963   499
24. The Constitutional Period Begins: 1963–?   559
25. Problems and Prospects   659

Appendices

A. Domesticated Plants in Afghanistan   669
B. Fauna in Afghanistan   670
C. Medicinal Plants in Afghanistan   672
D. Calendars Used in Afghanistan   674
E. Folk Music and Instruments (with Illustrations)   677
F. *Mémoires de la Délégation Archéologique Française en
   Afghanistan*   689
G. Afghan Cabinets: 1963–71   690
H. AUFS Reports on Afghanistan by Louis Dupree: 1959–71   695

Bibliography   699

Index   723

Epilogue (1973)   753

Epilogue to the Second Printing (1978)   761

Epilogue (1980)   769

ILLUSTRATIONS

1. Wakhan Corridor near Qadzi Deh   Facing Introduction
2. Pamir Knot   7
3. Durrani Pushtun nomads in Badakhshan   7
4. Central Mountains: Salang Pass   11
5. Central Mountains: Unai Pass   11
6. Eastern Mountains: Ghilzai Pushtun nomads   13
7. Central Mountains: *Lalmi* wheat and threshing areas   23
8. Hilmand Valley   27
9. Western stony desert   29
10. Southwestern sandy deserts   29
11. Northern Mountains and Foothills: Valley of Gurziwan   30
12. Turkestan Plains: Ghilzai Pushtun nomads   30
13. Eastern Mountains: Tajik village   34
14. Northern Mountains and Foothills: livestock trails   34
15. Durrani Pushtun at Dilaram   56
16. Kirghiz horsemen in the high Pamir   56
17. Seasonal workers in Kabul   56
18. Mangal Pushtun dancing   71
19. Durrani Pushtun near Qandahar   71
20. A red-bearded, blue-eyed Nuristani   73
21. A blind singer of epic poetry   73
22. An Uzbak farmer playing the *chang*   113
23. A Nuristani playing a four-stringed harp   113
24. A Besud Hazara playing the *dhamboura*   113
25. Winter quarters in Badakhshan   133
26. Eastern Mountains: village in Nuristan   133
27. Family compound, Kabul   135
28. Rooftop living in summer   135
29. A fortress-dwelling compound of the Mangal Pushtun   137
30. Multi-storied houses   137
31. Mud huts built under natural rock shelter   139
32. Beehive domed huts   139
33. A vertical windmill   141
34. Nuristanis at Wama   143
35. and 36. Construction techniques   149
37. Winter plowing near Qandahar   150
38. Uzbak farmers winnowing wheat   150
39. A covered bazaar, Khulm   154
40. Bazaar street, Qandahar   154
41. A part-time shoemaker and his son   162
42. Qandahar artisan making prayer beads   162
43. A tajik twine seller   162
44. An Uzbak farmer   167
45. Taimani Aimaq   167

vii

46. A Ghilzai Pushtun patriarch and his grandson   167
47. Distinctive Taimani rectangular tent   171
48. A Ghilzai Pushtun camp near Aq Kupruk   171
49. Portable huts in summer pasturage areas   173
50. A Taimani *chapari*   173
51. Uzbak *yurt*   175
52. A Tajik *kherga* in Aq Kupruk   175
53. Inside an Uzbak *yurt*   176
54. Constructing a *chapari*   176
55. Brahui in the Hilmand Valley   178
56. A Brahui matting hut   178
57. A Tekke Turkoman couple   182
58. Firozkohi Aimaq   182
59. Modern wooden grave markers in the Pech River valley   207
60. A Kafir grave effigy   216
61. A Baluch mosque at Chahar Burjak   216
62. A championship *buzkashi* match during the King's birthday celebrations   220
63. A Tajik farmer   225
64. Taking home a new bread oven   225
65. An ironmonger's shop in Qandahar; nomadic bread-baking   226
66. A Tajik butcher   228
67. Pushtun cooking *chapli kabab*   228
68. A fried-fish peddler   230
69. Outdoor cooking among the Uzbak   232
70. An Uzbak family   232
71. The distinctive dress of Nuristani women   234
72. Tara Khel Ghilzai nomadic woman preparing cheese   234
73. Palaeolithic relics   254
74. Painted pottery shreds of the Later Iron Age   270
75. The oldest sculpture found in Asia and other antiquities   273, 277
76. Ai Khanoum: a general view of the lower town from the acropolis   290
77. Ruins of the colonnade, Ai Khanoum   290
78. The staircase at Surkh Kotal   293
79. An inscription in cursive Greek at Surkh Kotal   293
80. Statue of Kanishka (?) at Surkh Kotal   294
81. The large Buddha of Bamiyan valley   304
82. The colossal Buddhas of Bamiyan valley   304
83. Ancient walls of Balkh   308
84. Lashkar Gah: the ancient palace-soldiers' bazaar   308
85. Bala Hissar, Kabul: the ancient seat of power   310
86. Amir Sher Ali Khan, with several sons, and advisers   412
87. Amir Abdur Rahman Khan   412
88. Amir Habibullah with some of his wives   436
89. King Amanullah in Europe   436
90. King Inayatullah and a Russian airplane   455

91. Habibullah Ghazi   455
92. King Mohammad Nadir during the Third Anglo-Afghan War   470
93. His Majesty King Mohammad Zahir   470
94. Sardar Mohammad Daoud Khan   521
95. The Constitutional *Loya Jirgah* in 1964   521
96. The Arghandab Dam   525
97. Modern Kabul   525
98. Coal miners at Darra-i-Suf   633
99. Qandahar International Airport   633
100. A modern apartment building in kabul   636
101. The Darunta hydroelectric project near Jalalabad   636
102. Textile mill at Gulbahar   639
103. Power plant at Naghlu   639

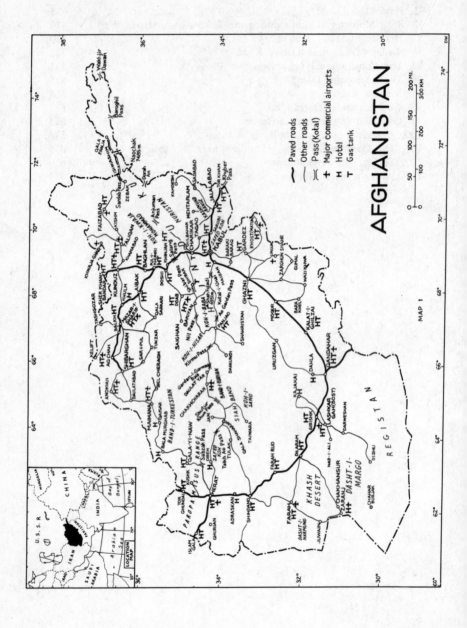

AFGHANISTAN

Paved roads
Other roads
Pass (Kotal)
+ Major commercial airports
H Hotel
T Gas tank

0   50 100 150 200 MI.
0 100 200 300 KM

MAP 1

MAPS

1. Afghanistan   x
2. Geographic zones   4
3. Relief map of Afghanistan   9
4. Four principal river systems of Afghanistan   32
5. Major areas under agricultural cultivation   46
6. Ethnic groups   58
7. Provinces of Afghanistan: before 1964   156
8. Provinces of Afghanistan: after March, 1964   157
9. Nomadic movements   165
10. Archaeological sites   265
11 a. Achaemenid satrapies, sixth century B.C.   275
   b. Alexander the Great's route and empire
12 a. Mauryan Empire under Ashoka   284
   b. Eurasia in the second century A.D.
13 a. Sasanian and Gupta empires   297
   b. Ghaznavid and Ghurid empires
14 a. Moghul and Safavid empires   320
   b. Empire of Ahmad Shah Durrani, A.D. 1762
15 a. Russian advances in Central Asia; British advances in India   342
   b. British retreat route, January, 1842

CHARTS

1. Climatic charts   15
2. Natural Vegetation: Central Mountains, Eastern Mountains,
   Southern Mountains and Foothills   20
3. Natural Vegetation: Northern Mountains and Foothills,
   Turkestan Plains   22
4. Agriculture: 1966–70   44
5. Domesticated Animals: 1966–70   48
6. Ethnic Groups in Afghanistan   59
7. Dari-Pashto Alphabets in Afghanistan   67
8. Villages in Afghanistan: 1963   144
9. Village Populations: 1963   145
10. Labor Force in Afghanistan: 1966-67   146
11. Distribution of Agricultural Land: 1963   147
12. Comparison of Provincial Systems   158
13. Towns in Afghanistan: 1969   160
14. Cities in Afghanistan: 1969   161
15. Nomads Seasonally Crossing into Pakistan prior to 1961   169
16. Kinship-Tribal Structure   184
17. Education: 1967–70   195
18. Literacy: 1960–61   248
19. The Prehistory of Afghanistan   257
20. Mundigak-Morasi Cultural Inventory of Artifacts   267
21. Political Fusion and Fission: 1747-1880   344
22. The Nineteenth-Century Struggle for Power   366
23. The Free Press in Afghanistan: 1965-71   602
24. Worker and/or Student Strikes and Demostrations: 1968   620
25. Exports by Commodity: 1966–70   625
26. Imports by Country: 1966–69   627
27. Exports by Country: 1966–70   627
28. Imports by Commodity: 1966–69   628
29. Foreign Assistance to Afghanistan: 1950–70   630
30. Third Five-Year Plan: 1967-72   646
31. Tourists in Afghanistan: 1969–71   656

DIAGRAMS

1. Turkestan Plains: Cross-Section of Topography   24
2. Cross-Section of the Hilmand Valley   38
3. Cross-Section of *Qanat* System   41
4. Indo-European Language Family   69
5. Nomadic Bread-Baking Method   226
6. Abdali (Durrani) Tribal Structure   333

1. Wakhan Corridor near Qadzi Deh. Snow-covered mountains in background are in U.S.S.R. August, 1966

Afghanistan Defined

YAGHISTAN, as the Amir Abdur Rahman Khan (1900, II, 157) referred to his country (particularly the tribal belt between British India and Afghanistan), has been variously translated: "Land of the Unruly," "Land of the Free," "Land of Rebels," and "Land of Insolence" (Coon, 1951b, 295–323).

The insolence of the Afghan, however, is not the frustrated insolence of urbanized, dehumanized man in western society, but insolence without arrogance, the insolence of harsh freedoms set against a backdrop of rough mountains and deserts, the insolence of equality felt and practiced (with an occasional touch of superiority), the insolence of bravery past and bravery anticipated.

The name Afghanistan simply means "Land of the Afghan." Some non-Afghans profess, at least half-jokingly, to believe that Afghan may have derived from the Persian word "afghan" (spelled the same as Afghan, افغان), defined as "noisy," "groaning," or "wailing," indicative of the way many Iranians have always felt about their linguistic and cultural cousins to the east.

The patterns of Persian poetry more probably account for the "wailing": originally, فغان meant "wailing." To improve the rhyme and rhythm, Persian poets added the *alif* or "a" (See Chart 7) to form the more poetic افغان. Another example is فرشته (angel), which poets changed to افرشته, *afristeh* (Shpoon, personal communication, 1969).

Variations on the word Afghan in reference to people may go back as early as a third century A.D. Sasanian reference to "Abgan" (Caroe, 1965, 79–80; A. Habibi, 1969). The earliest known reference to the Afghans in a Muslim source probably occurred in A.D. 982 (Caroe, 1965, 112), but tribes related to those of the modern Afghans probably have lived unrecorded in the region for many generations.

For millennia, the land now called Afghanistan sat in the center of the action, the meeting place of four ecological and cultural areas: the Middle East, Central Asia, the Indian subcontinent, and even the Far East, for the Pamir Mountains intrude into Chinese Sinkiang.

Palaeolithic man probably lived in the caves of northern Afghanistan as long as 50,000 years ago. North Afghanistan also possibly sits in the zone of the development of the domestication of the wheat/barley, sheep/goat/cattle complex, the Neolithic Revolution which gave man control of his food supply about 11,000 years ago, which led ultimately to the urban civilizations of the Nile Valley, the Tigris–Euphrates Valleys, and the Indus Valley. Post-World War II excavations in south–central Afghanistan point to intimate relationships with the Indus Valley civilization, fourth–second millennia B.C.

Another important event in world history occurred in the Afghan area as a result of Alexander's passage through the region in the fourth century B.C. Out of a mixture of the sensuous Indian, humanistic classical, and vigorous Central Asian–Sino-Siberian ideologies rose the Mahayana Buddhism practiced in most of the modern Far Eastern world. As a result of intensive contacts, particularly from the first to the fifth centuries A.D., the Mahayana (northern school) ideology and its attendant art styles traveled across Central Asia through the Dzungarian Gates to Mongolia, China, Korea, and eventually to Japan along the luxury trade Silk Route, which connected ancient Cathay with the Mediterranean classical world of the Roman Empire. During the early part of this east–west contact, Buddhist artists first began to depict the Buddha in human form, essentially an orientalized version of the Greek god Apollo.

The great civilizations of early Asia were based on the control and use of water, and great surpluses then created great civilizations and empires (Wittfogel, 1957).

Islam exploded into the region by the mid-seventh century A.D., and remains an important element in modern cultural and political patterns. Traditionally an area through which armies passed on their way to somewhere else, Afghanistan nevertheless witnessed the rise of several of its own indigenous empires. The Ghaznavid (tenth–twelfth centuries A.D.), probably the most important, was a true renaissance of juxtaposed military conquests and cultural achievements.

Political instability, brought on by the destructive Mongol and Turco–Mongol invasions of the thirteenth–fourteenth centuries A.D., and recurring localized, fraticidal wars broke up the Silk Route trade, and by the fifteenth century European navigators sought new sea routes to the East, which led to the rediscovery, exploitation, and development of a New World.

Asian imperialists (Persian Safavids and Indian Moghuls) fought over the Afghan area in the sixteenth–seventeenth centuries A.D. but in 1747 the last great Afghan empire rose under the leadership of Ahmad Shah Durrani, crowned king in Qandahar.

Fratricidal tribal wars and the intrusion of European imperialism into the area characterized nineteenth-century Afghanistan. Twice (1839, 1878) British armies invaded Afghan territories in response to real or imagined threats to India as Tsarist armies moved into the Muslim khanates of Central Asia, including lands claimed by the Afghan amirs.

The creation of modern Afghanistan began during the reign of Abdur Rahman Khan (1880–1901). While external powers (Britain, Russia) drew the boundaries of Afghanistan, the Amir attempted to spread his influence (if not actual control) over the myriad ethnic groups and tribal kingdoms included inside his boundaries, a process of "internal imperialism." Indeed, before 1880, the Afghans themselves referred to their area variously as Kabulistan (south of the Hindu Kush to the Indus River), Zabulistan (or Khorasan, including the Hindu Kush, Qandahar, and Herat), and Turkestan (north of the Hindu Kush and east of Herat) (Kakar, 1968, 1).

Most Afghan historians, followed sheeplike by western scholars, consider 1747 (Ahmad Shah Durrani) the beginning of the modern Afghan state.

I disagree, for, until 1880, the process of alternating fusion and fission dominated the political scene. By political fusion and fission, I mean the following pattern of events: A charismatic leader arises in a tribal society and, by military power, intrigue, and judiciously arranged marriages, unites several tribes into a confederation, which spreads as far as its accumulated power permits, creating an *empire,* not a *nation-state.* With (sometimes before) the death of the emperor, fission occurs, and the great empire once again segments into a multiplicity of tribal kingdoms. Later, another charismatic leader arrives and the process is repeated. (See Chart 21 for graphic representation of fusion and fission in later Afghan history.)

Ahmad Shah Durrani, therefore, created a Durrani empire, not a nation-state. Even before his death, the tribal wars and struggles for individual power within the various branches of the ruling family began, and they continued into the twentieth century.

British and Russian imperialism, however, blocked Abdur Rahman Khan, preventing him from spilling over into India, Persia, and Central Asia and creating another great Afghan empire. European imperialism had replaced Asian imperialism in the region.

The British, with at least the tacit consent of the Russians, controlled Afghan relations with other countries until 1919, when the Afghans gained the right to conduct their own foreign affairs after the Third Anglo–Afghan War. The Afghans consider 1919 as the year in which they truly became independent of foreign domination.

Three words characterize twentieth-century Afghanistan: non-alignment, independence, development, themes which, in varying degrees of intensity, describe the entire developing world today. The creation of new nations after World War II forced the major powers to realize that no nation, however remote, is unimportant. Post-World War II Afghanistan became an "economic Korea" and the interplay between the Soviet Bloc and the West (mainly the United States and West Germany) found Afghanistan serving as a catalytic agent to force both sides to shift from *de jure* competition to *de facto* cooperation, offering lessons in dynamics for the rest of the developing world. Naturally, the specifics of the Afghan experience cannot be transplanted to the heartlands of other developing nations, but a study of Afghanistan's recent history may help others understand the processes involved in changing from a tribal society to a nation-state.

In 1964, Afghanistan launched a new democratic experiment, and today tries to create a constitutional monarchy within a parliamentary framework. The real power, however, remains vested in a liberal king currently backed by a liberal army elite.

Created partly as a result of imperialism, but never a colony, Afghanistan, like all new states, now tries to build a stable nation, but with an overwhelming 90–95% non-literate population, a basically agrarian economy, and a peasant-tribal society with loyalties oriented locally and not nationally. The task of achieving stability may not be impossible, but it is certainly challenging.

ACKNOWLEDGMENTS

PRIMARILY a preliminary statement after twenty years of research and intimate relations with Afghanistan and surrounding areas, this book attempts the impossible: to present a study of a single piece of real estate through time, from one cell up, from the Stone Age to tomorrow. The approach, therefore, is micro- (or mini-), not macro-, like that of Oswald Spengler and Arnold Toynbee. Neither is the book meant to replace the classic modern works of Caroe (1965), Fraser-Tytler (1967), Klimburg (1966), or Wilber (1962). With no single theoretical bias, some discussions may appear out of proportion to others, but the main purpose should be kept in mind: this is an attempt by an anthropologist to ferret out the patterns, functional and dysfunctional, in the total synchronic-ecological-cultural sense.

Since 1949, when I first became interested in Afghanistan as a specific field of research, literally thousands upon thousands of people of many nationalities have contributed to this book, some in literature, others in personal communications, most in face-to-face situations. Eventually, I hope to be able to thank one and all in the traditional Afghan face-to-face manner.

However, some individuals read the manuscript (or parts of it) before publication and must be directly acknowledged. Dr. Donald N. Wilber did me the honor of reading and objectively criticizing the entire manuscript in draft form, and I am most grateful to him for his contributions. Abdul Raziq Palwal, Institute of Anthropology, Kabul University, also read the whole manuscript and offered many valuable suggestions.

I owe a great deal to Professor A. A. Michel (University of Connecticut), Professor Laurence H. Lattman (Pennsylvania State University), Dr. Alfred Schreiber (Niedersachsisches Landesamt für Bodenforschung, Hannover) for their comments on the geography and geology sections. Dr. Dexter Perkins, Jr., and Mr. Peter Edmonds supplied additional information on the fauna. Others contributing to and/or criticizing various sections are as follows: Professor Ludwig Adamec (Part IV); M. Paul Bernard (Chapters 14, 15); Mr. Winstanley Briggs (Chapter 24, the economic section); Mr. Abdul Qadir Fahim (Chapter 9); Mr. Qasem Ghazanfar (Chapter 7); Mr. A. G. Ghaznavi (Chapter 11); Dr. Thomas Gibson (Chapter 24, the economic and foreign assistance sections); Mr. H. Jadir (Chart 23); Professor M. Amir Kaify (Part IV); Professor Mohammad Hasan Kakar (Chapter 18); Dr. Abdul

ACKNOWLEDGMENTS

Kayeum (Parts I, II, IV); Said Mohammad Maiwand (Chapter 22); Dr. Leon Poullada (Part IV); Mr. Shafie Rahel (Chapter 24); Professor Mohammad Hussain Razi (Chart 23); Said Qassim Rishtya (Part IV); Mr. Mohammad Moosa Shafiq (Chapter 24, the constitutional section); Mr. Abdussattar Shalizi (general comments on selected sections); Mr. Saduddin Shpoon (Chapter 7); Mr. Wali Shah Wali (Chapter 11); Mr. Abdul Wahab Tarzi (Chapters 20, 21).

To Peter Gold (text) and David Schalliol (photographs) go my great thanks for Appendix E: Folk Music and Instruments. Sayyid A. Husani, Faculty of Letters, Kabul University, did the excellent calligraphy for Chart 7. Richard S. Davis assisted in tracing various elusive bibliographic references. Rafi Samizay, Faculty of Engineering, Kabul University, drew Diagrams 1–3 and 5 for which I thank him profusely. Nicholas Amorosi, Museum of Natural History, drew the implements in illustration 73.

The excellent maps were drawn by Mr. Douglas Waugh of the American Geographical Society, and the many thousands of words in this book would have little meaning without his contribution.

All photographs except the following were taken by the author: Afghan Films, 2, 18, 98–103; Professor Jimmy Bedford, 95; Délégation Archéologique Française en Afghanistan, 75e, 76–80; Nancy Hatch Dupree, 41, 54, 57, 68–70; Hubbard Goodrich, 33; H. E. Klappert, 74; *Life*, 75a; Ministry of Information and Culture, Government of Afghanistan, 16, 93–94; L. V. Peterson, 75f–i; Josephine Powell, 39, 60, 64, 75b, 81–82, 84; Khalilullah Enayat Seraj (KES) Collection in the National Archives of Afghanistan, 86 (KES 2), 87 (KES 15), 88 (KES 158), 90 (KES 1313), 91 (KES 2188), 92 (KES 804/9); private collection, 89.

Many institutions have materially contributed to my twenty years of Afghan research and I gratefully acknowledge each: American Geographical Society; American Museum of Natural History; American Philosophical Society; Arctic-Desert-Tropic Information Center (Dr. Paul Nesbitt, Director; Dr. Oliver L. Austin, Jr., staff scientist), Air University; The Pennsylvania State University; India Office Library and Files of the Commonwealth Office, London (with particular thanks to the Librarian, S. C. Sutton, and Martin Moir, Esq.); Kabul University; National Museum of Afghanistan, Kabul; the Ministries of Information and Culture and Education, Royal Government of Afghanistan; Social Science Research Council, New York; Wenner-Gren Foundation for Anthropological Research, Inc.; National Science Foundation GS 2459; Institute of Archaeology, Royal Government of Afghanistan.

The following very kindly gave permission to quote certain materials: Abdul Raouf Benawa (Chapter 7); S. Shpoon (Chapters 7, 17); Major J.C.E. Bowen (Chapter 7); D. MacKenzie, *Poems from the Divan of Khushal Khan Khattak,* George Allen and Unwin Ltd. (Chapter 7); E. Howell and O. Caroe, *The Poems of Khushal Khan Khatak,* Pashto Academy, University of Peshawar (Chapter 7); Sir Jogengra Singh, *The Persian Mystics,* John Murray (Publishers) Ltd. (Chapter 7); unpublished Crown copyright material in the India Office Records transcribed in this book (Chapters 17–18) appears by permission of the Secretary of State for Foreign and Commonwealth Affairs, United Kingdom.

The American Universities Field Staff (Alan Horton, Executive Director; Phillips Talbot and Teg Grondahl, former Executive Directors), for whom I now work, has permitted me unlimited freedom of research since 1959, and such a book as this would never have been possible without such unqualified support. In addition, Mr. Grondahl and Dr. Horton have given me permission to quote (or paraphrase) extensively from my *A.U.F.S. Reports* on Afghanistan, published between 1950 and 1971 (Appendix H).

For their patience and perseverance while editing and designing from 10,000 miles away, I owe special thanks to the staff at Princeton University Press, particularly R. Miriam Brokaw, Associate Director and Editor in Chief, who encouraged me from beginning to end; George Robinson, my gentle but persuasive editor; and Helen Van Zandt, designer, who appreciated the visual qualities of Afghanistan and the Afghans.

To my wife, Nancy, go general thanks and specific love for helping me plod through this manuscript. All of the things I could say to her in public have been said before, and all of the things we have said in private remain ours alone.

Note on Transliteration

In transliterating Persian terms into English, I have tried to follow as closely as possible (but without diacritical marks) the report from the Subcommittee on Transliteration (February 17, 1959) to the Committee on Near and Middle Eastern Studies, Social Science Research Council, New York, on "Transliteration of Persian for Library Cataloging Purposes," in conjunction with Steingass (1930) and S. Haim (1934–36). I hope that personal preferences which have crept in may be forgiven, since I make no pretense at being a language scholar. For Pashto, I attempted to agree with D. Mackenzie (1951).

ACKNOWLEDGMENTS

A phonemic note: The ‍و, usually transliterated "u," has more of an "o" sound in Afghan Dari than in Iranian Farsi. Therefore, I often use "o" rather than "u," simply because the latter more closely approximates the Afghan pronunciation. Besides, over ninety percent of the Afghan population is non-literate, and, to add to the complications, no adequate Afghan Dari-English dictionary exists, and many Afghan literates (including scholars) disagree on transliterations. Some of the terms used in this book have never been written down in Dari, for they constitute part of the folk language of the villager and nomad. Whenever possible, I have requested from individuals still living their own preference in the spelling of their names in English.

In conclusion, I must confess I go along with Col. T. E. Lawrence and his contempt for transliteration nit-pickers: "Arabic names won't go into English, exactly, for their consonants are not the same as ours, and their vowels, like ours, vary from district to district. There are some 'scientific systems' of transliteration, helpful to people who know enough Arabic not to need helping, but a wash-out for the world. I spell my names anyhow, to show what rot the systems are" (*Revolt in the Desert,* 1927, xv). Professor Richard N. Frye says practically the same thing about Persian in his classic *The Heritage of Persia* (1963, xviii–xix).

I hope that this book will establish guidelines for further investigation as well as present a reasonable survey of available data. Particularly, I hope platforms will be established from which Afghan scholars can launch research projects of their own.

Total responsibility for content, opinions expressed, false facts, and misinterpretations, however inadvertent, is mine alone. May Allah have mercy on me for my presumptuous insolence!

LOUIS DUPREE

PART I. THE LAND

HALF WAY around the world from the United States sits land-locked Afghanistan, a harsh, brutal, beautiful land, dominated by the disembodied mountainous[1] core of the Hindu Kush, the westernmost extension of the Karakorum Mountains, and the Himalayas, which push from the Pamir Knot into central Afghanistan in a general northeast–southwesterly trend to within one hundred miles of the Iranian border. The ranges stretch about 600 miles, or 966 kilometers, laterally, with the average north–south measurement being 150 miles, or 240 kilometers. The Pamir Knot contains more than 100 peaks which rise between 20,000 and 25,000 feet, or 6,100 and 7,620 meters, the highest in Afghanistan being Naochak (24,500 feet; 7,470 meters). The higher peaks in the central Hindu Kush[2] vary from 14,000 to 17,000 feet, or 4,270 to 5,180 meters. The highest peak, Shah Foladi, in the Koh-i-Baba range of the central Hindu Kush, reaches an altitude of almost 17,000 feet, or 5,140 meters.

Many passes cut through the central Hindu Kush mountains, and in the past provided the main routes north and south.

North of the Hindu Kush lie the Turkestan Plains, rolling semi-deserts with altitudes between 900 and 1,200 feet, or 270 and 370 meters. The flood plains of the Amu Darya (classical Oxus) River and its tributaries are relatively level and, in some places, marshy.

The dry western and southwestern sections of Afghanistan, extensions of the Iranian Plateau, rise gradually in altitude from west to east. In-

---

[1] Geographic names vary in time and space. I have attempted to use locally recognizable names. Coordinates in the index will help the reader locate most places mentioned in the text.

[2] Almost all references in Western language sources define Hindu Kush as "kills the Hindu," a grim reminder of the days when many Indians died in the high mountain passes of Afghanistan on their way to the slave markets of Muslim Central Asia. According to most Afghan scholars with whom I have talked, however, Hindu Kush is probably a corruption of *Hindu Koh,* name of the mountain range which, in pre-Muslim times, divided the area of dominate Hindu control to the south and southeast from the non-Hindu areas of the north, whose people were probably Zoroastrians and may have later developed into the modern Tajik. Another possibility is that Hindu Kush means "water mountains." The Avestan *Hindu* may be an equivalent of the Vedic *Sindhu,* which also means water or river.

1

hospitable stony deserts dominate, but sandy deserts of considerable size exist in Registan south and east of the Hilmand River.

Anyone flying over Afghanistan will be struck by the nakedness of the terrain. Bare rock dominates dramatically everywhere above 14,000 feet or 4,270 meters. Scrub vegetation and grasslands cover most lower altitudes. Occasional clumps of trees appear in the foothills of the northern slopes of the Hindu Kush. True forests exist only in eastern Afghanistan, mainly in the provinces of Paktya, Ningrahar, and Kunar.

Ecologically, most of Afghanistan is semi-desert, with bare patches of ground showing through the vegetative cover. Even the high-valley vegetational patterns of the Wakhan Corridor are semi-desert.

The lush vale of Jalalabad, often described as "subtropical," actually has a "dry-summer subtropical" or "Mediterranean" climate and needs extensive irrigation to grow citrus fruits, rice, and sugar cane. Probably the best climatic analogues in the United States exist in the Imperial Valley of California and the Arizona citrus-fruit areas (Michel, 1959, 29).

Although extensive and certainly not easily negotiable, the mountains of Afghanistan never truly served as barriers to cultural, economic, or political penetration, but merely funneled peoples and ideas along certain routes. Seasonally, the mountains and passes laden with snow could not be breached, so trading and raiding groups made end-arounds, skirting mountains until they reached the great gap between the Hindu Kush and Elburz Mountains (Iran). The terrain in the gap consists of lowland deserts, swamps, and plains extending from the Herat-Mashhad (Iran) line to Qandahar,[3] from which India lies open and vulnerable.

[3] Qandahar can also be transliterated Kandahar. According to Fussman (1966, 33), Qandahar is Farsi under Arabic influences; Kandahar, Pashto. I prefer Qandahar because the common spelling in modern Afghan literature continues to follow the Arabic "q" (ق).

CHAPTER 1

Geographic Zones

THE diverse geographic zones of Afghanistan are discussed from the point of view of total ecology, emphasizing lines of human contact and communication in reference to zones of accessibility and relative inaccessibility. Therefore, Map 2-A should be examined in conjunction with Maps 3, 4, 6, and 9, to understand better the criteria used to delimit the zones.

The Danish geographer Humlum (1959) divided Afghanistan into ten natural provinces: East, South, Central, West, Northwest, North, Nuristan, Badakhshan, Wakhan, Monsoonal Afghanistan (Map 2-B). Those who wish to savor Humlum's fine work and detailed descriptions of the geographic areas are invited to consult his volume, and recommended to read Michel's review (1960), in which he primarily disagrees with the inclusion of Jalalabad in Monsoonal Afghanistan. Michel feels that Jalalabad, with less than eight inches of rainfall, almost dry summers, and infrequent frosts, should, on the Köppen-Trewartha system, be called "subtropical steppe, dry summer" (Michel, 1960, 359–60).

Climate varies considerably, both diurnally and annually. Generally, however, Afghanistan has hot, dry summers and cold winters with heavy snowfalls in the mountains. In November, the snow line begins to creep down the mountains, and stops at about 6,000 feet (1,830 meters) above sea level. Average annual precipitation registers less than 13 inches (21 centimeters). Extremes vary from about two inches (3.2 centimeters) in the southwestern deserts to 13 inches (21 centimeters-plus) in the eastern part of Afghanistan. Maximum precipitation, about 36 inches (58 centimeters) annually, occurs in the Salang Pass area. As can be seen from Chart 1, the wettest months occur regionally at different times during the year, a phenomenon related to location, elevation, and exposure. Much of the rain falls during the winter months (December to February). In the Kabul Valley, however, summer Indian monsoons occasionally push rains into the area. Precipitation increases with elevation, and most water resources of Afghanistan result from the melt waters flowing out of the Hindu Kush.

From November to March, snow blankets the mountains. Peaks over 18,000 feet (5,500 meters) are permanently snow-covered, and several

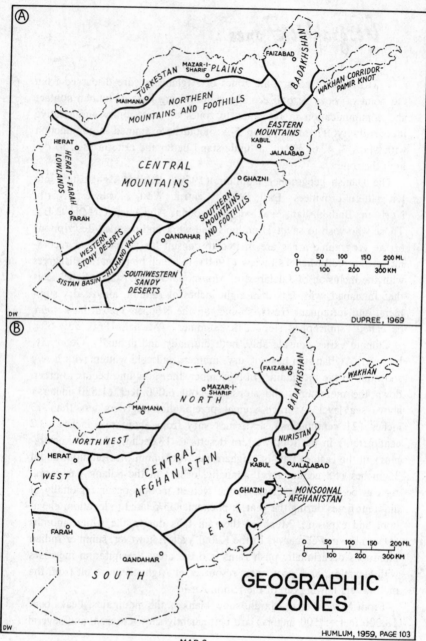

A — DUPREE, 1969

FAIZABAD
BADAKHSHAN
WAKHAN CORRIDOR—PAMIR KNOT
MAZAR-I-SHARIF
TURKESTAN PLAINS
MAIMANA
NORTHERN MOUNTAINS AND FOOTHILLS
EASTERN MOUNTAINS
KABUL
JALALABAD
HERAT
HERAT - FARAH LOWLANDS
CENTRAL MOUNTAINS
GHAZNI
FARAH
SOUTHERN MOUNTAINS AND FOOTHILLS
WESTERN STONY DESERTS
HILMAND VALLEY
QANDAHAR
SISTAN BASIN
SOUTHWESTERN SANDY DESERTS

0 50 100 150 200 MI.
0 100 200 300 KM

DW

B

FAIZABAD
BADAKHSHAN
WAKHAN
MAZAR-I-SHARIF
NORTH
MAIMANA
NORTHWEST
NURISTAN
HERAT
CENTRAL AFGHANISTAN
KABUL
JALALABAD
WEST
GHAZNI
MONSOONAL AFGHANISTAN
EAST
FARAH
QANDAHAR
SOUTH

0 50 100 150 200 MI.
0 100 200 300 KM

GEOGRAPHIC ZONES

DW

HUMLUM, 1959, PAGE 103

MAP 2

sizable glaciers still exist in northeastern Afghanistan. When snow begins to melt in March, the rivers begin to rise. Seasonal fluctuations occur simultaneously because the rivers get their waters from the same geographic source. Most rivers have maximum flow in the spring and minimum in summer, autumn, and winter. The major exception, the Wakhan Corridor, has maximum melt in late August, and daily fluctuations are spectacular. Small, fordable streams in early morning become torrents in the late afternoon, as water from snow melted by the midday heat flows down to the high valley plains of the Wakhan.

In many instances, minimum precipitation means drying up, or reduction of a river to a series of isolated pools in the stream bed. At times, premature warm weather or sudden rainstorms cause flash floods which catch and destroy whole semi-nomadic or nomadic camps as they pause seasonally in arroyos. Such a flash flood caught Alexander the Great during his invasion of the Afghan area (Burn, 1962, 164).

The Eleven Geographic Zones

The first six zones (the Wakhan Corridor–Pamir Knot, Badakhshan, Central Mountains, Eastern Mountains, Northern Mountains and Foothills, Southern Mountains and Foothills) relate to the Hindu Kush mountain system, young rugged ranges (like the Rocky Mountains) with sharp peaks, deep valleys, and many almost impenetrable barriers. The remaining five zones (Turkestan Plains, Herat–Farah Lowlands, Sistan Basin–Hilmand Valley, Western Stony Deserts, Southwestern Sandy Deserts) embrace the deserts and plains which surround the mountains in the north, west, and southwest (see Map 2).

The Wakhan Corridor and the Pamir Knot: This unique area belongs geographically to the greater Pamir Mountain system. The Anglo-Russian Boundary Commission of 1895–96 politically forced this zone on Amir Abdur Rahman Khan, so that at no point would British India and Tsarist Russia touch.

Many writers indiscriminately lump the Wakhan Corridor and the Pamir Mountains together and fail to distinguish between the sub-zones. In reality, the Corridor is one geographic entity and the Pamir Mountains another, although the Wakhan leads directly into the Pamir. I have been reminded (Michel, 1968) that "Pamir" actually refers to the high and relatively flat valleys between the mountain ranges, where the Kirghiz graze their flocks.

Two relatively wide valleys exist in Wakhan: one at Ishkashim (two miles across, three miles long); another at Qala Panja (less than a mile in all directions).

"Pamir Knot," although scientifically unacceptable to many, aptly describes the fist-like ranges which pivot off the Karakorum, Kunlum, and Himalayan mountains, shifting the trend from roughly southeast–northwest to northeast–southwest through Afghanistan. According to Humlum (1959, 17) 82.9 percent of the Wakhan–Pamir area is above 10,000 feet (3,000 meters), and 17.1 percent between 6,000 and 10,000 feet (1,800 to 3,000 meters). Perpetual snow covers all the Pamir above 16,500 feet (5,000 meters) above sea level. Many glaciers nestle at the higher elevations. Blue-green glacial lakes, such as Sar-i-Köl, shimmer. Passes thread through the high mountains at between 11,500 and 14,800 feet (3,500 to 4,500 meters), often 1,700 to 3,000 feet (500 to 1,000 meters) higher than the valley bottoms (Humlum, 1959, 112).

Mountain climbing in the Hindu Kush has increased considerably during the past few years. Several recent expeditions have climbed many peaks in the mountains south of the valley of the Ab-i-Panja (border with the U.S.S.R.), which later becomes the Amu Darya. In 1965, for example, at least twenty major foreign expeditions, including groups from West Germany, Japan, Poland, the United States, the United Kingdom, Czechoslovakia, Austria, and Italy, climbed mountains in the Afghan Hindu Kush.

Travel in the Pamir, which begins east of Qala Panja, is difficult, even with the hardy yak used by the Kirghiz nomads. In the sparsely populated Wakhan along the Ab-i-Panja, the people use the Bactrian (two-humped) camel and the horse. An unpaved, natural road follows the high, alpine valley of the Ab-i-Panja from the entrance of the Wakhan to Qala Panja. Trucks occasionally travel between Ishkashim and Qala Panja, and a Land Rover can breeze along the road at fifty kilometers an hour.

Often, however, the river narrows to less than one hundred yards and the ubiquitous Soviet watch towers stretch to cast shadows on Afghan soil, which accounts for the Afghan reluctance to permit foreign visitors to hunt in the home of the *Ovis polii* (Marco Polo sheep). Incidentally, even Russians have difficulty visiting the Pamir, because of the Afghan–Chinese border.

Several seasonally closed passes lead from Wakhan to Hunza and Chitral in Pakistan: Baroghil Pass; Dorah An (called Kach in Paki-

2. Pamir Knot. August, 1969. *Photo: Afghan Films*

3. Badakhshan. Durrani Pushtun nomads on way from Lake Shewa winter pasturelands in Turkestan Plains. August, 1966

stan) Pass. The Kilik (or Wakhjir) Dawan leads from Kashmir into Chinese Sinkiang and on to Tiwa and Urumchi, following former important trade and communication routes traveled by Marco Polo and earlier a flanking force of Genghis Khan, among others. In August, 1969, the Pakistanis, in cooperation with the People's Republic of China, reopened an old route between Chinese Sinkiang and Gilgit, which can be utilized only seasonally, however.

Badakhshan: Geographically, Badakhshan stretches from the entrance of the Wakhan to Kotal-i-Anjuman in the south and west, with the Amu Darya as boundary to the north. The Ab-i-Panja flows to the north near Ishkashim (entrance to the Wakhan) and cuts a large salient out of Central Asia as it patiently makes a parabolic swing to the west and south, thus avoiding the northeast mountains of Badakhshan.

High elevations over 10,000 feet (3,000 meters) constitute 27.5 percent of the terrain; 6,000 to 10,000 feet (1,800 to 3,000 meters), 36.2 percent; 2,000 to 6,000 feet (600 to 1,800 meters), 32 percent; 1,000 to 2,000 feet (300 to 600 meters), 42 percent, as one approaches the Turkestan Plains (Humlum, 1959, 17).

The sharp, rugged Koh-i-Khwaja Mohammad range in northern Badakhshan has been cut in many places by the Kokcha River 30 to 80 feet (9 to 25 meters) into the rock of the valley floor. The steep mountain slopes are covered with rockfall and talus. In the river valleys, up to three series of stream-laid gravel terraces occur, often cut several times by recurrent, spring melt-water floods.

An inhospitable but beautifully sculptured region, Badakhshan consists mainly of metamorphic and plutonic rocks, dissected by V-shaped valleys, which funnel most life into narrow trails.

Several of the open valleys surrounded by mountains and watered by streams, but mainly by springs, appear to have been glacial lakes during the Late Pleistocene. One such series of valleys lie west of Kishm, just north of the great mountain, Takht-i-Sulaiman (Throne of Solomon).

Several significant lakes exist in Badakhshan, the subject of many learned papers by British explorers in the nineteenth and early twentieth centuries. Thousands of nomads gather at the largest, Lake Shewa, in the summer, and return to the Turkestan Plains (near Chahar Darra, west of Kunduz) or eastern Afghanistan (Laghman), in the winter. Most Laghman nomads, however, go to the Central Mountains in the summer.

8

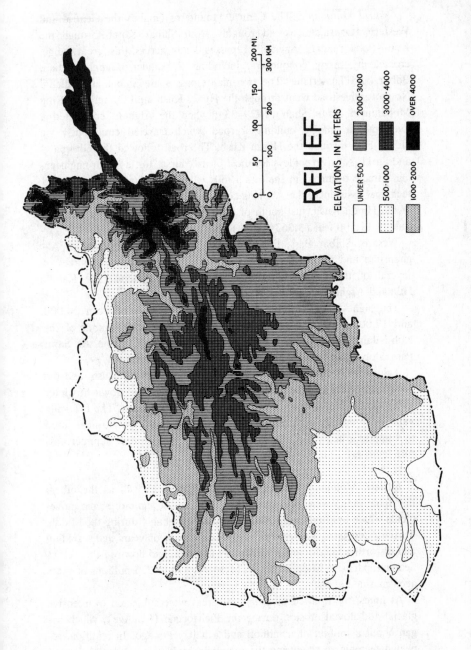

RELIEF

ELEVATIONS IN METERS

UNDER 500

500-1000

1000-2000

2000-3000

3000-4000

OVER 4000

0   50   100   150   200 MI.

0   100   200   300 KM

Central Mountains: The Central Mountains (mainly the Central and Western Hazarajat) extend roughly from Shibar Kotal through the Koh-i-Baba range. A series of passes leads across this great range, crossed by many conquerors, including Alexander, Genghis Khan, Babur, and Tamerlane. The two major passes are Shibar and Salang. No motorable road went through the Hindu Kush until the reign of King Mohammad Nadir Shah (1929–33), when the Afghans completed a long-time dream by building a road which traveled circuitously via Shibar Pass through the Hindu Kush. The road followed the Ghorband and Surkh Ab river valleys for most of its course. But a major engineering miracle occurred in the late 1960s when, with Soviet financial and technical assistance, the Afghans constructed a tunnel through the heart of the Hindu Kush, just south of the summit of Salang Pass at an altitude of 11,100 feet (3,363 meters) above sea level.

West of Shibar Pass, the Koh-i-Baba mountains, backbone of Afghanistan and a rugged, barren elevated tableland, contain sources of several of the country's more important river systems: the Kabul, Hilmand-Arghandab, and Hari Rud (see Map 4).

The highest peaks in the Central Mountains vary between 14,000 and 17,000 feet (4,270 and 5,180 meters), with the summit of the Koh-i-Baba range at Shah Foladi, about twenty miles from Ak Sarat Pass. Slopes on the north are gentler than those to the south.

Talus covers the lower mountain slopes of the Hindu Kush, and the river valleys are choked with boulders and gravels laid down in winter and moved along with great rapidity by spring snow melt. The few wide valleys are usually inhabited and cultivated or, if at high altitudes, used as summer grazing lands for livestock. These high altitude summer pasture lands are usually called *yilaq.*

Eastern Mountains: The Eastern Mountains (as well as the others in Afghanistan) were presumably subjected to the same orogenic movements which uplifted the Himalayas proper (probably during the Middle Tertiary and later, or between 15 to 40 millions of years ago), folding and distorting the original sedimentary deposits, laid down in the Tethys Sea and extensive Middle Eastern Mesozoic (70 to 225 millions of years ago) marine basins.

At times, the uplifted mountainous areas were subjected to intensive glacial and fluvial erosion during the Pleistocene (Ice Age), which began about a million or a million and a half years ago. In addition, repeated tectonic stress during the mountain building movements created

4. Central Mountains. Salang Pass looking southeast from southern end of Russian-built tunnel. August, 1966

5. Central Mountains. Unai Pass looking eastward. October, 1966

great fault systems. Most valleys (such as Ghorband, Kabul, Panjsher) are marked by fault lines created chiefly by Alpidi (Tertiary) movements. Although many valleys are narrow, some wider intermontane basins do permit agriculture. Frequent earthquakes, about fifty shakes of varying intensity per year, still occur.

To call the mountain systems of Afghanistan tortured is not trite, but concise.[1,2]

Four major valleys dominate the human geographic patterns of the Eastern Mountains.

Kabul (an area of high level basins, with altitudes varying from 5,000 to 12,000 feet—1,500 to 3,600 meters—filled with probable Neogene and Pleistocene sediments) is surrounded by mountains of old rugged crystalline and metamorphic Palaeozoic rocks. The Paghman Range sits northwest of Kabul, with the Safed Koh to the southeast and the Koh-i-Baba rising in the west. The Kabul River flows through Tang-i-Gharu, one of the more spectacular gorges in Afghanistan, to Jalalabad.

The second major valley, *Kohistan–Panjsher,* includes the wide basin of Koh Daman and Charikar and leads to the steepsided valleys of Nijrao and Tagao, where farmers practice terraced agriculture. This region consists mainly of faulted, dissected limestone, with some intrusive epliolites bordered by gneisses and igneous rocks in the east.

The Panjsher Valley serves as a major north–south route used by nomads summering in Badakhshan and wintering in the Laghman–Jalalabad area. Until 1961, many of these groups crossed the border into Pakistan to winter in the Peshawar Valley and points south.

The third major valley, *Ghorband,* lies in an east–west trend from Charikar to Shibar Pass. Here the sedimentary basin is flatter and with higher terraces than the Panjsher. Farther west, near Bulola, limestone, and near Bamiyan, sandstone and conglomerate, cliffs are encountered, but farther east, the formations become increasingly undifferentiated metamorphics.

Nuristan (formerly called Kafiristan), a region of wild, narrow mountain valleys, accessible only by foot trails except on the periphery where

---

[1] For more on geology: see Gannser (1964); Griesbach (1887); Wirtz (1964); Zeigler (1958). For geography, see *The Geographical Review of Afghanistan,* published since 1962 in Dari and Pashto with occasional articles in English as the semi-annual organ of the Institute of Geography, Faculty of Letters, Kabul University. Also see G. Arez (1970).

[2] For additional information on natural vegetation: *Afghanistan: B.I.S.* (1948); *Afghanistan: Field Notes* (1915); Furse (1956ab, 1966); P. and P. Furse (1968abc).

6. Eastern Mountains. Ghilzai Pushtun nomads near Anjuman Pass (Panjsher Valley) on way from Badakhshan to winter pasturage in Pakistan. Pakistan stopped such trans-border migrations in fall, 1961. October, 1950

new roads have been constructed, consists of five major north–south valleys (from east to west: Bashgal-Landai Sin-Kunar River complex;
Waigal; Pech-Parun-Kantiwa; Alingar-Kulam; Darra-yi-Nur), and
about thirty east–west lateral valleys leading into the major valleys.
Nuristan is a complex country of gneisses, dioritic and granitic pegma-
tites, undifferentiated metamorphics, some Mesozoic limestone beds,
slates, and recent deposits in the valleys. The five major north–south
valleys (Bashgal, Waigal, Pech, Alingar, Alishang) support streams
which swell the Kunar River as it flows southwesterly until it joins the
Kabul River. Many passes lead into Nuristan from all directions.

In addition, Kotal-i-Unai, a relatively easy pass, leads from Kabul
into the eastern Hazarajat. Several passes lead from Paktya into the
Kurram Valley of Pakistan, through Parachinar to Thal.

Snow usually begins to fall in October, blocking most mountain
passes for at least part of the winter. The permanent snow line varies
between 10,000 and 12,000 feet (3,000 and 4,600 meters) above sea
level. The winter snow line creeps down to about 6,000 feet (1,800
meters). Even in the summer, snow flurries occasionally occur at altitudes above 12,000 feet (3,600 meters). Snow fields and permanent
glaciers breed unfavorable conditions in some areas above 14,000 feet
(4,300 meters).

Blizzards dominate the winter months, and snow blocks most passes
above 7,000 to 8,000 feet (2,100 to 2,400 meters). Systematically accurate snow depths are not available, but drifts of ten feet (three
meters) and deeper have been reported. Winds accompanying winter
storms reach gale proportions and continue to slice down the valleys,
even when not transporting snow. Strong steady winds also occur in
spring, summer, and autumn, especially in the higher altitudes, but are
less fierce below 6,000 feet (1,800 meters). The local population knows
all the seasonal winds and has names for the more vicious and more
gentle ones.

In the spring (March–May), the snow melts and rushing streams become raging torrents. The winter months (December–March) are intensely cold and snowy in the Eastern Mountains, although much less
snow falls in the main basins, such as Kabul, Kohistan, and Ghorband.
Temperatures average around freezing but sometimes drop as low as
1°F. (−30°C.).

Spring temperatures increase tremendously (see Chart 1). Freezing
weather is found in April in the highest passes, but below 7,000 feet
(2,100 meters) temperatures are more comfortable, averaging 55° to

CHART 1
Climatic Charts

Geographic Region and Province; Degrees centigrade	1965			1966								
	Oct	Nov	Dec	Jan	Feb	Mar	Apr	May	June	July	Aug	Sept
BADAKHSHAN												
Mean Max. Temp.	25.2	17.3	10.9	14.4	13.1	13.4	18.7	24.5	34.7	36.0	35.3	29.5
Mean Min. Temp.	8.4	3.9	-5.2	-2.2	2.6	2.9	6.1	9.4	13.7	15.5	15.0	8.8
Mean Temp.	16.0	9.6	2.0	4.9	7.4	7.6	12.1	17.2	25.3	27.7	26.1	20.0
Relative Humidity	X	X	X	X	X	X	X	X	X	X	X	X
Total Rainfall in mm	8.9	37.4	8.6	15.0	72.3	103.5	100.8	31.8	1.0	0.9	0	0
BAGHLAN (Northern Mountains and Foothills)												
Mean Max. Temp.	26.7	18.4	11.0	15.2	14.9	15.5	21.1	29.4	37.8	37.5	36.5	31.5
Mean Min. Temp.	9.4	4.0	4.8	-1.8	4.8	6.2	10.4	13.3	17.9	19.1	17.4	12.1
Mean Temp.	16.9	10.1	1.5	5.0	9.1	10.2	15.1	20.7	27.3	27.5	25.9	20.0
Relative Humidity	64	76	73	69	82	83	81	62	48	46	51	55
Total Rainfall in mm	2.5	6.0	14.0	Tr	54.4	126.0	68.9	8.1	0	0	0	Tr
BALKH (Turkestan Plains)												
Mean Max. Temp.	26.4	20.1	13.7	17.1	16.6	16.6	23.5	31.5	39.5	39.2	38.8	32.1
Mean Min. Temp.	X	6.0	-2.5	X	X	X	13.7	17.5	24.8	26.8	25.4	17.2
Mean Temp.	18.8	11.9	4.5	7.5	10.3	11.7	17.4	25.0	32.3	33.4	31.7	24.4
Relative Humidity	46	57	53	55	73	69	58	45	45	43	46	35
Total Rainfall in mm.	0	1.0	2.0	1.0	44.5	65.4	16.5	0	0	0.2	0	0
FARAH (Herat-Farah Lowlands)												
Mean Max. Temp.	32.7	24.7	17.9	20.5	19.6	24.1	31.8	36.4	42.9	42.7	40.2	36.2
Mean Min. Temp.	12.6	6.1	-0.6	1.1	7.1	8.0	15.0	17.6	25.2	23.6	20.1	15.3
Mean Temp.	20.3	13.8	7.4	9.5	12.5	15.5	23.5	27.7	34.0	32.8	30.5	25.1
Relative Humidity	45	62	60	63	71	50	57	50	40	45	42	47
Total Rainfall in mm	0	13.0	1.1	10.3	54.7	0	0	0	0	0	0	0
FARYAB (Turkestan Plains)												
Mean Max. Temp.	24.4	18.5	12.7	16.7	14.0	14.6	20.8	28.2	36.2	35.5	34.6	29.3
Mean Min. Temp.	8.8	5.5	-1.1	2.4	3.4	2.2	7.0	11.0	17.6	18.5	17.4	12.1
Mean Temp.	16.0	10.6	4.8	8.3	8.2	8.5	14.2	19.8	26.8	27.1	26.0	20.7
Relative Humidity	X	X	X	X	X	X	X	X	X	X	X	37
Total Rainfall in mm	5.2	14.0	21.4	1.5	49.8	93.7	39.8	0.3	0	0	0	0

Source: *The Kabul Times Annual*, 1967, 87-90.

CHART 1 (*continued*)

Geographic Region and Province; Degrees centigrade	1965			1966								
	Oct	Nov	Dec	Jan	Feb	Mar	Apr	May	June	July	Aug	Sept
GARDEZ (Southern Mountains and Foothills)												
Mean Max. Temp.	20.5	12.2	5.2	5.1	6.9	10.1	14.1	21.7	27.5	27.8	28.9	24.4
Mean Min. Temp.	4.1	-0.3	-9.5	-8.6	-1.2	-1.1	3.5	6.7	11.7	14.1	13.7	8.5
Mean Temp.	12.3	4.8	-4.0	-3.5	1.8	4.0	8.5	14.9	20.8	21.1	21.0	16.4
Relative Humidity	42	58	48	60	78	67	68	44	50	52	51	49
Total Rainfall in mm	0	15.9	18.6	11.5	94.9	77.6	65.4	10.6	6.1	8.3	0	0.1
GHAZNI (Southern Mountains and Foothills)												
Mean Max. Temp.	22.5	13.7	5.7	5.3	8.9	12.4	15.8	23.9	30.0	30.8	30.8	25.9
Mean Min. Temp.	2.8	-2.0	-10.1	-12.3	-4.7	-3.9	1.0	7.8	13.0	15.4	14.2	9.0
Mean Temp.	12.2	4.9	-3.4	-4.3	2.4	4.7	8.8	15.9	22.9	23.0	22.1	16.8
Relative Humidity	61	71	73	69	81	68	70	55	53	59	56	52
Total Rainfall in mm	0	36.4	52.0	16.4	105.5	26.3	94.2	7.2	1.2	1.1	0	0
GHELMIN (Central Mountains)												
Mean Max. Temp.	22.1	14.4	6.5	7.7	9.4	–	15.7	22.3	28.2	28.6	28.3	24.1
Mean Min. Temp.	13	-3.4	-12.2	-10.8	-1.6	–	2.8	4.9	7.8	9.1	7.3	2.8
Mean Temp.	10.3	4.4	-5.2	-3.2	2.7	–	8.2	12.9	18.5	19.7	18.2	13.0
Relative Humidity	60	71	65	66	78	–	65	44	34	47	51	61
Total Rainfall in mm	0	8.5	14.7	Tr	39.6	–	94.0	2.8	0	0	0	0.1
GHOR (Central Mountains)												
Mean Max. Temp.	16.1	8.6	2.7	-1.5	3.0	4.3	8.7	16.7	24.0	24.9	24.4	20.0
Mean Min. Temp.	-3.2	-7.1	-15.8	-20.2	-8.7	-7.5	-1.8	0.1	3.4	4.5	2.6	-2.6
Mean Temp.	5.8	-0.5	-8.4	-12.2	-3.2	-2.4	3.2	8.7	14.9	15.9	14.9	9.4
Relative Humidity	60	67	62	71	82	76	82	64	62	60	49	52
Total Rainfall in mm	0	13.6	18.4	11.6	42.0	71.9	93.7	2.8	0	0	0	Tr
HILMAND (Sistan Basin-Hilmand Valley)												
Mean Max. Temp.	33.2	24.3	16.6	19.2	19.8	24.7	29.2	36.4	42.4	41.5	37.5	34.1
Mean Min. Temp.	12.7	6.5	-0.9	1.3	7.1	8.2	12.6	17.5	21.8	23.5	17.4	15.1
Mean Temp.	21.8	14.1	6.1	8.3	12.5	15.4	20.5	27.4	32.2	31.7	26.6	24.1
Relative Humidity	33	46	53	53	64	36	39	37	31	27	25	4
Total Rainfall in mm	0	10.2	13.5	0.7	41.0	0.4	1.9	0	0	0	0	0

CHART 1 (*continued*)

Geographic Region and Province; Degrees centigrade	1965			1966								
	Oct	Nov	Dec	Jan	Feb	Mar	Apr	May	June	July	Aug	Sept
HERAT (Herat-Farah Lowlands)												
Mean Max. Temp.	27.5	20.2	13.1	16.4	14.3	18.3	22.2	29.0	34.5	35.7	34.9	30.8
Mean Min. Temp.	10.0	3.9	-3.5	0.4	4.1	3.9	8.7	12.8	19.9	21.6	19.3	13.4
Mean Temp.	19.7	11.4	3.5	7.1	8.2	10.4	14.8	20.8	28.4	29.1	27.6	22.0
Relative Humidity	51	61	70	66	75	50	55	36	34	33	38	38
Total Rainfall in mm	0	7.8	13.8	21.6	73.8	27.6	100.8	0	0	0	0	0
JOWZJAN (Turkestan Plains)												
Mean Max. Temp.	25.3	19.1	12.5	15.2	14.8	16.0	23.2	31.2	38.4	36.9	37.0	31.2
Mean Min. Temp.	11.8	6.8	-0.1	3.0	5.5	6.6	10.8	14.5	21.2	22.1	20.7	15.8
Mean Temp.	18.2	12.3	5.9	8.3	9.8	11.4	16.6	23.1	29.5	30.1	28.9	23.7
Relative Humidity	44	61	69	61	71	66	59	33	32	36	29	24
Total Rainfall in mm	1.3	11.0	14.8	8.0	54.5	45.0	24.3	0	0	0	0	0
KABUL (Eastern Mountains and Foothills)												
Mean Max. Temp.	24.3	15.7	7.7	9.1	10.5	12.6	17.0	25.0	32.1	31.9	31.8	27.3
Mean Min. Temp.	4.9	-0.4	-8.3	-6.4	-0.7	-0.5	4.3	7.4	12.4	15.0	14.8	8.4
Mean Temp.	14.4	6.7	-2.7	-0.3	4.2	6.1	11.0	17.0	23.1	24.6	23.9	18.7
Relative Humidity	52	65	67	72	76	72	76	51	29	34	25	41
Total Rainfall in mm	0	40.0	6.2	13.1	83.4	79.7	70.8	11.9	0	3.5	6.8	3.0
QANDAHAR (Southern Mountains and Foothills)												
Mean Max. Temp.	31.4	22.9	15.4	18.5	18.9	22.7	26.9	34.8	40.3	39.9	38.5	34.1
Mean Min. Temp.	11.6	5.8	0.7	1.5	6.6	6.9	12.1	15.6	20.6	22.7	19.3	14.0
Mean Temp.	20.0	12.7	5.3	7.4	11.6	14.0	18.5	25.5	31.2	31.5	28.6	23.2
Relative Humidity	26	49	45	49	67	46	52	26	22	25	21	19
Total Rainfall in mm	0	8.8	44.2	3.1	76.5	11.6	27.4	0	0	0	0	0
KUNDUZ (Turkestan Plains)												
Mean Max. Temp.	26.0	18.7	11.0	15.4	15.4	15.7	21.8	30.6	39.0	38.9	37.2	31.1
Mean Min. Temp.	12.7	6.3	-2.8	0.9	5.7	6.5	10.9	15.2	23.0	24.0	22.8	16.3
Mean Temp.	18.8	11.8	3.4	7.3	10.2	10.7	16.1	23.0	31.3	31.5	29.8	23.4
Relative Humidity	60	74	64	61	77	80	72	51	X	38	39	42
Total Rainfall in mm	1.6	14.8	11.8	3.0	49.2	118.5	32.5	1.7	0	0	0	0

CHART 1 (*continued*)

Geographic Region and Province; Degrees centigrade	1965			1966								
	Oct	Nov	Dec	Jan	Feb	Mar	Apr	May	June	July	Aug	Sept
LAGHMAN (Eastern Mountains)												
Mean Max. Temp.	30.1	22.6	16.3	18.0	18.0	18.9	23.6	32.7	38.7	36.3	37.6	31.8
Mean Min. Temp.	13.0	7.3	-0.9	1.1	7.1	7.7	11.5	15.6	22.5	24.2	24.4	17.7
Mean Temp.	21.4	14.1	6.4	8.4	12.4	13.1	17.8	25.4	31.4	30.5	29.9	25.2
Relative Humidity	X	X	66	X	X	X	X	X	X	X	X	58
Total Rainfall in mm	12.2	24.1	20.4	0.7	65.7	142.6	62.5	5.8	Tr	Tr	0	0
NINGRAHAR (Eastern Mountains)												
Mean Max. Temp.	32.3	23.9	16.4	X	18.9	20.7	25.3	35.8	41.2	39.4	38.5	34.2
Mean Min. Temp.	15.7	9.6	0.6	2.2	8.8	9.9	13.8	20.0	26.8	26.4	26.7	20.6
Mean Temp.	23.3	15.2	7.1	8.6	13.4	14.2	19.1	28.4	34.1	32.2	32.0	20.4
Relative Humidity	47	60	67	58	70	67	64	31	30	49	47	53
Total Rainfall in mm	0	37.5	11.7	Tr	36.4	105.3	41.8	4.0	0	0	0	5.3
PAKTYA (Southern Mountains and Foothills)												
Mean Max. Temp.	27.7	20.5	14.4	16.4	15.4	18.1	21.9	30.9	34.7	32.5	32.0	28.8
Mean Min. Temp.	12.2	5.6	-1.5	0.6	4.9	6.1	9.7	14.5	20.9	21.3	20.7	16.5
Mean Temp.	19.6	12.2	5.0	6.0	9.5	11.4	15.4	23.2	28.2	26.1	25.9	22.2
Relative Humidity	50	63	55	53	74	70	71	42	44	63	67	59
Total Rainfall in mm	0	38.8	33.6	Tr	75.6	68.0	51.1	41.8	47.9	143.4	55.1	88.1
PARWAN (Eastern Mountains)												
Mean Max. Temp.	24.1	16.0	8.3	8.6	11.1	13.5	17.3	24.0	30.2	31.3	31.5	26.8
Mean Min. Temp.	14.7	7.2	-2.3	-0.5	4.2	5.4	9.3	15.2	21.9	22.8	22.2	17.7
Mean Temp.	18.8	11.5	2.2	3.0	7.4	8.7	13.0	19.8	26.3	26.7	26.4	21.5
Relative Humidity	32	44	44	63	59	53	53	30	24	23	21	23
Total Rainfall in mm	Tr	13.1	66.2	6.0	122.3	159.1	91.1	1.7	0	Tr	Tr	9.0
SALANG (Central Mountains)												
Mean Max. Temp.	6.5	1.0	-3.5	-2.1	-2.8	-2.1	2.6	6.3	12.9	13.5	13.3	9.4
Mean Min. Temp.	0.9	-7.0	-11.5	-10.8	-9.5	-10.0	-6.5	-2.2	3.8	5.0	4.4	0.1
Mean Temp.	2.3	-3.3	-7.7	-6.4	-5.7	-6.0	-1.9	1.8	8.0	8.8	8.5	3.9
Relative Humidity	86	80	47	48	72	72	72	72	67	63	66	70
Total Rainfall in mm	25.1	98.2	48.9	24.6	309.2	326.4	227.9	92.8	0	8.8	0.9	16.2

65°F. (13° to 18°C.) at noon. Actually, the high, dry, sunny climatic face of Afghanistan is more often comfortable than not in habitation areas. May is seasonally warm up to heights of 11,000 feet (3,350 meters), though the temperature fluctuates and freezing weather does occur.

Summers are relatively warm and comfortable. Autumn (October–November) brings intense cold to heights above 6,000 feet (1,800 meters). Snow filters down on the northern slopes, while the southern slopes still have warm (55°F., or 13°C.) days. Changes in altitude as well as season produce great temperature differences. A descent from 11,000 feet (3,350 meters) to 5,000 feet (1,520 meters) can involve a 70° to 80°F. (21° to 26°C.) change in a few hours. High in the permanent snow fields and glaciers, day temperatures can be warm (up to 65°F., or 18°C.) if no winds blow. The wind-chill factor becomes important as altitude increases.

Even when there is no snow lying, persons unaccustomed to high-altitude glare require sunglasses. Caravaneers consider western-style sunglasses as prestige items. Many, however, still utilize homemade types similar to those made by the Eskimo: a strip of leather or wood with thin slits cut to limit the amount of sunlight striking the eye. In addition, the epicanthic eyefold of the Central Asian Mongoloid serves as a natural biological adaptation to protect the eye against snow and sun glare.

Nuristan and Paktya are the most heavily forested areas in Afghanistan. The Panjsher Valley, as historical references attest (Le Strange, 1930, 350), had large forests until they were destroyed by the greedy hand of man, who cut down and burned trees to smelt silver, copper, and other ores during the heyday of the early Islamic period before the thirteenth-century Mongol invasions. Man remained, but the forests never returned.

Modern vegetation patterns in the Eastern Mountains consist mainly of thin grasses and stunted bushes. Actually, about 40 percent of all Afghanistan is covered with sparse greenery. Chart 2 gives a general picture of the vegetation by altitude in the Central Mountains, Eastern Mountains, and Southern Mountains and Foothills.

There is a geographic anomaly, the so-called Reg-i-Rawan, an area of sand dunes, near Begram, just south of Charikar.

Southern Mountains and Foothills: This region is formed as the river systems of the Kabul and Hilmand debouch into the plains, and semi-

CHART 2
Natural Vegetation
Central Mountains, Eastern Mountains, Southern Mountains and Foothills

Altitude	Characteristics
Above 14,000 feet	None
12-14,000 feet	Mountain meadows of short grasses and seasonally flowering plants.
10-12,000 feet	Mountain scrub, grasses and seasonally flowering plants, small scattered bushes (juniper, dwarf willow, rosebay, tragacanth, euphorbia).
Up to 10,000 feet	Dry scrub, semidesert bushy plants (feather grass, wormwood, saltwort, tragacanth, camel grass, tamarisk) and scattered clumps of pistachio trees.
Forest zones of Nuristan and Paktya:[a] 8 or 9,000 feet to 10-11,000 feet	Conifer forests of pine, cedar, fir, larch and yew with a few broadleafed trees (willow, poplar); ivy found only in Nuristan.
4,500-5,000 feet to 8-9,000 feet	Bushes and broadleafed forests of oak (including holly oak) with well developed undergrowth, and some walnut, alder, ash, juniper; above 5-6,000 feet, conifers included to form mixed forests.
Jalalabad region[a]: up to 4-5,000 feet	Subtropical scrub and flowering plants and shrubs, including some palm trees especially around Jalalabad town.
Valley floors and river banks	Plane trees, poplar, willow and mulberry thickets; much bush growth where land not cultivated.

[a] Distinctive floral zones. Chart highly schematic. Because of the varied terrain within each zone, many local variations occur.

desert becomes desert, with agricultural villages studding the "tooth-paste squeezes" of the rivers and tributaries. The area mainly embraces Qandahar, Ghazni, and much of Paktya.

Northern Mountains and Foothills: A broad zone of mountain plateaux and foothills north of the Hindu Kush watershed stretches from the 70°E. meridian west to the Iranian border. Low, bare limestone, shale, and sandstone mountains with rounded summits dominate. Soils are usually thin and stony, except on lower, recent flood-plains with silt, clay, and loess deposits. In winter and spring these soils turn into deep muds.

The Band-i-Turkestan Range rises south of Maimana to heights of 11,000 feet (3,350 meters), and runs almost due east–west for about 125 miles (200 kilometers). The northern slopes drop abruptly onto the Turkestan Plains. In the foothills a loessy-sand called *chol* covers the bare rock.

South of the Band-i-Turkestan Mountains lies the Murghab River valley, a rolling limestone region parallel to the mountains, and never more than six to eight miles wide.

To the east the Paropamisus (plus Koh-i-Changar and Firozkoh) Mountains cut off Afghan Turkestan from the high valleys of the Central Mountains, and are the northern extremity of the main watershed complex. The region, characterized by deep valleys and rounded summits, consists mainly of barren scarps of metamorphic rock with peaks up to 11,500 feet (3,500 meters).

East of the Firozkoh lie the Kunduz, Andarab, and Surkh Ab valleys, which vary from narrow gorges to broad flat-bottomed valleys. The Andarab Valley pushes east toward Doshi. Between Doab and Bulola, the Surkh Ab Valley moves through a series of narrow gorges. Above Bulola, the valley divides: Shibar Pass lies to the east, and Bamiyan, Nil Kotal, and Aq Ribat to the west.

For a schematic representation of the vegetation by altitude in the Northern Mountains and Foothills and the Turkestan Plains see Chart 3.

Turkestan Plains: The northern foothills abruptly drop from 4,000 to 6,000 feet (1,220 to 1,830 meters) into stony plains about 1,200 feet (370 meters) above sea level.

The elevation drops less than 1,000 feet (305 meters) in 50 miles (80 kilometers). Scattered dunes sometimes occur in the pebbly deserts and conversely. Sand drifts and dunes begin near Andkhui less than

CHART 3
Natural Vegetation
Northern Mountains and Foothills, and Turkestan Plains

Altitude	Characteristics
Above 13,000 feet	None
11,500-13,000 feet	Mountain meadows with short grasses and flowering plants.
8-10,000/11,500 feet	Mountain scrub of short grasses, flowering plants, and small bushes (tragacanth, milk vetch, *Astragalus* sp., euphorbia).
6-8,000 feet (west); 6-10,000 feet (east)	Scrub of scattered trees, grasses, flowering plants, small bushes in clusters. Oaks and conifers (including junipers); at higher levels willows and poplars, plus maple and hazel to the east.
3-3,500 to 6-6,500 feet	Scrub of grasses, small bushes, and pistachio trees.[a]
Up to 3-3,500 feet	Meadows of reeds and grasses with occasional pistachio trees.
Valley floors and river banks	Camel thorn (grass), plane trees, poplars, willows, mulberry trees where there is cultivation. Reeds along the Amu Darya.

[a] Pistachio trees common all over northern Afghanistan; usually about 10 feet high, diameter 4-6 inches; staggered about 15-25 feet apart; and, although wild, have appearance of cultivated orchard. Chart is highly schematic. Because of the varied terrain within each zone, many local variations occur.

7. Central Mountains. *a*) Hazarajat: *lalmi* (dry cultivated) wheat on loess-covered hillsides. November, 1961. *b*) Threshing area for *lalmi* wheat near Jam. October, 1961

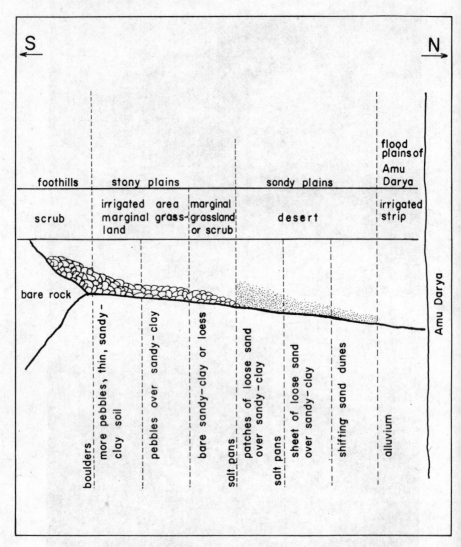

DIAGRAM 1
Turkestan Plains: Idealized Cross-Section of Topography

20 miles or (32 kilometers) from the Amu Darya. To the east, near Khist Tapa, the sand pinches out about 2 miles (3.2 kilometers) from the Soviet border. The long, shifting dunes reach heights of 30 feet (9 meters). Almost level, the floodplain of the Amu Darya varies from 2 to 10 miles (3.2 to 16 kilometers) in width. Marshy, alluvial terraces, 10 to 20 feet (3 to 6 meters) high, often separate the floodplain from the desert. West of Termez, U.S.S.R., a number of islands dot the river. North of Tashkurghan and southwest of Andkhui sit expanses of salt flats which become wet marshes in winter, but dry, crusty zones in summer.

Much variability in temperature occurs in winter (December–February) (Chart 1). A series of warm days (60° to 70°F., or 15° to 21°C.) gives way to a three- to four-week period of freezing weather.

Spring (March–May) exhibits great climatic variability. March and April temperatures often drop to freezing, and maximum readings for two consecutive days in May may vary as much as 50°F. (28°C.). Snow, sleet, and cold rain fall, but the snow seldom sticks. Throughout the spring, average temperatures increase gradually. Daytime temperatures sometimes exceed 80°F. (26°C.) in March, 90°F. (32°C.) in April, 100°F. (37°C.) in May.

Diurnal summer (June–September, the least variable of the seasons) temperatures still fluctuate greatly. Day temperatures often reach 105°F. (40°C.), with nights much colder. However, by the middle of September, nighttime freezing temperatures commonly occur.

Autumn (October–November), like spring, exhibits variable temperatures, and a shift from hot to freezing weather can strike abruptly.

Rain falls sporadically in autumn and winter, but most falls in spring as thundershowers, increasing the danger of floods. Disastrous floods sometimes result as snow melts in the mountains south of the plains during April and May. The average annual precipitation in the Turkestan Plains seldom reaches 10 inches (25.4 centimeters), however.

In late summer and early autumn soft winds from the north shift rich loess to the plains and foothills of north Afghanistan, permitting extensive highland agriculture. For centuries, this unscheduled aid program has been annually giving Afghanistan tons of top soil from the Russian Central Asian steppes. The loess often seems to hang in the air, and penetrates everything, skin and clothing, with an almost oily consistency, and sometimes even blocks out the sun in the afternoon. Such wind-blown, natural phenomena, however, cause grasslands to flourish into

25

farmlands and into seasonal flowering grasses to feed the flocks of the nomads.

Herat–Farah Lowlands: Actually an extension of the Khurasan Region of the Iranian Plateau, the Herat–Farah complex consists mainly of mountain ranges and low hills, sporadically rugged but generally rounded, separated by broad, flat valleys. The area is approximately enclosed by the Hari Rud to the north, the Khash Rud to the south, and the Central Mountains to the east.

The region is intensively cultivated where water is available.

The low hills near Herat are crystalline rocks and undifferentiated metamorphics of the Upper Palaeozoic, with Mesozoic limestones and shales north of the Hari Rud. Mesozoic limestones and shales, Tertiary sandstones, clastics, and basic to intermediate volcanic intrusions and extrusions abound in the south. Desert basins of sandy clay covered with loose gravels and pebbles surround the hills. Near the Irano–Afghan boundary exist a number of salt- and mudflats, more extensive than those of the Turkestan Plains.

Winter (December–February) finds freezing temperatures common at night. Warm spells do occur, however, and temperatures above 70°F. (21°C.) have been reported for December–January, and 80°F. (26°C.) in February. Spring (March–May), more variable than winter, has some freezing temperatures in March, but the average gradually increases to about 70°F. (21°C.) in May. Day temperatures in the hot, dry summer (June–September) sometimes reach 120°F. (45°C.). A June midnight temperature of 120°F. (45°C.) has been recorded at Farah. In September, a noticeable decrease in temperature occurs, and nights become chilly and even cold, although the days remain relatively warm. Transitional autumn (October–November) has decreasingly warmer days and increasingly colder nights, especially in the Herat area.

Annual precipitation averages 7 inches (18 centimeters) in Herat. Both snow and rain fall in the Herat area during winter, but snow melts and seldom remains on the ground for long. Although less rain falls in the spring, rivers swollen with melt-water often cause floods as early as February and climax in April. Summer thunderstorms and flash rains occur, but autumn is almost rainless.

Hilmand Valley–Sistan Basin: Most of the low lying (average elevation about 1,700 feet, or 520 meters) Sistan Basin lies in Iran. The

8. Hilman Valley. Tamarisk jungle to right. Stony desert in background. September, 1961

eastern boundary of the Sistan Basin penetrates the edge of the Dasht-i-Margo ("Desert of Death") along a sharp scarp with the height varying from 30 feet (9 meters) to several hundred feet. The Sistan Basin, a zone of intermittent lakes, fresh water and brackish marshes interspersed between stony and sandy deserts, forms a part of the great inland Hilmand drainage basin. The river flows into the Hamun-i-Hilmand, a series of marshes and connecting lakes. Fresh water overflows from the Hamun, and empties into the Gaud-i-Zirreh, an ephemeral brackish lake.

Level, fertile plains, the ancient beds of extinct lakes, surround the modern lakes. A number of volcanoes erupted in the early Pleistocene, covering much of the bottom with lava flows and caps. In well-exposed vertical sections, several layers of Neogene and Pleistocene sediments can be differentiated. Reddish and greenish clays alternate, interspersed with bands of gravels and sands. Gravel deposits and fine silts overlay the clays.

Spring floods often cover wide areas, and the uncontrolled Hilmand flushes downstream from the mountains. But the huge dams at Kajakai on the Hilmand and Dahla on the Arghandab have helped gain moderate control since the mid-1950s.

Tamarisk bushes grow in abundance along sections of the Hilmand flood plain not utilized for agriculture. The Afghans call such tamarisk groves, where wild boar still thrive, *jangal* (jungle).

The vicious *bad-i-sad-o-bist-roz* ("wind of 120 days"), a seasonal natural phenomenon, emphasizes the inhospitability of southwestern Afghanistan. Born of the differential pressures between the northern plains and the southern and southwestern lowland deserts, and blocked by the Central Mountains of Afghanistan and the Elburz of Iran, the winds whip down the natural corridor along the Irano–Afghan border, stirring up violent sandstorms from Herat to Pakistani Baluchistan. Velocities vary from day to day and week to week, but sometimes exceed 100 knots. Beginning in July, the winds gradually increase and blow through September.

Other strong, cold winds push out of the high-pressure areas south of Central Asia and the Turkestan Plains in autumn, winter, and spring, but seldom with the force of the *bad-i-sad-o-bist-roz*.

Another phenomenon of the lowlands of Afghanistan, both north and south, is the *khakbad* ("dust wind"), or small whirlwind of sand. At times, tens of these miniature tornados can be seen swaying across desert and semi-desert areas.

9. Western stony desert of Dasht-i-Margo, north of Hilmand River. August, 1949

10. Southwestern sandy deserts. Northern sector of Registan.

11. Northern Mountains and Foothills. Valley of Gurziwan south of Maimana. Camels of nomads grazing on freshly-reaped wheat stubble. August, 1970

12. Turkestan Plains. Ghilzai Pushtun nomads in winter pasturage near Andkhui. November, 1959

Western Stony Deserts: Mainly uninhabited and relatively unexplored, the Dasht-i-Kash, Dasht-i-Margo, and adjacent areas are hot, waterless, barren, varnished-pebble-strewn deserts, which (like the Southwestern Sandy Deserts) seldom rise over 3,000 feet (915 meters) above sea level, usually ranging between 1 and 3,000 feet (305–915 meters). Scattered lenses of volcanic ash a few inches thick alternate with volcanic lavas in the region. Spring flash floods cut deep depressions in the sandy clay and silt underlying the heavily cemented, blackish wind-polished basaltic pebbles. Seasonal overflow from the Hilmand creates shallow ponds throughout the fringes of the desert.

Great diurnal changes of temperature occur, and water sometimes freezes at night in summer in spite of noon maxima of 120°F. (45°C.), or higher.

Limited flora and fauna can survive in either the Sistan Basin, Western Stony Deserts, or Southwestern Sandy Deserts. Desert plants are xerophytic and adapt to extremes of aridity and salinity. Only thorny, deep-rooted plants exist perennially. The commonest and most widespread is camel grass or thorn, a member of the pea family, which is greenish-gray in color. Camel grass exudes a combustible sap which hardens on contact with the air and can be used as an emergency food. Some such *manna* must have assisted the Israelites in their trek through Sinai to Canaan. Camel grass itself can be used to quick-broil small animals and birds, for it burns rapidly at a very high temperature.

Southwestern Sandy Deserts: South and east of the Hilmand River lies Registan, the "Land of Sand," an area of shifting sand dunes with an underlying pebble-conglomerate floor. The moving dunes reach heights of between 50 and 100 feet (15 and 30 meters). However, some fixed dunes exist in central Registan. Level areas between the dunes, called *pat* (which also means desert in Baluchi) menace travelers. Treacherous, sandy-clay mush when wet, *pat* becomes a hard-topped pan when dry, but remains mushy underneath.

The Hilmand system to the north and west, the Chaman–Qandahar road to the east, and the Chagai Hills of Pakistan to the south enclose the sandy deserts.

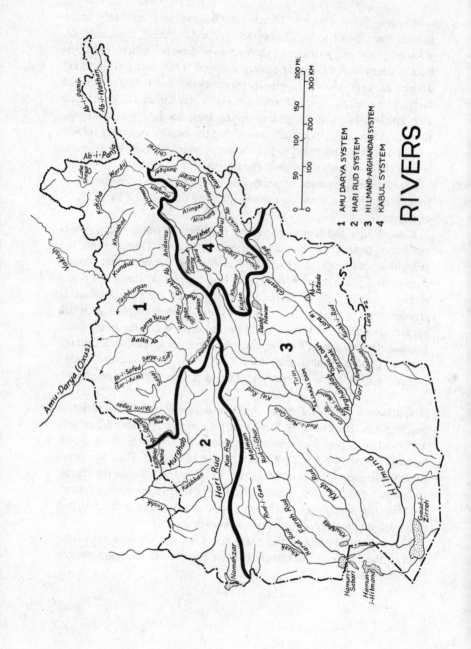

RIVERS

1 AMU DARYA SYSTEM
2 HARI RUD SYSTEM
3 HILMAND-ARGHANDAB SYSTEM
4 KABUL SYSTEM

CHAPTER 2

Water

WATER is the key to the distribution, proliferation, and perpetuation of animal and plant life, and its absence limits agricultural and pasture land (see Map 4). Its source in Afghanistan lies in the high watershed of the Central Mountains. Afghanistan's problem is not insufficient water, for enough exists to increase productivity of current acreage and to add many thousands of marginal acres to production. Control, not amount, is the difficulty. Most of the millions of acre-feet of water which seasonally pour down from the mountains disappears into the deserts, or is pirated away by the many uncoordinated irrigation intakes lining the rivers and tributaries.

Since all the rivers get their water from the same source at approximately the same time, seasonal fluctuations occur almost simultaneously. Most rivers have maximum flow in spring and early summer and minimum in late summer and winter. Minimum often means complete drying-up, or such a drastic reduction that rivers like the Khash Rud in the southwest shrink to unconnected pools in the stream beds.

Four main river systems exist: Amu Darya, Hari Rud, Hilmand–Arghandab, and Kabul. Only the Kabul River has an outlet to the sea; it joins the Indus system at Attock, Pakistan, but the other three are entirely inland systems.

The major perennial rivers are Amu Darya, Kabul, Hilmand, Arghandab, Panjsher, Logar, Hari Rud, and Kunar. Perennial tributaries are Laghman, Surkh Ab, Kunduz, Kokcha, Rud-i-Band-i-Amir (called Balkh Ab in its lower course).

Disastrous floods can occur anytime between February and July, washing away fields, drowning livestock and people.

Amu Darya (Oxus) System

The Amu Darya (the classical Oxus River), principal boundary with the U.S.S.R. (determined as middle of *thalweg*—deepest channel—in 1946), runs for about 680 miles (1,100 kilometers) before it pushes north into Russia and empties into the Aral Sea; its total length is about 1,500 miles (2,400 kilometers). Before becoming the Amu Darya, it

33

13. Eastern Mountains. Tajik village at north end of Khord Kabul Pass

14. Northern Mountains and Foothills. Eroded arroyo near Aq Kupruk south of Mazar-i-Sharif. Sheep-goat trails plainly visible. Hillsides bloom in late spring. October, 1959

has several local names. At its headwaters in the Pamirs, it is known as the Ab-i-Wakhan, but the name changes to Ab-i-Panja when the Ab-i-Pamir joins the Ab-i-Wakhan. In Russian Tajikistan, its name is Pyandzh. The Afghans call it Amu Darya when it is joined by the Kokcha. The Russians, however, reserve the name Amu Darya for the river when a more important tributary, the Vakhsh, runs into the Ab-i-Panja from the Soviet side.

Practically all along the course of the Amu Darya up to Kunduz the extremely precipitous and rocky Russian bank lies higher than the Afghan bank. Since 1955, the Russians have helped the Afghans develop three river ports, Sher Khan Bandar, Tashgozar, and Dagla Arosa (also called Kelift) opposite the Russian railheads of Nizhniy Pyandzh, Termez, and a Soviet town also named Kelift. The major Afghan port is Sher Khan Bandar (formerly called Qizil Qala and Imam Sahib), north of Kunduz. Goods to and from Afghanistan are transported across the Amu Darya by river steamer (some are paddlewheelers) and tugs pulling *ferrahot* (barges) which ply between the ports. Goods to and from Pakistan and India increasingly flow along these routes.

The Kokcha, 200 miles (320 kilometers) long and major tributary of the Amu Darya, rises on the eastern flanks of the Central Mountains and flows northerly, then westerly to join the Amu Darya. Several small tributaries empty into the Kokcha, among them, the Anjuman and Munjan at 'Iskarzar and the Warduj near Barak, or Baharak.

The 300-mile-long (480 kilometers) Kunduz, only other tributary of the Amu Darya in Afghanistan, has several local names. It is Bamiyan Rud from its source to Bulola, then Surkh Ab between Bulola and Doshi. Joined by the Andarab at Doshi, the stream becomes the Kunduz River. Other minor tributaries which join the Kunduz are the Khanabad, just south of Chahar Darra; the Kamard, which comes in from the west at Doab (Doab Mekh-i-Zarin); Saighan, a main headwaters tributary coming in a little south of the Kamard.

Several important local rivers flow into the Turkestan Plains between Tashkurghan and Aq Chah, but die out before reaching the Amu Darya. The Tashkurghan River, about 120 miles (190 kilometers) long, flows almost due north out of the northern slopes of the Hindu Kush, through the spectacular Tang-i-Tashkurghan, a steep, half-mile-long gorge, before it peters out in the Turkestan Plains north of Khulm (the new name for Tashkurghan; Khulm had been its medieval name).

A winding river, the Balkh Ab (about 300 miles, or 480 kilometers, long) originates in the Zard Sang (Sang-i-Zard) region of the Central

Mountains. Known as the Rud-i-Band-i-Amir until its confluence with the Darra Yusuf, the Balkh Ab twists down the mountains, surrounded by high cliffs most of the way, to the Turkestan Plains, where about twenty irrigation canals (each 12 feet, or 4 meters, wide and 45 feet, or 14 meters, deep), locally known as the Ishkabad canal system, drain off the water before it reaches the Amu Darya. The canal system embraces an area 25 miles (40 kilometers) north–south and 75 miles (121 kilometers) east–west.

The beautiful Band-i-Amir lakes sit near the source of this river.

The Sar-i-Pul River (about 200 miles, or 320 kilometers, long) rises northwest of the Balkh Ab near Qala Shahar (also called Faoghan), being milked dry by irrigation ditches before it reaches Shibarghan. Several smaller rivers feed the winding Sar-i-Pul as it approaches the Ab-i-Safed Tangi. From the right fork, the Darya-yi-Siah enters; from the left fork, the Sazai River enters south of Sar-i-Pul town. The Ab-i-Safed River departs the Sar-i-Pul River at Saiyidabad, then flows north–northwest and dies out a little beyond Shibarghan.

The final important river flowing toward the Amu Darya is the Ab-i-Qaisar, a 200-mile-long (320 kilometers) stream originating near Barqi Rajan (11,473 feet, or 3,500 meters, above sea level). It follows narrow valleys and high cliffs before pouring into the 28-canal Mirabad system of the Turkestan Plains near Daulatabad. From the southwest the Shirin Tagao joins the Ab-i-Qaisar north of Daulatabad; the Maimana River comes in south of Jalaogir.

Hari Rud System

The Hari Rud (about 420 miles, or 650 kilometers, long in Afghanistan) flows almost due west out of a narrow trough between two ranges of the central Hindu Kush mountains, cutting a fertile valley out of the rocks. North of Islam Qala, it turns north, becomes a part of the Afghan–Iranian border for about 100 miles (161 kilometers), and continues into the U.S.S.R. as the Tedzhen.

A single important tributary, the Kao Rud runs west and southwest through alpine meadow lands and enters the Hari Rud from the south near Obeh.

The other major river in the Hari Rud system, the Murghab (about 250 miles, or 350 kilometers, in Afghanistan; another 250 miles in the U.S.S.R.) does not join the Hari Rud but rises in the western Hindu Kush, flowing first north and then west. At Darband-i-Kilrekhta, the river leaves the Band-i-Turkestan mountains through a 180-foot-wide (60 meters) gap. At Bala Murghab the valley has widened to 2 miles (3.2 kilometers), surrounded by low hills to the northeast and high cliffs to the southwest. As Michel (1968) correctly points out, including the Murghab in the Hari Rud system is somewhat contradictory, since the two rivers do not meet. However, once again I plead that I have divided Afghan geographic zones and water systems with an emphasis on integrating culture and ecology.

Several tributaries (mainly the Karawal Khana from the east) meet in confluence south of Maruchak; the Kashan and the Kushk join the Murghab in Russian territory.

Hilmand–Arghandab System

The Hilmand system drains about 40 percent of Afghanistan's land area and may have great potential for development. Many believe that until the Turco–Mongol devastations of the fourteenth century A.D. the Hilmand Valley had been a great bread-basket, but recent unpublished research questions this contention.

The 800-mile-long (1300 kilometers) Hilmand rises out of the southern watershed by the Koh-i-Baba Range near Kabul, and flows in a generally southwesterly direction until it approaches the Iranian border, where it takes a sharp turn north and empties into the marsh lakes and lagoons of the Hamun-i-Hilmand, lying mainly in Iran. Distribution of the Hilmand water is still a major point of controversy between Iran and Afghanistan.

The Hilmand has no outlet to the sea, and millennia of evaporation have produced many salt flats, such as the Gaud-i-Zirreh in the Sistan Basin. Seasonal increments of snow-melt keep the rivers of the Hamun-i-Hilmand fresh, but the lakes overflow and spread salts to other parts of the depression.

The mountains of the Hazarajat hem the Hilmand into narrow valleys with gorge-like cliffs. Above Girishk, the topography changes and wide terraces or former flood plains dominate, until the river breaks out into the deserts of southwestern Afghanistan and flows to and across the Iranian border.

Several tributaries join the Hilmand: Kaj Rud and Tirin in the Hazarajat, Rud-i-Musa Qala south of Kajakai, and several intermittent streams south of Girishk.

The only other major river in the system is the Arghandab (about

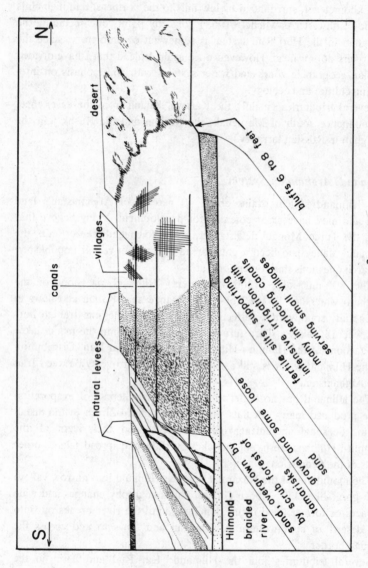

DIAGRAM 2
Idealized Cross-Section of the Hilmand Valley

350 miles, 560 kilometers, long). The headwaters of the Arghandab squat in the granitic masses of the eastern Hazarajat. Less than 50 miles (80 kilometers) north of Qandahar, the Arghandab flows into open country. A low line of hills separates the river from Qandahar and the Patao canal-system which supplies the city with water. The Arghandab eventually reaches the Hilmand at Qala Bist, considerably drained off by intensive irrigation along the way.

Two intermittent streams, the Kushk-i-Nakhud (colloquially pronounced "Kishk-i-Nakhud") and the Garm Ab west of Qandahar, feed into the Arghandab from the north. The Arghastan River, about 175 miles (280 kilometers) long, sits east of and parallel to the Arghandab. Joined by the Lora no. 1 and Kushk-i-Rud, the Arghastan hits the Dori River southeast of Qandahar, and the Dori then flows on to join the Arghandab west of Panjwai.

The Dori, about 200 miles (320 kilometers) long, is called the Lora (a second Lora) near its source in Pakistan. Its name changes to Kadanai as it enters Afghanistan, and the name Dori applies east of Spin Baldak. Irrigation largely dissipates both the Dori and Arghastan before they unite.

The Tarnak, about 200 miles (320 kilometers) long and sandwiched between the Arghandab and Arghastan, waters the Kalat-i-Ghilzai region. Most of the Tarnak has been diverted for irrigation before it joins the Dori.

The Ghazni Rud, about 150 miles (240 kilometers) long, mainly waters the Ghazni area, and its principal tributary, the Jilga, flows out of Paktya.

A brackish lake, Ab-i-Istada, 17 miles (27 kilometers) long by 5 miles (8 kilometers) wide, receives the runoff from the Ghazni Rud. The Ab-i-Istada, the source of Lora no. 1, freezes over in winter.

Farther west and north, the Farah Rud (about 200 miles, or 320 kilometers, long), which has its watershed in the Paropamisus Mountains, flows through the desert to the Hamum-i-Sabari (or Sabiri). The Rud-i-Ghor joins the Farah Rud near Kumrak before it debouches into the stony desert of the Dasht-i-Narmung. Near 32°50′ N., 63°15′ E., the Malmun River joins the Farah Rud.

Originating in the mountains southeast of Herat, the Harut Rud flows past Shindand and in spate reaches the Hamun-i-Sabari. The Rud-i-Gaz joins the Harut at Shindand, and the Khushk Rud, an intermittent stream, dribbles into the Harut during the flood season (December–March). Intensive irrigation by the Persian-speaking farmers considerably milks the Harut and its meager tributaries.

A final important, intermittent river, the Khash Rud (about 300 miles, or 480 kilometers; active only during the melt-water season), flows from its source in the western Hazarajat to Chakansur during the flood season. Near Dilaram, the Khash Rud becomes a series of isolated pools during the dry season. Even the more affluent Arghandab can dry up into a series of unconnected pools in unusually dry years.

Manmade water-systems called *qanat* (an Arabic term) in Iran and Afghanistan, and *karez* in Pashto,[1] exist throughout eastern, southern, and southwestern Afghanistan. Open-ditch irrigation is much easier to implement in the northern Turkestan Plains with its relatively shallow water-table. From the air, the *qanat* of Iran, Afghanistan, and West Pakistan look like neat lines of anthills leading from the foothills across the desert zones to the greenery of the villages and towns. Actually a line of "wells" (shafts) connected by tunnels to intercept the water table, the *qanat*-system brings water to the surface for use in irrigation (see Diagram 3). Part-time specialists (they are farmers first), such as the Andar Pushtun of eastern Afghanistan, dig the wells and tunnels, using lighted candles or lanterns to line up the excavators as they dig toward the next well. Excavators use hard ceramic hoops to reenforce weak strata. The *qanat* system must be cleaned annually because of silt accumulation. Goatskin buckets attached to a windless contraption haul the originally excavated dirt and the later accumulated silts to the surface.

The work is dangerous, for shafts of 30 to 50 feet (9 to 15 meters) are common. Some shafts reach depths of over 100 feet (30 meters), but without the extensive *qanat* system, agriculture in marginal areas would be greatly reduced. Only the highest shaft leading up the hillside intercepts the water-table. Then, guided by the tunnels, the water spills out onto the irrigation ditches and fields.

Kabul River System

The Kabul River System forms a part of the greater Indus River system. The Kabul River (about 225 miles, or 350 kilometers, long) flows from its headwaters at Sar Cheshma (or Sar Chisma) just east of the entrance to the Unai Pass (about 14,000 feet, or 4,270 meters, above sea level), through the Kabul Valley and then into some of the more treacherous Afghan territory, including the Tang-i-Gharu, on its way

[1] Called *foggara* in north Africa; *feledj* in Oman; also called *khariz* in Iraq and Iran. See Wolski (1965) for more details.

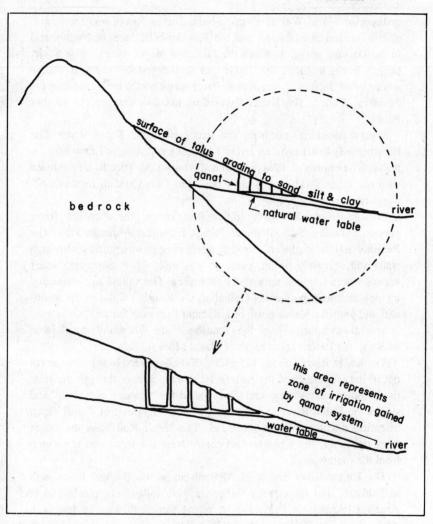

DIAGRAM 3
Idealized Cross-Section of Qanat System

to the post-World War II German-built dam at Sarobi and the hydro-electric station at Mahipar, and the Russian-built dams at Naghlu and in the Darunta gorge. Through the Jalalabad plains, where a new Soviet project hopes to make the desert and semi-desert bloom, near Dakka southeast of Jalalabad, the Kabul River turns north, then east into the Peshawar Valley. The Kabul River does not flow through the Khyber Pass.

Several tributaries reinforce the strong perennial Kabul River. The Panjsher and two Laghman rivers (Alishang and Alingar) flow into the Kabul River north of Jalalabad, and the Surkh Ab (not to be confused with the other Surkh Ab, part of the Amu Darya system in north Afghanistan) from the south.

Coming from an entirely different direction, the Panjsher River (about 200 miles, 320 kilometers, long) rises near Anjuman Pass. The Panjsher trends southward through alternating narrow gorges with high walls and relatively broad, open (⅓–¾ mile, ¾–1 kilometer, wide) valleys where terraced agriculture flourishes. The valleys are connected by high mountain passes. At Gulbahar, the Panjsher shifts to the southeast and joins the Kabul north of Lataband Pass near Sarobi.

Several tributaries join the Panjsher: the Ghorband near Jabal us-Seraj, the Parian Dara north of Dasht-i-Rewat.

The Logar River (about 125 miles, 200 kilometers, long) flows north out of the mountains of the eastern Hazarajat, courses through the relatively wide Logar Valley, sometimes called the "granary of Kabul," and strikes the Kabul River at 6.2 miles (4 kilometers) east of Kabul. Open irrigation ditches and *qanat* abound. The Shiniz Rud joins the Logar from the south, the Khawat Rud comes from the west, and the Kajao from the southwest.

The Kunar River begins in Afghanistan as the Bashgal River high in Nuristan, and flows lazily through a wide valley until pinched in at Arnawai (Arandu in Pakistan). A raging torrent through its length in Afghanistan, the Bashgal joins the Kunar River proper, pushing through the mountains of Chitral (also the name of a river) in Pakistan. Below Chiga Serai (now Asadabad), the river valley widens about 1½ miles (2.4 kilometers). The flood-plain near the Jalalabad Valley exceeds one mile. The Kunar feeds many canals and *karez*. The Kunar joins the Kabul near Jalalabad.

CHAPTER 3

cAreas Drastically cAffected by Man

STATISTICS on Afghanistan abound, but most consist of "intelligent estimates," i.e., wild guesses based on inadequate data, and practically all figures given in this book must be considered to be such intelligent estimates. With this caution in mind we can say that the total area (see Map 5) of Afghanistan is about 63 million hectares (245,000 square miles). Of the total area about 12 percent is cultivated annually because of water shortages.[1] The irrigated land is called *abi,* while dry farmed land is *lalmi.* The *lalmi* area consists of about 1.3 million hectares and supports wheat and barley primarily. (One hectare equals 2.47 acres, but some Afghan villagers measure land in *jerib,* or approximately .5 acres. Chart 4 indicates agricultural productivity from 1966 to 1970. For a list of domesticated plants in Afghanistan see Appendix A. Map 5 graphically illustrates the areas of intensive cultivation.)

The most extensive areas of cultivation currently exist north of the Hindu Kush mountains. Irrigation projects now being developed in the south and southwest could possible change this picture appreciably in the next decade or so. The geology of most inhabitable areas (e.g., the Kabul Valley, Hilmand–Arghandab Valley, Hari Rud Valley, and the Turkestan Plains of the Amu Darya) exhibits reasonably similar Neogene and younger deposits (conglomerates, gravels, sands, and loess), which should make it easier for planners and technicians to integrate regional and national projects.

[1] For a detailed discussion see Michel's chapter on "Agriculture" in Wilber (1962, 221–41). Three recent works are extremely important: *Agricultural Development in Afghanistan with Special Emphasis on Wheat* (1967); Pickett (1967); Dada and Pickett (1969). Also see Vavilov and Bukinich (1929) and Volk (1954).

43

CHART 4
Agriculture: 1966–70

Agricultural Area (in 000 of hectares[1])	1966-67	1967-68	1968-69	1969-70
Total possible cultivable area	14,000	14,000	14,000	14,000
Total under cultivation (including fallow land)	7,835	7,844	7,844	7,844
Total irrigated area	5,331	5,340	5,340	5,340
Total non-irrigated area	2,504	2,504	2,504	2,504
Main Crops				
Wheat	2,346	2,063	2,063	2,070
Corn	500	453	453	457
Barley	350	316	316	317
Rice	222	206	206	206
Cotton	48	55	55	55.1
Sugar beet	4	4.5	4.5	4.6
Sugar cane	2	2	2	2.5
Oilseeds	150	41	41	41.5
Vegetables	110	91	91	91.7
Fruit	78	135	135	136
Others	–	–	–	39

Source: *Survey of Progress: 1969-70*, Department of Statistics, Ministry of Planning, Royal Government of Afghanistan, Kabul, October, 1970, S-22. Note discrepancies in figures between 1966-67 and 1967-68, caused by the introduction of new statistical procedures, the accuracy of which remain to be tested through time.

[1] Based on land taxes collected, therefore, too low.

CHART 4 (*continued*)

Yield per hectare (in tons)	1966-67	1967-68	1968-69	1969-70
Wheat	0.9	1.1	1.1	1.2
Corn	1.4	1.7	1.7	1.7
Barley	1.1	1.1	1.1	1.2
Rice	1.5	1.9	2.0	2.0
Cotton	1.2	1.2	1.3	1.5
Sugar beets	14.0	14.0	13.7	14.8
Sugar cane	25.5	23.7	23.7	24.0
Oilseeds	0.4	.9	.9	.9
Vegetables	5.3	7.0	7.2	7.3
Fruit	4.7	6.0	6.1	6.3

Total Yield (in 000 tons)	1966-67	1967-68	1968-69	1969-70
Wheat	2,033	2,241	2,354	2,450
Corn	720	768	773	785
Barley	375	358	361	365
Rice	337	396	402	407
Cotton	61	69	71	85
Sugar beets	56	67	62	68
Sugar cane	51	57	57	60
Oilseeds	55	35	36	37
Vegetables	590	638	654	671
Fruit	372	826	834	842
Others	–	39	39	40

MAJOR AREAS
UNDER CULTIVATION

COINCIDENT WITH AREAS OF
MAXIMUM POPULATION DENSITY

ISHKASHIM

FAIZABAD

JALALABAD

KUNDUZ

KABUL

KHOST

BAGHLAN

DOAB

BAMIYAN

GHAZNI

MOQUR

MAZAR-I-SHARIF

SAR-I-PUL

KALAT-I-GHILZAI

ANDKHUI

SHIBARGHAN

QALA SHAHARAK

GANDAHAR

DAULATABAD

MAIMANA

JAM

OBEH

DILARAM

LASHKAR GAH (BOST)

SHINDAND

HERAT

FARAH

| 0 | 50 | 100 | 150 | 200 MI. |
| 0 | 100 | 200 | 300 KM |

CHAPTER 4

𝒟omesticated 𝒜nimals

DOMESTICATED animals also play a major role in modification to natural vegetation and the geographical scene in general (see Chart 5 for the numbers of livestock in the country today).

Horses (*asp,* Dari; *as,* Pashto, male; *aspa,* Pashto, female)[1]: Prestige animals, horses exist all over Afghanistan. The largest, about 14 hands, are found in the Herat region. Horses in Turkestan, Qataghan, and Badakhshan are little more than overgrown ponies, but are as sure-footed as mountain goats on precipitous trails. Hazarajat horses and some in the Turkestan plains may have an Arab strain. Highly prized Waziri horses (with diagnostic inward, crooked ears) are raised in Ghazni and Katawaz. Pack horses or small ponies, *yabu,* raised most commonly in Turkestan, can carry loads up to 200 pounds (91 kilos) at about 3½ miles (5.5 kilometers) per hour.

Donkeys (*khar,* D.; *khar,* P., male; *khra,* P., fem.): The most popular beast of burden in Afghanistan is the donkey. These little animals can transport about 150 pounds (58 kilos) at 2.5 miles (4 kilometers) per hour. They graze anywhere and require little fodder. The best breed is reputedly raised near Qandahar. Many villagers transport large loads on donkeys to town bazaars for sale and return riding bareback.

Mules (*jater,* D; *kacher,* P.): The army uses mules to haul its mountain artillery units. In the southern foothills Afghans use mules as pack

---

[1] In Dari, the term *madah* means female animal, and, in general, is used as a prefix: e.g., *madyan* (mare); *madah shotor* (she-camel). For female donkeys and bitches, the prefix *machah* can also be used: i.e., *machah khar* and *machah sag.* Exceptions exist: e.g., *gawmish* refers to both male and female water buffalo; *gusfand* (ram), *mish* (ewe).

Pashto nouns have gender, and the term for a specific female animal is usually formed by adding a suffix to the male root: *ukh* (male camel), *ukha* (she-camel); *wuz* (buck goat), *wuza* (doe). Again, exceptions exist: *peseh* (ram), *maygah* (ewe). For all terms, pronunciations vary with regional dialects: *horus* (rooster in Qandaharian dialect), *kharus* (rooster in Ningraharian dialect); *peshi* (tomcat in Qandaharian), *nerpish* (tomcat in Ningraharian); *peshei* (female cat in Qandaharian), *peshau* (female cat in Ningraharian).

In most areas certain animals have particular prestige (e.g., horses in the north) or economic (cattle and goats in Nuristan) importance. Many local names exist to differentiate the animal by sex, age, color, shape of horns, etc.

47

CHART 5
Domesticated Animals[1] (In millions of animals)

	1967-68	1968-69	1969-70
Sheep (excluding qarakul)	15.0	15.0	15.0
Qarakul sheep (Persian lamb)	6.0	6.49	6.5
Cattle	3.6	3.6	3.7
Goats	3.2	3.0[2]	3.2
Donkeys	1.2	1.3	1.3
Camels	.3	.3	.3
Horses	.3	4	.45
Hens	5.5	5.57	6.0

Source: *Survey of Progress: 1969-1970*, Department of Statistics, Ministry of Planning, Royal Government of Afghanistan, Kabul, October 1970, S-22.

[1] Based on livestock taxes collected; therefore, too low.
[2] Where those 200,000 goats disappeared to during 1968-69 is a mystery.

animals. Two types occur: the heavier *pindi* (named after the mules of the Punjab, i.e., Rawalpindi) and the lighter *kashmiri*. Both are raised in Chakari, a village of specialists in the Logar Valley.

Camels (*shotor*, D.; *ukh*, P. male; *ukha*, P., fem.): The classic transport of the Central Asian nomad is the camel, usually the one-humped dromedary. These nasty-tempered beasts can carry loads of 400 pounds (182 kilos) in the plains and 300 pounds (137 kilos) in the mountains. Some Bactrian, or two-humped, camels can be found in Badakhshan and Wakhan. Another famous breed of camel, the Baluchi, raised by the Baluch nomads of the southwest and west and noted for their endurance and speed, participated in the nineteenth-century, long-range raiding caravans of the Baluch into Central Asia. The British brought *pax Britannica* into the area and ended the raiding.

Sheep (*gusfand*, D.; *peseh*, P., male; *maygah*, P., fem.): Fat-tailed sheep and the more usual short-tailed sheep (*turki*) are common in Afghanistan. Most sheep usually have monochromatic black, white, gray, or brown wool; white sheep appear to be more common in the south and west. The Persian lamb (*qarakul*) of the north, one of Afghanistan's major exports, is either black, brown, gray, or, occasionally, white. The golden-brown is the most highly prized among the Afghans for making prestige hats.

Goats (*buz* D.; *wuz*, P., male; *wuza*, P., fem.): Afghan goats, short-horned and long-haired, are indiscriminately herded with sheep.

Cattle (*gaw*, D.; *ghwa*, P., male, *ghwaya*, P., fem.): Cattle types vary in geographic regions. On the eastern slopes of the Hindu Kush, they resemble the small-humped hill-cattle of India. The cows are good milkers, though the oxen, too small for heavy work, are used as light transport, plowing, and threshing. (Afghan peasants also use the horse and even the camel—sometimes in combination—for threshing.) In the north, cattle are larger, and the oxen prove to be good draft animals; the cows are poor milkers compared to those in the mountains. Cattle in Qandahar and Farah lowlands more closely resemble American breeds in type and milk potential.

Water Buffalo (*gawmish*, D.; *maykh*, P., male; *maykha*, P., fem.): Water buffalo exist primarily as plow animals in the Jalalabad and Qandahar areas. Twentieth-century Pushtun migrations to northern Afghanistan brought small herds of water buffalo into the Qataghan-Kunduz area.

Yak: Only the Kirghiz and other Pamiri peoples use the yak, mainly east of Qala Panja, the geographic dividing line between the Wakhan Corridor and the Pamir Mountains.

Chickens (*morgh*, D., general term; *horus*, D., rooster; *churgh* and *horas*, P., rooster; *churgha*, P., hen): Both villagers and nomads keep a rather scrawny variety of chicken. Eggs (*tokhm*, Persian; *hagheyeh*, P.) are important in the diet of the Afghan, and chicken is often an essential ingredient in pilau.

Ducks (*morghabi*, D.; *heylai*, P., one term): Occasionally, Afghans raise ducks, particularly the Peking duck, introduced in the 1950s by J. Christy Wilson, Jr., Protestant minister to the foreign community in Kabul.

Turkeys (*filmorgh*, literally, "elephant bird," D.; no Pashto term exists): Afghan farmers near Kabul raise turkeys mainly to grace the plates of foreigners.

Dogs (*sag*, D.; *spay*, P., male; *spie*, P., fem.): The Afghans seldom treat dogs kindly, because Muslim custom considers dogs unclean. Europeans have been known to spend time in local jails for taking issue with an Afghan flogging his dog. Three general types of Afghan dogs exist. Large mastiff-type creatures live in villages and travel with caravans as watchdogs. Two names are used for these dogs: *sag-i-ramah* (*da*

49

ramay spay, P.), "dog of the herd" or *sag-i-turkestani,* or Turkestan dog. The Afghan nomads sometimes paint the *sag-i-ramah* with the same ownership designs as sheep in order, so they say, to confuse wolves and other predators. Vicious animals, *sag-i-ramah* sometimes attack a man on horseback. In nomadic camps, a nomad cannot approach another man's tent in safety unless the owner holds his dog. These dogs, however, are afraid of rocks, and anyone approached should not panic and run, for he will be attacked immediately. The best defense is to pick up a large rock, or pretend to pick up a rock if none can be found. Usually, the dog stops advancing, but continues to snarl and howl. The owner will always come to check on the noise.

Afghans train *sag-i-ramah* for fighting, and often fight among themselves over disputed decisions or if anyone injures their dogs, an exception to their usual dislike of dogs.

An urban pet, called *papi,* at least superficially resembles the spitz of southern Siberia and farther north. The Afghan hound, *tazi,* exists in Afghanistan primarily as a desert hunting-dog and will be discussed later (p. 215).

Packs of dogs nocturnally roam the streets of the larger cities, particularly Kabul. Periodically, the police liberally distribute poisoned meat throughout Kabul. The survivors, however, live quite well off the land. I tend to grade the level of poverty in Asian cities by examining the state of the urban dog-population. Those in Kabul appear fatter and healthier than most I have seen elsewhere in Asia.

Cats (*peshak,* D.; *peshi,* P., male; *peshei,* P., fem.): The alley cat is most common, and usually subjected to the same treatment as dogs. Afghans prize true Persian cats, which receive the same good treatment accorded the Afghan hound.

CHAPTER 5

Fauna

AFGHANISTAN has few endemics (animals found there and nowhere else), but contains elements of the major surrounding faunal zones, according to Kullmann (*Science,* 1965), who states that the following assemblages are represented in Afghanistan: Palaearctic, Southwestern Asia, India, Turkestan, Himalayan. (Dr. Kullmann established a new zoo in Kabul, officially opened in August, 1967, which contains, among others, the following Afghan specimens: snow leopard and macaques from Nuristan, gazelle, ibex, markhor, wolf, fox, wildcat, hyena.) See Appendix B.

Most Afghans pride themselves on being outdoorsmen and hunting is a great pastime. Only among the Sayyad, the hunter-fishermen of the Hilmand, do such activities have major economic importance, although leopard, fox, otter, and other furs are sold either as blankets or coats in some city and town bazaars.

In general, the upland fauna of the Himalayas occupy the mountainous central core: snowcock, markhor, pica or piping hare, ibex, snow leopard, brown bear, with, in the Pamir, an occasional Siberian tiger, a much larger cat than its tropical cousin in Bengal. The Marco Polo sheep (*Ovis polii*) is also limited to the high Pamir.

The Turkestan Plains support a steppe fauna replete with bustards and susliks. The southern and western deserts exhibit an extension of the Iranian Plateau—Southwest Asian and Palaearctic fauna with strong elements of Caspian fauna: gazelle, coursers, swallow plovers, flamingo, and, in the *jangal,* wild pig. Along the southern borders and up into the Vale of Jalalabad penetrate some Indian fauna, including an occasional mongoose, leopard, and cheetah. The macaque also occupies the forested areas of Nuristan near the Pakistani border.

Fish (Berg, 1948; Edmonds, 1968) abound in the streams, but few are exploited. A variety of German brown trout (*Salmo truta oxenesus*), locally called *mahi-kholdar,* swims in the streams north of the Hindu Kush, with the exception of the Hari Rud. Since June, 1966, Bulgarian specialists at the Qargha fisheries, near Kabul, have released about 500,000 rainbow trout fingerlings in the Salang and Panjsher rivers. The rainbows average 6 to 8 inches' (15–20 centimeters') growth per year.

Barbels (carp: *Barbus capito conocephalus*) swim in streams both north and south of the Hindu Kush.[1] A tasty, but bony, fish called *shir-mahi* (milk fish), the local barbel, varies in color. The northern variety have yellow bellies; the southern, white.

The *laka* (*Glyptosternum reticulatum*), found in the warmer waters of the Amu Darya as well as the northern streams, is a primitive form of European catfish which grows up to seven feet in length.

Fresh-water crabs occur throughout the country and, along with many minnows and small fish, help keep the village canals (*juy*) and streams relatively uncontaminated.

The most widely distributed game-birds include such native upland, open-scrub species as the chukar partridge (*qawk*), a red-billed, red-legged species the size of a small chicken used for fighting as well as food. The little *sisi* partridge, scarcely larger than North American quail, and the even smaller *bodena* (a lark), also appear. Sparrows are also eaten.

In sparsely wooded areas, the francolin (black partridge) occurs, and pheasants live in some eastern and southern valleys. The large snow-cock, or snow-pheasant, breeds and feeds in the high mountain country just below the snow-line in the east. In winter, flocks of the little migratory quail come down from the north, and feed in the grassy plains and wetter valleys. The flamingo breeds in the Ab-i-Istada area during the winter.

Several species of the bustard (size of a small grouse), and the dove-like sand grouse, pass through Afghanistan.

About eighty species of wild pigeons and doves occur in Afghanistan, particularly in the plains and foothills, concentrated near human habitations and sometimes along the desert fringes. Waterfowl arrive during early-spring and early-fall migrations. The migratory birds usually take one of two routes from South Siberia, Pamir, and Badakhshan: either through the central mountain passes, or around the mountains along the western foothills. Many rest in Sistan (Hamun-i-Hilmand, Hamun-i-Sabari and other marshy areas) before continuing on their way south

---

[1] The Extension Department of the Ministry of Agriculture and Irrigation, with financial and technical assistance from the People's Republic of China, established a fish research and breeding center at Darunta in 1967. After introducing four varieties of carp, the center offered 70,000 kilos of fish for sale in the markets of Kabul and other urban centers, so the importance of fish in the diet may increase (*Kabul Times,* December 22, 1969).

to Arabia, East Africa, or India. They return along the same route in the spring. Ducks, geese, teals, snipes, plovers, pelicans, herons, grebes, storks, swans, and sandpipers gather in season. Among others, the white-headed Brahmani duck nests in Sistan. The dainty demoiselle crane simply rests while passing through.

The Sayyad (Baluch living in the Sistan swamps and specializing in hunting and fishing) net the birds coming and going. They hang nets in the marshy reeds and the birds become entangled on landing. The Sayyad use the same nets to catch fish from their reed or dugout canoes.

The birds flying the central route are often forced to low altitudes when fog or spring rain block the passes. In March, 1965, I tape-recorded a large flock of demoiselle cranes circling over Kabul because fog blocked its route over the mountains.

Birds of prey exist in sizeable numbers and species. Hawks, falcons, and owls occur almost everywhere, but particularly in the plains and scrub country. Large vultures idly circle the air looking for carrion, and many eagles (including the golden eagle) scan the hills and mountains.

The commonest small birds of the plains and semi-deserts include larks (*bodena* and others) and pipits. Near human habitations, crows (including the hooded crow), jays, and rooks abound. Where food is plentiful, myriad series of small birds, such as flycatchers, warblers, sparrows, swallows, shrikes, and others occur.

The nightingale (*bulbul*), fabled songster of Middle Eastern poetry, sings sweetly in the summer, and the colorful crested hoopoe adds a splash of color to the landscape. The magpie is ubiquitous throughout the area.

Paludan lists 389 species of birds recorded in Afghanistan, and he states that "231 [of these] may be assumed to breed in the country" (Paludan, 1959, 322). The bulk belong to the Palaeartic faunal assembly.

Large land turtles occur in Afghanistan, even in Kabul. Frogs and toads also exist in great numbers. A dozen or so species of lizards (including the large, up to six-feet-long, monitor lizard) can be seen in the desert fringes and dry foothills. Snakes are abhorred by Muslims and Christians alike for their sinister influence in the Garden of Eden and Afghanistan has two species of cobra, the little, deadly neurotoxic krait, and many vipers, including Russell's viper.

Insects abound. Mosquitoes spread malaria, and other potential menaces (fleas, ticks, lice, roaches) live parasitically in areas of human habitation. Flies and biting gnats cover the country, and the praying mantis twists and turns in the gardens of urban centers, as well as in the rural areas.[2]

Spiders (non-poisonous) and scorpions (poisonous) occur everywhere.

[2] For those interested in further details, thirty-four separate reports on the *Insecta, Chelicerata, Araneidea,* and *Pisces* collected by the Third Danish Expedition to Central Asia have been published in *Vidensk. Medd. fra Dansk naturh. Foren* in various issues from 1950 through 1966.

PART II. THE PEOPLE

AFGHANISTAN'S people[1] rival the topography in ethnic, linguistic, and physical variety. Basically, the country is a zone of predominately Muslim, Indo-European speakers of the Mediterranean sub-stock of the great Caucasoid race[2], which extends from Gibraltar and Tangier on both sides of the Mediterranean, and moves through Anatolia, Iran, and southern Afghanistan into northwest Pakistan. A Spaniard, Sicilian, Greek, Turk, Arab, or Sephardic Jew would be physically at home in most of Afghanistan. Only distinctive tribal and ethnic clothing, language, religion, and other cultural impediments make the difference.

But, like the United States, and for a much longer period, Afghanistan has been a cultural, as well as physical, melting-pot: Persian, Central Asian, Sino-Siberian, European (Hellenistic, Roman), Indian, Turkish, Arab, and Mongol influences rose, fell, and blended.

[1] Most writing on Afghan people and culture is simply a footnote to Elphinstone's classic work (1815). Writers on Afghanistan have either copied Elphinstone or copied those who have copied Elphinstone. Several post-World War II anthropological researches in Afghanistan (and neighboring areas of West Pakistan) have greatly added to our reservoir of knowledge. Among them: Amoss (1967); Bacon (1951, 1958); Barth (1956, 1959); Buddruss (1960); Cammann (1957); Davydov (1963, 1969); Demont and Centlivres (1967); Dupaigne (1968); L. Dupree (1954, 1955, 1956, 1961a, 1964c, 1965a, 1968c, *A.U.F.S. Report* LD-5-63); Edelberg (1960, 1965); Edelberg and Ferdinand (1955/56, 1958); Ferdinand (1956, 1957, 1959abcd, 1960ab, 1962, 1963ab, 1964, 1966/67); Grötzbach (1965, 1966); Hahn (1964, 1965); Janata (1962/63ab, 1963, 1969); Jeanneret (1964); S. Jones (1966, 1967); Kieffer (1967); Klimburg (1966); Kussmaul (1965); Palwal (1968, 1969abc); Pehrson (1966); Schurmann (1962); Siiger (1963); Snoy (1962, 1965). Russian-readers are referred to Kukhtina (1965) and the periodic catalogues of the Library of the Institute of the Peoples of Asia, the U.S.S.R. Academy of Science, Moscow.

[2] Race in this context is merely descriptive, referring to loosely identifiable physical features, and not meant to imply social, physical, mental, cultural, psychological, or sexual inferiority.

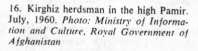
15. Nurzai Durrani Pushtun nomad at Dilaram. Sub-specialty of this group is raising Afghan hounds (*tazi*). December, 1950

16. Kirghiz herdsman in the high Pamir. July, 1960. *Photo: Ministry of Information and Culture, Royal Government of Afghanistan*

17. Besud Hazara from Panjao on left; Safi Pushtun from Laghman on right. Both are in Kabul to do seasonal work as construction laborers. November, 1963

CHAPTER 6

Ethnic Groups

AFGHANISTAN is not a self-contained ethnic unit, and its national culture is not uniform (see Map 6 and Chart 6). Few of its ethnic groups are indigenous. All Pushtun, for example, are not Afghan citizens. Almost an equal number live in the Tribal Agencies and the North-West Frontier Province of Pakistan. Tajik, Uzbak, Turkoman, and Kirghiz have their own Soviet Socialist Republics in the Soviet Union. Most inhabitants of the extreme western part of Afghanistan, geographically and culturally an extension of the Iranian Plateau, are simply Persian-speaking Farsiwan (also called Parsiwan or Parsiban) farmers. Baluch (or Baluchi, which usually refers to their language) live in the southwestern corner of Afghanistan, northwestern Pakistan, and southeastern Iran; several large groups also live in the Turkoman S.S.R.

The Brahui (Dravidian-speakers, often Australoid in appearance) live in the same general area as the Baluch. In Pakistan, the Brahui divide the Baluch of Kalat State into two major local groups.

Nuristani, Kohistani, Gujar, and other small groups of mountaineer sheep/goat herders, dairymen, and farmers occupy the rugged mountain zones of eastern Afghanistan and Pakistani Chitral. About 3,000 of the Chitrali Kafirs still practice a non-Muslim religion. The Wakhi-Pamiri groups overlap into the mountains of Pakistan, and the Barbari (or Berberi) of eastern Iran probably have an Aimaq or Hazara origin.

Three physical types are present in Afghanistan: Caucasoid (mainly Pushtun, Tajik, Baluch, Nuristani), Mongoloid (mainly Hazara, Aimaq, Turkoman, Uzbak, Kirghiz; see Woodd-Walker et al., 1967), and modified Australoid (Brahui). Most Dravidian-speakers (Dravidian is a major Indian language family) live south of the Narbada River in India. Mystery shrouds the comings and goings of the Brahui in Pakistan and southwestern Afghanistan. Either they were left behind when the Indo-Europeans invaded from the north in the second millennium B.C. (or earlier), or they filtered back after the situation somewhat stabilized. Many work today as tenant farmers for the overlord Baluch in southwestern Afghanistan, but the Brahui in Kalat State (Pakistan) still prize their relative independence from outside interference.

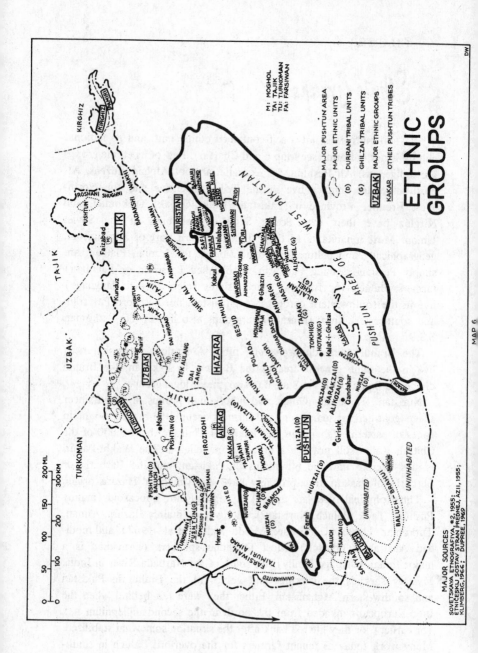

ETHNIC GROUPS

M: MOGHOL
TA: TAJIK
TU: TURKOMAN
FA: FARSIWAN

- - - MAJOR PUSHTUN AREA
MAJOR ETHNIC UNITS
(D) DURRANI TRIBAL UNITS
(G) GHILZAI TRIBAL UNITS
UZBAK MAJOR ETHNIC GROUPS
KAKAR OTHER PUSHTUN TRIBES

MAP 6

MAJOR SOURCES
SOVETSKAYA ETNOGRAFIYA #2, 1955;
ETNIČESKIJ SOSTAV STRAN PREDNEJ, AZII, 1955;
KLIMBERG, 1966; DUPREE, 1969

CHART 6
Ethnic Groups in Afghanistan

Ethnic Group[3]	Language[1]	Religion	Comments[2]
Pushtun[3]	Pashto dialects (I/E)	Hanafi Sunni, except Turi (Shi'a)	About 6.5 million in Afghanistan; approximately an equal number in Pakistan. Basic physical type: Mediterranean substock of Caucasoid stock.
Tajik	Dari, Tajiki dialects (I/E)	Mainly Hanafi Sunni; some (especially in north) Isma'iliya Shi'a	About 3.5 million in northern Afghanistan; concentrated in northeast where they usually refer to themselves by the valley or region in which they live. Those living in areas dominated by other ethnic groups simply refer to themselves as Tajik. Term "Tajik" from old Persian "Taz" or "Taj," meaning "Arab." Basic physical type: Mediterranean substock; Mongoloid attributes increase from south to north.
Farsiwan (Parsiwan or Parsiban)	Dari (I/E)	Imami Shi'a	About 600,000 mainly agriculturalists, living near the Iranian border, Herat, Qandahar, Ghazni, and other southern and western Afghan towns. Often mistakenly referred to as Tajik in literature. Basic physical type: Mediterranean substock.
Qizilbash	Dari (I/E)	Imami Shi'a	Primarily an urban group scattered throughout Afghanistan. Descendents of military and administrative personnel left behind by Nadir Shah Afshar in the 18th century A.D. Today many hold important bureaucratic and professional appointments. Among the more literate groups in Afghanistan. Some use, the Shi'a practice of taqiya (dissimilation) and pass for Sunni in order to escape discrimination. Basic physical type: Mediterranean substock.

CHART 6 (continued)

Ethnic Group	Language[1]	Religion	Comments[2]
Hazara	Hazaragi (Dari dialect, I/E)	Some are Imami Shi'a; some are Isma'iliya Shi'a; a few are Sunni	About 870,000. Probably arrived in Afghanistan between A.D. 1229-1447 (Bacon, 1951), and are not descendents of army of Genghis Khan, as popularly believed. Basic physical type: Mongoloid, some Mediterranean admixture in ethnic gray zones.
Aimaq	Dari dialects (I/E) with much Turkic (U/A) vocabulary	Hanafi Sunni	About 800,000 in Afghanistan. Usually incorrectly referred to as "Chahar" ("four" in Dari) Aimaq (Turkish "tribe"). People themselves never use "chahar," unless prompted by interrogator. They refer to themselves with tribal designations (Map 6). Some slough over into Iran and are called "Barbari" or "Berberi." Basic physical type: Mongoloid (less so than Hazara), much Mediterranean admixture.
Moghol	Many speak Dari (I/E) today, but vocabulary contains many Mongolian loan words. Old men and women still consider Mogholi (U/A) to be mother tongue of group. Some southern Moghol speak Pashto	Hanafi Sunni	Originally concentrated in Ghor, several thousand Moghol now live scattered through central and north Afghanistan, probably breaking up about 125 years ago (Schurmann, 1962, 15), or even earlier (Ferdinand, 1964, 176). The Moghol may be the descendents of the armies of Genghis Khan. Basic physical type: Mongoloid with occasional Mediterranean admixture; i.e., blue or mixed eye combinations with blond or reddish hair.

CHART 6 (*continued*)

Ethnic Group	Language[1]	Religion	Comments[2]
Uzbak	Uzbaki (or Jagatai) Turkic (U/A) dialects	Hanafi Sunni	About one million (mainly sedentary agriculturalists) in north Afghanistan. Refer to themselves with old tribal names: Haraki, Kamaki, Mangit, Ming, Shesh Qara, Taimus (also see Jarring, 1939). Basic physical type: Mongoloid with much Mediterranean admixture in ethnic gray zones.
Turkoman	Turkic (U/A) dialects	Hanafi Sunni	About 125,000 (primarily semisedentary and seminomadic) in north Afghanistan. Brought in *qarakul* sheep (Persian lamb) and Turkoman rug industry in the 1920s during the Basmachi revolts against the Bolsheviks. Major groups are: Tekke, Yomud, Tariq, Lakai (Herat area); Tekke, Ersari (Aq Chah area); Saroq, Chakra (Andkhui); Salor (Maimana); Ersari, Mawri (Daulatabad); Salor (Maruchak). Basic physical type: aquiline Mongoloid.
Kirghiz	Kipchak Turkic (U/A) dialects	Hanafi Sunni	Several thousand transhumants live in the Afghan Pamir Mountains. Basic physical type: Mongoloid.
Pamiri (Ghalcha or Mountain Tajik)	Various Pamiri or East Iranian (I/E) dialects	Some Isma'iliya Shi'a; some Hanafi Sunni	Several thousand mountain farmers, living mainly in Badakhshan, Wakhan. Major groups: Parachi, Munji, Roshani, Sanglichi, Shughni, Yaghnobi, Ormuri, Wakhi, Iskashimi. Basic physical type: Mediterranean substock, with Mongoloid admixture.

CHART 6 (continued)

Ethnic Group	Language[1]	Religion	Comments[2]
Baluch (Baluchi)	Baluchi (I/E)	Hanafi Sunni	About 100,000 in Afghanistan. Caravaneers, nomads (and slavers until the British ended slavery in the 19th century), the Baluch are now semisedentary or seminomadic; some live in NW Afghanistan, others travel from Sistan to Herat in summer, returning to Sistan in winter. Most Baluch are Rakhshani, and main sub-groups include: Sanjarani, Nahrui, Yamarzai, Sumarzai, Gumshazai, Sarabandi, Miangul, Harut, Salarzai. A specialist Baluch group of hunter-fishermen (called the Sayyad) live in the Sistan swamps. They are not a separate ethnic group as previously reported. Some Sayyad are Farsiwan. Another Baluch group, the Gaudar, specializes in cattle raising. Basic physical type: Mediterranean substock with more brachycephalic tendencies.
Brahui	Brahui (D); most also speak either Pashto or Baluchi	Hanafi Sunni	About 200,000 in southwestern Afghanistan, usually tenant farmers or hired herders for Baluch or Pushtun khans. Main Brahui groups include: Aidozi, Lowarzi, Yagizi, Zirkandi, Mamasani. Brahui often refer to themselves as a Baluch sub-group. Basic physical types: Veddoid, with much Mediterranean admixture.
Nuristani	Kafiri (I/E) dialects	Hanafi Sunni	About 100,000 in eastern Afghanistan. Amir Abdur Rahman Khan forcibly converted the Afghan Kafirs to Islam in the late 19th century A.D. Refer to themselves by the valleys or region in which they live: e.g., Waigali, Wamai, Krueni (G. Robertson, 1900). Basic physical type: Mediterranean, with about one-third blondism in the population.

CHART 6 (*continued*)

Ethnic Group	Language[1]	Religion	Comments[2]
Kohistani	Dardic (I/E)	Hanafi Sunni	Distinct linguistic groups on the southern fringes of Nuristan: Pashai, Gawarbati, Sawoji, Deghani, Kuwar (Gabr).[4] Most also speak Pashto. Basic physical type: Mediterranean.
Gujar	Dialect related to Hindustani (I/E)	Hanafi Sunni	Cattlemen-farmers on eastern fringes of Nuristan. Most also speak Pashto. Basic physical type: Mediterranean.
Jat Guji (called Gujar in North) Changar Musali, Chalu, Sheikh Mohmandi (traders only; claim Arab descent)	Dialects related to Hindustani (I/E)	Hanafi Sunni	"Gypsy-like" bands of tradesmen, tinkers, musicians, fortune tellers. Most speak Dari and/or Pashto. Many claim to be of "Arab" descent. Basic physical type: Mediterranean.
"Arab"	Primarily Dari (I/E) or Pashto (I/E)	Hanafi Sunni	Many have reported Arabic-speakers in Afghanistan. I have yet to meet a group with Arabic as mother tongue. Many groups, however, call themselves "Sayyid," claim Arab descent, and speak some Arabic (S), or an arabized Persian. Basic physical type: depends on area, either Mediterranean, Mongoloid, or admixture.
Hindu	Mother tongue either Hindustani (I/E), Punjabi (I/E), or Lahnda (I/E)	Hinduism	About 20,000, found mainly in urban centers as merchants, traders and moneylenders. Basic physical type: North Indian.

CHART 6 (*continued*)

Ethnic Group	Language[1]	Religion	Comments[2]
Sikh	Same as Hindu; mainly Punjabi or Lahnda.	Sikhism	About 10,000 scattered throughout cities and towns of Afghanistan as merchants, traders, and moneylenders. Both Hindus and Sikhs speak Dari and/or Pashto, most are Afghan citizens, and worship without undue interference. Basic physical type: Mediterranean with extreme hirsuteness; Sikhs are world's hairiest people.
Jew (*Yahudi*)	Few speak Hebrew (S); all speak Dari (I/E) and/or Pashto (I/E)	Judaism	Several thousand, living in Kabul, Qandahar, Herat, as merchants, traders, and moneylenders. Several hundred went to Israel, but most subsequently returned. Evidence of early Jewish contacts (ca. 5th century A.D.) with Afghan area recently discovered (Bruno, 1963; Gnoli, 1962; Rapp, 1965). Basic physical type: Mediterranean.

[1] Major language families: Indo-European (I/E), Uralic-Altaic (U/A), Dravidian (D), Semitic (S).

[2] Population figures derived from official Afghan estimates for provinces (*Kabul Times Annual*, 1967, 94-152), and interpolations from my estimates of the percentage of ethnic groups in each province, data gathered from 1949-68.

[3] Several sources list the major (and sometimes minor) Pustun tribes. Among them: *Afghanistan*: B.I.S. (1948); *Afghanistan: Field Notes, General Staff* (1915); Caroe (1965); Davies (1932); L. Dupree (1953); Fletcher (1966).

[4] The Munji groups call the Kafirs Gabr.

Few Afghan groups maintain racial homogeneity outside the Pushtun areas of the south and east, and even there breakdowns appear on closer analysis (Debets, 1966c, 1970; Maranjian, 1958). Many groups have practiced miscegenation for centuries and composite communities exist in broad bands of ethnic gray zones. When long contact has existed between Caucasoid and Mongoloid groups, particularly in north Afghanistan among Tajik and Uzbak, red or blond hair, blue- or mixed-eye combinations occur in association with epicanthic folds and high cheekbones. Many darker-skinned[1] Baluch and Brahui also have blue, green, or mixed eyes.

Blondism, however, occurs at a high frequency among the more remote Nuristani, and several regions I have visited in Nuristan exhibit at least 30 percent blondism (blue or mixed eyes, and blond or red hair combinations). Professor Debets' recent (1965) research (also see D. Hughes, 1967) on the fringes of Nuristan indicate a great mixture with Mediterranean-Indian types, but a different situation exists in the central Nuristani area.

---

[1] To determine true skin color, a researcher must examine the armpit, a shaded spot untouched by the sun.

CHAPTER 7

Language

THREE, and possibly four, major language families (Indo-European, Uralic-Altaic, Dravidian, and possibly Semitic) are spoken in Afghanistan. The literature, however, uses a modified Arabic script (Chart 7), and most of the 30,000 Hindus and Sikhs, mainly merchants in the cities and towns, write in the Arabic script of the Lahnda (Western Punjabi) dialects. Only a few Afghan Jews know how to write Hebrew; most of the people calling themselves "Arab" speak little Arabic and the majority are non-literate.[1] Some Arabic-speaking groups have, however, been reported near Maimana (Schurmann, 1962, 102), Kunduz, Aq Chah, and Balkh (Ferdinand, 1964, 194; Jarring, 1939, 17, 20; Tolstova, et al., 1962–63, II, 582–96). Recent research by Farhadi, 1967, 84; 1970) delineated the following groups of "Arabs" (who speak a Persianized Arabic): west of Daulatabad (Khushalabad), near Balkh (Yakhdan), Aq Chah (Sultan Aregh), and Shibarghan (Hassanabad). Farhadi estimates the population of the areas to be approximately 5,000. Many religious leaders, often themselves non-literate, recite the *Qor'an* in Arabic without knowing what they say, and their listeners remain in great ignorance.

The two principal languages of Afghanistan are Indo-European (Diagram 4): Persian (or Farsi) and Pashto. The 1964 Constitution names both Dari (or Afghan Farsi) and Pashto as official languages. Dari, an old term, literally means "language of the court."[2] In reality, Dari (still the court language in Afghanistan as it was in Moghul India) serves as the *lingua franca,* although the Constitution designates Pashto as the "national language." A special committee, appointed in 1964, continues to study ways of promoting the growth and spread of Pashto.

An attempt to Pashto-ize all governmental inter-office memoranda

---

[1] I personally abhor the term "illiterate," which has a pejorative connotation in literate countries. In this book, I use non-literate to mean a society with a great body of literature but most of whose population are unable to read and write.

[2] Some Afghan linguists have communicated to me that they believe "Dari" originally meant "language of the valley" (*darra*). However, Frye (1966, 282) convincingly derives "Dari" from "language of the court" (*dabar or dar*).

CHART 7
Dari-Pashto Alphabets in Afghanistan*

DETACHED	INITIAL	MEDIAL	TERMINAL	TRANSLITERATION
١	ا	٠	ـا	ANY VOWEL OR DIPTHONG REQUIRED
ب	بـ	ـبـ	ـب	b
پ	پـ	ـپـ	ـپ	p
ت	تـ	ـتـ	ـت	t
ث	ثـ	ـثـ	ـث	s̲
ج	جـ	ـجـ ، ـج	جـ ، ـج	j
چ	چـ	ـچـ ، ـچ	چـ ، ـچ	ch
ح	حـ	ـحـ ، ـح	حـ ، ـح	ḥ
خ	خـ	ـخـ ، ـخ	خـ ، ـخ	kh (x)
د	د	٠	ـد	d
ذ	ذ	٠	ـذ	z̲
ر	ر	٠	ـر	r
ز	ز	٠	ـز	z
ژ	ژ	٠	ـژ	zh
س	سـ	ـسـ	ـس	s
ش	شـ	ـشـ	ـش	sh
ص	صـ	ـصـ	ـص	s̲
ض	ضـ	ـضـ	ـض	z̲
ط	طـ	ـطـ	ـط	t̲
ظ	ظـ	ـظـ	ـظ	z̲
ع	عـ	ـعـ	عـ ، ـع	ʻ
غ	غـ	ـغـ	غـ ، ـغ	gh
ف	فـ	ـفـ	ـف	f
ق	قـ	ـقـ	ـق	q

CHART 7 (*continued*)

DETACHED	INITIAL	MEDIAL	TERMINAL	TRANSLITERATION
ک ، ك	ك ، کـ ، گ	کـ	ـك ، ـك	k
گ ، گ	گ ، گـ	گـ ، ـگـ	ـگ ، ـگ	g
ل	ا	لـ	ـل	l
م	مـ ، مـ	مـ ، ـمـ	م ، ـم	m
ن	ذ	ـذ	ـن	n
و	و		ـو	u, v, o, w
ه	هـ	ـهـ ، ـحـ	ـه ، ـه	h
ي	یـ	ـیـ	ـي	i, y
		ـئـ		HAMZA USED TO BREAK i,y SOUNDS

	ADDITIONAL	PASHTO	PHONEMES	
ټ	ټـ	ـټـ	ـټ	t̂
څ	څـ	ـخـ ، ـغـ	ـخ ، ـڅ	ts, dz
ډ	ډ	.	ـډ	d̂
ړ	ړ	.	ـړ	r̂
ژ	ژ	.	ـژ	z̧, ǧ
ښ	ښـ	ـښـ	ـښ	x̌, ṣ
ڼ	ڼـ	ـڼـ	ـڼ	n̂
ی ، یٔ		.	ـیٔ ، ـیـ	ey, ei
ې		ـېـ	ـې	e

---

* NOTE THAT THE WRITTEN LETTER SYMBOLS ARE WRITTEN DIFFERENTLY DEPENDING ON WHERE THEY COME IN A WORD: AT THE BEGINNING (INITIAL) THE MIDDLE (MEDIAL) OR AT THE END (TERMINAL).

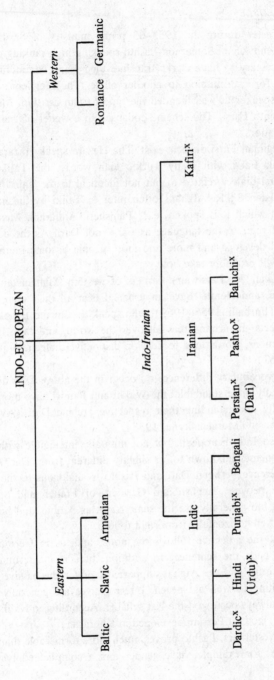

DIAGRAM 4

The Indo-European Language Family
(simplified)

INDO-EUROPEAN

Western

Romance   Germanic

Eastern

Baltic   Slavic   Armenian

Indo-Iranian

Indic

Dardic[x]   Hindi (Urdu)[x]   Punjabi[x]   Bengali

Iranian

Persian[x] (Dari)   Pashto[x]   Baluchi[x]

Kafiri[x]

[x]Spoken in Afghanistan

came to disaster during the 1953–63 prime ministry of Sardar Mohammad Daoud Khan. Some non-Pashto-speaking high-ranking officials found it necessary to have clerks translate their Farsi communications into Pashto for transmission to another office. The recipient, often a non-Pashto-speaker as well, handed the report to an assistant for translation back into Farsi. The scheme collapsed in a welter of translation and retranslation.

Several regional Farsi dialects exist. The Hazara speak Hazaragi; the Aimaq speak Farsi with many Turkic loan words; the Tajik speak Tajiki, a Farsi dialect related to but not identical to the Tajiki spoken in the Tajikistan S.S.R. Afghans often refer to Tajiki by the name of the valley in which it is spoken; e.g., Panjsheri, Andarabi. Most rural Afghans still refer to the language as Farsi, not Dari. As the constitutional period develops and more and more people become literate, the name Dari will probably take hold.

The Farsiwan (or Parsiwan) farmers of western Afghanistan speak Iranian Farsi, and Heratis have an urban dialect all their own. So do the Kabulis (Farhadi, 1955, 1969), who speak the slurred Brooklynese of Dari dialects. In urban areas all over the world, and even internal wards or sections, words tend to develop distinctive dialectical qualities (Wilber, 1967).

Although vocabulary differences do occur in the above Dari dialects, all are mutually understandable; the Wakhi and Pamiri have more difficulty mutually understanding their respective archaic Dari (Avestan) dialects, however (Morgenstierne, 1938).

Pashto, also Indo-European, but not mutually intelligible with Dari, has nine phonemes unknown to, or slightly different from, Dari (Chart 7). The difference between Dari and Pashto is analogous to the range of difference between English and German, or French and Spanish. Farsi and Pashto generally use the same script as Arabic, and both are therefore written horizontally from right to left.

In Persian, the adjective follows the noun, and, as in German, the verb usually ends the sentence. In addition, time is indeterminate in many verb forms, and the Afghans apparently prefer the passive to the active in writing as well as speech. Interrogatives are generally tonal. Word-stress always occurs on the last syllable. According to Najib Ullah (1963, 219), modern Persian developed in Khurasan.

To most Westerners, Pashto proves much more formidable than Dari. Pashto nouns, for example, have gender and a complicated two-case,

18. Mangal Pushtun from Paktya province dancing the *Attan*. Typical eastern Pushtun clothing and long hair. Men in background wearing *qarakuli* hats are government officials. Summer, 1970. *Photo: Afghan Films*

19. *a*) Popolzai (Durrani) Pushtun village near Qandahar. *b*) Same group eating pilau. Clothing typical of western Pushtun. Note *tawwiz* (amulets) worn around necks. June, 1960

71

two-number declension system.[3] Syllabic stress is more varied in Pashto than Farsi. Most linguists divide Pashto into two dialects, the soft Pashto ("Pushtu") of the Qandahar area, and the harsher "Pukhtu" of Peshawar and the North–West Frontier Province and most of the Tribal Agencies of Pakistan. However, the eminent Soviet linguist, N. A. Dvoryankov (1963), differentiates a third dialect in Afghanistan with a phonemic structure intermediate between the Peshawari and Qandahari dialects in Paktya, particularly in the Khost area, and possibly over into Parachinar. He calls the dialects Qandaharian (western), Ningraharian (eastern), and Paktyan (southern). D. Mackenzie (1959) summarizes four different dialects: Southwest (Qandahar); Southeast (Quetta); Northwest (Central Ghilzai); Northeast (Yusufzai).

Another Iranian language, Baluchi, is spoken in southwestern Afghanistan. The Brahui, Dravidian-speakers living among the Baluch, speak Baluchi as a second language, using the South Indian language almost exclusively in the home.

The separate Kafiri and Dardic dialects (Morgenstierne 1929ab, 1932, 1934, 1944, 1949, 1956) exist primarily in and surrounding Nuristan and include several disparate groups. Often each village or valley tends to attach a specific name to its dialect: Ormuri, Pashai, Deghani, Wamai, Waigali, Kami, Kati (Bashgali or Kamdeshi), Prasun (Vermir), Ashuni.

Often, in two valleys less than a day's walk apart in Nuristan, the groups have different terms for such important kin designations as father, mother, brother, and sister, remarkable cases of linguistic resistance to acculturation in order to perpetuate a society's cultural ethos. Peripheral Nuristani groups have had sustained contact with the outside world which, however, seldom comes to Nuristan. Many individual Nuristani leave their mountain homes to visit the plains and urban centers or to serve in the army.

The second most important language family, Uralic–Altaic, is represented by Altaic (Turkic dialects), and concentrated north of the Hindu Kush among the Uzbak, Turkoman, and Kirghiz (Jarring, 1939). Dialects vary from group to group, but most are mutually intelligible. Many Persian words exist in the Uzbaki of Afghanistan; the closer the

[3] For detailed discussion of Persian and Pashto see: Chavarria-Aguilar (1962); Dvoryankov (1960, 1963); Farhadi (1955); Lambton (1967); Levy (1923); D. Mackenzie (1959); Morgenstierne (1927, 1940); Penzl (1955, 1963); Roos-Keppel (1901); Wilber (1962, 1967).

20. Red-bearded, blue-eyed Nuristani, Darra-i-Nur. Living near Safi Pushtun, he has adopted Pushtun headgear. April, 1960

21. Blind Zinjarani Baluch and son singing epic poetic history of tribe. Blind poet on right playing bowed *sarinda* or *sarud*. At Chahar Burjak in Afghan Sistan. March, 1962

relations between the groups, the more Persianized the Uzbaki becomes. As do the Indo-European languages, the Turkic languages of Afghanistan use the Arabic script. However, just across the border (*pay-i-darya;* immigrants from north called *pay-yi-daryai*) in the U.S.S.R., both Indo-European and Turkic languages have been transposed into the Cyrillic alphabet during the Soviet period.

First mentioned by Leech (1838) and later studied briefly by Ferrier (1857), von der Gabelentz (1866), Ramstedt (1906), Ligeti (1955), and A. Franklin Mackenzie (personal communication, 1955), the Moghol were rediscovered by H. F. Schurmann and Shinobu Iwamura in 1954. Schurmann later (1962) did an extensive ethnography of the Moghol and their neighbors. In addition to Schurmann and Ferdinand's review of Schurmann (1964), several other short works on the Moghol exist: Mariq (*D.A.F.A.* xvi, 77–78, 1959), Heissig (1969), and Weiers (1969). Moghol villages have been reported scattered through Ghor, the Hazarajat, and as far east as Badakhshan, almost to the entrance of the Wakhan. Several villages exist near Herat. Few people, except the older men, remember much of the old language. I recorded on tape several old men at Turkabad in 1961. They deplored the fact that younger men became more Persianized with each generation, and most Moghol (although many proudly identified themselves with this tribal designation) speak Farsi, even at home. According to Schurmann, the breakdown of Mongolian as a language and the Moghol as an integrated ethnic group in Ghor probably began in the middle of the nineteenth century A.D. (1962, 16). Mongolian is also Uralic-Altaic.

At the Twenty-fourth International Congress of Orientalists held in 1957, a committee (G. Redard and C. N. Kieffer to supervise in Afghanistan) on Iranian languages was formed to undertake the systematic study of languages in Iran, Afghanistan, and Soviet Central Asia. An Institute of Linguistics, headed by Nur Ahmad Shaker, is now recording languages all over Afghanistan.

Literature

In discussing the peoples and culture of Afghanistan, society must be divided into literate and non-literate segments and these implications considered. Afghanistan, like most Muslim (and other developing) nations, has a literate *culture,* but a non-literate *society.* Culture, for the purposes of this book, may be defined as the way a people live; the totality of their tool-kit, material and non-material. Society is the action component, people who live in a certain way, using part, but seldom all, of the available tool-kit. Most individuals in a non-literate society do not, however, have access to the great literature of their culture. And some of the world's finest literature (philosophical and scientific, as well as poetry) has been written in Arabic, Turkish, and Persian. Pashto has a limited, though important, literature in the area. Many non-literates in Afghan society, however, can recite Persian poetry by the hour (Mohammad Ali, 1958b, 1965). Most have at least passing acquaintance with the greater classical Persian poets: Rumi, Jami, Firdausi (who lived in Ghazni during the heyday of the Ghaznavid Empire). Some Afghans even remember some verses of the minor Muslim poet, Omar Khayyam.

Most literate or non-literate Afghans, be they Persian-, Pashto-, or Turkic-speakers, consider themselves poets. Poetry, essentially a spoken, not a written, art, gives non-literates the same general opportunities for expression as the literates in a society. Afghanistan, therefore, is fundamentally a nation of poets.

To savor the flavor of Persian, Turkish, and Pashto poetry, we must examine some translations, roughly in chronological order.

The following short poem by Hanzala of Badghis, who lived in Nishapur during the first half of the ninth century A.D. in the court of a Tahirid ruler, expresses a central theme in Afghan culture:

> If leadership rests inside the lion's jaw,
> So be it. Go, snatch it from his jaws.
> Your lot shall be greatness, prestige, honor and glory.
> If all fails, face death like a man.
>
> (Translated by S. Shpoon)

Another poet of the same general period, Mahmud Warraq, wrote a love quatrain, probably dedicated to a slave girl. This sad poem deals with unrequited love, and the quatrain may possibly be one of the first of its kind.

> My beauty, I cannot exchange you for the cash of my life.
> You are priceless. I will not sell you so cheap.
> I hold your skirt with both my hands.
> I may loosen my hold on my life, but not my hold on your skirt.
>
> (Translated by S. Shpoon)

75

A tenth-century A.D. poet, Abu Shukur of Balkh, wrote the following during the Samanid period.

> A tree with a bitter seed
> Fed with butter and sugar
> Will still bear a bitter fruit.
> From it, you will taste no sweetness.
> (Translated by S. Shpoon)

One of the greatest poets of the early Islamic period, Rodaki of Samarkand, was, like many poets, blind. The following poem illustrates only a minute segment of his wide ranging interests:

> Ode (*Qasida*) to the Mother of Wine (Grapes)
> The mother of wine must be sacrificed,
> And her son caught and thrown in jail.
> But who would dare take the son away
> Unless the mother be crushed and her soul extracted?
> Even then it is not fair to snatch the baby
> From his mother's milk and breast.
> He should be starved for seven whole months,
> From the first of Odibehest until the end of 'Aban.*
> Only then, out of fairness and piety, should
> The child be put in prison and his mother put to death.
> For the first seven days he will sit stunned and bewildered
> in his narrow cell.
> Then he will revive and, writhing, burst into tears.
> (Translated by S. Shpoon)

Following this, Rodaki describes the complicated process of wine making, and the ceremonial aspects of serving wine, particularly in the court of the Amir of Bokhara. Actually, the whole poem evolves into praises of the Amir.

Daqiqi of Balkh began the first *Shah-Namah,* eventually incorporated in the great work of Firdausi. Like the other Persian poets of the tenth century, Daqiqi wrote many allegorical poems about love.

* Odibehest and 'Aban are Iranian Persian terms respectively for *saur* (April/May) and *aqrab* (October/November).

O my idol! A cloud from Paradise
Has bestowed an emerald gown on the earth.
Deserts are like blood-stained silk
And the sky has the fragrance of musk.
With a mixture of musk and red wine
An artist has drawn an image of my love on the deserts.
The world has become peaceful
For both the tiger and the deer.
For such occasions, we need a sun-faced idol,
And a moon, leaning on a cushion of sun.
We must have an idol with cheeks like rubies,
And red wine to match the cheeks.
The world has become a peacock,
With roughness here and smoothness there.
Mud smells of roses,
As though kneaded with rose water.

From among all the good and bad things of the world,
Daqiqi has chosen four:
Ruby-red lips, the wail of the flute,
Blood-colored wine, and the Zoroastrian religion.

(Translated by S. Shpoon)

Possibly the greatest culture climax in the Afghan area occurred during the Ghaznavid period. In the court of Mahmud of Ghazni lived 400 poets and a total of 900 scholars. Probably the greatest of these was Abdul-Qasim Firdausi. The classic *Shah-Namah, Book of the Kings of Persia,* had 60,000 couplets (Levy, 1967). Anticipating a sizeable gift, Firdausi dedicated the work to Mahmud with a very flowery ode (Najib Ullah, 1963, 242). For his trouble, however, Firdausi received only a pittance of what he thought he deserved. He changed the introduction to one of great satire, and had to flee from Ghazni. He died about 1025 at Tus in Khurasan.

The first woman known to compose poetry in both Arabic and Persian was Rabi'a Balkhi, whose brother ruled Balkh during the tenth century. She fell in love with a Turkish slave, and he gave her a rose. Her brother discovered several poems Rabi'a had written to her lover. Angry, he threw her into a *hamam* (steam bath), and had her veins

---

[4] A technical discussion of the various forms of poetry can be found, among other places, in Najib Ullah (1963, xi–xxi).

slashed. Before she bled to death, legend says, Rabi'a wrote the following poem in Persian on the wall of the *hamam,* with her own blood:

> I am caught in Love's web so deceitful
> None of my endeavors turned fruitful.
> I knew not when I rode the high-blooded steed
> The harder I pulled its reins the less it would heed.
> Love is an ocean with such a vast space
> No wise man can swim it in any place.
> A true lover should be faithful till the end
> And face life's reprobated trend.
> When you see things hideous, fancy them neat,
> Eat poison, but taste sugar sweet.
>
> (K. Habibi, 1967)

Once a religion approaches ritual stagnation and an internal logical or rationalistic philosophy evolves, mysticism inevitably arises. Laymen, whether intellectuals or non-literates, often find the monotonous regularity of the ritual and the maddeningly simple one-two-three-four of the logic fail to yield spiritual satisfaction. Men wish to know the Supreme Being as a personal, not an impersonal, god, but orthodoxy usually tends to be abstract and impersonal. In Islam a number of mystical orders arose to satisfy this need: the Sufi, or Tasawwuf.[5]

The term Sufi probably derives from the Arabic *suf* (wool) and refers to the wearing of woolen robes (*labs-al-suf*) by early (and often later) Sufi ascetics.

The Sufi orders usually did not pretend to replace orthodoxy, but offered a way to seek the Supreme Being through personal experience (*ma'rifat*) and to achieve momentary union with God, thus, in general, rejecting knowledge (*'ilm*), rational and theoretical. Sufi seekers often sound superficially like agnostics, or, with their emphasis on personal experience, like existentialists. They are different, however, in that they not only seek, but they find God. Actually, Sufism embodies only a few ideas (the unity of mankind; predestination; the possibility of momentary union of man with God), but the personal experience of Sufis suggests multitudinous varieties of poetic expressions to describe and define their experiences. The continual efforts to coin new poetic phrasings

---

[5] For those who wish to pursue the study of Sufism, I recommend the following: Arberry (1942, 1950, 1953, 1961); Gibb (1949); Nicholson (1914, 1921, 1923); Pfannmuller (1923); C. Rice (1964); Winsinck (1940).

at least partly account for the many philosophical contradictions found in Sufi literature.

Almost all the founders of the Sufi orders and philosophies[6] turned to Sufism after reaching the limits of rational knowledge and finding their search for the Truth still unfulfilled.

Abu Isma'il 'Abd Allah ibn Mohammad-al Ansari, known commonly as Sheikh-ul-Islam-Khwajah (religious titles) Abdullah Ansari, or the Pir of Herat, was born in Quhandiz, a quarter of old Herat, in about A.D. 1005 and died in the same city about A.D. 1088. Ansari poetically expresses his pilgrimage from orthodox theology to mysticism, and this excerpt demonstrates the odyssey from the unknown to the known, then a new reliance on the mystical:

> From the unmanifest I came,
> And pitched my tent, in the Forest of Material existence.
> I passed through
> Mineral and vegetable kingdoms,
> Then my mental equipment
> Carried me into the animal kingdom;
> Having reached there I crossed beyond it;
> Then in the crystal clear shell of human heart
> I nursed the drop of self into a Pearl,
> And in association with good men
> Wandered round the Prayer House,
> And having experienced that, crossed beyond it; .
> Then I took the road that leads to Him,
> And became a slave at His gate;
> Then the duality disappeared
> And I became absorbed in Him.
>
> (J. Singh, 1939, 19–20)

[6] Major Sufi leaders and teachers include: al-Muhasibi (born in Basra, A.D. 781; died A.D. 857 in Baghdad), probably the first Sufi philosopher with complete theological training; al-Ghazzali (born in Tus, modern Mashhad, Iran, A.D. 1059; died A.D. 1111 in Tus; traveled over most of the Muslin world), one of the more original Sufi thinkers; Sana'i (dates unknown, but all reliable estimates vary between eleventh and twelfth centuries A.D.; born and died in Ghazni, Afghanistan, but was well traveled), wrote the first mystical epic in Persian; 'Attar (*ca.* A.D. 1136–1230), an original, vigorous, imaginative poet and an artistic link between Sana'i and Rumi; Ibn 'Arabi (born in Murcia, Spain, A.D. 1172 or 1173; died in Damascus, A.D. 1240), monist and pantheistic philosopher. Sa'di (*ca.* A.D. 1184–1292; well traveled), a great lyrical poet, author of the

In common with mystics in most religions, Sufis believe in the oneness of man with God, or, as succinctly put by G. M. Wickens (1953, 159–60), "the soul's exile from its maker and its inborn longing, nourished or surpressed in the face of other attractions, to return and lose itself in Him." Because of this, orthodox Muslim religious leaders initially declared Sufi thinking heretical. Sufis were persecuted and sometimes executed, but the piety, austerity, passion, and personal participation inherent in Sufi ritual kept the orders alive. Eventually orthodoxy tolerated Sufism so long as its followers accepted orthodoxy in matters of religious law, and Sufism became grafted on to the religious body of Islam. Today few Muslims escape its impact and ideas.

To achieve this momentary union with God, the Sufi must create the proper atmosphere. Some achieve this with repeated prayers and chants; some with artificial stimulants, including drugs; some by meditation. The Mawlawiya Order of Rumi (the so-called "Whirling Dervishes") produce ecstasy with their whirling dances. Thus, the Sufi can seek God in individual or group ecstasy. But all Sufis resort to poetry during their trips.

Persian, the court language of the Moghul Empire, found its Indian master in Mirza Abdul Qadir Beidel, born in Patna (A.D. 1644) and died in Delhi (A.D. 1720). His family had come from Turkestan, and he maintained lifetime contacts with Sufis in the Afghan–Persian world. The following is an example of his poetry, and is the first *Ghazal* from his *Divan,* or compiled works.

Only humility can bring you to the high seat of God.
Bow down just a hair, and before Him wear proudly your hat.
The solemn palace of love cannot permit joking gestures.
The eyes, like dew, should receive the seal of a dab of tears.
Non-existence has an image and a world of its own.
Realities are sometimes created in the footprints of passersby.
No one could help rid me of my dual self.
I lowered my head and took refuge in my solitary, inner self.

---

famous *Gulistan* (*cf.* Rehatsek trans., 1966) and *Bustan;* Rumi (born in Balkh, Afghanistan, A.D. 1207; died in Rum A.D. 1273) probably the greatest of all Sufis, founder of the Mawlawiya Dervishes; Hafez (born in Shiraz in A.D. 1326; died in Shiraz, A.D. 1389), author of four thousand couplets, often criticized hypocrisy of religious leaders (for flavor see Avery and Heath-Stubbs, 1952); Jami (born in Herat, A.D. 1414; died in Herat, A.D. 1492, after widespread travels), the finest Sufi poet of the fifteenth century.

Vain was my search for Joseph in lust's land of Canaan.
Perhaps I, too, should go into myself and dig a well inside.
If, within your heart flows the never-ending blessing of morning light,
Your days will never know darkness, though all existence turns into
night.

(Translated by S. Shpoon)

The sixteenth, seventeenth and the first half of the eighteenth centuries produced many Afghan poets, as literacy increased in the upper
classes, but the political situation militated against great poetry being
written during most of the time, particularly in Persian. Among the
more famous Afghan poets writing in Persian were Kahi (born in
Kabul, studied in Herat, died in India in A.D. 1577); Abul-Faizi Hazrat
(a seventeenth-century poet from Badakhshan); Sa'aduddin Ansari of
Kabul, a seventeenth-century Sufi poet.

The sixteenth- and seventeenth-century A.D. tribal leaders in the Afghan area wrote extensive poetry, just as did many European monarchs
of the same period. The first great Durrani emperor, Ahmad Shah
Durrani (A.D. 1747–73: period of rule) wrote great Pashto and occasional passable Persian poetry. He wrote:

By blood, we are immersed in love of you.
The youth lose their heads for your sake.
I come to you and my heart finds rest.
Away from you, grief clings to my heart like a snake.
I forget the throne of Delhi
When I remember the mountain tops of my Pushtun land.
If I must choose between the world and you,
I shall not hesitate to claim your barren deserts as my own.

(Translated by S. Shpoon)

Shah Shuja, grandson of Ahmad Shah Durrani, left behind a collection of poetry, as did his father, Timur Shah.

Several nineteenth-century Afghan poets writing in Persian deserve
mention. Mehrdel Khan Mashriqi, brother of Amir Dost Mohammad
Khan, patterned his poetry after the ancient classics. For example:

My perpetual pain is the source of my bliss.
My miseries are my *Id** festivals.

* *Id* festivals refer to religious holidays.

My love, have a few more rounds of wine.
It will quench your last night's thirst.
All the cups of the world are filled, the roofs of nine skies sag.
How long will the clouds of my eyes keep pouring?
A jug of wine on my shoulder, a cup in my hand,
Can the wise man forgive the repeated folly of youth?
O morning breeze, tell my love, whose Christ-like lips give life,
That, although I live, I am away from her, and thus foolhardy am I.
Mehrdel has a breast tatooed with arrow wounds.
His red tears are witnesses to his love.

(Translated by S. Shpoon)

A political exile, Ghulam Mohammad Tarzi, a noted poet and epigrapher, excelled in *shekast* (literary, *shekastah*), or broken-line poetry, written in his own beautiful script on specially treated paper. In a period when family names were almost unheard of in Afghanistan, he chose "Tarzi" (meaning "stylist") as his pen name. Actually, some collateral members claim that his father, Rahmdel Tarzi, used the term first. Ghulam Mohammad Tarzi was a nephew of Mashriqi.

Oral epic poetry has long existed in Afghanistan, but few examples have been written down. In the mid-nineteenth century Hamid of Kashmir (then a part of Afghanistan), wrote a long narrative concerning the first Anglo-Afghan War (which he entitled the *Akbar-Namah*), a highly imaginative and, on the whole, relatively accurate poem.

The body of the nineteenth-century Muslim modernist, Jamal ad-Din al-Afghani (1838–97) lies buried on Kabul University grounds under a magnificent shrine. His role as Islamic reformer has recently been challenged by several specialists (S. G. Haim, 1962; Keddie, 1962, 1965, 1968; Kedourie, 1966). Keddie, in her latest work, takes a much more balanced view than Kedourie, however. The evidence presented, although it indicates that al-Afghani was probably born in Persia as a Shi'ite, simply, in my opinion, enhances his stature as a modernist. He used his religion for political purposes (a legitimate exercise in any non-literate, tradition-ridden society); he may have considered all organized religions to be bad, and at times revealed a tendency toward agnosticism. But effective, non-violent change can occur only when the innovators work *within* cultural patterns. Therefore, al-Afghani, Mohammad Abduh (his chief disciple), and their modernist successors should not be considered "subverters" (Kedourie, 1966, 63) of the *essence* of Islam (see Chapter 8 below), but rather antagonists to the perpetuators of a traditionalist orthodoxy, derived from a manmade, not divinely inspired, *Shari'at*. For an excellent balanced short discussion, see Kenny (1966) and A. Ahmad (1969), both of whom agree that al-Afghani used religion "as an instrument for the achievement of pre-eminently political goals" (Kenny, 1966, 20).

Pashto as a literature tends to get short shrift even in Afghanistan.[7] In his excellent survey of *Islamic Literature,* (1963), Najib Ullah (Afghan scholar and diplomat, whose last name was Toraviana) almost completely neglected Pashto. However, two recent volumes deal exclusively with the *Divan* (collected poetry) of Khushal Khan Khattak (Howell and Caroe, 1963; D. Mackenzie, 1965).

The authenticity of the *Puteh-Khazaneh,* published in Qandahar in 1749 and claiming to contain several eighth- and ninth-century poems, has been recently questioned (Wilber, 1967, 412). No matter, for Pashto literature does not come into its own until the seventeenth century, but then seems to move along at a relatively uninspired pace until the twentieth century.

The two great seventeenth-century Pushtun poets were Khushal Khan Khattak and Rahman Baba.

Khushal (1613–90) epitomizes the Pushtun warrior-poet, the ideal personality type in Afghan culture. Although constantly at war with other Pushtun or the Moghuls, the Khattak chieftain constantly found beauty in nature and man. English translations of his poetry tend to vary with time periods and individual translators. Here, for example, are three translations of one of Khushal's great poems: *Adam Kheleh Afridei* ("The Maidens of the Adam Khel Afridi").

C. Biddulph (1890, 98) gave the verses a Victorian touch:

> The Adamkheyl Afridee maidens are red and white;
> Many and varied are the charms that are theirs,
> Great large eyes, long eyelashes, broad eyebrows,
> Sugar-lipped, rosy-cheeked, moon-like foreheads,
> Tiny mouths like a Rose-bud, even teeth;
> Their heads girt with dark tresses, fragrant as Amber,
> Their skins as smooth as ivory, bare of hair;
> Straight their figures, like Alif; fair their complexions.
> Like the Hawk has been my flight along the mountains,
> Many a partridge there has been my prey;

[7] For survey in English, see A. Habibi, (1967, 1968ab.).

The Hawk, whether young or old, seeks its quarry,
But the swoop of the old Hawk is the most unerring.
O! of Lundi's streams the water, and of Bari,
Is sweeter to my mouth than any Sherbet.
The Peaks of the Matari Pass rise straight up to the heavens,
In climbing, climbing upward, one's body is all melted.
I came to the Adamkheyls in Tirah,
Then I parted with them at Khwarrah with sad heart.
Love's troubles are like fire, Khush-hal,
What though the flame be hidden, its smoke is seen.

One of the world's great contemporary Pashto scholars, D. Mackenzie, rendered the poem (1965, 91):

> The Adam Khel Afridi maids
> Are both rosy and fair;
> Among them there are many beauties
> With every kind of charm.
>
> With great bright eyes, long curling lashes
> And eyebrows arched and wide,
> With honey lips and rosy cheeks
> And foreheads like the moon;
>
> With tiny mouths like budding roses
> And teeth even and white,
> Their heads all clad in blackest tresses
> Fragrant as ambergris;
>
> Their bodies smooth as any egg,
> Without a trace of hair,
> Their feet petite, with rounded heels,
> Their haunches plump and wide;
>
> Their stomachs slim, their bosoms broad,
> Their waists perfectly narrow,
> Their figures straight as letter "I"[8]
> And shining silver-white.

[8] D. Mackenzie prefers "I" to *alif*, for the first letter in the Pashto alphabet is upright and not curvaceous.

Although I wander, like a hawk,
About the barren hills
Many a pretty little partridge
Has fallen prey to me.

Young and unskilled, or old and sly,
A hawk always seeks prey,
And an old hawk's stoop is surer
Than that of a young bird.

Either the waters of Landdai[9]
Or the Bara stream
Taste sweeter, more refreshing both,
Than sherbet in my mouth.

The peaks that flank Matari pass
Rise straight up to the sky;
In climbing, ever climbing them
One's angles soon gain strength.

I came into Tirah country
Among the Adam Khels;
Now, sad at heart, I've taken leave
Of all these gentle souls.

All love's affairs are well portrayed
By fire, O Khushal:
Although you cover up its flames
The smoke will still be seen.

The final, shortened, version is by Bowen (1966, 79), an army officer who served along the frontier in the waning days of empire:

The Lasses of the Adam Khel,
    As every lover knows,
Are delicately coloured—like
    The petals of a rose;
My Love a snowy partridge is,
    Who chooses winter time
To seek among the stony fells
    A cloak of silver rime.

[9] Kabul River.

My Love, my Bird, remember that
A hawk, when he grows old,
Becomes more subtle in the chase,
His stoop becomes more bold:
Surrender then to me, for though
I seem no longer young,
The fervour of my love will taste
Like honey on your tongue.

I think the contrasting translations are instructive from both the points of view of English and Afghan personality types and values.

Khushal could never be accused of modesty (certainly not a modern Pushtun personality trait either) when he wrote:

When Khushal first began to write
Poetry in his mother tongue
He gave the Pashto language much
Of beauty that it lacked before.
(D. Mackenzie, 1965, 59)

Khushal Khan Khattak was a political as well as a poetic animal. The following poem shows his feelings toward his chief Moghul antagonist, Aurangzeb:

Ra ma'lum shu da Aurang 'adl u insaf
I know all that I want to know
Of Aurangzeb's justice and right,
The orthodoxy of his faith
And his devotional retreats;
His brothers german, one by one,
All put to death at his command,
His father overcome in battle
And flung into a prison cell.

Although a man prostrate himself
With face to earth a thousand times,
Or bring his navel to his spine
By dint of fasting endlessly,
As long as he does not intend
To act justly and righteously

His adorations and devotions
Will be of no avail to him.

May he whose tongue travels a road
Quite different from that of his heart
Suffer the torments of the damned,
His vitals be ripped by the knife.
The serpent outwardly appears
Handsome in body, sleek and lithe,
But inside it harbours all kinds
Of venom and impurity.

A brave man's he whose deeds are many
And whose words modest and few;
From cowards one seldom sees deeds
But boasts enough for twenty men.
Although Khushal is powerless
To reach the tyrant here and now,
On the Day of Resurrection
May God not grant him His grace!
                    (D. Mackenzie, 1965, 66)

Khushal subtly thrusts at narrow religious leaders and beliefs:

> *'Arif sarhai haghe dai . . .*
> The knowing, the perceptive man
> Is he who knows about himself,
> For in self-knowledge and insight
> Lies knowledge of the Holiest.

If in his heart there is no fear,
His deeds are not those of the good,
Pay no heed to the one who's skilled
In quoting the Koran by heart.

The wrongful actions of the self
Are a misfortune in your home:
If you're not Satan to yourself
No other Satan need you fear.

Abandon greed and leave desire,
Covet no thing or person more,

Then you will need no other name—
You'll name yourself the king of men.

Unless God set him on the way
Talking alone will not suffice,
Even if He should resurrect
The Sage Luqman to be his guide.

Jesus, by means of miracles,
Gave blind men power to see again,
But in this life no single fool
Was made a wise man by his prayers.

Although he has nothing but this,
Let him not grieve if he be wise:
Khushal Khattak will swear to it,
The wise man need have no regret.

(D. Mackenzie, 1965, 98–99)

Of Pushtun character, Khushal Khan Khattak was very perceptive. He recognized the destructiveness of the tribal schisms on potential Pushtun (Pathan) unity:

Of the Pathan that are famed in the land of Roh,
Now-a-days are the Mohmunds, the Bangash, and the Warrakzais, and the Afridis.
The dogs of the Mohmunds are better than the Bangash,
Though the Mohmunds themselves are a thousand times worse than the dogs.
The Warrakzais are the scavengers of the Afridis,
Though the Afridis, one and all, are but scavengers themselves.
This is the truth of the best of the dwellers in the land of the Pathans,
Of those worse than these who would say that they were men?
No good qualities are there in the Pathans that are now living:
All that were of any worth are imprisoned in the grave.
This indeed is apparent to all who know them.
He of whom the Moghuls say, "He is loyal to us,"
God forbid the shame of such should be concealed!
Let the Pathans drive all thought of honour from their hearts:
For these are ensnared by the baits the Moghuls have put before them.

(C. Biddulph, 1890, 119)

A consummate warrior, Khushal nevertheless did not neglect his sex-life:

> *Leka badzen che halwa khwri*
> As a greedy man eats sweetmeats
> The lover takes his queen's fair mouth.
>
> Let none take him to task for it,
> For he consumes only his own.
>
> I'd always taste her sugary lips
> Though other men eat quails and manna.
>
> Both her breasts are round as pears
> Fit only for kings to taste.
>
> There is no bravery in him
> Who'll let the sword fall on his neck.
>
> The lover dies thus at your hand
> And still swears by his love for you!
>
> When does a hungry man pay heed
> To whether what he eats is lawful?
>
> Take her mouth, Khushal, in secret;
> The falcon steals flesh from the game.
>   (D. Mackenzie, 1965, 199)

But, politically or sexually, Khushal Khan Khattak was indeed, as he put it:

> *Da Afghan puh nang mi utarlah turah,*
> *Nang yali da zamane Khushhal Khatak yam.*
> My sword I girt upon my thigh
>   To guard our nation's ancient fame;
> Its champion in this age am I,
>   The Khatak Khan, Khushhal my name!
>   (Howell and Caroe, 1963)

Rahman Baba, a contemporary of Khushal Khan Khattak, was more mystic than warrior. But his mysticism, born of Sufism, also touches the Pushtun cultural essence. Not so proud and fiercely militant as

Khushal Khan Khattak, Rahman Baba continually warned the ambitious and proud of their base earthly origin:

> Live not with thy head showing in the clouds,
> Thou art by birth the offspring of this earth.
> The stream that passed the sluice cannot again flow back,
> Nor can again return the misspent time that sped.
> Consider well the deeds of the good and bad,
> Whether in this thy profit lieth or in that.
>
> (Translated by Qazi Sarwar)

A major three-volume work on modern Pashto literature, written by a noted Pushtun poet, Abdul Rauf Benawa (1961–62, 1967–68), covers Pushtun writers on both sides of the Durand Line (see below, pp. 426–29), and includes such well-known poets as Sayyid Mian Rasul Rasa (a Pakistani diplomat with long service in Kabul, now Director, Pashto Academy, Peshawar University) and Ghani Khan (son of Khan Abdul Ghaffar Khan, known as the Frontier Gandhi). Some of the younger poets deal with modern social and political themes, breaking the traditional rhyming and rhythmical rules, but many still follow the old forms.

An interesting non-rhyming form, *landay*,[10] exists in the Pushtun areas of Afghanistan and West Pakistan. Both men and women compose and sing *landay,* as well as knowing hundreds of traditional couplets, passed on from generation to generation (Shpoon, 1968). The first line of the *landay* must have nine syllables, the second thirteen. Below are a few examples.

> Your face is a rose and your eyes are candles;
> Faith! I am lost. Should I become a butterfly or a moth?
>
> (Benawa, 1958, 27)

> My beloved returned unsuccessful from battle;
> I regret the kiss I gave him last night.
>
> (Benawa, 1958, 42)

---

[10] In addition to the *landay,* three other types of Pashto folk songs are popular: *kakarri gharri* (also called *da buri zhaghuna* and *da shin khalo taki*), couplets with eight syllables on each line, sung by both men and women; *atann* (varied styles), three lines with 11-7-11 syllabic scheme, sung only by women; *sharora* (also called *babulala* and *khorsadi*), three lines with 8-8-8 syllabic scheme, sung only by women. Many traditional songs exist; others are composed spontaneously.

If you don't wield a sword, what else will you do?
You, who have suckled at the breast of an Afghan mother!

(Benawa, 1958, 36)

Shame on you, old man.
Don't wink at me.
Are you drunk with hashish?

(Sphoon, personal communication, 1970)

Give me two things.
Then let the British come.
A gun to fight with
that won't jam.
A girl to fight next to
who will love.

(Sphoon, personal communication, 1970)

Call it romance, call it love,
You did it.
I'm tired now, pull up the blanket.
I want to sleep.

(Sphoon, personal communication, 1970)

An anonymous poem quoted by Bowen (1968, 98) serves as a fitting end to this rapid survey of themes in Pashto poetry:

> A Pathan Warrior's Farewell
> Beloved, on a parchment white
> With my heart's blood to thee I write;
> My pen a dagger, sharp and clean,
> Inlaid with golden damascene,
> Which I have used, and not in vain,
> To keep my honour free from stain.
>
> Now, when our house its mourning wears,
> Do not thyself give way to tears:
> Instruct our eldest son that I
> Was ever anxious thus to die,
> For when Death comes the brave are free—
> So in thy dreams remember me.

Turkic-speakers in Afghanistan have mainly oral traditions, but during the fifteenth century, a great Chagatai and Uzbaki Turkic literature grew up in Turkestan. The greatest writer, Ali Sher Nawai, was born in Herat (A.D. 1440), but traveled widely throughout the area. Nawai died in A.D. 1501 and lies buried in Herat in a plain, unadorned tomb. A large statue of him exists in Tashkent, capital of Uzbakistan S.S.R. The Turkish writing of the period modeled itself after the Persian, and Ali Sher Nawai wrote fluently in both Persian and Chagatai Turkic, but constantly championed Turkic over Persian.

The novel as found in the West is rare in the Middle East and virtually unknown in Afghanistan. One well-known leftist journalist, Nur Mohammad Taraki, is considered to be a budding Persian-language novelist, however. Prose-writing usually concerns history, social problems, culture, religion, and, increasingly, current politics. However, much of this prose tends to use poetic imagery, even in letters to editors in local newspapers. Among the better-known modern historians, essayists, and journalists (usually also poets and unless indicated otherwise, mainly Persian writers), one must include Mahmud Beg Tarzi, Ghulam Muhayuddin Afghan, Maulawi Saleh Mohammad, Abdul Hadi Dawi, Ahmad Ali Kohzad and his younger brother, Mohammad Nabi Kohzad, Said Qassim Rishtya, Abdul Rahman Pazhwak, Salauddin Seljuki, Fikri Seljuki, Osman Sidqi (Ambassador to China), Abdul Hai Habibi (President of the Afghan Historical Society), Professor Mohammad Ali, Mohammad Din Zhwak (mainly Pashto), Habibullah Tegai (mainly Pashto), Mohammad Hassan Sapai (mainly Pashto), Sayyid Ihsanullah Hir (mainly Pashto), Mohammad Qadir Taraki.

Among the more important twentieth-century Afghan poets are (D = Dari; P = Pashto) Akbar Nadim (D; died in 1916); Abdul Ali Mustaghni (PD; died in 1934); Abdul Kader Bedel (D; very influential on younger poets); Abdullah Qari (D; poet laureate; died in 1944); Sufi Abdul Haq Beitab (D; became poet laureate in 1942; died in 1969); Khalilullah Khalili (D; currently Ambassador to Iraq); A. R. Pazhwak (DP; former President of the U.N. General Assembly, 1966–67); Abdul Rauf Benawa (P); Gul Pacha Ulfat (P); Sayyid Shamsuddin Majruh (P); Ghulam Ghaus Khaibari (P); Mohammad Ghulam Ningrahari (P); Najiba Nazhand (D; woman); Abdullah Bakhtanai (P); Zia Qarizada (D; a leading experimenter); Mohammad Ibrahim Khalil (D; writes memorial verses for tombs); Mohammad Asef Suhail (D); Aziz Rahman Mamnoon (P); Mahjuba Herawi (D; woman); Qasim Wajid (D); Mahmud Farani (PD; the major experimenter); Wasif Bakhtari (D); Mohammad Rahim El-Ham (PD); Saduddin Shpoon (P for poetry; D for prose). Other important critics and poets include Abdul Hamid Makhmoor (D; died in 1964); Goya Etemadi (D; died in 1968); Shayeq Jamal (D); Karim Nazihi (D); Haider Zhobal (D); Sulaiman Layeq (PD; a well-known leftist journalist).[11]

It must, however, be remembered that most Afghans still do not have access to their literate culture. The 5 to 10 percent literate Afghans are generally a remarkable group. Most speak not only their mother tongue, but one or more other Afghan languages, and more often than not at least one Western or non-Afghan Eastern language. Commonly, one meets Afghan officials speaking five languages: Dari, Pashto, English, French or German, and Urdu. A small number trained in Japan before World War II speak Japanese. Some now speak Russian. A few speak Chinese, having been to the People's Republic of China as exchange students. Afghans usually speak non-Afghan languages with little trace of an accent.

French was the non-Afghan *lingua franca* among the intelligentsia before World War II, but now English dominates. Russian slowly increases in importance, and some signs (barber shops, general stores, tailors, etc.) announce their services in both English and Russian, as well as Farsi or Pashto or both.

Afghans with advanced education obtained outside their homeland often complain of the inadequacy of Farsi and Pashto for modern technology. Foreign technical terms are sometimes introduced into everyday conversation, but not to the extent one finds in Pakistan and India, where a welter of linguistic diversity makes Afghanistan seem a sea of simplicity and forces the elite to use English as a medium of communication.

National ethnic pride often encourages attempts to modernize a language, and the Afghans have a Pashto Academy (*Pashto Tolaney*), directed by Sadiqullah Rishtin, which systematically purges foreign words and replaces them with Pashto, often inventing new compound Pashto words as replacements.[12] The simple term "rocket," for example, becomes *torghunday,* "a black mound which flies up in the sky."

---

[11] The discussion of twentieth-century Pashto literature taken from personal communication with M. A. Qasem Ghazanfar, who is currently preparing a Ph.D. dissertation on the subject at Columbia University, and S. Shpoon of the *Pashto Tolaney* (Pashto Academy). Also see D. Wilson (1969).

[12] The Pashto Academy is now a section in the combined Afghan Academy,

In spite of efforts by the several innovators previously mentioned, the general state of modern Afghan literature can only be described as sterile and unimaginative. Probably the main reason relates to the mutual antagonism between Dari and Pashto writers, with growing discontent among the few Turkic authors. The groups suffer from combined superiority-inferiority complexes, and blame each other for the current malaise. The flood of quality and pulp Iranian Farsi literature further inhibits potential innovators. So Dari and Pashto writers suspiciously eye each other and the government eyes both groups, and modern Afghan writers sit in a cultural limbo, pens silent, as social, political, and economic reforms push ahead. The rise of the free press since 1966, however, could act as a catalytic impetus, and move Afghan authors, regardless of linguistic bias, toward the creativity of which they are capable.

---

founded in October 15, 1967. The Afghan Academy also includes the Historical Society of Afghanistan (A. Habibi, 1968c); the Ariana Encyclopedia Department; the Book Publishing Institute; the Public Libraries Department; the Press Awards Bureau. The Afghan Academy comes under the jurisdiction of the Ministry of Information and Culture.

CHAPTER 8

Religious Non-Literacy in a Literate Culture

IN NO INSTITUTION does the disparate attitudinal dichotomy of literate *vs.* non-literate have as much cogency or meaning as it does in religion. Islam is not a simple "conversion or the sword" doctrine. The roots of Islam were watered in the same philosophical and geographical garden as Judaism and Christianity. Muslims consider Jews, Christians, and Zoroastrians (Gaudefroy-Demombynes, 1968, 123) *ahl-i-kitab* ("people of the Book," i.e., those with divinely inspired written scriptures).

The same wall dividing Judaism from Christianity also splits Christianity from Islam: the role and nature of Christ. The Jews still wait for the Messiah; the Christians have Christ as their personal Saviour and the Divine Son of God; the Muslims, however, simply look on Jesus (or 'Isa) as the Prophet before Mohammad.

Islam developed out of the Judaic–Christian matrix, theoretically eliminating (at least for the Muslim) contradictions in the earlier theological mathematics (one plus one plus one equals one). To the Muslim, only Allah (roughly, "the God") is divine. He is the Yahweh or Jehovah of the Jew and Christian. Like all organized religions, Islam has a codified system of ritual (commonly called the Five Pillars of Islam) for initiation and permanent identification.

1. *Shahadat*[1] ("profession of faith"): A single statement by which a man identifies himself as, or becomes, a Muslim: "Ashhadu anna la ilaha illa llahu, wa anna Muhammadan rasulu-llah—I give witness that there is no God but Allah, and Mohammad is the Messenger of Allah."

---

[1] All terms are those commonly used in Afghanistan and sometimes vary from the Classical Arabic in both form and meaning. The same applies to the historical and theological interpretation discussed in the text. Those interested in comparing the Afghan terms, definitions, and interpretations with Classical Islam and Muslim history are invited to consult, among others, Brockelmann (1947), Coulson (1964), Gaudefroy-Demombynes (1968), Gibb and Kramers (1953), and Hitti (1949), as well as the continuing series, *Encyclopedia of Islam.*

Most Afghans prefer a shortened version: "La-ilaha-illa-llah, wa Muhammad rasulu-llah." Muslims attribute no divinity to Mohammad; he is simply a prophet or messenger. Therefore, Muslims insist they not be called "Mohammedans," for this term, by analogy with the "Christ-" in "Christianity," seems to them to imply divine attributes in the Prophet.

2. *Salat* or *Salah* ("prayer"): After ritual ablutions, devout Afghan Muslims pray facing Mecca, five times each day: dawn (*sobh*), noon (*chast*) or early afternoon (*pishin,* when the shadow of a pole equals one-fifth of its height or before the length of a man's shadow equals his height), mid-afternoon (*digar*), dusk (*'ishan*) and early evening, before retiring (*koftan*). All these terms are in general use in Afghanistan; they vary in other Muslim countries.

The *Hanafi* call to prayer in Afghanistan is:

Allah o akbar (God is most great)
Allah o akbar
Allah o akbar
Ashhadu anna la ilaha illa-llah (I testify that there is no God but Allah)
Ashhadu anna la ilaha illa-llah
Ashhadu anna Muhammad rasulu-llah (I testify that Mohammad is the messenger of God)
Ashhadu anna Muhammad rasulu-llah
Hayya 'lla 's-sala (Come to prayer)
Hayya 'lla 's-sala
Hayya 'ala 'l-falah (Come to prosperity)
Hayya 'ala 'l-falah

In some larger cities, public address systems and even recorded calls to prayer have been recently introduced, although not to the extent to which they are found in Pakistan and Iran.

3. *Zakat* ("almsgiving"): Considered a purifying act. Every Muslim should annually give a certain percentage of his negotiable, debt-free wealth to the poor, either directly or indirectly. In Afghanistan, the traditional amount is two and a half percent. The custom of *zakat* helps account for the tolerance of beggars in the Muslim world; they are necessary to the individual who wants to see where his charity goes and is not content simply to send a check to a mass-media campaign office. *Zakat* also partly justifies the lack of taxation for social welfare in certain areas of the Muslim world.

4. *Sawm* ("fasting," called *ruzah* in Afghanistan): Although widely practiced throughout the Muslim world, the ritual fasting during Ramzan (Ramadan) cannot be justified from a careful study of the *Qor'an* (von Grunebaum, 1951, 51–65). Ramzan occurs in the ninth month of the Muslim religious calendar (See Appendix D for the interpretation of the various calendars used in Afghanistan). From sunrise (theoretically when a white thread can be distinguished from a black thread, but now astronomically determined in most areas) to sundown (white thread and black thread indistinguishable), no food, liquid, tobacco, *chars* (marihuana), opium, or other foreign bodies, even spittle, may pass the lips of the true believer (Pickthall, 1954, 49; *Qor'an,* Surah II:187). The dawn is called *sahari,* sunset *'iftar.* The month of fasting follows the lunar calendar and therefore occurs eleven days earlier each year, which creates great hardships for the devout when Ramzan falls in summer.

Exempt from the fast are suckling children, travelers, soldiers in the field, the sick, the pregnant. All but the children, however, must make up lost days at other times of the year.

In most towns and villages, a mullah's call to prayer begins and ends the fast. Today in many areas of the Muslim world government-sponsored mullah announce the new moon over the radio, which annually causes arguments among members of the religious community about the validity of the audible pronouncement of a visual sighting. In Kabul, the cannon on Sher Darwaza hill (which announces noon daily) is fired an hour before sunrise, so that those fasting may get up and eat; the second time the cannon fires, people stop eating. The cannon also announces the end of fasting in Kabul. Most Afghans break the daily fast by first eating dates or raisins, excellent quick energy food, before consuming mountains of pilau and gallons of tea.

The fasting ends with three days of celebrations called Little *'Id* (*'Id-il-Fitr, 'Id-i-Ramzan,* in Turkic *Shaher-i-Bairam,* and in Pashto, *Qamqai Akhta*). Most people (especially the children) get new clothing, and friends visit one another. Little *'Id* begins on the first of *Shawwal,* Muslim lunar calendar.

An optional fast day is *'Ashura',* 10th of *Muharram,* or Martyrs' Day, primarily a Shi'a festival. It lasts from sunset to sunset. Many important historical events presumably occurred on *'Ashura'.* Jews celebrated the holiday as their Day of Atonement long before Islam. Noah supposedly disembarked from the ark on *'Ashura'.* In Islam, Husain (grandson of the Prophet Mohammad) was killed on October 10, 680; his body lies buried in Kerbala, Iraq, and his head is honored in Cairo at the Mosque of the Hasanain. The sizable Shi'a populations in Iran and Pakistan hold large celebrations on *'Ashura'*, little observed in Afghanistan, however, because of its small Shi'a minority.

5. *Hajj* ("pilgrimage"): All Muslims are supposed to make a pilgrimage to the sacred city of Mecca in Saudi Arabia. Those who make the trip are called *Hajji* and enjoy a respected status throughout the Muslim world. The traditional time to make the *Hajj* is *Dhu'l Hijra,* the twelfth month in the Muslim lunar calendar. Mecca had been a holy pilgrimage place long before Mohammad, and he simply adopted the custom for Muslim usage. Today, many Afghans annually fly to Mecca, primarily with the national airlines, Ariana Afghan Airlines. In April/May, 1968, 216 Afghan pilgrims made the *Hajj* to Mecca in a 14-bus caravan, which included medical and cooking facilities. In 1969 and again in 1970, 1,500 pilgrims made the trip in buses, 5,000 by air.

The major festival during the *Hajj* is the ritual slaying of sheep on the tenth day of *Dhu'l Hijra* or *'Id al-Kabir,* Big *'Id*, also called *'Id-i-Qurban* or, in Turkish, *buyuk bairam.* The day is also called *'Id-i-Duha* or *'Id-i-Adha* (or *Azha*) in Afghanistan. Of the slaughtered sheep, one third goes to the sacrificer's family, one third to kin, one third to the poor. The ritual slaying is in memory of Abraham's slaying of a sheep in place of Isaac at the command of Allah. The festival usually lasts four days, but is a less festive occasion than Little *'Id* because of the solemnity of the memorial situation. During *'Id-i-Qurban* friends usually exchange presents.

The final important religious holiday is the birthday of the Prophet Mohammad (*'Id-i-Milad-i-Nabi*), which occurs on the twelfth day of *Rabi' ul-awal.* The Prophet also died on this day, which increases its importance and solemnity.

Nawruz, March 21 (1 *Hamal* on the Afghan solar calendar), the first day of spring, is also the first day of the Afghan New Year, an important festival, and ecologically more consistent than the wintery January 1 of the Christian world. The Achaemenids shifted *nawruz* from the summer equinox (June 21) to the vernal equinox (March 21), according to Wilber (1958a). Another logical time-keeping device used in Afghanistan is that the new day begins at sundown, instead of at midnight. This confuses foreigners occasionally, because when an Afghan invites you to his home on Friday night it would be Thursday night in the Western way of reckoning.

When *nawruz* begins, 'Ajuzak, an ugly old woman, roams abroad. She may be the ugly aspect of the matrilineal spiritual base of all societies. If it rains on *nawruz*, 'Ajuzak is washing her hair, and the spring planting will prosper. Another version is that 'Ajuzak has a swing and if she falls to the left on *nawruz* it will be a dry year; if to the right, wet. Infants must be hidden away from the evil eye of 'Ajuzak to prevent illness.

In addition to the comforting oneness of universal group rituals, a codified way of life must be spelled out in detail for the faithful in an organized religion. Often, as in Christianity, the flock should try to emulate the life of the founder. Later interpretations expand, elaborate, and "modernize." Mohammad never claimed divinity or even perfection, although many later Muslim theologians, in competition with the Christians over the goodness of Christ, claimed human perfection for the Prophet.

The codified beliefs of organized, literate Islam are found in the *Qor'an,* the *Hadith,* and the *Shari'at,* all interpreted by men who attempt to divine Allah's message and will, men appointed either by themselves or those in religio-secular power.

In attempts to find analogies between Christianity and Islam, some have equated Mohammad with Jesus, the Bible with the *Qor'an.* Possibly better pairs would be St. Paul and Mohammad (both were Prophets announcing the arrival of the "message"); Jesus and the *Qor'an* (the messages); the Bible with the *Hadith* (interpretations and elaborations of the message) (W. C. Smith, 1959, 25–26).

Mohammad received the *Qor'an* from Gabriel who, along with the Archangel Michael, are only two of the many *dramatis personae* found in both the Bible and the *Qor'an.* A partial list includes the following (the four major prophets, *Sharif,* before 'Isa and Mohammad are identified with *):

Qor'an	*Bible*
Adam*	Adam
Nuh*	Noah
Ibrahim*	Abraham
Ishak	Isaac
Musa*	Moses
Ya'kub	Jacob
Irmiya	Jeremiah
'Ayub	Job
Yusuf	Joseph
Yusha'	Joshua
Yahya	John the Baptist

I have already mentioned the role of 'Isa (Christ) in Islam. In addition, Muslims believe in the virgin birth, and greatly revere Maryam (Mary).

To the Muslim, the *Qor'an* is the word of God, not Mohammad, just as, to Jews and Christians, the Ten Commandments are the word of God, not Moses.

The *Hadith* (actions and traditions or sayings of the Prophet) supplement the *Qor'an*. Often, *Hadith* resemble the parables so familiar to Christians. The most reliable *Hadith* come from the Companions of Mohammad. Christ had his Disciples, who developed His image and passed it on to Europe; Mohammad had his Companions, divided into thirteen grades. Mohammad's closest friends belonged to grade I; anyone catching a glimpse of the Prophet is in grade 13. Three categories of reliability arose, and naturally those farthest away from the Prophet became suspect. The term *ashab* loosely means "companion," and T. Hughes (1885, 24) estimates a total of 144,000 existed. The *Hadith* recorded immediately after the death of Mohammad are considered to be the most reliable, particularly when written by a Companion, first grade, in this manner: " 'Ali [son-in-law of the Prophet] said, The Prophet, peace and blessings of Allah be on him [this, or a similar phrase, is always added after a mention of the Prophet] said: Obedience is due only to that which is good" (M. Ali, n.d., 397). In modern terms, this *Hadith* represents a clear call for civil disobedience when secular law violates the essence of the "absolute good." Many instances are cited to justify the *Hadith*. For example, Khalid, a troop commander, ordered his officers to execute some prisoners. The officers refused, and the Prophet later approved their action (M. Ali, n.d., 397).

Gibb (1949, 79) indicates that al-Bukhari (d. A.D. 870, an early *Hadith* collector) may have examined at least 200,000 *Hadith,* out of which he approved 7,300 (actually only 2,762 if duplicates are eliminated).

The *Hadith* have often been used to justify non-Muslim customs later adopted by specific groups. *Hadith* stretch credulity when quoted thus: "Abu Kuraib said to us that Ibrahim ibn Yusuf ibn Abi Ishaq said to us from his father from Abu Ishaq from Tulata ibn Musarif, that he said, I have heard from Bara ibn Azib that he said, I have heard that the Prophet said, Who ever shall give in charity a milch cow, or silver, or a leathern bottle of water, it shall be equal to the freeing of a slave" (Coon, 1951b, 99).

Theologians usually accepted those *Hadith* with an unbroken word-of-mouth chain connected by a maximum of five links. Any break in the chain made the *Hadith* unreliable. Many *Hadith,* obviously later accretions and designed to justify different interpretations of Islam, partly led to the creation of the separate *Shari'at,* or Codes of Theological Law.

Islam, like Christianity, is divided into two major sects, born primarily because of disputes over political succession, rather than religious differences. The problem of succession to the leadership of the Muslim community arose after the death of the Prophet Mohammad in 632. One group thought the leader (*Khalifa,* or Caliph) should be elected from the Quraish tribe of the Prophet; another thought 'Ali should succeed his father-in-law (Mohammad left no male heirs); yet another group opposed the establishment of any formalized leadership institution.

The first three caliphs were companions and age peers of the Prophet Mohammad, members of the Quraish, and kin related to him in one way or another: Abu Bakr (632–34), the father of the Prophet Mohammad's favorite wife, 'A'isha; 'Umar (634–44), father of the Prophet Mohammad's wife Hafsa; 'Uthman (644–56), the Prophet's fifth cousin and son-in-law, who married two of Mohammad's daughters.

With the murder of 'Uthman, the mantle of Caliph fell on 'Ali (656–61) son-in-law, cousin, and foster brother of the Prophet Mohammad. During 'Ali's short reign, the already shaky Muslim Empire began to disintegrate in a disastrous process of political fission. Within a quarter of a century after the death of its founder, therefore, Islam began to crumble as a cohesive political force.

Islam quickly split into two major groupings: the Sunni and the Shi'a. Very roughly, the Sunni can be considered the orthodox line (*sunna* means "custom," or the way of life propounded by the Prophet), the Shi'a, as breakaway sects. Generally, the Shi'a repudiated the first three Caliphs, and accepted 'Ali and his line as the logical successors to the Prophet Mohammad. The Shi'a began to split among themselves, as did the Sunni, until three major sub-sects of the Shi'a survived, and four sub-sects of the Sunni, each attempting to justify its doctrinaire position through the medium of *Hadith.* So the *Qor'an* and *Hadith,* plus commentaries (*Tafsir*) on the two, equaled the rise of the various Sunni and Shi'a *Shari'at,* religiously oriented and inspired codes of law. By the tenth and eleventh centuries A.D., relatively rigid *Shari'at* set the pattern for the next 1,000 years.

The largest sub-sect of Shi'a Islam is found in Iran, where the Ithna

'Ashariya ("the Twelvers") dominates and is the official state religion. The Twelvers are also known as the Imami (Imam = caliph or religious leader) because they recognize twelve successive imams beginning with 'Ali (Coon, 1951b, 121). Other Imami live in Iraq and Afghanistan, particularly near the Iranian border and in the Hazarajat, and in the urban centers where great numbers of Qizilbash reside.

The Zaidiya Shi'a rejected the fifth imam and, instead, accepted his brother Zaid as Imam. The Zaidiya dominate Yemen, but the present Imam, a direct descendant of Zaid, no longer sits on the throne, for a civil war rages as this book is written. If the Republican government gains total control, what will happen to the Zaidiya Shi'a religion? Will a new sect arise? Will the government become completely secular and attempt to dismiss Islam as unimportant? Each political change in the Near and Middle East brings about attendant changes in the dominant religion.

The Isma'iliya reject the sixth imam and accept Isma'il, the elder son of the fifth imam. After Isma'il's son, Mohammad, substitute or "concealed" imams have succeeded one another, the real imams remaining invisible. The Muslim tradition of succession in a given family, but not necessarily according to primogeniture, was graphically and poignantly demonstrated when the Agha Khan III, spiritual leader of the Isma'iliya, died in 1957, having first appointed a grandson, Karim, a Harvard graduate, Agha Khan IV, instead of his internationally famous playboy son, Ali Khan.

The Isma'iliya have a wide geographic spread: Negro Africa, East Africa, India, Pakistan, and Afghanistan. Many are important entrepreneurs, financiers, and bankers, and the Isma'iliya operate a fantastically successful welfare program, including education, public health, recreation, and insurance for believers. The objects (diamonds, gold, etc.) used annually to give the Agha Khan IV a birthday gift go to the welfare fund and not to his personal fortune.

Sunni Afghan villagers often look on neighboring Isma'iliya as "devil worshipers" because of their use of the peacock to symbolize the hidden Imam. The peacock represents the *shaytan* (devil) in the non-literate iconography of many Muslim areas. An Iraqi ethnic group called the Yazidi ("devil worshipers") by their neighbors call the peacock *Malik Tawwus* (King Peacock), and believe the peacock saved Christ from the cross (al-Jadaan, 1960).

Afghan Isma'iliya include many Wakhi (Nizaris), Shigni, Ishkamishi, Sanglechi, Munji, and Pamiri peoples of Badakhshan, as well as many Hazara, in spite of the common belief that all Hazara are Imami Shi'a.

The rest of the Afghans (aside from the Imami mentioned earlier), or about eighty percent of the total population, are Hanafi Sunni, also dominant in Pakistan, India, and Lower Egypt. In fact, the Hanafi *Shari'a* is the most common of the four sub-sects of Sunni Islam. The other three are the Maliki (North Africa, Upper Egypt, the Sudan); Shafi'i (Hadramaut and Indonesia); Hanbali (Saudi Arabia). The four schools vary only in interpretation of the *Qor'an* and *Hadith*, and do not concern themselves with the succession of imams. Only the extremely conservative, juristic Hanbali refuse to admit equality for the other three sub-sects of Sunni Islam.

To complicate the religious scene further, many Sufi *tarika* (or *tarikat;* plural, *turuk;* sub-subsects, "roads," or "pathways") occur within each *Shari'a,* some being founded as late as the early nineteenth century, for example, the Senusiya of Libya (Evans–Pritchard, 1949: L. Dupree, 1958b). Sub-subsects often redivided into branches (or sub to the third power sects): the Ahmadiya of Egypt (founded in the thirteenth century A.D.) initially proliferated to 16 branches, but now only three are active (Gibb and Kramers, 1953, 575).

Often a *tarika* revolves around local customs or cults integrated into the body of Islam; at other times, the personal charisma of a single man could shape the rules and ritual. Usually the *tarika* are associated with mystic Sufism. Of the about two hundred *tarika* founded in Islam since the ninth and tenth centuries, only about seventy-five are still active, including the Pir-Hadjat in Herat, whose basis is the life and writings of Ansari. Only two major *tarika* remain centralized in their areas of origin: the Senusiya in Libya and the Mawlawiya in Turkey. Most Pushtun follow the *tarika* of Pir Baba (also called Ghaus-ul Azam Dashtagir), whose real name was Abdul Qadir al-Jilani, and who is buried in Baghdad.

Islam has given much to the West, and during the so-called Dark Ages of Europe (fifth to thirteenth centuries)—although they were not so dark as once painted—the Muslim world made great and lasting contributions to medicine, philosophy, geography, literature, painting, architecture, and mathematics (Southern, 1962). The West currently uses a modified system of Arabic numerals (Wright, 1952).

All these ritualized aspects and codified beliefs can be destroyed or modified *without* destroying the essence of Islam, with Soviet Central Asia as a classic example (Bennigsen and Lemercier–Quelquejay, 1967; Nova and Newth, 1967; Pipes, 1955; G. Wheeler, 1966). Islam lives in the Muslim republics of the U.S.S.R.; the ethics remain, more or less, even after the ritual has become atrophied.

The essence of Islam, stripped of turgid liturgicism and *Hadith*-baiting, reduces itself to three major themes: belief in Allah, the equality of men before Allah (not necessarily before other men), and social justice (the right of a man to live among other men and exploit his talents). From another viewpoint, the essence of Islam defines man's relationships to the universe (order does exist), man's relationship to God (all men are equal in the eyes of Allah), and man's relationship to man (social justice).

Contrary to popular belief among most westerners and many literate Muslims, the essence of Islam (as interpreted by Modernists) is *not* fatalistic or predeterministic. *Insha'llah*—"If God Wills"—a common Muslim expression, seems to imply divine manipulation which can be neither changed nor influenced. The term "Islam" means "submission," but not blind submission to a computerized fate programed by an impassive source. On the contrary, a Muslim submits to a way of life (or essence) after careful examination.

Islam in essence is not a backward, anti-progressive, anti-modern religion, although many of its interpreters, the human, action component, may be backward and anti-progressive. Religions interpreted by man constantly change in day-to-day functioning, but their essence remains unchanged and unchanging. Christianity, for example, embraces existentialism, the Ecumenical Council, and the snake-cults of the hills of the American South. The essence remains the same; only interpretations differ. Here literate and non-literate Afghans find themselves poles apart.

The Islam practiced in Afghan villages, nomad camps, and most urban areas (the ninety to ninety-five percent non-literates) would be almost unrecognizable to a sophisticated Muslim scholar. Aside from faith in Allah and in Mohammad as the Messenger of Allah, most beliefs relate to localized, pre-Muslim customs. Some of the ideals of Afghan tribal society run counter to literate Islamic principles. The Pushtunwali (traditional code of the Pushtun hills), for example, demands blood vengeance, even on fellow Muslims, contradicting Sura 4:92–93: "It is not for a believer to kill a believer unless it be by mistake. He who hath killed a believer by mistake must set free a believing slave, and pay the blood-money to the family of the slain, unless they remit it as a charity" (Pickthall, 1954, 88).

In practice (but not in theory) Islam loosely accepts "saints," and the cults of saints, although forbidden, abound throughout the Muslim world. Almost any stone thrown in Afghanistan will hit the shrine (*ziarat*) of a *pir, khwajah,* or other name-saint. Pilgrims flock to *ziarat* to ask for the intercession of a particular saint with Allah for specific favors. In Afghanistan, for example, a saint's tomb near Jalalabad specializes in curing insanity; another near Charikar cures mad-dog bites; and in the valley of Paiminar, just north of Kabul, are forty-odd shrines, all dedicated to fertility. Women desiring children visit Paiminar to buy amulets (*ta'wiz*) from the *ziarat* caretakers, each guaranteeing a son or daughter as the case may be. At one tomb, women actually fondle the bones of *shahed* (Muslim martyrs, particularly those killed in warfare against non-Muslims) and eat a pinch of earth, probably reflecting a very ancient belief in impregnation from mother earth.

The caretakers of the various shrines throughout Afghanistan sell *ta'wiz* for practically anything a man or woman might desire: control over a loved one; increased sexual prowess; protection from bullets in a feud; general good luck; protection from the evil eye, and others. Many *ta'wiz* consist simply of magical formulas or verses copied from the *Qor'an*, which are folded and sealed in a cloth, leather, or metal triangular or square packet, and then sewn to the clothing of the purchaser.

Supplicants use several devices to remind the saint of their requests. Usually an object is left behind: a lighted candle, a piece of cloth tied to a pole, a ball of clay to harden in the sun. At the Ashukhan and Arafan shrine in Kabul, believers drive nails into the threshold. Driving nails into selected trees scattered throughout Afghanistan (the shrine of Khwajah Ansari near Herat, for instance, and another near Chahardeh-i-Ghorband) can achieve cure for toothaches. Often women will leave small toy *charpayi* (string beds) or construct small hammocks at fertility shrines to remind the saint to intercede. In addition to purchasing *ta'wiz,* pilgrims leave money with the caretaker to help support the shrine.

A special festival (*jandah bala kardan,* "raising of the standard"), held on *nawruz* at the tomb of Hazrat 'Ali in Mazar-i-Sharif, offers the faithful a chance to gain religious merit. The standard of 'Ali is raised in the courtyard of the shrine and the devout scramble over one another to touch its staff. Those who touch the staff first gain extra merit. The *jandah* (standard) remains standing for forty days, and thousands of pilgrims visit the shrine. Many sick and crippled persons touch the pole, hoping for a miraculous cure (N. Dupree, 1967a, 54).

Another Mazar-i-Sharif festival with pre-Muslim fertility connotations occurs about forty days after *nawruz,* when the standard comes down. At this time, a distinct red species of tulip blooms and disappears shortly after. People visit friends and wish each other long and happy lives and large families. Any pre-Muslim ritual accompanying the birth and death of the red tulip has long been forgotten.

Several thousand white pigeons live in the shrine complex of the Sharif 'Ali in Mazar-i-Sharif. Afghans believe that one in seven is a spirit (*arwa'*) so they feed the pigeons when they visit the shrine, hoping to gain religious merit points. If a man kills one of the pigeons in which the *arwa'* resides, the *arwa'* will return to haunt his dreams.

Many other examples of non-Islamic practices can be cited (I. A. Shah, 1928): black magic, shamanism, and types of voodoo (sticking sharp objects into dolls, for example) are practiced, and witches (*koftarha*), usually old women past childbearing age, exist throughout the country, and are occasionally killed. The witch not only uses wax, clay, and other materials to represent the victims, but incorporates the victim's hair, or fingernail- or toenail-parings into the effigy. Even dirt from under the nails can be used, and villagers have told me that they bury their shorn hair and parings in secret.

Parents frighten small children by saying that a wicked witch named *madar 'ol* will steal them away if they are disobedient.

The practitioner of black magic (*seher*) relies on the assistance of *arwa'-yi-khabisah* or *arwa'-yi-palid* (unclean spirits). Positive and negative charms and spells exist in the realm of religio-magic.

When black magic exists in a village or camp, white magic must be on hand to fight the evil. Often the mullah (Islamic religious leader) will serve as a shaman to counter the black magic. In fact, he may know these better than he does formal Islamic rites. Charms and spells are usually referred to respectively as *nuri* (Arabic for heavenly light; and *nari* (Arabic for fire, also associated with *shaytan,* Satan). Bullets which have wounded but not killed, for instance, are positive charms and have great prophylactic, protective powers, and Afghan warriors pay high prices for them.

Several supernatural creatures harass the Afghan. The *jinn,* indefinable spirits, try to possess the living; some are evil, some merely jokers, but a person possessed by a *jinn* must be exorcised, because *jinn* are considered to be the main cause of insanity. Impersonal spirits created from smokeless fires, *jinn* return to fire as man does to dust, and infest all Afghanistan, causing mischief, such as tripping people in the dark and causing disease. The *jinn* replaces the scientific "germ" for the non-literate Afghan.

Arwa', spirits or ghosts, tortured souls of the improperly-buried dead, or those cursed by Allah or man, can be visible or invisible, and take either human or non-human form. *Pari* are beautiful fairies, who fly from the Caucasus to steal bad children for slaves. *Dehyu, bohyu,* ugly giants (with horns, tails, and thick hides), protect the *pari* from the evil eyes of man. *Sayyid,* in this sense referring to the souls of pious men, return to earth to warn evildoers to repent. They can take any shape, including human.

A special group of individuals called *malang* wander about the countryside. They are holy men thought to be touched by the hand of Allah. Some go naked, moving with the season; others dress in women's clothes; still others wear elaborate, often outlandish, concoctions of their own design. Usually Afghan, Iranian, Pakistani, or Indian Sufi Muslims, *malang* travel from place to place, fed, honored, and at times feared by the local population, or at least held in awe. Often, they spout unintelligible gibberish, words they claim to be from Allah or a local saint. At other times, they quote from the *Qor'an,* usually incorrectly. The *malang* seem to be decreasing in number as Afghan society becomes more mobile, and modern processes give wider latitude for dissidents to adjust to new occupational opportunities outside the village and nomadic camp. The *malang* visually symbolizes the smouldering dissidence which often burns in individuals and which group action suppresses in the tightly knit peasant-tribal society of Afghanistan.

Since no one willingly leaves the protective matrix of the socio-economic relationships of kin and village, the *malang must* (in the Afghan view) have been touched by the hand of God, and, therefore, be tolerated. He is another example of the wonder and power of Allah. Sometimes a *malang* performs a local miracle and settles down in a specific village, often under a large tree. When he dies the villagers build a *ziarat* around his tomb, and he becomes their very own saint, a *pir* to intercede personally for them, thus bringing a more localized, personalized meaning to their religious lives.

The traditionalists feed fuel to the peasant-tribal beliefs in predestination, aided and abetted by religious leaders on every level. Those at the bottom of the hierarchy, the village mullah, often non-literate farmers, often function as part time religious leaders. Technically, Islam has no organized clergy, and every man can be a mullah. Anyone can lead in prayer. But where two men exist, hierarchies rise, and so they did in Muslim countries. At times informal, but often formally associated with the power élite, *'ulama* (bodies of religious leaders) assisted the rulers of city-states, tribal groups, or empires to maintain control over the masses, and interpreted the law.

Thus the essentially non-Islamic belief of the non-literate Muslim that Allah planned all in advance excuses tyranny, and prepares men to accept whatever fate hands them.

The Afghan *Jam'iyat ul-'ulama,* founded in 1931 by King Mohammad Nadir Shah, originally had seventeen members, usually one chief religious leader from each province. In its heyday, the *'ulama* advised the executive and legislative branches on Islamic matters, literally controlling the courts and the schools, as well as watching over and commenting on public and private morality and customs. After Mohammad Daoud Khan became prime minister in 1953, however, the political power of the *'ulama* began to wane.

The government-paid hierarchy of religious leaders remains substantially as created by Amir Abdur Rahman Khan in 1896, when he abolished most *waqf* (religious trusts) and transferred their holdings to government control.[2] *Waqf* usually support mosques, schools, hospitals, or other religiously oriented institutions with the income derived from land or shops donated in perpetuity by devout Muslims. Often, the donor would continue to receive the income from the property during his lifetime, the funds reverting to the *waqf* at his death. Occasionally, individuals or families donated land or buildings for use by a trust.

Sometimes, both the religious leaders administering the *waqf* and the donor violated the intent of the trust by diverting at least part of the income to their personal use. Since *waqf* are exempt from taxation, the government lost considerable revenue, which partly accounts for Abdur Rahman's seizure of many *waqf,* and his demand that the rest account publicly for all expenditures.

The *imam jum'a* or *khatib* (orator who delivers the Friday sermon, *khutba*) sits at the top of the hierarchy and serves as religious leader to the large *masjid-i-jum'a* or *masjid-i-jami'* (Friday mosque) of the big cities. Kabul has about twenty *masjid-i-jum'a* and a hundred or so minor mosques (Wilber, 1962, 68), served by two lesser grades of *imam.* Afghanistan has a total of about 15,000 mosques, according to Wilber.

The government appoints an *imam* after consultation with local re-

---

[2] In December, 1969, Prime Minister Nur Etemadi appointed a commission to advise on *waqf* management, in an attempt to eliminate inequities in the system.

ligious leaders and, in principle, secular authorities cannot dismiss an *imam.*

The muezzin (*mu'adhdhin*) calls the congregation to prayer. Any Muslim, however, can give the call to prayer, and the government-paid muezzin works only in the cities and larger towns, functioning as an assistant to the *imam* (Wilber, 1952).

The *khadim* works as caretaker and janitor at the mosque and, although paid by the government, usually expects baksheesh from worshippers and visitors.

Mudaris are teachers of religious subjects at mosques, *madrasa* (religious schools), paid either by the government or privately. Those with the title *Qar'i Sahib* can recite the *Qor'an* well; anyone knowing the *Qor'an* by heart (often blind men) is referred to as *Hafiz.*

The *qazi* (mentioned earlier and to be discussed in detail later), although paid by the government, remain outside the religious hierarchy but are deeply entrenched in the government hierarchy. They function as judges for the Ministry of Justice. Slowly and irrevocably, however, secular law is replacing the orthodox decisions of the *qazi.*

Several honorific titles, some inherited, some achieved, are in common usage in Afghanistan: *Sheikh-ul-Islam,* a title reserved for renowned mystics and members of the *'ulama,* once bestowed exclusively by the Caliphs of Baghdad; *Maulana,* the usual title given in Afghanistan to a member of the *'ulama,* a renowned mystic, or a great scholar in Islamic studies; *Khwajah,* the title of a teacher leaving behind a school of followers, or a brotherhood (often such men become saints after death); *Hazrat,* a title for respected religious leaders who are primarily, though not necessarily, scholars. Among the more noted recent religious leaders in Afghanistan are the Hazrat Sahib of Shor Bazaar (a member of the Mujadidi family, which arrived in Afghanistan from Chinese Sinkiang after the post-World War I, anti-communist Basmachi revolts), and the Sayyid-i-Kayan, who maintains tight control in the eastern Hazarajat. In some villages, the title *Hazrat* refers to those who consider themselves descendants of 'Uthman, the third caliph; in others of 'Uman, the seventh caliph.

The most common religious term is *Sayyid* (*Sa'adat,* plural) referring to the descendants of the Prophet, who are therefore descendants of Fatima[3] and 'Ali. Both Sunni and Shi'a *Sa'adat* exist.

---

[3] Daughter of the Prophet Mohammad. All Mohammad's sons preceded him in death. See Guillaume (1955) and Jeffery (1958) for the life of Mohammad. Naturally, many other accounts exist.

Khoja (Arabic; also means eunuch, so Afghans use *Khwajah* in Farsi), in north Afghanistan, refers to those who claim to be the descendants of Abu Bakr, the first caliph.

The utilization and function of these honorific terms vary throughout the Muslim world and even inside Afghanistan.

In spite of the increase of secularization since 1953, religious leaders still maintain their extra-curricular vested interests: many own extensive tracts of land (often disguised as *waqf*); most have local political influence; others control educational institutions; some, along with certain tribal leaders, hold power of life and death over their followers, and the government dare not interfere.

But the essence of Islam remains progressive, and the modernists steadily strengthen their secular position by building on Islam and not destroying it (see Chapter 24).

Several sizeable non-Muslim ethnic groups live and work in Afghanistan.

Historically, the Hindus played an important role in shaping the destiny of Afghanistan, especially in the eastern and southern areas. The Mauryan Empire spread into Afghanistan during the fourth and third centuries B.C.; another great dynasty, the Gupta, controlled parts of Afghanistan in the fourth and fifth centuries A.D. The militant Hindu Shahi kings ruled parts of Afghanistan in the eighth to tenth centuries A.D., and some Afghan Hindus claim Hindu Shahi ancestry.

Two groups of Indian origin currently exist: about 200 Indian nationals, and 25,000 Afghan nationals, by their own estimates. Most engage in commercial activities. In modern times, the first 10 Hindu merchants came to Kabul about 65 years ago. The group grew perceptibly larger after the 1947 Partition of the Indian subcontinent into India and Pakistan. The migrants worked previously in the region now known as West Pakistan, and most lost their businesses in the wake of the communal riots which racked the area following the partition.

Sikhs, however, constitute the majority (about 15,000) of Afghan nationals of Indian origin. Like the Hindus, they primarily engage in commercial activities, and few Afghan towns exist without their quota of Hindu and Sikh businessmen. The Sikhs generally exhibit the "five K's," though somewhat modified in form, of warrior (*akali*) Sikhdom and maintain their ethnic identity: the protective, thick, long, uncut hair (*kesh*) held with a comb (*kangha*) and the distinctive shorts (*kachaba*) remain the same, but the two weapons, *kirpan* (two-edged dagger or sword) and *khakra* (steel quoit, 5″ to 12″ in diameter and worn in the turban), have become diminutive. The Sikh businessmen of Afghanistan wear a miniature silver *kirpan* around their necks and a steel bracelet (*kara*) on the left wrist as a possible substitute for the deadly quoit. The "five K's" have also undergone miniaturization among the Sikh business community in India.

Both Hindus and Sikhs actively practice their respective religions and maintain their distinctive temples. Most still speak Hindi or Punjabi.

Indian nationals operate under an Afghan–Indian barter agreement. Afghan nationals of Indian extraction, however, work under Afghan laws, and sometimes suffer discrimination of varying degrees in government offices. Their young men perform national service, but while on active duty, Sikhs are permitted to wear the "five K's."

Small Jewish (*Yahudi*) business communities with active synagogues exist in Kabul, Herat, and Qandahar. Many Jews initially emigrated to Israel, but most returned because of the discrimination they and other Sephardic and oriental Jews suffered under the dominant European Ashkenazim. Many have since emigrated to the U.S.A.

To my knowledge, only a few Parsee (Zoroastrians) businessmen live and work in the Indian commercial community.

Since, legally, the Afghan government wisely permits no proselytizing, only rarely do Afghan Christians surface.

CHAPTER 9

Folklore and Folk Music

AFGHAN folklore and legend often intimately relate to Islam, although much of the corpus definitely preceded Islam. Of course, all religions, however sophisticated, build on neighboring earlier faiths and adapt existing legends to fit new needs. Folktales and folk songs in Afghanistan, as in other non-literate and pre-literate societies, are group reinforcing, and psychologically satisfying to the individual.*

Folk poets constantly rise from the Afghan milieu and are honored. Malang Jan Besudi, a modern example, lived hard and died young in a motor accident in 1957, but his poems have been printed, sung, and remembered. Literate Afghans always find a verse to fit any situation or, better yet, compose a couplet on the spot. All Afghan verse is rampant with *double entendre,* be the topic political, psychological, or sexual.

Folklore and folk music in a non-literate society have many functions, but all revolve about instruction and entertainment. They explain and justify the group's existence. They define the ideal personality type, and describe ideal interpersonal, in-group and extra-group relations. Afghan folk songs and folktales tend to perpetuate, not protest, the existing order.

Just as written history reflects the culture in which it is written and interprets facts subjectively in any given period, so does folklore. In reality, history tends to be accepted fiction at any given time by a specific people. For example, Russian and American historians of World War II and the rise of the Cold War vary considerably in their discussion of the role of their respective nations. If written history tends to be subjective in time and space, how much more true of non-literate folklore?

I have collected hundreds of folktales in Afghanistan, and have reached some tentative conclusions concerning the patterns and functions of folklore in non-literate Afghan society. Several are discussed here.

* (See Appendix E for discussion of Afghan musical instruments.)

22. Uzbak farmer (part-time mullah) playing *chang* ("Jew's-harp") at Aq Kupruk. August, 1962

23. Nuristani playing four-stringed harp (*waj* or *wunz*) on rooftop in Wama. Note log ladder connecting houses. Houses of logs with chinked stone and plaster, and timber roof held down with stones. April, 1963

24. Besud Hazara playing *dhamboura* in Kabul, where he has come to work as a carpenter during the off-agricultural season. October, 1963

113

The Accordion Effect: Folktales seldom observe correct chronological sequence, but historically verifiable incidents generally compare favorably with written accounts.

The Skewed Evolutionary Aspect: Technological advances (such as the automobile) often find themselves included in events which occurred centuries ago.

The Educational Aspect: Group reinforcing values are stressed. In the origin myths, the uniqueness and superiority of the group over other groups are stressed. The ideals of the culture are described and pitted against the reality of social living.

Social Control: The individual is told by illustration what he or she can or cannot do, and what rewards and punishments await the individual in response to his or her deeds.

The Entertainment Aspect: In a society with no television, few radios, no movies except in the large cities, and no friendly neighborhood bars, the entertainment value of folklore and folk music cannot be overemphasized. Villages with folktellers who give excellent personalized performances consider themselves lucky, and they invite neighboring villagers to attend sessions. Often the folkteller will interject personal experiences into the tale, particularly if he (or she[1]) is elderly. The audience seldom sits passively through a performance, but shouts approval, encouragement or dissent over various points, and sometimes arguments break out over conflicting versions of a tale. Sometimes a tale will be partly told, partly sung, using either two-line (*ghazal*) or four-line (*charbayti*) stanzas (Najib Ullah, 1963, xi–xxi).

The folktale serves as a great emotional safety valve in any non-literate society.

For the purposes of this book, I have divided the folktales of Afghanistan into five, somewhat overlapping, categories: religion, history and legend, love and jealousy, virtue and morality, and, for lack of a better term, *jokes.*

Religion: Village and nomadic-camp Islam, as examined earlier, often only superficially resembles the literate Islam of the *Qor'an, Hadith,* and *Shari'at.* In general, the villagers know the *dramatis personae* and many of the incidents related in the *Qor'an,* but give both a local twist. To reinforce his beliefs, the rural Afghan localizes his religion. In addition, pre-Islamic saints become Muslim saints, complete with Muslim

---

[1] Important women folktellers exist in the Hazarajat (Ferdinand, 1959b, 38). For a discussion of a group of part-time "folkplay" performers near Herat, see Baghban, 1968ab).

names, and, often, rites and rituals connected with the pre-Muslim saint remain almost unchanged.

To bring Islam even closer to the Afghan, several important Islamic figures are believed to be buried in Afghanistan or, like 'Ayub (Job), are said to have passed through the country. A healing hot spring, Chashmah-yi-'Ayub, bubbles forth at a spot where the Balkh River emerges from the mountains in north Afghanistan.

More important, 'Ali ibn Abi Talib, the fourth caliph, cousin, son-in-law, and foster-brother of the Prophet Mohammad, is "entombed" under a magnificent structure at Mazar-i-Sharif, "Noble Tomb" or "The Shrine of the Sharif 'Ali." Afghan legend states that after 'Ali's assassination at Kufa, his followers tied his body to the back of a white female camel.[2] 'Ali had given instructions to bury his body at the exact spot the camel died. At what is now Mazar-i-Sharif, the camel expired, and 'Ali was buried. Other (probably more accurate) traditions have his body interred near Kufa, where the town Najaf (now called Mashhad 'Ali) grew up around his tomb.

But to many Afghans and other Muslims, 'Ali *is* buried at Mazar-i-Sharif, Afghanistan, and their belief is what is important. If one doubts that 'Ali visited Afghanistan, the believer can show concrete proof in many places where unusual basaltic, granitic, or other dikes zigzag through the mountainous landscape. "Hazrat 'Ali killed these dragons and Allah turned them into stone," they will say. 'Ali is the Muslim Gilgamesh or St. George, the dragon-slayer. Most areas have legends concerning his dragon-slaying prowess and, according to some, by drawing his fingers through the earth, 'Ali created most of the mountains and valleys in north Afghanistan.

If one continues to doubt, the believers indicate oval or semicircular depressions in horizontal rock outcrops and say, "See, the hoofprints of the great horse of 'Ali, Daldal!" Actually, Daldal was the horse of Husain, but never mind, the proof of the importance of Afghanistan to early Islam is clear and undeniable to the believer. 'Ayub slept here, and 'Ali lies buried in Mazar-i-Sharif. Some believe the Prophet Mohammad ascended to Heaven on Daldal, and that the Milky Way is the stardust raised by Daldal as he galloped across the sky. According

---

[2] The camel fascinates both east and west. Much folklore has developed concerning this obstreperous beast in Muslim countries. For example, Allah has one hundred names (or attributes) and man knows only ninety-nine. The camel, however, knows the 100th, but will not tell it, which accounts for his constant superior (supercilious ?) mien.

to Afghan legend, *barq* (electricity) is named after the Prophet's true horse, *Baraq,* because of the Milky Way exploit.

Another interesting attempt to connect Afghanistan with Qor'anic text concerns the *Ashab al-Kahf* (in Arabic, People of the Cave, Sura 18: 9–27, in the *Qor'an.* See Pickthall, 1954, 213–214). The Qor'anic *Ashab al-Kahf* tells of a number of men seeking the "truth," in the company of their faithful dog, several centuries before the Prophet Mohammad. Allah, in His mercy, put the "seekers" to sleep in a cave to await the Revelation.

The traditional site of "The Cave" is in Jordan or Iraq, but one also exists near Maimana in Afghanistan, watched over by a group calling themselves "Arab" and *Sa'adat* (Descendants of the Prophet). They do not speak Arabic, however, although some know much of the Arabic *Qor'an* by heart. A blind "Arab" *Sayyid* told me this story in Persian (I paraphrase):

In the days before Mohammad, peace and blessings be upon his name, all people were Kafir [heathen], and Allah, the Merciful, the Compassionate, the All-Knowing, waited to give His Messenger the Message.

There were several young men who began to seek the truth, but the true message was not yet. They traveled for many years accompanied by their faithful dog, and one day, weary from the search, they entered this cave and fell asleep. The dog slept outside to protect them. Allah, knowing they were good men and wishing them to be witnesses for Him, placed the men and their dog in a magic sleep to await the revelation of the Message.

Six hundred years passed and the men slept, and, at last, Allah sent Gabriel with the Message to Mohammad, blessings be on his name. Mohammad, may his name be blessed, heard the story of the Sleepers, and sent four of his intimate Companions ('Ali, Abu Bakr, 'Umar and 'Uthman) to announce the coming of the true Message to the Sleepers. The Companions flew[3] to the *Ashab-i-Kahf.* Allah had awakened the Sleepers before the arrival of the Companions, and they, being hungry, sent one of their number to the bazaar for food. The shopkeeper would not accept their strange money, and the Sleepers began to realize they had slept much longer than just one night.

[3] Magic carpet?

The arrival of the Companions cleared up all their questions. The Companions instructed the Sleepers in the true Message.

The Companions offered to return the Sleepers to Arabistan, but the Sleepers looked at each other and said, "What have we to offer when we have gained so much? Allah has preserved us to learn the true Message, so all that remains is Paradise."

So the Sleepers returned to the Cave with their dog, and Allah in His wisdom put their bodies to sleep and transported their spirits to Paradise.

The Companions flew back to Mohammad, may his name be blessed, and informed him of the miracle they had seen.

The Prophet, peace be upon him, asked, "How many Sleepers were there?"

While all listened in wonderment, Hazrat 'Ali said, "Four." Abu Bakr said, "Five." 'Umar said, "Six." And 'Uthman said, "Seven."

The Prophet, peace be upon him, said simply, "The ways of Allah are wonderous, and only He knows how many Sleepers there are. Only He knows when one will awaken. The world is full of seekers and only Allah knows their number and when they will awaken."

This tale essentially parallels that found in the *Qor'an*, but for the doubter, the "Arab" *Sayyid* caretaker reports an accretionary localized tale:

About a thousand years ago, an Afghan king doubted the story of the *Ashab-i-Kahf*, so he desired to visit the cave, count the bodies—if any truly existed—and put an end to the nonsense. He left with his whole court, with his favorite *tazi* [Afghan hound] and *baz* [falcon], for he planned to hunt *ahu* [gazelle] along the way.

As the King's party approached the night's camp, a large, beautiful *ahu* appeared in the distance. Swiftly the King unhooded the *baz* and unleashed the *tazi,* and those experienced companions of the hunt sped toward the fleeing target. Soon after, they disappeared and night fell just as the camp was pitched.

The King did not worry unduly, for the hunt had often been long, and the *tazi* and *baz* sometimes returned at night. This time, they did not return, which even more angered the King as he mounted to go to the *Ashab-i-Kahf* the next morning.

When the King reached the cave, he leaped from his horse and threw open the wooden door leading to the burial chamber. And there, just inside the entrance, were three mumified objects: his *baz,* his *tazi,* and the *ahu.* The king believed and left the cave without counting the Sleepers. To this day no one save Allah knows how many Sleepers are in the cave.

"If," the "Arab" *Sayyid* concluded, "anyone is rash enough to try to count the bodies, Allah will strike him blind and mad, and he will wander these hills cursed by all until he dies. Listen tonight and you will hear a blind, mad pilgrim howling at the moon. Last week, he tried to count the Sleepers."

I received permission to enter the cave to view the Sleepers by candle-light. Another pilgrim had tacked a gaudy-colored print of the Ka'ba, like those the Hajjis buy as soveniers in Mecca, over the door. The plastered entrance bore grafitti of generations of pilgrims. To the right of the door, the shrine of the dog of the Sleepers had been piled high with goat and sheep horns, more evidence of the persistence of the prehistoric, possibly totemic, "goat cult" of Central Asia and the Middle East. I stepped through the door and into the void.

In the darkness lit only by an unstable candle, I could see a platform covered with muslin. Several humped hillocks pressed snugly against the muslin. I lifted one edge of the covering cloth, gently, and with some apprehension. Underneath I could see several mummified bodies, so I just as gently lowered the shroud. I did not bother to count the number of bodies for the prospect of wandering blind through the Afghan hills overcame my curiosity. So presumably, only Allah still knows the correct number.

History and Legend:[4] Most historical legends deal with inter-tribal and extra-tribal fights. Warfare plays a major role in most non-literate societies, either its pursuit or avoidance.

Students of warfare often ignore the relation of leisure time to fighting in the ecological cycle. Wars, naturally, be they tribal feuds or world holocausts, must be justified by the men who fight them. Blaming wars on the aggressive animal instincts in man satisfies no one, so variations on territorial or property integrity or group honor arise within the cultural patterns. Actually, in-group tensions account for much out-group aggression, particularly in non-literate societies. When the agricultural

[4] Also see Hackin and Kohzad, 1953.

off-season occurs and the nomads are not moving, long hours of boredom result. Young men sitting idle in villages and nomadic camps rapidly find suppressed anxieties rising to the surface, and violence easily erupts. How much better for group survival if this explosive violence could be channeled *away* from the village or camp, and directed at "outsiders." Relatively few people are killed in tribal fighting, but the safety valve aspect cannot be underestimated. Group unity, threatened by individual outbursts of violence, is curtailed, and the bored human animal has an outlet for his passion. After all, we must remember that the non-literate villager or tribesman has little in the way of entertainment apart from his legends and his legendary heroes, whom he hopes to emulate. Even most Afghans with western educations tend to identify with the warlike traditions of Afghan tribal society.

Sporadic feuding also performs an important biological function: it helps maintain population control. During a visit to a Pushtun village in Paktya in 1962, I witnessed attempts by another tribal group to steal some trees (trees are valuable in this part of Afghanistan) and a feud which had been dormant for ten years flared up anew. Within a week 10 of the 100 adult males in the village had been killed.

All Afghan groups with which I am familiar look on themselves as bold warriors, and their folklore reflects this attitude. However, each group *always* wins. Neighboring groups often tell the same stories about an identical tribal war with only the ending slightly modified; the group of the folkteller always wins. In the real sense, each group *does* win, for the fighting usually ends with approximately equal amounts of blood spilled and of property destroyed on both sides. Often, tribal fights are described as individual combats, in which the legendary hero of one group defeats another in single combat.

Another important function of the folkteller is genealogical. Many folktellers can recite the entire genealogy of the group's important khans and, as the recitation takes place, intertwine folk songs and folktales. The life of each hero epitomizes a period in time.

Different ethnic groups sometimes have distinct legends of origin and development, but many tales overlap and often spread far beyond the boundaries of Afghanistan. The Turkic-speakers in north Afghanistan usually have variations of *Geser,* the epic of the Mongols. The Uzbak relive their days of greatness in several epics, which tell the story of the Golden Horde and the Central Asian Khanates as reflected by the lives of their great leaders: Alpamysh, Koblandy, Yer-Targyn, Yedigy (who led the attack on Moscow).

The Kirghiz epic, *Manas,* greatly influenced later Islamic historical folklore with its emphasis on the horse-cavalry complex.

One historical folktale I collected in Kohistan illustrates these various points. The historical event described is relatively accurate, but note that the folkteller, a Tajik, plays up the Tajik folk hero, Bacha Saqqao, rather than the Pushtun hero, General Mohammad Nadir Khan (King of Afghanistan from 1929 to 1933). Official Afghan histories, of course, report this incident with different emphasis. The tale traces the actions of Bacha Saqqao after he had been surrounded by Marshal Shah Wali, *Fateh-i-Kabul* ("Conqueror of Kabul"), and the events leading to the death of Bacha Saqqao a few months later:

Bacha Saqqao walked through the entire army of Shah Wali with his wife on his back, and no one in the thousands upon thousands dared lift a weapon against his fierce look. Bacha gathered a few followers around him in his Kohistani home and unsuccessfully attempted to regain the throne. But he remained such a menace that the new king, Mohammad Nadir Shah, invited Bacha Saqqao to come to Kabul and rule Afghanistan jointly with him.

The loyal followers of Bacha Saqqao pleaded with their leader not to trust the Pushtun king for the proverb goes: "Trust a snake before a harlot, and a harlot before a Pushtun."

But the Bacha said, "It was written that I would be a king, and king I was, and king I shall be again, if Allah wills. I go to Kabul to be king again, or to die."

King Mohammad Nadir Shah threw Bacha Saqqao into a dungeon and a few days later, ex-King Habibullah Ghazi (for such was Bacha Saqqao called when he ruled Afghanistan) was executed by a firing squad. He laughed and joked until the shots were fired, and those with him asked, "Oh, Bacha, do you not know your last hour is here?" Bacha replied, "I do not need for you to tell me that. It has been decreed by Allah." A mullah asked why Bacha did not pray as did the others.

"Why should I raise my voice to Allah? He has given me more than I asked for in life, He has made me king. What else shall I ask of Allah? I have always been in his hands."

In another Kohistani village I collected the following variation:

Amanullah was a good king, but he had bad ideas for the people of Afghanistan, and when he was overthrown by Bacha Saqqao, everyone in the country accepted the Bacha as a good king. Some people said he was.Tajik, but this is not true. Bacha Saqqao was an Arab of the purest strain.

He was really named Habibullah Ghazi, and he destroyed all the bad opposition in the country. Shah Mahmud and many members of the Durrani became his supporters. Habibullah Ghazi asked Nadir Khan to come back to help him form a modern army. Nadir Khan agreed, but when he reached India, he talked the Pushtun people into revolting against the true king, Habibullah Ghazi. The British helped Nadir Khan or the Bacha would not have been defeated.

Before his defeat, Bacha sent Shah Mahmud to ask Nadir Khan why he had turned against him after he had offered him the job of commander-in-chief of the army. Shah Mahmud then joined his brother, Nadir Khan, instead of returning to report to the Bacha.

A traitorous general told Nadir Khan about an unguarded pass to Kabul. Shah Wali took a force to Kabul, and found Bacha Saqqao in the *arg* [fort] with only 400 men. Forty thousand of the army of Shah Wali surrounded the *arg*. Bacha Saqqao came forth alone with machine-guns and drove off the entire force. After two days, deserted by all his faithless companions, the Bacha walked out of the *arg* with his wife, I think it was his second wife, on his back. Not a single one of the Pushtun tribesmen dared to fire into that masculine glare.

He marched straight to Charikar and Gulbahar and into the Nijrao area, where he was joined immediately by 60,000 loyal followers.

Frightened, Nadir Khan once again sent Shah Mahmud to beg the Bacha to come to Kabul and discuss who should be King and who of the two should be Prime Minister. Bacha Saqqao was at first against the plan. He asked Shah Mahmud why he had deserted him after he had been so good to him in Kabul.

Bacha's followers, however, were not so bold and brave as Bacha. They wanted to negotiate. After a little thought, the Bacha laughed and said, "Come, let us go to Kabul because I have been king, and am not afraid to die, for if we go to Kabul, the treacherous Durrani will surely kill us. So do not be afraid, it will be as Allah desires. I return to Kabul either to be king or to be a corpse." So Bacha Saqqao and some of his closest companions went to Kabul, and were immediately admitted to see a nervous, floor-pacing Nadir Khan, who had not slept all night. The two great men greeted each other with hugs and kisses. Nadir Khan begged to be excused immediately, claiming to be very sleepy.

Soldiers entered and immediately arrested a laughing Bacha Saqqao and his followers. "Prepare to die," he said.

The next day, shot down by thirteen soldiers, the Bacha died laughing. All the bodies of Bacha and his followers were hung in the Chaman for a week.

Love and Jealousy. In a society where romantic love—though not forbidden—often takes a back seat to family-arranged marriages, legends of passion and jealously serve both as safety valves and to remind men and women what punishment to expect if they violate the code. The preferred marriage for a man is to his father's brother's daughter, or as near that relation as availability permits. Afghan attitudes toward women permeate these tales.

One story will be sufficient to illustrate their flavor. Naturally, the tale has several variations, a common phenomenon in folklore. I collected the following version of a Silas Marner-type tale in a Pushtun village near Qandahar.

Three brothers had children born the same year: to Mohammad Ayub, a son named Khadi; to Mohammad Akbar, a son named Aslam; to Mohammad Sufi, a daughter named Marghalai. Mohammad Akbar and Mohammad Sufi were wealthy farmers, but Mohammad Ayub had lost all his land in a flash flood by the Khash Rud, and worked for his two brothers.

As Khadi and Marghalai grew up together they fell in love, and would meet often in a clump of trees near Koh-i-Duzdan [Mountain of Thieves]. Their love was as pure as they were young, and one day Khadi asked his father to ask his uncle for Marghalai in marriage. The father gently tried to dissuade the son, but could not. So he set out on his impossible task, for he knew that Marghalai had already been promised to her wealthy cousin, Aslam.

When the lovers met the first time after the sad news, they both wept, and Khadi announced his decision to leave and seek his fortune in Hindustan.

"I shall return wealthy and we shall be married," he said, and left in the darkness, followed by the eyes of Marghalai, flooded with tears.

Years passed, and a rich caravan from Hindustan approached. The leader was Khadi, now wealthy and handsome by the grace of Allah. The caravan camped near the same clump of trees, and Khadi, disguised as a peddler, entered the village and asked about Marghalai.

The people told him, "She is well and happy, the wife of Aslam, and the mother of Jamila, 'Ayub, Akbar, and Khadi. Allah has been gracious to her."

"And what of Mohammad Akbar?"

"Dead, many years ago. He died of a broken heart because his son, Khadi, left without a word, the ungrateful wretch!"

Khadi sadly returned to the clump of trees. The caravan left and slowly made its way to Hindustan with its riches, and with Khadi and his broken heart.

This tale contains many recurrent themes found in Afghan folklore: unrequited romantic love; respect for age; filial piety; acceptance of parental authority; the joys of having children; riches and happiness can be attained only if Allah permits.

Many other popular Pashto romances exist, with the hero being a selfless lover who sacrifices himself, and the heroine, his sweetheart, who sacrifices herself. They actually sacrifice each other to each other. Most of these revolve around a Romeo and Juliet theme and among the more common are: *Adam aw* [and] *Durkhani; Fateh Khan aw Rabia; Momen Khan aw Shirini; Shanhdi Khan aw Bibu; Turdalai aw Shahi; Saiful Maluk aw Badri Jamaleh; Sharif Khan aw Mabaie; Farhad aw Shirin; Yusuf aw Zulaika.*

One of the more popular Romeo and Juliet tales in Persian concerns Leila and Majnun, told many times by many poets, both as oral folklore and as literature. Among the Persian poets writing the story of Leila and Majnun were Nizami in the twelfth century and Jami in the fifteenth century (Arberry, 1958, 124, 126, 447–48). The story of Leila and Majnun is basically an ancient Arabian story, and the theme deals with the love of the poet Qais bin-Amir, called Majnun or "Mad One," because his passionate love for the beautiful Leila, daughter of a great nomadic chieftain, drove him insane. Leila, forced to marry another against her will, dies. His arms embracing her gravestone, a heartbroken Majnun follows her in death (Nazimi, 1966).

One tale, with variations, reaches back to the familiar Old Testament story of Joseph and Potiphar's wife. Note this pre-Muslim tale hints at adultery (to be considered later), but really points at the hypocrisy of man (and woman):

> Yusuf [Joseph], son of Ya'kub [Jacob], son of Ibrahim [Abraham] was the youngest son, but the most beloved. He went with his brothers on a trading caravan from Caanan, somewhere in Arabistan, to Egypt. The brothers dumped Yusuf in a well, killed a sheep, wrapped up the sheep in a cloak, then took the bloodied cloak to Ibrahim. A caravan came along, looked in the well, dragged out Yusuf, and sold him as a slave in Egypt.
>
> The handsome young slave became the favorite of the Pharoah's wife, Zulaika. Tongues among jealous females began to wag, so Zulaika held a banquet for her lady friends. She served apples with knives. Then Zulaika asked Yusuf to come in with some grapes. All the lady guests began to swoon and accidentally cut their wrists while looking at the beautiful Yusuf. Zulaika then said, "See, you are just as guilty of secret lust as I am."

Omissions in folklore often reveal as much as the tales themselves recount explicitly. Usually, omitted themes would release disruptive forces if individuals even admitted such thoughts. Probably the most important omitted theme is adultery, because in spite of statements to the contrary, much extramarital dallying goes on in the villages and nomadic camps.[5] Heavy penalties result in discovery: the guilty couple can be stoned to death by the wife's husband and his relatives.

Because of the prevalence of such rural goings-on, however, it seems strange that folktales denouncing the practice do not exist in large numbers, if at all. Several plausible reasons may account for this. Cowardice in battle, a public act, disgraces the group as well as the individual; adultery, a private act between consenting parties, endangers group equilibrium only when made public, and then it disgraces the cuckolded husband's manhood, and, by extension, violates potential property rights of his younger brothers (the levirate). So all the husband's immediate kinsmen become involved in a matter of honor and property.

Possibly the psychological root of the problem goes back to a simple biological fact which has obviously disturbed man for millennia. A

---

[5] For those who wish to read additional documentary proof of the prevalence of marital infidelity, see Chaudri Mohammad Ali (1966); Pehrson (1966, 52–70).

woman always knows she is the mother of her children, but a man can never really be sure he is their biological father.[6] In a tribal-peasant society with the existence of common promiscuity, permissive or non-permissive, sociological fatherhood becomes more important than biological. The sociological father assumes economic and political rights and obligations, as defined by the society, toward the son, and *vice versa*. The unsure biological equation probably helped precipitate the continued efforts of man to prove his superiority over women, carried to extremes in non-literate Islam. I personally believe all the world is a matriarchy, although some societies (or individuals) will not accept this.

By ignoring adultery—or refusing to admit its widespread existence—Afghan villagers and nomads perpetuate group survival. In addition, women play their public economic and social roles as inferiors faithfully, and only in a choice of extramarital sexual partners can they exercise genuine free will in a society which often tends to regard them as simply a form of livestock. Discovery can mean death for the woman and her paramour, and the group would lose two valuable politico-economic creatures, another reason for ignoring the adulterous activities in the villages.

Women, however, sometimes crack under the strain of combined boredom, frustration, and mistreatment and suffer various forms of female hysteria. Often, their families will take them to a shrine near Jalalabad which specializes in such maladies. The woman is trussed up and left overnight at the shrine, cared for and prayed over by the resident brotherhood. Such treatment usually brings her back to normalcy quickly.

Virtue and Morality: These tales articulate the values of the society in both positive (he who does what he should is rewarded) and negative (he who does what he shouldn't is punished) aspects. Although folktales in all five categories emphasize, in one way or another, the idealized basic personality type (a warrior-poet), the virtue and morality themes constantly epitomize the *chevalier preux, sans peur*.

The general traits which characterize the Afghans can be categorized thus: their suspicion of outsiders is modified by a traditional code of

[6] Could this possibly be one of the deep-rooted unconscious reasons for men's aggressive tendencies (assuming they exist) toward one another? In warfare, then, is a man, in blind atavistic jealously, killing the thing which woman can produce and he cannot? By extension, is he killing his own father (whoever he may be) and his own son (whoever the son's father may be)?

hospitality; they believe but seldom worship; they are ruggedly ir-religious unless an outsider challenges their beliefs; their brutality is tempered with the love of beauty; dynamic when work is to be done, they are easily swayed to indolence; their avarice is combined with im-petuous generosity; conservative in their mountain homeland, they adapt quickly to new ideas and techniques when citified; they have an anar-chistic love of individual freedom softened by the accepted rule of their aristocratic khans; their masculine superiority complex tacitly recognizes women's rights; their love of isolation is overlaid by curiosity about the outside world.

The ideals found in folktales, however, focus on key themes expressed in the *Pushtunwali* (or *Pukhtunwali*) and other codes of the hills. Major themes are *melmastia* (being a genial host; giving lavish parties), *mehrmapalineh* (hospitality to guests), *nanawati* (the right of asy-lum, and the obligatory acceptance of a truce offer), *badal* (blood revenge), *tureh* ("sword," i.e., bravery), *meranah* (manhood; chivalry), *'isteqamat* (persistence; constancy), *sabat* (steadfastness), *imandari* (righteousness), *ghayrat* (defense of property and honor), *namus* (de-fense of the honor of women).

I have been collecting local versions of the *Pushtunwali* for many years, and the following paraphrases the major or generally accepted features of the code:

> To avenge blood.
>
> To fight to the death for a person who has taken refuge with me no matter what his lineage. [Example: If a man, rich or poor, kills a man of another lineage, he can force anyone outside the slain man's lineage to help him simply by killing a sheep in front of that individual's hut or tent.]
>
> To defend to the last any property entrusted to me.
>
> To be hospitable and provide for the safety of the person and property of guests.
>
> To refrain from killing a woman, a Hindu, a minstrel, or a boy not yet circumcised.
>
> To pardon an offense on the intercession of a woman of the offender's lineage, a *Sayyid* or a mullah. [An exception is made in the case of murder: only blood or blood-money can erase this crime.]
>
> To punish all adulterers with death.
>
> To refrain from killing a man who has entered a mosque or the

126

shrine of a holy man so long as he remains within its precincts;
also to spare a man in battle who begs for quarter.

This is a stringent code, a tough code for tough men, who of necessity
live tough lives. Honor and hospitality, hostility and ambush, are paired
in the Afghan mind. The values of the Pushtun and of the Muslim religion, modified by local custom, permeate in varying degrees all Afghan
ethnic groups.

The warrior-poet, brave in battle, will also be articulate in the *jirgah,*
able to speak on any subject, evoking poetic imagery and illusion on
specific points. Few men fulfill the idealized requirements to become
great warrior-poets; when they do, however, they become the heroes of
their age, as did Khushal Khan Khattak.

Afghan village and nomadic society has little room for dissidence.
The folktales emphasize this. Some tales describe what happens when
a coward returns home: his mother disowns him. It is almost always
the mother who rejects the coward—again emphasizing the importance
of woman in the society. A coward killed running away from a fight
will not be buried in the Muslim rites. He becomes a ghost, never to
reach Paradise.

This Baluch folktale illustrates many of the themes mentioned in most
virtue and morality tales:

The tents had been pitched and the women prepared the evening
meal. As dusk approached, so did a rider out of the desert. He
rode to the tent of the Khan and threw himself from his horse,
prostrated himself at the Khan's feet, and demanded protection.
He was being followed, he claimed, by a large band of horsemen
with whom his family had a blood feud. The old Khan, wise beyond years, and as pure as his white beard, granted the supplicant
asylum. The man was led to the guest tent and there fed, and told
to prepare himself for the evening.

The Khan's young son came to his father and cried, "Oh my
father! That is Badshah Gul, who but two months ago slew my
brother and your son."

"Yes, my son, but now he is a guest in our camp. He has asked
for asylum. We have given him asylum. And remember, my son,
even if it takes a hundred years, your brother's death, my son's
death, will be avenged."

The young son, inflamed, left his father's tent and, taking his brother's dagger from its honored place, crept to the guest tent and buried the dagger into the breast of the guest, as they had buried his brother two months before.

The next morning, amid cries and lamentations, the body of the guest was discovered. Tearing his clothing, ripping his turban in agony, the old Khan cried, "Who could have done this? Who could have brought dishonor on the name of our family? The camps of the Baluch will forever condemn us for this dishonor!"

The young son threw himself at his father's feet and begged forgiveness, saying that in a moment of blind rage, he had dishonored the group.

The old Khan took the knife which had killed the guest and plunged it into the heart of his son.

The Baluch camps still tell of the killing in the guest tent, but they tell the story with honor.

Afghan parents often scare children into obedience and respect by threatening them with bogeymen (*jinn,* fairies, giants) who will spirit them away. In Nuristan, children learn early of an "abominable snowman" type of creature, and some adults actually claim to have been attacked by the beast.

Kalilah-wa-Dumnah, Persian versions of animal fables (resembling those of Aesop), have long been used in Afghan schools to teach moral values. Villagers and nomads know many more in the oral tradition.

Jokes: This category of folkloric themes includes those "safety-valve" tales which attack certain institutions by using individuals as butts of the jokes, often filled with *double entendre.* Many can only be called dirty stories. Peasants and nomadic herdsmen, living close to nature, have earthy, descriptive, foul but flowery ways of expressing poetic images in everyday intercourse, a talent carefully hidden from casual visitors. Current political jokes also serve as outlets for the literate Afghan as his country moves, for some much too slowly, toward a democratic system of government.

Religious leaders, usually behind their backs, become the butt of jokes in villages. But who can say whether or not these religious men do not possess the power to curse in the name of Allah? The Afghan feeling of independence and equality is strong in these jokes. A common figure of fun throughout the Muslim world is the Mullah Nasruddin. At times a sharp operator who outwits all his opponents, he sometimes becomes trapped in his own net of intrigue. At other times the Mullah slyly attacks Muslim ideas and society to make specific points.

Two stories concerning the Mullah Nasruddin will illustrate these types of stories:

The Mullah Nasruddin had a beautiful daughter, the desire of all the evil eyes of the men living in his village. Everyone sought the hand of the fair maiden, but the Mullah Nasruddin protected her from the outside world, saving her for the wealthy young Khan who lived just outside the village.

At last the young Khan came to ask for the hand of the beautiful maiden. The Mullah Nasruddin drove a hard bargain and was to receive the highest bride-price ever bargained for in the entire region. With the usual Muslim regard for ceremony, the Mullah Nasruddin insisted on a long waiting-period before the wedding vows could be taken.

It seems that the young and beautiful daughter of the Mullah Nasruddin had a mind and a body of her own. She fell in love with a young stalwart ne'er-do-well in the village, who constantly showered her with attention as she went to the nearby well to gather water in the morning and at dusk. Her trips to get water began to take longer periods of time. Most people in the village knew what was happening, but no one dared tell the Mullah Nasruddin.

The time for the wedding approached and the young, wealthy Khan came to collect his bride. Mullah Nasruddin brought her to greet her betrothed. Lo and behold! She was well pregnant by this time. The young, rich Khan was horrified, and turned on the Mullah Nasruddin, demanding to know why such a thing had occurred. And when the Mullah Nasruddin merely replied that such things are normal when people get married, the young, rich Khan stormed out of the Mullah Nasruddin's compound, and said that he withdrew his offer of marriage to the young and beautiful daughter of the Mullah Nasruddin and therefore would expect a return of the down payment on the bride price.

The Mullah Nasruddin, genuinely shocked, called after the young, rich Khan and the young Khan returned. "Let us be sensible about this," pleaded the Mullah Nasruddin. "Actually, I should double the bride price now that my daughter is truly pregnant and can give you a son."

The young Khan, even more horrified, stuttered and asked, "In the Name of Allah, why?"

The Mullah Nasruddin calmly replied, "Why just last week I delivered a cow to a man to whom I had sold the cow several months before. In the interim period, the cow became pregnant, and when I delivered the cow, I demanded and received twice the original amount. Now what is so different between a cow and a daughter?"

*

Nasruddin heard that there was a banquet being held in the nearby town, and that everyone was invited. He made his way there as quickly as he could. When the Master of Ceremonies saw him in his ragged cloak, he seated him in the most inconspicuous place, far from the great table where the most important people were being waited on hand and foot.

Nasruddin saw that it would be an hour at least before the waiters reached where he was sitting. So he got up and went home. He dressed himself in a magnificent sable cloak and turban and returned to the feast. As soon as the heralds of the Emir, his host, saw this splendid sight they started to beat the drum of welcome and sound the trumpets in a manner befitting a visitor of high rank.

The Chamberlain came out of the palace himself, and conducted the magnificent Nasruddin to a place almost next to the Emir. A dish of wonderful food was immediately placed before him. Without a pause, Nasruddin began to rub handfuls of it into his turban and cloak.

"Your Eminence," said the prince, "I am curious as to your eating habits, which are new to me."

"Nothing special," said Nasruddin; "the cloak got me in here and got me the food. Surely it deserves its portion." (Paraphrased from Idris Shah, 1967, 42).

The final tale, a morality joke with personality implications, comes from Laghman:

One night, three thieves of the Ut Khel tribe approached a peddler riding a donkey. After salaams, two of the thieves walked on either side of the peddler, regaling him with enchanting stories, while the third walked behind, jabbing the donkey with a pointed stick to keep him moving at a steady pace. The two thieves then gently lifted the saddle of the weary peddler, while the third led away the donkey, heavily laden with bazaar goods. The peddler eventually fell asleep and the Ut Khel thieves lowered him to the ground and hastily left to join their fellow thief.

CHAPTER 10

Settlement Patterns

SEVERAL factors, among them ecology, technology, and historical accident, influence settlement patterns and crystallize Afghan ethnic groups into two general categories, sedentary and non-sedentary. The interactional complex includes sedentary villages, towns, and cities, and their relationships to nomads, semi-nomads, and semi-sedentary groups.

Village

The terms *qaryah* (Dari) and *keley* (Pashto) are usually used to mean village. *Deh* also means village, but today it is particularly used to compound names to refer to specific villages, e.g., Deh Morasi, Qadzi Deh.

Two types of completely sedentary village settlement-patterns exist: linear and nuclear. The linear type, common in Southeast Asia (Ahmad, 1956), occurs along the major rivers, clinging to the watercourses. The nuclear pattern, in which villages cluster about a town, and several village-town clusters surround a city, is more common in Afghanistan. Villages usually grew in response to needs for water and defense.

The villages, generally self-sufficient subsistence units, must obtain certain items (tea, sugar, salt, iron implements, cloth, mirrors, trinkets, kerosene, lamps and lamp chimneys, matches, etc.) from either a town bazaar or itinerant peddlers. Until recently, the Afghan village had two interesting peculiarities when compared to other Asian villages: no bazaars and no wheels. Therefore, few full-time specialists live in the village. A man is a farmer first and foremost, although some farmers do function as part-time specialists: carpenters, masons, bricklayers, butchers, shoemakers, and mullah. These men practice their subspecialties after completing their daily or annual farm work. Occasionally, regional part-time specialists seasonally travel from area to area on the off-agricultural season; the Andar Pushtun, for example, are experts in constructing and repairing the *qanat* in winter; some Wardak Pushtun travel to eastern Afghanistan to construct *qal'ah* (Dari, fortress-residences with watchtowers; called *kalah* in Pashto). In the West most people spend their days as professional specialists or technicians, but

25. Badakhshan. Uzbak *qishlaq* (winter quarters) of Chenar-i-Baba, Darwesh near Kishm. Semisedentary pattern. August, 1966

26. Eastern Mountains: village of Wama in Nuristan. Note house types, typical of region. April, 1963

Afghans on the whole are generalists, following diurnal and annual ecological cycles.

The wheel, primarily on bicycles, now appears in some villages within
the infrastructured zones of easy accessibility. But the pre-World War
II Afghan village had no wheels for transport. The only wheel in the
countryside was the potter's wheel, usually in the towns and city
bazaars. Even today, small groups of semi-sedentary or semi-nomadic
potters pause seasonally in various villages.

The principal manner of transport has always been on foot (most
common), or on horses, donkeys, and camels. Some villagers, particularly among the sedentary Pushtun, use cattle as beasts of burden to
haul logs and to bring reaped cereals from the fields to the threshing
and winnowing areas.

The Afghans use hand-drawn ferries extensively to cross rivers and
streams, but only the Sayyad Baluch of the Sistan Basin regularly use
dugout or plank boats and canoes (*tutin*) constructed from the reeds
which grow in the swamps. They also make huts of the reeds.

House types vary with terrain and available building material, but
almost always occupy non-productive land (Alberts and Dupree, ms.).
The most common house type in high, dry Afghanistan is square or
rectangular, made of sun-dried brick covered with a mud and straw
plaster. The bricks are made in wooden molds, then placed on the
ground to dry. Flat roofs of rammed earth interlaced with twigs are
supported on mat-covered beams. Stone foundations commonly occur
in mountainous areas. Although slanted tin roofs are becoming more
popular in Kabul, most Afghan houses continue to have flat mud roofs,
which must be shoveled free of snow in the winter and remudded every
fall or they will leak.

In the west, both in the Turkestan Plains and along the Irano–Afghan
border, a squarish dome-roof variant exists, possibly related to the conical beehive dwellings found in central Anatolia and northern Syria. A
roof opening (*badgir*) admits air and light and expels smoke. Many
villages in western Afghanistan consist of such interconnected beehive
huts, and the villagers construct additional segments as new nuclear
families come into being. A post-World War II variant in southwestern
Afghanistan extends into Iranian and Pakistani Baluchistan and has a
rectangular floor plan with a tunnel-vault roof and with or without
frame windows. In Baluchistan, semi-circular reed huts are made by
some Baluch and Brahui groups, particularly semi-nomadic and semi-
sedentary peoples. They do not plant trees and bend them over, as de-

27. Family compound, Shahr-i-Naw (the "New City"), Kabul. March, 1960

28. Hazara family, living on rooftop in summer, Kabul. June, 1965

scribed in some of the literature (Fairservis, 1961, 28), or, rather, they do not do so in modern times. They may have done so in the past. They do, however, use *chapari* (mats spread over poles) as temporary huts.

Particularly south and west of the Hindu Kush, crushed limestone or gypsum are first fired and then mixed with water to form *gatch,* an adequate plaster used in construction.[1]

Mud walls of varying heights line meandering lanes and enclose the small compounds of the houses. Some newer houses in villages do not have compound walls, but these are rare. Traditionally, walls ensured privacy, and corralled the livestock at night. The compound usually includes storage sheds, animal pens, cooking areas, a general area for family work and play, and sometimes a small pool, or *juy* (artificial stream, small canal), for ablutions, and washing dishes or clothing. Women and girls often transport water home several times a day from a local stream, *juy,* or well, in porous pottery jugs which cool water by evaporation. The trip to communal sources of water gives the women a chance to leave the compound, to socialize with each other, and to flirt with the men. Various size tin cans up to five-gallon kerosene tins increase annually in popularity for water collecting and storage.

Typically, a village residence has two or three rooms, carpeted with rugs, or *gelim,* if the owner can afford them. Most villages have guest rooms or guest houses for the traveler. The village mosque often serves this function, as well as being the *jirgah* meeting place, and seasonal school. At other times, villages hold meetings under large trees in open communal gardens. Household furnishings consist mainly of cooking utensils, pots, cups, and saucers, religious mementos, inherited heirlooms (guns, sword, old basins, *aftabah,*[2] etc.), storage chests and containers, stone or clay lamps, *'alekan* (kerosene lamps) or *gazlamp* (new "Persian" words), and samovars among the more affluent.

Grains are often stored in large pottery bins which sit off the floor on sturdy pottery legs to keep insects and chickens from raiding the food supply. The cloth stopper commonly used to seal the opening at the lower end proves ineffective, however, and I have seen chickens casually peck out the stopper and eat their fill. Prehistoric designs identi-

---

[1] See Wulff (1966) and Mitsukuni and Kihei (1966) for excellent technological discussions of house-building and other technical aspects of material culture.

[2] Usually brass or tin-plated copper, the *aftabah* (water jug) has a long curved neck and is used to wash before meals and before prayers, as well as after relieving oneself.

136

29. Mangal Pushtun *qala* (fortress-dwelling compound). Paktya. August, 1960

30. Multi-storied houses, *pisé* walls, stone foundations, in middle Panjsher Valley, Bazarak. March, 1963

cal to those on steatite and copper seals from Deh Morasi Ghundai
(L. Dupree, 1963a) and Mundigak (Casal, *D.A.F.A.* xvii, 1961, see
Appendix F), have been deeply incised on the outside of most storage
jars.

Occasionally, a villager will own a *charpayi* (rope or string bed with
wooden frame), but in most places rolls of mattress-bedding, stacked
neatly during the day, are laid out nightly. The flat rooftops usually
serve for summer sleeping, drying fruits and vegetables, and as auxiliary
work areas. At times a tamped-earth platform in front of the hut is
similarly utilized. If weather permits, cooking takes place outside the
huts. Charcoal, *busah* (or *butah,* oily roots and branches), and dung
patties are the chief fuels. Women and children gather all animal refuse
and the women shape it into cakes about ten or twelve inches in diameter. They slap the dung patties, each with a handprint in the middle,
onto the outside of the house or onto flat rock surfaces to dry.

In some areas, smoke holes are pierced through the center of the
roof or in a corner of the room. In other areas (such as Nuristan),
smoke holes seldom exist, and eyes smart as the thick smoke seeks an
exit.

Many village huts, particularly south of the Hindu Kush (Kabul Valley, Maidan, Logar, Ghazni, Ningrahar), have a type of forced hot-air,
tunneled, heating system (*tawkhanah*) under the floor. A *busah* fire built
at one end quickly heats the floor. Nightime winter chill dissipates and
sleep comes more comfortably. The villagers carefully control the fires
to prevent their spreading.

Afghans place small, low, wooden tables over *manghal* (charcoal
braziers), and spread a blanket out over the table so that it drapes to
the floor. Then whole families sit around the *sandali* (as the system
is called), covering legs, arms, and much of their bodies under the
blanket to absorb the heat. *Bukhari,* Central Asian style wood-, char-
coal- and sawdust-burning stoves, are popular in urban centers.

Numerous departures from these general characteristics exist. In both
north and south, as one moves from the plains up the mountainous valleys, stone gradually replaces mud-brick and *pisé* (pressed mud) construction. For example, north of Charikar in the Panjsher Valley, we
first encounter foundations of stone. Moving up the valley the transition
is gradual, and the stone walls creep slowly up from the foundation
until, at Kotal-i-Khawak on the lower slopes of the Hindu Kush, all
four walls consist of stone, often rounded river boulders, chinked with
mud plaster. Most houses in the Panjsher have two stories, and in the

31. Mud huts built under natural rock shelter. Hazarajat. November, 1959

32. Farsiwan (Persian-speakers of Western Afghanistan) beehive-domed huts between Herat and Qala-yi-Naw. July, 1969

winter, animals sleep inside on the ground floor. As the heat rises from their bodies, the upper floor becomes warmer.

A peculiar type of structure (called *sayagi khanah* in Kohistan north of Kabul and *kishmish khanah* around Qandahar) dries green grapes into raisins. These mud-brick buildings have rectangular loop-holes for air circulation, and often look like block houses. Inside, bunches of grapes hang from wooden poles. Grapes dried outside in the sun become red raisins.

Windmills in western Afghanistan sit along the Iranian frontier from north of Herat all the way into Sistan. (N. Wolfe, 1966, 44. See also Ferdinand, 1963b, 1966–67; Wulff, 1966.)

Windmills have been a part of Herat's landscape since the seventh century when they were first described by Arab geographers. From these sources we know that the entire area around and along the eastern borders of Iran, the area, that is, of ancient Khorasan, was liberally dotted with windmills. Furthermore, early twentieth-century travelers also describe ruined windmills around Kabul and Ghazni and as far east as the Indus River. But even then they were but relics of the past. Though these first windmills antedate the appearance of windmills in Europe and China, the question as to whether the latter were inspired by those of Khorasan, or whether they were independently invented, has not been settled with absolute certainty. Many, however, are firmly convinced that the windmills of ancient Khorasan were indeed the source of inspiration.

The windmills of Herat operate only during the period locally referred to as 'the time of the 120 days' wind' which normally blows from June to September. This is also the time of the wheat harvest. During this period the mills work day and night.

Outside Herat the mills are built singly or in pairs, but in other parts of the province, as for instance at Ghorian, it is not uncommon to find a line of ten to twelve mills adjoining each other. Early twentieth-century reports record as many as 50 and 75 mills built together in single long rows. These mills are at first not readily recognizable to the Western eye for they do not have the huge wheeled arms with which Don Quixote fenced. The lower half consists of a square mud-walled room. Here one finds the millstones which are fed by means of a wooden feeder from a larger hopper built into the side wall. Resting against the upper millstone and

33. Vertical windmill, Herat. May, 1965. *Photo: Hubbard Goodrich*

the feeder there is a small rod known as the vibrator-stick. The movement of the turning stone vibrates this rod which in turn shakes the grain from the feeder. Against the other wall there is a long trough for the collection of the milled flour after it is thrown out from between the two millstones.

The mill-shaft is made from white poplar and rises from the center of the millstones through the arched roof of the mill-house. To this shaft are attached six sails to each of which two reed mats are affixed. These sails spin between walls on two sides forming a well which aids in funneling the wind. At Herat the outer edges of this well are attractively stepped. (Quoted from N. Wolfe, 1966).

Pigeon towers to collect droppings are at least five hundred years old in the Iranian plateau (Beazley, 1966), the manure being used for fertilizer and tanning. The towers are mainly found in western Afghanistan, but some exist near Kabul and other major cities.

Only in the relatively heavily forested areas of Nuristan and Paktya do complicated wooden houses exist. A special class of artisans called Bari build the Nuristani houses, which perch on high mountain slopes, the dwellings strung together like a DNA helix. One man's roof is another man's work and play area. The Bari artisans perform all their complicated carpentry using adzes and knives.

Mountain-dwelling Pushtun in Paktya often build two-story mud-brick and stone houses, roofed with slate, staggered one on top of the other, much like the Pueblo dwellings in the southwestern United States. Ladders must be used to climb from roof to roof.

In flatter areas, however, men stand atop circular watchtowers overlooking the vineyards, orchards, and grain fields, which surround most Pushtun villages, and give warning of approaching raiders, bandits, or animal predators. Often, individual compounds have their own watchtowers.

Some sedentary cave-dwellers exist in Afghanistan, particularly in the Hazarajat, where the people build large sun-dried brick and *pisé* structures inside the openings of large rock shelters found along the river terraces.

Although I previously decried the lack of adequate statistics available for Afghanistan, we do have several general censuses which help clarify the sedentary *vs.* non-sedentary picture, at least in the gross quantitative sense. Charts 8, 9, and 11 are taken from *Population and Agricultural*

34. Nuristanis at Wama. Distinctive daggers are expensive prestige items. Twenty-foot-long leggings protect legs from brush. Knee-length pantaloons also unique to Nuristan. Men often go barefoot all winter. April, 1963

CHART 8
Approximate Number of Villages in Afghanistan, 1963

Province	Total number of villages in province
Kabul	1,323
Herat	1,329
Qandahar	1,576
Mazar-i-Sharif	763
Qataghan	1,417
Ningrahar	1,103
Paktya	534
Farah	584
Maimana	483
Badakhshan	649
Parwan	668
Ghazni	1,706
Girishk	381
Shibarghan	498
Ghor	649
Uruzgan	379
Bamiyan	162
Total:	14,205

CHART 9

Reported Occupations of Village Population: 1963

Province	Percentage males listing an occupation	Percent of occupied males who are:						
		Religious Teachers	Farmers	Shepherds	Blacksmiths	Carpenters	Barbers	Other
Kabul	34.9	6.7	86.6	1.9	0.4	1.9	1.5	1.0
Herat	30.2	8.6	79.2	10.9	0.4	0.1	0.6	0.2
Qandahar	59.5	7.8	65.7	1.4	0.1	0.1	0	24.8
Mazar-i-Sharif	32.0	6.8	76.2	12.6	0.7	0.9	0.6	2.2
Qataghan	28.5	12.4	75.7	6.7	0.9	1.1	1.4	1.8
Ningrahar	28.3	2.0	94.2	1.5	0.2	0	0.4	1.6
Paktya	17.4	9.4	74.0	11.1	4.1	0.3	1.1	0
Farah	20.5	12.7	69.9	7.7	1.9	2.7	3.5	1.2
Maimana	18.8	11.0	72.8	4.1	2.0	3.7	4.4	0.8
Badakhshan	48.2	5.7	78.5	6.0	0.3	0.2	0.1	9.1
Parwan	51.5	9.5	89.1	2.5	0.5	0.7	1.1	3.6
Ghazni	41.0	6.5	89.2	2.0	0.5	0.4	0.6	0.7
Girishk	18.3	12.8	77.2	7.5	0.3	1.0	0.9	0
Shibarghan	–	–	–	–	–	–	–	..
Ghor	32.0	9.9	85.7	0	4.4	0.3	0.3	0
Uruzgan	27.3	9.1	85.8	3.4	0.7	0.8	0.3	0
Bamiyan	35.5	5.2	84.2	7.3	0.4	0.4	0	2.5
Weighted average, all provinces using estimated total village population for weights	35.5	8.5	80.3	5.4	1.1	1.0	1.0	3.4

CHART 10
Distribution of Labor Force in Afghanistan: 1966–67

Total Estimated Population of Afghanistan: 15,400,000

Sector	Numbers	Percentage
Agriculture	2,942,000	77.0
Industry, handicrafts	231,000	6.0[1]
Construction and Mines	83,000	2.2
Transport and Communications	30,000	0.8
Education	12,000	0.3
Health	6,000	0.2
Trade	106,000	2.8
Civil Service	60,000	1.6
Miscellaneous activities in rural areas (undefined)	350,000	9.1[1]
	3,820,000	100.0

Source: *Survey of Progress, 1968-1969,* Department of Statistics, Ministry of Planning, Kabul, September, 1969, p. 37.

[1]If these figures (indicating part-time work) are added to Agriculture Sector, population engaged in farming and herding approximates 90% (author's note).

CHART 11
Estimated Distribution of Agricultural Land by Form of Tenure
by Province: 1963

Province	Percent of total land which is (derived estimates):			
	Sharecropped	Mortgaged	Owner operated	Other
Kabul	16.1	6.6	74.9	2.4
Qandahar	9.1	7.5	54.1	29.3
Herat	13.4	0.7	62.7	23.2
Mazar-i-Sharif	23.6	1.5	60.0	14.8
Ningrahar	5.4	43.6	45.1	5.9
Paktya	2.0	3.7	94.3	–
Qataghan	22.2	5.8	63.2	8.7
Ghazni	8.1	11.2	79.6	1.1
Girishk	6.4	5.7	18.7	69.2
Farah	24.1	11.2	60.1	14.3
Maimana	2.4	0.6	75.2	21.8
Shibarghan	–	–	–	–
Badakhshan	1.3	0.8	75.4	22.4
Parwan	5.8	9.1	80.0	5.1
Bamiyan	1.6	0.6	73.9	23.8
Uruzgan	13.3	5.8	79.8	1.1
Ghor	12.1	1.2	75.8	10.9
	13.8	5.5	60.5	20.2

Av. for all prov. except Shibarghan

Survey of 500 Villages (*1963*), undertaken by the Ministry of Planning. The Department of Statistics and Research admits wide margins for error on several of the interpolations, primarily because of the reluctance of villagers to answer questions concerning ownership of property and livestock (they feared increased taxes) and the number of sons (they feared conscription), in spite of assurances of annonymity given by the poll-takers.

However, the number of villages (Chart 8) tends to coincide with rough field-counts I have made in several provinces on the ground and with the use of aerial photos. This is also true of the percentage of land (Chart 11) owned by cultivators (about 50 percent) and the lack of non-agricultural occupational specialization in villages (Chart 9). I suspect that any villager listing an occupation other than farmer-herder still functions primarily as a farmer, which is certainly true in the villages I have studied. Therefore, with these warnings, I present several tables from the survey. Chart 10 must also be considered with the same precautions in mind.

In addition to the Ministry of Planning reports, about 8 to 10 percent of the villages in Qataghan and Badakhshan have been surveyed by the WHO Malaria Eradication teams (Dr. Korkut Kardas, personal communication, 1959). From a study of 190,000 houses, the following tentative conclusions were reached: 1) living space per person inside the huts averaged 65 square meters, compared to approximately 50 square meters per head for the rest of the country; 2) an average of one nuclear family per room or ten people per house existed.

Land Tenure (Chart 11): "Land systems determine social attitudes, social satisfaction. They are interwoven with national tradition, even with national character." (Warriner, 1955, 21.)

As an anthropologist, I take mild issue with the word "determine," but none can deny the important correlation between land ownership and the total cultural patterns in any society. Transient journalists and self-styled reformers often whip themselves into pseudo-religious frenzies over the inequities of absentee landlordism, but seldom does anyone objectively consider the complex, functional interrelationships which comprise land tenure systems.

Basically, agricultural production in Afghanistan involves five elements: land, water, seed, animal or mechanical power, and human labor. Theoretically, whoever contributes one of the elements receives one-fifth of the resulting crop. Land and water rights often go together. Usually, the landowner also supplies the seed. Animal or tractor power

35. and 36. Construction techniques, beehive-domed huts near Aq Chah. September, 1969

37. Alikozai Durrani Pushtun, winter plowing near Qandahar. November, 1950

38. Uzbak farmers winnowing wheat with wooden fork and shovel. Zarshoy, south of Maimana. August, 1969

for plowing and cultivation may be provided by the landlord, the cultivator, or a professional oxen or water buffalo owner. In many instances, the individual who plows, plants, weeds, tends, reaps, and winnows the ·crop receives only the one-fifth due for labor. With this, he supports his family and usually dreams unfulfilled dreams of buying his own farm.

Land ownership often, though not always, leads to a higher standard of living and increased political power.

Little beyond the landlord's own personal integrity curbs his exploitive tendencies. Largely immune to social pressures and far from being restrained by Islamic ethics (as interpreted by conservative religious leaders), he often uses them to manage more efficiently his God-fearing, predeterministically-oriented tenants. In addition, many religious leaders themselves are large landowners.

Absentee ownership, an outgrowth of the land tenure system, fosters and perpetuates certain abuses. The large owner normally controls holdings through resident lieutenants often referred to as headmen (*malik*) or overseers (*arbab;* at times refers to actual owners), with some loyalty to both owner and tenants. At times, the rent collector-headman takes advantage of his position and extorts unreasonably high shares from the tenants. The landlord seldom visits his villages, inspects the overseer's accounts, or questions his methods as long as he delivers the proper quotas. The landlord tends to become remote and the peasant more subject to abuses when village lands are leased or sub-leased to speculators, who install their own professional overseers.

Many ask why the peasant docilely accepts his condition. Several factors reinforce the *status quo:* the failure of periodic revolts; the peasant's belief in the predeterministic aspects of a man's existence; and such peasant traits as strong individualism and non-cooperation outside the family, skepticism, and suspicion of neighbors as well as outsiders, pride and vanity, all preclude easy mobilization of the villagers for concerted non-religiously oriented action.

Other factors which help keep the peasant in line include the relative lack of mobility within the class system, the lack of positive alternatives, and the threat of expulsion or economic sanctions. Many landlords rotate tenants periodically to frustrate the formation of local clique alignments.

However, all landlords should not be stereotyped as mercenary tyrants. Viewed from within the total cultural milieu, the landlord becomes a major entrepreneur, juggling extensive operations and tremendous capital, understandably wishing to advance the interests of his class and leave his son or sons a worthy inheritance.

The relationship between landlord and tenant, landlord and overseer, and overseer and tenant involves much give and take, however. Many landlords in Afghanistan take a paternalistic interest in their peasants. The wise landlord or overseer listens to the recommendations of the community's respected *rish-i-safidan* ("white beards" or elders) in minor matters. Such permissiveness usually does not indicate weakness on the landlord's part, however, and he would not hesitate to drive a recalcitrant peasant from one of his villages.

In fact, peasants are seldom as docile as they appear to outsiders. Generations of exploitation have taught them many survival techniques not obvious to the casual eye. Laxity, stubbornness, stealing, false reporting of productivity, hiding a part of the crop, and conniving with the overseer against the owner constitute but a few methods of a not-so-passive resistance to a lopsided land tenure system.

In any event, kinship, peer-group affiliations, territorial identification, and common grievances tend to cement the peasantry psychologically, if not physically, and generate an *esprit de corps* which neither landlord nor his agent can stifle without the risk of upheaval or, more important, declining profits.

On the positive side, landlords and agents serve as buffers between the state and the peasant, who still prefers to remain as remote as possible from any government institution. Simple land reform, or giving the land to the peasant, is not the answer. Integrated approaches must be taken so that when the peasant does receive land of his own, he can adequately cope with outside as well as inside pressures, which build up to deprive him of his newly acquired land.

Land reforms, without adequate protective measures, lead to another type of land ownership, in which city opportunists will lend money to the peasant and very shortly gain the land, or traveling nomads, with relatively great wealth, will do the same. In addition, sharp peasants living in the village will themselves take over land from their less technically efficient peers.

Land reform can occur by accident. For example, after the December, 1959, Qandahar land-tax riots in Afghanistan, the Government surreptitiously released rumors that land reforms would follow shortly, and that no one could own more than 30 *jerib* (15 acres). Many large landholders immediately began to sell land to their landless peasants, and land reform by rumor was accomplished. Generally speaking, only the more competent and energetic peasants who had been able to save large sums of capital over the years were able to purchase land. Few of these new landowners, gaining land through a competitive system, have lost their land. Most peasant sharecroppers still remain perpetually in debt to landlords and moneylenders. Actually, a major absentee landlord problem does not exist in Afghanistan, and according to 1968 estimates, fairly reliable I think, only about 30 individuals in Afghanistan own over 1,000 *jerib* of land.

Town

Towns (*shahr*) generally occur where several major trails intersect, usually near a large river. Since 1953, new asphalt roads have been built within a day's walking distance of most towns.

The town is usually the lowest commercial, administrative, and communications entity. Villagers often bring raw materials, local village products, and agricultural produce to the town by donkey, horse or on their own backs. The goods are then shipped to the cities by truck, camel, or donkey. Many of the larger towns have horse-drawn, two-wheeled *gawdi* (similar to the Indian *tonga*) for local transportation. The lower-grade civil servants and quasi-military police have their headquarters in the town, and landlords who own land in the surrounding villages often live in the town. Trucks transport finished goods from cities to towns, which always have a bazaar street along the main, and frequently the only, street. Full-time specialists—iron-mongers, potters (Demont and Centlivres, 1967), weavers, dyers, carpenters, masons, general storekeepers, bicycle repair men, automotive repair men, caravansarai owners—generally live above their shops in the bazaar, thus occupational-residential unity exists (L. Dupree, 1968c).

Many structures in towns, particularly government buildings, are now constructed with bricks (*khist-i-pokhtah*) baked in kilns.

The town bazaar, especially the *samovar,* also acts as an important disseminator of news. Although *samovar* is the common name for teahouse in Afghanistan, the Iranian Farsi term, *chaykhanah,* has come into popular usage (particularly among foreigners) since World War II. No longer must the Afghans depend on a face-to-face, word-of-mouth situation as a primary spreader of rumors and news. All *chaykhanah* have

39. Covered bazaar,
Khulm. March, 1966

40. Bazaar street, Qandahar. Women on right wearing traditional *chadri*. Mosque
on left. July, 1969

transistor radios capable of picking up most stations from Radio Peking to the Voice of America. Radios have also made multiple appearances in the villages and only the remoter areas lack at least one transistor radio. Even some nomads tend their flocks to the tunes of a small radio. Many *chaykhanah* have a hand-cranked phonograph, which blares out 78 r.p.m. recorded music, which is primarily Hindu film music. Indian films are very popular in Afghanistan in towns and cities where film theaters exist: Kabul, Jalalabad, Qandahar, Herat, Mazar-i-Sharif, Maimana, Kunduz, Pul-i-Khumri.

The new provincial system promulgated in March, 1964, forced the creation of many new provincial capitals with "new" administrative towns constructed separately from the "old" towns. Often, the ubiquitous rivers needed to supply a town's water needs neatly divide the "old" and "new" urban centers. Villages have grown into towns, and towns reverted to village status as the post-1950 infrastructure developed, and road systems shifted.

Afghanistan's new provincial system attempts to decentralize in order to speed up economic and political development, and the towns serve as the links up and down the administrative chain.

The Afghan government divided the 7 major and 7 minor provinces (Map 7) into 28 provinces (Map 8), all technically of equal rank. Originally, the 1964 plan called for 29, but Urgun–Katawaz Province still exists only on paper and in reality remains divided between Ghazni and Paktya. (Map 7).[3] As old roads and trails improve and new ones penetrate the less accessible areas, some neighboring provinces will probably join to form larger units and the total number will reduce from the present 28.

At first, the concept may seem illogical, but on closer examination it reveals a realistic approach. The provinces vary in size; the more accessible the area to roads and telecommunications, the smaller the province; generally those geographic regions with forbidding zones of inaccessibility are much larger.

A three-phase process appears to be evolving: 1) increase the number of provinces to encourage local involvement with provincial representatives of the central government; 2) as the infrastructure breaches zones of relative inaccessibility, further increase the number of provinces to increase development potential; 3) decrease the number of provinces

---

[3] See the *Kabul Times Annual* (1967) for complete list of provinces and outline sketches concerning each.

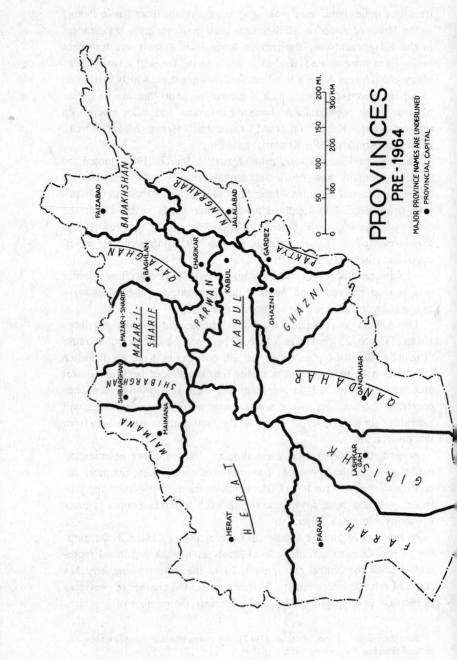

PROVINCES
PRE-1964

MAJOR PROVINCE NAMES ARE UNDERLINED
● PROVINCIAL CAPITAL

200 MI.
300 KM
150
100
50
0

FAIZABAD

BADAKHSHAN

NINGRAHAR

JALALABAD

QATAGHAN

BAGHLAN

CHARIKAR

GARDEZ

PAKTYA

PARWAN

KABUL

MAZAR-I-SHARIF

GHAZNI

GHAZNI

SHIBARGHAN

SHIBARGHAN

QANDAHAR

QANDAHAR

MAIMANA

MAIMANA

GIRISHK

LASHKAR GAH

HERAT

FARAH

HERAT

FARAH

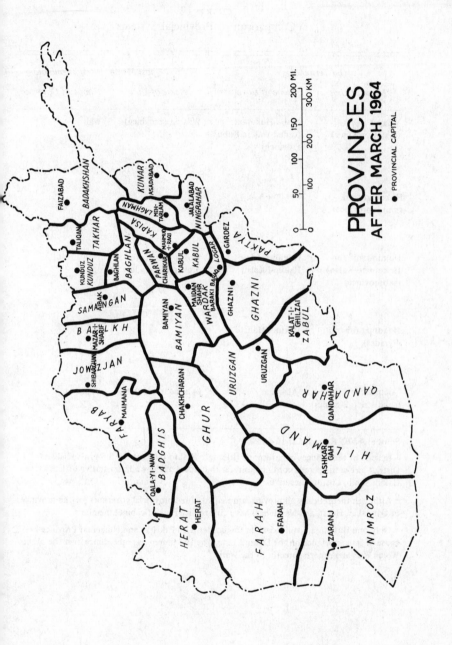

PROVINCES
AFTER MARCH 1964

● PROVINCIAL CAPITAL

CHART 12

Comparison of Provincial Systems

Old Terminology		New (post March, 1964) Terminology	
Name of Unit	*Name of Governor*[2]	*Name of Unit*	*Name of Governor*
Wilayat (major province)	Naib-i-Hukumat (called Wali in Kabul Province)	Wilayat (province)	Wali
Hukumat-i-a'la (minor province)	Hakim-i-A'la		
Hukumrani[3] (or Hukumat-i-Kalan) (subprovince)	Hukumran (or Hakim-i-Kalan)	Wolus Wali[1] (sub-province; 4 grades)	Wolus Wal
Hukumat (district; 4 grades)	Hakim-i-Mahalli		
'Alaqadari (subdistrict; 2 grades)	'Alaqadar	'Alaqadari (district)	'Alaqadar

Source: *A UFS Report,* LD-10-66

[1] In spite of the changes in governor's titles into Pashto terms at the Subprovincial and District levels, the people continue to refer to holders of these administrative offices as Hakim Sahib. Custom dies hard.

[2] Although theoretically all provinces are equal, three provincial governors (of the provinces of Qandahar, Herat, and Ningrahar) have civil service rank of cabinet members.

[3] Only one Hukumrani still exists on the border with Pakistan and Ningrahar Province because of its importance on the Durand Line. The Hukumran has precedence over the other Wolus Wals and reports directly to the Wali.

as the entire country becomes readily accessible and centralization of efforts possible.

Theoretically, a man can reach his provincial capital in one day on donkey, horse, or foot; previously it took several days in most provinces. However, even today, for example, the trip from remoter Hazara villages in Wardak–Maidan Province to its capital, Maidanshahr (or Kot-i-Ashro), requires two, and sometimes more, days.

At the present time, young, energetic, usually western-educated provincial, subprovincial, and district governors (see Chart 12) actively try to spread the New Democracy introduced by King Mohammad Zahir Shah's accession to power in 1963 and the promulgation of the new Constitution in 1964. Previously, the *hakim* and *'alaqadar* governed with little check from the center, although the "eyes and ears of the King" (the ancient Achaemenid custom of having royal spies among civil servants) generally kept the provincial governors in line and discouraged them from seeking too much personal power or wealth, although corruption was (and is, in some areas) a major problem.

In order to obtain the relative number of towns, I have totaled the number of administrative centers from the lowest *'alaqadari* to provincial capitals, with the exception of the five true cities listed on Chart 14. The total 309 (Chart 13) is probably an overestimate because a number of the lower range administrative centers in Paktya, Ningrahar, and Kunduz serve more as security-oriented, military outposts than real towns with a full range of commercial as well as governmental activities. Most, however, do fulfill two-thirds of the critical definition that they be administrative, commercial, and communication centers. Almost all towns have government schools, usually only the first three grades; no true villages have government schools. The quality of teaching is spotty and depends largely on the individual teachers involved.

In some larger towns, "ward" part-time specialization exists outside the bazaar. For example, at Ruka, a Tajik town in the Panjsher Valley north of Kabul, with twenty separate subdivisions, the farmers of four "wards" are seasonal, part-time artisans: i.e., ironmongers, potters, weavers, cloth dyers. These specialists bring their wares to the central bazaar through which the main road passes.

City

When the main commercial routes meet and permit access to the out-

CHART 13
Towns in Afghanistan: 1969

Province	Number of Towns
Badakhshan	13
Baghlan	9
Badghis	6
Balkh	9
Bamiyan	7
Farah	10
Faryab	12
Ghazni	22
Ghor	6
Herat	12
Hilmand	12
Jowzjan	11
Kabul	11
Kapisa	8
Kunar	13
Kunduz	6
Laghman	6
Logar	7
Nimroz	7
Ningrahar	20
Paktya	35
Parwan	9
Qandahar	15
Samangan	6
Takhar	11
Uruzgan	9
Wardak-Maidan	8
Zabul	9
Total:	309

side world, cities spring up, all within a few hours by road from international boundaries. Five cities exist in Afghanistan:

CHART 14

Cities in Afghanistan: 1969

	Population
Kabul	435,203[a]
Qandahar[b]	115,000
Herat[b]	86,000
Mazar-i-Sharif[b]	50,000
Kunduz[b]	40,000

[a] According to first census, taken in 1967, *Survey of Progress 1967–68:* an overestimate, many surrounding villages included arbitrarily because the 25-year-plan for the city of Kabul includes them.
[b] Only an estimate; no censuses taken yet.

Maimana, now transitional, may well become a city within the next decade, and the growing industrial complexes at Baghlan and Pul-i-Khumri should also develop into cities. Jalalabad, because of its increasing commercial importance, geographic position, and site as center of a large new irrigation project should soon achieve cityhood.

The city, therefore, is a major commercial, administrative, and communications center, linking the interior with the outside world.

Large guild-like groups of specialists live in separate sections of the bazaar of the "old city." Individual artisans and, more recently, factories produce items for export and for sale in the town bazaars.

In addition, particularly in the off-agricultural season, certain groups move into the urban centers, particularly Kabul, in great numbers (Groetzbach, 1969). About 2 to 3,000 Hazara from Besud and Jaghori come into Kabul and engage in the manufacture and sale of *roghan* (butter and lard), wood, and charcoal. Many have settled in or near Kabul and now virtually control the winter sale of wood; others have become artisans working in aluminum, making pots and pans, etc. (Amoss, 1967). Most Hazara, however, work at coolie labor, gathering each morning at specific points in Kabul, to which labor foremen come to enlist their day's requirement of workmen. In the city as well as the countryside, the Hazara are low men in the ethnic peck-order. Man must always find a rational reason for his discrimination against fellow men, and non-Hazara Afghans use two counts against the Hazara: 1) they are physically Mongoloid and, by tradition, descendants of the destructive army of Genghis Khan; 2) most are Shi'a Muslims.

The relative peck-order from top to bottom of the major ethnic groups is: Pushtun, Tajik, Nuristani, Uzbak, Turkoman Aimaq, Hazara.

41. Uzbak farmer (part-time shoemaker) and son (wearing colorful *chapon* overcoat) at village of Chenar-i-Baba Darwesh. near Kishm, Badakhshan. July, 1966. *Photo: Nancy Hatch Dupree*

42. Qizilbash artisan in Qandahar making *tasbeh* (prayer beads) from highly-prized semi-precious stone called *sang-i-Shah Maqsud.* July, 1969

43. Tajik twine-seller in Aq Kupruk bazaar, south of Mazar-i-Sharif. August, 1965

Many Tajik come into Kabul, primarily to work as servants in the foreign community or as *motorwan* (drivers). Most maintain roots in their villages, however, and use their surplus monies to purchase land or trucks, and go into the transportation business.

Some Pushtun from Paktya and Ningrahar come to Kabul. Only a few work as servants. Most work as seasonal specialists, such as making *buryah* (matting from *nyi,* a fibrous grass); many as *motorwan.*

Provincial officials (the governor, his staff, commanders of major army garrisons), normally live in the "new city," and increase in number as the administration tightens its procedures and expands its operations. Each ministry involved with development has a representative in the office of the governors, subgovernors, and often district administrators. A crucial chain of command exists in this situation. The Ministry of Interior appoints the governor, but his development staff is appointed by the ministries involved, making coordination difficult as jealousies over rights and prerogatives develop. The primary ministries represented in various administrative government offices are Public Works, Public Health, Education, Finance, Communications, Justice, Interior, Information and Culture.[4]

In the capital city of Kabul, a central government administration exists, and a two-house, partly-elected parliament meets to pass laws. Courts administer justice under the new Constitution and the present transitional secular-*cum*-Islamic law situation.

The new sections of Kabul continually spread into the countryside or rise upward with multi-storied buildings which now probe the skyline. A plethora of new restaurants, general stores, supermarkets, and garages cater to the swollen foreign colony and growing Afghan middle class. A new Russian-constructed prefab factory belches out duplicate structures, which some Kabulis have put up inside their compounds as second houses.

Hydroelectric power or large gasoline- or diesel-powered generators offer unstable (though rapidly improving) facilities to the residents of Kabul and other cities and some larger towns. No cities yet have potable piped water; the Japanese, however, are currently building such a system for Kabul at the perfect time to catch the beginnings of a population

---

[4] Wilber (1962, 164) lists the following as "typical members of a provincial governor's staff": Financial Commissioner, Commandant of Gendarmerie, Commandant of Police, Director of Customs, Director of Education, Director of Health, Press Director, Director of Records, Director of Communications, Judge of the Appellate Court, Director of Agriculture, Director of Industry. The Gendarmerie functions primarily as the maintainer of law and order in the countryside and police usually remain in the towns and cities.

expansion, an excellent example of developmental timing. Modern plumbing, however, remains a curiosity for most urban Afghans, and all the world serves as an outdoor toilet.

The city grows rapidly; the town follows more slowly; the villages continue as always (Neolithic subsistance pattern in an Early Iron Age technology), sending surplus crops and population to towns and cities.

Nomads and Modern Trends

About two million Afghans remain either fully nomadic or semi-nomadic, and an increasing number of these two types join the already numerous semi-sedentary groups. It must be borne in mind that all ethnic groups have fully sedentary villages and at least some semi-sedentary elements.

Having defined the sedentary village-town-city trinity, we must now define the symbiosis and strain which exist between sedentary farmers, semi-sedentary farmers, nomads and semi-nomads.

Sedentary Farmers: These are agriculturists who live permanently in the same village and leave only when forced or to accept a better farming opportunity.

Semi-sedentary Farmers: This group comprises agriculturists who own enough livestock to be moved in the summer to highland pastures by a few people (less than 50 percent) and return to permanent villages in the winter; or agriculturists who move with their families to their fields at harvest time and live in portable huts, a phenomenon most common among the central and eastern mountain farmers extending into Badakhshan. The movement is primarily vertical, not horizontal.

Nomads: These are herdsmen who move as a group from summer to winter pasturages and back again. (See Map 9 for major routes.) Most nomads are either Pushtun, Baluch, or Kirghiz. The Pushtun and Baluch move more horizontally than vertically; but the Kirghiz in the Pamir Mountains move more vertically than horizontally.

Semi-nomads: They are herdsmen who practice some agriculture. A sizeable portion (more than 50 percent) of a semi-nomadic group will move with the livestock to summer pasturages (*yilaq*), while the remainder tend crops in the winter headquarters (*qishlaq*). Their movements, primarily vertical, usually cover much shorter distances than those of the true nomads. Again, semi-nomadic groups are mainly Pushtun and Baluch.

For years, most sources estimate two million nomads for Afghanistan.

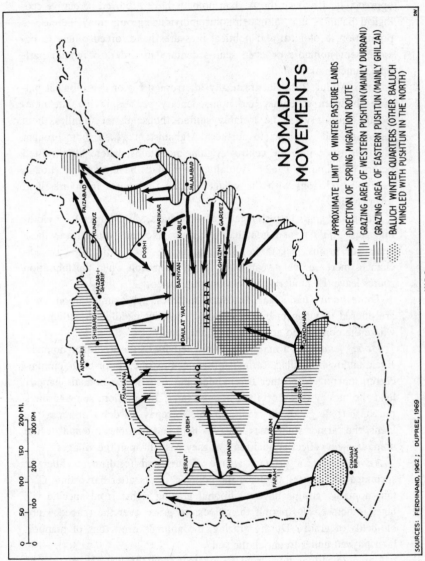

NOMADIC
MOVEMENTS

— APPROXIMATE LIMIT OF WINTER PASTURE LANDS

↑ DIRECTION OF SPRING MIGRATION ROUTE

GRAZING AREA OF WESTERN PUSHTUN(MAINLY DURRANI)

GRAZING AREA OF EASTERN PUSHTUN (MAINLY GHILZAI)

BALUCH WINTER QUARTERS (OTHER BALUCH
MINGLED WITH PUSHTUN IN THE NORTH)

MAP 9

SOURCES: FERDINAND, 1962 ; DUPREE, 1969

0   50   100   150   200 MI.

0   100   200   300 KM

FAIZABAD
KUNDUZ
DOSHI
CHARIKAR
BAMIYAN
KABUL
JALALABAD
GARDEZ
GHAZNI
HAZARA
MAZAR-I-SHARIF
SHIBARGHAN
ANDKHUI
MAIMANA
DAULAT YAR
AIMAQ
QANDAHAR
OBEH
GIRISHK
HERAT
SHINDAND
DILARAM
FARAH
CHAHAR
BURJAK

DW

Probably Wilber (1962) was the first to arrive at this figure, and I suspect the number to be as close to correct as possible, and not increasing appreciably. I believe the Afghan nomads have achieved a relative ecological balance, and, although some individual groups may increase in population, ecological and political pressures have forced others to become semi-nomadic or even semi-sedentary in order to remain part-time, functional nomads.

Amir Abdur Rahman drastically interrupted regional ecological balances between sedentary and non-sedentary peoples in the late nineteenth century when he forcibly shifted thousands of families, both sedentary and nomadic, to northern Afghanistan. These shifts brought intensive trade into the central Afghan mountains, where little existed before (Ferdinand, 1962). Actually, the nomads have many functional, symbiotic relations with the villagers along the routes from grassland to grassland.

Sheep and goats furnish meat, dairy products, wool (sheep) for clothing, rugs (*qalin*), and goat hair for tents. Nomads often trade these items for grains, vegetables, fruit, and nuts, and although cash exchanges increase every year, barter is still common when the migration routes leave the modern lines of communication.

Trade items (tea, sugar, kerosene, matches, guns, ammunition, etc.) are offered to villagers by the nomads; itinerant peddlers function *only* where the nomads do not control the monopoly.

Money lending is a major economic activity of the wealthier nomads. Even landowning village farmers often need extra cash for birth, circumcision, marriage, or other ceremonies and rituals; the nomads happily lend the money at exhorbitant interest rates. In addition, some farmers purchase trade goods on credit. Unable to repay his debts or repay the loans, the farmer sometimes loses his land and becomes a tenant to the nomads, who collect annual rents as they pass through the villages.

Animal dung, a primary source of fuel and fertilizer, is liberally sprinkled on farmers' fields by the nomads' flocks after harvesting. Certain nomadic groups have traditional grazing rights from specific villages; others pay to permit their flocks to graze over the reaped, stubble-fields of grains. During grazing, the animals drop tons of manure, later plowed under to enrich the soil.

Communications flow from region to region through the mouths of the nomads. Although the transistor radio (even among the nomads) enlarges the national and world views of the non-literate Afghan, nomads still function as communicators of local and regional news.

44. Uzbak farmer at Aq Kupruk. August, 1965

45. Taimani Aimaq from Qala Shaharak. October, 1961

46. Ahmadzi Ghilzai Pushtun patriarch and grandson near Baghlan. Group had been moved north by Amir Abdur Rahman Khan. October, 1959

The nomads also serve, contrary to popular belief, as the *maintainers and perpetuators of marginal grasslands*. Sheep and goats do not overgraze, but actually add fertilizing manure to the hilly marginal grasslands as they move. Withdraw them and marginal grasslands become inhospitable semi-deserts with little vegetation. Such grasslands have, over the centuries, become natural soil banks which can be utilized for agriculture if provided with adequate irrigation, an almost impossible feat if the grasslands become semi-deserts or true deserts. Witness the failure of the "Virgin Lands" scheme in the Kazakhstan Soviet Socialist Republic. Soviet planners in the 1930s considered the nomads totally parasitic, and collectivized or eliminated them from the countryside. The grasslands of Kazakhstan became virtual deserts, and Soviet attempts to make them bloom have yet to succeed. Some Soviet theoreticians maintain that no real conflicts existed between nomads and settled villagers, but rather between semi-nomads and farmers as both competed for land (L. Dupree, AUFS Reports, LD-3-64).

Intelligently conceived, vigorously implemented range-programs to supplement land reclamation and improved agricultural practices would benefit both nomads and villagers, but the elimination of the economically valuable goat, or his replacement by sheep, will probably not appreciably improve the situation.[5] It is worth repeating that the nomads live in a symbiotic, not parasitic, relationship with man and nature in Afghanistan.

Two other important historical events, one internal, one external, since the late nineteenth century affected nomadic patterns. Post-World War II development programs in Afghanistan have been notable in several ways. Unfortunately, however, the Afghan Government, listening to well-meaning foreign advisers wearing cultural blinders, believed that nomads and their flocks were non-productive and parasitic on the landscape, and wanted to settle them down, forcibly if necessary. Presumably the Afghans never heard of—or digested—the difficulties experienced by Reza Shah Pahlavi in his attempts to break up the migrations of the Zagros Mountains nomads in Iran, nor the bloody maneuvers necessary for the Soviets to collectivize the Central Asian nomads. Many Afghan officials believe that nomads genuinely desire to settle down if given the opportunity. Nomads, however, look on themselves as superior beings, envied and feared by villagers. Any nomad desiring to settle down would be considered psychopathic by his peers.

[5] For a discussion of similar patterns in Turkey, see Kolars (1966).

CHART 15
Nomads Seasonally Crossing into Pakistan Prior to 1961

Major Groups	Where Spent Winters	Numbers to Pakistan in Fall
Sulaiman Khel Ghilzai	Ghazni	82,973
Ahmadzai Ghilzai	Logar	72,040
Ahmadzai Ghilzai	Paktya	46,112
Taraki Ghilzai	Moqor	46,250
Various Ghilzai and Durrani elements	Qandahar	43,125
Andar Ghilzai	Kalat-i-Ghilzai	27,500
Total:		318,000

Source: Department of Tribal Affairs, Royal Government of Afghanistan, 1962.

All presently identifiable Afghan ethnic groups have had nomadic pasts and still romanticize about them. In fact, we now have evidence that nomads settle down only if, for one reason or another, they have lost their flocks, and must either attach themselves to other nomadic groups as *hamsayah* (clients) or work as seasonal farm labor. Wealthy nomads may own land and eventually build *kalah* (houses in a compound), but they make the annual trek with their nomadic or seminomadic companions as long as physically able.

The external trouble, however, the problem of "Pushtunistan," caused a complete shift of the migration patterns of about 200,000 Pushtun nomads (Chart 15). The Durand Line between Afghanistan and Pakistan closed in 1961, and the *powindah*,[6] as they are known in Pakistan, had to readjust their migration routes entirely *inside* Afghanistan. During the first year, and then with lesser intensity in 1962, nomads actually fought with each other as they competed for new winter grasslands, and farmers resisted the nomads who established winter quarters near their villages. The government supported the villagers, but helped

[6] *Powindah* literally means "nomad" or "grazer," not "trading nomad" as it is usually mistranslated. For detailed discussion, see Ferdinand (1962, 157–58).

the nomads feed their flocks with airdrops of forage during the lean 1961 and 1962 winters. By 1966, the internal routes had shaken down, and the ecological balance once again seems secure. Many Afghan nomads are still bitter, however, for some own land in the tribal territory of Pakistan, still inaccessible to them because the border remains closed to them—though not to normal commerce.

The Pakistani economy also initially suffered. The *powindah* worked as seasonal winter labor in the sugar cane fields of the North–West Frontier Province and smuggled goods back and forth into both countries, a lucrative operation for many thousands of legitimate businessmen, who depended on these illegitimate items for great profits. In addition, some of the Pushtun and Baluch nomads also worked in the coal mines near Quetta during the off-herding season.

But the image of the modern Afghan nomad would not be complete without a recent, though still rare, transportation innovation. Several nomadic groups with whom I am familiar have purchased or hired trucks to assist them in their movements from one pastureland to another. The bulk of the baggage, women, children, and elderly people travel by truck, while the young men and women still move along the traditional mountainous trails with the grazing flocks.

Fully nomadic groups, a diminishing breed, live either in tents or in various forms of portable huts in both *qishlaq* (winter quarters) and *yilaq* (summer quarters). Semi-nomadic groups occupy a mixture of tents, portable huts (yurts, etc.) and permanent mud huts in the *qishlaq,* but fully portable types in the *yilaq.* Semi-sedentary groups (primarily transhumants), who constitute the next stage in the evolution from fully nomadic to fully sedentary, move vertically to summer pasturages where they live in portable huts or tents.

The differential distribution of tent and hut types can "be used as important indices for cultural connections as well as give hints about the peoples' origins" (Ferdinand, 1964, 187).

Black goat's hair tents (*kizhdei* or *kigdei,* Pashto; *palas* or *ghizdi,* Dari): Three major types have wide distribution: the southern and western Durrani Pushtun type; the eastern and northern Ghilzai type; the barrel-vaulted type of Baluchistan (Ferdinand, 1959c, 1960a, 1960b). A fourth type, *arabi,* localized among the Taimani Aimaq and seldom found north of the Hari Rud (Ferdinand, 1964; Hatt, 1945), is rectangular in shape. All four types belong to Ferdinand's "guy-rope tents" which "have no self-supporting structure framework" (Ferdinand, 1964, 188), unlike the yurt types.

170

47. Distinctive Taimani *Arabi* rectangular tent in winter quarters near Sar-i-Chasmeh south of Jam. October, 1961

48. Ghilzai Pushtun nomadic camp near Aq Kupruk on Balkh River. July, 1962

171

The black tent provides a functional portable dwelling for desert and semi-desert environments. At first, the practicality of a black tent in the white-hot, summer sun might seem minimal, because black absorbs heat. A black covering gives much more shade than white, however, and the sides of the tent can be rolled up to permit the ubiquitous Afghan winds to circulate and cool the interior. The resulting sensible temperature inside the black goat's hair tent often falls about 20° to 30°F. below the outside temperature.

Yurt Types[7]: Several names are used to identify north and central Afghan yurts, among them *kherga* (Dari), *khedga* (where Uzbak–Tajik are mixed), *üi* (pronounced *ooee;* Turkic). The classic Afghan portable yurt has a latticework wooden frame, covered with reed matting and a number of colorful woven bands (*bildaw*) wound around the latticework frame and outside the matting. A series of long poles tied with special knots support the poles at the top of the wooden frame foundation. They are curved to fit into a slotted, hollow, wooden disc (*tughlugh*) at the summit of the yurt. Felt (*namad*), often elaborately decorated, is tied over the top of the roof, the designs usually on the inside of the yurt. A two-part, wooden frame door, often carved with designs, serves as the entrance.

Almost all the yurt-using semi-sedentary and semi-nomadic peoples (Uzbak, Turkoman, Hazara, Tajik, Aimaq) of northern Afghanistan use this type of conical mobile structure. The nomadic Kirghiz of the Pamir are the major exceptions and live in *üi* with more rounded roof poles, as do some of the eastern semi-nomadic Hazara, who winter near Chahardeh-i-Ghorband and often tend the flocks of their sedentary Qizilbash neighbors as well as their own.

In many sedentary Turkoman, Uzbak, Tajik, Aimaq, Hazara, and mixed ethnic villages in the northern Afghan mountains, foothills, and plains, true yurts sit inside compound walls, serving functionally as summer huts as well as sentimental reminders of nomadic days past. Nuclear family transhumants among the groups seasonally move from village to agricultural fields, often for several weeks. Usually, the families live in *chapari,* yurt-like structures constructed in a variety of ways, but unlike the yurts in that they have no lattice-work foundation. Curved or straight poles are either placed in the ground or braced and then usually sided with matting and roofed with matting or felt. Sometimes a center

---

[7] See Ferdinand (1964), Gafferberg (1953), and Schurmann (1962) for descriptions of and conflicting viewpoints about yurt types. For the classic study defining yurts, see Kharuzin (1896).

49. Taimani Aimaq *chapari* (portable huts) in summer pasturage near Jam. October, 1961

50. Close-up of Taimani Aimaq *chapari* near Jam. Straight poles sunken into ground form framework of walls; straight sticks bound together at top form conical roof. Structure covered with felt reed matting. October, 1961

pole is used for additional support. Certain groups (e.g., Taimani Aimaq) use a *chapari* as a cooking area.

Mat (buryah) shelters (kappa'): These shelters are generally localized south of the Hindu Kush, but particularly where *nyi* grass (a type of reed) is found in abundance. They are usually lean-to in type, although the Baluch and Brahui construct more elaborate huts.

Miscellaneous: Branch and twig huts often stand beside communal threshing, winnowing, and storage areas. Guards nightly sleep in the huts to protect against thievery, animal and human. In order to check theft, many Afghan and Iranian peasants use a unique type of "lock": globs of clay are applied about twelve inches apart to piles of grain and then impressed with a wooden seal, carved with the owner's mark. The clay hardens. Grain removal breaks the seal thereby revealing the theft, if not the thief.

*

To get the full flavor of the villager-nomad symbiotic relationships, one might examine the area of Darra-yi-Suf in north Afghanistan. Many nomads, about 80 percent Pushtun and 20 percent Baluch, pass through Darra-yi-Suf in late spring. Most Pushtun nomads in this region are Mandozai, a branch of the Ghilzai tribe which originally lived in eastern Afghanistan until Abdur Rahman forcibly moved the groups north in the 1890s. The nomads string out like ants along the narrow trails, moving from the dry, hot, parched Turkestan Plains, west of Mazar-i-Sharif, up into the cool mountains in search of grass. Seldom does a single segment have more than a hundred black goat's hair tents. On the move, the sheep, goats, camels, cattle, and people often clog up the narrow passes, so that motor vehicle movement must be measured in increments of sheep, not horse, power, although few vehicles, in fact, travel these roads.

The long arcs of migration usually swing north before reaching Bamiyan. The nomads travel slowly to winter quarters in the Turkestan Plains, and pitch their tents in traditionally defined grassy areas south of the Amu Darya (Oxus River). Some, however, continue to move westward to the Shibarghan and Maimana area.

The nomadic movements resemble intricate military operations. When the mountains are not too steep and rocky to be covered with grasses or wheat stubble, the sheep and goats use the high trails, grazing as they stump along, tended by the younger shepherds. From a distance they look like disjointed snakes, moving in parallel lines. Other livestock,

51. Uzbak *ooee* (Uzbaki Turkic) or *kherga* (Dari Persian) from Imam Sahib, south of Maimana. September, 1968

52. Tajik *kherga* in Aq Kupruk, showing framework. Note wooden, rounded rooftop. August, 1965

53. Inside an *ooee*, showing how curved roof poles are attached to lattice-work wooden foundation wall. Poles are not tied directly in crotch, but just below, in a sling-type knot to make the whole structure flexible yet secure. September, 1968

54. Framework of Uzbak *chapari* near Mirza Walang, south of Sar-i-Pul; completed, felt-covered *chapari* to left. September, 1969. *Photo: Nancy Hatch Dupree*

older men, women, and children plod the lower valley trails. Camels shuffle along with the unconcern of their species, secure in the knowledge that only they, of all creatures, know the hundredth name of Allah. The packs creak as the heavily laden animals move with tents, poles, pots, pans, five-gallon kerosene containers, clothing, wooden and leather *sanduq* (boxes filled with worldly possessions and trade goods), iron cooking-trivets, and tambourines. Small children, lambs, kids, chickens, and even puppies often sway polyhedrically, safely tied on the camel packs. Donkeys, and sometimes cattle, also serve as beasts of burden. Horses proudly snort and stamp; the only burdens they ever feel are human. A small boy will walk alongside the trail, holding one of the band's most precious possessions: a *'alekan* (kerosene lantern, a corruption of the term hurricane lamp). Large, savagely trained, mastiff-like dogs accompany the nomads and guard both the lower and upper trails. When camp is set up, these fierce dogs will let neither man nor beast approach the tents without their masters' consent. Nomads say they clip the ears and tails of these dogs for two reasons: to prevent illness and to give them the advantage in a fight—no ripped ears or torn tails for the Afghan nomad's dog.

Because the various sections of the moving subtribe must mesh their movements to prevent confusion on the trail, scouts from each segment stay in touch with those ahead and behind. The groups occupy traditional camping grounds, often outlined by stones, pausing for a night or several nights as the situation demands. Occasionally, one group may graze for three or more days while the group ahead moves rapidly to the next grass. While in camp, the nomads daily move their herds in separate groups to mountain pasturelands. Each subsection within a moving band paints distinctive designs on the tails and backs of its sheep. These designs may also have a magical, prophylactic function. Sometimes the nomads tattoo the same design on their women.

A group may move only two or three miles in a day; or it may move up to fifteen miles a day over barren passes to reach a fertile camping ground. Often, the groups camp outside villages on the plowed fields. When the nomads stop for the night, the women set to work immediately. The men stand guard and get the sheep and goats ready for the night, tying the lambs together by their forelegs in long lines. Most work is woman's work. They make the tents, put up the tents, take down the tents, load the camels, unload the camels, cook the food, make the butter, weave and sew, bear the children and help raise them. The men play at being men. They sing songs of love and war. They plot

55. Brahui near Rudbar in Hilmand Valley. March, 1962

56. Brahui matting hut (*kappa*) near Rudbar in the lower Hilmand Valley. Logs hold roof on in face of high summer winds. June, 1960

blood-feud revenges and carry out raids from their winter quarters. At times, they hire nearby villagers to watch over their flocks at night, or day and night in winter grasslands. I have sometimes asked nomadic men: "What work do you have?" They quickly and invariably reply: "*Hich!*" ("Nothing!") Other Afghans envy the life of the nomad. Of course, the life is much more difficult than the nomads admit but like many men who live with and against nature, they prefer to laugh at their hardships and would not give up their way of life for all the farming land in Afghanistan—especially if they had to farm it.

The Afghan government slowly encroaches on the green grasslands of the nomad in the Turkestan Plains and elsewhere, however. Where agriculture once proved impossible because of fluctuating annual precipitation, irrigation now permits year-round water control, and farmers move in. When nomads return from the spring-summer cycle of movement, they sometimes find part of their grazing land occupied by pioneering farmers. Resistance proves useless because the government, with its largely Russian-equipped army, backs the farmer. Many marginal grasslands still exist in the loess-covered foothills of the north, however, so the nomads seek out new areas. In Afghanistan, unlike Iran, the nomad does not *own* grazing land, but simply depends on *traditional* grazing *rights,* for which he sometimes pays. Often the search for new grass throws the group off its time schedule: in 1962, the last nomads passed through Darra-yi-Suf about three weeks late.

Many nomads, realizing that time and the government are against them, make a compromise. They get permission to buy and farm the grasslands of their traditional winter quarters and become semi-nomadic. Part of the group remains behind to raise some crops when the bulk begins its warm weather cycle. Those left behind continue to live in black tents and initially refuse to build mud huts. Eventually, however, a subtle change occurs. To make the tents more comfortable, the erstwhile nomads dig into the ground inside the tents and begin to build low walls outside the edges of the tents as protection from the weather. The *pisé* wall grows gradually higher, and in a few years the occupants take down the tents, put on a roof, and have a hut to live in. The group which moves with the flocks, however, often continues to live in tents or yurts in both *yilaq* and *qishlaq*.

The nomad continues to look on the farmer with contempt. Even after he becomes semi-nomadic, semi-sedentary, and eventually fully sedentary, his pride of nomadic ancestry makes him feel superior to his agelong farmer neighbors.

As of the summer of 1969, Pushtun and Baluch nomads still moved up and down the passes and valleys of Darra-yi-Suf, seeking green grass for their flocks, and serving as the most important link of many Hazara, Tajik, Aimaq, Turkoman, and Uzbak villagers with the outside world. (Total sedentary male population of Darra-yi-Suf is about 30,000.)

As the nomads bring in news and trade goods, the search for grass has its commercial side. In fact, several nomads have told me they consider herding secondary to trading. The system involves both cash and barter, with barter more important than cash in some areas. Items brought in by nomads include kerosene, matches, cloth, sugar, tea, spices, peppers, guns, ammunition, iron tools, milk and milk products, livestock, hides, leather, rugs, carpets, and *roghan* (fat of the fat-tailed sheep, used in cooking). In exchange for such goods, the farmers offer grains, fruits, nuts, and vegetables. The nomads' sheep and goats also perform a symbiotic function with the farmers' fields. They graze over the stubble of freshly reaped fields, depositing manure, which, when plowed under, helps fertilize the fields.

Many farmers remain in perpetual debt to nomadic traders. Some eventually sign over their farms to nomads and become tenant farmers. Violence may occur if a farmer delays too long in paying his debts or a nomad pushes a farmer too far.

Several sub-groups of nomads exist in Afghanistan. They disdain both agriculture and herding for more opportunistic vocations. These groups include roaming, gypsy-like bands, usually called *Jat* or *Musali* in the south, and *Guji* (also pronounced *Gujar* or *Gujur*) in the north. They traditionally practice ironsmithing, fortune-telling, entertaining, even prostitution, as they travel from sedentary village to city. Many have obvious Indian origins and bring dancing monkeys as well as musicians along with them. A distinctive group of itinerant traders, the Shaikh Mohammadi (claiming Arab descent), travels in the north. Most of these groups live in either white tents or black goat's hair tents which have been repaired many times and resemble patchwork quilts.

Altogether, Coon's mosaic concepts (Coon, 1951b) have never been more amply and graphically illustrated than in the current varieties of peoples and patterns in Afghanistan.

CHAPTER 11

Life Cycle

THE groups described in the preceding pages consist of individuals, and they, as do we all, pass through life as single units, no matter how irrevocably they or we remain bound to the groups and institutions which represent society. Naturally, the individual life cycle in Afghanistan varies from group to group, and often within each group, but the patterns are similar enough to permit generalization. In rural areas, large families (especially the numbers of males) are desirable for economic (more hands to work in the fields or tend the flocks) and political (the more warriors, the more power) reasons.

The key here, as in much of Afghan life, is kinship, that reciprocal set of rights and obligations which satisfies and, in other ways, limits an individual's status and role in relation to others in his group and outside his group. Although Afghan society can be pigeonholed as patriarchal (authority in the hands of old men), patrilineal (inheritance through the male line), patrilocal (girl moves to husband's place of residence on marriage), the idealized picture is greatly modified by certain elements which perpetuate matri-influences. For example, the preferred marriage for a man is to his father's brother's daughter, which keeps most females in the group. Intimate aunt-niece relationships, as well as daughter-in-law and mother-in-law closeness, strengthens the already strong matri-core in the society. Although women formally have little power, they are informally quite strong, not only in home-decision making, but often in extra-family economic activities, such as the sale of homemade items. Women have, in fact, always been politically strong in Afghanistan, as is well illustrated by the following quote from Vigne (1840, 256–67): "Muhammad Afzal Khan, the eldest son. . . . I heard a very good account of him, but he is motherless, and has fewer friends in the Zunana," (i.e., harem or women's quarters), therefore he had less power than his half brothers.

The levirate, still common in some areas, keeps the matri-core intact in the family, as does the low divorce rate. Polygyny, when it (uncommonly) occurs, usually serves as a cohesive factor, for the multiple wives are often close kin. Personality clashes can and do occur, natu-

57. Tekke Turkoman and wife in Herat. May, 1965. *Photo: Nancy Hatch Dupree*

58. Firozkohi Aimaq from north of the Hari Rud. October, 1961

rally, but the family generally manages to keep in-group conflict behind mud walls and presents a front of solidarity to outsiders.

No genuinely stratified class system exists in Afghanistan, although family connections usually determine leader and follower status. This arrangement tends to be flexible, however, and the 1964 Constitution established for the *first time* accession to the throne by the king's eldest son.

Vertically, an Afghan kin-system stretching from nuclear family to nation can be described. Equivalent Afghan-English terms are not always identifiable, and Chart 16 is grossly idealized, because villagers and nomads in Afghanistan do not articulate the system in this fashion. In fact, I have never met an Afghan who could articulate the *system,* although all could, in varying degrees of comprehension, discuss *functions* (rights and obligations or lack thereof). Political loyalties usually become so diffused as to be unrealistic by the time subtribe is discussed, and are strongest at the levels up to section, with the present peak of intensity found among the Pushtun nomadic groups. Tribe has, in general, degenerated into a term of identification when away from one's own village or area.

The system involves a genealogy of real or assumed ancestry, and the blood aspect permeates the entire fabric, for even the blood-feud is inherited. (For detailed discussions see Caroe, 1965; Spain, 1962.)

Non-Pushtun groups often refer to themselves with geographic rather than kin-tribal designations. Tajik, for example, call themselves Panjsheri, Andarabi, etc. Uzbak still use the old names of political units, popular during the great days of their power in Central Asia (Jarring, 1939).

Often, when two Afghans meet and complete the first formalized salutations, they compare kinship affiliations. The begin with major ethnic group, and go down the line until they find a common term to relate or not relate to one another. Their subsequent interactions are defined by this exercise in identification.

The *nuclear family,* foundation and primary perpetuator of most societies, consists (from ego's point of view) of father, mother, (and possibly stepmothers), siblings, and half-siblings, when applicable. A nuclear family can generally be defined as one which eats food prepared at the same hearth. At times this may include ego's parents or even grandparents, particularly in the urban scene.

Aside from some literates (mainly Western trained), few Afghans

183

CHART 16
Generalized Kinship-Tribal Structure in Afghanistan

Pashto (P), Dari (D)[2] Terms	Kin-Political Unit	Approximate English Equivalent
Watan (D); Mamlakat (D); Heywad (P)	Afghanistan as a geographic entity; a nation with boundaries	Nation-State
Wolus (P); Mellat (D)	In the cultural sense, Afghanistan or an individual ethnic group; in the political sense, everyone in Afghanistan	Nation or Ethnic Group
Hukumat (D)	Afghanistan: Government in the administrative sense	Bureaucracy
Dawlat (D)	Afghanistan—the three branches: executive, legislative, judicial	Government structure
Tayfa (D); Takun (P)	Ethnic group by physical type; e.g., *tayfa-yi-Hazara*	Ethnic Group (racial connotations)
Pushtun[3]	Qaum (D, P); Qabila (D; more formalized Arabic term); Tabar (P)	Ethnic Group in the political sense
Durrani	No special term	The Durrani and the Ghilzai, largest Pushtun tribes, are simply referred to by name
Zirak[4]	Qabila preferred; but Qaum also used; Tabar (P); Khater (D, mainly Tajik)	Tribe
Smaller tribes: e.g., Wardak, Jaji, Mohmand, Shinwari	Qaum preferred; Qabila also used	Tribe

CHART 16 (*continued*)

Pashto (P), Dari (D)[2] Terms	Kin-Political Unit	Approximate English Equivalent
Barakzai	Qaum (D,P); Tabar (P); Khater (D)	Section
Mohammadzai	P'sha (P); Khater (D)	Lineage (if residential unity still exists, a clan)
Yahya Khel	Khel (D,P)	Sublineage
Kurani (P); Khanawada (D)	Plarghaney (P) if ego's father or uncle head; Nikaghaney (P) if grandfather is head	Extended Family with residential unity, and intensive, reciprocal social, economic, and political rights and obligations
Kahol (P); Kurani (D)[5]	Group with which grandfather lives called Nikaghaney; units without grandfather called Plarghaney	Extended Family with no residential unity, but with at least residual social, economic, political rights and obligations
Various family names when they exist	Famil; hastavi (D,P); aulad (Arabicized D,P)	Nuclear Family; mainly found among urban literates

[1] The terms used are fuzzy because it is difficult to generalize for all groups, or even within specific groups. The people in the various units can seldom define or describe the structure, but they live it functionally all their lives.

[2] The terms used by Dari speakers are often Arabic.

[3] Examples given from Ethnic Group to Sublineage will follow the kin-political structure of the current Royal Family.

[4] In this category are the main tribal units of both the Durrani and Ghilzai. Durrani: Achakzai, Alikozai, Alizai, Barakzai, Nurzai, Popalzai. Ghilzai: Ali Khel, Andar, Hotaki, Kharoti, Nasir, Sulaiman Khel, Taraki, Tokhi. The Ali Khel and the Sulaiman Khel still retain the "khel," although they have grown into full-fledged tribes.

[5] Kahol especially disruptive to women, who must leave to join husband's household. In extended family units, ego refers to his paternal uncles and cousins collectively as tuburghaney.

have family names, but call themselves "son of so and so." Family names, however, relate to the necessity to identify oneself beyond the extended family group for some—but not all—bureaucratic purposes. Many conscripts still retain the "son of so and so" designation. While in the army, they will have small brass finger rings crudely engraved in Arabic script with their names and use the seals for identification purposes.

Family names become necessary, however, to those Afghans who leave the country for overseas educations. Others, particularly writers and scholars, choose to select personal identifications. Some adapt geographic names: Panjsheri, Ghaznavi, or Kohzad ("of the mountains"); some open a book and with eyes shut point to a word; still others adopt an adjective which relates to their occupations or interests, e.g., Tarzi ("stylist").

At times, the new names make life complicated, when two full or halfbrothers select *different* family names. Dr. Abdul Zahir (once Ambassador to Rome and former President of the first freely-elected *Wolesi Jirgah*—Lower House of Parliament—under the 1964 Constitution) and his brother, Dr. Abdul Kayeum (former Second Deputy Prime Minister and Minister of Education) have never adopted similar family names, and their respective children continue to use Zahir and Kayeum.

Another set of politically important brothers, Said Qassim Rishtya and Mir Mohammad Siddiq Farhang, actually tried to adopt a family name. Farhang had been named after Mir Mohammad Hashim, an uncle, and Rishtya after their father, Said Habib, giving both of them parallel name structures. The brothers early became noted writers and adopted pen names which they still use: Farhang (Dari; "knowledge, culture, wisdom"), and Rishtya (Pashto; "truth"). They (and their sister, Roqia Abubakr, who served as an elected member in the *Wolesi Jirgah,* 1965–69) announced their intention to adopt Habib as a family name in response to a request from the local telephone company, which wished to eliminate the plethora of Mohammad Alis, Ghulam Rasools, etc. However, because of their close identification with their pen names, their efforts were ignored, even by the compilers of the Kabul telephone directory. So they remain Mir Mohammad Siddiq Farhang and Said Qassim Rishtya.

Individuals are often referred to by their formal status titles (even after they cease to perform the attendant role): *Wazir Sahib* (cabinet minister); *Wali Sahib* (governor); *'Alaqadar Sahib* (district governor);

Mastufi (or *Khan*) *Sahib* (finance official, tax collector). Such informal titles as *Qar'i Sahib* (one who knows the *Qor'an* by heart in Arabic, usually a mosque teacher) are also used instead of nicknames or proper names.

Nicknames in the nuclear and extended family usually refer to kin relationship. Terms exist for younger and older brothers and sisters, and a close friend outside the family may be called *bradar-jan* ("dear brother" in Persian) or *lala* ("elder brother" in Pashto). A man referred to as "uncle," *kaka,* particularly in the modern urban context, need not necessarily be a consanguineal relative, but simply an older friend, upon whom one can call for social, economic, or political advice or assistance. Such informal relationships have tended to expand in importance with the growth of urbanism in Afghanistan.

Pashto makes distinction between paternal (*kaka,* same as Persian for both paternal and maternal uncle) and maternal (*mama*) uncles. Kinship terms, therefore, reflect the masculine bias of the society, with the emphasis on the patrilineal side. Ego's mother and her sister (often married to ego's father's brother and the mother of ego's wife), however, have always been embraced in ego's kin-system. In addition, ego's mother's sister (maternal aunt) will become his stepmother under the levirate.

When two ethnic groups live in a gray zone and begin to intermarry, the kinship terms reflect the process, and the terms of the dominant group are adopted by the "lesser" group. Almost always, men of the dominant group will take wives from the lesser, and almost never will a man from the lesser group marry a woman from the dominant. In many areas of the north now occupied by the Pushtun, Pashto kinship terms tend to replace Turkic or Persian terms, as informal channels of communication between the two groups rapidly become formalized.

As an example, during Amir Abdur Rahman's forced migration of many sublineages of the Ghilzai Pushtun in the late nineteenth century, the following process developed in several villages with which I am familiar. When the Ghilzai first arrived, they constructed separate villages near the Uzbak or Tajik villages. If mates of close kin could not be found in the north, young men would return to their lineage homes in south-central Afghanistan to seek out brides. Very quickly this system broke down. The Ghilzai who remained in the south did not want to see their daughters move away from the localized, extended family unit, for the very foundation of parallel cousin-swapping is reciprocity. So the northern-based Ghilzai males had to look elsewhere for brides, and began to take daughters from the neighboring Uzbak and Tajik, and relations between the involved villages intensified.

Even today, Uzbak men rarely marry Pushtun women, but the Uzbak elders now meet with the Ghilzai elders to form an inter-village council. The *malik* (headman), however, remains Pushtun. The term *khan,* used very indiscriminately in Afghanistan and the North–West Frontier of Pakistan, usually identifies a man as from a respected family, and not as royalty. Many have adopted the term *khan* simply as a prestige symbol in urban society.

Post-World War II voluntary migrant Pushtun (primarily Shinwari) to the Kunduz area were at first horrified at the Pushtun–Uzbak or Pushtun–Tajik miscegenation, but some have already begun to follow the same marital patterns as the earlier migrants. These processes, among others have tended to make the nuclear or extended family the most important economic and political institution. Until Amir Abdur Rahman's forced migrations in the 1880s and 1890s, the clan community (Murdock, 1949, 74–76) existed in many areas of easy accessibility, especially among the Pushtun in western and south-central Afghanistan. The clan evolved, in Murdock's terminology, into a sib, a group with a name but no residential unity, called a sublineage in Chart 16. In addition, the shifting of extended families from village to village by Abdur Rahman's provincial governors further dismembered the clan community. Many villages which contained only one clan before 1880 (Temple, 1879) today have several lineages and sublineages represented.

Muslim custom permits a man four wives and all the concubines (*surati*) he can support. Several important figures in nineteenth-century Afghanistan kept large numbers of *surati,* and the progeny of their unions include the genealogies of the more prominent families in modern Afghanistan and gave rise to hundreds of new nuclear families. Issue of *surati* have equal rights with legitimate children, which partly accounts for several vicious nineteenth-century struggles for power.

Throughout Afghan society, but more prevalent in the nineteenth-century power elite, is the *ghulam-bachah* institution, under which the ruling amir keeps a son or sons of tribal and ethnic leaders in his court, ostensibly to train them in the ways of government but also as hostages.

In another situation, an individual becomes a functional stepbrother (*bradar-andar*) or stepsister (*khwar-andar* if he or she shares a common "milk mother" (*madar-i-reza'i* or *madar-i-shiri*). Men and women in such relationships cannot marry.

By general consent, an outsider can become a member, or a blood brother, of a group. Sometimes a family with no sons, but surplus daughters, invites a vigorous bachelor outside the family to take the hand of a daughter and move in with them, the groom becomes the "son" of the family, with the same inheritance rights as a legitimate son.

The *extended family* currently serves as the major economic and social unit in Afghanistan, particularly among non-literates, although eventually the nuclear family may take over. Residential unity characterizes the extended family, and usually includes ego, ego's wife or wives, ego's children, ego's siblings, their wives or husbands and offspring, ego's parents, ego's parents' siblings and families (i.e., uncles, aunts, cousins of ego), ego's grandparents.

Sometimes residential unity is within the village rather than a single compound. Occasionally, the nuclear families which make up an extended family reside in neighboring villages, particularly among non-Pushtun groups of the north, but exchange frequent visits and jointly participate in life crisis ceremonies. In addition, a new complication arose in the urban scene after World War II. Often, younger sons left villages for military service and remained in towns and cities to seek a fortune or obtain work on one of the myriad development projects. As a result, the families of two or more brothers in an extended family will not have residential unity, but, at least for the present, maintain intact their traditional rights and obligations. Naturally, lack of proximity places strains on these relationships. More strain actually occurs, however, when ego's parents and/or grandparents move to the city to live with him. Readjustment proves generally overwhelming for the older generation, and some take to opium or marihuana for solace, for once in the new urban situation, most older people have no roles to perform.

Another set of relationships comes under heavy strain when transferred to the urban scene. Male first cousins are often competitors for the daughters of their paternal uncles, but in the villages and nomadic camps they usually have little to do with actual mate selection, which is undertaken by their elders, thus preventing potential conflict. As mentioned elsewhere (Chapter 9), seasonal intergroup feuds permit an externalization of the internal, interpersonal tensions which build up during the annual cycle. When segments of extended families (often brothers and their children) move into the same tightly compressed compounds of the city, however, violence becomes internalized, particu-

189

larly between competing male cousins. So intense is the connection that one word for enmity, *tuburganay,* is derived from the Pashto term for cousin, *tubur.*

The dominant pattern is for the extended family to live in a single village or valley, or travel with the same nomadic group. Intensive social (especially parallel cousin marriages) and economic cooperation reinforces the importance of the extended family on the modern scene. Political loyalties also focus more on the extended family, replacing the nineteenth century emphasis on the lineage and sublineage among larger units, where clan communities and villages once existed.

Many educated young Afghans deride the value of the extended family in a developing society, but until the government can assume overall responsibility for social security and welfare, the extended family performs valuable functions in these spheres.

Few non-urban Afghans today use kinship designations above the *sublineage,* which, however, still retains residual economic and political functions, resorted to only after those of the extended and nuclear family have been exhausted. Few sublineages maintain any semblance of residential unity today, except in some zones of relative inaccessibility, such as mountainous Paktya. Groups which have voluntarily or forcibly migrated from their tribal homelands often can remember ancestors only as far back as grandfathers. Included in the sublineage are all collateral kin extending down from grandfather and his brothers, their children and grandchildren.

From *lineage* up on Chart 16, the ties become more and more genetically tenuous, and named ancestors normally end at the subtribal or tribal levels, and functional rights and obligations correspondingly lessen. Only in times of imperialistic drive, when *tribes* moved from loose confederation to empire did the tribe replace the lineage and sublineage as the most important political institution. The constant local warfare (blood feuds, raiding parties) usually occurred between sublineages (clan) or lineages, and only between tribes when they existed as smaller, relatively isolated units (e.g., the Mangal and Zadran), or long-term struggles for major regional power erupted (e.g., the great tribal wars between the Durrani and Ghilzai). Tribe and subtribe, in particular, remain basic territorial designations (with real or imaginary borders), however, for even a displaced Durrani or Ghilzai points to his homeland in the southern and central parts of Afghanistan as his place of origin, a reality of the mind, if not geographic location (see Caroe, 1965, 3–24, for the classic genealogies).

All the above reach peaks of intensification among the nomadic groups, with political importance still in the lineage, or functional camp. Economic importance is dictated by the size of the winter and summer camps, and the fairly strict yet informal power structure which exists. This includes the famous trading camps of the nomads in the central mountains of Afghanistan (Ferdinand, 1962).

I have specifically suggested some changing patterns in the idealized system in Chart 16 and hinted at others. Although most literate Afghans continue to articulate the ideal system, the functions of the kinship structure have already obviously shifted in several directions in the twentieth century:

1. The forced migrations of certain Pushtun groups in the late nineteenth century caused a breakdown in the clan community, the ending of the sublineage and lineage as important political entities, and a decline of the integrated section.

2. A shift of the economic functions from the clan village to the extended family occurred, in spite of the loss of proximal residential unity among many groups. Whenever a man is away from his extended family, working on a development project or in the city, he maintains close economic ties with his extended family, sending them money and seeking out jobs for his close kin. Some of the surplus village labor force moves to the towns and cities, thus helping maintain the ecological balance in rural areas. The more relatives a man has in the city, the more important he becomes in the localized, newly introduced work groups.

3. Shifts in population also resulted in intergroup marriages between neighbors. Generally Pushtun males marry non-Pushtun females, but seldom do non-Pushtun males marry Pushtun females.

4. Development projects brought about a gradual post-World War II movement from rural areas to urban centers. Forced and hired labor and conscripted army and labor corps service thrust young men into contact with opportunities outside the kin-oriented, socio-economic-political structure. In many cases, the returnees have drifted into informal groupings within their villages, and their accepted leaders, although outside the formalized power structure, influence decisions, especially when development projects enter the area. Factory workers and truck drivers have developed their own

leader-follower patterns outside the kin structure, and they exhibit the attributes of incipient unions. The same is true of the miners of the Pul-i-Khumri and Darra-yi-Suf areas.

Kinship, however, still substitutes for government in most areas, and social, economic, and political reciprocal rights and obligations function effectively within the extended family. For how long, depends on the imagination and vigor with which the central government pushes progressive development programs and the degree of acceptance by the village-nomadic power elites, which slowly realizes that acceptance means the survival of their own local power—at least in the short run.

Birth and Childhood

From birth, the individual begins his inevitable total integration into the group. Traditional, conservative, non-literate Islam is present at the beginning and remains to perpetuate in-group attitudes to the end. In the traditionalist view the use of religion to create individual conformity and lessen group tensions is no vice. The life cycle and its ritualized aspects naturally vary from region to region and from group to group, but the scheme presented here gives a generalized picture for the entire country.

Each village or nomadic group usually has at least one midwife who assists at childbirth. When a first child is born, the family holds a day-long celebration, the opulence of the family determining its extent. The occasion becomes especially auspicious if the child is a boy, for this establishes the virility of the father, the fertility of the mother, and gives the family an heir to its property and—more important—family honor.

Guns are fired, drums beaten, and food given to the poor, again more elaborate if the child is a boy. Often the family foregoes the ritual of driving away evil spirits when a girl is born. Deliberate female infanticide rarely exists, but in large rural families, girl babies reportedly have died from neglect.

Usually on the third day after birth, the child is given his or her official name. Before the third day, the family refers to the baby by a substitute name to prevent evil *jinn* from stealing the infant by calling its name. In many non-literate societies supernatural figures can gain control of an individual's soul or inner being simply by calling his or her name.

A religious leader (mullah) whispers *"Allah-u-akbar!"* ("God is Great!") four times into the infant's ear, informs the child of its illustrious ancestry, and exhorts it to be a good Muslim. The mullah may name the child, but often the father's oldest brother (paternal uncle of the infant) decides on a name, especially if the child is male. In many urban literate families the parents name the child or get a consensus from the family residing in general proximity. These literates hold a christening ceremony, not dissimilar to that of the West.

Among nomads, the paternal uncle generally gives the child a name, for he becomes the boy's sociological father if the child's father dies, and one of the uncle's sons will probably marry the child if it is a girl.

Urban Afghans usually have a *shaw-yi-shesh* (seventh night after birth) celebration. Relatives and friends bring gifts for the infant and most of the activity (singing, dancing) takes place in the women's quarters. Sometimes, the child receives its name at this ceremony. The child, regardless of sex, remains with the mother and the women.

A baby is swaddled, and the mother carries it around on her hip, using her shawl, a garment of many uses. The cradle used by most Afghan groups can be either put on the ground, hung from a nomad's tent pole, a villager's roof, or a tree. Boys wear wooden penis holders which look like pipes and drain through a hole in the cradle. Girls also have urine drains with a slit instead of a "pipe" head. Baby boys often run around naked, but girls almost always wear clothing (loose pantaloons or dresses).

Mothers breast feed babies until they begin to chew the nipples raw, or another baby is born. Weaning is a brutal process, and the mother cuts the child off without warning. In some groups, mothers place black goat's hair over the nipple, and when the child comes 'for milk, she shows the horrible-looking thing to him and accuses him of being responsible. Tantrums commonly result.

Mothers table and toilet train their children at an early age. They must also swing the heavy hand of discipline, because fathers are usually loving and indulgent. The mother maintains considerable influence in a son's life. The harem atmosphere exists in every household or camp where females of two or three generations must compete for affection. Quite early in life, the young boy learns he must bargain well and sell his attributes high in order to survive in the village or tribal struggles for power. One is tempted to relate (at least partly) the ability of Muslim statesmen to gain concessions from both East and West to the lessons learned in the harem atmosphere.

An older brother or sister carries the child, often piggy-back, soon after he learns to toddle. The child also helps to watch over the grazing livestock of the family. Children learn early where their socio-economic-political obligations lie. Separate kinship terms differentiate elder brother and elder sister from younger brother and younger sister. In addition, special age terms refer to females, different for each major life-crisis: pre-puberty; post-puberty; when married but childless; with children but no son; when son is born and finally called "woman"; past-menopause.

Fathers usually bathe boys and help them dress until they reach the age of five or six years. Boys are generally circumcised by their seventh year, at which time they begin to become men. They should know how to dress themselves, and are permitted to wear a turban cloth over their turban caps. Itinerant barbers often perform the circumcision. A feast accompanies the ceremony if the family can afford it. The festivities might include sporting events, such as *buzkashi* (see below, p. 218), wrestling, and tent-pegging. The father gives prizes to the winners, usually money or expensive turban cloths or both.

The youngest son, always the favorite, sits with his father when visitors arrive and the ritualized, defensive hospitality of the village runs its formalized course. Older sons must quickly learn to take subsidiary roles in parental affections when a new son arrives. The psychological strains are obvious and great.

In most areas, no official ceremony marks puberty for girls, but in some areas (such as parts of Nuristan) huts still exist to isolate menstruating women from the society, which considers them unclean. In certain Pushtun areas of Paktya, *gur,* unrefined molasses or a kind of brown sugar, is passed around among close women relatives of a girl when she reaches puberty.

Subteen boys begin to assist their fathers in the fields, or, if nomadic, learn to ride, shoot, and herd. They can no longer play freely with female counterparts. Childhood is over; adulthood begins. One major feature of child-socialization in the Afghan non-urban society is that children have no adolescence, no transitional, educational period among their contemporaries away from their families to prepare them for the world they enter as adults. The young Afghan boy from 10 to 12 (or even younger) moves directly into an adult world. Adolescence is primarily a function of a literate, pluralistic society, which can afford to waste half a man's life in socialization, or preparing him to live as a productive member of his society. Some Westerners remain in adolescence until past thirty, undergoing training or graduate studies to enable them to take their places in the adult world. Others never achieve adulthood, but once the American child enters the public school system, he

CHART 17
Education in Afghanistan: 1967–71[1]

Kabul University	1967-68	1968-69	1969-70
Afghan teachers	450	568	763
Foreign teachers	98	183	225[2]
Students (total)[3]	4,264	5,445	5,757
Male	3,531	4,647	4,913
Female	733	798	844

All Other Schools	1967-68	1968-69	1969-70
Schools (total)	2,581	2,628	2,904
For boys[4]	2,249	2,313	2,556
For girls	332	315[5]	348
Students (total)	497,879	540,737	579,955
Boys	429,549	469,606	503,594
Girls	.68,330	71,131	76,361
Teachers (total)	11,640	13,529	15,533
Men	11,640[7]	11,623	13,421
Women	no data	1,906	2,112
Avg. no. teachers per school[6]	4.5	5.1	5.4
Avg. no. students per school[6]	193	244	200
Ave. no. students per teacher[6]	43	40	37[8]

Source: *Survey of Progress: 1969-70*, Department of Statistics, Ministry of Planning, Kábul, October 1970; Planning Department, Ministry of Education.

[1] For prior statistics, see Louis Dupree, *Afghanistan: 1966* [LD-4-'66], Fieldstaff Reports, South Asia Series, Vol. X No. 4, 1966 and *Afghanistan: 1968*, Part II, [LD-5-'68], Fieldstaff Reports, South Asia Series, Vol. XII, No. 5, 1968.

[2] Increased foreign teachers relates directly to rising enrollment in the Russian-sponsored Polytechnic Institute, which opened in 1967 with about 120 students, and now has 700 students. Interestingly, the Ministry of Information has statistics on the Polytechnic Institute, but the *Survey of Progress* (Chart S-29) indicates that statistics are unavailable.

[3] Large annual jumps in Kabul University students caused by rule which admits all who pass entrance exams.

[4] A few urban schools are coeducational (as is Kabul University), but none is listed as such in the annual statistical reports.

[5] Unexplained drop in girl's schools; Ministry of Education insists it must be a typographical error.

[6] It is difficult to accept these figures uncritically, because I have visited many rural schools with a fewer than 50 per cent of the teachers (or students) listed in the official statistics.

[7] The figure apparently embrances men and women.

[8] An important figure, indicating (at least on paper) a gain in the number of teachers per student.

spends more time away from his nuclear family than with it. He develops new sets of interpersonal, institutional relationships, and usually these change constantly through life, whereas, on the whole, the rural Afghan child keeps the same interpersonal institutional relationships within his immediate kinship unit.

A sub-pubescent Afghan girl helps look after her younger brothers and sisters, as well as the village livestock. Before she reaches nine or ten years of age, her mother teaches her to grind wheat and corn, fetch water, cook, mend and wash clothes, make dung patties, gossip at the fire, well, or stream, and a thousand other odds and ends a woman must know to be a good wife and mother.

Few village schools exist in Afghanistan, and most are mainly experimental and near the larger cities. Even the recent figures from the Ministry of Education (Chart 17) probably do not represent a true picture, for it is often the case that where schools exist, no teachers are available. At times opposition to new schools comes from within the village or tribe. The headman of one village typified this attitude when he asked me, "Why should a farmer learn to read?" This was in 1951, but attitudes have been slowly changing, and monumental since 1963.

In villages where mosque schools exist, local mullah teach young boys the *Qor'an;* older women perform the same task for girls. Classes are unscheduled and held only during the agricultural off-season.

The education (or socialization other than economic activity) of the child is mainly in the hands of the grandparents or, if its grandparents are dead, older uncles and aunts. Three generations of social symbiosis exist, each symbolizing various stages of the society. The grandparents represent the past and, with other elders in the village, are the walking encyclopedia of the society, the distilled knowledge of the ages. In Persian they are called the *rish-i-safid,* and in Pashto *spin-giray.* They pass on their knowledge to the young in the verbal, folk traditions of Afghanistan. Ego's parents, intimately engaged in the present, are the economically producing generation, often too busy to teach non-material aspects of the culture to the children, symbols of the future, the guarantees of continuation and continuity.

The grandchild-grandparent relation, therefore, early becomes intensely important and lasts long. The closeness is emphasized by the terms of endearment used by the grandchild and grandparent, sometimes the *same term,* thus, in a general way, equating the two generations, the reservoir of knowledge and the recipient.

Sibling rivalry will out, however, as older brothers and sisters bring down the heavy hand of discipline on the younger ones. Each sibling works off his or her frustrations on the next youngest, an effective way to train children who must live and work together as adults to perpetuate the society. Older brothers pick on younger brothers, with the youngest brother, although the parental favorite, usually receiving more than his share of the slaps and licks.

Friendship (*dosti:* to be friends) outside the kinship structure does occur, but mainly among the literate groups. The extra-kin hierarchy of friendship generally assumes a certain line (naturally, levels of emotional intensity vary and terms specifically can vary from region to region).

Bradar (brother in Dari); *khwar* (sister in Pashto); *kaka* (all uncles in Dari, paternal uncle in Pashto); *mama* (maternal uncle in Pashto): such terms identify an individual's best friends, who can be counted on for help of any kind at any time. The term *kaka* (Dari) refers to someone in the generation above ego; *lala* (Pashto for elder brother) is also used. Friends may also refer to each other by placing *jan* (dearest friend or darling) as a suffix to a name, e.g., Yaqub-*jan*, Razi-*jan*, Palwal-*jan*.

Dost: used by both men and women for either sex. A type of second-line friendship; the *dost* will usually help in any situation except an emergency which might get him involved against his own or his family's interests.

Rafiq: someone who has been close at some period of life or another, e.g., school-chums, fellow office-workers, comrades in military service. The *rafiq* will help officially, and even unofficially, if the aid involves no inconvenience to his person. The term encompasses both men and women.

Ashna: simply an acquaintance.

Only at the best friend level (*bradar, khwar,* etc.) do we find a differentiation between female and male. In urban society, the formal term *sahib* is used for both adult men and women, a not-too-confusing contradiction when one remembers that, although ideally male dominated, females often in reality have great influence.

Marriage

In addition to the technically permitted four wives and all the concubines a Muslim man can support, the Shi‘a have a custom called *mut‘a* in Arabic (temporary marriage), *sigha* in Persian, by which a man can contracturally take a woman as wife for a specified time for specific remunerations. Along certain caravan routes the custom still exists as a convenience to caravaneers. Actually a form of prostitution, the arrangement keeps a man happy away from home. The female cooks and cares for him for a short period, and he is better prepared to perform his primary economic functions. Prostitution in major Afghan urban centers occurs much more commonly than is believed or admitted by the local population.

Much talk centers on homosexuality, both male and female. Presumably the customs are widespread, though more among the urban than rural classes. Boredom has led women in harems to lesbianism. A shortage of females encourage male homosexuality. Proverbs, folktales, and folk songs often deal with homosexuality. "A woman for mating, a boy for love" is one example. A song tells a sad tale in which "A beautiful boy with a bottom like a peach stands across the river, and I can't swim!"

Males often kiss when they meet, or walk down the road hand in hand, but these gestures are usually simply manifestations of friendship, not homosexuality. Much friendly—and at times not so friendly—banter takes place between males concerning homosexual activities. Some male prostitutes do exist, mainly young dancing boys who dress like women and wear make-up. Also, truck drivers sometimes carry young lovers with them on long trips. As in most societies, however, there is probably more talk about doing than actual doing.

Preferred mate is still parallel cousin (father's brother's daughter), but as the society becomes more urbanized and the nuclear family (or segmented fragments of the extended family) replaces larger units as the basic socio-economic-political unit, individual preference increases to be the pattern. "An intelligent boy should select a girl of his own family status, or rather a degree below himself," an older friend will advise an urban young man thinking of marriage.

Competition for brides has been increasing, and the "bride price" (shir-baha, Dari; wulwar, Pashto) is so high (rates vary from about 500 to 40,000 afghanis, with the average being 10 to 15,000 afghanis) that few Afghans can support more than one wife, so although polygyny is permissible, in practice monogamy is the rule. Many men, unable to furnish the wulwar before middle age, marry late, and often obtain brides from families in need of money. Instances of men over 60 marrying girls of 12 or 13 have been reported in rural areas, but the usual ages of marriage are from 18 to 20 for men and 15 to 17 for girls.

Wealthy men (particularly before this century) eagerly bought up young, pretty girls spotted by their agents in the countryside. Girls from Astanah in the Panjsher (among other areas) were especially prized for their beauty.

Most non-urban marriages, however, still strive to maintain lineage and tribal solidarity. The present royal family vividly illustrates this attitude: all the king's four married sons and two married daughters are married to first cousins.

At times, brothers will agree to exchange offspring before birth, a real genetic gamble. An in-family marriage is a relatively simple affair to arrange. Consent between the families (not the bride and groom) is all that is necessary. The family often forgoes the bride price, particularly in cases of residential unity. Today, however, as brothers move away from village to town or city, the bride price becomes important.

Actually, the English term "bride price" gives a mistaken connotation to what is essentially an economic exchange. If the girl leaves the vicinity of her extended family, they lose a valuable, economically producing member of the team, and the money (or livestock or combination of both) compensates the bride's family for its loss.

The dowry (*jahiz,* Dari; *khawkul,* Pashto) from the girl's family, written into the marriage contract along with and sometimes equal to the bride price, includes clothing, bedding, and other household utensils the couple will need. Among urban literates, the *khawkul* will also include a refrigerator, electric range, washing machine, and other modern amenities. Traditionally, the *khawkul* should last the couple for about fifteen years.

In both in- and out-group marriage, the procedure is approximately the same (also see Janata, 1964a; I. A. Shah, 1928). When the parents of a boy or girl decide their offspring are ready for marriage, they engage a kinsman or kinswoman as go-between (*ru-yi-bar,* Dari; *wasta,* Pashto) to handle the delicate financial negotiations, which may go on for months. Among modern literate Afghans two families normally enter into direct, short negotiations. Often boys and girls of such families become directly involved in the choice of a mate. Should either boy or girl express extreme distaste for the match, public condemnation sometimes forces the parents to break off negotiations. Parental authority is still so strong, however, that, once begun, the marriage plan continues to move toward its irrevocable conclusion, with no consent necessary from the principals, the bride and groom.

If the engaged are parallel cousins, they probably know each other pretty well, particularly in a village or a nomadic camp. If not close kin, the bride and groom find out about one another as the sisters of the boy and brothers of the girl spy out information.

After informal inquiries by the go-between have been successfully concluded, both sides set a date for the *labs-griftan* ("to get the word," or "promise"). Several respected ladies (usually elderly) of the boy's family go to the girl's house for tea and sweets. They accept a tray of sweets and a special, conical, sugarloaf (*qand*), varying from 12 inches to 2½ feet in height and 6 inches or more at the base, and an embroidered kerchief to symbolize acceptance of the match. The sugarloaf and kerchief play important roles in later ceremonies related to the marriage.

Within a week, the boy's family returns the tray filled with money and the betrothal is announced. Often the elderly ladies have decided on the amount of money on the returned tray to prevent charges of stinginess—marriages have been called off for less in Afghanistan.

The next ceremony, (*shirin-i-griftan,* Dari; *khwalish-khwari,* Pashto—"taking or eating sweets"), act of official engagement, may occur after a delay of several months or shortly after the return of the tray, depending on the situation. In the villages and nomadic camps announcement occurs immediately· Traditionally, only the women attend this ceremony at the home of the bride's family, and the women of the groom's family bring several dresses (at least four or five, a year's supply), some jewelry, and the three-piece silver ladies' toilet-set which includes tweezers, ear-cleaner, and toothpick. If they can afford it, the groom's family offers the engaged girl a silver necklace with fish pendants, ancient symbols of fertility. Another common jewelry symbol, the circle (related to the sun or sunburst), guarantees the couple good luck.

Close relatives break the conical sugarloaf over the bride's head (to make her disposition sweet?) with a ceremonial sugar axe, usually decorated with a stylized bird of life (ancient sun-bird) motif. According to legend, the sun-bird, omen of good fortune in the prehistoric Middle East and elsehere, brought divine nectar (*homa*) from heaven; thus sweets are constantly connected with the wedding rituals (Cammann, 1957, 6–7).

If the sugarloaf breaks into many fragments, it is a good sign and indicates a long and happy marriage. The bride's family keeps the bottom section of the cone to make the *sharbat* (sherbert) and *malida* (a sweet wheat pudding) served at the actual wedding. The wedding *sharbat,* thick, colorless, and flavored with rosewáter, is full of seeds (fertility symbols again?) traditionally called *tokhm-i-riyan* or *tokhm-i-biryan.* A sweet omelette, *wiskel,* may also be served.

Thus the *shirin-i-griftan* makes the engagement official and also helps the females of the two families get acquainted.

Many urbanized families pass over the *shirin-i-griftan* as a separate ceremony, and either ignore it completely or combine it with the wedding ceremony, called *'arusi* in Persian and *wadeh* in Pashto. But the gifts of bridal clothing and jewelry will be delivered before the wedding by the women in the groom's family. The silver (or gold) wedding jewelry usually includes *karah* (wrist bracelet), *churi* (arm bracelet), *halhal* (ankle bracelet), *selselah* (necklace of small silver fragments which make a hissing sound as it moves), *tik* (forehead pendant), *guluband* (pendant locket), *gushwarah* (earrings), and *angeshter* (finger rings). The *halqa-yi-bini* (nose ring), once popular, is going out of style, particularly in the urban centers.

Traditionally, the wedding takes place over a three-day period. The boy's father (or a combination of paternal relatives) pays the bills, including payments to musicians, dancers (female impersonators), and singers. Games often accompany the festivities and skills tested between members of the families involved. Chess, wrestling, and mock sword battles are among the more popular games.

On the first day, the bride's male and female kin, dressed in their colorful finery, go to the groom's home to talk and socialize. On the next day, the groom, usually on a horse wearing a finely decorated blanket, leads a procession of his kin, accompanied by musicians and dancers. At intervals, the male kin fire rifles in the air to announce the coming of the groom.

While the muscians entertain the men, the women prepare the bride for the *muybafi,* her removal to the groom's house. The women anoint her hair with perfume and tie it in braids, using cloth with seven colors of the rainbow for good luck. Other women sing double-meaning songs, keeping time with a *dayrah* (tambourine).

Both bride and groom often wear traditional dress, handed down in their respective families. On third day a feast is held at the groom's house, men and women eating separately. Musicians and dancers continue to perform; guests play games and banter with the groom. In the late afternoon the procession winds back to the groom's house. The veiled bride rides on horseback in front of the groom, probably the only time she will ever be in front: after marriage, the man will ride, the woman will walk, or if both walk, she will remain several paces behind her husband. The origin of this custom not so much symbolizes female inferiority, as it gives her a buffer against the oncoming world, and her husband a chance to protect her against attack.

The *nikah-namah* (signing of the contract) and *shaw-yi-khinah* (or *takht-i-khinah*, the actual marriage ceremony) take place on the third night. For the *nikah-namah*, representatives of the bride and groom act as witnesses and sign the marriage contract which, among other things, specifies the bride price, the *mahri-mu'ajjal* (which she can demand at any time), and the *mahri-mufassal* (which she receives on the death of her husband). If the male divorces the female, she can demand both. The details have been previously discussed between the families but final protests can be made and the contracts readjusted.

The agreement signed, the officiating mullah recites from the *Qor'an.* Guests throw sugared almonds and walnuts at the groom (planting the seed of life in his groin?). Single males, just as bridesmaids in some Western countries try to catch the bride's bouquet, scramble to recover almonds from the groom's clothing.

At the *shaw-yi-khinah,* myrtle leaves, mixed with water and blended into a thick paste, form the henna. (Henna is also used to dye gray beards red, to give old men a youthful appearance, or so they like to believe. In addition, old men who have made the *hajj* to Mecca sometimes dye their beards with henna.) The groom's closest paternal relatives lead him to a raised platform (*takht,* or throne), where, seated in a mass of cushions, he awaits the bride.

The bride, surrounded by female relatives, approaches the groom, usually to the strains of the traditional wedding-song, *ahestah-buro* ("go slowly"). A sister or cousin precedes the bride carrying the red henna in a tray, elaborately decorated with flowers. Close relatives hold a *Qor'an* wrapped in several layers of fine cloth over the heads of the couple. The bride's veil is lifted by a close female relative, and bride and groom read the *Surat-i-Fatwa.* This section of the ceremony is called *aynah-masaf* (*masaf* refers to *Qor'an*). A mirror (*aynah*), placed before the two principles, theoretically permits the couple to see each other for the first time. The mullah asks the boy if he will take the girl, provide for her, and make her happy, etc. He answers yes. The girl, however, often (traditionally, at least) hesitates several times before agreeing to her part of the bargain.

A male relative paints the groom's little finger with henna and ties a piece of embroidered cloth to the finger. The groom repeats the act with his bride. (Could this symbolize the deflowering, since henna is red?)

The groom then tastes the *sharbat* and *malida* and spoonfeeds some to the bride. Sugared almonds again rain on the newlyweds.

Both the *nikah-namah* and the *shaw-yi-khinah* involve elaborate rituals, and most Afghans cannot remember the meanings of the symbolic acts, lost in pre-Islamic mists. I have merely hinted at a few parenthetically.

Two final ceremonies prepare the couple for the *rokhsati* ("departure"; also means "holiday"). Close relatives cover the bride with seven veils during a ceremony called *plughut*. The final veil, usually silk (*abrisham*), has one of four objects (saffron, crystalline sugar, cloves, and a coin) tied in each corner. The objects respectively symbolize marital happiness, family prosperity, individual purity, and collective security. Four male relatives of the bride hold the seventh veil over her, untie and remove the objects, then lower the veil over her head.

The bride's father (or nearest male relative) performs the *kamarbandi*. He knots the seventh veil together with a green turban cloth (symbol of the parental turban, i.e., authority), and ties the connected lengths around his daughter's waist, thus symbolically releasing her to the husband, insuring him of her purity, and reminding her to shine with honor always for the family's sake.

The couple goes to the groom's house and retires. The party continues. In the last century, parties often lasted a week or even longer. Traditionally, in some areas, the girl's virginity must be proved intact on her wedding night, and the groom's closest male relatives checked the bedding for evidence. If not a virgin, the bride could be killed by the groom, and the girl's family would have to replace her with a sister. (If, after the *shirin-i-griftan,* the engaged girl dies, the family produces a sister or a suitable replacement. If a man dies after marriage, a brother of the husband takes the girl as wife, even if he already has a wife. This, of course, is the levirate. The growing Afghan middle class seldom observes these old customs, however.)

A variation on these wedding customs (primarily Kabuli) exists in Qandahar and elsewhere. *Shaw-yi-khinah* is the wedding eve and the marriage takes place on the first night, when the groom's kin take the bride to his house. She rides on a horse behind the groom. On the evening of the third day, the bride's kin come to her new home to bid her farewell.

As indicated earlier, little premarital sex occurs, but in the event a girl is not a virgin, she may resort to the time-honored custom of bringing a small, blood-filled, membranous sheep-gut pouch to bed, and break it during intercourse. In few areas, however, do Afghans still make the virgin-bed check.

The custom of *ru-yi-namayi* ("seeing the face") is still popular. Relatives and close friends visit the couple two days (or on another specified day) after the ceremony and leave behind gifts or cash to help the young couple launch their married life—a "shower," in reverse order to American practices. The couple serves the guests (segregated by sex in most homes but the more Westernized) tea and cake, or *sharbat* (sometimes ice cream) if in summer. Close relatives and latecomers stay for a dinner of pilau. Often, however, all guests remain for a meal.

Today in Kabul, most upper-class families combine the *shirin-i-griftan, nikah-namah* and *shaw-yi-khinah* into one gala evening at such chic places as the Kabul Hotel, Khyber Restaurant, or Bagh-i-Bala (the old Moon Palace of Amir Abdur Rahman, now restored in nineteenth-century style). The growing urban middle class in Kabul now has the public ceremony performed in one of the many semi-westernized restaurants popular in Shahr-i-Naw and other sections of the city. Close male relatives of the groom send out invitations to other men; mothers or close female relatives of the groom invite the female guests.

Several modern gimmicks have become associated with the combined ceremonies: paper flowers instead of natural ones, and often the henna tray has battery-powered, blinking, electric lights attached. Upper-class weddings no longer segregate the sexes, and both men and women wear Western evening dress. Often, only the bride wears a traditional, family, hand-me-down dress (usually of red or green velvet); the groom wears a tuxedo. A bride may also choose to wear an elaborate Western-style white wedding-gown, complete with veil and train.

Afghan law currently requires couples to register weddings at offices of the nearest *qazi* (government-trained, religious-*cum*-secular judge), before witnesses (two female witnesses equal one male witness). Some couples do this before the ceremony, others after, but the *nikah-namah,* a large impressive decorative document, must be procured, even by foreigners who marry in Kabul, in order to make the marriage legal. The *qazi* asks the same questions asked during the actual religious ceremony, and repeats the beautiful koranic marriage injunctions to the couple.

Among the Turkoman, simulated bride-capture often takes place. The kinsmen and friends of the groom "forcibly" take the bride from her father's yurt, under a barrage of eggs thrown by the girl's relatives, possibly another atavistic fertility gesture. Wife-stealing was important as late as the nineteenth century, and, even today, if a Turkoman boy and a girl run off together, their parents must accept the *fait accompli* and arrange a "bride price" and dowry. In the rest of tribal Afghanistan, on the contrary, such an event brings disgrace on the families involved.

September is a favorite month for marriages all over Afghanistan, but custom prohibits weddings in the period between the two *'Ids* (p. 98). This custom has rural roots, where weddings usually follow the end of the season's reapings. Food is plentiful and families have surpluses for the festivities accompanying the rituals. Before the fall planting of crops, human seeds can be planted to assure the family's perpetuation.

Another ritual relating to the non-Islamic ceremonial fertility aspect of Afghan society occurs among certain nomadic Pushtun groups: a female relative of the groom drives a wooden stake into the ground inside the tent where the couple will spend their first night.

In spite of the time, money, and energy spent on the marriage, divorce (*talaq*) for the male is theoretically easy. He simply repeats in public "I divorce thee" (*tu-ra talaq-mekumam* or *ta-talaqawam*) three times, and the marriage dissolves. According to a tradition called (*bah-seh-sang*), the man drops a stone each time he says the phrase. The divorcee returns home, and must (in the usual sexual discriminatory pattern) wait three months before remarrying. The male can remarry immediately. The three-month waiting period for the woman does have an important practical application, however. In the event that she had been pregnant at the time of the divorce, her condition would be apparent in three months and the child will belong to the former husband, even though he may not be the biological father.

The literate, urban "new woman" (post-World War II) in Afghanistan, however, has much more to say about choice of mate and divorce than commonly believed, though she still must gain support of her closest male relatives. A husband's sterility, cruelty, or repeated adultery will usually cause a woman's family to support her plea for divorce. The three main causes for divorce are barrenness in the wife, or no son produced; a nagging or ill-tempered wife; non-payment of dowry. Family and public pressure plus private pride, however, help hold the divorce rate very low in Afghanistan.

Death and Inheritance

Islam demands ritual purity in death as in life. The body of a man or a woman buried without proper Muslim rites will, according to belief, be horribly mangled and its bones crushed by its own grave, thereby robbing the soul of a body for the call on Judgment Day. Before the Prophet Mohammad, Allah changed dead men into turtles, elephants, and monkeys; the belief probably relates to extremely early Hindu influences.

When a man approaches death, lamentations (*sugwari,* Dari; *wir,* Pashto) begin. Although a few may quietly read the *Qor'an,* most women scream, moan, cry, and tear their hair and clothing, even though the dying man may demand peace and quiet. Neighbors send in food and money as well as sympathy. Death, like life, becomes a public act.

After a man's death, his close male relatives wash his corpse, often assisted by a mullah, who offers prayers to Allah and proclaims the dead man to have been a good Muslim while alive. The mullah intones: " '*Inna 'lillahi wa 'inna 'illayhi raji'un*" ("We come from God, to God we return.").

Rosewater (*ab-i-gulab*) is sprinkled on the corpse. The burial must take place before sundown, never at night. If a man dies at night, he will be buried as soon as possible after sunrise.

Six close relatives and/or friends transport the body, on a *charpayi,* dressed in new white clothing, head and feet covered (rarely bare), with big toes tied together, to a mosque, where a mullah says the *jenazah* (Prayer for the Dead) in Arabic. Sometimes, the mullah recites the *jenazah* at the graveside instead of at the mosque. At other times the body remains at home (often the practice in urban society today) and the friends and relatives of the deceased gather at the *masjid* (mosque) for the *jenazah.*

Slightly different ceremonies are held for women. A dead woman is washed by her woman relatives in the female quarters.

Traditionally (and still the practice outside the more modernized sections of the major cities), a person meeting a funeral procession should follow for forty paces, saying the Prayer for the Dead.

Graves (*qabr*) should be about six feet deep, and, in some areas, have an L-shape called *lahad.* Orientation varies, but usually the feet point toward Mecca, so that on Judgment Day, the body can sit up facing the Holy City. At other times, the feet point toward the south, the head north, and the face toward Mecca. To allow the dead person

59a-d. Modern wooden grave-markers at southern end of Pech River valley. Note stylized anthropomorphism in a and b, and horse-like shape of c and d. April, 1963

to sit up in his grave at the Last Judgment, the chamber is about two feet high, and sometimes higher. Wealthy families line the graves with baked brick, but many non-literates shudder at this practice, feeling the resurrected body will have too difficult a struggle to escape the grave.

In other areas corpses are laid on their right side in a north–south orientation with the face turned toward Mecca. A mat is placed over the corpse, the chief mourners throw in a few handfuls of dirt, then the hole is filled and rocks piled on top. Where wood is available (e.g., Koh Daman), lattice-work railings often enclose the graves. Modern head and foot markers in Nuristan and surrounding areas look suspiciously like stylized hangovers of the anthropomorphic grave effigies carved during Kafir times.

In some areas, particularly among the Pushtun groups, women are discriminated against even in death. A man's foot and head stones sit perpendicular to the body line, a woman's parallel.

Mourners place small pottery or stone lamps on the grave. Occasionally the head stones will hold niches for the lamps or for candles, particularly if the deceased had been a holy man or a respected figure in the community. Another interesting custom, again mainly Pushtun, involves the white cloth used to lower the body into the grave. A narrow strip of the cloth is tied over the grave from head to foot. When the strip breaks, the soul escapes to purgatory, to be joined by the body on Judgment Day. The damned souls of improperly buried persons can kill humans or enslave other souls, and can at times be controlled by the practitioners of black magic.

One Afghan graveyard custom is economically harmful. Villagers and nomads collect any combustible plants (e.g., camel grass, tamarisk) for cooking and winter fuel. They never remove any vegetation from a graveyard, however, because they believe someone in their immediate family will die, or a malevolent *jinn,* long imprisoned in the root of the plant, will escape.

Nomads bury their dead along their routes of migration, and cover the graves with cairns.

The living still have several obligations to the dead, however. Depending on the family, for up to a year after the burial, friends and relatives gather on Thursday evenings at the home of the deceased for a pilau. Thursday evening is early Friday (*Jum'a*) by Afghan reckoning, so the custom is called *Jum'aragi.* In addition, wealthier families will hire their own personal mullah to pray for the soul of the deceased for a year. On the fourteenth day after the interment, close relatives and friends return to the grave, light the lamps or bring new ones, and return home to a big pilau. A similar visit and ritual is held on the fortieth day (*ruz-i-chel* or *chehel*).

The one-year anniversary of a death (*sali* in Persian, *tlin* in Pashto) is celebrated at home, and friends drop in for a final memorial ceremony. Often the mourning women (mothers, wives, and daughters of the deceased), who have been wearing the white of mourning for the past year, visit the grave and ask the corpse to release them from mourning so that they may wear colored clothing again.

A 1950 (distinct from the 1967 marriage law) law banning ostentatious life-crisis ceremonies prohibits many of the expensive aspects of birth, circumcision, marriage, and burial rituals. The law limits the funeral ceremony from eight to twelve A.M. in a *masjid* on the day of death, or the following day. The law further attempts to prevent wailing, scratching of faces, and other wasteful and painful practices by mourning women. No *khyrat* (large amounts of shared food) can be given to the poor during the ceremonies, and parties at the various post-burial ceremonies (fourteen days, forty days, and one year) are forbidden. The rising urban middle class largely ignores the letter of the law, and villagers and nomads continue to go into debt if necessary to meet their traditional ritual obligations.

One Western custom has crept into the urban funeral ceremonies: the wearing of a black armband or tie.

Life must go on and the inheritance system guarantees continuity. The ratio of inheritance of land and money is two to one, in favor of males. Girls, however, usually get much of the household goods. The eldest son sometimes receives the farm intact to prevent a continual splitting-up into smaller parcels of land. A ten-*jerib* (five-acre) farm would otherwise be cut into infinitesimal slices in several generations. Younger sons now often receive cash instead of land, or several brothers will jointly work the land and share its proceeds. The dowry of unmarried girls is held in escrow by elder brothers until they marry. The residue of the dowry of a widow goes to her sons and daughters in the usual two to one ratio, for the dowry had been property jointly held with the husband.

Sports and Games

Like other individual aspects of a total cultural environment, play and recreational activities reflect the values, the ethos of the society. Are they games of skill or brute strength, mental exercise or violent contact, physical or mental coordination? Do they involve the quietness of the hunt until erupting in terminal violence, the wild dissonance of a bull-fight with its hushed dripping of blood at the end, the seated furor of observer sports, or the participation of a thousand horsemen galloping on the plains of Turkestan? Is cheating accepted or at least the attempt respected? Does chance or luck control, or is strategy the key?

Afghan sports and games, therefore, reflect many aspects of Afghan culture by age, sex, ethnic group, literate versus non-literate segments, although some overlap does occur. Infant games, for example, may appear one-way, but they assist the infant as he interacts with the adult to identify the outside physical world and his inner mental world. Inter-play between adults and infants reinforces the close contacts necessary to generate mutual need and affection. The young children begin as *tabulae rasae,* and explore their own physical geography under the tutelage of father, mother, grandparents, brothers, sisters, or other close consanguineal relatives. The outside world also comes into proper focus during the simple games played before the child can walk. Some child psychologists (and other social scientists) consider the young child's role as passive, but can a learning process ever be truly passive?

Almost as soon as the child begins to walk, he participates in his second phase of gamesmanship, in games which last until—and usually throughout—adulthood. The Afghan child becomes an adult in his or her early teens, and rapidly develops into a group-oriented individual, performing a full range of economic, political, and social tasks. So there is little wonder that the adolescent team competitions so prevalent in Western literate societies are rare in Afghanistan, except in special cases to be noted and elaborated.

The most popular children's games are the informal games of tag ("You're It"), Blind Man's Bluff, and the unstructured fighting found all over the world.

For a society as fundamentally warlike as the Afghan and where the ideal personality type is the warrior-poet, boys do not play war games like Western children's Cowboy and Indians, Cops and Robbers, Communist vs. Capitalist, and so forth, found in technologically ad-vanced, literate societies. I believe several factors affect this lack of interest in relatively formalized copies of the real thing. At the age when American boys, for example, receive their first air guns, an Afghan tribal boy gets a rifle and is taught by his father to use it properly. War in Afghan society relates to the family, tribal, kin-blood honor, and is not an amorphous, ill-defined, loosely implemented ideology with built-in contradictions (the Four Freedoms, democratic society, socialism, communism, capitalism, etc.), but is an immediate face-to-face confrontation with a real, nearby enemy, a confrontation involving *zar, zan, zamin* (gold, women, land). Afghans do not play at war; they make war within the strictures of their cultural patterns. In addition, self-identification with a group is important, and what Ghilzai Pushtun would play the role of a Durrani, or what Mangal would be a Zadran or would any Afghan be a *farangi* (foreigner generally, but specifically, and pejoratively, the British)? Pride of group is too great.

In pluralist American society, by contrast, individuals switch loyalties in stage-like identities in childhood's war games, a pattern which often continues throughout real-life adulthood.

Non-urban Afghan children begin their group responsibilities early and have limited time for games, so their repertoire remains within the range of tag, and a few other games, all with locally available objects. A peasant or nomad father may carve a crude doll for a daughter, make or buy a sling and slingshot for a son, which, as well as providing sport, helps prepare the children for later responsibilities. The girl plays house and mother; the boy sharpens his eye with the sling and slingshot to kill small animals for food, or drive them away from the fields.

All over Afghanistan in both urban and rural areas, boys and girls play *bujul-bazi*,[1] a game resembling marbles (also played in cities), but played with sheep knucklebones (*bujul*) or similar shaped objects.

One universal sport, *pahlwani* (wrestling), varies little from region to region, and is one of the few rural sports to involve inter-group competition. The rules are simple: the wrestler may grab arms or clothing, but not legs. Much clothing is ripped and occasionally must be replaced before the match can continue. Spectators gladly loan *chapan* to be torn to shreds, for, after all, the honor of the village rests on the outcome. Balance is all important. Usually, the wrestlers grab one another's forearms in overlapping grips, and move sideways in a crablike, rocking motion, testing each other's strength and trying to catch each other off balance. Often, a man will leap high into the air, trying to toss his opponent with a judo hip-throw. To counter this, the other wrestler will twist in midair and end up behind his opponent with a headlock. Some-

[1] *Bedey* in Pashto. When goat astraguli are used, the game is called *bizai*. Many more regional variations exist in Afghan sports and games than in the West, because widespread non-literacy makes it impossible to write down and disseminate uniform rules.

times only one such move as this ends the match. The whole object is to throw the opponent and pin his shoulders to the ground. When it seems apparent that one man has another pinned, the coach of the winner lifts his man by the waist and runs around the circle of spectators. The victor clasps his hands over his head and the crowd applauds.

As would be expected, a greater diversity of children's games exists in urban centers. Hoop racing (unknown in villages because few wheels exist in rural Afghan life) is popular. Another important fun game easily recognizable to Westerners is the scissors-stone-paper game played with the hands.

Kite fighting (*gudi-paran-jangi;* literally "flying puppet" or "doll fighting"), a favorite urban sport, weather permitting, provides boys with great opportunity for individual competition. Contestants cover the kite strings (*manji*) with a mixture of powdered glass and rice flour (*shisheh*), sold in small discs. They try to outmaneuver each other in order to cut the string of an opponent's kite by rubbing the strings together. To increase maneuverability, Afghan kites have no tails. Children of all ages run over rooftops and compound walls in hazardous attempts to recover a falling kite. A loser, at times, will hide and tie a string to a stone, toss the stone over the victor's string, and pull the kite down. Others tie a stone on either end of the string and use the result like a gaucho's *bola* (*chilak*). In season, telephone lines and trees in Kabul blossom with colorful kites.

Many boys in Kabul (and other urban centers) keep flocks of pigeons (*kawtareh,* Pashto; *kabutar* or *kaftar,* Dari) in special houses on rooftops, and periodically release them for exercise. Pigeon-rustling is a great sport, another manifestation of the gambling syndrome in Afghan culture. Pigeon owners take great pride in their flocks, usually consisting of two types: *argheh* (tail and wings same color; flies in a straight line) and *lutum* (colorful types which fly in circles, dive, and tumble).

Released pigeons fly together and return together, but neighborhood boys try to lure the pigeons to their compounds with calls and whistles and Judas-pigeons. Others trap neighbors' birds with nets. Several alternative fates await the captured pigeon. If a boy captures a close friend's (*sayad-band*) pigeon, he returns it. Others' (*sayad-waz*), he sells in the bazaar, or clips the wings if it is a good breeder. Some pigeons end up in pilau.

Two games (*tup-dandeh; chub-dandeh*) combine certain elements of cricket and stickball and occupy much of the young boys' leisure time in the narrow dirt streets of Afghan cities.

Girls and occasionally boys play a brand of hopscotch called *juz-bazi*. Winter brings out the ingenuity of Afghan children. They have no sleds, skates, or skis, and must invent games. Naturally snowball fights are common, and both boys and girls slide on the frozen lakes, streams, and *juy* (small irrigation canals or ditches) instead of skating. Using skins or wooden boards, they slide down frozen hills. Some make snow-men, but the old custom of *sherbashi,* the sculpturing of leopards, lions, and other animals in the snow, common a generation ago, now exists only in Nuristan and parts of Badakhshan. A few of the Germans and Italians employed in Afghanistan before World War II skied informally, but now a ski lodge exists near Kabul. Many Afghans educated in Europe and the U.S. join the foreign colony in weekend skiing.

Adults play a surprise game (*barfi*) when the first snow (*barf-i-awal*) falls in Kabul. Friends try to anticipate one another in sending a note to each other: "Snow comes continuously from above; snow is mine and *barfi* is yours." If the couplet, usually brought by a servant, reaches the addressee, he must give a complete pilau (large meal) for the sender. Many Afghans avoid answering the door during the first snow-fall with the agility of summons dodgers. If the recipient catches the messenger before he can reach home, the sender must give a pilau and the messenger as well submits to a symbolic beating.

A favorite memory game involves the breaking of the chicken wish-bone (*chenaq*). It matters not who receives the larger fragment. A wager is made (usually a pilau), and, at any time in the future, when one of the players hands the other an object (any object), the recipient must immediately say, *"Mara yad ast"* ("I remember"). The game con-tinues until one participant forgets, and must pay the forfeit. The winner announces: *"Mara yad, tura faramush–"* ("Memory for me, forgetful-ness for you!").

Festivals usually include several rides for children, such as ferris wheels, and carrousels, on which boys imitate *buzkashi* riders. Bursting balloons with pellet guns is also popular at festivals. *Gise* or *tas* (a dice game combining liar's dice and poker) dominates the festival gambling, and the rustic croupiers seldom lose.

Afghans love gambling, which takes many forms. For the Afghan, often living at a survival-subsistence level, all life is a gamble. Boys risk their pocket change on *tokhm-jangi* (egg fighting) as they try to smash each other's hard boiled eggs by end-to-end bumping. Young boys selling *qaymaq,* a curd-like food in small pottery dishes, often gamble all their earnings by betting on who will sell out first. Odds and

Evens (*joft-o-taq*) is played with candy, small coins, and dried fruits. A child holds a number of objects behind his back, and his opponent guesses odd or even. A correct guess and the objects change hands.

Urbanized adults play myriad card games, including bridge and a poker-pinochle derivative called *falash* (flush), and many upper-class women with little else to do (like certain groups of Helen Hokinson's American women) gamble incessantly and sometimes put their spouses irretrievably into debt. Men will occasionally gamble away all their property and even put up unmarried daughters as stakes, a practice frowned upon but still practiced.

The rules for parcheesi, caroms, and chess (invented somewhere in the area), played in both cities and rural areas, tend to vary. I have sometimes had new rules tossed at me as a checkmate (my opponent's) appeared inevitable. For example: if a player is down to one pawn, his queen, and his king, the queen cannot be taken! Afghans often play chess in gardens, or under trees in villages.

Probably because of the martial aspects of Afghan society and its male orientation, ubiquitous hunting and informal target-shooting exist. Weapons range from matchlocks or flintlocks (with eighteenth- and nineteenth-century British Tower firing mechanisms) and percussion-cap rifles to modern high-powered arms, or reasonable imitations, made at Darra (Kohat) in the tribal area of Pakistan, where, protected by separate laws governing the six Tribal Agencies of Pakistan, Pushtun artisans produce by hand everything from Bren and Sten guns to brand name automatic pistols, complete with manufacturer's marks. But the most popular weapon in Afghanistan is the muzzle-loading, percussion-cap rifle or the late nineteenth-century breach-loading Enfield. Either can be used as rifle or shotgun depending on the size of the load.

Game birds (duck, partridge or quail, grouse, snowcock) are the usual victims of the hunter's gun. Seasonally, ducks and other migratory birds pass through Afghanistan, and, using live Judas-ducks or decoys, hunters prowl the edges of Afghan lakes and artificial ponds near villages. Whether the decoys are indigenous or derivative from British decoys brought up in the nineteenth century is unknown, but three types exist. The more frequent, a crude, but aesthetically pleasing, two-part (body and neck-head) wooden decoy (*muli*), exists mainly in the Panjsher Valley. Another, found in shallow lakes and marshes near Kabul and in the southeastern valleys, consist of duck shapes sculptured from mud and straw, which sit on platforms of mud on the surface and harden in the sun. Hunters in southwestern Afghanistan (Hilmand–Arghandab valleys and Sistan) make decoys from interlaced reeds (*lukhi*).

Larger game hunted include various wild sheep and goats (such as ibex and markhor) in the mountains, gazelle in the deserts, and snow leopards (*palang*) and bears (*khers*), which occasionally slip in among the domesticated animals and carry them off. Few hunt these larger predators for sport. Most villages have part-time hunters, who have enviable kill records and often wear scars which bear witness to missed shots. Village hunters, usually superb stalkers, mimic the animal being pursued. The ancient weaponry used by most hunters makes it necessary for him to be as close as possible to his target before firing. I have watched Nuristani hunters stalk turkey-sized snowcock up a mountainside, moving with the grace of the bird, and come within twenty feet of this flighty creature before delivering the death shot. In Badakhshan, some stalking hunters wear masks with rabbit ears. West of Badakhshan, hunters use a large square (seven feet) cloth (*chireh*), painted with mythological and real animals, to lure birds. Holes cut into the cloth permit vision and firing. At times, hunters dig shallow foxholes before covering themselves with the camouflaged cloth.

Probably the best known game animal for the international sportsman is the Marco Polo sheep (*Ovis polii*). In addition, huge Siberian tiger occasionally roam the high Pamir. The Siberian tiger makes the lowland Bengal tiger look like a tabby cat by comparison.

Many graves and tombs in Afghanistan are literally covered with the horns of slain animals. The local people usually describe the habit as "custom," but I suspect the practice relates to the pre-Islamic, and even prehistoric, totemic identification of certain groups with the virility and independence of the wild mountain sheep or goat. The former function of the horns on graves was probably to pass on some of the strength, cunning, and agility of the slain animal to the individual buried on the spot.

Afghan hounds (*tazi*) abound in Afghanistan. Shorter-haired and longer-brained than his showy counterpart in the United States and Europe, the *tazi* is so highly regarded by the Afghans that he is not considered a mere dog (*sag*). Afghans often mistreat ordinary dogs, but never the *tazi*. (The name *tazi* probably comes from a Persian term for Arab, *taz*). He sleeps in the tent or hut with his master, wears a quilted coat of his own in winter, and in return assists in the hunt, particularly for gazelle and rabbit. A hunter in the plains, the *tazi* has an underdeveloped olfactory sense but superior eyesight. He hunts by sight

60. Kafir grave effigy, brought to Kabul by Amir Abdur Rahman Khan after defeat and conversion of Kafir (now called Nuristani) to Islam in 1895-96. About 6½ feet tall. Now in Kabul Museum. *Photo: Josephine Powell*

61. Goat horns (ibex, gazelle) decorate Baluch *masjed* (mosque), Chahar Burjak. Custom dates from prehistoric times. March, 1962

and not smell. Some have clocked *tazi* at fifty miles an hour, but they do not depend on speed alone to catch the slippery gazelle, who runs a complicated zig-zag pattern when chased. The *tazi* runs in a straight line, and, computer-like, bisects the angles of the turns. The fatigued gazelle drops, the *tazi* hamstrings the animal, and waits for his master to come up for the kill. A Muslim cannot eat meat unless the animal has been properly slaughtered (*halal*), i.e., the throat must be cut before the animal dies. Other meat is *haram* (unclean).

Most Afghan groups trap small animals and birds, using a variety of simple devices. Netting is popular in most areas, either by means of a small net held up by sticks with a drawstring attached to the center stick and the trap baited with grain, or with Judas-birds staked out in cages to lure birds into huge nets controlled by the trappers. Some birds are eaten, but two types are also used for fighting: *qawk* (rock or chukar partridge) and *bodena* (small, lark-like bird). The Afghans highly prize their *qawk-i-jangi* (fighting partridge) and train them carefully, feeding them a fattening diet of raisins and almonds. The proud owner takes his *qawk* for walks, sings to him, and preens his feathers. The *qawk* is kept in a cage covered with a brightly embroidered cloth.

During the *qawk* fights, the birds seldom fight to the death, and rules prohibit lethal spurs and other artificial appendages. An experienced referee, selected from among the aficionados, serves as arbiter. He and the owners must agree which two birds can fight. Unequal matches between small and large birds are not permitted. Birds selected, the owners remove the detachable bottoms of the cages, and, keeping the *qawk* caged, vertically move a bottom up and down between the cages to agitate the birds, who begin to peck at the cage bottom and each other. The owners lift the cages and the *qawk* begin their fight. Each owner has four time-outs (a total of eight) and can place his cage over his bird if he appears to be losing. The cage agitation begins anew. When one bird obviously gains advantage over the other, the fight ends. The birds, cages covered, rest in the shade. Two other participants come forward. Afghans (particularly the Uzbak near Kunduz) raise and fight large cocks, but do not use spurs or other blood-drawing equipment.

Other animal fights (camels, rams, dogs, even captured hyena in Qandahar) occur during national holidays and other festivals. The dogfights usually get rather bloody, and often take place on Fridays in Kabul. Much money passes hands during the bird and animal fights, another example of the gambling aspect.

Buzkashi,[2] like baseball to the American, cricket to the British, and soccer to the French, characterizes and often caricatures the essence of Afghan culture. *Buzkashi* literally means "goat-grabbing," but now players commonly use calves. According to tradition, the game developed on the plains of Mongolia and Central Asia, where nomadic horsemen of the region are said to have used prisoners of war instead of goats or calves, dismembering the hapless creatures and reducing them to masses of hominid jelly during the play.

New rules promulgated by the Afghan Olympic Federation recently toned down the game for official functions in order to make it safer. Now mounted referees call two types of fouls: intentionally hitting your opponent with a whip or trying to force an opponent off his horse. Flagrant violation of either of these two rules can result in expulsion from the game, and, as in ice hockey, leave a team short a player for a specified period of time. The new rules also limit play to one hour with a ten-minute break at halftime, and determine the size of the field (400 × 350 meters), as well as the number of players on each team (5 to 15).

In the north, *buzkashi* thrives as in the old days, with no rules and a few simple principles, substituting, however, a calf for a man, much to the disappointment of many elderly enthusiasts. *Buzkashi* forms a major part of the extracurricular lives of the people of northern Afghanistan. It constantly reminds the sedentary farmer of his former heroic nomadic ancestry, and helps the nomad relive the greatness of his past cavalry victories. After the late-summer reaping of wheat and barley and the early-fall plowing, many Uzbak, Tajik, and Turkoman play *buzkashi* on the plowed fields. The horses inadvertently contribute to soil fertility. When snow comes, the games cease, but the horsemen renew their contests after the spring planting, particularly near *nawruz* (March 21), the first day of the Afghan year. A fine match can be seen annually at this time in Mazar-i-Sharif.

Buzkashi continues intensively during the spring and summer as teams practice for the *jeshn* holidays. Now, practically all northern provincial centers and many sub-provincial towns have *buzkashi* on *nawruz* and *jeshn*. Provincial champions then meet in October for the national championship during the King's birthday celebrations in Kabul.

Actually, anyone can arrange a *buzkashi* match by sending out word that he will pay the winner of a match and give prizes for goals scored

[2] For an interesting novel on *buzkashi*, see Joseph Kessel's *The Horsemen* (1968).

by individual players. The amount of the prize for a goal is announced before the beginning of play and paid after each goal. Money, turban cloths, or a *chapan* will be the usual prize. The custom now is to give money for all but the final goal, when the sponsor donates a fine turban cloth.

The rules of northern *buzkashi* are quite informal. The headless carcass of a calf is placed in the center of a circle and surrounded by the players of two opposing teams, which have been known to number as many as 1,000. I have heard of games with even more. Naturally, only a few *chapandaz* (master players) ever get their hands on the calf. The rest ride spare horses, and from time to time a *chapandaz* rides outside the play and remounts. Some riders merely join the fun for a close-up of the action; others are novices learning the game, and give their horses experience before they join in the central melee. And melee it is.

Scoring a goal can be simply described, not so simply executed. At a starting signal, traditionally a rifle shot but often a blast on a whistle or shout from the match's sponsor, the first-string *chapandaz* push their horses, rearing and snorting in formation, toward the center of the circle. Each man attempts to lift the calf to his saddle, a difficult task with horses' hoofs, slashing whips, and the weight of the carcass combining to complicate the problem. Horse and man function as one being, a joy to watch. The sport is dangerous, but injuries are infrequent because of the excellent training of the horses and the coordination between man and mount. Often I have seen men fall in a maelstrom of flailing hoofs and not be touched. Training and instinct combine to keep the horses' hoofs clear of a dismounted rider.

The training, however, is long and arduous. *Chapandaz* or *mehtar* (special trainers) carefully work with the horses. Most *chapandaz* own their mounts. Horses remain in training for five years before being committed to action on the *maydan* or *dasht,* in the great plains of the north. Good horses play for twenty years, and many Afghans claim the better *chapandaz* must be at least forty years old. The diet of the horses, sometimes better than that of many Afghan peasant, consists of barley twice a day, melons in season, and occasional meals of barley mixed with raw eggs and butter.

The lengthy training pays off. Horses seldom step on a fallen rider, and also swerve away from collisions without a gesture from their riders. The old Afghan saying stands: "Better a bad rider on a good horse than a good rider on a bad horse." When both are good, a *chapandaz* is born.

After a rider grabs the calf, lifts it to his saddle, and secures the calf's leg under his own leg against the pommel, he heads for the turning-point, carrying his whip in his mouth. He must circle this predetermined spot, sometimes two to three miles away, but more often under a mile, then return and drop the carcass inside the original circle or another near it. After each goal, the calf must be carried around the turning-point before another goal can be scored. If the carcass slides outside the circle, no goal is scored. When a *chapandaz* thinks he has *bord* (scored a goal), he lifts his whip high in the air and the sponsor of the match (and all the spectators) quickly and very vocally decides whether or not the rider has scored and therefore rates a prize.

Naturally, the other riders attempt to snatch the calf from any opponent clinging to the carcass. Often, like intricate flowers, folding and unfolding, riders in a circular mass, arms dangling to the ground, will hover over the calf, trying to grab the fallen corpse. When a rider picks up the calf the action begins anew. Strung out like cavalry after an initial clash of arms, the riders whiz across the landscape, exhibiting breathless skill. Sometimes, two or three *chapandaz* simultaneously grasp the calf, and attempt to wrest it one from the other, at times literally clinging to their mounts by their stirrups, whips clenched in teeth.

If the carcass breaks, riders with various parts of the anatomy gallop to the circle and drop the grisly remains. The sponsor and judges (usually retired *buzkashi* riders) must decide who controlled the largest portion. Play continues until the sponsor or sponsors of the match run out of money and prizes. Even then someone else · often pays the prize money for a few additional goals.

Not only is *buzkashi* played on the *maydan* (open plain) but also in the river, *buzkashi-yi-darya*. A greased pig is probably easier to manage than a wet, slimy 50- to 100-pound calf carcass. The game rules of *buzkashi-yi-darya* continue the same as on the *maydan,* but the play is more difficult. Over river bank and cobble beds, through water over their heads, gallop the riders.

Teamwork supposedly plays an important role in *buzkashi,* and it does in the more sanitized matches held by the Afghan Olympic Federation. But in the mountains the play continues to characterize the main themes in Afghan culture, best described as close cooperation within a framework of fierce, individual competition.

Informal horse races and tent-pegging (*naiza bazi,* literally "lance game," a practical cavalry maneuver in past centuries) sometimes share the spotlight with *buzkashi* and *pahlwani* on national holidays, religious festivals, and personal *rites-de-passage* (life-crisis ceremonials such as birth, circumcision, and marriage). The number of wrestlers and *buzkashi* players varies with the wealth of the family involved.

Another warfare training (now disappearing), *chub bazi* (stick playing or fighting), relates to sword training. Two or more men, each holding a stick in either hand, alternately hit each other's sticks in a traditional pattern. If one misses a beat, his fingers or another part of his body will get a vicious whack. At times a small shield about two feet in diameter replaces one of the sticks.

One interesting recreational institution, *'askari bazaar* (the soldiers' bazaar), grew up in response to the need for cheap entertainment for the low-paid Afghan soldiers stationed in the Kabul area. Every Friday or *Jum'a* (the Muslim equivalent of the Sunday holiday in the West), off duty *'askar* gather in the large open field (*chaman*) near Ghazi Stadium or in the new Zarnegar Park near the tomb of Amir Abdur Rahman Khan to sing and dance, watch *qawk* fights, or engage in general roughhousing, including *pahlwani*. Few Afghan soldiers have enough maney to attend the local movie theaters, so the *'askaribazaar* is always crowded.

The cultural uniqueness of Nuristan extends to its sports and games. Several variations of *bujul,* wrestling, and ballgames exist. Whereas most Afghan groups avoid body contact sports in order that no blood may be spilled, both Nuristani men and boys revel in a team sport which more or less resembles rugby. The men choose an equal number for each team, select two goals (trees or rocks), establish boundaries, and the play begins. The opposing teams face one another, and the blocking, grabbing, and tripping begin. One man on each team tries to dash past the blockers and cross the goal line. His opposing number tries to prevent him. Balance, speed, and blocking ability are necessary for this bone-rattling game.

In some Pushtun areas, *khusay* resembles the Nuristani game, but each player must hold one foot behind his back and hop toward the goal. A player is disqualified if he drops the foot to the ground, giving the other team a numerical advantage. The group teases a leg-dropper, saying he is like a cow who has given birth to a calf, not a flattering simile.

Among the several Greek-like elements in Nuristani cultural patterns is a field-hockey game (*wakranea*) played with a stick, which has a cylindrical, bulbous head and is used to hit a wooden ball or an opponent. Since a contingent of Kafir (meaning "heathen" in Arabic, the pre-Muslim name for the Nuristani) fought with Alexander in his Indian campaign, it is not surprising that they brought back soldiers' games with them, a common acculturation process in armies, past and present.

Much rough-and-tumble wrestling, ballgames and field hockey takes place on rooftops in Nuristan, with drops of thirty feet or more for those who fall off. Few do, but outside observers shudder as the participants roll to the edge and lean over, much like the antagonists in western movie cliff-hanger fights. But the Nuristanis laugh at the danger and remain as surefooted as the mountain goats they stalk so realistically.

Western-type sports began in the rarified upper-class atmosphere during the reign of the Amir Habibullah (1901–19), an avid gadgeteer, who introduced the automobile to Afghanistan, was a good amateur photographer, and an admirer of Jules Verne. He also introduced tennis, cricket, and golf to the country. A Scots engineer, James Murray, employed by Habibullah to construct a bridge near Jalalabad, the Kabul woolen mills, and a dam at Ghazni, also constructed two or three golf courses.

Probably the most important trend since World War II has been the introduction of organized team sports and individual sports which demand physical coordination. A special type of hand-to-eye coordination needed in a mechanized society is not required in an agricultural-pastoral milieu. Physical coordination is, after all, a product of cultural conditioning as well as individual ability. A body or any part of it reacts in an eye-to-mind-to-relevant-muscle sequence. Watching a villager or tribesman cross Kabul's increasingly crowded streets illustrates this. His peripheral vision tells the villager something moves toward him, but his cultural experience leads him to expect a slow-moving camel or donkey, or possibly a fast-moving horse. Unfortunately, in Kabul, it would probably be an automobile. The villager will take an extra step or two, actually looking at the car, but not reacting. Many accidents occur in this way. In addition, self-trained Afghan motorists often have difficulty in judging time-motion ratios.

Several contact sports have been recently introduced, new to the Afghan way of competition, but the fierce competitiveness and desire to win (group and individual pride) and do honor for family and tribe have given impetus to such team sports as basketball, soccer, volley ball and field hockey (in which several Nuristanis have made great names for themselves). Olympic wrestling and weight-lifting, easily related to informal rural contests, have become very popular, and the Af-

ghans have sent field hockey, wrestling and weight-lifting teams to several Olympiads since World War II.

Although neither a game nor a sport, picknicking is a great Afghan
pastime, and on *Jum'a* and other holidays, whole families take to the
fields and gardens, to loll about or wrestle, to drink tea and eat, to listen
to the *bulbul* (nightingale), transistor radios, watch the hoopoe, to pick
and garland flowers.

But in both sports and games, be they traditional or modern sports
introduced from the outside, the Afghan, product of a harsh, inward-
looking, group-oriented society, plays to win. To paraphrase an American ideal: It's not how you play, but whether you win the game. (Deep
down where it counts, I suspect American athletes—and particularly
their coaches—feel the same way).

Diet

Man does not live by religion, folk music, and folktales alone; he must
also have bread, and the varied diets of Afghanistan deserve rather detailed treatment, for they once again emphasize the melting-pot aspects
of total Afghan culture. The foods of Central Asia, China, Tibet, the
Iranian Plateau, Pakistan, and India blend in Afghanistan. Food is
neither too hot for Westerners, nor too bland, nor too monotonous, but
has enough regional specialization to delight the most fastidious, adven-
turous gourmet.

The Afghan may not live on bread (*nan*) alone but he comes mighty
close to it. At least eleven terms for bread exist in Pashto. Throughout
much of Afghanistan, the term *nan* refers to food in general. Hot *nan,*
as most experienced gourmets agree, is one of the world's great foods.
The specifics of diet vary from region to region according to local resources, but almost anything which can be ground by a watermill or
in a mortar is used to make unleavened or lightly leavened bread: wheat
(*abi*—irrigated—and *lalmi*—highland, non-irrigated), barley, maize,
millet (particularly in Nuristan), even dried mulberries and peas. Distinctive shapes and types of bread characterize various parts of the
country. The more common bread, oblong in shape, somewhat resembles a racetrack. The bread of the north tends to be more oval.

Special types of bread, such as *bolani* (bread with leeks or potatoes
baked in the center), occur throughout Afghanistan.

Bread ovens also are distinctive. The most common, the pottery *tandur* (see photo), is buried in the ground with coals at the bottom. The

224

63. Tajik farmer
at Aq Kupruk.
August, 1965

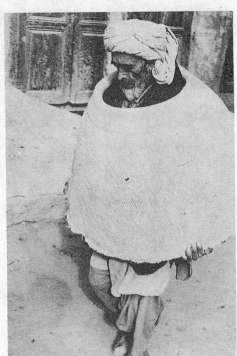

64. Newly purchased pottery
tandur (bread oven), Khulm
Photo: Josephine Powell

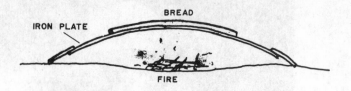

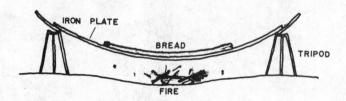

DIAGRAM 5
Nomadic Bread-Baking Method

65. Ironmonger's shop, Qandahar. Bread-baking plates (see Diag. 5, above) hang in entrance. January, 1951

bakers slap the flattened dough against the inner wall for baking. A team smoothly delivers the bread from dough to customer. Some nomads use a portable, curved, circular iron plate, placed in one of two positions (see Fig. 65 and Diag. 5).

Nomads on the move and shepherds in the hills sometimes cook *nan-i-kak,* prepared by covering a heated stone with kneaded flour-and-water dough. The stone and dough are placed near hot coals and turned occasionally as the bread browns. When done, the bread is easily broken from the stone for eating.

In Kabul, a distinctive custom developed, particularly among the seasonal workers (such as the Hazara). Every morning the workers and other urban poor make the rounds of the *hotel* (which means restaurant, not hotel) to sell or trade *gandanah* (leeks) for *nan* left over from the previous evening's pilau. Such juice-soaked *nan* is called *sabuz.* The people joke with one another and ask what type of pilau they are eating, from the residual tastes left on the *nan.*

Many types of pilau (rice, usually served with meat and/or vegetables) exist. Several varieties of rice grow in the wetter areas of Afghanistan: Jalalabad, Laghman in the east; Kunduz in the north (Ferdinand, 1959a). The Afghans cook most of these dishes in *roghan-i-dumbah* or *roghan-i-zard.* They often refer to *roghan-i-zard* (a clarified butter) as *ghi,* a Hindi term which many believe to be English. *Roghan-i-dumbah* is a lard rendered from the tail of the fat-tailed sheep. Recently, however, the use of vegetable shortening (called *roghan-i-nawati*) has increased with major exports from Pakistan, India, Iran, and Western Europe. Two local factories, at Bost and Kunduz, also provide part of Afghanistan's vegetable oil needs.

All pilaus have some sort of boiled meat buried in the center of the rice. Side dishes of vegetables (*qormah*), with or without meat but often with a tomato (*bonjan-i-rumi*) base, supplement the pilau to give added flavor and body. Some curries are used in areas near Pakistan. The vegetables include spinach (*sabzi* or *palak*), potatoes (*kachalu*), peas (*mashong*), eggplant (*bonjan-i-sia*), carrots (*zardak*), turnips (*shalgham*), and squash (*kadu*). Yogurt (*mast*) also is served as a side dish and at times mixed with the rice. Sometimes an eggplant with sour cream (*qruti*) dish called *burani* is eaten with the *chilaw* or pilau. Of the many types of pilau, these are, perhaps, the most common:

Chilaw: plain rice with a large hunk of mutton or a chicken buried in the center.

227

66. Tajik butcher in
Aq Kupruk bazaar.
August, 1965

67. Shinwari Pushtun cooking *chapli kabab* at Hadda near Jalalabad. Note leather
chaplis (sandals) to right. April, 1964

Qabli (not "Kabuli," as commonly believed by many foreigners) pilau: with raisins, shredded carrots, almonds and pistachio nuts. To serve a guest *qabli* indicates great respect.

Sabzi (or *zamarud*) pilau: with spinach.

Mashong pilau: with small green peas.

Yakhni pilau: with mutton (different from *chilaw* in that the mutton is steamed with the rice).

Reshta pilau: with eggs.

Bonjan-i-sia pilau: with eggplant.

Morgh pilau: with chicken.

Naranj pilau: a sweetish pilau with dried orange peels.

Kala-pacheh pilau: with the head (including eyeballs, usually served to the honored guest) and feet of a sheep.

Landi pilau: with dried meat prepared like jerky; a favorite winter dish.

A mixture of pickled vegetables (baby eggplant, carrots, beans, chilis) called *torshi* is normally served with pilau. In Jalalabad and Kabul, a special hot chili sauce, *chutney-morch,* is highly prized, especially by the upper classes. Often, sour oranges (*naranj*) from Jalalabad are squeezed on any pilau for added flavor. From the Peshawar Valley of Pakistan come the highly-prized, tarty-sweet, blood-red *malta* orange, eaten after the meal.

Afghans often use the term "pilau" to mean "food" in general, because of the importance of the dishes in the culture, and wager one, two, three, or more pilaus when arguments occur. In bargaining with workmen, archaeologists sometimes have to agree to a pilau (or its monetary equivalent) as part of a day's wages.

Pilau and other foods are eaten with the right hand. Sauce from the *qormah* dishes helps hold the individual grains of steamed rice together. The fingers curve the mass into a ball and the thumb shoves the ball into the mouth. The left hand is reserved for less palatable natural functions (e.g., washing after relieving oneself), and what problems these culturally determined eating habits have caused genetically left-handed children forced from early childhood to conform remains to be studied.

Several thick, gummy rice (*kichri*) dishes are popular (called *shuleh* in general), particularly for convalescents and as desserts. Usually, a hole is dug in the center of the *kichri* and mixtures of ground meat and *qruti* or *ghi* poured into the well. Another thick rice dish, *berenj-* (word for rice) *i-lak* is made by mixing rice with *nakhod.* a type of

68. Fried-fish peddler in central bazaar, valley of Gurziwan, south of Maimana.
August, 1970. *Photo: Nancy Hatch Dupree*

chick pea, also roasted in hot sand and seasame oil and eaten like popcorn (*palah* or *jowari,* Dari; *ninah,* Pashto), another popular dish.

A thick dessert paste, *faludah,* also served to the ill, is prepared by mixing milk and wheat flour in a porous bag and then boiling for ten to twelve hours. The Afghans place boiled rice-spaghetti syrup (*mirwayi*) in the middle of the *faludah.*

An American-type white rice (*batah*) which requires more water for cooking is growing in popularity. Stuffing ground meat mixed with rice into eggplant, squash, and green peppers has become common in most urban centers.

Dampok, rice boiled in water and oil (which are not drained off after cooking), is a well-known and well-liked dish in both rural and urban areas.

Another important item in Afghan diets (particularly in urban centers) are *kabab* types, usually alternately skewered lean mutton cubes and small pieces of fat broiled over charcoal and served on the *sikh* (skewer). The results are called *sikh-* or *parchah-* (cubed) or *tikah-* (cubed) *kabab.* At times onions and small tomatoes divide the meat. Normally, a *salad* of chopped fresh onions and tomatoes are served as a complementary dish. For added flavor the Afghan dips most *kabab* in crushed grape seeds, paprika, and black pepper. *Kuftah-kabab* (meat balls with onions ground with the meat, cooked either in a pan or on skewers over charcoal) is often cooked as *qormah* and served as a side dish with pilau. *Shami-kabab,* possibly of Kashmiri origin, resembles *kuftah-kabab,* but has raw eggs and ground boiled potatoes mixed with the meat. *Shami* are prepared on *sikh,* but removed before serving. The *sikh* hole remains visible. A highly-spiced, hamburger-like patty, *chapli-kabab,* found mainly in the Jalalabad area but spreading, has obvious connections with the hotter dishes of Pakistan.

Other types of *kabab* include *lolah* or *qimah* (oblong, skewered meatballs served on the *sikh*); *karayi* (mutton meatballs or cubes mixed with onion, tomato and a dropped egg, cooked and served in a round metal pan called *karayi*); *pashti* (skewered meat with bone fragments from any part of the sheep still attached); *dashi* (pan-browned mutton with humerus and femur bone fragments still attached); *qabr-ghayi* (skewered mutton with rib or backbone fragments still attached); *naychayhi* (small mutton cubes on bamboo slivers).

Afghans eat hot soups, *shorwa,* especially in winter. At times, they use communal wooden spoons to eat the soup, as well as for a favorite summer dish, sour milk and cucumbers (*badrang*). Most soups use mut-

69. Summer outdoor cooking at Uzbak village of Chenar-i-Baba Darwesh. Large gourd container to right. August, 1966. *Photo: Nancy Hatch Dupree*

70. Uzbak family in typical long, roofed porch. Woman is making *dugh* (buttermilk) in skin bag. July, 1966. *Photo: Nancy Hatch Dupree*

ton stock, however. The afghans tear up *nan,* toss it into the *shorwa* to soak, and eat the soggy mass by hand. The Uzbak of the north prepare a hearty cattle-blood soup, mixed with tomatoes, after a cattle slaying; they also eat a horsemeat sausage called *qazi.*

A pasta complex spreads from the Far East to Italy, and on to Western Europe and America, having its origin somewhere along the Silk Route. Sinologists are unsure of the area of the origin of pasta, but in north Afghanistan and in southern cities, a type of minestrone (noodle-vegetable soup) called *ash* exists, as do several types of ravioli (*ashak*) with either cheese (*panir*), meat (*gusht*), or leek (*gandanah*) fillers. The Afghans eat both *ash* and *ashak* with *chakah* (drained yogurt) or *qruti* (sour cream). A second type of *ash,* popular among the Uzbak and Turkoman of the north, is made by mixing *qruti* with the already cooked pasta, and then eaten with meat and vegetable sauces (*qormah*).

A steamed meat-dumpling called *mantu,* probably of Tibetan origin, also occurs in north Afghanistan. The Tibetans use the same term for a similar dish.

Du-payazah ("two onions"), a mixture of cooked and raw onions poured like soup over chunks of *nan,* is popular.

Dairy products from cows, sheep, and goats play a major role in the diet of both villagers and nomads. Everything from fresh milk to all sorts of boiled milk and regional cheeses are eaten. Major milk products include *panir-pokhtah* (a crudely pasteurized cheese), *panir-chakah* (unpasteurized, a cottage cheese type), *dugh* (sour milk), *mast* (yogurt), *qrut* (hard, dehydrated curd-balls). *Qruti,* a favorite winter dish, is made by melting *qrut* in boiling *roghan-i-dumbah* or *zard,* and then soaking hunks of *nan* in the soupy, greasy mixture. The Afghans also top many dishes with *qruti* made by softening the dehydrated curd in water.

Chicken and eggs are widespread and widely eaten. Other domesticated fowl include guinea hens, ducks, and turkey. Afghans prefer their boiled eggs either tepid or practically raw. When eating boiled eggs, they tap the small end off the egg, put salt and pepper in the top and drink down the egg in one gulp. Scrambled eggs with tomatoes and/or onions are cooked in *roghan.*

More and more Afghans eat fish, and they have always prized game, particularly gazelle, ibex, markhor, duck, quail, pigeon, and partridge. In some areas the people net an interesting small bird, *qazalaq,* about the size of sparrow (which are also eaten). Defeathered, degutted,

71. Nuristani woman in Wama. Clothing distinctive from rest of Afghanistan. Note cornering of building. April, 1963

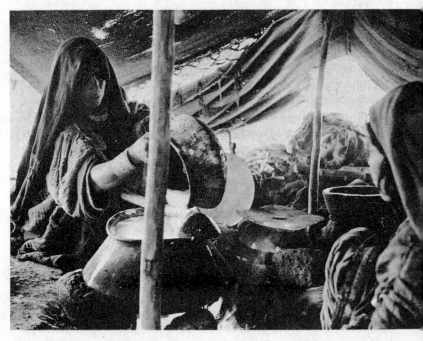

72. Tara Khel Ghilzai nomadic woman preparing cheese in tent, near Paiminar, east of Kabul. May, 1960

cooked in *roghan,* the birds are eaten with their delicate skulls still attached. The head is bitten off first. In the northern part of the country,
where crows grow fat eating maize, the Afghans hunt and literally eat
crow.

Tea (*chay*), a staple with meals, serves as the in-between meal hospitality drink of Afghanistan. Among the urban classes in Kabul and
larger towns, *soda* (including Coca-Cola from Peshawar and a new Coke
plant now operating in Kabul) grows in popularity with each passing
summer. Specialty shops manufacture the *soda* in heavy, marble-capped
bottles, using large cylinders of compressed CO_2. Venders cool the *soda*
with snow, which villagers cut into blocks and bury underground in winter, transporting it for sale to the nearby bazaars in skins to minimize
melting. Various flavored *sharbat* are also made from snow.

Two types of tea, black (*chay-sia,* popular south of the Hindu Kush)
and green (*chay-sabz,* popular north of the Hindu Kush), are available
at all teahouses (*chaykhanah* or *samovar*), and consumed throughout
the country. Often, the Afghans prepare green tea with cardamon. A
prestige tea, *qaimak-chay,* includes lumps of boiled curds, and has a
distinctive salty flavor. *Qaimak* can also be eaten separately in small
pottery jars, and is particularly popular at breakfast time. Those who
can afford sugar serve it in tea, but in the *samovar* a customer must
ask for sugar, for it costs extra. Seldom does one find tea drunk with
milk, the popular drink in most of South Asia.

Many Afghans simply soak sugar cubes (*qand*) in tea, and then eat
the *qand* or hold it in the mouth as they drink. Also taken the same
way are locally made hard candies and sugar-coated nuts and other
foods: *noql-nakhod* (chick peas); *noql-pistah* (pistachio nuts); *noql-
badam* (almonds); *noql-khashtah* (peach pits).

Traditionally three cups of hospitality tea should be drunk. A guest
commonly will have his handleless cup filled at least halfway with sugar,
an indicator of welcome and hospitality. The first cup assuages thirst,
the second pledges friendship, the third is simply ostentatious. Formalized Afghan hospitality demands conspicuous consumption, and guests
eat prodigiously to indicate their appreciation to the host. A few loud
belches at the end of a meal are considered polite and please the host.
Except in the more Western-oriented homes, Afghans eat sitting on the
floor, clustered around several dishes of food.

Sweets, excellent quick-energy foods, are widespread, and include raw
sugarcane and sugar beets, *jelabi* (deep-fried, pretzle-shaped wheat and
sugar twists soaked in syrup, and traditionally eaten with fried fish),

gur (unrefined molasses lumps), and *shur-nakhod,* a mixture of beans, raisins, and sweet-sour syrup (*serah*). Puddings, especially caramel, are popular in urban centers, as well as *firni,* a rice pudding with almonds and cardamom and a silver foil topping. Thin, crisp *gush-i-fil* (elephant ears) are a favorite Afghan pastry, as are *kolcha,* locally made cookies.

Fresh and dried fruits (many varieties of melons, grapes, apples, apricots, plums, cherries, mulberries, etc.) and nuts (walnuts, almonds, pistachio, pine nuts, etc.) form a major part of the Afghan diet and are exported in large quantities. Travelers often carry dried fruit-nut combinations as quick-energy snacks tied in the end of their turban cloths, including *chakidah* (walnuts and dried mulberries), *talkhun* (mulberry cakes), and a mixture of nuts, raisins, and dried mulberries. Growing more popular is corn roasted over charcoal, which can be purchased from hawkers in the bazaar, along with fried *shir-mahi* (milk fish).

On special occasions such as weddings (already discussed) Afghans prepare distinctive foods. On *nawruz,* for example, two special dishes are *samanak,* a mushy dessert made of wheat and sugar which takes two and a half days to prepare, and *haft-mewah* (seven fruits, to symbolize spring), a compote of walnuts, almonds, pistachio nuts, red raisins, green raisins, dried apricots, and a local fruit known as *sanjet* (jube jube).

Nuristan continues to be culturally aberrant. Many women do not know how to boil rice, for the people live mainly on dairy products and corn and millet breads. They prepare a special cheese fondue in butter (also a medium of exchange), and soak it up with bread. Before conversion to Islam in the 1890s, Kafirs made wines extensively. Some Nuristanis continue to make wine today.

Few non-literates in Afghanistan drink alcohol, but the Western-educated (as well as those educated in the U.S.S.R.) Afghans (though not all) make up for everyone else in the country. Most Afghans smoke, and tobacco is widely grown for local consumption in the *chelem* (water pipe). Urban Afghans smoke imported American, German, Russian, British, Pakistani, or Iranian cigarettes. Often, when an Afghan first begins to smoke cigarettes, he holds the cigarette between the index and middle fingers and puffs through his fist, so that his lips do not touch the tobacco.

The smoking of *chars* (marihuana) is widespread, but I have met few habitual users in my years of residence and research in Afghanistan. Usually habitual users are old men approaching senility, who have passed their biological and economic usefulness as mature adults and no longer enjoy political power as *rish-i-safid.* Most Afghans who smoke the resinous substance from *Canabis* do so at the end of a hard day's work in the fields or with the flocks, so the few puffs actually represent the equivalent of several suburban martinis after a day's tensions in Western cities. A few communal puffs of the *chelem* at the local meeting-ground with kinsmen and friends ended, the men go home to the evening meal, prayers, sex, and sleep. Seldom does the smoking of *chars* interfere with the daily socio-economic activities of an individual.

Teryak (opium), smoked and grown mainly in the northeast, usually becomes detrimental only in the same situation as *chars*. I have met several addicts in Kabul, older men who moved to the city to live with their sons or other close relatives. Under the new urban situation they had lost their influence and active participation in family affairs. Disoriented, they turned to the solace of *teryak*.

More sophisticated Afghans prefer *mufarah,* a tasty concoction of the essence of *teryak,* resin of *chars,* plus ginger and other spices, blended like *halwah* or *baklawah.* The Afghans claim *mufarah* makes an individual laugh for hours, but it also disrupts time-motion senses and causes a floating sensation.

Pork (*gusht-i-khuk*) is the object of the major dietary prohibition followed by most Afghans. Abstinence from pork in early Islamic Arabia, where trichinosis was rampant, made good dietary sense, but not so in high, dry Afghanistan. However, some Western-trained Afghans will not eat pork, although they drink alcohol.

Urban eating habits, particularly in Kabul, have been drastically changed in the past fifteen years with the great influence of foreigners and the return of Western-educated Afghans. The Khyber Restaurant, for example, a cafeteria and restaurant, offers solid American construction-camp food. The manager of the Khyber Restaurant had been trained by American engineer construction camp cooks in the late 1940s and early 1950s. Other Afghans, trained in Germany, have opened rotisseries.

Several newer hotels offer other cuisines—the Spinzar, Central European; the Faiz, American; Intercontinental, luxury, with New York cut steaks and snails flown in periodically.

In many urban centers, men shop for food in the bazaar, and often claim to be better cooks than their wives.

In rural Afghanistan people eat two meals a day, breakfast and dinner, with many in-between snacks (dried nuts, fruits, bread). Dinner sometimes includes rice, with meat only occasionally, but tea and hot bread come with most meals. Leftovers often serve as breakfasts.

Whenever a large animal (cow, oxen) is killed, for whatever reason, the Afghans practice a custom called *khyrat*. Everyone in the village or camp gets an equal share of the meat, no matter who owns the beast. In times of stress (e.g., a cholera epidemic) the wealthier families contribute animals and other food for a feast in attempts to oppose and drive away the evil spirits. All in the village receive an equal share of all the food prepared, an obvious group attempt to protect itself through in-group interactions.

Gastro-intestinal diseases (especially forms of diarrhea, generically called *pych*) are common because of lack of sanitation, the continued use of contaminated water supplies, and improperly prepared food.[3]

Dress and Ornaments

In all societies, literate and non-literate, clothing serves symbolic as well as practical purposes. Also, all societies adopt non-functional clothing from outsiders, which identifies them as members of a developing class, usually literate.

In a pluralistic society like the United States, much overlap occurs at all levels, and clothing habits change throughout the lives of individuals and groups, but in Afghanistan ethnic pride leads toward acceptance of a specific mode of dress for group identification. Much of the clothing, however, remains similar because of similar individual work-patterns: peasant-farmer, nomad or town artisan.

In north Afghanistan, among the Turkic-speaking Uzbak, Turkoman, Kirghiz, and Persian-speaking Tajik, Hazara, and Aimaq, men shave each other's heads about once a month. Each man has his own razor, and squats patiently while a friend scrapes the bristles from his scalp, and then reciprocates. Some villages have part-time barbers who perform the services to a specific clientele in return for cash or kind.

South of the Hindu Kush in eastern Afghanistan, men generally prefer long hair, cut neat and square at the level of the earlobe, a kind of masculine bob. When they perform the *atan* (the so-called national dance, but primarily Pushtun), their long, often oiled, black hair whips and swirls with the exciting savagery of the dance.

In the remoter parts of Nuristan some men and most boys still leave a lock of hair on the back of the head, which facilitated the taking of heads or scalps in pre-Muslim days.

[3] Afghan toilet habits are somewhat different from those of the West. For example, Afghan males squat to urinate, and, instead of toilet paper, use clods of earth or chunks of sun-dried bricks.

Full beards are still popular outside the major cities, as signs of manhood, and as the beard whitens, so does the venerability of the man: *rish-i-safid* (white beard) refers to an elder, *rish-i-safidan,* the informal village council. Among the urban literates, mustaches are preferred, sometimes accompanied by a compromise goatee.

In some areas, young boys have their heads shaven except for a forelock by which, according to tradition, the boys may be snatched to Paradise if they die young.

Women seldom cut their hair, except in mourning, when some shave their entire heads. Body hair, including pubic hair, however, is painfully plucked with a looped string. Although girls go through no official puberty rites, this type of depilation may echo some such pre-Muslim ritual.

Afghan women wear their hair in various braided pigtail combinations, one, two, or several, at times straight, at other times coiled, the mode varying with the ethnic group. Among some Pushtun, unmarried girls wear their hair in two braids which hang down their backs. Other groups have three or several braids hanging on the back, decorated with embroidered cloth woven through the braids. When married, a woman will braid her hair into many braids toward the back of the head to indicate marital status. Among the upper and middle classes, the popularity of Western hairstyles of all varieties has led to a proliferation of modern hairdressing salons, particularly in Kabul.

Most Afghans dress similarly from the neck down according to sex. However, young boys sometimes wear dresses until shortly after they learn to walk (or even older), which facilitates toilet training.

Headgear, however, varies from group to group, and is the last piece of traditional clothing to go as a man becomes westernized. Even literate religious leaders may adapt Western dress, but they usually retain their distinctive turbans. Specific types of turban caps (*kolah*) and ways of tying the turban cloth (*lungi* or *dastar*) identify various groups among the Pushtun, Tajik, Hazara, Aimaq, Baluch, and Uzbak. White used to be the favorite turban cloth, although many, particularly among nomads, used black, a color which hides dirt. The post-World War II influx of cheap multicolored Indian and Japanese textiles made more colorful *lungi* popular in all groups.

The longer the *lungi,* the more fashionable. Often, a man's turban cloth will be more meters long than he is tall. All but the Pushtun groups usually tuck the ends of their turban cloths into the turban; the Pushtun leaves one end dangling over the shoulder, a pattern being adopted by others. The turban cloth has many functions. It protects the head from blows, intended or accidental; the end can be pulled across the face for protection against sand and snow storms. It can be used to transport small objects (eggs, sugar, rice, tea, etc.). The turban cloth is used in certain games such as high jumping. Snacks (*qrut* or raisins) can be tied in the loose end, to be eaten as desired. Afghans also utilize the turban cloth to lift objects from one level to another.

Just as the *lungi* can be distinctly tied to identify a group, the turban cap (*kolah*) is even more distinctive (Centlivres and Centlivres, 1968) Each ethnic group or region embroiders easily recognizable designs onto the semicylindrical or rounded caps, usually made by women in the home. Some, particularly in the west among the Persian-speaking villagers (Farsiwan) or in the north among some of the Turkic-speaking peoples, wear caps of bare felt. Other caps, however, are elaborately decorated, particularly among the Uzbak and Tajik. One of the more highly prized *kolah,* cylindrical and richly embroidered with gold and silver thread and sequins, is made by male bazaar specialists in Qandahar. Women in the Qandahar region now produce and peddle *kolah* decorated with brightly colored Pakistani glass beads. Some eastern Pushtun (Afridi, Mohmand, Mahmund) wear pointed turban caps. Others, farther south, like the Mangal and Jadran (sometimes spelled (Zadran), wear tall, cylindrical straw *kolah.*

Most farmers wear turban caps in the field, although some prefer to wind a turban cloth without a cap around their heads as protection against heat and dust. Boys usually wear turban caps until circumcised, and then proudly display their first *lungi,* which, like their rifle and dagger, is a symbol of manhood.

Turkomen wear distinctive tall, trapezoidal *qarakul* caps. The Kirghiz in the Pamir wear felt skull caps under fur-trimmed, floppy-eared quilted hats.

Another regional piece of headgear is the flat, pork-pie Nuristani cap (*pawkul*), commonly called the Chitrali cap, for most are brought into Nuristan from Chitral. The *pawkul* looks like a rolled up paper bag in summer, and can be rolled down in winter to protect the ears.

The modified cylindrical *qarakuli* (now popular in certain American urban centers) is the prestige headgear for all who can afford them.

The universal head-covering for women is the shawl (or *chadar*), which, like the *lungi,* performs many functions. The shawl keeps the dust from the hair, and permits the woman a modicum of modesty, for she can clutch a corner between her teeth when a stranger passes, thus partly covering the face. Babies can be wrapped and fed in the privacy of one end of the *chadar*. Small items can be tied in a corner and transported. At times women wear turban caps under the *chadar*, particularly for ceremonies and festivals.

Turkoman women wear the most distinctive hats in all Afghanistan, tall and covered with silver ornaments. Some hats, usually worn on special occasions, are often one and a half to two feet high. For daily work activities, Turkoman women wear peaked cloth turbans or head shawls in summer, but the same floppy quilted hats as the men in winter. Women's hats in Nuristan are sometimes covered with cowrie sheels, which served as a medium of exchange until the early twentieth century.

Most Afghan males wear slipover, loosely fitting, long-tailed cotton shirts, which reach the knees (or lower) and are buttoned at one shoulder. The shirt-tail flaps outside the baggy trousers, but can be tucked up inside the waist drawstring while the farmer works in the field. Qandahar specializes in white and brightly embroidered (small mirrors often sewn into the design) shirts for both men (*ghara*) and women (*ghangai*).

The horseriding groups of the north (particularly Turkoman, Uzbak, Tajik, Kirghiz) wear more form-fitting trousers, which befits horsemen. Fitted trousers probably originated in the plains of Central Asia and Mongolia in response to the development of horseback riding.

Nuristani men wear heavy wool, V-necked shirts and kilt-like shorts which often end just below the knee. The shorts have a drawstring.

Most Afghan males wear a sleeveless *waskat* (waistcoat or vest) over the shirt. Although the *waskat* is usually locally made and distinctly embroidered, many Afghans with access to town bazaars prefer to buy second hand American or European items, often locally embroidered. Quite a bit of the second-hand clothing of the United States ends up in Afro-Asia. The sale of second-hand clothes has become big business in the U.S.A. since World War II. Several American factories also reweave the old clothes to meet the peculiar or particular tastes of certain developing countries, but tons of unaltered second-hand clothing of all types turns up in Afghanistan. American businessmen buy the clothing by the warehouse-load from various charitable organizations which collect old clothes from contributors. The organizations use the resulting funds for operational and charitable purposes, so everyone benefits.

The major city bazaars in Afghanistan all have large sections which handle second-hand clothing, and when a new shipment arrives, men and women rush from far and wide to a veritable paradise of old clothes. Labels appear from reputable, and sometimes fashionable,

241

American clothing stores. World War II military tunics are especially popular with the martial Afghan males, who often dress in the traditional way, with the exception of an 8th Air Force tunic complete with embroidered captain's bars, silver wings, the DFC (Distinguished Flying Cross), Air Medal with three oak leaf clusters, plus the ETO (European Theater of Operations) ribbon with battle stars. Another Afghan will sport an army "Big Red One" (First Infantry Division) jacket; others wear the First Marine Division tunic. I have seen West Point capes, R.A.F. greatcoats, United States Merchant Marine Academy "blues," and even a tunic from Fishburne Academy, a private military school in Virginia.

Village women usually wear white or colorful cotton (cloth of Indian, Japanese, or local manufacture) shirts, baggy trousers, or ankle-length skirts. The more affluent and leisurely inclined the woman, the more cloth used in the pleated trousers, often up to twenty meters. Women in the north prefer the brightly colored tie-dyed silks, or Russian cotton chintz with gay, bold, flowered designs.

Among some Pushtun nomads, unmarried girls wear long cotton black *kamis, kamiz,* or *gamis* (also called *payran* or *payrahan;* a long, loose shirt) and a red *shalwar* (Dari; *tomban* or *yizar,* Pashto) or baggy pantaloons, to indicate their status. Married women wear a *kamis* which reaches to within six inches of the ankle, flowing blue pantaloons, a head covering called *parvani* in Dari or *poraney* in Pashto, and often leggings (*paychah*).

Wives and daughters of *maldar* (wealthy nomads) dress in bright wine and green velvet, heavily embroidered in gold. Coins of various denominations and ages (some as old as the Indo–Bactrian dynasties) sewn or woven into the garments worn by nomadic women make these creatures walking banks. Much of the family money surplus is literally tied up in women's clothing. Woman-stealing, still a favorite pastime among the nomadic Pushtun, is as much for fiscal as sexual reasons.

Nuristani women wear heavily embroidered blouses and full skirts, and, more rarely, narrower pantaloons than those worn by women of other ethnic groups.

In colder weather Afghans wear one of several heavy coats: *pustin* (dressed sheepskin, worn with fleece inside, often embroidered); *pustinchah* (sleeveless waistcoat made like *pustin*); *kusay* (short-sleeved coat of white raw wool, elaborately embroidered in Paktya); *paysawal* (long cloak with sleeves blocked; worn draped over shoulders); *chapan* (quilted cloak of many colors made in the north, but now exported to major Afghan cities for sale); *gopichah* (mainly Uzbak, a pullover cloak buttoned at one shoulder, quilted for winter wear). A short *chapan* is worn while riding. The Kirghiz and Kazakh of the high Pamir wear cloaks heavily padded with wool and fur. Even on the hottest summer days, village Afghans visiting the city wear heavy coats, *chapan,* or *kusay,* with Western suit coats and vests.

Afghan terms for types of Western clothing have been interestingly shifted from original meanings. For example, *jampar* refers to a lady's blouse or, at times, a man's or woman's sweater; *jaket* (with stress on second syllable) refers to either a sweater, a sport coat, or a business-suit coat. Often a *kamarband* (cloth belt of varying widths and thicknesses) encompasses the outer coat; the Afghans seldom support their baggy pants with anything but a drawstring.

Afghans sleep in their clothing. Some males strip to the waist when engaging in hard labor, but most remain fully clothed. When bathing in a stream, men will remove the long shirt, and loosen their baggy trousers to wash their private parts. Modesty is still the pattern. *Payjama* (a Hindi word referring to the baggy trousers and long shirts of Asia), usually of Western manufacture, are worn in urban centers. Many wear gaudy *payjama,* considered in good taste, in the street during warm weather.

Footgear varies from place to place and with the season. Open-toed and open-heeled leather or straw (*nyi* grass) sandals (often with tire-rubber soles) are the more popular footgear with villagers and nomads in the plains and foothills south of the Hindu Kush. Straw sandals occur mainly in Paktya, where large quantities of *nyi* grass can be collected. Other areas of *nyi* exist in the valleys leading into the Amu Darya west of Badakhshan. The usual term for sandal is *chapli.* In Kabul and other urban centers, cheap colorful plastic sandals from Pakistan, India, and Japan are growing in popularity.

Northern Afghans, particularly the Turkic-speaking horseback riders of the Turkestan plains and foothills, wear various types of boots. For walking and working, many wear open, boat-shaped, leather, shepherd's shoes (*borma*), laced with homemade string or leather thongs. Two kinds of walking boots called *maksis* exist, which can be either one-quarter or one-half leg in height: one has hard leather sole and heel, the other soft leather. In urban areas and some rural areas, Russian, Czech, Indian, or Pakistani manufactured rubber overshoes have replaced the leather sole-covers worn over the soft-soled boots when walking outside but removed on entering the home. Some wear rubber overshoes on bare feet. Another calf-high boot, *chamus,* has a soft sole. A popular knee-high boot (*muza*) with hard sole and high heel for hooking in stirrups is also worn.

Mountain peoples, particularly the Hazara and Aimaq, knit knee-length, thick wool stockings (with traditional designs) to wear inside boots in winter. The Hazara also knit and sell gloves with the same designs. In the high mountains of the Hindu Kush and the Pamir, people often wear fur-lined boots.

The Tajik make and export high wooden clogs to wear in mud. The clogs are carved with traditional designs (Andreev, 1927, 1932).

Nuristani men and women, in keeping with their cultural uniqueness, wear distinctive woolen leggings (*kutpula'un* in the Waigali dialect; *paitawah* in Dari) up to twenty feet long, tied with twisted wool string. (Elsewhere Afghans wear shorter *paitawah,* not only around the ankles but to support wrists.) Often the Nuristani goes barefoot, even in winter snows, but always wears leggings to protect his or her legs from the thick undergrowth. The Bari[4] artisans of Nuristan also make a buskin-type boot of cowhide for winter wear. Dried grass and straw packed inside the boot help keep it dry. Goatskin jackets or heavy serape-like cloaks (*kucha'ok*), fastened around the waist with a silver-studded dagger belt, are also worn by Nuristanis in winter. Women wear a long cloak (*sanah*), gathered at the waist by a narrow, fifteen foot long *Kamarband,* called *jagori* in Waigal. The total configuration of Nuristani clothing possibly relates to those of a belt of Eurasian mountaineers stretching from the Carpathians of Central Europe to Chitral.

In addition to the *ta'wiz* (see above, p. 105) all Afghans, men and women, are fond of ornaments. Patai's (1952) discussion of the importance of the aesthetic in the daily life of the Middle East especially applies to Afghanistan. The monotonous life of the village peasant and the mobile immobility of the nomad are constantly enlivened by man-made sights and noises. A seasonally drab landscape and repetitive ecological calendar breed a mania for contrasting color and design which extends beyond individual clothing. Probably the love of colorful flowers relates to this. Nomads with rifles slung at the ready will have several flowers in their turbans or in the lapels of their waistcoats, and often flowers burst forth from rifle barrels. Villagers, in town on

---

[4] The Bari artisans are considered inferior by the mountain shepherd-cattlemen of Nuristan, and until World War II, many Bari lived as virtual slaves. Even today, Bari find it difficult to move from one village to another without the consent of the dominant Nuristanis.

bazaar day, pick and sniff flowers as they pass a garden. Artists paint truck body-panels with gaudy, colorful scenes of fountains, mountains, mosques, lions, horsemen, flowers, guns, locomotives, trains, a hand on a telephone, a jet or conventionally powered aircraft. Horses wear elaborate trappings and colorful blankets, particularly in the north. In the urban centers, horse-drawn two-wheeled *gawdi* roll colorfully and noisily down the street, the horses gaily bedecked with crimson pompoms, bells, and yak-tail fly whisks. The proud *maldar* (wealthy nomad) dresses his camels with gaudy trimmings.

Jewelers, silversmiths, and goldsmiths laboriously manufacture items for individual use. Customers give face-to-face orders, the future owner approves the plans, and the artisan executes the job with an individualistic flair. The emphasis on individual skills and the artisan's pride in the artistics as well as function reminds one (at least superficially) of the *mana* (impersonal power), which is transmitted from the artisan to his tool and then on to the object in Oceania (Malinowski, 1954). The Afghan artisan also does more than make an artifact; he incorporates a part of himself into it.

Paradoxically, emphasis on individual·artisan effort does not produce perfect end-products. Since only Allah is perfect, everything made by man is imperfect, so even the most beautiful Mawri Turkoman rugs, Uzbak saddlebags, Istalif blue-glazed pottery, and Kabuli silverware will have at least one flaw purposely constructed into the design. In addition, increasing urbanization and the demands which follow this process always find quality deteriorating in favor of quantity, a growing problem among Afghan artisans.

Women (or their husbands), even after marriage, purchase as much gold, silver, and brass jewelry as they can afford, some set with precious or semi-precious stones (lapis lazuli, carnelian, etc.), but often just colored glass. The Turkoman women of the north wear the most distinctive and elaborate gilded silver jewelry in Afghanistan. The well-dressed Turkoman lady will be bejeweled from head to toe: front and back headbands and plaques which hang from the headdress, armbands, bracelets (some with a ring and a thimble for each finger), breast and back plaques (rectangular, square, and triangular), rings, necklaces, and anklets.

The fish (at times with wings), a common fertility symbol, appears frequently in jewelry (Cammann, 1957). Other important prehistoric symbols are the sun-bird (phoenix) and the tree of life, found not only on jewelry but woven into the rugs of Afghanistan.

245

Men often wear one or more rings. Urban non-literates usually have their personal seals or script spellings of their names on a ring which substitutes for signatures. Afghan soldiers use such rings to sign official military documents. One interesting ornament pinned to many a male peasant and nomad contains five functioning toiletry tools: nose-hair cutter, fingernail clipper, ear-wax cleaner, toothpick, and fingernail cleaner.

Some men wear a gold ring on one earlobe or the other, usually the result of a parental committment when a child is deathly ill. The parents pray and ask Allah to save the child's life. If the child lives, the parents place a gold earring on his ear as a reminder of Allah's compassion. Some Afghans, however, state they wear a gold earring because it is sexy. Others insist it identifies practicing homosexuals.

Wristwatches serve many non-literates simply as status items, for sometimes the conspicuously worn watches are broken. Some non-literates also sport fountain-pen tops in their waistcoat pockets for the same reason.

The custom of tattooing (using copper sulphate, charcoal, and pin pricks) women among certain Pushtun nomadic groups has never been adequately explained. Cammann (1957, 17–18) reports that tattooing may occur at weddings, but he expresses doubts of this custom as reported, and I can only echo his distrust. Rather, from what I have been able to gather, the tattoos on forehead, forearms, sometimes hands, and even breasts relate more to tribal property symbols. Similar signs, often a type of stylized bird, occur on camels and horses.

Cosmetics used by most women include the so-called *haft-rang* (seven colors): *khinah* (henna) for hands and feet; *wasmah* (indigo) for the eyes; *sorkhi* (red powder) for the face; *safidah* (white powder) for the face; *sormah* or kohl (purplish-black paste) for eye-liner; *zarnik* (gold dot for the forehead); *ghalya* (musk, ambergris, oil) for the body.

Modern trends in dress include exchanges of clothing types by overlapping groups in ethnic gray zones. Mushwani Pushtun, for example, dress like their Nuristani neighbors, except for their long-tailed Pushtun shirt; at many places in north Afghanistan, Tajik and Uzbak live in the same valley and wear each other's headgear types, where at one time distinctive *kolah* existed for the different groups. Other current trends are the gradual Westernization of dress in the major cities, and the movement of the *chadri* (or *borq'a*) from the city to the town.

The *chadri*, though still present, began to disappear from Kabul in 1959, particularly among the literate class where Western clothing, sometimes from Paris and Rome, had dominated underneath the *chadri* since at least World War II. The *chadri,* a sack-like garment of pleated, colored silk or rayon, covers the entire body from head to toe, with an embroidered lattice-work eye-mask to permit limited vision. The women who came out of the veil in 1959 first wore a uniform consisting of a scarf, dark sunglasses, heavy coats, gloves, and cotton stockings. Nylon hosiery soon replaced the cotton stockings, the gloves and sunglasses gradually disappeared, and the coat was made of thinner and thinner material until it, too, was discarded. Today even the scarf is being left at home and miniskirts, worn by pert school girls, blossom on the streets of Kabul and on the Kabul University campus. Upper-class women still import high fashions from the West, but a number of Afghan ladies, trained as dressmakers in Europe, have opened salons and cater to an ever-growing middle-class clientele. Underwear and brassieres have been introduced into many general stores in Kabul.

Women in the cities continue to come out of purdah (*pardah*) and remove the veil, but a strange reversal of attitudes has occurred in villages becoming towns, brought about by the massive shifts of the transport and communication networks in the 1960s. Village and nomadic women seldom wore the *chadri* in the past because it would have interfered with their many daily economic functions. Now, however, if a village grows to town status, complete with a bazaar, and a man gains enough wealth to hire servants, his wife often insists on wearing a *chadri,* for she believes the custom to be sophisticated and citified—not realizing her city cousins have opposite attitudes. In addition, many young girls in the cities and towns wear the *chadri* briefly after puberty to indicate they have become bona fide women, ready for marriage.

Actually, the *chadri* originally had two functions: it put all women in public on an equal basis (a plain *chadri* could cover the most inexpensive clothing) and it kept women (i.e., personal property) from being coveted by other men. However, some *chadri* were made in the richest silks and also used for clandestine assignations, thus defeating the original purposes.

CHAPTER 12

The Inward-Looking Society

ALL THE FOREGOING DISCUSSIONS about the people of Afghanistan lead us to some generalizations concerning the nature of the peasant-tribal societies which dominate the world scene today. One primary attribute is *non-literacy* (Chart 18). Therefore the bulk of the population in most developing societies has no direct access to the rich literatures of their cultures, and must depend on interpretations, usually by vested-interest religious and secular leaders.

Another key factor is economic: in peasant-tribal societies, most of the people spend most of their time *engaged in basic-food production*. In Afghanistan, for example, over 90% of the population are farmers, herdsmen, or a combination of the two. In Pakistan and Iran, 75 to 80% engage in basic-food production activities. The usual figure given

CHART 18

Percent of Population Which Was Literate in 1960–1961*

Kabul	5.9%
Qandahar	0.9
Herat	3.0
Mazar-i-Sharif	3.4
Ningrahar	2.1
Paktya	0.8
Qataghan	3.4
Ghazni	3.3
Girishk	1.3
Farah	3.6
Maimana	0.7
Shibarghan	(no answer)
Badakhshan	2.6
Parwan	1.5
Bamiyan	3.8
Uruzgan	0.6
Ghor	3.1
Weighted average for all provinces except Shibarghan	3.1

* Source: *Population and Agricultural Survey of 500 Villages*, Research and Statistics, Ministry of Planning, Kabul, 1963, .6. No reliable estimates on literacy are available.

for the U.S.S.R. is still about 45%. In the U.S.A., by contrast, less than 6% of the population actually produces food. The percentage of non-literates and basic-food producers tends to be almost identical in most developing societies.

Lack of mobility is also a big factor. Occupationally, a man in a peasant-tribal society will probably follow the occupation of his father, normally farming or herding. Politically, a man will be a leader or a follower depending on the status of his family. Socially, a man usually marries within his tightly defined group; in Muslim society, a man's pre-ferred mate is still father's brother's daughter, parallel first cousin. Economic, geographic, and social mobility do exist, but in a limited sense, when compared to mobility in the literate, pluralistic, developed societies of the West. I am making no value judgment concerning these patterns, simply describing them. Even nomads, although they may sea-sonally move, lack real mobility. They travel from winter to summer pasturelands and back again. Any deviation from their traditional routes would bring conflict with other groups until adjustments could be made.

The village builds a "mud curtain" around itself for protection against the outside world, which has often come to the village in the past. Sustained relations with the outside world have seldom been pleasant, for outsiders usually come to *extract* from, not bring anything into, the village. Items extracted include rent, taxes, conscripts for armies, women for the harems of the rich and powerful. The process, therefore, has generally been one way, *away* from the village. As a consequence, most villagers simply cannot believe that central governments, provincial governments, or individual local or foreign technicians want to introduce permanent reforms. Previous attempts have generally been of short duration and abortive, for once the "modernization" teams leave, the villagers patch up the breaks in the "mud curtain" and revert to their old, group-reinforcing patterns. Most villages listed in governmental records of the developing world as "developed" have never been re-visited or rechecked, and the "development" exists only on paper.

Local and foreign experts cannot really be blamed for being duped by villagers, who, over many generations, have developed excellent de-fensive mechanisms to protect themselves from the outside world. For example, villagers willingly accept any and all suggestions for techno-logical change, because they realize that the sooner they accept, the sooner the "developers" will leave.

In addition, an outsider seldom meets the true power elite of a village unless he remains for an extended period. When outsiders approach, the village leaders disappear behind mud walls, and the first line of defense (second line of power) come forward to greet the strangers with formalized hospitality, which surprisingly enough also serves as a defensive technique. If the central government identifies the village or tribal elite, control becomes easier as the zones of relative inaccessibility evaporate with the creation of an effective infrastructure. The formalized hospitality of the villager can quickly develop into hostility unless the outsider becomes a functioning member of the society.

Contrary to popular belief, villagers are fundamentally non-cooperative creatures outside their kin group, and not communally oriented. I say non-cooperative, not uncooperative, for villagers will build farm-to-market roads or improve irrigation and drainage systems if *forced to* by the government or *paid* for labor rendered. Seldom can villagers be persuaded to work for (to them) an abstract, distantly (for the benefit of future generation) achieved common goal. The villager wants to benefit now.

Locally oriented religious beliefs serve not only as rationale for existence, but justifications for the perpetuation of a predeterministic *status quo,* in which a man who performs his given (not chosen) roles in society can expect Paradise as a reward.

All these attributes perpetuate an "inward-looking" society, which simply means a society into which a man is born into a *set of answers.* In developed nations, a man is born, at least technically, into an "outward-looking" society, or a *set of questions,* but the answer to any given question breeds another set of questions, so the half-truths of tomorrow continually replace the half-truths of any given today.

Developing and developed societies, therefore, have polar scales of attitudes, values, and time, and these as well as technology must be altered to bring about permanent change. Whether this is good or bad remains for the historian to interpret, and is not for the anthropologist to accept or reject at this stage. For example, if a woman dies because of a *jinn* or the will of Allah, instead of childbed fever, introduction of public health measures *alone* will help but little. If a tractor runs because of the will of Allah instead of preventive maintenance, breakdown renders the tractor useless.

All development programs are essentially attempts to create a nation-state. If we institutionally define a nation-state as having a set of reciprocal economic, military, and even social (integration, social security, Medicare, etc.) rights and obligations, it becomes obvious that a modern nation-state is as much a state of mind as a geographic entity.

250

Today, kinship rights and obligations replace government in most developing countries.

A major key to development, then, is involvement.

But getting the villager involved in his own development constitutes only one facet of the overall problem. The other is to get the 5 to 10% literate class, particularly government officials, involved with the villagers. Government officials form an outward-looking group, and generally they look *away from,* not *toward,* the village. They prefer to remain in the national capital and reap the benefits of their literate status: good government or business jobs, social prestige, extensive foreign contacts. In addition, when promotions, choice assignments, or overseas boondoggles come up, those at the center usually benefit, not the officials assigned to the subprovince, district, and subdistrict levels. The key action component, motivation, remains only partly solved. However, motivation for both the villager and the literate official revolve about improved status and adequate financial remunerations. The new provincial system and Constitution discussed below both give wider opportunities for alternative social, political, and economic activities and help create an emergent middle class.

We have placed the people on the landscape. Now we must find out how they got there and, possibly, where they are going.

PART III. THE PAST

"For me, archaeology is not a source of illustration for written sources, but an independent source of historical confirmation, no less valuable and important, sometimes more important than the written sources." (Rostovtzeff, 1922, viii)

Few places epitomize the truth of Rostovtzeff's statement like Afghanistan. We must combine archaeology and history[1] to establish a reasonably valid outline of prehistoric and historic patterns, especially since the literate sources usually glorify any dynasty in power at any given moment, thereby distorting the historic and cultural whole. In addition, over ninety percent of the Afghans remain non-literate.

[1] For a survey of Persian, Pashto, and Arabic sources on Afghan history, see A. Habibi, 1968c.

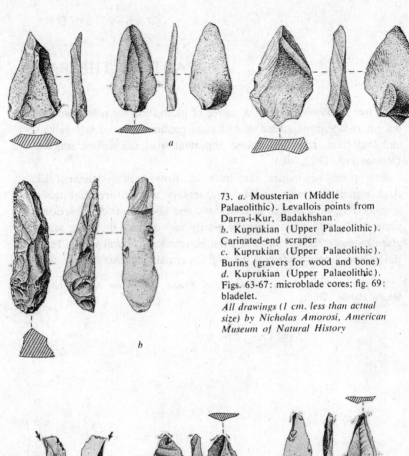

73. a. Mousterian (Middle
Palaeolithic). Levallois points from
Darra-i-Kur, Badakhshan.
b. Kuprukian (Upper Palaeolithic).
Carinated-end scraper
c. Kuprukian (Upper Palaeolithic).
Burins (gravers for wood and bone)
d. Kuprukian (Upper Palaeolithic).
Figs. 63-67: microblade cores; fig. 69:
bladelet.
*All drawings (1 cm. less than actual
size) by Nicholas Amorosi, American
Museum of Natural History*

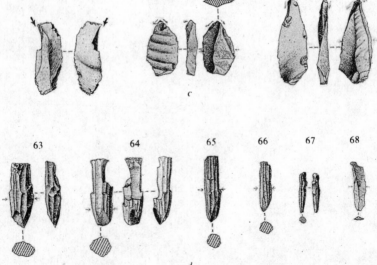

63   64   65   66   67   68

d

CHAPTER 13

The Prehistoric Sequence

CA. 50,000 B.C.–SEVENTH CENTURY B.C.

UNTIL the post-World War II period, archaeologists largely neglected the prehistory of Afghanistan, partly because of the richness of historic finds, partly because of the relative lack of interest of European and American scholars in Central Asia. Some work, however, was done. Dr. Roman Ghirshman, now Chef du Mission, Délégation Archéologique en Iran; sunk test pits at Nad-i-Ali in Sistan (southwest Afghanistan) just before World War II and excavated materials probably dating from the first millennium B.C. Aside from Ghirshman's work (1939), however, the prehistoric periods of Afghanistan remained unplumbed, and few could have predicted the rich finds to come after 1949, the date of the first archaeological survey specifically undertaken to identify prehistoric sites.

Flavorful newspaper accounts of "Lost Cities" resulted in some unpleasant publicity from the Afghan point of view (Kohzad, 1950a), but the First Expedition (1949) of the American Museum of Natural History recorded a series of potential prehistoric mounds in Afghanistan (Fairservis, 1950a,b), and the Second Expedition (1950–51), led by Walter A. Fairservis, Jr., did primer work in the prehistory of Afghanistan and West Pakistan (Fairservis, 1956). After Fairservis tested the mound of Deh Morasi Ghundai near Qandahar and moved on for additional surveys in Sistan (Fairservis, 1961), Louis Dupree made more extensive excavations and uncovered a series of Chalcolithic (Copper Age) occupational levels dating from the fourth to the first millennia B.C. The site possibly represents a semisedentary situation, common in that part of Afghanistan today: a part of the people seasonally move into alpine pastures in the Hazarajat with flocks of sheep, goat, and cattle, while the bulk remain in the village area to farm the adjacent land (L. Dupree, 1963a).

As Dupree completed his work at Deh Morasi Ghundai, Jean-Marie Casal began a series of excavations (1951–58, 10 field seasons) at Mundigak, a Bronze Age site about 50 kilometers north of Deh Morasi

Ghundai. The two sites (Deh Morasi Ghundai and Mundigak) seem to complement one another.

Prehistoric research remained relatively quiescent after the completion of the Mundigak digs until 1959, when Dupree returned to Afghanistan. During this period, however, systematic cave archaeology began. Professor Carleton S. Coon, University Museum, University of Pennsylvania, a pioneer in scientific cave research in the Middle East, excavated Kara Kamar near Aibak and discovered at least two, and possibly four, Stone Age levels (Coon, 1957).

In November–December, 1959, Dupree and Abdul Rauf Wardak of the Kabul Museum surveyed most of the limestone hills of the north Hindu Kush and recorded 100 caves and 150 mounds of archaeological interest (L. Dupree, 1964b; L. Dupree and Howe, 1963). The summer field seasons (1962, 1965) of excavations at Aq Kupruk at four localities produced a typological sequence leading from the Upper Palaeolithic to a Nomadic Iron Age complex. The uppermost levels included material from the Kushano–Buddhist periods of the mid-fifth to seventh centuries A.D. A series of multilated Buddhist wall-paintings occurred in association with the Kushano–Buddhist material.

An Italian archaeologist, Salvatore M. Puglisi, reported some "Clactonian" implements near Hazar Sum in the Aibak area (Puglisi, 1963), and has personally informed me of an Upper Palaeolithic industry like that found at Aq Kupruk, but to date little has appeared in print.

In the summer of 1966, at Darra-i-Kur in Badakhshan, near the village Chenar-i-Baba Darwesh off the road from Chenar-i-Gunjuskhan, Dupree and Afghan, American, and French colleagues found four cultural levels: Middle Palaeolithic; a late Siberian-type Neolithic (see Ranov, 1962); Iron Age (Kushan?); an Islamic level with some fifteenth-century A.D. Timurid pottery.

Archaeologists have just scratched the surface of prehistoric research in Afghanistan, but an increase in activity and the phenomenal wealth of the finds deserves a preliminary inventory. No definitive conclusions can be drawn, but from the evidence, certain inferences can be made (L. Dupree, 1967b, 1969a; Masson and Sarianidy, 1969). The terminology used does not imply contemporaneity with other Eurasian or African archaeological periods, but simply pigeonholes the industries *typologically* (see Chart 19).

CHART 19
The Prehistory of Afghanistan: A Tentative Chart

	Aq Kupruk I (Snake Cave)[1]	Aq Kupruk II (Horse Cave)[1]	Aq Kupruk III (Open air site)[1]	Aq Kupruk IV (Skull Cave)[1]	Deh Morasi Ghundai[2]	Mundigak[3]	Nad-i-Ali[4]	Sistan Sites[5]	Darra Dadil Darra Chakhmakh[6]	Kara Kamar[7]	Hazar Sum[8]	Darra-i-Kur (Cave of the Dead Sheep)[15]
Later Nomadic Iron Age Hv 426: 1390 ± 60 B.P.[10] Hv 427: 1340 ± 70 B.P.	X	X		X							X	
Early Nomadic Iron Age Hv 1359: 1635 ± 70 B.P. Hv 1360: 1645 ± 70 B.P. Hv 1361: 1635 ± 65 B.P.	X	X		X	X	X	X	X			X	X
Goat Cult Neolithic GX 0910:[11] collagen: 3780 ± 130 B.P. carbonate: 3425 ± 125 B.P.												X
Mundigak-Morasi Bronze Age 5000-3000 B.P. P-1493 (Morasi II: 2597 ± 55 B.C.)[12]					X	X		X				
Gap												

CHART 19 (continued)

	Aq Kupruk I (Snake Cave)[1]	Aq Kupruk II (Horse Cave)[1]	Aq Kupruk III (Open air site)[1]	Aq Kupruk IV (Skull Cave)[1]	Deh Morasi Ghundai[2]	Mundigak[3]	Nad-i-Ali[4]	Sistan Sites[5]	Darra Dadil	Darra Chakhmakh[6]	Kara Kamar[7]	Hazar Sum[8]	Darra-i-Kur (Cave of the Dead Sheep)[15]
Aq Kupruk Non-Ceramic Neolithic Hv 425: 8650 ± 100 B.P. Hv 1355: 10,210 ± 235 B.P. R-274: 9475 ± 100 B.P.[16]	X	X										X[16]	
Kara Kamar "Mesolithic" 10,580 ± 750 B.P.[13]	X	X									X		
Kuprukian B (Upper Palaeolithic) Hv 1358: 16,615 ± 215 B.P.	X	X										?[16]	
Kuprukian A (Upper Paleolithic) ca. 20,000 B.P.[9]	X	X'									X	?[16]	
Kara Kamar "Aurignacian" ca. 34,000 B.P.[13]													
Middle Palaeolithic GX: 1122: Baba Darwesh 30,300 - 1900 B.P. + 1200 B.P.[14]									X			?	X

CHART 19 (continued)

Kara Kamar "Aurignacian"
ca. 34,000 B.P.[13]

Middle Palaeolithic
GX: 1122: Baba Darwesh
30,300 - 1900 B.P.
+ 1200 B.P.[14]

1 L. Dupree, 1964b; 1968a.
2 L. Dupree, 1963a.
3 Casal, *DAFA* XVII, Appendix F, 1961.
4 Ghirshman, 1939.
5 Fairservis, 1961.
6 L. Dupree and Howe, 1963.
7 Coon, 1957.
8 Puglisi, 1963.
9 L. Dupree, 1968a.
10 Hv are C-14 dates from Niedersächsisches Landesamt für Bodenforschung, Hannover, West Germany. Before Present (B.P.) refers to before 1950.

11 C-14 dates from Geochron Laboratories, Inc., Cambridge, Mass.
12 B.C. date from University of Pennsylvania, University Museum, Applied Science Center for Archaeology.
13 C. Coon and E. Ralph, 1955.
14 Probably contaminated and older; date from Geochron Laboratories, Inc.
15 Dupree, Lattman, and Davis, 1970.
16 Date from Rome laboratory, *Radiocarbon* (1967): rock shelter near Hazar Sum named Darra Kalon, which seems to have sequence as shown on Chart, but we need more data from Puglisi. Possibly only Aq Kupruk Non-Ceramic Neolithic and Kuprukian B represented, or possibly Kuprukian B and Non-Ceramic Neolithic are phases of same complex.

Middle Palaeolithic

The flake tools found in 1959 by Dupree and Wardak in Darra Dadil, Darra Chakhmakh, and elsewhere indicated the probable existence of Middle Palaeolithic industries in north Afghanistan. Now stratigraphic evidence exists at Darra-i-Kur (Cave of the Valley) in Badakhshan and Ghar-i-Mordeh Gusfand (Cave of the Dead Sheep) near Gurziwan, south of Maimana. At Darra-i-Kur, the excavators found about 800 implements and *débitage* made of locally available blackish and yellowish-green stones as yet unidentified, but probably types of impure flint or chert. The tool kit of the Darra-i-Kur Mousterian included cores, Levallois flakes, handaxe types, various scraper types, flake-blades, and Levallois points.

Similar Mousterian tool types have been found at the Cave of the Dead Sheep, but the raw material used was siliceous limestone (Dupree, Lattman, and Davis, 1970).

The few bones found in the Baba Darwesh Middle Palaeolithic levels could be identified only as from wild sheep or goat and one possible large bovine specimen. The excavators located no definable hearths, but uncovered many flakes of charcoal in the zone between the swamp backwash clays and the lower cave gravels. A major roof-fall now blocks over one-half of the Middle Palaeolithic occupation area, and presumably the underlying hearths and bones have remained undisturbed for millennia.

Often, Middle Palaeolithic industries have occurred in association with Neanderthal Man, the nearest to Darra-i-Kur being in Uzbakistan S.S.R. at Teshik-Tash (Movius, 1953a), Bisitun and Tamtama (Coon, 1951a) in Iran, and Shanidar in Iraq (Solecki, 1966; Stewart, 1962). In the Darra-i-Kur Middle Palaeolithic levels, the excavators discovered a large fragmentary human temporal bone, studied by Dr. J. Lawrence Angel of the Smithsonian Institution, who states he believes the fragment to be nearer to modern man than to Neanderthal Man (personal communication, 1968).

However, the Middle Palaeolithic industry at Darra-i-Kur with its suggestions of Upper Palaeolithic elements, plus the possible *Homo sapiens sapiens* skull fragment, have interesting inferences. Pradel (1966) recently discussed the transition from Middle to Upper Palaeolithic, in which he attempts to relate stone industries to skeletal remains and hints that such ingredients may be found in the Near East. The Darra-i-Kur finds support his speculations. In other words, north

Afghanistan may be in a zone where a variety of modern man developed physically and, with the advent of an Upper Palaeolithic blade industry, began to revolutionize Stone Age technology.

Upper Palaeolithic

Archaeologists have identified Upper Palaeolithic blade industries at three Afghan localities; Kara Kamar (Coon, 1951a), Aq Kupruk (L. Dupree, 1964b, 1968ab) and Hazar Sum (Puglisi, 1962). Coon's Kara Kamar "Aurignacian" has several C-14 dates averaging 32,000 years before 1950 (Coon and Ralph, 1955). However, the small sample of 82 implements from the Kara Kamar "Aurignacian" make it impossible to define the industry, hence the quotes surrounding "Aurignacian." Of the 82 implements, 52 were nose scrapers. Other tools consisted of "Aurignacian-type" blades, unutilized microlithic blades, one drill, and three bone awls. No burins (gravers or engravers) were found. The Kara Kamar "Aurignacian" peoples apparently subsisted mainly on wild sheep and horses. Tortoise shells also appeared in all levels.

About 20,000 Upper Palaeolithic flint implements have been excavated from three localities at Aq Kupruk, about 50 kilometers west of Kara Kamar. The *Kuprukian* industry, as the excavators call it, is stratigraphically divided in two phases at two of the three sites: *Aq Kupruk II* (Horse Cave or *Ghar-i-Asp*) and *Aq Kupruk III,* an open-air site on a river terrace. A thick (up to 1.5 meters) layer of sterile, windblown loess separates the two phases: Kuprukian A (the older) and Kuprukian B. The homogeneous flint used to manufacture the Kuprukian tools is brown or brownish-red, a very fine, easily worked material in contrast to the impure, silicious chert, limestone, and other raw materials used in the Middle Palaeolithic.

The Kuprukian A assemblage consists of a mixture of two Upper Palaeolithic industries: a blade-flake tradition and a microlithic tradition. The blade-flake facies contains cores, utilized and retouched blades and flakes, side and end scrapers, keeled scrapers, nose scrapers, points, burins (engravers), and combination tools such as end scraper-burins. Some small, flake handaxes or cleavers also occur. The microindustry includes cores, points, burins, and bladelets, but *no geometrics,* often one of the hallmarks of later Mesolithic industries (Coon, 1951a, 1957; Huckreide, 1961). Upper Palaeolithic (and earlier) blades-plus-micro industries have been frequently found in the Near East and

261

Europe, particularly since World War II. (Among others: Movius and Judson, 1956; Kökten, 1963; Higgs, 1965.)

The faunal finds of Kuprukian A, as identified by Dr. Dexter Perkins, Jr., are *Cervus elaphus* (Red deer), *Ovis orientalis cycloceros* (Urial), *Capra hircus aegagrus* (Bezoar); wild cattle; jackal (personal communication, 1968).

The Kuprukian B assemblage closely resembles that of Kuprukian A but separated in time by the sterile loess. However, the number of micro-tools apparently increases in comparison to the number of blade-flake implements. More bone points, awls, punches, and other perforator types of fragmentary bone tools also occur in Kuprukian B, in addition to several incised bone fragments. The faunal list according to Perkins includes Urial, Bezoar, horse, jackal, fox.

The excavators found an interesting *objet d'art* in Kuprukian A, *Aq Kupruk II,* an oblong limestone pebble with incisions apparently meant to represent a human face, possibly the oldest sculptured piece from Asia and one of the older specimens found anywhere (L. Dupree, 1968b).

The nearest Upper Palaeolithic sites to Aq Kupruk and Kara Kamar are found in Iraq (Braidwood and Howe, 1960; Solecki, 1966), but further research in Iranian caves will undoubtedly produce similar industries. In fact, none have been found in India (Wheeler, 1959), but some may occur in Soviet Central Asia according to Ranov (1963, 1964ab, 1967; Movius, 1953b; Litvinski, 1968).

"Mesolithic"

Coon (1957) identifies a "Mesolithic" at Kara Kamar which yielded 58 tools, primarily microlithic cores and blades, but no geometrics. According to R. Davis (1970), the microlithic industry of Kara Kamar was manufactured using different techniques from those of the Upper Palaeolithic Kuprukian.

Gazelle, wild sheep, and mole vole were dietary favorites in the "Mesolithic."

Non-Ceramic Neolithic

Domesticated sheep and goats have been identified from the first (A) phase of the Non-Ceramic Neolithic at *Aq Kupruk* I (Snake Cave or

Ghar-i-Mar). The plant remains (including carbonized materials) have yet to be studied, along with an interesting pocket of sheep or goat dung. Flint implements abound in both the Non-Ceramic Neolithic phases A and B, but a wider variety appears in the upper levels: sickle blades, cores, end and side scrapers on blades, points, and burins. Polished bone points also occurred.

If subsequent C-14 dates approximate the ones on Chart 18, and if the plant remains prove to be transitional or domesticated, the foot-hills of the Hindu Kush mountains in north Afghanistan must be con-sidered one of the early centers for the domestication of plants and animals, the Neolithic Revolution (Childe, 1946), which permitted man to control his food supply and create surpluses which led to specializa-tion and ultimately to civilization and nuclearization.

Probably the wheat/barley–sheep/goat complex developed in a gen-eral latitudinal (34°–40°N), altitudinal (500–750 meters above sea level) zone, and spread quickly throughout from north-central Afghan-istan to Anatolia and possibly the Aegean area. Most early Asian Neo-lithic sites of 9 to 11,000 years ago fall within this latitudinal-altitudinal ecological zone. Today, a slow walker, traveling 15 kilometers a day, can cross this area easily in about six months, and prehistoric man was not the homebody hypothesized by past generations of anthropologists.

From my studies of modern nomads and peasants since 1949, I sug-gest that pastoral nomadism (emphasizing sheep/goat economy) may have developed when dissidents in the incipient farming, sedentary groups broke away because they could not stand the boredom of settling down, and returned to a compromise between sedentary agriculture and the preceding hunting and gathering nomadic cultures, in which man was simply an animal chasing other animals.

The Non-Ceramic Neolithic faunal list compiled by Perkins includes sheep/goat and possible cattle.

Ceramic Neolithic

A change in stratigraphy at *Aq Kupruk I* and *II* heralded the introduc-tion of pottery into the area. Two types have been identified: a crude, software, with limestone, shred, or chaff temper and simple, rounded rims and flat bases; a better fired ware with zigzag incisions character-istic of the Neolithic pottery of Russian Turkestan (Tolstov, 1962). The software Neolithic of Hotu and Belt Caves in Iran offer close parallels to the Aq Kupruk Ceramic Neolithic (Coon, 1957). Other cultural finds included limestone hoes, manos, metates, polishers, celts, stone bowl fragments, carved turtle-shell fragments, and many chert tools including cores, sickle blades, micro-points, bladelets, drills, and a unifacially pressure-flaked point.

The following faunal remains have thus far been identified by Perkins: onager and domesticated sheep, goat, cattle.

The "Goat Cult" Neolithic

A different type of Neolithic occurred above the Middle Palaeolithic at Darra-i-Kur. More closely related to the later Neolithic of Kashmir (B. Lal, 1964) and South Siberia, the "Goat Cult" Neolithic of Darra-i-Kur has a diagnostic software (less than 5 hardness on the Moh Scale) pottery which I propose to call the Baba Darwesh Black Ware. Decorations include striated, punctated, and incised chevrons, parallel lines, triangles, ladder motifs, cross-hatchings, and zigzags. Some base sherds have interior basket or fiber impressions. Others have finger-impressed rims. Several pottery discs are perforated. The rare flint implements (several sickle blades and a single point) were of a brown and brownish-red homogeneous flint, completely unlike the ratty black material of the underlying Mousterian. Three polished stone axes were found (one with a pecked, worked butt), along with bone awls, polishers, spatulas, gouges, and polished sheep astraguli. A slate knife and pendant, a long limestone knife, basaltic hammerstones, slate scrapers, quartzite pebble tools, a perforated shell, a limestone bead, a steatite spindle whorl, a polished obsidian (?) bracelet fragment, and a partly finished pendant of a local stone called sang-i-Hazrat Sayyid give witness to the diversity of the Goat Burial Neolithic assemblage.

More importantly, postholes appeared in the soil, possibly to hold up tents or even subterranean huts. The most spectacular finds, however, relate to the fauna. The excavators uncovered three pit burials containing articulated bones of domesticated goats, two with heads missing (purposely decapitated), one in association with fragments of two or three children's skeletons. The burials possibly have ritual significance, relating to the Goat Cult which has existed in Central Asia from Mousterian to modern times (Movius, 1953a, 55–58).

Other fauna identified by Dr. Perkins include domesticated sheep; domesticated cattle; Gazella subgutturosa; onager and Equus przewalskii; Vulpes vulpes (red fox); martes sp. (marten); Canis aureus (jackal); Canis lupus (wolf); bird and fish bones.

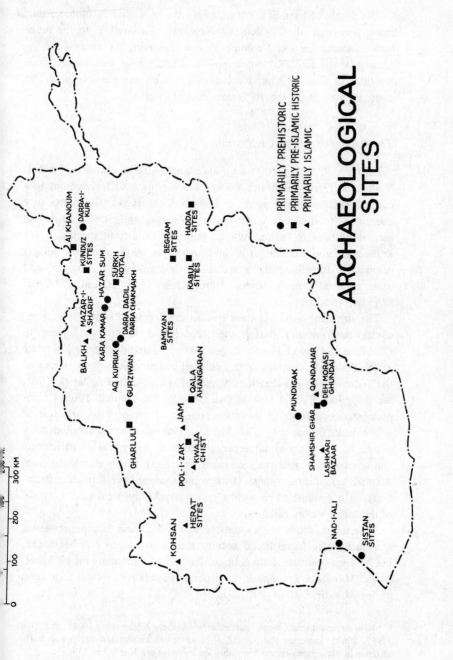

ARCHAEOLOGICAL SITES

PRIMARILY PREHISTORIC ●
PRIMARILY PRE-ISLAMIC HISTORIC ■
PRIMARILY ISLAMIC ▲

AI KHANOUM ■
DARRA-I-KUR ●
KUNDUZ SITES ■
HAZAR SUM ●
SURKH KOTAL ■
MAZAR-I-SHARIF ▲
BALKH ▲
KARA KAMAR ●
DARRA DADIL ●
DARRA CHAKMAKH ●
AQ KUPRUK ●
GURZIWAN ●
BEGRAM SITES ■
HADDA SITES ■
KABUL SITES ■
BAMIYAN SITES ■
GHARLULI ●
QALA AHANGARAN ▲
POL-I-ZAK ▲
JAM ▲
KWAJA CHIST ▲
MUNDIGAK ●
QANDAHAR ■
DEH MORASI GHUNDAI ●
SHAMSHIR GHAR ■
LASHKARI BAZAAR ▲
KOHSAN ▲
HERAT SITES ▲
NAD-I-ALI ●
SISTAN SITES ●

300 KM
200
100
0

The South Siberian-South Russian-Northeast Afghan Neolithic occurs much later than the Aq Kupruk Neolithic which relates to the much earlier Middle Eastern Neolithic. A line separating the area of the beginning of the foothill Neolithic of the Middle East and the mountain Neolithic of Central Asia (including Kashmir) can possibly be drawn approximately along the 70°E. meridian of longitude.

The Bronze Age and Civilization

Between 3000 and 2000 B.C., as urban civilizations rose in the Nile Valley, the Tigris–Euphrates Valleys, and the Indus Valley, peasant agricultural villages served as the backbone of the economy. Control of a guaranteed food surplus was necessary to support the growing cities with their multitudes of fulltime religico-political and artisan specialists. We know more about the larger urban centers than we do about the villages responsible for filling the granaries of Mohenjo-daro, Harappa, and other regional centers (Dales, 1966; Khan, 1958; B. Lal, 1962–63; Wheeler, 1968a).

The first true urban centers rose in the Iranian Plateau (which includes Afghanistan) during the Achaemenid Empire, according to Ghirshman (1954).[1] However, two sites in Afghanistan probably relate to the elaborate complex of agricultural communities which supported the Indus Valley Civilization. Mundigak (Casal, DAFA XVII, 1961, see Appendix F) and Deh Morasi Ghundai (L. Dupree, 1963a) complement one another in the interpretation of the protohistoric role of Afghanistan (Chart 19). Deh Morasi represents a small semisedentary village with a transitional economic base of wheat/barley agriculture and sheep/goat/cattle transhumance. Mundigak slowly developed from a small agricultural village (with some evidence for semisedentarization) to a genuine town with a granary, possibly a provincial capital of the Indus Valley civilization.

A series of crude sherds appear below the main occupation levels at Deh Morasi. Casal found nothing similar to *Morasi I* at Mundigak, but he does postulate a nomadic or seminomadic economy for his lowest levels, *Mundigak I,* followed by a period of relative cultural stagnation during *Mundigak II.*

---

[1] New archaeological work, particularly Lamberg-Karlovsky (1969) and Tosi (1967, 1969), indicates the possibility of an urban civilization in Iran as early as those in Mesopotamia and the Indus Valley. Also see K. Fischer (1969).

CHART 20
Mundigak-Morasi Comparative Cultural Inventory of
Important Artifacts

(Casal, *DAFA* XVII, Appendix F, 1961; L. Dupree, 1963a)

Morasi	Mundigak
IV Copper compartmented seal; red-slip pottery Post-1500 B.C.	VII Flint projectile points; granaries; iron in quantity; steatite seal; alabaster; terracotta dogs; stone hoes; bronze awls, bronze trilobate arrowheads; red- and gray-slip potteries
	VI Flint projectile points; bronze projectile points; stone hoes; stone and baked-clay spindle whorls; bronze awls, fragments of iron first appear; alabaster; red-slip or red-surface pottery with violet designs
III Terracotta female figurine, late style; red-slip pottery; baked bricks Ca. 2000-1500 B.C.	V Massive Monument; red-slip pottery; steatite seals; bronze awls, seals, projectile points; flint projectile points; stone and baked-clay spindle whorls; alabaster; stone hoes, pottery bird head; terracotta female figurine (late)
	IV The "Palace" and "Temple"; Zhob terracotta female figurines; terracotta male figurines; bronze seals; flint blades, projectile points; stone hoes; stone discs; mortars; sculptured limestone head; flint microliths; terracotta bulls, goats, dog or pig; alabaster; bronze awls; pins; bird figurine vases, bronze lancehead; pottery and baked-clay spindle whorls
II Copper tubing and handle fragments; steatite spindle whorl; steatite seals; bone awls, scrapers, polished pendant; stone sling projectile?; metate-pestle; dibble weight; alabaster; faience? bead; pottery discs; animal figurine; clay figurine; clay spindle whorls, tube, missile; Zhob terracotta mother goddess figurine; copper pin; celts; sun-dried brick, pisé; shrine complex Ca. 3000-2000 B.C.	III Pottery drains; terracotta human and bull figurines; stone and bone seals; clay and stone spindle whorls; alabaster; flint microliths, blades, projectile points; stone hoes; bone awls, needles, bone tube; copper and bronze awls, adzes, hoe, chisel, pins; baked brick
	II Terracotta human and bull figurines; stone seals; flint projectile points, blades; copper pins, needles, awls; clay spindle whorls; clay missile; bone awl; stone hoe
GAP	
	I Stone hoes; copper awls; terracotta bull figurines; clay spindle whorls; alabaster; bone awls; pisé and sun-dried brick
I Coarse Ware pottery Ca. 4000 B.C.	

Outside influences, probably from southern Iran (Casal, DAFA, XVII, 1961; L. Dupree, 1963a; Dales, 1966; Lamberg–Karlovsky, 1967), initiated a great period of development during *Mundigak III–Morasi II,* the phase of emergent semisedentary and sedentary villages. Probably the most important find of this period is the shrine complex of sundried brick at Morasi, in association with a terracotta "Mother Goddess" figurine of the Zhob Valley type (Fairservis, 1959), a painted goblet, a compartmented steatite seal, copper tubing fragments (for drinking?), a pair of domesticated goat horns and a scapula, and a magnetite nodule, all conceivably relating to a fertility cult. The bricks were rectangular (18 × 16 × 12 cm.), with the exception of the topmost, which were plano-convex. The upper bricks had faint matting impressions, and, when broken the central top brick contained a fist-sized mass of semicarbonized barley (a six-rowed domesticated variety) and an *Aegilops* sp., possibly one of the ancestors of modern wheat (*Triticum*), according to Chowdhury (in L. Dupree, 1963a, 126–31). The presence of wild grains mixed with domesticated barley in the center of the brick offers additional credence to the thesis that the *Morasi II* people were semisedentary and that the shrine complex was fertility oriented.

Most of the Sistan surface collections of Fairservis (1961) are probably approximately contemporaneous with *Mundigak III–Morasi II.*

Mundigak, a much larger site (20 meters high and 150 meters at its widest point) than Deh Morasi (6 meters high and 50 meters long) developed into a full-fledged town during *Mundigak IV.* Early in the phase, however, invaders from northern Iran destroyed the incipient town, but its inhabitants appear to have immediately rebuilt on the ruins and reached a cultural climax which included the construction of a "palace" and a "temple." A sculptured limestone head (male) found in *Mundigak IV* resembles the limited finds of sculpture in the Indus Valley of approximately the same period (Dales, 1966, 273–74). The invaders may have been nomads, content with destroying, looting, and departing, a not uncommon pattern in the protohistoric Middle East. *Morasi II,* probably still semisedentary, seems to have escaped destruction, possibly because it was not wealthy enough to attract the avaricious eyes of the raiders.

Another invasion, postulated from Ferghana (Russian Central Asia), occurred during *Mundigak V,* but again the energetic inhabitants rebounded (as had their ancestors) to another climax, constructing a "massive monument," possibly a religious edifice where human sacrifice may have been practiced (Casal, *DAFA,* XVII, Appendix F, 1961) to a prehistoric Kali? Several specialists have commented that the hideous-faced, handsomely-bosomed female figurines of Baluchistan and south–central Afghanistan may represent such a diety (L. Dupree, 1963a; Fairservis, 1959; Piggott, 1960). The *Morasi III* people plodded along, probably still semisedentary, although baked bricks do appear for the first time.

Mundigak VI–VII and *Morasi IV* appear to have been occupied only periodically by nomads and seminomads after the mid-second millennium B.C., a time of troubles when Indo–European-speakers apparently swept down from the north.

A gap now plagues the excavator, but history does begin to enlighten us, at least partly, about mid-first millennium B.C.

Early Nomadic Iron Age

Before moving into history, however, we must consider the archaeological evidence for the nomads who ranged throughout Afghanistan and surrounding areas in the early centuries A.D., with particular reference to the evidence from the excavations in the caves and rock shelters of Shamshir Ghar (L. Dupree, 1958a) and *Aq Kupruk I, II,* and *IV* (L. Dupree, 1964b, 1968a). In discussing this period, scholars sometimes tend to ignore the nomads' material culture and emphasize the great artistic, political, religious, and social achievements of both Eastern and Western civilizations. I shall not neglect these important elements (to be discussed in the next section), but since nomads have always been important features on the Afghan cultural landscape, they merit special consideration in each period. I shall not attempt to link up specific tribal, ethnic, or political names with specific archaeological levels at Aq Kupruk, but may do so eventually if subsequent excavations permit more definite identifications. For those interested in sources which identify various tribal and ethnic groups with art styles of the same period, I suggest (among others): Altheim, 1959, 1960; Jettmar, 1967; McGovern, 1939; Phillips, 1965; T. Rice, 1965.

The Early Nomadic Iron Age finds include several excellent bronze, trilobate projectile points, bracelets and bracelet fragments, rings, and earrings. An extensive painted-pottery series was found, including black-on-buff surface but with red-on-buff dominating. Motifs included dot-tipped rosettes; free, flowing repeated spirals; wavy lines; checkerboard designs; naturalistic and stylized animals, primarily ibex and other goat types; stylized plants. Several terracotta figurines were found. A

74 Later Iron Age. Painted pottery, red on buff, from Aq Kupruk I (Snake Cave). Ca. A.D. 300 *Photo: H. E. Klappert*

realistic representation of a sheep is especially worthy of note, along · with a bearded human figurine, probably a bowlegged horseman, wearing leather armor. A highly stylized, completely degenerated, particularly when compared with the Morasi–Mundigak finds, female figurine also occurred in the Aq Kupruk Early Nomadic Iron Age. Other finds included carnelian beads, a clay spindle whorl (?), flint end scrapers, and side scrapers on blades.

Dr. Perkins has identified domesticated sheep, goat, cattle, and horse in the Early Nomadic Iron Age levels of *Aq Kupruk I*.

Later Nomadic Iron Age

The Later Nomadic Iron Age, represented chiefly by a burial containing about ten individuals uncovered at *Aq Kupruk IV* (Skull Cave), also occurs at *Aq Kupruk I* and Shamshir Ghar (L. Dupree, 1958a). Much grave furniture accompanied the Skull Cave burials, some of which had been disturbed by animals and possibly by later water action. The cultural finds included a bronze mirror (possibly South Siberian in origin), bracelets, rings, and projectile points. Iron objects included points, daggers, and horse trappings. A silver ring with a lapis lazuli setting was also uncovered, as well as carnelian and other beads. Pottery included two complete plates of red-streak burnished patterned ware, unguent jars, lamps, a cup, and many scattered sherds.

Cultural items from *Aq Kupruk I* included a two-bar loom, wooden projectile point, textile and basket fragments, querns, pounders, and more iron than bronze points. Large storage jars occurred in association with other utilitarian ware in both *Aq Kupruk I* and *II*. In addition, a large variety of painted wares (red or black on buff surface being dominant; repeated spirals the major motif) were discovered.*

* While I was reading page proofs, the following monograph of interest to archaeologists was published: L. Dupree in collaboration with J. Angel, R. Brill, E. Caley, R. Davis, C. Kolb, A. Marshack, D. Perkins, Jr., A. Solem: "Prehistoric Research in Afghanistan (1959–1966)." *Transactions of the American Philosophical Society,* new series, vol. 62, pt. 4, 1972.

$\mathcal{E}$ast and West $\mathcal{M}$eet and $\mathcal{M}$ingle

SEVENTH CENTURY B.C. TO SECOND CENTURY A.D.

SOME HISTORIANS have attempted to identify references to the Afghan landscape in the *Rig Veda* (Mohd. Ali, 1957; A. Kohzad, 1946, 1953a, 1954; Najib Ullah, 1961). Others (e.g., Frazer–Tytler, 1967, 17) believe the first identifiable mention of the area now called Afghanistan can be found in the *Avesta* (E. Wilson, 1945, 55–65), the canonical scriptures of the Zoroastrians plus the teachings (*Gatha*) of Zarathustra (Iranian name for Zoroaster, which is Greek), its founder. Later accretionary commentaries on the *Avesta* are called *Zand* and *Pa-Zand*.

Mystery clouds Zarathustra's life (Duchesne–Guillemin, 1966; Henning, 1961; Zaehner, 1961), and proposed dates for his birth range from 1000 B.C. to the early sixth century B.C. He may have been born in Media (Ghirshman, 1954, 161), eastern Iran (Porada, 1965, 271), or, according to local legend, northwest Afghanistan. Most historians agree with the tradition that Zarathustra was killed in or near Balkh about 522 B.C. during a nomadic invasion from Central Asia (Olmstead, 1960, 105).

The *Avesta* was probably first written down in the reign of Cyrus the Great (559–30 B.C.), who helped spread Zoroastrianism rapidly throughout the Achaemenid world (Map 11A). Fundamentally, the Parsee (as it is frequently called) religion is an "impure monotheism" (Ghirshman, 1954, 162), a belief in the duality of Good (*Ahura-Mazda*) and Evil (*Ahriman*), and their constant struggle for control of the universe. Humans can assist Good to win through a combination of Good Thoughts, Good Words, Good Deeds, as defined in the *Avesta*. Today, surviving pockets of Zoroastrian adherents reside in Iran as successful businessmen at Tehran and in trade and farming in Yazd and Kerman (50,000), with another 125,000 living in India, Pakistan, and parts of East Africa, mainly as members of the business and professional community.

About 556 B.C. Zarathustra reputedly converted Queen Hutaosa

75. *a*. Kuprukian (Upper Paleolithic). Limestone sculpture: 6.5 cm., ca. 14,000 B.C.: oldest sculpture in Asia. *Photo:* Life *magazine*

b. Mundigak (Bronze Age). Limestone head: 10 cm., ca. 2500 B.C. *Photo: Josephine Powell*

c. Deh Morasi Ghundai (Bronze Age). Terracotta "female goddess" figurine: ca. 6.5 cm., ca. 2800 B.C.

d. Alexander the Great. Ca. 2.5 cm. diameter, 4th century B.C. Private collection.

(Atossa) and her husband, King Vishtaspa (also known as Hystaspes), ruler of Hyrcania (northeast Iran) and Parthia (eastern Iran and northwest Afghanistan). Later, about 545 B.C. (Olmstead, 1960, 103), Vishtaspa became a satrap of Cyrus the Great, who conquered as far east as the Punjab.

The first son, Darius, born to Vishtaspa and Hutaosa, shortly after their conversion, usurped the throne and became the greatest Achaemenid of them all (Ghirshman, 1954, 161; Olmstead, 1960, 102–03, 107). Wilber (1962, 11), however, refers to Queen Hutaosa as his paternal grandmother. No matter what his antecedents, Darius the Great (522–486 B.C.) consolidated and expanded the Achaemenid Empire to its greatest lengths, including several satrapies in and around Afghanistan (Map 11A): Aria (modern Herat); Bactriana (Balkh and Mazar-i-Sharif, called the "Siberia of the Persian Empire," by Woodcock, 1966, 62); Margiana (Merv); Gandhara (Kabul, Jalalabad, Peshawar); Sattagydia (Ghazni to the Indus River); Arachosia (Qandahar and Quetta); Drangiana (Sistan). Darius subdued the small Afghan tribal kingdoms only after bitter fighting, and constant revolts forced the Achaemenids to maintain strong garrisons in the eastern satrapies.

In spite of the enmity between the hill tribes and the Persians, the Bactrians under the satrap Bessus supplied a cavalry force of one hundred for the battle of Gaugamela, where Alexander the Great (336–23 B.C.) won his final, decisive victory over Darius III (336–30 B.C.). Classical historians[1] identify the Bactrians among the more formidable antagonists to face Alexander.

The Asian Greek colonists, allies of the Achaemenids, also bitterly opposed the young Macedonian upstart, in spite of the fact that one of Alexander's announced intentions for marching east was to "liberate" the Greeks under Persian rule (Fuller, 1958). The satrapy system of the Achaemenids, however, permitted each people in the empire to exist under their own leadership, the first known attempt to create a "One World" (Olmstead, 1960). So the Greek colonists in Asia did not wish to be liberated and resisted fiercely. The desire for personal power and public vengeance against the Persians for their prior incursions into the Greek world probably served, at least initially, as primary motivations for Alexander's conquests.

---

[1] Among them: Arrian (Flavius Arrianus; see Robson, 1961; de Selincourt, 1962); Plutarch; Diodorus Siculus; Quintus Curtius; Justin. See Tarn, 1948, Part II, for a definitive discussion on these sources.

274

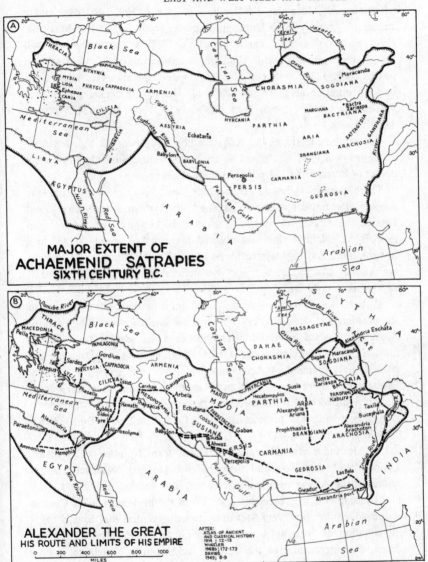

A

MAJOR EXTENT OF
ACHAEMENID SATRAPIES
SIXTH CENTURY B.C.

B

ALEXANDER THE GREAT
HIS ROUTE AND LIMITS OF HIS EMPIRE

0   200   400   600   800   1000
MILES

AFTER:
ATLAS OF ANCIENT
AND CLASSICAL HISTORY
1914 ; 12-13
WHEELER
1968b; 172-173
DAVIES
1949; 8-9

MAP 11

275

The story of Alexander has been told and retold, part history, part legend. Specialists have devoted lifetimes of scholarship debating the "Romance of Alexander." According to Tarn (1962, 144) over eighty versions in twenty-three languages, ranging from England to Malaysia, exist. Folktales about Iskander (as most Middle Eastern groups call Alexander)[2] are still told in the villages and camps of Afghanistan, and in this book, I shall only consider Alexander's operations in Afghanistan and surrounding areas (Map 11B). (For complete details and controversies, see Griffith, 1966; Tarn, 1948, 1951, 1962; R. E. M. Wheeler, 1968b.)

The military might of the Achaemenids was destroyed by Alexander at Gaugamela (331 B.C.), and he burned down the cultural and political center of Persepolis (331 B.C.) during a drunken orgy.

Three satraps (Bessus, Barsaentes, and Satibarzanes) from the Afghan area murdered Darius III, the living symbol of the Achaemenid Empire, near Shahrud by the Caspian Sea. Alexander buried his rival as befitted a fellow king and pointed his army of about 30,000 men toward India and the eastern limits of the Persian Empire. He entered the Afghan area in 330 B.C. and met fierce resistance while on the trail of Darius' murderers.

Satibarzanes (Satrap of Aria) asked for forgiveness for his part in the murder, and Alexander not only forgave but reappointed him satrap. Alexander headed for Balkh when he heard that Bessus (now calling himself King Artaxerxes, the Great King, and wearing the upright pointed tiara, symbol of Achaemenid royalty) was gathering a force. Satibarzanes, however, revolted in his rear, so Alexander, with his usual alacrity, turned swiftly to meet the threat and surprised Satibarzanes, who barely escaped to join Bessus (Tarn, 1962, 61; Burn, 1962, 130–31).

"If Alexander wanted cities in eastern Iran, he must build them" (Tarn, 1962, 60), so build them he did. He first constructed Alexandria-of-the-Arians near modern Herat, and continued to build cities and cantonments to protect his rear. From the beginning of his Central Asian adventure, however, Alexander failed to realize that he was fighting a nationalist war, not simply destroying an empire. The tribal kingdoms, no longer allies of the defunct Achaemenids, fought to protect their own form of mountain independence and were an important factor

---

[2] Iskander is identified with an heroic Persian king, and also with the Two-Horned Prophet, Dhu'l-Qarnayn in the *Qor'an*.

75. *e*. Ai Khanoum. Unfinished limestone statue of an athlete-scholar: 35 cm. high,
ca. 3rd century B.C. *Photo: Délégation Archéologique Française en Afghanistan*
f. Begram. Bronze head, possibly a weight: ca. 9 cm., ca. 2nd century B.C. *Photo:*
L. V. Peterson
g. Hadda. Stucco head of donor: ca. 3rd-4th centuries A.D. *Photo: L. V. Peterson*
h. Hadda. Stucco head of Buddha: ca. 4th-5th centuries A.D. *Photo: L. V. Peterson*
i. Tagao. Marble head of Durga: ca. 20 cm., ca. 7th-8th centuries A.D. *Photo:*
L. V. Peterson

which eventually forced Alexander to retreat to Babylon as his troops grew ever more tired and finally rebellious.

He moved against Barsaentes in Drangiana (along the Hilmand Valley). Barsaentes, also caught off guard by Alexander's swift movements, fled to eastern Arachosia, but the Indians, alarmed by all they heard of Alexander, sent Barsaentes in chains as a gift to the young Macedonian general. Alexander executed the unfortunate satrap, probably more for rebellion than for the murder of Darius III.

Alexander paused at Phrada (capital of Drangiana), probably near modern Nad-i-Ali (called Faranj or Zaranj in later sources), to deal with an unsuccessful plot to assassinate him (Tarn, 1962, 62). In the late autumn of 330 B.C., Alexander marched against some relatively isolated tribes in northern Gedrosia (Baluchistan) called the Ariaspians (Pushtun or Baluch?), nomads never subdued by the Persians and governed by their own chiefs, and whose government resembled the open councils of the Greeks. Arrian (III, xxvii, 4) states that the tribal assembly (*jirgah*) of the Ariaspians so impressed Alexander that he permitted them to continue their way of life unhampered by Macedonian administrators.

Alexander refused to remain in a winter camp, feeling that idle hands would be his worst enemy, and he wished to have it out with Bessus. Within a short time the satrapies of Carmania, Gedrosia, and Arachosia submitted to Alexander, who split off Drangiana and joined it with Aria. His winter campaign in climatically mild southwestern and south-central Afghanistan carried him up the Hilmand–Arghandab River system toward Ghazni, and he founded his second Alexandria on the Tarnak River. Tarn (1962, 65) believes the site to be at Ghazni. However, others like Burn (1962, 135), Woodcock (1966, 27), and R. Wheeler, 1968b, 65) feel, probably correctly, that the site of Alexandria in Arachosia is nearer Qandahar. Still moving, Alexander pushed into the central mountains near Kabul, and established another strategic Alexandria near the confluence of the Ghorband and Panjsher Rivers (about fifty miles north of Kabul) in order to provide a base for his march over the mountains. Alexandria-ad-Caucasum (i.e., Parapomisus) is thought by Ghirshman (*DAFA*, XII, 1946, 3–4, see Appendix G) to be near the site of Begram, at Bordj-i-Abdullah.

In the spring of 329, Alexander's troops, suffering from frostbite and snow blindness, slogged over snow-covered Khawak Pass. The soldiers rested between marches in the stone and mud huts of the Afghan hillsmen. Sheep and mules (often eaten raw), and plants called "silphium" (Rawlinson, 1912, 38) or "terebinths and asafoetida" (Arrian, III,xxviii, 6–7) furnished food for the weather worn troops.

The Bactrian army practiced a "scorched earth" policy from the Bamiyan and Andarab Valleys north to Aornos (possibly—though far from proven—modern Khulm, also called Tashkurghan), where Bessus waited for Alexander. The Bactrian king expected the Greeks to wait until the snows melted and then cross the central mountains over the Shibar Pass. He hoped to engage Alexander's force in the narrow Tang-i-Tashkurghan.

Once again, Alexander's speed and daring caught his opponents by surprise. He played his usual flanking game and attacked Bessus and his Sogdian allies, Oxyartes and Spitamenes, from the east, out of Drapsaka (modern Kunduz).

Defeated, Bessus retreated across the Oxus to Sogdiana, burning his boats on the north bank of the river. Hardly pausing at Bactra (possibly near modern Balkh), Alexander ordered the Zoroastrians to close down their *dakhmas* "Towers of Silence," on which Parsees expose their dead to be devoured by carrion birds (Rawlinson, 1912, 39–40). In addition, he refused to be bothered by a new revolt in Herat led by Satibarzanes, who was killed by Erigyiues, whom Alexander sent to deal with the revolt.

Alexander led his men across the Oxus near Kelift (modern town across the river in the U.S.S.R.) on either skins "stuffed with rushes and padding" (Tarn, 1962, 67) or "rafts made of the leather bivouàc tents stuffed with dry grass" (Burn, 1962, 1936; Arrian, III, xxvix, 3–4). The entire army crossed the Oxus in five days. The troops probably used inflated skins, still common in parts of Afghanistan. No matter what the mode of transport, the oppressive summer heat plagued Alexander's army as it plunged deeper into the *terra incognita* of Central Asia, where it established outposts and lines of communications. With each mile, the army got thinner, literally and figuratively.

Spitamenes, now thoroughly frightened, turned over Bessus to Alexander and fled farther north. Alexander imposed a horrible revenge on Bessus for regicide. Stripped naked and wearing a dog collar (Arrian, III, xxx, 3), Bessus was lashed as Alexander's army marched past, and then sent to Bactriana. Later, Alexander ordered Bessus' nose and ears cut off and sent the unfortunate Bactrian patriot to Ecbatana (modern Hamadan, Iran), where he was mercifully executed. The death of

Bessus did not satiate Alexander, as the Sogdians and other nomadic groups in Central Asia had hoped. Alexander pushed on to the outer limits of the Achaemenid Empire, and occupied Marcanda (Samarkand, summer capital of Sogdiana). At Kojend, Alexander built his northern-most city, Alexandria-Eschate or "Alexandria at the End of the World." Wounded in the fighting (fibula: Burn, 1962, 136; or tibia: Arrian, III, xxx, 11), near Kojend, Alexander issued angry orders for all local nomadic leaders to swear fealty to him. Instead, the proud nomads at-tacked Alexander's outposts at all points, and Spitamenes besieged Samarkand. From that time until he departed the Central Asian steppes, Alexander knew no peace. A stone hit him in the head during the fight-ing at Cyropolis, temporarily impairing his sight.

At Alexandria-Eschate (a mud-walled affair, completed in twenty days) on the Jarxartes River, Alexander observed the tactics of "Scythians" (Burn, 1962, 137) or "Sakae" (Tarn, 1962, 168), prob-ably the finest light cavalry in the known world at that time. Alexander appreciated the excellent martial qualities of the horsemen of the steppes, and later replaced his cavalry losses with Central Asians.

Alexander's artillery (catapulters and giant spear-throwers) fired across the river and from boats, but the nomads, bent on invading the settled areas to the south (until recently an annual event among many Middle Eastern nomadic groups), simply moved out of range, not with-out some casualties, however, including a leader skewered by a feathered javelin (Burn, 1962, 137).

In spite of evil omens and warnings from his priests, Alexander once again crossed the river on rafts made of bivouac tents. The slingers and archers led the amphibious assault, followed by the infantry. Then the vaunted heavy cavalry of Alexander had its first unpleasant taste of nomadic cavalry tactics, which resembled those of the American Plains Indians. Alexander's speed and mobility defeated the ponderous armies encountered in Western Asia, but the mobile tactics of the mountain guerrillas of central Afghanistan and the riders of the Central Asian steppes constantly snatched victory from his grasp. The nomads rode circles around various elements of Alexander's forces, firing arrows from many positions, even under the bellies of their horses (Fuller, 1958).

Confused accounts exist, but Alexander did force a truce and was not ignominiously defeated, like the relief column he sent earlier to Samarkand, where nomadic tactics (ambush, encirclement, massacre) overwhelmed a column commanded by Pharnuches (Tarn, 1962, 69). The defeat of Pharnuches was the major defeat of Alexander's career, and he went to great pains in order to keep news of the debacle from his army.[3]

Alexander, ill with gastrointestinal ailments, personally led a fast-moving relief column to Samarkand, covering 170 miles in slightly over three days and three nights, only to find Spitamenes had judiciously vanished. Alexander wintered (329–28 B.C.) in Bactra (Tarn, 1962, 70; also called Zariaspa: Burn, 1962, 139), his army tired after two years of solid fighting. Spitamenes rested in Bokhara, the winter capital of Sogdiana. Both men collected their forces and wits for the spring encounters which must come.

Five columns of Alexander's army crossed the Oxus and marched into Sogdiana after Spitamenes. Many costly small battles were fought with the elusive nomads, but Spitamenes remained free and Alexander remained frustrated. The wily Spitamenes even raided as far south as Bactra. As summer drew on, the nomads (as some in Afghanistan still do annually) withdrew to the steppes and plains with their flocks.

Alexander wintered (328–27 B.C.) in Nautaka (Bokhara ?) (Burn, 1962, 144) in order to apprehend Spitamenes if he returned. Spitamenes did and found the countryside either ravaged or controlled by Alexander's army, which had defeated the nomads in open battle. His allies deserting, Spitamenes retreated. Hearing of Alexander's pursuit, the "Scythians" cut off Spitamenes' head and sent it to the "Great One" as a present. Thus died Alexander's most formidable opponent. Alexander obviously respected the slain patriot, for he gave Spitamenes' daughter, Apama, to Seleucus, ruler of the Persian zone after Alexander's death.

The spring of 327 saw Alexander hard in combat, subduing the remainder of the Sogdian towns. Many guerrillas holed up in the heretofore impregnable Sogdian Rock (Sisimithres) near Derbent. Surrounded by sheer, snow-topped cliffs, the Rock did indeed seem impregnable, and the guerrillas, when Alexander demanded surrender, taunted him to look for "winged soldiers" (Burn, 1962, 145). Alexander did just that. He asked for 300 volunteers to scale the cliffs under cover of darkness, promising 300 gold pieces to each man and 12 talents for the first man to reach the top. Using ropes and iron tent pegs as pitons about 270 men reached the top. Thirty fell to their deaths in the attempt, but the early morning light revealed Alexander's "airborne" troops

[3] For Alexander in Turkestan, see Litvinski (1963), Vorobevya (1963) and von Schwarz (1893). I am indebted to Paul Bernard, Director, Délégation Archéologique Française en Afghanistan, for calling my attention to these references.

standing on the skyline above the startled guerrillas, who immediately surrendered.

Among the prisoners was Roxane, the lovely (according to most accounts and particularly Afghan folklore) daughter of Oxyartes, a leader in Bactriana. Alexander fell in love with her, but refused to force his attentions. Oxyartes, impressed by Alexander's courteous behavior (and possibly with an eye on a valuable political alliance), also surrendered. Possibly to cool his passions, Alexander, accompanied by Oxyartes, moved against another Rock: the Rock of Chorienes "on the Vakhsh River south of Faizabad" (Tarn, 1962, 76). The Rock of Chorienes fell after Alexander, again the brilliant military engineer, built a causeway across the deep ravine protecting the fortress. Oxyartes conducted the truce negotiations for Alexander.

Shortly thereafter, Alexander married Roxane in a partly Persian, partly Macedonian ceremony. Alexander, following Macedonian custom, cut a wheat cake with his sword, and both he and Roxane ate morsels.

Much has been made of the romantic love of Alexander and Roxane, particularly in Afghan folklore. Many Afghan parents name their daughters Roxane. One tale has her at Alexander's bedside as he dies of fever in Babylon. Tarn, however, always a doubter of Alexander's heterosexual powers, says of the marriage: "It was a marriage of policy, intended to reconcile the eastern barons and end the national war. Tradition naturally represents him as in love with her, but it is doubtful he ever cared for any woman except his terrible mother." (Tarn, 1962, 76; for a new, more virile view of Alexander, see R. E. M. Wheeler, 1968b, 24–28).

Before leaving for India, Alexander rebuilt Bactra as another Alexandria, in addition to Alexandrias at Merv and Tarmita (possibly modern Termez). In addition, he put down another conspiracy, brought about by his attempts to declare himself a god. He left for India in the early summer of 327 B.C.

Traveling through Bamiyan and the Ghorband Valley (Tarn, 1966, 88), he reached Alexandria-ad-Caucasum in ten days. Near Jalalabad, Alexander split his army into two major groups: the baggage and equipment followed the Kabul River into India; the fighting force, led by Alexander, moved north to protect the flank and to pacify the mountainous tribes. Alexander can be called many things by his admirers and detractors, but never "peace-loving."

His troops poured through Laghman and followed the Kunar River into Bajaur and Swat, fighting all along the way, meeting on equal terms such warlike groups as the Aspasii (Bajauri) and the Assaceni (Swatis, with capital at Massaga), who wounded him in the ankle. The Kafirs (Edelberg, 1965) living near Nysa (not Swat as suggested by Tarn, 1962, 89) in Kunar (Koh-i-Mor, traditionally founded by Dionysius) sent 300 cavalry to fight with Alexander against Poros (the Paurava Rajah of the Punjab) whom Alexander defeated with great skill at the battle at the Jhelum in 326 B.C. (Fuller, 1958).

The end was near. Alexander's troops mutinied at the Beas River as he tried to drive them on beyond the limits of known classical geography. Obsessed with conquest, Alexander still professed interest in creating One World. Sulkily, Achilles-like, he retired to his tent for three days. He finally gave in, and turned his army toward Babylon. The largest element marched by way of Makran to Kerman; the elephants lumbered along the Hilmand Valley and Sistan; the rest of the units sailed along the Arabian Sea coast via Bandar Abbas under the command of Admiral Nearchus.

More fights, more wounds, more deserts, more thirst, more mountains, then Babylon and death, even as he planned an Arabian expedition. On June 13, 323 B.C., fever (was it malaria ?) killed one of the great charismatic leaders of all time before he reached age 33, and he had already ruled for 12 years and 8 months.

The death of his political empire and the birth of cultural Hellenism rapidly followed Alexander's death. Fission split his empire, never too well fused. Three major divisions finally boiled up out of the cauldron of intrigue: Seleucus took over the Persian world; Ptolemy, the Egyptian; Lysimachos, the Graeco–Macedonian. In Greece and Macedonia, however, the political successors bloodily fought for power after 321 B.C. (Burn, 1962, 181–93). Small kingdoms rose and fell with frightful regularity. Even Roxane's young son, born June 28, a short time after Alexander's death, was proclaimed King Alexander II. Roxane had a rival, Stateira (Darius III's daughter, and also wife of Alexander) murdered and thrown into a well. She and her young son suffered similar fates in 310 at the hand of Kassandros, then the power in Macedonia.

Local rebellions broke out in the Bactrian and Indian provinces almost immediately after Alexander's death. Many of Alexander's Greek and Macedonian colonists, homesick, unsuccessfully attempted to return home, blocked by the Seleucids in Iran. Initially, the eastern, Greek-controlled satrapies remained nominally loyal to the Selucids, but in

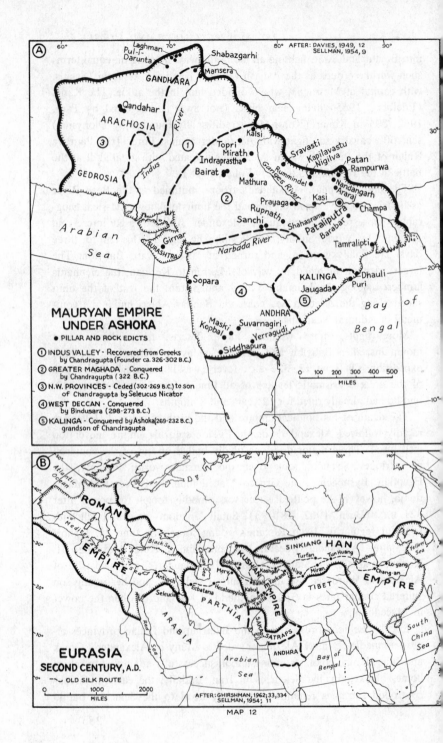

MAURYAN EMPIRE UNDER ASHOKA

● PILLAR AND ROCK EDICTS

① INDUS VALLEY - Recovered from Greeks
   by Chandragupta (Founder ca. 326-302 B.C.)
② GREATER MAGHADA - Conquered
   by Chandragupta (322 B.C.)
③ N.W. PROVINCES - Ceded (302-269 B.C.) to son
   of Chandragupta by Seleucus Nicator
④ WEST DECCAN - Conquered
   by Bindusara (298-273 B.C.)
⑤ KALINGA - Conquered by Ashoka(269-232 B.C.)
   grandson of Chandragupta

Ⓐ AFTER: DAVIES, 1949, 12
SELLMAN, 1954, 9

0 100 200 300 400 500
MILES

Ⓑ

EURASIA
SECOND CENTURY, A.D.
~∼~ OLD SILK ROUTE

0 1000 2000
MILES

AFTER: GHIRSHMAN, 1962; 33, 334
SELLMAN, 1954; 11

MAP 12

256 B.C. (Narain, 1962, 181; I shall use Narain's dates for the Greek kingdoms) the Satrap Diodotus declared independence. Thereafter, Greek power in the Afghan–Indian area lasted about 200 years with varying degrees of success (Tarn, 1951; Narain, 1962; Woodcock, 1966).

Two great Greek kingdoms arose in the east: first the Bactrian (north of the Hindu Kush) and later the Indo–Greek to the south. Many scholars (among them Rawlinson, 1912; Rostovtzeff, 1922, 1941; Tarn, 1951; Narain, 1962; Woodcock, 1966) have unsuccessfully attempted to follow the tortuous successions of the Bactrian and Indo–Greek kings as they overthrew one another and in between managed to march from Central Asia to the Arabian Sea, across northern India to Patna on the Ganges. Dynasties rose and fell, but we know the kings primarily from their coinage, one of the great minor art forms of all time (Bivar, 1955; Cunningham, 1888; Curiel and Fussman, *DAFA* xx, 1965; Curiel and Schlumberger, *DAFA* xiv, 1953; Narain, 1955; Prinsep, 1836; Rapson, 1898). The names on the coins ring out loud and clear the Greekness of their origin: Diodotus, Euthydemus, Demetrius, Pantaleon, Agathocles, Menander, Strato, Apollodotus, Eucratides, Heliocles, Hermaeus.

Therefore, from the death of Alexander to the beginning of the Central Asian nomadic invasions in about 130 B.C. (R. E. M. Wheeler, 1968b, 162), a patchwork of Greek royal dynasties and city-states existed. Into this confused political situation rode the nomadic Parthians who penetrated Sogdiana from the west in about 248 B.C. The Parthians replaced the Selucids in Iran, and controlled the area from about 129 B.C. to A.D. 226.

Rome pushed into Anatolia and prepared for later confrontations with the East. The Mauryans (324–184 B.C.) left the heat of the Indo–Gangetic plains for the cool mountains of Afghanistan. The mingling of these groups laid the groundwork for the great expansion of trade and the cultural renaissance which followed.

The Archaeological Evidence

Gradually, but with particular intensity since World War II, evidence has accumulated to give substance to the scanty historical references to the Afghan world of the early centuries B.C. and its contacts.

About 255 B.C. the Mauryan Emperor Ashoka (ca. 269–32 B.C.) established a series of Rock and Pillar Edicts (also called "Pillars of

Morality") throughout his empire (Map 12A) in attempts to proselytize his subjects to Buddhism. Ashoka, originally a militant Brahman, had indiscriminately slaughtered about a hundred thousand innocents (by his own admission) during the conquest of Kalinga. Horrified at his acts, Ashoka wept and became a fervent Buddhist, enforcing peace on his people with the same vigor with which he had practiced warfare.

Three extremely important Ashoka Rock Edicts have been found near Qandahar[4]: one in 1958 (Schlumberger, et al., 1958; Carratelli, et al., 1964; review of Carratelli by Levine, 1967); the second was a fragmentary inscription in Greek, purchased in the Qandahar bazaar in 1963 by Dr. W. S. Seyring (Schlumberger, 1964); the third, also purchased in the Qandahar bazaar in 1963, is 24 × 18.5 cm., and consists of seven lines of Prakrit and Aramaic (Benveniste and Dupont–Sommer, 1966; Caillat, 1966). The 1958 Rock Edict was uncovered by workmen[5] near the Chehel Zina ("40 steps"), a complex which includes an incomplete series of inscriptions describing the conquests of the great Moghul Emperor Babur (A.D. 1526–30), completed—and possibly added to—by his son, Humayun (A.D. 1530–56) (Shakur, 1947, 94–98). The Rock Edict now sits unprotected, enclosed by a compound wall, but it has been translated and studied so that a great body of literature now exists (for partial bibliography, see Carratelli, et al., 1964, 29–30, 41). The Edict, 55 by 49.5 cm., has 13½ lines of Greek text and 8 lines of Aramaic, official language of the Achemenid Empire, and *lingua franca* for much of Western Asia until replaced, first by Greek and then local Iranian languages (Ghirshman, 1954, 204, 229–30).

Several important facts emerge from the many studies of the Chehel Zina Edict, among them the importance of Greek in the Afghan area at the time of Ashoka; the lingering of Aramaic long after the fall of the Achaemenids; hints of humanitarianism similar to the later Western variety. In addition, the Edict represented—until later finds at Surkh Kotal (where an inscription in Greek script, but not language, was found) and Ai Khanoum—the easternmost Greek inscription, the only Greek inscription attributed to Ashoka, the only complete Aramaic in-

---

[4] For a superb study of Qandahar through time, see K. Fischer, 1967.

[5] This remarkable inscription would probably have been destroyed if Abdul Bay Ashna, school principal in Qandahar, had not immediately notified Ahmad Ali Kohzad, noted Afghan historian and President of the Afghan Historical Society at the time. Several of the workmen thought the script English, left behind by the British to commemorate their victories in the Anglo-Afghan wars (Carratelli, et al., 1964, 41).

scription west of the Indus,[6] the first evidence of the spread of Buddhism so far to the West, and it roughly identifies the western limits of Ashoka's empire.

Translations of the Chehel Zina Greek and Aramaic indicate some differences, but the flavor remains the same. Both exhort men to kill animals only for food and not sport, and to abstain from evil doings. The following translation of the Greek is by Carratelli (1964, 29–39; also see Schlumberger, et al., 1958, and R. E. M. Wheeler, 1968b, 66):

> Ten years [of reign, or since the consecration] having been completed, king Piodasses [Piyadassi[7]] made known [the doctrine of] Piety to men; and from this moment he had made men more pious, and everything thrives throughout the whole world. And the king abstains from [killing] living beings, and other men and those who [are] huntsmen and fishermen of the king have desisted from hunting. And if some [were] intemperate, they have ceased from their intemperance as was in their power; and obedient to their father and mother and to the elders, in opposition to the past also in the future, by so acting on every occasion, they will live better and more happily.

G. Garbini (Carratelli, et al., 1964, 41–62; also see Schlumberger, et al., 1958; Levine, 1967) made the Aramaic translation and the text is essentially the same as the Greek.

Another Ashoka Rock Edict was added to the Chehel Zina Edict in 1963, with the purchase of another Greek inscription, presumably originally from the Old City of Qandahar (Zor Shar in Pashto; Shahr-i-Kona in Farsi). The 1963 Edict, a rectangular limestone block, 45 by 69.5 cm., contains 22 lines of an incomplete Greek inscription, yet sufficiently complete to permit scholars to relate the find to Ashoka.

---

[6] Fragmentary finds have occurred at Taxila (Herzfield, 1928; Majumdar, et al., 1961, 101–102) and in the vicinity of Pul-i-Darunta near Jalalabad (Henning, 1949–50) consisting of words in Aramaic and Prakrit or Gandhari (Bailey, 1943, 46). Other Ashoka Edicts were all written in Prakrit and Brahmi, except those at Mansera and Shahbazgarhi written in Kharosthi (Carratelli, et al., 1964, 6).
Four new Ashokan inscriptions were found in the Laghman area between Shatalak and Qargha by Jean and Danielle Bourgeois on November 22, 1969 (reported in *The Kabul Times,* January 1, 1970). Three of the inscriptions are reported in an Indic (Prakrit?) language, the fourth in Aramaic.

[7] Piodasses (Piyadassi) refers to Ashoka, and literally means "of amiable appearance." Only on the Maski (Majumdar, et al., 1961, 103) and Gujarra (Sircar, 1956) Rock Edicts is Ashoka mentioned by name.

The English translation here is taken from R. E. M. Wheeler (1968b, 68), but Schlumberger (1964) did the original translation from Greek into French.

> . . . piety and self-mastery in all the schools of thought; and he who is master of his tongue is most master of himself. And let them neither praise themselves nor disparage their neighbours in any matter whatsoever, for that is vain. In acting in accordance with this principle they exalt themselves and win their neighbours; in transgressing in these things they misdemean themselves and antagonize their neighbours. Those who praise themselves and denigrate their neighbours are self-seekers, wishing to shine in comparison with the others but in fact hurting themselves. It behoves to respect one another and to accept one another's lessons. In all actions it behoves to be understanding, sharing with one another all that each one comprehends. And to those who strive thus let there be no hesitation to say these things in order that they may persist in piety in everything.
>
> In the eighth year of the reign of Piodasses, he conquered Kalinga. A hundred and fifty thousand persons were captured and deported, and a hundred thousand others were killed, and almost as many died otherwise. Thereafter, pity and compassion seized him and he suffered grievously. In the same manner wherewith he ordered abstention from living things, he has displayed zeal and effort to promote piety. And at the same time the king has viewed this with displeasure: of the Brahmins and Sramins and others practising piety who live there [in Kalinga]—and these must be mindful of the interests of the king and must revere and respect their teacher, their father and their mother and love and faithfully cherish their friends and companions and must use their slaves and dependents as gently as possible—if, of those thus engaged there, any has died or been deported and the rest have regarded this lightly, the king has taken it with exceeding bad grace. And that amongst other people there are . . .

Schlumberger (et al., 1958, 5) and R. E. M. Wheeler (1968, 69), on the basis of the 1958 and 1963 Greek inscriptions, now positively identify Shahr-i-Kona as a "full blown Alexandria."

Inscriptions are fine, but cities would be better, and for more than forty years the Délégation Archéologique Française en Afghanistan (*DAFA*) sought monumental evidence of the Greeks. Where were the cities, the Alexandrias and Bactra, called the "Mother of Towns" (Barthold, 1928), capital of Bactriana? An early French Mission directed by A. Foucher dug several *sondages* at modern Balkh, traditional site of Bactra, but could identify no Greek remains. The excavators abandoned Balkh in 1925 for more fruitful research farther south, particularly at Hadda and Begram. The French never gave up their dream of finding Greek cities, but not until the post-World War II period did they make another attempt at Balkh, where Professor Daniel Schlumberger sank one hundred test pits, but the elusive Bactra remains undiscovered.

In 1953, an American team under Professor Rodney Young (1955), University Museum, University of Pennsylvania, excavated in the lower city at Balkh. An Islamic wall and a possible Kushan (ca. second century A.D.) wall were uncovered.

In November, 1963, the French finally located their Greek city at Ai Khanoum ("Moon Lady" in Uzbaki Turkic), where the Kokcha River meets the Darya-yi-Panj. Several exciting preliminary reports (Schlumberger, 1965; Schlumberger and Bernard, 1965; Bernard, 1966, 1967, 1968ab, in press) have been written so far, and excavations will continue for several years at this easternmost genuine Greek city. The town plan compares favorably with Dura-Europos, a Hellenistic city in Syria (Rostovtzeff, et al., 1943–49), and these complexes have been identified by the French: the upper town, with a huge citadel (Bala Hissar) situated at its northern extremity; a lower town with residential and administrative areas, including a palace with a peristylar courtyard; a *gymnasium,* the Greek-style university which emphasized balanced intellectual and physical development; a funerary *heroön;* a large private home with at least a three-phase occupation; an Oriental temple, again reminiscent of Dura-Europos.

Equally important are three examples of Graeco-Bactrian marble statuary, the first ever found. One, uncovered in the *gymnasium,* represents a cloaked, bearded male with his right hand clutching his cloak. Bernard (1967, 319) dates this find provisionally in the third century B.C. A small statue of a nude male athlete was also discovered, in addition to a marble foot wearing a Greek sandal. Several fragments of stucco or clay were found in the palace and the temple. Identifiable objects include lion heads and paws, a horse's leg, and human figures, both clothed and naked.

Bernard, now Director of *DAFA* since Schlumberger's retirement in 1966, relates the Ai Khanoum ceramics and terracotta roof-tiles to most

76. Ai Khanoum. General view of the lower town from the acropolis. Amu Darya (Oxus) in upper center. Probably 4th to 2nd centuries B.C. *Photo: Délégation Archéologique Française en Afghanistan*

77. Ai Khanoum. Ruins of the colonnade. southwest porch. *Photo: Délégation Archéologique Française en Afghanistan*

Hellenistic sites of Western Asia (Seleucia on the Tigris, Dura-Europos, Antioch, Tarsus, Samaria, Pergamon, Alishar Huyuk) and other Greek colonies (Olbia, Olynthus, Priene), as well as sites on the Greek mainland, all dating from the end of the fourth century B.C. to the end of the second century B.C.

Two important Greek inscriptions in stone have been found at Ai Khanoum. One is a dedication in the name of two brothers to Hermes and Heracles (Hercules), the two patrons of the *gymnasium,* respectively representing the mental and physical aspects of the classical Greek educational institution. The second stone specimen, uncovered in the *heroön,* contains two side-by-side, contemporaneous (beginning of the third century B.C.) inscriptions. The essence of the two inscriptions (as well as the script) reemphasizes the overall Greekness of the site. A certain Clearchos (identified as a disciple of Aristotle) had transcribed, in the *temenos* of Kineas (an important personage and possibly founder of the city), a partial list of Delphic precepts, copied originally by Clearchos in Delphi itself. According to Bernard, complete lists of the maxims are available in contemporary literary sources, and an epigraphic copy has been discovered at Miletopolis in Turkey. The precepts define the qualities admired by the Bactrian colonists (and the Greek mainlanders) for the various stages of a man's life[8] (Robert, 1968).

Corinthian capitals and Persian-style bases lie scattered and mixed in the courtyard. Practically the entire upper levels are covered with evidence of widespread destruction by fire (Bernard, 1967, 323), when the Śaka or possibly even the Kushans first invaded the area. But why did the site remain unoccupied after Central Asian nomads had destroyed it at the end of the second century A.D.? The question becomes even more puzzling because of the undoubted strategic importance of Ai Khanoum, located between two major rivers. Schlumberger and Bernard (1965) give us a possible answer. Destruction of the local irrigation system by the invaders, coupled with the prevalence of malaria in the area, may have rendered the region uninhabitable. Only recently, in the 1960s, did joint Afghan-World Health Organization efforts eliminate malaria as a major health menace in north Afghanistan.

Bernard had this to say about his site in 1966: "Ai Khanoum will

---

[8] A loose translation is as follows:
As children, learn good manners./ As young men, learn to control the passions./ In middle age, be just./ In old age, give good advice./ Then die, without regret.

at long last unveil in all its wealth and magnificence the much sought after Graeco-Bactrian civilization which radiated its brand of Hellenism to Maurya India, and the Kushan and Gandharan arts which developed afterwards in Afghanistan, Pakistan and India" (personal communication, 1966). He is right to wax poetic about his site, which may be Alexandria-on-the-Oxus (Bernard, 1967, 322–23). Whatever its name, the city slept with its secrets for 2,000 years, and the French at last found their Greek city after 42 years of arduous research.

Surkh Kotal, another important site excavated by Schlumberger from 1952 to 1963, lies 9.5 miles north of Pul-i-Khumri, and offers the first definite evidence of an indigenous Bactrian art, possible inspiration for the later Gandharan style (Schlumberger, 1953, 1955, 1959, 1961; Ghirshman, 1962). The massive site consists of a hilltop complex containing a principal temple and a *cella* (square area marked by four column bases). A secondary temple leans against the exterior wall of the main temple and contains a square fire altar (Zoroastrian), its cavity filled with gray ash. A staircase of monumental proportions reaches from top to bottom of the high hill-temple complex, connecting four distinct terraced embankments.

The discovery of numerous coins helped date the temple in the era of the great Kushan kings of the early second centruy A.D., Kanishka and Huvishka. The splendid inscription in cursive Greek found in 1957 also confirms this date. Probably the most important single specimen from Surkh Kotal, the 25-line inscription is in the eastern Iranic or "Bactrian" language, according to Professor W. B. Henning (1960). The inscription, still not satisfactorily deciphered (Rosenfield, 1967, 158), does mention Kanishka, and refers to repairs of the sanctuary by a successor of Kanishka. The French also found fifty or so limestone blocks with fragmentary Greek script. The blocks probably initially greeted the visitor near the entrance of the staircase, and had been removed later to line the deep well at the foot of the complex.

Culturally, the finds at Surkh Kotal throw new light on the respective debts of East and West to each other (Girshman, 1962, 2–5; Rosenfield, 1967, 154–163). Foucher (1905, 1918, 1922, *DAFA*, I 1942, *DAFA*, I 1947, 1951), however, had already postulated earlier that the Gandharan art style developed out of a localized Indo-Greek style.

Later, scholars such as Rowland (1966a) and R. E. M. Wheeler (1949, 1955) believed the Gandharan style at least partly the result of "Roman" influence which mingled with Buddhism along the Silk Route. However, Schlumberger at Surkh Kotal revealed an already ad-

78. Surkh Kotal. The staircase, 55 meters high, 2nd century A.D. *Photo: Délégation Archéologique Française en Afghanistan*

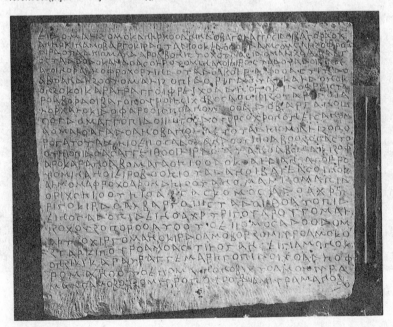

79. Surkh Kotal. Inscription in cursive Greek script in limestone tablet. *Photo: Délégation Archéologique Française en Afghanistan*

80. Surkh Kotal. Statue of Kanishka (?): 115 cm. high, 2nd century A.D. *Photo:*
Délégation Archéologique Française en Afghanistan

vanced "Bactrian" style, which possibly developed independently (relatively speaking, of course, in this mixed-up zone) in eastern Persia and northern Afghanistan after the death of Alexander and *before* the intensification of the great Silk Route trade. Obviously, later Roman and Central Asian influence did make great impacts, but the concept of an indigenous Graeco-Bactrian (or Graeco-Buddhist) art style cannot be taken lightly after Surkh Kotal and Ai Khanoum (Dani, 1968, 22–26; Ghirshman, 1962, 4; R. E. M. Wheeler, 1968b, 171).

CHAPTER 15

Invasions and Commerce

THE RISE AND FALL OF THE SILK ROUTE SECOND CENTURY A.D.–EIGHTH CENTURY A.D.[1]

AFTER Ashoka, militant Brahmanism ended the political force of Buddhism in India, but the Mahayana Buddhism (the Greater Vehicle) which gestated in Gandhara spread along the commercial Silk Route to Turkestan, Mongolia, China, Korea, and ultimately Japan. Various Mahayana sects dominate the Buddhist world today, and of the earlier Hinayana sects (Lesser Vehicle), only the Theravada (Doctrine of the Elders) survives in Ceylon, Burma, Thailand, and Cambodia (Humphreys, 1962).

Great art and great ideas mingled in Gandhara, feasted on one another, and spread in all directions. The mystical humanitarianism of Hellenism (foreshadowed by some of Ashoka's Pillars of Morality) the pragmatism of Rome, and the dynamic realism of the Sino-Siberian art, mingled with the gentle, sensual contradictions of Mauryan (ca. 324–184 B.C.) and later Gupta (ca. A.D. 320–544) Indian styles.

The climax occurred in Gandhara, where Gandharan art appears in the late first century A.D. and vigorously dominates the area until about the middle of the fifth century A.D. For the first time, artists portrayed the Buddha in human form. Previously, representations of the Lord Buddha had been symbolic: a foot, handprint, lotus, wheel, and swastika, among others (Rowland, 1963). The Gandharan manifestation of the Buddha, essentially a mixture of the artistic and ideological genes mentioned earlier, is an Orientalized version of the Greek Apollo.

Earlier, however, the Graeco-Bactrians in Afghanistan and northwest India first felt the impact of Central Asian nomadic invaders about 130 B.C., when the Śaka (or another group) pushed them out of northern Bactria. The Śaka (variously called Śaca, Śacae, Śacaruli, Śacaraucae

[1] Chapters 15 and 16 attempt to correct and slightly expand historical perspective (second century B.C. to A.D. 1222) in L. Dupree (1958a, 276–82).

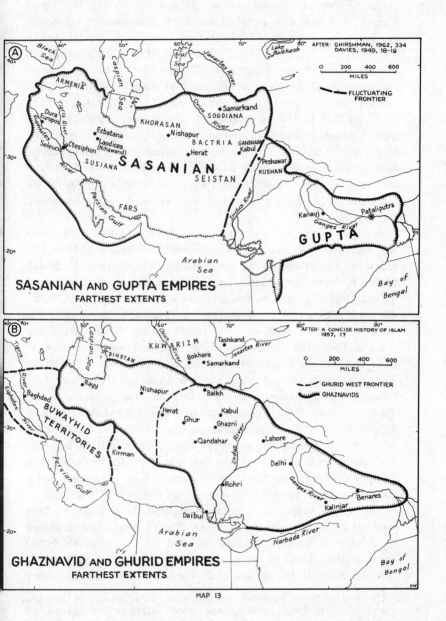

Map A:

AFTER: GHIRSHMAN, 1962, 334
DAVIES, 1949, 18-19

0   200   400   600
MILES

‒ ‒ ‒ FLUCTUATING FRONTIER

Black Sea

ARMENIA

Caspian Sea

Aral Sea

Jaxartes River

Lake Balkhash

Dura Europos

Tigris River

Euphrates River

Seleucia

Ctesiphon

Ecbatana

Laodicea (Nihawand)

SUSIANA

Nishapur

KHORASAN

Oxus River

SOGDIANA

Samarkand

BACTRIA

Herat

GANDHARA

Kabul

Peshawar

KUSHAN

SASANIAN

SEISTAN

FARS

Persian Gulf

Indus River

Kanauj

Ganges River

Pataliputra

GUPTA

Arabian Sea

Bay of Bengal

SASANIAN AND GUPTA EMPIRES
FARTHEST EXTENTS

Map B:

AFTER: A CONCISE HISTORY OF ISLAM 1957, 17

0   200   400   600
MILES

‒ ‒ ‒ GHURID WEST FRONTIER
〜〜〜 GHAZNAVIDS

Tigris River

Euphrates River

Baghdad

Caspian Sea

DIHISTAN

KHWARIZM

Oxus River

Bokhara

Samarkand

Tashkand

Jaxartes River

Rayy

BUWAYHID TERRITORIES

Nishapur

Balkh

Herat

Ghur

Kabul

Ghazni

Qandahar

Indus River

Kirman

Lahore

Delhi

Rohri

Daibul

Arabian Sea

Ganges River

Kalinjar

Benares

Narbada River

Bay of Bengal

GHAZNAVID AND GHURID EMPIRES
FARTHEST EXTENTS

MAP 13

in Indo-European classical sources; Se Sewang, Se-jung in Chinese sources) had been slowly pushed west by a chain reaction originating on the western frontiers of Ch'in Dynasty China in the second century B.C. Previously, during the third century B.C., the two strongest groups in the Far East, the sophisticated Han Dynasty Chinese and the nomadic confederation of the Huingnu (Hsiung Nu) waged constant war with one another. The great Ch'in Emperor, Shih Huang-ti, began to build the Great Wall in 214 B.C. in order to contain these marauding herdsmen. A pattern of raid-retaliation had been established by the beginning of the second century B.C. The Huingnu invaded the Chinese borderlands at will, however, forcing the Chinese to send armies to drive them out. As a result the Huingnu could not permanently occupy the looted land, but neither could the Chinese *limes* system keep the nomads in the steppes.

A subject people of the Huingnu, the Yueh-chih,[2] attacked their masters about 165 B.C., starting the chain reaction mentioned above. Defeated by the Huingnu, but still powerful, the nomadic Yueh-chih packed up horses, tents, and baggage and with their flocks moved west, the only logical route. The Huingnu controlled the north; the Chinese, the south and east. A small group of the Yueh-chih (called the Little Yueh-chih) moved southwest and settled among the war-like Kiang tribes of Tibet. The majority, the Great Yueh-chih, moved north of the Gobi and into the lands of the Wusun, a numerically inferior group. The Wusun subsequently moved north, and attached themselves to the Huingnu for protection. Constantly searching for pasturelands, the Yueh-chih moved west, near Lake Issik-Kul (now Lake Balkhash; 40°35′ N, 76°00′E) in the Dzungarian Basin, and drove out the Śaka, who fled in two directions: one group crossed the Oxus River into Bactria; another moved westward into Iran, now controlled by the Parthian Dynasty (249 B.C.–A.D. 224), also of steppe origin. The chain reaction soon began again, and the Yueh-chih did not remain long in Bactria.

The Wusun, supported by the Huingnu, pushed the Yueh-chih from the Lake Issik-Kul region about 140 B.C. The Yueh-chih, in turn, pushed the Śaka from Bactria. The Śaka occupied Śakastan (modern Sistan) and founded a kingdom which extended, for a brief period, from the Hilmand River to the Persian Gulf. Then the great Parthian soldier-

---

[2] In referring to the Yueh-chih, Kushans, et al., I am speaking of the ethnic groups that took group action to meet specific situations. For example, not *all* the Śaka migrated to Sistan, nor to Pakistan. Many stayed behind in Parthian Iran to serve as mercenaries or to settle down as agriculturalists. Also, the term Kushan refers to the ruling section of the five-sectioned Yueh-chih nation.

king, Mithradites II (ca. 124–88 B.C.), reconquerered Śakastan and once again made it a Parthian satrapy.

The Śaka nobility became satraps and furnished garrison troops for most of the eastern Parthian Empire. Gradually, the Śaka satraps of Gandhara (including modern Peshawar and Jalalabad), Mathura (modern Muttra in India), Kaccha (modern Kutch), Surashthra (Kathiawar), and Arachosia (Qandahar) made themselves virtually independent kings, while still swearing fealty to Parthian rulers.

By the beginning of the Christian era, most Greek states[3] south of the Hindu Kush had fallen to the Śaka-Parthian kings. The last to fall was the Kingdom of Kabul under Hermaeus (75–55 B.C.[4]). Whether Kabul fell to the Śaka or the Yueh-chih is still questioned.

Parthia's hold on its eastern empire weakened, and finally collapsed between A.D. 45 and 64. The rise of Kushans, one of the five principal Yueh-chih tribes (the other four were Humi, Sewangi, Hitum, and Koruto), precipitated this collapse. The Kushans united the Yueh-chih into a powerful military machine during the early first century A.D. (McGovern, 1939, 248).[5] Middle Eastern, Indian, and Western sources after the first century A.D. refer to the Caucasoid, Indo-European (probably Iranian)-speaking Yueh-chih as the Kushans, but the Chinese continue to use the older name (McGovern, 1939, 111, 120). Although I shall call this empire and people Kushan, it should be remembered that Kushan and Yueh-chih are probably interchangeable.

In the first century A.D., Kujula Kadphises (Kadphises I) and his son Vima Kadphises (Kadphises II) spread Kushan control from the lower Indus Valley (minus Surashthra) to the Iranian frontier, from Chinese Sinkiang to the Caspian and Aral Seas. Sometime after the death of Kadphises II, Kanishka I founded the Second Kushan dynasty, possibly in the early second century, A.D.

Kanishka is certainly one of the two or three really great figures in Indian history. Not only was he a great soldier, but it was undoubtedly due in no small measure to his influence, that Gandhara,

---

[3] The Indo-Greek kingdoms of 130 B.C., as seen by Narain (1962, 103), consisted of seven parts, roughly as follows: Badakhshan, Kabul, Ghazni, Gandhara (with Pushkalavati also called Purushapura or Charsada, as capital, see R. E. M. Wheeler, 1962), Swat, Taxila, Jammu-Sialkot.

[4] Narain's dates (1962, 153–62, 181). Bivar (1955, 6) dates Hermaeus as early as 90 B.C. or earlier.

[5] The Kushans had ousted the Śaka from the overlordship of Bactria shortly after 130 B.C., *or,* alternately, they may have been the 130 B.C. invaders instead of the Śaka (McGovern, 1939, 249). In any event, the process of political fission (Parthia) and fusion (Kushan Empire) began.

the seat of his government, became a potent and vital center of literary and artistic activity. He was also a magnificent patron of religious learning, and the northern Buddhists looked upon him in the same manner as the eastern Christians looked upon Constantine. Numerous monuments and coins dating from his reign have been reported, but so lacking are the Indians in historical tradition that we are still in some doubt as to when his reign actually took place (McGovern, 1939, 251–52).

No matter when he lived and died (see Basham, 1968, and Rosenfield, 1967, 253–58 for discussions), Kanishka left an indelible mark on the Indian, Afghan, Iranian, and even Chinese cultural landscape, for it was during his reign that Buddhism rose to its apogee in Central Asia and subsequently spread to the Far East and parts of Southeast Asia. Kanishka's armies marched down the Ganges at least as far as Banares and Ghazipur. He established satrapies down to the mouth of the Indus, conquered Śaka-controlled Surashthra, Kashmir, Chinese Sinkiang, Kashgar, Yarkand, Khotan, and all the Chinese provinces north of Tibet and east of the Pamir (Map 12B). He moved his major capital from Bactria to Pushkalavati (or Purushapura), possibly near Charsada in the vicinity of modern Peshawar. Kapisa (Begram), north of Kabul, became a summer capital. The north Indian capital was Mathura. The death of Kanishka, like his origins and life, remains shrouded in mystery. Tradition holds that his own officers, tired of being military exiles from their homes and families, assassinated him.

The Kushan Empire held its own under the last two Second Dynasty kings, Huvishka and Vasudeva (who probably died about A.D. 220). The empire broke up into independent and semi-independent states, but its legacy had been great. The first two Kushan Dynasties were periods of great artistic and intellectual achievements (Ghirshman, 1957; Rosenfield, 1967; Rowland, 1966b, 175–122).

As mentioned previously, a great increase in East–West trade accompanied Kushan rule. Land and sea routes both permitted an exchange of goods from China to Rome (Map 12B). Overland routes were more important during the first few centuries of the Christian era, but some seaborne trade existed between India and Rome, conclusively proved by the excavations at Arikamedu on the southeast coast of India (Wheeler, Ghosh and Deva, 1946).

The major East–West land-route from China skirted the Gobi and entered Chinese Turkestan (Sinkiang) from Tun Huang, south of the

Dzungarian Gates. Here the route branched. The southern section moved through the Tarim Oasis via Niya, Khotan, and Yarkand to Kashgar. The northern segment skirted south of Lake Balkhash, Turfan, and Urumchi (Tiwa) to Kashgar. The route then wound its way through Ferghana to Bactra, a major transhipment point. From Bactra (Balkh), an important subsidiary route led south through Aq Kupruk, Bamiyan, Begram, Jalalabad, Purushapura, and past Taxila to the Indian Ocean and the sea-routes.

The main land-route continued westward from Bactra across Parthian (and later Sasanian) Iran through Merv and Ecbatana (Hamadan) to Seleucia, Petra, Palmyra, or Tadmor (Syria), or Antioch, among the more important storehouses of goods for transhipment to Rome or China.

Major items of export from the Roman Empire (including Syria and Egypt) were gold and silver plates, woolen and linen textiles, topaz, coral, amber (also from the Baltic), frankincense, glassware, and wine. From India came cotton cloth, indigo, spices, semi-precious stones, pearls, ivory, Kashmir wool, steel swords, and furs. Central Asia (including Afghanistan) contributed rubies, lapis lazuli, silver, turquoise, various gums, and drugs. China sent raw silk to Rome, and embroidered silks to Central Asia and India. Furs and gold from Siberia and Manchuria and many spices from the east traveled to both India and Rome (among others, see: Boulnois, 1966; Hedin, 1938; Mahler, 1966; Miller, 1969; Stein, 1921, 1928). The ultimate markets are indicated by discoveries of Roman glass in China, Indian pottery at Pompeii, Chinese pottery in Roman tombs of the European Rhineland (R. E. M. Wheeler, 1950, 52).

While the Kushans covered the Central Asian steppes and India and the Parthians held sway in most of the Iranian Plateau, several Persian tribes clung to their pristine Zoroastrianism and faded into the southern Zagros mountains. As the Kushan Empire broke up into independent and semi-independent fragments, the Zagros tribes emerged as an indigenous Persian dynasty, the Sasanian (A.D. 224–651) and quickly overthrew the intruder Parthians. Ardashir I (A.D. 224–41), the founder, overran the Kushan states from Sogdiana to the Punjab (Map 13A), and a violent nationalistic reaction against Greek, Roman, and Central Asian influences erupted. By the death of Ardashir, however, most Kushan states were semi-independent and only nominally recognized Sasanian overlordship. The early phases of the Kushano–Sasanian period in Afghanistan lasted until about the mid-fifth century A.D. with the arrival of the Hephthalites (or Ephthalites).

From the beginning, however, the Sasanians considered the Byzantine Empire their main foe. They fought many wars against the Romans, first marching west in A.D. 229. The political and economic effects of this East–West struggle for control were far-reaching and long-lasting. Seaborne trade across the Persian Gulf, Arabian Sea, and Indian Ocean gradually replaced much of the overland trade routes because of the instability created by the fighting. The upsurge in the sea-trade did not totally close down the caravan trade, however, and as the Romans and Sasanians wore each other out militarily, land-routes reopened and the Sasanians themselves often served as the land-trade middlemen (Shepherd, 1966).

A native Indian dynasty, the Gupta (ca. A.D. 320 to the seventh century A.D.) established itself in north and central India (Map 13A). The Gupta, as pro-Indian as the Sasanians were pro-Iranian, attempted to expel the Śakas and Kushans from western and northwestern India, succeeding in the former, but only partially defeating the Kushans, who retained control of the upper Indus Valley.

The small, disunited Kushano-Sasanian states in Afghanistan could not meet the sudden threat to Bactria in the latter half of the fifth century A.D. as the Hephthalite Huns rode out of Central Asia. The Hephthalites, as much a mystery people as the early Śaka and Kushan, cannot be precisely dated. History first records the Hephthalites as clients of the Avar Mongolian Empire about the end of the first century A.D. Probably wishing to be free of their overlords, the Hephthalites moved through Chinese Turkestan and Sogdiana, extorting tribute en route. Crossing the Oxus, the Hephthalites drove out the Kushans, ruled by Kidara, a Fourth Dynasty Kushan king. The military aristocracy of the Bactrian Kushans fled south and, forced east by the Sasanians, passed through Qandahar and eventually conquered parts of Gandhara. The Kidarites (or Little Kushans, as the Fourth Dynasty kings are sometimes called) ruled northwest India, the Punjab, and southwest Afghanistan for about a decade until the Hephthalites once again displaced them.[6]

The Hephthalite Empire in Afghanistan and northwest India lasted about a century (ca A.D. 450–565), extending from Chinese Sinkiang to Sasanian Iran, from Sogdiana to the Punjab. More than thirty separate semi-independent kingdoms had been conquered. The Hephthalites,

---

[6] Among others, see the following for different points of view on the dating of the Hephthalites and the Kidarites: Herzfeld, 1930; Ghirshman, *DAFA* XIII 1948, 1957; Curiel and Schlumberger, *DAFA* XIV, 1953.

however, had no peace during their reign, and the Sasanians were their chief antagonists. Several Sasanian monarchs, frustrated in wars with the Byzantine Empire, turned east. Initially successful, they were ultimately defeated by the militarily adroit Hephthalites about A.D. 484 (Porada, 1965, 261).

However, about A.D. 565, the Hephthalites succumbed to attacks by the combined forces of the Sasanians and the Western Turks, who made their appearance in the political arena about A.D. 552, when they rebelled against and crushed the Avar Empire in Central Asia (McGovern, 1939, 417–18). The Turks became masters of all the Hephthalite territories north of the Oxus. The Sasanians ruled south of the Oxus, but the Turks would later greatly affect the history of Central Asia, the Middle East, and North Africa.

Thus at the beginning of the seventh century A.D., most of Afghanistan lived under Sasanian control, divided into provinces governed by Hephthalite satraps in the north and Kushan satraps in the south and southwest.

The Sasanian Empire crumbled as a result of Arab attacks in the second quarter of the seventh century, and anarchy and minor invasions again swept Afghanistan. Each new satrap had to fight his neighbor to maintain his position. To further complicate the picture, the Hindus and Western Turks kept pushing at the frontiers of the petty states, south and north respectively, absorbing a few, accepting tribute from others. The Hindu-Shahi Dynasty established itself in Kabul and controlled much of eastern Afghanistan until the ninth and tenth centuries A.D.

The Archaeological Evidence

Archaeological work has materially increased our knowledge of the late centuries B.C. and the early centuries A.D. in Afghanistan. Among the more important sites are[7]: Bamiyan (N. Dupree, 1967b; Gardin, 1957; A. Godard, Y. Godard and Hackin, *DAFA* II, 1928; Hackin and Carl, *DAFA* III, 1933; Rowland, 1938; Hackin, et al., *DAFA* VIII, 1959); Hadda (Barthoux, *DAFA* VI, 1930, *DAFA* IV, 1933; Mustamandi, 1968ab; Mustamandi and Mustamandi, 1968); Begram (Ghirshman, *DAFA* XII, 1946; Hackin and Hackin, *DAFA* IX, 1939; Hackin, Hackin, et al., *DAFA* XI, 1954); Fondukistan (Hackin, et al., *DAFA* VIII, 1959); Balkh (Dagens, LeBerre, and Schlumberger, *DAFA* XIX, 1964; Foucher, 1942; Gardin, *DAFA* XIX, 1964; Shamshir Ghar (L.

[7] For an excellent general survey, see Rowland, 1966b.

81. Bamiyan. Large Buddha:
53 meters high, 5th century A.D.
Note paintings above head. *Photo:*
Josephine Powell

82. Bamiyan Valley. Left, large Buddha; right, small Buddha, 35 meters high,
second half of 3rd century A.D. Hundreds of pilgrims' caves along sandstone face
of cliff. *Photo: Josephine Powell*

Dupree, 1958a); Khair Khaneh (Hackin and Carl, *DAFA* VIII, 1936); other Kabul sites (N. Dupree, 1972).

Bamiyan: Located about 205 miles (330 km.) northwest of Kabul and 8,200 feet (2,500 meters) above sea level, Bamiyan straddles the ancient route from Balkh to Taxila.[8] The caravanserais, caves, and two spectacular sandstone statues of the Buddha (175 and 120 feet, or 53 and 35 meters, high respectively), well known to early Chinese and Korean pilgrims as well as nineteenth-century European travelers (Mirsky, 1964; N. Dupree, 1967b), still delight the eye as one of the unnumbered wonders of the ancient world. According to Rowland: "These two statues present us with the first appearance of the colossal cult image in Buddhist art" (1966a, 98); the small Buddha "is really a gigantic magnification of a Gandhara image" (1966b, 95), the large Buddha "an enlargement of an Indian Buddha statue of the Gupta period" (1966b, 97).

The French conducted extensive investigations at Bamiyan from 1922 to World War II. Arguments between art historians thunder through academic journals but the principal Bamiyan finds probably date as follows: the 35-meter Buddha, second half of the third century A.D.; the 53-meter Buddha, fifth century A.D.; wall paintings and stucco decorations, late fifth to early seventh centuries A.D., with possibly a few earlier melanges of Sasanian-Gupta elements of the fourth and fifth centuries A.D. Possibly all these dates are wrong, but most scholars agree about the site dates in the Kushano-Sasanian period, or ca. A.D. 300–700 (L. Dupree, 1958a, 284). The total configurations of Bamiyan indicate an eclectic hybrid mixing of Indian, Central Asian, Iranian, and Classical European art styles and ideas (Rowland, 1938).

Kakrak, another Buddhist site about 2.5 miles (4 km.) southeast of the Buddhas, has a standing Buddha about 10 meters high, and a sanctuary exhibiting frescoes of a centrally seated painted Buddha surrounded by circles of smaller seated Buddhas, "one of the earliest representations of the Mahayana Buddhist concept of one of the celestial Buddhas surrounded by his magic emanations" (Rowland, 1966b, 98), the *mandala* of esoteric Far Eastern and Tibetan Buddhism. The Kakrak finds probably date about fifth or sixth centuries A.D., or even later.

[8] Located in the Punjab region of West Pakistan. An important political, religious, and commercial center from at least the fourth century B.C. to about the mid-fifth century A.D. (Marshall, 1951; R. E. M. Wheeler, 1950, 1955, 1968b.)

Hadda: Between 1923 and 1928, the French excavated at Hadda (primarily Tapa Kalan stupa), located some five miles (8 km.) southeast of Jalalabad at an elevation of about 1,500 feet (457 meters) above sea level. Although extremely popular with nineteenth-century European looters, Hadda's stupas and caravanserais still hold many art objects for the excavator to uncover, as witnessed by the 23,000 limestone, schist, and stucco (lime plaster) heads of all sizes uncovered by the French. The heads included serene Buddhas and Bodhisatvas, complaisant donors, grinning demons, helmeted soldiers, ascetics, monks, as well as representations of many contemporary ethnic groups. Limestone and schist bas-reliefs and sculpture also occurred in abundance.

Since 1965, a young Italian-trained archaeologist, Dr. Shahibye Mustamandi (his name is also spelled Mostamindi, Moustamindy, Mustamindi), Director of the Afghan Institute of Archaeology, has been excavating Tapa Shotor and other areas at Hadda (Mostamindi and Mostamindi, 1969; Moustamindy, 1969; Mustamandi, 1968a; Mustamindi and Mustamindi, 1968). Tapa Shotor stupa has yielded several important pieces of Buddhist statuary and an unique "Fish Porch" niche with an elaborate stucco marine scene with both real and imaginary sea creatures, probably dating second or third century A.D. (Mustamandi, 1968b; 1969). The "Porch," 2.40 meters by 2.20 meters, portrays a scene from the life of the Buddha: i.e., the conversion of the Snake King who lived in an underwater cave near Hadda.

Begram (Kapisa): Excavated twice (1936–40 by Hackin; Ghirshman, 1941–42), Begram sits about 50 miles (80.5 km.) north of Kabul at the confluence of the Panjsher and Ghorband rivers, about 5 miles (8 km.) west of the modern town of Charikar at an elevation of about 5,000 feet (1,524 meters) above sea level. For the first few centuries A.D., Begram must have been an extremely important commercial, strategic center, sitting at the juncture of two main trade routes cutting off from the major Silk Route: one from Balkh to Bamiyan to Peshawar to Taxila; the other leading down the Panjsher Valley from Badakhshan, Turkestan, and Chinese Sinkiang.

Hackin excavated in both "la nouvelle ville royale" (Begram proper) and "la vielle ville royale" (or Bordj-i-Abdullah). In the new royal city, Hackin found some of the most spectacular museum pieces of the twentieth century. Scattered pell-mell in two rooms were many profane luxury goods side by side with rare Buddhist objects: carved ivories from India; vases and lacquer ware from Han Dynasty China; classical Graeco-Roman bas-reliefs, plaster-cast medallions; Graeco-Egyptian bronzes, including a 24.1 cm.-high statue of Serapis–Hercules; Phoenician glassware from Tyre and Sidon; and a vase depicting a scene from the Iliad. Most of the magnificent finds probably date in the first two centuries A.D.

In 1941–42 Ghirshman attacked Begram again in order to establish a stratigraphic sequence for the first time in Afghan archaeology. Ghirshman identified three major occupation periods: I (second century B.C. to middle of second century A.D.) equated with the Indo-Parthian levels of Taxila and possibly capital of the last of the Indo-Greek kings (Rowland, 1966b, 24); II (mid-second century to mid-third century A.D., probable destruction by the Sasanian Shapur I in 241 A.D.); III (mid-third century A.D. until fifth century, Hepthalite invasion).

The ornamental jewelry of Period II tells a story of widespread trade. For example, a gold bracelet with sockets for 46 worked rubies (20 still intact) was discovered, and gold earrings inlaid with turquoise, and undecorated bronze earrings. All these specimens closely resemble others found in South Sarmatian tombs (second century B.C. to first century A.D.) and fifth-century Merovingian France (Ghirshman, *DAFA* XII 1946). Other jewelry came from India, Rome, Egypt, and Central Asia. Dionysius is represented on Period II seals.

Other sites in the Begram area include: Paitava (Rowland, 1966a), a stupa about five miles south of Begram, containing several Buddhist stucco heads with Parthian elements and bas-reliefs in schist of the third–fourth centuries A.D.; Shotorak (Meunié, *DAFA* X, 1942), a Buddhist *sangharama* (monastery), including 7 or 8 stupas, about 4.5 miles east of Begram, probably dating first–third centuries A.D.; another stupa at Koh-i-Mori (Mustamandi and Mustamandi, 1968).

Fondukistan: In a small valley subsidiary to the Ghorband Valley, about halfway between Begram and Bamiyan, sits Fondukistan, another *sangharama,* probably late sixth or early seventh centuries A.D. on the basis of Hephthalite[9] and Sasanian (Khusrau II: about A.D. 590–628) coins. At Fondukistan, clay modeling of heads and torsos completely replaced the earlier use of schist, and the colorful painting which accompanies the sculpture reflects intensive Indian influences, even though clothing and hair styling remains oriented toward the Sasanian, sometimes with Hellenistic undertones.

Balkh: A. Foucher, first Director of D.A.F.A., unsuccessfully sought the site of Bactra for eighteen months during 1924 and 1925.

---

[9] Also see R. E. M. Wheeler, 1968b, 150.

83. Ancient walls of Balkh, traditional site of Bactra, "Mother of Towns." July, 1965

84. Lashkar Gah, a 10th-11th-centuries A.D. Ghaznavid palace-soldiers' bazaar complex near the confluence of the Hilmand and Arghandab Rivers. *Photo: Josephine Powell*

Twenty years later, Daniel Schlumberger was appointed Director of D.A.F.A. He renewed the search for classical Bactra, and he and his colleagues sank over one hundred test pits (Gardin, *DAFA* xv, 1957, Fig. 1: map by LeBerre) in the Balkh area during two field seasons in 1947. The elusive Bactra remains undiscovered, but Gardin identified three pre-Islamic ceramic complexes (pre-Kushan, fifth–third centuries B.C.; Kushan, first century B.C. to third century A.D.; Sasanian, third–ninth centuries A.D.[10]). Schlumberger and D.A.F.A.'s superlative architect since 1945, Marc LeBerre, have defined three major architectural building periods at the site, the first two pre-Muslim.

Shamshir Ghar[11]: A unique cave site about fifteen miles west-southwest of Qandahar, Shamshir Ghar ("Cave of the Sword") long afforded haven to refugees from invaders, and yielded a four-period ceramic and stratigraphic sequence, three pre-Islamic occupations: I (pre-Kushan, pre-first century B.C.; II (Kushan, first century B.C.-mid-third century A.D.; III (Kushano–Sasanian, the major cultural levels, periodically occupied from mid-third to late seventh centuries A.D.).

Khair Khaneh: The importance of regional Hindu hegemony (see p. 303) in parts of eastern Afghanistan is emphasized by the excavations of Khair Khaneh, a Brahmin[12] temple about 7.5 miles from the center of Kabul. Khair Khaneh is situated in the pass separating the Kabul Valley from Kohistan (which includes Begram). Kushano–Sasanian and early Hindu art motifs mingle in a whitish-gray marble statue of the Sun God (either Surya or Mithra) seated on a throne, attended by two acolytes, Danda and Pingala. Underneath the throne, the sculptor carved a small Sun God representing dawn driving a two-horse chariot across the sky.

At one corner of the temple, a skeleton, possibly the result of an earlier human sacrifice, perhaps to dedicate an earlier temple, has been found.[13] The importance of the area continued to modern times, and the present government sponsors annual Farmers' Day celebrations and competitions to greet the New Year (first day of spring) at Khair Khaneh.

[10] Gardin realizes the Sasanians collapsed politically before the ninth century, but their ceramic traditions continued (*DAFA* XVIII, 1957, 95, footnote 9).

[11] This paragraph includes corrections and reevaluations of my monograph (1958a, 283–85), based on personal research, and those of Gardin (*DAFA* XV, 1957), K. Fischer (1967), and Leshnick (1967).

[12] Rowland (1966b, 107), however, considers the temple dedicated to an Iranian cult, and dates the site post-241 A.D.

[13] Personal observation.

85. Bala Hissar, Kabul. Ancient seat of power. Oldest walls probably Ephthalite (ca. 6th century A.D.). These walls later, and added to until late 19th century. November, 1970

Several isolated finds attest to Hindu presence in other areas. These include a marble Śiva head from Gardez; a whitish gray marble Durga head from Tagao in the Laghman Valley; a marble bas-relief sculptured in an unknown province showing Durga conquering Mahisasura (a demon); a provincial three-headed deity from the Mazar-i-Sharif museum, reputed from Saozma-Kala, twenty-five miles southwest of Balkh (K. Fischer, 1957; Rosenfield, 1967, 93–94). Tucci (1968), however, advises caution in accepting the Saozma-Kala head as genuine.

On the limestone wall in the darkness of the Fifth Chamber at Shamshir Ghar, the excavators discovered four tridents, painted red, in association with a series of red dots (L. Dupree, 1958a, 179, 273–75).[14] Calcite covered much of the paintings indicating some antiquity. I suggest that Hindu (or possibly Buddhist) refugees from the Sasanian invasions (Period III) may have established a temporary temple in the Fifth Chamber.

Other sites: Several other sites of the period under discussion deserve mention, particularly Tapa Maranjan in Kabul (Hakin, et al., 1959); the Buddhist site of Tepe Sardar near Ghazni excavated by the Italians (Taddei, 1968); the Japanese Buddhist stupa excavations at Kunduz (Mizuno, et al., 1964); the French investigations at the stupa of Guldara (Hackin, et al., 1959) near Kabul, and studies of Takht-i-Rustam, a stupa-monastery-cave complex near Aibak (K. Fischer, 1959; Mizuno, 1962); the unique (in Afghanistan) Sasanian wall paintings at Dukhtar-i-Nushirwan (A. and Y. Godard, J. Hackin, *DAFA* II; Rowland, 1946).

[14] Tridents have also been found at Surkh Kotal on limestone blocks relating to the lower section of the staircase (Bernard, personal communication, 1969).

CHAPTER 16

Islam Spreads Its Banner

A THOUSAND YEARS OF CENTRAL ASIAN IMPERALISM: EIGHTH TO NINETEENTH CENTURIES A.D.

THE Muslim Arabs broke Sasanian power at Qadisiya in A.H. 16/A.D. 637[1], and delivered the coup de grâce at Nihawand (near Hamadan) in 22/642. Subsequently all eastern Iran fell into Arab hands. The first big Arab raid through Qandahar and central Afghanistan took place in 80–81/699–700, when the Arab governor of Sistan was sent to chastize the Hindu-Shahi king of Kabul, who had refused to pay tribute. Even though defeated, the Hindu–Shahi (possibly former Kushans) continued to rule Kabul as vassals of the Umayyid Caliphs (41–132/661–750).

At this time T'ang dynasty China, which had defeated the Turks about 9/630, also covetously eyed the Afghan area. From 45–97/665–715 the Chinese, unable to fight actively for control of Afghanistan because of internal difficulties, helplessly watched Arab raids for booty give way to permanent military garrisons. The Muslims permitted local native rulers to retain their thrones, but assigned Arab military governors and tax collectors to assist them.

The Early Islamic Periods: Eighth to Thirteenth Centuries A.D.

When the Abbasid Caliphs came into power revolts occurred all over the Islamic world (132/749). But al-Mansur, the second Caliph

[1] See Appendix D for a discussion of the complicated calendar used in modern Afghanistan. Dates follow Bosworth (1967), Freeman-Grenville (1963), or Hazard (1951) wherever possible. First date refers to (Qamari = lunar) A.H. (After Hijra), or A.D. 622, the date the Prophet Mohammad left Mecca for Medina. The second date refers to A.D. For example: 387/997 means 387 A.H. and A.D. 997. Some confusion still exists concerning many dates and I have tried to select those which appear the most accurate, but certainly will not swear by them.

312

(136–58/754–75) of this dynasty, secured the empire. By 236/850, however, the Abbasids began to crumble, and many petty independent Muslim states sprang up from the Mediterranean to Central Asia. The first three semi-independent, eastern dynasties were of local Iranian or Afghan origin; the *Tahirid* (205–59/821–73), capital at Nishapur, penetrated Afghanistan, only in the extreme west, bordering Khurasan; the *Samanid* (204–395/819–1005), capital of Bokhara, ruled Sistan, Qandahar, Khurasan, and Transoxiana; the *Saffarid* (253-ca. 900/867–1495), capital at Nimroz, broke the power of the Hindu–Shahi in Kabul, the Buddhist Kushans in Zamindawar, Bost, Ghor, and Qandahar, and even survived as vassals in Sistan under later dynasties.

The eastern dynasties swore nominal fealty to Baghdad but, in reality, fought for power in turn (Saunders, 1965). Although the intellectual center of Islam remained at Baghdad, the Samanid capital of Bokhara and neighboring Samarkand witnessed the rise of Persian over Arab scholarship in these areas. By the end of the Samanid dynasty, both these cities ranked with Baghdad as centers of learning and art.

Also during the Samanid period, the Turks of the north, gathering strength since the beginning of the Chinese Sung dynasty (349/960), thrust themselves into the Islamic limelight for the first time. In 380/990 the Ilek (Ilaq) Khan (Qarakhanids or Toquz–Oghu) Turks of Turkestan captured Bokhara, and nine years later finished off the Samanids, dividing the Samanid domains with the Ghaznavids, who, under Subuktigin, had seized Khurasan south of the Oxus in 384/994.

With the *Ghaznavid* or Yamini Dynasty (366–582/977–1186), the Turks began a climb to power in Iran, Afghanistan, and India (Bosworth, 1963). Alptigin, Turkish "slave" commander of the Khurasan (capital at Nishapur) garrison of the Samanids, attempted a coup in 350/961. As had happened before and would happen again many times, the "slaves" of western Asian ruling families slowly and subtly (and often not so subtly) exchanged status (as well as role) with their masters.[2]

This time the coup failed, however, and Alptigin fled to Ghazni with a few loyal Turk followers, where he and several successors ruled, but still as vassals of the Samanids in Bokhara.

---

[2] Gibb and Bowen (1951) have published a brilliant study of the "ruling slave" phenomenon in the late Ottoman Empire.

The real founder of the Ghaznavid Empire, Nasir ad-Dawla Subuktigin (366–87/977–97), was son-in-law and one-time "slave" of Alptigin.
Only with Subuktigin's son, Yamin ad-Dawlah Mahmud (388–421/
988–1030), however, did the Ghaznavids embark on empire building, which also led to one of the great renaissances of the Early
Islamic period (Habib, 1951; Khalili, 1954).

A great general, Mahmud conducted at least seventeen successful
campaigns against India. He added northwest India and the Punjab to
his empire, and enriched his treasury by looting wealthy Hindu temples.
Probably more important, Mahmud's mullahs converted many Hindus
to Islam, beginning a process which still plagues the subcontinent. He
also overthrew the ruler of Ghor, an independent mountain kingdom
in central Afghanistan, in 393/1002 (Elliot and Dowson, 1953; Bosworth, 1963). The Ghurid ruler, of east Persian descent, was possibly
one of the last of the Kushans.

At this time, the Sunni Abbasid Caliph was virtually a prisoner
of the Shi'ite Buwayhid ruler of western Iran. Sunni Mahmud invaded Iran and sliced Isfahan, Ray, and the Makran coast from
Buwayhid control (Map 13B). The Caliph, al-Qadir (381–422/991–
1031) showed his appreciation by titling Mahmud, Yamin ad-Dawlah
(The Right Arm of the State). Despite his reputation for military
ferocity, Mahmud filled his capital and other cities with men of great
learning, and became a patron of the arts. Among these 900 scholars
were the scientist-historian al-Biruni, the poet Firdausi, and the historian
al-Utbi.

At the death of Mahmud the familiar pattern of the breakdown of
central authority occurred (McGovern, 1939, 116–17). Small independent states sprang up in the Indian provinces, while the Qarakhanids
(382–607/992–1211) in the north and the Seljuks (who had replaced
the Buwayhids in 447/1055) from Iran nibbled away at the frontiers.
The death blow came from the Ghurids in 582/1186, when they defeated the last Ghaznavid prince in Lahore.

Two excellent post-World War II excavations have added significantly to our knowledge of the Ghaznavid Period. From 1949 to 1952,
Schlumberger and his colleagues excavated five seasons at the fortress-
residence site of Lashkari Bazaar (Gardin, *DAFA* XVIII, 1963; Kohzad,
1953b; Schlumberger, 1949, 1950, 1952ab). Three palaces (North,
South, Central) and two mosques were surveyed, measured, and tested,
as was the mile-long section of the soldiers' bazaar.

The Italians under Professor Guiseppe Tucci, Director of the Istituto Italiano per il Medio ed Estremo Oriente (I.S.M.E.O.), have excavated and undertaken restoration at the royal city of Ghazni, the capital of the empire, and uncovered thousands of objects, including marble statues of Hindu gods worn smooth by the feet of Muslim worshippers. Mahmud or his successor had placed the idols under the threshold for use as stepping stones into the principal mosque. Among the preliminary reports on Ghazni are Bombaci, 1959, 1966, and Scerrato, 1959, 1962. Other reports have appeared sporadically in *East and West* (new series), a journal published by I.S.M.E.O.

In addition, the two "Towers of Victory" at Ghazni (one dating during the reign of Masud III, 493–508/1099–1114, the other Bahram Shah, 512–47/1118–52) probably served as models for the magnificent, sixty-meter-high structure (a minar?) at Jam (dating sixth century A.H./twelfth century A.D.) and the Qutb Minar (a "Tower of Victory" dating from the late sixth-early seventh centuries A.H./thirteenth century A.D.) in Delhi. The Jam tower not only gives evidence of the cultural climax of the Ghurids in central Afghanistan, but also provides an (as yet) unsolved enigma: why is the structure isolated so far from obviously intensively occupied areas on the main route farther south? For conflicting views, see Mariq and Wiet (*DAFA* XVI, 1959), Trousdale (1965) and Leshnik (1968).

In the last half of the sixth century A.H/twelfth century A.D., therefore, Turkish dynasties controlled all the eastern caliphate. Much of Afghanistan, eastern Iran, and modern Pakistan were ruled by the Turkish Ghurids (ca. 390–612/ca. 1000–1215). Parts of central and western Iran remained in the hands of the Seljuk Turks (429–590/1038–1194), until the Turkish Khwarazm Shahs came out of Transoxiana to overthrow them. Originally satraps of the Seljuks and earlier dynasties, the Khwarazm Shahs came into their own about 596/1200.

The Abbasid caliph was caliph in name only, and the Arabs no longer controlled western Asia as the year 1200 approached. The invincible Khwarazm Shah Turks loosely ruled an empire stretching from India to Turkey but rumors filtered out of Central Asia that a savior was on the way. The Christians believed that "Prester John" would save them from the Muslims; the Caliph hoped the new invader would reestablish the glory of a centrally powerful caliphate.

The man who came out of Mongolia in 617/1220 was not a noble savior on a white horse but a brutal,[3] brilliant, military tactician on a scraggly Mongol pony, leading an army which seemed to be part horse. Genghis (Chinggis) Khan (ca. 550–624/1155–1227) made history by destroying the finest civilizations of the thirteenth century A.D. He carved an empire from the China Sea to the Caspian Sea, but it was a transient empire and the emperor slept in a tent instead of a palace. The results, however, were not transient.

Genghis Khan was the atom bomb of his day; and western Asia still bears the scars, still suffers from the economic impact. The atom bombs on Hiroshima and Nagasaki destroyed much and killed many, but the cities are rebuilt, even if the dead cannot be returned, nor the effects of the fallout completely dissipated from the minds and bodies of men. The silted canals and destroyed cities in western Asia sit as Genghis Khan's monuments (Barthold, 1928; Grousset, 1938, 1941; Vladimirtsov, 1930, 1948). Among the scars in Afghanistan are the silent ruins of Sar Khoshak, Shahr-i-Zohak and Shahr-i-Gholghola near Bamiyan (N. Dupree, 1967b, 60–73).

But Islam did not die in the rubble. "In the darkest hour of political Islam, religious Islam has been able to achieve some of its most brilliant

---

[3] Although not so brutal as popularly believed. It must be remembered that most contemporary sources are hostile to any invader. For example, the following physical description (Blake and Frye, 1949, 295–97) occurs in the *History of the Nations of the Archers* (*The Mongols*):

> Now, however, we shall also tell what these first Tat'ars resembled, for the first who came to the upper country were not like men. They were terrible to look at and indescribable, with large heads like a buffalo's, narrow eyes like a fledgling's, a snub nose like a cat's, projecting snouts like a dog's, narrow loins like an ant's, short legs like a hog's, and by nature with no beards at all. With a lion's strength they have voices more shrill than an eagle. They appear where least expected. Their women wear beautiful hats covered at the top with a head shawl of brocade. Their broad faces were plastered with a poisonous mixture of gum. They give birth to children like snakes and eat like wolves. Death does not appear among them, for they survive for three hundred years. They do not eat bread at all. Such were the first people who came to the upper countries.

In addition the authors of the *History* assess the Mongols (ibid., 303–05):

> . . . their cavalry . . . took the unconquered towns and castles, plundering and taking captives. They killed without mercy men and women, priests and monks, making slaves, taking the deacons as their slaves, and plundering the churches of the Christians without fear. Stripping the precious relics of the holy [martyrs] and the crosses and holy books of their ornaments, they cast them away as of no value.

successes" (Hitti, 1949, 475) for, "less than half a century after Hulagu's (a grandson of Chinggis Khan, who ruled 654–63/1256–65) merciless attempt at the destruction of Islamic culture, his great-grandson, Ghazan[4] (694–703/1295–1304), as a devout Muslim, was concentrating much time and energy on the reunification of the same culture" (Hitti, 1949, 488).

The Timurid Period: (771–912/1370–1506)

Between the death of Genghis Khan and the rise of Tamerlane a period of fission descended over much of Central Asia, a pause between storms. The eleven Mongol khans (sons and grandsons of Genghis Khan) ruled most of the middle East until the time of Timur-i-Lang (or Tamerlane). During this confused period the Karts (643–784/1245-1381), a Tajik Dynasty, rose in Herat, swearing fealty to the Il-Khanid Mongols, successors to Genghis in Iran. However, in 733/1332 the Karts gained *de facto* independence which lasted until smashed by Tamerlane in 783/1381.

Tamerlane (771–807/1370–1405), a Turco-Mongol claiming descent from Genghis Khan, ended the fissionable period by fusing an empire from India to Turkey. The Turco-Mongols of this period can probably be considered ethnographically Uzbak. Tamerlane, the consummate conqueror, died as he prepared to march on China. His empire began to die with him, but his successors became patrons of the arts par excellence as epitomized by the many structures still standing at Samarkand and Herat, which actually served as capital during the reign of Shah Rukh (807–50/1405–47), son of Tamerlane. Ulugh Beg (850–53/1447–49), Shah Rukh's son and an astronomer, built a large observatory outside Samarkand and made many contributions to modern astronomy.

During the reign of Husain Baiqara (875–912/1470–1506), the last great Timurid, poets (such as Jami), artists (such as the famous miniaturist Behzad) and other scholars flocked to his capital in Herat. The late fifteenth century A.D., therefore, was one of cultural renaissance in Central Asia and northwest Afghanistan.

Several structures still standing in Herat (as well as Samarkand and elsewhere) offer tangible evidence for the architectural greatness of the Timurids (Pugachenkova, 1970; Seljuki, 1962; Wolfe, 1966). The

---

[4] Both were Il-Khanids, a dynasty which controlled Iran from 654–754/1256–1353.

Masjid-i-Jum'a (Friday Mosque), probably begun by Ghiyasuddin Ghuri (who lies buried inside the mosque) about 597/1200, was reconstructed and redecorated by Shah Rukh and Mir Ali Sher Nawai, also a great poet and statesman (political adviser to Husain Baiqara) in 904/1498.

Queen Gawhar Shad (wife of Shah Rukh) commissioned the great Persian architect, Qavam-ud-Din, to construct a combination *musalla* (place of worship)-*madrasa* (school or place of learning). Two tall minars stood on either side of the *madrasa* front portal, and the architect inconspicuously placed Gawhar Shad's mausoleum in one corner. The flowery light-blue-green mosaics on the outer fluting of the dome still impress one with their delicate beauty. Inside the dome, blues, reds, and gold leaf weave intricate designs. The blues are colored by lapis lazuli. The interior of the tomb forms a square chamber with axial niches. Actually, three domes soar over the tomb, a middle dome covers and protects the painted inner dome.

Gawhar Shad lies inside the mausoleum in select company with the following identified from tombstones by Seljuki (1962; Wolfe, 1966, 43): her favorite son, Prince Baisunghur (who died in 837/1433 of alcoholism); her favorite grandson, son of Baisunghur (died 864/1459); a great-grandson, Mirza Ahmad (died 849/1445); Mirza Shah Rukh (died 899/1493), son of her slayer. (She was murdered in 862/1457, over eighty years old, but lively enough to be considered a threat to the waning power elite). An unknown number of others were buried in Gawhar Shad's mausoleum, for many tombstones have disappeared from the site.

Of the original four minars at the corner of the *musalla* of Gawhar Shad, only one remains.

Sultan Husain Baiqara added several edifices to the scene, including a *chahrsu* (covered bazaar), a hospital, and a *madrasa* with four minars.

In 1885, the British, at the insistence of Amir Abdur Rahman Khan, destroyed most of the Timurid structures of the *musalla* complex to clear fields of fire because of a threatened Russian invasion of Herat. The Russians did not come, and only the mausoleum of Gawhar Shad and nine of the ten minars remained standing. Two minars fell during the 1931 earthquake, another in 1951. The remaining six soar precariously 150 feet skyward.

The Gazargah complex three miles east of Herat also contains several notable Timurid remains, as well as the tomb of the celebrated (in Afghanistan) eleventh-century A.D. Sufi poet and philosopher, Khwaja

Abdullah Ansari Herawi (de Beaurecueil, 1957; Seljuki, 1962; Wolfe, 1966, 48–57).

By 905/1500, the Timurids had frittered away their power in Central Asia, and the end came when the Mongol-Uzbak, Mohammad Shaybani (903–16/1500–10), conquered Herat and ended "the last great Islamic dynasty of steppe origin" (Bosworth, 1967, 167). The Shaybani dynasty controlled Transoxiana until the beginning of the seventeenth century A.D.

In the south and west, however, powerful states arose to compete in the Afghan area.

Moghuls and Safavids: ca. A.D. 1500–1747

For over two hundred years the Persian Safavid Dynasty (907–1145/1501–1732)[5] and the Muslim Indian Moghul Dynasty (932–1274/1526–1707) fought for control of Afghanistan. Both utilized military tactics based on the use of gunpowder to establish bases of firepower and permit mobility, one reason no further cavalry-oriented, steppe-based empires spread from Central Asia.

Babur, founder of the Moghul Dynasty, was a Chagatai Turk, descended from Tamerlane on his father's side, Genghis Khan on his mother's. The Shaybani Uzbaks drove Babur from his father's satrapy in Ferghana to Kabul in 910/1504. Babur loved Kabul and only moved into India when frustrated in his attempts to regain Ferghana. He left Kabul in November 933/1525 and marched against the Lodi Sultan, Ibrahim II (ca. 923–32/ca. 1517–26). On April 21, 933/1526, at Panipat, Babur challenged the power of the Lodis. His mobile, aggressive army of 12,000 destroyed a ponderous military machine of 100,000. But Babur still pined for Kabul and wrote: "The climate [of Kabul] is extremely delightful, and there is no such place in the known world" (Majumdar, et al., 1961, 430).

Humayun, Babur's son and successor, ruled for two distinct periods (937–47/1530–40; 962–63/1555–56). The fifteen intervening years saw the Suri Afghans on the throne in Delhi[6] (Rahim, 1961). Afghan

---

[5] Safavids reigned in parts of Iran until about A.D. 1800 but the last effective Shah ruled about 1145/1732.

[6] The Delhi Sultans were basically the successors of the Turkish Ghurids of Afghanistan and ruled as follows in Delhi: Mu'izzi (Slave) Dynasty (602–89/1206–90); Khaljis (689–720/1290–1320); Tughluqids (720–817/1320–1414); Sayyids (817–55/1414–51); Lodis (855–932/1451–1526); Moghul interlude; Suri Afghans (947–62/1540–55); Humayun returns (Hanifi, 1964; Neamat Ullah, 1965).

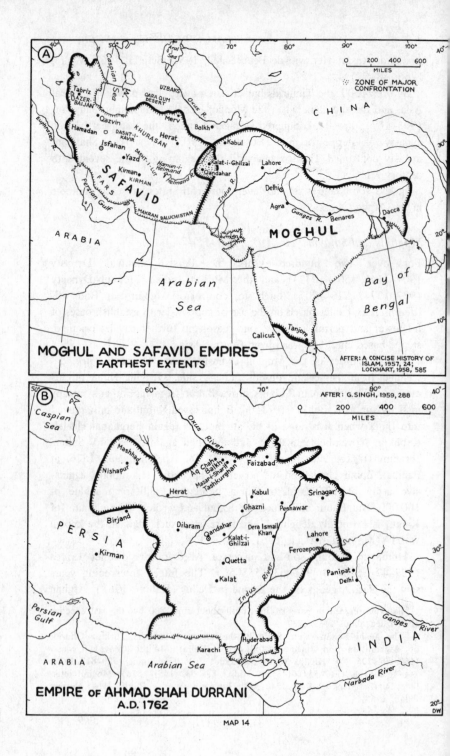

MOGHUL AND SAFAVID EMPIRES
FARTHEST EXTENTS

AFTER: A CONCISE HISTORY OF
ISLAM, 1957, 24;
LOCKHART, 1958, 585

EMPIRE OF AHMAD SHAH DURRANI
A.D. 1762

AFTER: G. SINGH, 1959, 288

MAP 14

influence and rulers remained in Bengal, however, until 1576, when the Moghuls at last gained control of this area (Majumdar, et al., 1961; Rahim, 1961).

Several great emperors ruled the Moghul Empire after Humayun: Akbar (963–1014/1556–1605), Jehangir (1014–37/1605–27), Shah Jahan (1037–68/1628–57), Aurangzeb (1068–1118/1658–1707). Technically the Moghuls ruled in Delhi until A.D. 1858, but their power waned and became impotent shortly after the death of Aurangzeb in A.D. 1707. Aurangzeb conquered most of India, the only time the Indian subcontinent had been close to union until A.D. 1947 (Map 14A).

In the sixteenth century a three-cornered fight developed among the Uzbaks (north), the Moghuls (south) and the Safavids (west). Another Turkic-speaker (probably ethnically a Kurd), Shah Ismail I (907–30/1501–24) created the Safavid Empire in Persia which competed with the Moghuls and Uzbaks for Central Asia. All three continually bumped against each other in a line running from Kabul to Qandahar. Tribalism continued to prevail in the Afghan region during the sixteenth and seventeenth centuries A.D. and at least 345 separate named tribal units existed (Rahim, 1961, 34–35).

Kabul came under Moghul control in 910/1504, but Safavid Persia ruled most of western Afghanistan by 1007/1598. In 966/1558 the Safavids under Tahmasp I (930–84/1524–76) occupied Qandahar; in 1584 the Uzbaks seized most of Badakhshan. Akbar recaptured Qandahar in 1003/1594. Shah Abbas I (Safavid, 996–1038/1588–1629) drove the Uzbaks out of Herat and recaptured Qandahar in 1032/1622. The pendulum swung again and in 1048/1638 Shah Jahan retook Qandahar from the Persians. Murad, Shah Jahan's son, reconquered Badakhshan from the Uzbaks, and the Moghuls controlled Balkh and the north until 1057/1647. But the fierce Uzbaks constantly harassed the Moghul garrisons. In despair the Moghuls abandoned north Afghanistan in 1058/1648.

Shah Abbas II (1052–77/1642–66) moved against the weakening Moghuls and in 1058/1648 annexed Qandahar, which the Moghuls never recovered. Aurangzeb, the last great Moghul, tried to retake the lost territories, but the truculent mountain Pushtun tribes revolted in 1069/1658, and fought against the Moghuls until 1086/1675.

Although the Afghans were not masters in their own land, neither were they completely subdued. Many tribes remained independent, and the symbol of the age is Khushal Khan Khattak, the warrior-poet, who epitomizes all the best in the Afghan ideal personality type. He spent his life fighting Moghul encroachment, and at the same time carried on his tribal blood feud with another major Pushtun tribe, the Yusufzai, centered in Swat, Pakistan. (For Khushal Khan Khattak, see above, pp. 83–89.)

The forty years between the death of Aurangzeb (1119/1707) and the rise of Ahmad Shah Abdali to the Durrani throne in Qandahar witnessed many exciting events. Most of the northern and eastern Afghan tribes remained independent or gained independence as the Moghul Empire deteriorated. At Qandahar and Herat major rivalries developed between the Abdali (later Durrani) and the Ghilzai[7] Pushtun, a rivalry still not completely eradicated. Herat remained in Safavid Persian hands until the rise of the Abdali, who had been driven from power in the Qandahar region by the Ghilzai in 1129/1716.

All during the Moghul-Safavid rivalry, the Ghilzai played off one against the other, but because of the liberal religious policy of Shi'i Safavids (although the Ghilzai were Sunni), the Ghilzai preferred the Persians and actually supported them militarily in the last serious attempt by the Moghuls to retake Qandahar in 1064/1653. However, the grandson of Shah Abbas II, Shah Sultan Husain I (1105–1135/1694–1722), altered the tolerant policies of the past, which culminated in the appointment of a Georgian apostate, Abdullah Khan, as Safavid Governor-General of Qandahar in either 1110/1698 or 1111/1699 (Lockhart, 1958, 83). The new Governor-General proved more grasping than any of his predecessors, and, contacted by the Moghul Governor in Kabul, Shah Alam, actually considered supporting the Moghul claims to Qandahar. Before the Ghilzai could act, however, the Baluch, under Mir Samander, attacked the Safavid garrisons in Qandahar in 1115/1703. They defeated Abdullah Khan's army and killed his son.

Sultan Husain, now thoroughly alarmed, ordered Giorgi XI, a Georgian mercenary, to Qandahar as Governor-General. Giorgi defeated the Baluch, but immediately decided that Mir Wais Khan, the Hotaki Ghilzai chieftain and nominal mayor of Qandahar, was a much more formidable rival than Mir Samander. Mir Wais, ostensively subservient to Giorgi, deplored the brutal suppression of his people by the Georgian troops. He led a revolt which the jubilant Giorgi put down with ever-increasing ferocity. The Georgian sent Mir Wais to Isfahan under heavy guard, a grave mistake for the Safavids (Benawa, 1956).

---

[7] More correctly called the Ghilji, but I follow "Ghilzai" in conformity with the bulk of references in European sources.

Mir Wais was not only a brave soldier and devout patriot, but a skilled tribal politician. He was also very wealthy. Through judicious flattery and subtle bribes, he gained much favor in Sultan Husain's court. The Shah actually permitted Mir Wais to make the Hajj to Mecca, where the wily Ghilzai secured a *Fatwa* (religious interpretation) which indicated the righteousness of a Sunni revolt against the "heretical" Safavid Shi'a. Armed with the *Fatwa* (which, naturally, he failed to show Sultan Husain), Mir Wais returned to Qandahar, heaped with honors from the Shah and with orders to check on the activities of Giorgi.

While in Isfahan, Mir Wais realized that the Safavid court was basically weak, and that a successful revolt in Qandahar would guarantee the Ghilzai independence for many years. In 1121/1709, the Ghilzai rose under Mir Wais and slaughtered the hated Georgian and his small garrison, while most of the Safavid occupation troops were on a punitive expedition against the Kakar Pushtun tribe (Lockhart, 1958, 87). How Giorgi met his death is unknown, but Sultan Husain could only impotently send a message of protest to Mir Wais, who arrested the messenger. A second protest messenger arrived in Qandahar, and was also thrown into prison by Mir Wais.

Shah Sultan Husain then ordered Kai Khusrau with his Qizilbash and Georgian troops to retake Qandahar and punish the rebels. Abdullah Khan Saddozai, an Abdali chief, aided Kai Khusrau and the combined army met the Ghilzai at Farah in November 1122/1710. For reasons unknown (possibly intrigue at Isfahan prevented Kai Khusrau from receiving the necessary troops and supplies to complete his mission), Mir Wais and Kai Khusrau agreed to a truce, but in 1123/1711 the Safavid commander moved on Qandahar. Attacked on two fronts, Mir Wais sent a strong force to confront and subsequently defeat the Abdali, but Kai Khusrau defeated the Ghilzai and laid siege to Qandahar. The siege failed.

For about four months, the Ghilzai and Baluch under Mir Wais continually harassed the Georgians, and laid waste the countryside. Unable to gather supplies, the Safavids and their Abdali allies retreated. The Ghilzai attacked and inflicted a crushing defeat on them. Kai Khusrau was killed. The victory proved a great morale-builder for the Afghans, for a proverb popular at the time said "The Persians are but women compared with the Afghans, and the Afghans but women compared with the Georgians." (Lockhart, 1958, 146).

Mir Wais died peacefully in 1128/1715, and lies in a mausoleum outside Qandahar. He never proclaimed himself king, but simply *Vakil* (Governor or Regent) of Qandahar.

Meanwhile the Abdali, erstwhile allies of the Safavids, revolted in Herat. Abdullah Khan Saddozai and his son, Asadullah, defeated at least four Persian armies sent against them, and by 1130/1717 proclaimed Herat an independent state.

Events in the south, however, led to another inevitable Ghilzai-Abdali clash. Abdul Aziz, Mir Wais' brother, succeeded him as *Vakil* and ruled Qandahar for about eighteen months. An atypical Ghilzai, Abdul Aziz wished to make peace with the Persians and make Qandahar once more a Safavid province. Mir Mahmud, the eldest son (18 years old) of Mir Wais, murdered his uncle and seized power in 1130/1717.

In 1130/1718, Asadullah, appointed Governor of Farah by his father (Abdullah Khan Saddozai), moved against Mahmud. He wished to regain Qandahar, which the Abdali had controlled until the late seventeenth century. The two armies met at Dilaram, and the Ghilzai decisively defeated the Abdali. Mahmud sent the head of the slain Asadullah to Sultan Husain, and reported he had engaged the enemics of the Safavids and defeated them. Impressed, the Safavid Shah heaped honors on the young Mahmud.

Meanwhile the defeated Abdali in Herat began a deadly game of fratricidal musical chairs. Khan replaced khan with unprecedented frequency, and instability really governed in Herat and Farah.

Just as his father had done, Mahmud correctly sensed the helplessness of Shah Sultan Husain, and he marched into Persia in 1132/1719, moving against Kerman, which he occupied almost without opposition. Mahmud brutally oppressed the population (mainly Zoroastrian), and exhibited the cruelty which characterized his short, stormy life. After about nine months, however, Mahmud returned precipitously to Qandahar and put down a revolt by the governor left in charge, Bijan Sultan.

The Safavids reoccupied Kerman and rapidly improved the defenses. Mahmud appeared once again outside Kerman, in October 1134/1721, and easily reoccupied the city, but the improved citadel, commanded by the brilliant Governor-General, Rustam Mohammed Sa'dlu, held out until the end of January 1135/1722, when Sa'dlu died, and the new commander agreed to pay Mahmud a fee to withdraw. The Ghilzai, excellent in ambush and mobile campaigning, tired of the siege, so Mahmud accepted and moved on Yazd.

Repulsed in his frontal assault on Yazd, Mahmud simply marched straight for Isfahan. A Persian force of about 42,000 men and 24 cannon, commanded by the French artillerist, Philippe Colombe, met the Afghans at Gulnabad. Mahmud was thus outnumbered about two to one (Lockhart, 1958, 136). On March 8, 1135/1722, Mahmud sealed the fate of the Safavids. The Persians fled to Isfahan, leaving about 5,000 men dead, including M. Colombe and his 24 cannon. The Afghans lost about 500 (Lockhart, 1958, 42).

Mahmud surrounded Isfahan and settled down to a six-month siege, which reduced the population to a diet of dogs, cats, old shoes, and horse dung, among other things (Lockhart, 1958, 165).[8] When Sultan Husain finally capitulated in April 1134/1722, probably about 80,000 people had died of disease and starvation, another 20,000 in battle. The city of Isfahan never recovered its former political importance, but few of its exquisite buildings had been damaged (Pope, 1938–39, Vol. II; Lockhart, 1958, 169–70). The population diminished further as Mahmud and his viceroy, Ashraf, continued bloody repressions. Even today, Isfahan is only about one-third its peak population, which reached 650,000 in the early seventeenth century.

The exchange of power between the defeated Sultan Husain and his cruel usurper, Mahmud, provides insights into the classic Islamic theory of government: a man rules with divine sanction, not by divine right. The following meeting took place between the victor and vanquished:

> After they had exchanged greetings, Shah Sultan Husain said, "My son, since the Supreme Being does not wish me to reign, and the moment has come which he has decreed for you to ascend to the throne, I cede my empire to you with all my heart, and I wish that you may rule it in prosperity." . . . Mahmud evidently felt pity for Sultan Husain for he addressed him as follows: "Let no grief take up its abode in your heart. Such is the mutability of human grandeur. Allah, who disposes of empires as he wishes, causes authority [over them] to pass from hand to hand and from

---

[8] Several Europeans lived through the siege of Isfahan and left behind observations. Lockhart (1958) uses these sources extensively, including Ange de Gardane, French consul; Joseph Apisalaimian, Armenian secretary and interpreter to the French consul; Petros di Sagis Gilanentz, another Armenian chronicler, who though not in Isfahan, obtained much of his data from Apisalaimian; Rev. John Frost, Chaplain of the English East India Co.; Mattheus van Leijpzig, accountant, the Dutch trading company; Reverend Tadeusz Juda Krusinski, a Polish Jewish missionary; Nicholaus Schorer, Chief Merchant, Dutch Trading Company in Isfahan.

one nation to another, as it pleases him. However, I promise to look upon you always as my own father and to undertake nothing in the future without taking your advice." . . . Sultan Husain, alluding to what Mahmud has said replied, "The rule is Allah's" (Gilanentz, quoted in Lockhart, 1958, 172–73).

On October 25, 1135/1722, Mahmud entered Isfahan in great pomp. In an attempt to legitimize his accession to the Safavid throne, Mahmud later married a daughter of Sultan Husain.

Mahmud, his head never secure politically, also literally had an unbalanced head which grew worse and worse. Only twenty years old and a ruler of Isfahan, Kerman, and Sistan (although the lines of communications were constantly interrupted), he only had another six years to live. Mahmud imprisoned Sultan Husain and all his sons, except the profligate Tahmasp, who escaped and declared himself Shah at Qazvin on November 10, 1135/1722.

In January 1136/1723, Mahmud bloodily occupied the city of Qazvin, which had abjectly surrendered after the drunken Tahmasp fled with his ministers and courtiers to Tabriz. Shortly after, the Qazvini revolted against their treatment by the Afghans. The brave citizens of Qazvin killed about 1,200 Afghans, and the survivors fled to Isfahan.

One result of the Qazvin uprising would later prove fatal to Mahmud. His cousin, Ashraf (son of the murdered Abdul Aziz), chose this moment to desert Mahmud's service, return to Qandahar, and attempt to seize power. Mahmud ordered his cousin to return to Isfahan. Ashraf refused.

Afraid the successful Qazvin revolt would encourage the Isfahani, Mahmud undertook to intimidate further the already cowed populace. He called a cabinet meeting (he had kept most of Sultan Husain's ministers in the court) and slaughtered them. Estimates vary from between 148 to 300. Mahmud then killed the sons of the ministers, and executed 3,000 Qizilbash guards (Lockhart, 1958, 198).

Some of the Ghilzai, never known for excessive gentleness, and appalled at the sheer numbers of the slaughtered, began to plot against Mahmud. After the failure of Mahmud's subsequent spring campaign against recalcitrant Persian cities, his soldiers forced him to send for Ashraf in 1137/1724. Men obeyed Mahmud out of fear and because of his personal charisma, but they loved Ashraf and wanted him to command them in battle. The suspicious and unstable Mahmud, however, soon placed Ashraf in prison.

Mahmud, convinced he needed, and deserved, divine assistance, secluded himself, in accordance with custom, in a vault or cave for forty days. Already mentally unbalanced, he came out utterly mad. Despondency led to persecution complexes and finally his mind snapped over a simple matter. Rumor reached Mahmud that one of Sultan Husain's children had escaped. In a frenzy of blood, Mahmud, with two assistants, hacked the sons of Sultan Husain to death, including the alleged escapee.

Hearing the screams, Sultan Husain rushed to the courtyard and watched helplessly as the blood of his blood flowed into the ground. His sons, hands tied behind their backs, were butchered. Only two sons still lived as Sultan Husain watched the ghastly scene. The two surviving small children fled to their father, who took them in his arms to protect them. Sword raised, angry Mahmud struck and wounded the old man. Mahmud, shaken by the sight of his father-in-law's blood, spared the two children. Reports of the number killed vary from 18 to 180. Lockhart (1958, 208) favors the number 39 given by Sheikh Mohammad Ali Hazin.

Mahmud sought the advice of all available doctors, and the Armenian clergy seem to have succeeded in partly restoring Mahmud to sanity, but only for a short time.

Meanwhile, Ashraf, in prison, had been in correspondence with Tahmasp, offering to join forces if Tahmasp would promise himself and his followers their lives and lands. Tahmasp agreed, but soon after his troops defeated an Afghan force near Qum. The Afghan commanders, leaderless because Mahmud's condition worsened daily, agreed among themselves to depose the mad Shah and place Ashraf on the throne of Isfahan.

On April 25, 1137/1725, Mahmud's agonies came to an end. In the weeks before his murder, he continuously flagellated and lacerated his own flesh. Some say he had leprosy; others, that he was partially paralyzed. Would cancer have caused such terrible actions? A brain tumor? Advanced syphilis? We shall never know, nor shall we know the cause of his death. Natural causes? Beheading? Suffocation? Strangulation? (Lockhart, 1938, 210).

In any event, the next day Ashraf proclaimed himself Shah, and therefore effectively cut himself off from Qandahar, for the brother of Mahmud, Husain, and other kinsmen would never accept the twenty-six or twenty-seven-year-old Ashraf as Shah.

Ashraf proved to be the bloody equal of his cousin and his first òfficial act was a blood bath. He executed many of Mahmud's intimates. Ashraf initially offered the throne to the bereaved Sultan Husain, but the old man, completely broken, refused. The new Shah expressed regret over the treatment of Sultan Husain by Mahmud, and ordered the bodies of the slain princes, still festering in the courtyard, to be properly buried.

Later, however, in 1139/1726, Ashraf ordered Sultan Husain executed, because the Ottoman Turks declared Ashraf to be a rebel, and asked how he could claim to be Shah while the old Shah lived. In 1140/1727, the Ottomans recognized Ashraf as Shah of Persia, after the Afghans decisively defeated the Turks near Hamadan. In return, Ashraf recognized the Sultan of Ottoman Turkey as titular leader of the Muslim world. A small war (1140–41/1727–29) with Russia diverted Ashraf temporarily. In a treaty, signed at Resht in February 1141/1729, he agreed to exchange ambassadors with the Russians. Each party agreed to protect traders and commercial interests of the other inside their respective boundaries, establishing a framework for peaceful coexistence.

The Safavid claimant, Tahmasp II, without a home to call his own, bounced as a political shuttlecock from adventurer to adventurer for ten years (1135–45/1722–32). The two major rivals were Fath Ali Khan Qajar, an important Khan of the Qajar Turks, and an Afshar (Chagatai) Turk, Nadir or Tahmasp Quli Khan ("Slave of Tahmasp"), a man who rose from cameleer to outlaw king with a large personal army. He would eventually leave his temporary imprint on Delhi, but he had an indelible impact on Persia.

In the contest for control of Tahmasp, Nadir won,[9] for he intercepted a letter from Fath Ali Khan to another rebel, Malik Mohammad, asking his assistance in a struggle against Nadir and Tahmasp II. Actually, Nadir had planned to make the same proposal to the same rebel chief! The enraged Tahmasp wanted to execute Fath Ali Khan, but Nadir objected, fearing a great tribal war with the Qajar would result. But behind Nadir's back, Tahmasp had Fath Ali Khan beheaded, thus eliminating Nadir's chief rival for power.

Before this, however, Mashhad, governed by the rebellious Malik Mohammad, fell to Nadir in November 1139/1726. Now only time stood between Nadir and the overthrow of the harem-oriented Tahmasp II, who constantly tried to wriggle out from under Nadir's thumb. Nadir proposed to destroy the Abdali (then engaged in internecine wars)

[9] The Qajars, however, eventually ruled Persia from 1193/1779 to 1342/1924.

power in Herat before moving against the Ghilzai Shah, Ashraf, at Isfahan. Tahmasp II agreed, for he and his effete courtiers hoped the Abdali would cancel out Nadir's implicit threat to the throne, and then return to their harmless (to the Safavids) fratricidal warfare. Nadir, however, cleverly refused to leave Tahmasp II alone with his court.

The rival Abdali leaders, Allah Yar Khan and Zulfiqar Khan, quick to recognize the menace of the gathering force at Mashhad, temporarily put aside their struggle for power and agreed that Allah Yar Khan would be Governor of Herat and Zulfiqar Khan Governor of Farah. Farther south, Husain, the brother of Mahmud, ruled Qandahar and remained hostile to the Abdali and to Ashraf in Isfahan.

With Tahmasp II in tow, Nadir moved to Islam Qala, where Mohammad Zaman Khan (father of Zulfiqar) had defeated the Safavids in 1132/1719 and thereby gained a decade of bloody independence and fratricidal wars for the Abdali.

Nadir destroyed the fabled invincibility of the Afghans by defeating the Abdali, many of whom then marched with the Persians to help destroy the Ghilzai at Isfahan. Allah Yar Khan swore loyalty to Tahmasp II and remained in Herat as Governor. But Zulfiqar Khan, assisted by the Ghilzai ruler of Qandahar, Husain Sultan, revolted as Nadir later campaigned against the Ottoman Turks, drove Allah Yar Khan from Herat, and marched on Mashhad in 1143/1730.

In September 1142/1729, however, Nadir and Tahmasp II turned toward Isfahan, and a now thoroughly worried Ashraf came to meet them. Nadir's hard-trained and battle-hardened Persians showed their mettle, and although greatly outnumbered, their newly instilled discipline and confidence produced a great victory. Ashraf and his Ghilzai (who had fought well as usual) retreated. After a rest, Nadir faced Ashraf once again and defeated him. The Ghilzai fled to Isfahan, leaving behind guns and baggage. Safe inside the city walls, Ashraf followed the example of Mahmud in defeat: he executed 3,000 of the most prominent Isfahani religious and civil leaders to cow the populace. Reinforced with guns and troops from Baghdad, Ashraf sallied forth to meet Nadir at Murchakur, north of Isfahan. Again, Nadir's superior generalship and the new ferocity of his army won the day. Ashraf fled from Isfahan and the rest of his short life would be spent on the run. After four and a half years, Ashraf, hunted by both Nadir and Husain Sultan of Qandahar (Ashraf's cousin), was probably killed by Husain south of Qandahar in February 1142/1730. Although proclaimed Shah in Qazvin in November 1135/1722, Tahmasp II had never ruled anything but his harem. Crowned again in Isfahan in December 1142/1729, Tahmasp II sat on the throne for two and a half years, and then Nadir forced him to abdicate, because Tahmasp's abortive campaigns with the Ottomans lost much of the territory Nadir had gained. Tahmasp's infant son (two years old) became Shah Abbas III, with Nadir as Regent.

The revolt of Zulfiqar Khan at Herat forced Nadir Khan to turn once again to the east and fight the tribe he so much admired, the Abdali Pushtun. The Ghilzai from Qandahar joined the Abdali at Herat to fight the Persian invader. The two Pushtun tribes might fight each other to the death for control of Herat, Farah, and Qandahar, but any external invader welded them together in a common cause. Nadir Khan would not be denied and in July 1144/1731, Zulfiqar submitted. His Ghilzai allies had already recently slipped away (G. Singh, 1959, 12). Nadir Khan, the victor, agreed to proposals by the defeated Abdali khans to appoint Allah Yar Khan as Governor of Herat. Within a few months, however, Allah Yar, again assisted by a Ghilzai army, raised the flag of independence. Afghan duplicity wore out the patience—though not the admiration—of Nadir Khan. When Allah Yar surrendered in February 1144/1732, Nadir permitted him to leave for Multan (in Pakistan where many Durrani still live today) and appointed a Persian to govern Herat (G. Singh, 1959, 13).

Zulfiqar and his younger brother, Ahmad Khan, fled from Farah to Qandahar, where Husain Sultan threw them into jail. Nadir Khan decided to transport the most dissident groups of the Abdali to Khurasan, as a minority group in the midst of previously migrated loyal Afghan Turks and other Iranian tribes (G. Singh, 1959, 13). But many Abdali joined his army and his admiration for these militant Pushtun continued to grow.

Nadir Shah finally moved against Qandahar in 1149/1736, assisted by the Abdali. He occupied much of southwest Afghanistan and southeast Persia before Qandahar surrendered in March 1150/1738. Husain Sultan had ruled the city since 1138/1725. Nadir Shah found Zulfiqar and his brother, Ahmad Khan, still in the Ghilzai prison at Qandahar. He released them and, pleased with the way his Abdali mercenaries had served him, Nadir Shah brought back the exiled Abdali groups from Khurasan and permitted them to resettle in Qandahar. In a change-about, the Ghilzai were exiled to Khurasan. The present disposition of the Pushtun tribes of western and southcentral Afghanistan were thus determined (Map 6).

Inevitably, Nadir Shah set out on the path pioneered by the Achaemenids, Greeks, Parthians, and Mongols. Although not geographically the same, the path was one of conquest, of subduing his fellow men. Ostensibly, Nadir took Delhi because the Moghul emperor, Mohammad Shah (1131–61/1719–48), mistreated some Persian envoys. National honor often serves as a springboard to war.

However, as Mahmud correctly gauged the decay of Safavid Persia, so Nadir measured the Moghuls. Nadir Shah fought and defeated the Pushtun tribes near Gandamak on his way to Jalalabad. He outflanked the Khyber. Pass, followed the Kabul River, and descended on Peshawar, which surrendered. The Punjab, governed by the influential Zakaria Khan at Lahore, collapsed before the Persian lion in early 1152/1739. The road to Delhi and the riches of the Moghul purse lay open to be purloined.

The Moghul court in Delhi which faced Nadir resembled the Safavid court in Isfahan which had faced Mahmud. Pleasure-loving and laden with "carpet knights" (Majumdar, et al., 1961, 532), the Delhi court hoped that Nadir would simply give up, but he pushed on rapidly. Uncomfortably girding themselves for battle and without the equivalent of the tough Georgian and Qizilbash mercenaries of the Safavids, the Moghul army commanders staggered to Karnal, twenty miles from Panipat, traditional battleground for settling the future of north India.

The inevitable defeat followed. Conqueror and conquered entered Delhi together. At first relatively lenient, Nadir finally instituted a blood bath when certain citizens of Delhi murdered some Persian soldiers, after a false rumor concerning Nadir's death spread throughout the city. Probably at least 20,000 people perished. In spite of this and other ghastly slaughters, Indian history has always been one of fertility reigning supreme over hostility.

Nadir departed Delhi after two months in mid-May 1152/1739. Laden with the treasures of the Moghuls, the Peacock Throne of Shah Jahan, the crown jewels (including the famous Koh-i-Nur diamond), clothing, furniture, priceless illuminated manuscripts, 300 elephants, 10,000 horses, 10,000 camels, 15 crores (one crore equals 100,000) rupees in cash, Nadir reached Qandahar in 1153/1740 (Majumdar, et al., 1961, 533). Losing interest in the hot Indian plains, Nadir returned control of his conquered territories south and east of the Indus to Mohammad Shah, the Moghul, as compensation for his financial losses.

In the autumn of 1153/1740 Nadir pushed past Herat (picking up volunteers from among the Abdali, who hoped to gain loot) and took

Samarkand, Bokhara, and Khiva. He returned to Mashhad, which he made his capital in 1154/1741.

Increasing brutality marked the final years of Nadir Shah. Convinced his son, Raza Quli, wanted to assassinate him and seize the throne, Nadir had him blinded. The killing of the light of his son's eyes diminished Nadir's own inner light, and he killed and killed. He grew more morose and suspicious. He alienated his previously loyal Persian, Qizilbash, and Turk followers (Lockhart, 1938).

Mistrusting many in his camp and suspecting a plot against his life, Nadir Shah ordered young Ahmad Khan (second son of Mohammad Zaman Khan), commander of a body of Afghan cavalry while his elder brother, Zulfiqar Khan, campaigned for Nadir in Mazanderan, to arrest most of the officers in the camp at Quchan. The plotters learned of the counter-ploy and struck the night before they were to be arrested— and probably executed. The beheaded body of Nadir Shah greeted the dawn.

Ahmad Khan and his 4,000 horsemen escaped the camp while the erstwhile followers of Nadir Shah the Great looted the camp. Ahmad Khan, a treasury official, however, lifted much of the Shah's portable treasury,[10] including the Koh-i-Nur diamond, which Nadir Shah had worn on his sleeve (G. Singh, 1959, 18–19). Pursued, Ahmad Khan threw off his pursuers by sending a small diversionary force toward Herat while he led the bulk of his troops toward Qandahar (Mohd. Ali, 1958b, 57).

Freed of Persian, Indian, and Uzbak domination, the Abdali Afghans ultimately dominated most of their empires. But first, the Abdali needed a leader, and who but the young Abdali warrior, Ahmad Khan? Near Qandahar, the army selected a paramount chieftain for the Abdali, not, as indicated by some Afghan historians[11] and parroted by most Western scholars,[12] king of Afghanistan, a position and title which did not exist at the time. Each section wanted its leader to be selected paramount khan. The *jirgah* lasted for nine days and two chief contestants emerged: Hajji Jamal Khan of the Mohammadzai lineage and Ahmad Khan of the Saddozai.

[10] Nadir Shah believed in bribing his enemies whenever possible, and fighting only as a last resort, so he always transported considerable sums with his royal camp.

[11] Among them: Mohd. Ali, 1958b; Ghubar, 1943, 85–90; A. Habibi, 1967a; Khafi, 1957; Kohzad, 1950b, 38–40; Najib Ullah, in Young (ed.), 1961, 6.

[12] Among them: Caroe, 1965, 255; Fletcher, 1966, 42; Fraser-Tytler, 1967, 61; G. Singh, 1959, 341; Sykes, 1940, 367; Wilber, 1962, 17.

DIAGRAM 6* †

Abdali (Durrani) Tribal Structure

Abdali (later Durrani)

|
Zirak

| Popalzai | Alikozai | Barakzai | Achakzai |

Saddozai
(in power,
A.D. 1747–1818)

Mohammadzai
(in power
since A.D. 1826)

* (after Caroe, 1965, 12)   † (also see Chart 21, p. 344)

But for the act of a bootlicking follower of the twenty-five-year-old Ahmad Shah, the leadership may have gone to Hajji Jamal, who controlled the most powerful section. Mohammad Sabir Khan, however, a noted *darwish* (holy man), who had earlier predicted that Ahmad Khan would be leader of the Afghans, rose in the *jirgah* and said: "Why all this verbose talk? God has created Ahmad Khan a much greater man than any of you; his is the most noble of all the Afghan families. Maintain, therefore, God's work, for His wrath will weigh heavily upon you if you destroy it." (G. Singh, 1959, 25–26). Ahmad Khan reputedly hesitated to accept the open decision of the *jirgah,* so Sabir Khan again intervened. He placed some wheat or barley (G. Singh, 1959, 27) sheaves in Ahmad Khan's turban,[13] and crowned him, *Badshah, Durr-i-Dauran* (Shah, Pearl of the Age). On the basis of a dream, Ahmad Shah Abdali changed his title to Ahmad Shah, *Durr-i-Durran* (Pearl of Pearls), or Ahmad Shah Durrani. Since 1160/1747, therefore, the Abdali have been called Durrani (Ghubar, 1943).

The other Abdali section chiefs accepted the leadership of the young Shah for varying reasons. He was, and let no one doubt this point, a genuine charismatic leader. Practical reasons, however, cannot be ignored. He did come from the most distinguished section of the Abdali, and was a direct-line descendant of Saddo, founder of the line and ambassador to the Safavid court of Shah Abbas. Not even Hajji Jamal could match such claims. In addition, the relatively small size of the Saddozai section may have prompted some khans to throw their support

---

[13] As an anthropologist, I cannot resist speculating that this fertility symbol must have an ancient prehistoric root in Afghanistan.

333

to Ahmad Shah, thinking (falsely) that they would be able to control the young man's actions. One must not forget that Ahmad Shah controlled the most effective fighting force in the area, 4,000 veteran cavalrymen, and this fact must also have helped in the final decision.

But what of the Ghilzai, traditional enemies of the Abdali, and the greatest potential threat to the new Shah? The defeat of the Ghilzai by Nadir Shah and their subsequent resettlement had sapped most of their political strength. More important, a large number of Ghilzai served with the Afghan contingent of Nadir Shah and followed Ahmad Shah to Qandahar. The Ghilzai, once masters of this part of the world, chose to bide their time and work with a winner, but they never again reached their previous pinnacle of power. The Durrani still rule.

What of the other Afghan (Pushtun) tribes, still in the hills, nursing their fragile, independent kingdoms, hoping the Abdali would not unite? Most preferred to see an internecine struggle between the Mohammadzai and the Saddozai, but Ahmad Shah Durrani combined incredible luck with consummate skill to create the last great Afghan empire.

Arriving outside Qandahar, Ahmad Shah met resistance from several quarters, but a gratuitous circumstance helped him consolidate his position. A single day prior to his arrival, a treasure-laden caravan reached Qandahar on its way to Persia. The new Shah seized the caravan of his dead master and spread the wealth among his retinue, the khans and their followers. The Qizilbash escort of the treasure convoy also joined the army, and proved excellent mercenaries and administrators in the service of Ahmad Shah. Their descendants still occupy high positions on the modern Afghan scene.

Inside Qandahar, Ahmad Shah executed several dissidents and potential dissidents, including a maternal uncle, Abdul Ghani Khan, governor of Qandahar for Nadir Shah Afshari (G. Singh, 1959, 31).

Qandahar purchased and coerced, the march of empire began.

The Durrani Empire: A.D. 1747–1793

Thus began another period of fusion, which, in its heyday, would extend from Central Asia to Delhi, from Kashmir to the Arabian Sea (Map 14B). Next to the Ottoman Empire, the Durrani was the greatest Muslim Empire in the second half of the eighteenth century.

Ghazni, the final important Ghilzai stronghold, fell; then Kabul, commanded by Nasir Khan, who had gone over to the Moghuls on the death of Nadir Shah Afshari, submitted. Asia's newest conqueror met little resistance as he took Pehsawar, crossed the Indus, and seized Attock. The Moghul governor of the Punjab, Hayatullah Khan (also called Shah Nawaz Khan), fled Lahore, and Ahmad Shah, sensing victory, spurred on his small, tough, mobile force of 12,000 men toward Delhi and the hapless Moghul Emperor, Mohammad Shah (1131–61/1719–48). So far, so good, but the final military gasp of the Moghuls briefly interrupted Ahmad Shah's imperialist ambitions.

Another Ahmad Shah (crown prince of the Moghuls) met Ahmad Shah the Durrani with a much stronger force at Manupur, and with the assistance of an able general, Mir Mannu, bitterly defeated the young Afghan. Ahmad Shah Durrani retreated as rapidly as his mobile force could travel to Qandahar, where he executed his nephew, Luqman Khan, who, left behind as governor, had declared independence.

Mohammad Shah died in Delhi 1161/1748. Ahmad Shah, his son, became emperor (1161–67/1748–54) and appointed the redoubtable Mir Mannu as Governor of the Punjab. In November 1162/1784, Ahmad Shah Durrani returned and would not be denied. Mir Mannu received no assistance from Delhi, so Lahore submitted to the Afghans. To save his kingdom, Ahmad Shah (Moghul) ceded all territories west of the Indus River to Ahmad Shah Durrani, and agreed to send specified taxes to Qandahar, which, however, were seldom sent. Mir Mannu remained as Governor of the Punjab for Ahmad Shah Durrani. The Pushtun khans of Dera Ghazi Khan and Dera Ismail Khan, and the Brahui Khan of Kalat, swore fealty to the Durrani Shah as he passed through their regions on the way home.

Back at Qandahar, Ahmad Shah discovered an assassination plot against him and executed not only the plotters, but ten members of each tribal section involved, selected at random (G. Singh, 1959, 81). Almost every time the Shah departed Qandahar, plots to overthrow him surfaced. No Pushtun likes to be ruled by another, particularly someone from another tribe, subtribe, or section.

Ahmad Shah Durrani now gathered a new force of 25,000 men and moved against Herat, still in Persian hands and governed by Amir Khan, an Arab in the service of Shah Rukh (grandson of Nadir Shah Afshari), nominal ruler of Khurasan from 1161–1210/1748–95. Herat fell after a siege of about nine months, but not without bitter, bloody fighting.

The Afghan Shah marched to Mashhad, capital of Shah Rukh, who, incidentally, had been blinded by an earlier rival, now dead. General Mir Alam actually controlled Khurasan, but the Afghan army defeated and killed him outside Mashhad, which Ahmad Shah subsequently besieged. The 16-year-old Shah Rukh surrendered to Ahmad Shah, and impressed by his young, blind adversary, the Durrani Shah left him ruler of Khurasan and proceeded to Nishapur, where the Afghans suffered a major defeat, retreating to Herat (G. Singh, 1959, 91).

In the spring of 1164/1751, Ahmad Shah invaded Nishapur again, supported by heavy artillery, including a cannon, cast on the spot, which could fire a projectile weighing almost 500 pounds. At the first shot, the gun exploded, but the devastating results in Nishapur frightened the city fathers and they surrendered. The Afghans, still smarting from the humiliations of their past defeat, looted and destroyed the town, indiscriminately slaughtered much of the population, and carried off many others as slaves.

Returning to Herat via Mashhad, Ahmad Shah once again had to pacify Khurasan, for Shah Rukh opted for independence after the failure of the Afghans to take Nishapur in their earlier attempt. The resilient Shah Rukh remained ruler of Khurasan after the pacification, but agreed to consider his kingdom a part of the Durrani Empire, under the protection of Ahmad Shah (G. Singh, 1959, 98).

Ahmad Shah returned to Qandahar, but sent an army to bring the area north of the Hindu Kush under his imperialistic wing. The Turkoman of Asterabad, the Uzbak of Maimana, Balkh and Kunduz, the Tajik of Khanabad and Badakhshan, and the Hazara of Bamiyan accepted the suzerainty of the Durrani Shah.

For the third time Ahmad Shah Durrani invaded India in 1165/1751 because Mir Mannu, taking advantage of Ahmad Shah's Persian and northern adventures, reaffirmed his loyalty to Delhi and refused to send the requisite taxes to Qandahar. Ahmad Shah Durrani defeated his old enemy in battle, and once again proved magnanimous in victory. He retained Mir Mannu as governor of the Punjab, but decided not to invade the plains of northern India because of the approaching summer.

The Moghul Emperor, still Ahmad Shah, once again agreed to cede the Punjab to the Durrani Ahmad Shah, and to pay "50 lakhs of rupees again in lieu of their surplus revenue" (G. Singh, 1959, 123).

On the way back to Qandahar, Ahmad Shah Durrani dispatched an expedition to integrate Kashmir into the Empire.

Shortly after, in 1167/1753, Mir Mannu died, and the Moghul Emperor appointed his own 3-year-old son as governor of the Punjab, and Mir Mannu's 2-year-old son as deputy. An internal struggle for control of the Punjab occurred, and Mir Mannu's widow, Mughlani Begum, a strong-willed, oversexed woman, emerged as Regent. She ruled from a bedroom with "caprice, and created disorder and anarchy" (Majumdar et al., 1961, 535). *Farman* (royal decrees) from both Ahmad Shahs, one in Qandahar, one in Delhi, failed to smooth the troubled waters, and, feeling her little empire collapsing around her, Mughlani Begum attempted to marry off her daughter to a nephew, Ghazi-ud-Din, also Wazir (Chief Minister and real power) to the Moghul Emperor Ahmad Shah. Ghazi-ud-Din removed his licentious aunt from Lahore to Delhi, and made Mir Moman Khan, a local noble, governor of the Punjab.

Ahmad Shah Durrani could not allow this challenge to his authority in the Punjab to go unanswered. For the fourth time, he roared into India and without serious opposition retook Lahore and entered Delhi in January 1170/1757. Ahmad Shah Durrani permitted the new Moghul emperor, Alamgir II (1167–73/1754–60) to remain on the throne, as he acknowledged Afghan rights in Kashmir, Punjab, and Sind. The previous Moghul emperor, Ahmad Shah Bahadur, had been deposed in 1167/1754.

Before summer arrived, Ahmad Shah Durrani sent a force to subdue the obstreperous Mahrattas and Jats, and his army marched to the easternmost limits of his empire at Agra. Then he appointed his son, Timur, to Lahore, and arranged for Timur to marry a daughter of Alamgir II, who gave the Afghans Sirhind as part of the dowry. In addition, Ahmad Shah gave Timur the title of Shah. Cholera and heat drove Ahmad Shah Durrani back to his beloved Afghan area. Another in a series of warrior-poets who delightfully stud Afghan history, the Shah wrote of his beloved hills:

> Whatever countries I conquer in the world,
> I would never forget your beautiful gardens.
> When I remember the summits of your beautiful mountains
> I forget the greatness of the Delhi throne.
>
> (A. Habibi, 1968a, 60)

Timur, however, neither a warrior nor a poet, watched ineffectively as the Punjab and other north Indian provinces collapsed in a frenzy of revolt. The Sikhs rose and attacked Amritsar, but the great Afghan general, Jahan Khan, put them down. Adina Beg Khan (Governor of Jullundur Doab) called on the emerging Mahrattas for support in his attempts to drive out the Afghans. These martial Hindus responded and a Mahratta army under Raghunath Rao combined with the Sikhs to expel the Durrani from Lahore in April 1171/1758. Returning home to Maharashtra, Raghunath Rao left Adina Beg as Governor of Lahore.

Nasir Khan, a formally loyal Brahui chieftan, also declared his independence, and a Brahui-Baluch confederation centered in Kalat State threatened Ahmad Shah Durrani. The Durrani Shah dealt with this threat with more diplomacy than might, for he wished to save his strength for the Mahratta threat. He allowed Nasir Khan to rule locally, in return for the right to ask for troops to serve in time of wars, and Nasir Khan agreed not to harbor the enemies of Ahmad Shah Durrani. In the usual act of sex-linked diplomacy, Nasir Khan gave a cousin in marriage to Ahmad Shah, with Quetta and Mastung as wedding gifts.

For the fifth time, Ahmad Shah Durrani returned to India in October 1759 (note that all Ahmad Shah's invasions of India occurred in the fall, the off-agricultural season in Afghanistan and the cool season in India), and reconquered the Punjab. He followed the retreating Mahrattas and after many battles, on January 14, 1174/1761, destroyed their power at Panipat, traditional battleground for the control of Delhi and north India. The defeat of the Mahrattas made it easier for the British to become the paramount power in India. Therefore, by destroying the Mahratta force (assisted by French mercenaries), the Afghans inadvertently aided the penetration of the British toward the northwest and, more immediately, the rise of Sikh power in the Punjab. If Ahmad Shah Durrani's successors had been warrior-poets or diplomatic soldiers, the final chapters of the story may have been different, however.

Before leaving India in the spring of 1174/1761, Ahmad Shah Durrani tried to stabilize the shaky Moghul throne. The youngest son, Aurangzeb, succeeded the murdered Shah Alamgir II in 1173/1760 as Shah Jehan II (or according to Bosworth, 1967, 210, Shah Jehan III), but remained a puppet of those around him. With the support of Ahmad Shah Durrani, Shah Alam II (1173–1221/1760–1806, except for 1202/1788, when Bidar-bakht briefly deposed him) proclaimed himself Emperor. Ahmad Shah sent *farman* to most Indian provinces and to Robert Clive in Calcutta, requesting they recognize the rightful emperor, Shah Alam II, son of Alamgir II. Most, including the English, acceded.

A year of artificial peace graced Qandahar and the Punjab. Ahmad Shah Durrani had reached his peak with the defeat of the valiant Mahrattas. Then began a series of events which weakened the Durrani Empire even before the death of its founder. Kinsmen constantly threatened his throne in Qandahar, and the Sikhs at last rose in strength in the Punjab, so Ahmad Shah hurried down to India for the sixth time in February 1175/1762. He besieged Lahore, overwhelmed and massacred thousands of Sikh men, women, and children, and systematically desecrated and destroyed much of Amritsar, holy city of Sikhdom. The undaunted Sikhs, however, quickly recovered, and within two years established themselves as masters of the Punjab.

Ahmad Shah's seventh excursion into India began in October 1178/1764. He quickly reoccupied Lahore but failed to force a decisive battle. The wily Sikhs simply waited for the Afghans to return to Qandahar, and harassed them with guerrilla attacks all along the Punjab route of march.

The Durrani Shah made another attempt to subdue the Sikhs in 1180–81/1766–67, however, when he moved into India for the eighth time. He even reoccupied Lahore without opposition. The Sikhs dispersed and reverted to their effective methods of guerrilla warfare. Once again, Ahmad Shah vented his frustration on Amritsar, destroying the city and slaughtering many of its inhabitants. Even the Moghul Emperor and the Indian princes refused to pay Ahmad Shah the homage he felt due his august person. The encouragement of the British in Bengal may have stiffened the backbone of the Indians, and the oncoming summer heat convinced the Afghans to return to Qandahar, constantly harassed along the way by the Sikhs. Trouble at home and potential mutiny among his unpaid troops (a classic problem in Muslim military history) sped Ahmad Shah toward Qandahar.

The Sikhs reestablished themselves and remained masters of the Punjab until the British destroyed their power in 1266/1849. Slowly the Indian provinces of the Durrani Shah gained independence or were absorbed by the rampaging Sikhs. Twice more, the last time in 1183/1769, Ahmad Shah tried to recover the Punjab, and failed.

With cancer eating away his face,[14] Ahmad Shah's enemies ate away at his empire. Instability reigned in the northern provinces. Some regions had declared independence and the Amir of Bokhara claimed others. Qandahar and Bokhara did not fight, but agreed to accept the Amu Darya as the boundary dividing their interests. The Amir of Bokhara, Murad Beg, also presented a *kherqa* (cloak supposedly worn by the Prophet Mohammad) to Ahmad Shah. Delighted, the Durrani Shah had a special mosque constructed in Qandahar to house the garment. Both the mosque and *kherqa* still exist.

Mashhad, scene of earlier triumphs, now began to plague Ahmad

---

[14] G. Singh calls the malady an ulcer and states the Shah wore an artificial silver nose after his own had been eaten away (1959, 325).

Shah. The ambitious son of Shah Rukh, Nasrullah Mirza, wanted independence and sought assistance from other Persian groups, such as the Zards (ruling in Shiraz) and the Kurds. Ahmad Shah moved into Khurasan in 1183/1769–70 and besieged Mashhad. The outnumbered Afsharids capitulated. Ahmad Shah, always generous with blind Shah Rukh, permitted him to remain as ruler of Khurasan. Shah Rukh, to seal the bargain, gave Timur Shah a daughter to add to his harem.

Death approached and Ahmad Shah designated his second son, Timur Shah, as his heir. Ahmad Shah went to the Sulaiman Mountains, east of Qandahar, to die in peace and in agony: "Maggots developed there [in the upper part of the nose] and they dropped into his mouth when he ate or drank." (G. Singh, 1959, 326). Peace came in October 1186/1772.

Ahmad Shah rose to greatness in the tradition of Afghan warrior-poets, a charismatic leader who fused but left fission in his wake. He ruled wisely in consultation with the Saddozai Khans of the nine major sections of the Durrani tribe. Paramount chieftain among equals, he listened to his supra-council, his loose parliament.

The immediate successors of Ahmad Shah Baba (Baba = Father, i.e., Father of his nation) ruled neither wisely nor well. Timur Shah (1186–1207/1772–93), saddled with the many wives his father had procured for him, still managed to meet his first test of strength. His elder brother, Sulaiman Mirza, supported by his father-in-law, Shah Wali Khan, declared himself Shah at Qandahar. Timur returned from Herat, where his father had made him governor, and Sulaiman Mirza, deserted by his followers, scampered to India.

Timur refused to pardon Shah Wali Khan and ordered him executed, along with two of his sons, and act which began to alienate the inept Shah from the local Pushtun for they considered him more pro-Persian than pro-Afghan. Timur Shah reciprocated the feeling and moved his capital to Kabul in 1189/1775–76. He further alienated the Qandahari Pushtun groups by utilizing a force of Shi'i Qizilbash cavalry as his personal bodyguard and trouble-shooters throughout his trouble-shot empire.

Although calmer than what would follow, Timur Shah's twenty-year-reign proved less than tranquil. Several threats came from Pushtun tribes, systematically suppressed by the Qizilbash mercenaries. Revolts occured in Sind, Balkh, Sistan, Khurasan, and Kashmir, however, and all these regions wiggled outside Kabul's net of power between 1189/1775 and 1196/1781. A new Uzbak dynasty, the Mangit, founded in

Bokhara under the Amir Masum in 1199/1784, lasted until 1340/1921, and often competed with the Durrani for control of the north.

In 1791, a plot by the Mohmand and Afridi Pushtun almost succeeded. The khans hoped to place Iskander, Sulaiman's son, on the throne. The tribesmen penetrated the Bala Hissar (High Fort) at Peshawar, and Timur Shah hid in one of the towers while his Qizilbash mercenaries dispatched the conspirators. Two captured plotters, Mohammad Khan and Faizullah Khan, swore fealty to Timur Shah on the *Qor'an,* but the Amir immediately ordered them tortured to death, a breech of the Afghan code of honor for which Timur Shah is widely remembered in the tribal areas.

Timur Shah spent his final few years hovering from the north to the south, trying to plug up the dikes of rebellion, giving way at each instance until his death in 1793. He lies buried in an unfinished tomb at Bagh-i-Umumi, Kabul.

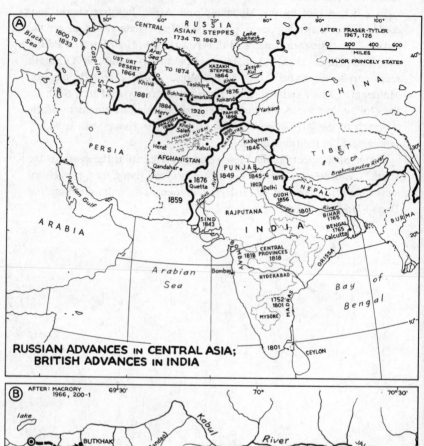

RUSSIAN ADVANCES IN CENTRAL ASIA; BRITISH ADVANCES IN INDIA

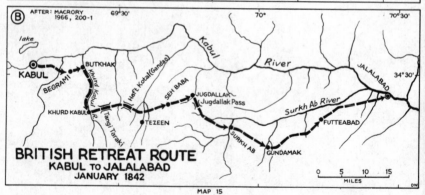

BRITISH RETREAT ROUTE
KABUL TO JALALABAD
JANUARY 1842

MAP 15

CHAPTER 17

The Age of European Imperialism

NINETEENTH CENTURY A.D.[1]

FROM the death of Timur Shah to the rise of the Abdur Rahman Khan (1880–1901), two themes dominated the Afghan scene: internal disorder and external invasions and pressures. The final dismemberment of the Durrani Empire occurred. Punjab, Sind, Kashmir, and most of Baluchistan were irrevocably lost, as the Mohammadzai (Barakzai) and Saddozai princes (both Durrani Pushtun) fought for regional control. Within each region, father fought son, brother fought brother, half brother fought half brother, uncle fought nephew in a never-ending round-robin of blood-letting and blindings. They contested for four major areas, Kabul, Qandahar, Herat, and the northern Uzbak Khanates, usually either independently or in alliances to contest each other for power.

For brief periods, the three important khanates of Kabul, Qandahar, and Herat were united. Many smaller independent or semi-independent Pushtun units rose and fell, among them, Ghazni, Farah, Jalalabad, Girishk, Kalat-i-Ghilzai. Non-Pushtun areas (such as the Hazarajat, Kafiristan, Badakhshan, Baluchistan) usually maintained their independent tribal integrity. During these unstable times, the Amir of Bokhara often made claims to territory south of the Amu Darya, or supported or assisted in revolts against Pushtun control.

The complexities of the internal disorders can best be described in chart form (Chart 21) and I leave it to those interested to seek out the details. An excellent modern Persian source covers these tribal machinations in great detail (Rishtya, 1958).

Civil wars, however, were but one factor which encouraged the external invasions. The simple geographic location of Afghanistan made it important for the control of the Indian subcontinent, defensively as well as offensively.

[1] Beginning with Chapter 17, dates are all A.D. unless otherwise specified by the usual A.H./A.D., because few dates in the nineteenth and twentieth centuries are controversial.

343

CHART 21
Political Fusion and Fission in Afghanistan 1747-1880

REIGN	KABUL	QANDAHAR	HERAT	NORTH AFGHANISTAN
Durrani Empire 1747-d.1772	*1747 end*: Taken by Ahmad Shah Durrani.	Capital 1747-75.		
			1750: Captured early in year. Khurasan reluctantly accepts paramountcy of Ahmad Shah.	Maimana through Badakhshan submitted by early 1750.
Timur Shah 1772-d.1793		*1772*: Opposed by eldest brother Sulaiman Mirza. Durrani-Ghilzai revolts.		
	1775-76: Capital transferred from Qandahar because of tribal opposition.	Sistan revolts from 1775.	Revolts throughout Khurasan from 1775.	
				Various revolts from 1780; treaty concluded with Bokhara recognized Afghan authority south of Oxus.
Zaman Shah 1793-1800	*1793*: Zaman Shah (5th son of Timur Shah) succeeds to throne assisted by Payinda Khan Barakzai of Qandahar	*1793*: Humayun (1st son of Timur Shah) revolts; occupied by Zaman Shah. Humayun later returns and is blinded by Zaman Shah.	*1793*: Shah Mahmud (second son of Timur Shah) retained as governor after initial revolt.	*1793*: Invasion of Balkh by Bokhara; peace terms concluded by Timur Shah reestablished. Virtually independent local khans compete for power.
			1795: Persians invade Khurasan.	
			1797: Shah Mahmud revolts; Zaman Shah occupies; Shah Mahmud flees to Persia; Qaisar (son of Zaman	

PESHAWAR	PUNJAB	KASHMIR	BALUCHISTAN: EASTERN PROVINCES (Dera Ghazi Khan, Dera Ismail Khan, Multan, Kalat, Bannu, et al.)	SIND
Taken end 1747.				
	1748: Lahore 1st occupied; constant revolts; 8 campaigns; finally lost to Sikhs in 1767.		Acquired 1748; uneasy suzerainty; opposed by Mahrattas, Sikhs, Baluchi and Brahui.	*1748*: Acknowledged Ahmad Shah.
		Acquired 1752.		
	1773: Sikhs control from Lahore to Attock.		*1772*: Sikhs gain Multan; regained by Timur, 1779.	
1781, 1791: Mohmand revolts.		Revolts.	Revolts throughout.	Revolts; virtual independence under Talpurs by 1786.
Shah Shuja (full brother of Zaman Shah) governor.		*1793*: Renewed revolts, suppressed.	*1793/94*: Khan of Kalat gives refuge to Humayun; revolts in Bahawalpur and Baluchistan; virtual independence from Afghans throughout.	
	1795: 1st expedition by Zaman Shah.			
	1797: Zaman Shah takes Lahore.			*1797*: Zaman Shah exacts tribute by force; hurries to Herat (in revolt).

CHART 21 (*continued*)

REIGN	KABUL	QANDAHAR	HERAT	NORTH AFGHANISTAN
			Shah) becomes governor.	
	1799: Qizilbash plot against Zaman Shah discovered.	*1799*: Execution of Payinda Khan Barakzai by Zaman Shah; Fateh Khan (son of Payinda Khan) joins Shah Mahmud in Persia.	*1799*: Shah Mahmud with Persian army invests unsuccessfully, leaves for Bokhara, and then Persia.	
Shah Mahmud 1800-1803	*1800*: Zaman Shah imprisoned, blinded; Shah Mahmud succeeds to throne.	*1800*: Taken by Shah Mahmud; Zaman Shah moves on, defeated; Shah Mahmud moves on Kabul.	*1800*: Fateh Khan joins Shah Mahmud in Persia; advance on Qandahar via Sistan.	
	1801/02: Ghilzai revolts at Kabul and Ghazni; Shah Shuja attempt to take fails in 1801.	*1801*: Ghilzai revolts.		Holds out for Zaman Shah.
	1803, June: Sunni-Shi'a riots; Shah Shuja invited in by anti-Mahmud forces. July: Fateh Khan defeated, Mahmud imprisoned.	*1802*: Shah Shuja attempts to take; defeated by Fateh Khan.		Revolt in Balkh in 1802.
Shah Shuja 1803-1809	*1803, June*: Shah Shuja succeeds to throne.	*1803*: Taken by Shah Shuja; Qaisar (son of Zaman Shah) appointed Governor.	*1803*: Firozuddin (full brother of Shah Mahmud, gov.; Kamran (son of Shah Mahmud) takes refuge here.	Local khans continue to compete for power among themselves throughout.
	1804: In hands of insurgents for one month; Shah Shuja regains; defeats Qaisar (moving up from Qandahar).	*1804*: Fateh Khan incites Qaisar to move on Kabul; Kamran (from Herat) takes; retaken by Qaisar; Shah Shuja occupies, reinstates Qaisar as gov. Qaisar rejoined by Fateh Khan,	*1804*: Fateh Khan incites Firozuddin to move on Qandahar. Firozuddin attacks but retires back to Herat.	

PESHAWAR	PUNJAB	KASHMIR	BALUCHISTAN: EASTERN PROVINCES (Dera Ghazi Khan, et al.)	SIND
	1798: Zaman Shah retakes Lahore; appoints Ranjit Singh gov.; returns to Herat (threatened by Persia and Shah Mahmud).			
1801: Shah Shuja declares himself Shah, marches on Kabul, defeated Sept., 1801. *1802, Mar.*: Attempt by Shah Shuja to take fails.	*1801*: Zaman Shah granted refuge by British in Ludhiana. Ranjit Singh proclaimed Maharaja; Punjab lost to Afghans.			

CHART 21 (*continued*)

REIGN	KABUL	QANDAHAR	HERAT	NORTH AFGHANISTAN
		who fails to incite Qaisar to march again on Kabul. Fateh Khan then joins Kamren. They occupy Qandahar and move on Kabul.		
	1805: Shah Shuja faces Kamran at Ghazni; Persian attack on Herat causes withdrawal of Kamran to Qandahar.		*1805*: Persian attack on Herat fails.	
		1805: Shah Shuja occupies.		
	1807/08: Plot to raise Abbas (son of Timur Shah) to throne fails; Shah Mahmud escapes; Qaisar proclaimed ruler, marches on Peshawar.			
	1808: Shah Shuja regains; moves on Qandahar.	*1808*: Shah Mahmud occupies. Shah Shuja reoccupies, moves on Herat.	*1808*: Shah Shuja confirms Firozuddin as gov.	
	1809: Shah Mahmud occupies; moves toward Peshawar.	*1809*: Taken by Shah Mahmud; Kamran appointed gov.; Mahmud moves on Kabul.		
Shah Mahmud 1809-18	*1809*: Shah Mahmud succeeds to throne; Fateh Khan appointed as Wazir and is actual power.			

PESHAWAR	PUNJAB	KASHMIR	BALUCHISTAN: EASTERN PROVINCES (Dera Ghazi Khan, et al.)	SIND
1805, Apr.: Shah Shuja arrives from Sind, leaves for Kashmir.		*1805*: Revolts by Abdullah Khan; put down by Shah Shuja.		Shah Shuja collects unpaid tribute-taxes.
	1806: Treaty of Lahore between British and Ranjit Singh.			
				1807/08: Expedition to Sind cut short by revolt of Qaisar and occupation of Peshawar.
1808: Qaisar ocpies; Shah Shuja reoccupies; moves on Kabul.				
1809, Jun.: Shah Shuja signs treaty with Elphinstone; British Mission in Peshawar since Feb. Shah Shuja moves toward Kabul; defeated at Nimla on 29th; flees to hills.	*1809*: Anglo-Sikh Treaty of Amritsar restricted Ranjit Singh to west of the Sutlej River.			*1809*: British treaty with Sind; Persian-French envoys also active against Afghan interests.
Kamran occupies; Azim Khan (full brother of Fateh Khan) appointed gov. *1810/12*: Shah Shuja gains and loses city several times; imprisoned and sent to Kashmir.		*1809*: Shah Shuja attempts to take; fails.		

CHART 21 (*continued*)

REIGN	KABUL	QANDAHAR	HERAT	NORTH AFGHANISTAN
			1817: Persia threatens; Fateh Khan takes; Dost Mohd. flees to Kashmir after harem scandal.	1817: Murad Beg becomes paramount Uz-bak Khan of north on death of Khilich Ali Beg; north inde-pendent of Kabul. Balkh taken by Bokhara.
	1818: Dost Mohd. occupies; sets up Sultan Ali (son of Timur Shah) ignoring Ayub in Pesha-war (now puppet of Azim Khan). Mahmud and Kamran ap-proach from Qandahar, sud-denly retire, kill Fateh Khan near Ghazni.	Occupied by Purdil Khan (brother of Fateh Khan) while Mahmud and Kamran advance on Kabul.	1818, May: War with Persia; in-decisive victory; Kamran blinds Fateh Khan. · 1818, end: Mah-mud and Kamran move on Kabul. Mahmud and Kamran return; control Herat.	
Barakzai Sardars 1819-26 *Civil War*	Azim Khan de-poses Sultan Ali, installs Ayub; Azim, as domi-nant Sardar ap-portions terri-tory: Kabul to Azim Khan; Ghazni to Dost Mohd. (brother of Fatch Khan also.)	Qandahar Sar-dars (brothers of Fateh Khan, all full brothers) in control; Sherdil as chief.	Sherdil occupies for short period; retaken by Shah Mahmud; Shah Mahmud deposed by Kamran. Mah-mud dies of cholera in 1829.	

PESHAWAR	PUNJAB	KASHMIR	BALUCHISTAN: EASTERN PROVINCES (Dera Ghazi Khan, et al.)	SIND
1813: Attock Fort surrendered to Sikhs by Afghans.	*1813*: Shah Shuja virtual prisoner at Lahore.	*1813*: Fateh Khan, allied with Ranjit Singh, defeats gov.; Shah Shuja returns with Ranjit Singh to Lahore; Azim Khan appointed gov. Kashmir.		
		1814: Sikhs attempt to take; fail.		
	1816: Shah Shuja joins Zaman Shah at Ludhiana; becomes British pensioner in 1818.	*1815*: Shah Shuja attempts to take; fails.		
		1817: Dost Mohd. held prisoner by Azim Khan on order of Fateh Khan following harem incident in Herat.		
1818: Dost Mohd. occupies; proclaims Ayub (son of Timur Shah) as ruler of Kabul; moves on Kabul. Azim Khan invites Shah Shuja to take throne; Shah Shuja deposes Ayub, fights with Azim and is defeated; Azim Khan moves on Kabul with Ayub.		*1818*: Dost Mohd. released after blinding of Fateh Khan; moves on Peshawar.	*1818*: Multan annexed to Punjay by Ranjit Singh.	
Peshawar Sardars (brothers of Feteh Khan, all full brothers) in control; Yar Mohd. and Sultan Mohd. as chiefs.		*1819, Jul.*: Annexed by Ranjit Singh; permanently lost to Afghans.	Sikh power extended to Dera Ghazi Khan, Dera Ismail Khan, Baluchistan, by 1823 all permanently lost to Afghans.	Shan Shuja attempts to raise army to regain throne; dispersed by arrival of Azim Khan.

CHART 21 (*continued*)

REIGN	KABUL	QANDAHAR	HERAT	NORTH AFGHANISTAN
	1823: Azim Khan dies; Ayub deposed; Habibullah (son of Azim Khan,) raised to throne, soon deposed. Dost Mohd. besieges; Sherdill of Qandahar emerges as dominant Barakzai and reapportions territories: Kabul to Sultan Mohd. (Peshawar Sardar); Kohistan to Dost Mohd.			
	1826: Dost Mohd. gains control; Sultan Mohd. returns to Peshawar.	*1826*: Sherdil dies; Purdil succeeds as chief Qandahari Sardar.		
Dost Mohd. 1826-39	Dost Mohd. continues to put down numerous revolts and foil intrigues by his brothers.			
			1832: Persia moves into Khurasan.	
			1833: Persians then threaten Herat; retire on death of Persian Shah.	
		1834, July: Shah Shuja defeated with aid of Dost Mohd.		
	1836: Dost Mohd. takes title of Amir.			
	1837, Sept.: Burnes Mission arrives.		*1837, Nov.- 1838, Sept.*: Persians besiege.	

PESHAWAR	PUNJAB	KASHMIR	BALUCHISTAN: EASTERN PROVINCES (Dera Ghazi Khan, et al.)	SIND
1823: Ranjit Singh occupies; retains Peshawar Sardars to govern.				
				Rhamdil (of Qandahar Sardars) governs; Mirs revolt; Sind lost permanently by Afghans.
1828: Local revolts put down by Sultan Mohd. with aid of Sikhs.				
1832: Sikhs occupy; Sultan Mohd. kept on as puppet gov.				1832: British force Mirs to sign treaty guaranteeing transit rights.
1834, May: Formally annexed by Sikhs.	1833, Mar.: Treaty of Assistance between Shah Shuja and Ranjit Singh; Shah Shuja marches on Qandahar.			1833/4: Shah Shuja opposed by Mirs: he defeats them in Jan., 1834, and proceeds to Qandahar.
1835, Spring: Dost Mohd's attempt to gain fails				
1836, Apr.: 2nd attempt by Dost Mohd. to gain fails				

CHART 21 (*continued*)

REIGN	KABUL	QANDAHAR	HERAT	NORTH AFGHANISTAN
		1838, Dec.: Shah Shuja marches on.		
		1839, Apr.: Shah Shuja arrives; moves on Kabul in July.		
Shah Shuja 1839-d.1842	*1839, Aug.*: Shah Shuja occupies; succeeds to throne.	Fath Jang (son of Shah Shuja) governs 1839/40; 1840/42: Crown Prince Mohd. Timur (son of Shah Shuja) governs.		Dost Mohd. flees to Bamiyan; attempts to raise army in Khulm fail; leaves for Bokhara.
	1840: Tribal revolts throughout; Nov.: Dost Mohd. battles with British in Kohistan then unexpectedly surrenders and is exiled to India.	*1840*: Tribal revolts.		*1840, Summer:* Dost Mohd. returns; tribal unrest throughout; on death of Murad Beg of Kunduz c. 1840, power returns to Khulm.
	1841, Sept.: Major plot against British begins.	British garrisons under sporadic attack.		
	1842, Jan.: British retreat; Apr.: Shah Shuja murdered; civil war; Fath Jang officially proclaimed Amir. Sept.: British return; Oct.: evacuate city; Fath Jang leaves with British; Shahpur (son of Shah Shuja) Amir until he fled to Peshawar end 1842; Akbar Khan (son of Dost Mohd.) in control awaiting return of father.	British relieved in May, evacuate city in Aug. leaving Safdar Jang (son of Shah Shuja) in charge; Safdar Jang forced out by returning Qandahar Sardars led by Kohandil.	*1842, Mar.*: Kamran suffocated by Wazir Yar Mohd. Alikozai who assumes absolute control.	
Dost Mohd. 1843-d.1863	*1843, Apr.*: Dost Mohd. returns;	Armed opposition to Dost		Local khans continue to jockey

PESHAWAR	PUNJAB	KASHMIR	BALUCHISTAN: EASTERN PROVINCES (Dera Ghazi Khan, et al.)	SIND
	1838, Jun.: Tripartite Treaty signed (Shah Shuja-Ranjit Singh-British); Oct.: Simla Manifesto announces war against Afghanistan.		*1838*: Bannu ceded to Ranjit Singh in Tripartite Treaty; Nov.. Army of the Indus arrives at Ferozpore; departs for Qandahar in Dec.	
	1839, Summer: Ranjit Singh dies.		*1839, Nov.*: British forcefully annex Kalat and other territories in area to Shah Shuja; independence restated later.	
Tribal revolts in Khyber region.				
				1843, Apr.: British annex Sind.

CHART 21 (*continued*)

REIGN	KABUL	QANDAHAR	HERAT	NORTH AFGHANISTAN
	authority extended to Ghazni, Jalalabad to Hazarajat. Sporadic uprisings successfully dealt with.	Mohd. by Qandahari put down by Akbar Khan.		for power; Dost Mohd. extends control only to Bamiyan and Mazar.
	1845: Akbar Khan dies.			
		1846: Farah fought over by Herat and Qandahar.		*1846*: Wazir Yar Mohd. of Herat occupies Maimana; retreats when Farah threatened.
				1849: all of north, except Badakhshan, accepts authority of Kabul; sporadic revolts in 1850.
		1851: Kohandil dies.	*1851, Jun.*: Yar Mohd. dies.	
		1855: Annexed by Dost Mohammad.	*1856, Oct.*: Persians besiege.	
			1857, Mar.: Treaty of Paris; Persians withdraw.	*1859*: Badakhshan recognizes authority of Kabul.
			1863, May: Annexed by Dost Mohd.; Jun.: Dost Mohd. dies; Sher Ali proclaims himself Amir.	
Sher Ali 1863-66	Opposing brothers attempt to gain control; Sher Ali victorious.	Mohd. Amin (full brother of Sher Ali) governs in opposition to Sher Ali	Mohd. Yaqub (son of Sher Ali) gov.	Mohd. Afzal (half brother of Sher Ali) governs in opposition to Sher Ali; defeated by Sher Ali; imprisoned.
		1865: occupied by Sher Ali.		
	1866: Sher Ali defeated by Ab-			

PESHAWAR	PUNJAB	KASHMIR	BALUCHISTAN: EASTERN PROVINCES (Dera Ghazi Khan, et al.)	SIND
	1845, Dec.-1846, Feb.: 1st Anglo-Sikh War; British occupy Lahore. *1846, Dec.*: Lahore ruled by Sikh Durbar under British Resident. *1849, Mar.*: Annexed to British India after 2nd Anglo-Sikh War.	*1846 Mar.*: Ceded to British by Sikhs; "sold" to Maharaja Gulab Singh, Mar. 16.	*1847, Nov.*: Bannu occupied by Sikh army led by British. *1849, Jan.*: British take Multan.	
1855, Mar.: Anglo-Afghan Treaty.				
1857, Jan.: Anglo-Afghan Treaty of Friendship.	*1857, May-1858*: War for Indian Independence (Indian Mutiny).		*1859*: Baluchistan annexed to British India.	

CHART 21 (*continued*)

REIGN	KABUL	QANDAHAR	HERAT	NORTH AFGHANISTAN
	dur Rahman (son of Mohd. Afzal); Mohd. Afzal released from prison.			
Mohd. Afzal 1866-d.1867	*1866, May:* Mohd. Afzal occupies; proclaimed Amir.		Sher Ali joins Mohd. Yaqub; their move on Mazar repulsed.	Numerous khans join Sher Ali; repulsed by Abdur Rahman.
	1867, Oct.: Mohd. Afzal dies.	*1867, Jan.:* Mohd. Afzal occupies.		
Mohd. Azam 1867-68	*1867, Oct.:* Mohd. Azam (full brother Mohd. Afzal) succeeds to throne.			
	1868: Mohd. Azam flees to Persia.	*1868, Apr.:* Occupied by Mohd. Yaqub from Herat; moves on Kabul with Sher Ali.		*1868, end:* Abdur Rahman defeated by Mohd. Yaqub at Bamiyan; flees to Bokharaı
Sher Ali 1868-d.1879	*1868, Sept.:* Occupied by Sher Ali.			
	1870: Mohd. Yaqub rebels; flees to Persia.		*1871, May:* Mohd. Yaqub occupies; confirmed as gov. by Sher Ali.	
	1874: Mohd. Yaqub imprisoned.		*1874:* Rebellion by Mohd. Ayub (full brother of Mohd. Yaqub) fails; Ayub flees to Persia	
	1878, Nov.: British invade Afghan territory; Dec.: Mohd. Yaqub released and appointed Regent; Sher Ali leaves for Mazar.	*1879, Jan.:* British occupy.		*1879, Feb.:* Sher Ali dies in Mazar.

PESHAWAR	PUNJAB	KASHMIR	BALUCHISTAN: EASTERN PROVINCES (Dera Ghazi Khan, e. al.)	SIND
	·1869, Mar.: Sher Ali attends Ambala Conference with British.			
	1873: Simla Conference attended by by Afghan and British delegations.			
1877, Jan.: Anglo-Afghan conference at Peshawar.				

CHART 21 (*continued*)

REIGN	KABUL	QANDAHAR	HERAT	NORTH AFGHANISTAN
Mohd. Yaqub 1879	*1879, Feb.:* Mohd. Yaqub succeeds to throne; May: Treaty of Gandamak with British; July: British Resident arrives with Mission; Sept.: British Mission killed; Oct.: British occupy; Yaqub abdicates; Gen. Roberts assumes control; Dec.: General tribal uprisings.		*1879*: Mohd. Ayub returns from exile in Persia, assumes control.	
			1880 Jun.: Mohd. Ayub moves on Qandahar.	*1880, Feb./Mar.:* Abdur Rahman returns; gathers troops around Kunduz; Maimana holds out.
Abdur Rahman 1880-d.1901	*1880, July:* Abdur Rahman proclaimed Amir; Aug.: British withdraw.	*1880, July:* Mohd. Ayub defeats British at Maiwand; Sept.: Gen. Roberts defeats Mohd. Ayub at Qandahar.		
		1881, Apr.: British forces withdraw; July: Mohd. Ayub moves on; Ayub defeated by Abdur Rahman and flees to Persia.	*1881, Sept.:* Occupied for Abdur Rahman by Abdus Quddus.	Abdus Quddus subdues north for Abdur Rahman; Maimana last to submit in Apr., 1884.

PESHAWAR	PUNJAB	KASHMIR	BALUCHISTAN: EASTERN PROVINCES (Dera Ghazi Khan, et al.)	SIND
1879: Kurram, Khyber, Michni placed under British protection by Treaty of Gandamak; permanently lost to Afghans.			*1879*: Pishin, Sibi placed under British protection by Treaty of Gandamak; permanently lost to Afghans.	

The Encroachment Begins*

The Napoleonic invasion of Egypt in 1798 really begins our story. Bonaparte, a charismatic leader in his own right, dreamed of restoring lost French prestige in India, his ultimate goal. The Muslim world, having reached several regional climaxes (Afghanistan, Ghaznavid; India, Moghul; Central Asia, Timurid; Persia, Safavid; Arab Near East, Umayyad; Turkey, Ottoman), now slowly erroded. Fission penetrated Islam and became the major pattern. The economic and intellectual growth, stunted by external forces which destroyed the hydraulic bases (Wittfogel, 1957) of the societies, virtually stagnated. Internal intellectual schisms proved debilitating. Lacking natural resources, technology in the Muslim world lagged behind that of the more affluent West. No empires last forever, no nation has *the* answer, so the pendulum had swung from the East to the West, where today it hangs in the balance. The beginning was the end. All roads led to India.

Sustained European contact came to India with the age of the sail and exploration, a result of the collapse of the overland trade routes. The English, dominant Europeans in India by the end of the eighteenth century, entered its age of Asian imperialism on December 31, 1600, when Queen Elizabeth I granted a "Charter to the Governor and Company of Merchants of London Trading in the East Indies," the East India Company. Previously, Portugal virtually controlled European trade with the East, but in 1580 Spain occupied Portugal, which then lost its monopoly to the Dutch and English. In 1664, however, the French East India Company was chartered, providing further competition for both the Dutch and English, especially the English. The last half of the seventeenth century saw the greatest period of the Moghul Empire under the Emperor Aurangzeb. Internal decay had long been at work, however, and after Aurangzeb, the empire rapidly fell apart. Under the great Moghul Emperor, European traders had been kept under close control. Their "factories" (trading posts) now sought and easily obtained greater power, and, although essentially an economic enterprise, the East India Company built the mighty British Indian Empire by force of arms.

By the middle of the eighteenth century, English commercial competition with other European countries (France, Portugal, Holland, and Denmark) developed into intense political competition. The trading companies of various European nations allied themselves with the dis-

* Map 15A.

362

united Indian princes, who constantly warred among themselves, and, as a consequence of the new alliances, extensions of European wars were fought thousands of miles from the seats of power. The same thing occurred in North America at the same time. The successive rulers of the now impotent Moghul Empire watched hopelessly as foreigners and their Indian allies split the subcontinent into spheres of economic and political influence.

Gradually the British, under the brilliant leadership of Robert Clive, gained control of all important areas and destroyed French power in India. Under the 1763 Treaty of Paris, the French and Portuguese, however, maintained a few enclaves, which lasted until after the 1947 partition of India. The Indians violently seized the last Portuguese territory in 1959 (L. Dupree, *AUFS Reports,* LD-3-1962; see Appendix H).

The rise of Napoleon brought about a renewed interest in Asia and India in Europe. At first successful in Egypt and Syria, Napoleon sent a mission to the Qajar Shah of Persia, Fath Ali Shah (1797–1834). M. Jaubert, Napoleon's chief envoy, tried to convince the Qajars to seize Georgia from Russia. The French sent a military mission to train the Persian army. In 1807, however, the Russians defeated the Persians at Arpatch. Under the Treaty of Fars, Qajar Persia lost more territory to Tsarist Russia, and lost faith in the French.

Great Britain responded in two ways. The British resident in Basra offered the Qajars 120,000 rupees and several diamonds from George III to fight the Russians. The British also sent Mountstuart Elphinstone to Peshawar, winter capital of Shah Shuja, the ruler in Kabul and son of Timur Shah. Shah Shuja signed a treaty of mutual defense with the British Mission in 1809.

The first threat collapsed at Waterloo in 1815, and Napoleon took his dreams into exile with him to St. Helena, where he died in 1821, still mentally commanding his legions. Even before the end of the First Empire of Napoleon I, however, the Tsarist Russians, former allies of the English against Napoleon, replaced the French as the major imperialist rivals of the British in Asia.

Since the time of Peter the Great (1682–1725), Russia coveted warm water ports to the south, either on the Dardanelles, in the Persian Gulf, or in the Indian Ocean. The Russian drive to the east began in 1734 with movements in Kazakhstan, and ended only when the great Asian empire of Russia reached the shores of the Pacific, and went on to Alaska and California.[2]

[2] Many similarities can be cited between the Russian drive to the East and

With the Treaty of Gulistan (1813), after the disastrous defeat of the Persian army at Aslanduz, Persia relinquished almost all its territorial claims in the Caucasus and agreed to withdraw its warships from the Caspian Sea. To contain Russia, the British signed a mutual defense agreement with the Qajar Shah in 1814, promising military and financial (£5 million) aid if a foreign power attacked Persia.

A Persian force, which included British advisers and was commanded by Abbas Mirza Qajar, the Crown Prince, tried to recover part of the Caucasus in 1826, but suffered another disastrous defeat at Canja. The Qajar army retreated. The British, busy elsewhere (particularly India), never fulfilled their formalized commitments to Persia (Singhal, 1963, 3; Lobanov-Rostovsky, 1951, 110).

The Treaty of Turkmanchai (1828) gave the Russians full control of the south Caucasus. The Persians also paid an indemnity equal to $15 million, and granted extraterritorial rights and commercial advantages to the Russians (Lobanov-Rostovsky, 1951, 110–11). The Qajars never recovered as a power in the Middle East, and "the moral ascendency achieved by their [Russian] victories and the supineness of British policy increased Russian influence at Tehran." (Fraser-Tytler, 1967, 81).

---

the American drive to the West (Lobanov-Rostovsky, 1951, 10). Both conquered non-literate hunters, nomads, or primitive agriculturalists. No match for the superior technology (particularly the firepower) of the Russians and Americans. the "primitives" of North America and Siberia fell rapidly.

The Russian *kreposts* look surprisingly like the log forts of the old American west, and the Cossack adventurers, who led the imperialist parade, resemble the American trapper, pioneer, and cowboy. Colonists followed the explorers and exploiters, but accidents of history permitted the Americans to develop their conquered lands more rapidly than the Russians, now just beginning to utilize their valuable and extensive Siberian resources on a large scale.

The Americans, although they fought a bloody civil war, had no real competitors in imperialism in the western hemisphere after the American Revolution. The Tsarist Russians, however, had to deal with the Ottoman Turks, the French, and the British, and later with an imperialistic, united Germany.

The Russians reached the Pacific in the late eighteenth century, but the Americans completed their drive to the west after the Mexican War of 1846–48, when the American government annexed Mexican territories in California and New Mexico. (The Russians had abandoned their settlements in California by 1844.)

In 1869, the Russians dumped their North American colony, Alaska, on the U.S. for $7,200,000, called "Seward's Folly" at the time. American sailors and seal-hunters established fishing posts in Siberia in the mid-nineteenth century, and asked the U.S. to claim this area as American territory. The agreement after "Seward's Folly" ended these claims, but if the United States had occupied parts of Siberia, the effect on history could have been staggering.

Civil Wars and Alarums: 1793–1839

Meanwhile, in the Afghan region, Zaman Shah, Timur Shah's fifth son, succeeded to the throne of the tottering Durrani Empire when his father died in 1793. Revolts sporadically fragmented the empire, but parts of Punjab and Sind remained uneasily under Kabul's control. Contemporary accounts (Majumdar, et al., 1961, 748–49), however, indicate that the British took Zaman Shah more seriously than do most modern researches. The British maintained a sizeable army in Oudh under Sir J. Craig to thwart an anticipated Afghan thrust toward India. Revolts at home and Persian pressure on Herat forced Zaman Shah to return from Lahore (much to the relief of the British), where he had moved in 1798, hoping to follow in the footsteps of his predecessors to Delhi.

The Barakzai Qandahari Sardars (Diagram 6; Chart 22), under Payinda Khan Mohammadzai alternately supported and threatened Zaman Shah. Without Payinda Khan's initial support, Zaman Shah would never have become ruler of Kabul.

Suspicious of Payinda Khan and under the influence of a rival Popalzai, Wafadar Khan, Zaman Shah had the Mohammadzai chief and other tribal leaders executed. Fateh Khan, Payinda's eldest son, then joined Zaman's chief rival and brother, Shah Mahmud, Governor of Herat, to overthrow and blind Zaman Shah. Oedipus-like, the deposed Shah wandered friendless through Central Asia and ultimately to India. The sympathetic British, once fearful of the might of Zaman Shah, pitied him in his blindness and pensioned him to die in Ludhiana.

The fratricidal in-fighting now began in bloody earnest. The Abdali-Ghilzai doings in the eighteenth century served only as a preliminary to the nineteenth century, when the Abdali (now Durrani) Sardars scrambled over one another for power like American ward politicians. (See Chart 21, which graphically illustrates the nineteenth-century game of dynastic musical chairs. Kin relationships can be found on Chart 22.)

The capable Barakzai Sardars, led by Fateh Khan, found Shah Mahmud, Zaman's brother and successor (1800–03), a tractable puppet. Another son of Timur Shah and full brother of Zaman Shah, Shuja Mirza, seized the throne in 1803, and ruled uneasily until 1809. A few weeks after he and Elphinstone signed a treaty of mutual assistance against the French and the Persians, the Barakzai placed Shah Mahmud on the throne for the second time (1809–18). Shah Shuja first went to Ala Mohammad Khan, Governor of Kashmir, who refused to help, but tried to pry the Koh-i-Nur diamond from the deposed Afghan. Shah

CHART 22

Genealogy of the 19th-Century A.D. Struggle for Power

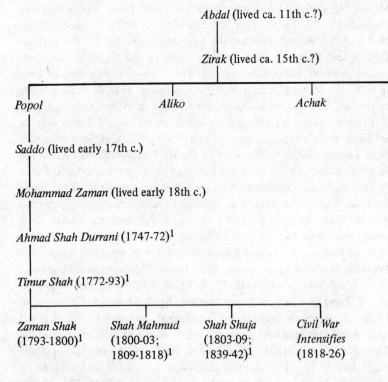

Abdal (lived ca. 11th c.?)

Zirak (lived ca. 15th c.?)

Popol	*Aliko*	*Achak*

Saddo (lived early 17th c.)

Mohammad Zaman (lived early 18th c.)

Ahmad Shah Durrani (1747-72)[1]

Timur Shah (1772-93)[1]

Zaman Shah (1793-1800)[1]	*Shah Mahmud* (1800-03; 1809-1818)[1]	*Shah Shuja* (1803-09; 1839-42)[1]	*Civil War Intensifies* (1818-26)

[1] Unless otherwise specified, dates in parenthesis refer to period an amir or king ruled in Kabul.

[2] The brothers of Rhamdel Khan (Kohendel Khan, Purdel Khan, Sherdel Khan, Mehrdel Khan) actively participated in the struggle for power.

[3] Sultan Mohammad was one of five brothers holding Peshawar who actively participated in the struggle for power.

[4] Dost Mohammad Khan, youngest brother involved in the struggle for Kabul, had a Qizilbash mother. He was, however, the favorite of Wazir Fateh Khan, whose murder brought the Barakzai into the field against the Saddozai.

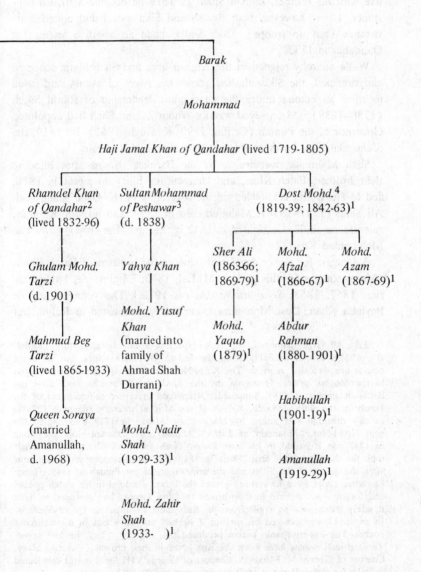

Barak

Mohammad

Haji Jamal Khan of Qandahar (lived 1719-1805)

*Rhamdel Khan
of Qandahar*[2]
(lived 1832-96)

*Sultan Mohammad
of Peshawar*[3]
(d. 1838)

Dost Mohd.[4]
(1819-39; 1842-63)[1]

*Ghulam Mohd.
Tarzi*
(d. 1901)

Yahya Khan

Sher Ali
(1863-66;
1869-79)[1]

*Mohd.
Afzal*
(1866-67)[1]

*Mohd.
Azam*
(1867-69)[1]

*Mohd. Yusuf
Khan*
(married into
family of
Ahmad Shah
Durrani)

*Mahmud Beg
Tarzi*
(lived 1865-1933)

*Mohd.
Yaqub*
(1879)[1]

*Abdur
Rahman*
(1880-1901)[1]

Queen Soraya
(married
Amanullah,
d. 1968)

Habibullah
(1901-19)[1]

*Mohd. Nadir
Shah*
(1929-33)[1]

Amanullah
(1919-29)[1]

*Mohd. Zahir
Shah*
(1933-   )[1]

Shuja fled in 1813 to Lahore, and Ranjit Singh agreed to assist him. In the bargain, Shah Shuja surrendered the Koh-i-Nur to Ranjit.[3] The Sikh emperor, a master of intrigue as well as a great warrior, procrastinated, and the humiliated Shah Shuja traveled to Ludhiana in 1816 to live with his brother, Zaman Shah. In 1818 he became a British pensioner. Later, however, with British and Sikh moral and material assistance (but no troops), Shah Shuja made an abortive attempt at Qandahar in 1833.

While anarchy reigned in the Afghan area and Shah Shuja schemed and dreamed, the Sikhs flashed across the pages of history and fused together an empire under the charismatic leadership of Ranjit Singh (1780–1839), the one-eyed warrior whom Zaman Shah had appointed Governor of the Punjab (Griffin, 1890; K. Singh, 1962). By 1819, the Sikhs controlled northern Punjab, Peshawar, and Kashmir.

Shah Mahmud, overthrown by the Barakzai Khans after blinding their brother, Fateh Khan, and later cutting him into pieces in 1818, fled to Herat and acknowledged the suzerainty of the Qajar Shah, Fath Ali Shah (1797–1834). Mahmud died in 1829, and his son, Kamran, ruled Herat until assassinated in 1842 by his able, but cruel, *wazir,* Yar Mohammad Khan.

A struggle for power developed between the brothers of Fateh Khan. (Major sources for this period: M. Lal, 1846; Elphinstone, 1815; Ferrier, 1857, 1858; *Seraj-uttawarikh,* ca. 1912.) The youngest son of Payinda Khan, Dost Mohammad, eventually dominated in Kabul, but

---

[3] Like all large diamonds, the Koh-i-Nur has a fascinating history (Mohd. Ali, 1961). It was probably from the Indian Golconda mines, but its exact origins are shrouded in myth. The Koh-i-Nur first becomes real when presented to the Moghul prince, Humayun, by the survivors of Ibrahim Lodi after the Battle of Panipat (1526). Supposedly, Humayun prevented mistreatment of the family of the slain monarch. A part of the Moghul treasury, the huge (279⁹⁄₁₆ carats) diamond was seized by Nadir Shah Afshar in 1739 who named the gem Koh-i-Nur, "Mountain of Light." Ahmad Shah Durrani stole the stone in 1747 and it passed to his sons Zaman Shah and Shah Shuja. Ranjit Singh took the diamond from Shah Shuja in 1813. The British appropriated the gem after the defeat of the Sikhs and the annexation of the Punjab in 1849. Henry Lawrence (later Lord Lawrence) placed the boxed diamond in his watch pocket and forgot about it until later informed that the Viceroy had arranged to have it safely transported as a gift from the East India Company to Queen Victoria. In panic, Lawrence asked his servant if he had noticed a box in his waistcoat pocket. The imperturbable Indian produced the piece of "glass" he had saved. Three British queens have worn the Koh-i-Nur in their crowns (Victoria; Mary, Consort of George V; Elizabeth, Consort of George VI), for it is still considered unlucky for males. Recut in 1852, the gem now weighs 106¹⁄₁₆ carats.

other brothers under Kohendel Khan often ruled independently in Qandahar, and elsewhere another brother, Sultan Mohammad Khan, actually ruled for the Sikhs in Peshawar. By 1826, however, the family at least tacitly recognized Dost Mohammad as titular head and he proclaimed himself Amir, never *Badshah* (or *Padshah,* king). Instability in Afghanistan created independence elsewhere. The Mirs of Sind, the Khans of Baluchistan, and the Uzbak Begs of the north broke away from the control of Kabul, and the Amir of Bokhara, driven by imperialist ambitions, moved across the Amu Darya to seize Balkh. During Dost Mohammad's first reign as Amir, he effectively controlled only Kabul and Ghazni, with periodic submission in other areas.

Dost Mohammad Khan, troubled by tribal revolts and the resistance of his brothers to his rule, sought British assistance to recover Peshawar from the Sikhs. In 1836, Dost Mohammad's army, led by his soldier son, Mohammad Akbar Khan, defeated the Sikhs near Jamrud and killed the great Sikh general, Hari Singh. A cautious Dost Mohammad neglected to follow up the victory with the occupation of Peshawar. Instead, he sought British acceptance of the deed, believing he could only be safe from renewed Sikh attacks with British assurance (Mohd. Ali, 1959, 14).

Therefore, Dost Mohammad Khan sent a congratulatory letter to the new Governor-General of India, Lord Auckland (1836–42), and asked for assistance in settling Afghan-Sikh differences, with particular reference to Peshawar. Auckland replied that the British government followed a consistent policy of non-interference in the affairs of independent nations. Subsequent history made this declaration one of the more laughable events in a series of unlaughable blunders.

Lord Auckland and his associates responsible for the First Anglo-Afghan War are not alone in their stupidity concerning Anglo-Afghan affairs. To quote an articulate British diplomat and historian (Fraser-Tytler, 1967, 84–85):

> We must deal fairly with Lord Auckland. He made mistakes enough in all conscience, and later historians have followed the example of contemporary writers in seeing in him and his policy no redeeming features whatsoever. Perhaps they are right. It is at any rate certain that the sins of the Government of India during the unhappy years 1838 to 1842 were visited on the heads of their successors for many succeeding generations. But in fairness one must point out that Lord Auckland and his advisers are by no

369

means the only rulers of India who have blundered over Afghan affairs. The policy of the Government of India in the 1870s, culminating in the Second Anglo-Afghan War, was an unhappy blend of myopia and impatience, and there are other examples of similar ineptitude. Even Lord Curzon and his advisers showed by their attitude during the Afghan treaty negotiations of 1904–5 a failure to grasp the fundamentals of the Afghan problem or to understand the mentality of the Afghan ruler.

A recent book by Norris (1967) also does much to dispel Kaye's ready insistence on blaming the entire fiasco of the First Anglo-Afghan War on Lord Auckland. Norris believes Auckland essentially served as a pawn in the meaningful (though often misguided) Whig policies of Lord Palmerston to contain Russian advances in Central Asia.

Also in response to the Amir's letter, Auckland dispatched Captain Alexander Burnes, who had already traveled extensively in Central Asia (Burnes, 1835), to Kabul in September, 1837. Burnes had orders to investigate the potentials of commercial relations between India and Central Asia "to work out the policy of opening the River Indus to commerce" (Kaye, 1874, I:181). In reality the economic institution served as a front for his real mission: to bring about a rapprochement between Ranjit Singh and Dost Mohammad, and to conclude a mutual security agreement with the Amir based on the Shah Shuja-Elphinstone Treaty of 1809.

Other external events drastically affected internal Afghan history at this stage. Russian intrigue and influence in the court of the weak but ambitious Qajar Shah, Mohammad Shah (1834–48), brought about the siege of Herat, nominally ruled by Kamran from his harem, but actually under the able guidance of his *wazir* (prime minister), Yar Mohammad Khan. As Burnes traveled toward Kabul, a Persian army led by the Qajar Shah, Mohammad Shah, approached Herat. A regiment of Russians commanded by a General Sampson moved with the Qajar army (Kaye, 1874, I:236), and seconded Russian officers gave unlimited advice on the conduct of the siege. Norris (1967, 179) mentions a battalion of Russian deserters commanded by a Polish officer, Berowski. The Qajar army appeared outside Herat on November 22, 1837, and the siege officially began on November 23.

We have much first-hand data on the nine months' investment of Herat because of the presence of a young British subaltern, a hero with the unlikely name of Eldred Pottinger, Bengal Artillery. Lt. Pottinger, one of many intrepid peripatetic, walking, horseback-riding British U-2s of the nineteenth century, assisted the Heratis in the improvement of their fortifications.[4] The Heratis themselves, led by Yar Mohammad Khan, deserve the lion's share of the credit for the successful defense of their city. The inept generalship of Mohammad Shah, the Qajar, also contributed to the success of the Heratis.

A Russian agent of Lithuanian extraction, Capt. Ivan Viktorovich Vitkevich (also spelled Vicovich, Vickovich, Vitkievitch), arrived in Kabul in December, 1837, with letters from the Russian Ambassador in Tehran, Count Simoultch Simonich, and an unsigned letter purported to be from the Tsar himself. Probably, the imperial letter did come from the Russian cabinet in St. Petersburg (Habberton, 1937, 12). Like Burnes, Vitkevich came to Kabul ostensibly to discuss commercial relations with the Afghans.

Dost Mohammad Khan, however, still obsessed with Peshawar, showed a "neutral" preference for the British, whom he hoped would help in his efforts to recover Peshawar from the Sikhs. The Amir ignored his brothers at Qandahar, who, in early 1837, threatened by the Persian move on Herat, allied themselves with the Qajar Shah for their own protection. Later, Captain Vitkevich guaranteed the alliance Russian support, probably overstepping his authority (Kessler, 1960).

Gradually, Dost Mohammad Khan began to realize the British would do nothing to upset their alliance with the Sikhs, particularly after Burnes delivered the following ultimatum (*Parliamentary Papers,* 1859, 177) on March 6, 1838:

> You must desist from all correspondence with Persia and Russia; you must never receive agents from [them[5]] or have aught to do with him without our sanction; you must dismiss Captain Vickovitch with courtesy; you must surrender all claims to Peshawar on your own account, as that chiefship belongs to Maharaja Runjeet Sing; you must also respect the independence of Candahar and of Peshawar, and co-operate in arrangements to unite your family. In return for this, I promise to recommend to the Government that it use its good offices with its ancient ally, Maharaja Runjeet Sing, to remove present and future causes of

[4] Pottinger left behind no published memoirs, for he died of typhus at the age of 32 in Hong Kong. Those wishing to pursue his exploits further should read Diver's (1914, 1924), highly romanticized, but entertaining, accounts.

[5] Published in previous *Parliamentary Papers* as "other powers."

differences between the Sikhs and Afghans at Peshawar; but as that chiefship belongs to the Maharaja, he may confer it on Sultan Mahomed Khan, or any other Afghan whom he chooses, on his own terms and tribute, it being understood that such arrangement is to preserve the credit and honour of all parties.

The Amir agreed and simply asked the terms, particularly with reference to Peshawar, be put in writing, but the British refused. His patience at an end, Dost Mohammad Khan entered into negotiations with Captain Vitkevich as Captain Burnes left for India in April, 1838.

With the departure of Burnes, the first major face-to-face Russian-British confrontation in Central Asia came to an end. The two young men met only once, Vitkevich had called on Burnes and left his card. In response, Burnes invited the Russian for Christmas dinner, 1837. The dinner went well and the competitors parted in good spirits. Both would die violently within five years (Norris, 1967, 134).

On his part, Dost Mohammad Khan had favored the Englishman at first and informed him of all that transpired between Vitkevich and himself (*Parliamentary Papers,* 1859, 90, 148–51). After Burnes left for India, the Amir set the balance straight by informing Vitkevich about his conversations with Burnes.

While the negotiations aimed at restoring Peshawar to Durrani control dragged on, the siege of Herat continued. Things went badly for the Persians, for although the local populace had been reduced to a diet of horseflesh, the city held out (Kaye, 1874, I:269). Exasperated, Count Simonich appeared at the Qajar camp in April 1838, with more money and additional Russian advisers. After this, the Russians virtually controlled operations until the end of the siege. Cavalry forays continued to have little effect on the besieged, and several frontal assaults (the major attack being on June 24) failed. June 1838, was to be the turning-point and the starting-point for several decades of Central Asian and South Asian history.

The rise of Russian influence in the Persian camp precipitated a rise in British anxieties over Tsarist intentions. St. Petersburg continued to issue honeyed assurances, repeating that the Russians had no designs on Kabul or India. But the reports of Russian activities in Herat, Kabul, and Qandahar forced the British to make an agonizing reappraisal of their policy in the area. British reaction set the course of Central Asian and Indian history for the next hundred years.

In June, Lord Auckland sent an armed force to the Persian Gulf to occupy Kharg (Karrack) Island and threaten the Qajar rear. Also in June, the deposed Saddozai Shah, the Sikh Emperor, and the Governor-General of British India (underwriter of the entire scheme) agreed to a "Treaty of Alliance and Friendship executed between Maharaja Ranjit Singh and Shah Shuja-ool Moolk, with approbation of, and in consent with, the British Government" (Kaye, 1874, I:332; *Parliamentary Papers,* 1839). Under the treaty's provisions, Shah Shuja would rule again in Kabul and Qandahar, enthroned with material assistance from the Sikhs and the British, in return for recognition of Sikh control over the former Durrani provinces in the Punjab and the North–West Frontier. Herat would remain independent.

Shah Shuja objected to the terms (including the annual monies and gifts he would have to send to Ranjit,[6] but the smell of the throne proved too strong. He sealed his fate, and agreed to return to Kabul with the British, although his interpretation of the treaty often clashed with that of the British. Shuja merely wanted British officers to assist, train, and advise a joint Sikh-Afghan expedition.

Lord Auckland, however, in November, began to gather a large British force, known as the Army of the Indus, at Ferozepore. Supposedly created in response to the threat to Herat, the Army of the Indus became a tragic instrument of aggression, and paid with its life for the miscalculations and misunderstandings of Lord Auckland, his advisers, and his superiors.[7] Wily Ranjit Singh, on the other hand, never intended

[6] "The Maharaja will yearly send to the Shah the following articles, in the way of friendship: 55 pieces shawls, 25 pieces of muslin, 11 doopullahs, 5 pieces of kinkaub, 5 sirrums, 5 turbans, 55 loads of baret rice, peculiar to Peshawar [paragraph 8]. . . . When the Shah shall have established his authority in Cabul and Candahar, he will annually send the Maharajah the following articles; viz. 55 high-bred horses, of approved colours and pleasant paces, 11 Persian scimitars, 7 Persian poniards, 25 good mules, fruits of various kinds, both dry and fresh, sirdars or musk melons of a sweet and delicate flavour (to be sent throughout the years), by way of Cabul River to Peshawar; grapes, pomegranates, apples, quinces, almonds, raisins, pisters or chesnuts, an abundant supply of each; as well as pieces of satin of every colour, chogas of fur, khinkabs wrought with gold and silver, Persian carpets, altogether to the number of 101 pieces. All these articles the Shah will continue to send every year to the Maharajah [paragraph 5]." In addition, Shah Shuja had to pay exhorbitant sums for Sikh assistance in the coming war to regain his throne, and 15 lakhs of rupees annually (paragraph 16, *Parliamentary Papers,* 1839).

[7] See Norris, 1967 (p. 173), for a balanced account of the picture vis-a-vis British-Russian confrontations in Eurasia. But even Norris says of the record: "All this was clear to Palmerston and most of his colleagues in the summer

to send his *Khalsa* (army) to fight a foreign war but cleverly encouraged Lord Auckland to take the not-so-rosy path to Afghanistan.

Colonel Charles Stoddart, who was to die horribly in Bokhara later,[8] delivered an ultimatum to Mohammad Shah Qajar outside Herat in August. The note bluntly stated the British would consider the occupation of Herat a direct threat to India. The Shah, looking for an excuse to end the unsuccessful, humiliating siege, broke off contact with Herat on September 9, 1838, and returned to Tehran. On November 8 the British Government of India received official notice that the siege had been lifted (Kaye, 1874, I:383).

In addition, St. Petersburg had already repudiated its representatives in Persia (A. O. Diugamel replaced Count Simonich in Tehran) and Afghanistan. Captain Vitkevich deserved better. He carried out a dangerous assignment, and, recalled to St. Petersburg in April 1839, requested an audience with Count Nesselrode, the Foreign Minister, only to be informed that the Count "knew no Captain Vickovich, except an adventurer of that name, who, it was reported, had been lately engaged in some unauthorized intrigues in Caubul and Candahar."[9] Vitkevich committed suicide.

---

of 1838. They were involved by Russian restlessness in two simultaneous Eastern crises. They knew it to be their duty to keep the peace in Europe. They must somehow defeat the Russians without openly offending the Emperor and his Government in St. Petersburg. Palmerston saw how it could be done. He would try to make the great powers jointly responsible for the protection of the [Ottoman] Sultan, since this was in their joint interest. But Russia was one of the great powers, and it would be necessary to coax her into joining the others and relinquishing the ambition to protect Turkey alone. There was all the more reason, then, why the crisis in Persia and Afghanistan should be handled with great diplomatic delicacy. The value of the interests at stake would fully justify a certain amount of deception. In the author's view, it was the British Government's determination to avoid European war at all costs that disguised the truth and doctored the record of events in Persia and Afghanistan in 1838. The disguise has hampered historians ever since."

[8] After a long imprisonment, Colonel Stoddart, along with a fellow prisoner, Captain Arthur Conolly, was beheaded in Bokhara in June, 1842, at the behest of the Amir Nasrullah (1826–60). The story of the two (and other) British agents can be read in Maclean (1958).

[9] This story, reported by Kaye (1874, I:209) and parroted by most writers since, runs counter to certain sources, summarized by Kessler (1960). According to Kessler, Count Nesselrode not only received Vitkevich immediately, but promised to restore his Lithuanian noble title, to promote him in the Imperial Guards Regiment, and to give him a large stipend for his services (Kessler, 1960, 14–15). Only eight days after his arrival in St. Petersburg, however, Vitkevich burned all his invaluable notes and shot himself. After examining the Russian evidence,

The siege lifted, the main reason for a possible British military movement into Afghanistan disappeared. To quote an excellent chronicler (Kaye, 1874, I:384–85) of the First Anglo-Afghan War:

> When the Persian army was before Herat—when the Afghan garrison was on the eve of surrender—when the chiefs of Cabul and Candahar were prostrating themselves at the feet of Mahomad Shah, the expedition for the restoration of Shah Soojah was one of doubtful honesty and doubtful expediency. The retrogression of the Persian army removed it at once from the category of questionable acts. There was no longer any question about it. The failure of Mahomad Shah cut from under the feet of Lord Auckland all ground of justification, and rendered the expedition across the Indus at once a folly and a crime.

As the siege of Herat ground into history, a conference at Simla shaped the fate of the Afghan area. The "hawks" on Auckland's staff, John Colvin, William Macnaghten, and Henry Torrens,[10] won over the "doves," and the Governor-General decided to implement the Tripartite Agreement with Ranjit Singh and Shah Shuja, i.e., place a British puppet on the throne at Kabul, even though Burnes and John MacNeill (British Ambassador to Tehran) recommended the British support Dost Mohammad Khan in his desire to unify (minus Peshawar) the Afghan area.

Burnes, however, like many intelligence officers past and present, hedged his bets in the same letter in which he praised Dost Mohammad: "As for Shooja-ool-Moolk, the British Government have only to send him to Peshawar with an agent and two of its own regiments, as an honorary escort, and an avowal to the Afghans, that we have taken up his course to insure his being fixed for ever on his throne." (*Parliamentary Papers,* 1859, 242; Kaye, 1874, I:356; Fraser-Tytler, 1967, 99).

Kessler concludes that Vitkevich, formerly active in movements to free Lithuania and Poland from Russian rule, "found he could not continue to live, probably because of his disenchantment with the role he had been playing and a feeling that he was responsible for the events in Persia. The underlying reasons for his decision to end his life probably will never be known" (Kessler, 1960, 17).

[10] Majumdar, et al. (1961, 754), mention Colvin and Macnaghten; Kaye (1874, I:351) implicates Colvin and Torrens; Norris (1967, 237–38) feels Torrens could have had little or no influence on the Governor-General's decision.

According to Kaye (1874, I:356, 500), Burnes crossed out his original statement: "of Shah Soojah-ool-Moolk personally, I have—that is, as ex-King of the Afghans, no very high opinion." To his credit, Burnes did end the letter with high praise for Dost Mohammad and a plea that, after careful analysis, the British would do well to support the Dost (*Parliamentary Papers,* 1859, 242–43):

> He [Dost Mohammad Khan] is a man of undoubted ability, and has at heart high opinions of the British nation; and if half you must do for others were done for him, and offers made which he could see conduced to his interests, he would abandon Persia and Russia tomorrow. . . . Government have admitted that at best he had but a choice of difficulties, and it should not be forgotten that we promised nothing, and Persia and Russia held out a great deal.

Although Dost Mohammad felt uneasy about his brothers at Qandahar and Peshawar, he said this of Shah Shuja: "As for the ex-King himself, I fear him not; he has been too often worsted to make head, unless he has aid from the British Government, which I am pretty certain he will never receive." (*Parliamentary Papers,* 1859; Kaye, 1874, I:202.)

Dost Mohammad might have worried more if he had known what the Governor-General planned for him. Auckland decided to march across the Indus, and on October 1, 1838, issued a "Declaration on the Part of the Right Honourable the Governor-General of India"—the so-called Simla Manifesto, which bluntly spelled out British intentions: the invasion of Afghan territory and the restoration of the Saddozai ex-Shah, Shuja ul-Mulkh (Kaye, 1874, I:369–74; Macrory, 1966, 78–81).

Auckland also announced a civilian team to advise the court of Shah Shuja. Political in-fighting had surfaced the two chief contenders. Envoy and Minister to the Court of Shah Shuja would be Sir William Macnaghten, and "Captain A. Burnes [subsequently knighted and promoted to Lt. Col.] of the Bombay establishment, who will be employed, under Mr. Macnaghten's directions, as Envoy to the Chief of Kalat, or other States" (Kaye, 1874, I:374). ("Kalat" refers to the Kalat Baluch-Brahui confederation in Baluchistan, not Kalat-i-Ghilzai in Afghanistan.) The tacit understanding seemed to be that Burnes would replace Macnaghten as envoy once Shah Shuja sat safely on the throne of Kabul.

376

The British Invade Afghanistan: 1839–42

The Army of the Indus[11] camped at Ferozepore in November, 1838, one month after the end of the siege of Herat. Seldom, if ever, does an army gather for a war and not fight, even in the face of sustained criticism and opposition at home.[12] Many British newspapers in India and England attacked the Simla Manifesto and opposed the war from beginning to end. Those against the war in England included this illustrious roster: Duke of Wellington (who initially supported the venture), Lord Wellsley, Sir Charles Metcalfe, Mountstuart Elphinstone, and the Court of Directors of the East India Company (whose company actually conducted the war). A Chairman of the Court of Directors, as early as 1834, commented cautiously on the first suggestions to send Burnes to Kabul: "I declined then to propose or to concur the appointment of Lt. Burnes to a commercial agency in Caubul, feeling perfectly assured that it must soon degenerate into a political agency, and that we should as a necessary consequence be involved in all the intanglements of Afghan politics" (Kaye, 1874, I:180–81).

In addition, a dispatch dated September 20, 1837, from the Court of Directors to Lord Auckland stated: "With respect to the states west of the Indus, you have uniformly observed the proper course, which is to have no political connection with any state or party in those regions, to take no part in their quarrels, but to maintain so far as possible a friendly connection with all of them" (Kaye, 1874, I:380).

Many in England intimately connected with India were horrified at the march across the Indus. Lord William Cavendish-Bentinck (first Governor-General of India under the Charter Act of 1833) supposedly exclaimed: "What! Lord Auckland and Macnaghten gone to war; the very last men in the world I should have suspected of such folly!" (Kaye, 1874, I:316). Even though Lord Auckland claims "concurrences of the Supreme Council of India" in the Simla Manifesto, Kaye casts grave doubts on this assertion (Kaye, 1874, I:381).

The unpopular war would become more unpopular as time passed.

---

[11] The Army of the Indus consisted of Bengal contingent: 9,500; Bombay contingent: 5,600; Shah Shuja Force: 6,000; Camp Followers: 38,000; Camels: 30,000; plus baggage of the officers (one brigadier, for example, had 60 camels for his baggage and General Sir John Keane, C.O., used 260 for himself and his staff (Macrory, 1966, 861). Also see Hough (1841, 5–8), Kaye (1874, I:404–06), and H. Biddulph (1941).

[12] As the First Anglo-Afghan War develops, note the many similarities with the American involvement in Vietnam.

Ranjit Singh not only reneged on his agreement to send Muslim levies to fight with the Army of the Indus (which departed Ferozepore on December 10, 1838), but refused to permit the Army of the Indus, commanded by General Sir John Keane, to march through his territory. With much difficult fighting and marching (Havelock, 1840; Hough, 1841) the massive body of British and Indian troops moved through Sind and Baluchistan (former Durrani territories), rapidly denuding the countryside of supplies. The Army reached Quetta, jumping-off point for Qandahar, on March 26, 1839.

The Army of the Indus passed into the territories of the Qandahari Sardars on April 25, 1839, and occupied Qandahar without a fight on the next day (Hough, 1841, 428). After a dilatory two-month stay in Qandahar, with deadly bouts of fever, dysentery, and jaundice, the army moved north. The day after General Sir John Keane led his troops toward Ghazni, a major actor in the drama, Ranjit Singh, died, and the Sikh Empire lived but a short time after his death.

In a series of brilliant military engagements and forced marches, General Keane decisively defeated the Afghan forces of Haider Khan (son of Dost Mohammad) at Ghazni on July 22, 1839, and occupied the town. The British arrived outside Kabul on August 6. Dost Mohammad Khan, deserted by his followers, fled to the north to try to continue his fight against the invaders by raising the Uzbak to his standard. The independent-minded Uzbak refused, and Dost Mohammad went to Bokhara, where he became a virtual prisoner of the infamous Amir of Bokhara, Nasrullah Khan.

Shah Shuja, after thirty years in exile and accompanied by Macnaghten and Burnes dressed in their diplomatic finery, entered a largely quiet Kabul on August 7, 1839. The short, unhappy second reign of Shah Shuja began, propped up by British bayonets, supported by British gold, sustained by British and Indian blood. By most contemporary accounts, Shah Shuja, never popular with his people, encouraged further enmity as the glaring presence of the *farangi*[13] bayonets increased hatred and distrust.

The British found in Kabul one Dr. Josiah Harlan, an American adventurer, who, after serving as a General in the Sikh army of Ranjit Singh and as an agent for the exiled Shah Shuja, tried, with little success, to find suitable employment under Dost Mohammad Khan. Probably

---

[13] *Farangi* literally means Frank or foreigner in Persia. The Afghans, however, use the term *haraji* for foreigner in general, and reserve *farangi* (a pejorative term) for the British alone.

the first American to visit the area, Dr. Harlan emerges from contemporary British sources as either a mountebank (Grey and Garrett, 1929, 240–64) or a fascinating *homme engagé* (R. Kennedy, 1840, 118–20). Harlan was obviously a little of both, as were many European adventurers of the period. He described his exploits in a book: *"A Memoir of India and Afghanistan* with observations upon the exciting and critical state and future prospects of those countries. With an appendix on the fulfillment of a text of Daniel in reference to the present prophetic conditions of Mahomedan nations throughout the world, and the speedy dissolution of the Ottoman Empire, by Josiah Harlan, Late Counsellor of State; Aide-de-Camp, and General of the Staff of Dost Mahomed Khan, Ameer of Kabul."[14]

Although the Simla Manifesto called for the withdrawal of British troops once Shah Shuja sat on the throne in Kabul, it became obvious that he would be unseated without their support. Macnaghten, with Auckland's acquiescence, decided to maintain a British garrison in Afghanistan until the situation stabilized. A group of the Bombay division departed on September 18, 1839; a larger unit under General Keane departed for Bombay on October 15, leaving General Sir Willoughby Cotton military commander in Kabul. Keane, unlike Macnaghten, saw nothing but disaster ahead if the British remained in Kabul, and remarked to young Lt. Henry Durand: "I wish you to remain in Afghanistan for the good of the public service; but since circumstances have rendered that impossible, I cannot but congratulate you on quitting this country; for, mark my words, it will not be long before there is here some signal catastrophe" (Kaye, 1874, II:23).

Macnaghten, however, felt so confident that his wife came up late 1839, complete with crystal chandeliers, choice wines, formal finery, and literally hundreds of servants. Other families followed, both the "ladies" of the officers and the "European women" of the common soldiers. A brown flow also flooded in from India. The families of the Sepoys, plus all stripes of camp-followers, made Afghanistan their home. For most, it would also be their graves.

Pax Britannica, so Macnaghten thought, permeated the land of the Amir, which included Kabul, Jalalabad, Ghazni, Kalat-i-Ghilzai, Qandahar, and north to Bamiyan. The rest of what we call Afghanistan today continued to consist of independent tribal kingdoms, mostly non-Pushtun (Yapp, 1962, 1963). Most of the former Durrani domains

---

[14] For an edited version of Harlan's verbose book (the text continues in the same vein as the title), see Ross (1939).

would come under British control before the end of the nineteenth century: Sind, 1843; Kashmir, 1846; Punjab, 1849; Baluchistan, 1859; North–West Frontier, 1895 (Map 15A).

Macnaghten, however, thought not only in terms of *Pax Britannica* for the Afghans, but dreamed of annexing Herat, and conquering Bokhara and parts of Central Asia. He saw almost no limits to the prowess of British arms. Fortunately, even Lord Auckland refused to foster such grandiose adventures in imperialism.

The Tsarist Russians did not sit idly as the British moved. In 1839, in response to the British drive into the Afghan area (as well as to annex territory and free Russian slaves), a Tsarist expedition marched against the Khan of Khiva. Disaster struck the Russians earlier than it did the British. Out of a force of 5,000 men, 22 guns, 10,000 camels, and 2,000 Kirghiz porters, only 1,000 men survived. Yet not one battle had been fought against Khiva. General winter once again prevailed (Lobanov-Rostovsky, 1951, 153–54).

It is difficult to blame either Tsarist Russia or Great Britain for their counter-actions in Central Asia. Both were imperialists driving for territory, natural resources, and international power, so the onus of such imperialism should be equally divided. The Russian manifesto issued to justify the Khiva fiasco makes more sense to me than the Simla proclamation, however. In part the manifesto declares (Kaye, 1874, II:34–35):

> The rights of Russia, the security of her trade, the tranquility of her subjects, and the dignity of the state, call for decisive measures; and the Emperor has judged it to be time to send a body of troops to Khiva, to put an end to robbery and exaction, to deliver those Russians who are detained in slavery, to make the inhabitants of Khiva esteem and respect the Russian name, and finally, to strengthen in that part of Asia the lawful influence to which Russia has a right, and which alone can insure the maintenance of peace. This is the purpose of the present expedition; and as soon as it shall be attained, and an order of things conformable to the interests of Russia and the neighboring Asiatic states shall be established on a permanent footing, the body of troops which has received orders to march on Khiva will return to the frontiers of the empire.

The tone of the manifesto, more forthrightly imperialistic than that of the British, bluntly states that the Russians wish to extend their zone of influence politically.

To secure the kingdom of Shah Shuja, the British occupied and forti-
fied, for varying periods of time, several areas: Qandahar, Ghazni,
Jalalabad, Charikar, Bamiyan, Kalat-i-Ghilzai. Other groups explored
the far reaches of the Afghan area (Wood, 1872). To secure communications and supply lines to India, British troops also occupied Quetta
and Ali Masjid (in the Khyber Pass). A double government came into
being. Ostensibly, Shah Shuja ruled, but seldom attempted to gain the
confidence of his people, even his closest relatives. His tax-collectors
actively collected taxes; his executioners actively executed his enemies,
both real and potential. The British, however, held the purse strings
and the guns, so many Afghans came to Macnaghten and his representatives for decisions which should normally have been in the province
of the Amir. Macnaghten lavishly dispensed cash subsidies to various
tribal chiefs, hoping to gain their loyalty. When Auckland drastically
cut the funds available for such chicaneries, loyalty withered in direct
proportion to the diminished grants.

In spite of the optimism of Macnaghten's reports to Lord Auckland,
revolts against the presence of the British began early and lasted long.
The only appreciable lull occurred during the winter of 1840, when
Shah Shuja and his government, along with Macnaghten, wintered in
Jalalabad, a practice still common in Afghanistan among those who can
afford it. This·period of relative calm followed the departure of Dost
Mohammad Khan for India and what many believed to be permanent
retirement. The former Amir had escaped from Bokhara in August
1840, and proceeded through north Afghanistan gathering supporters.
Many were not so much pro-Dost Mohammad as anti-*farangi*. The
Uzbak, led by Mir Wali (Beg at Khulm, also called Tashkurghan), accompanied him to Bamiyan, where the British defeated the reluctant
forces of the ex-Amir. The Uzbak, plus the hired mercenaries, deserted
the Dost and returned home (Yapp, 1962, 514). But, as the usually
sanguine Macnaghten described the situation: "The Afghans are gunpowder, and the Dost is a lighted match" (Kaye, 1874, II:83). He felt
better after the British victory at Bamiyan; "The Dost had only one
weapon and that was religion.[15] . . . I think the Oosbegs will now
abandon him" (Kaye, 1874, II:85–86).

Dost Mohammad Khan, however, ever resilient ("I am like a wooden

---

[15] Probably Yapp (1962, 513) more correctly assesses the situation: "Undoubtedly religion and a feeling of obligation to Dost Muhammad played some part
in his [Mir Wali Beg's] conduct but the dominant motive seems to have been
the desire to extend his power over the petty chiefs, south of the Oxus, who
were patronized by the British."

spoon, you may throw me hither and thither, but I shall not be hurt."),
gathered the tribes of Kohistan about his person and gallantly led them
to defeat the British on November 2, 1840 (Kaye, 1874, II:86). Then,
with success dangling its fickle charms before him, Dost Mohammad
traveled to Kabul with a single companion, Naib Sultan (Rishtya, 1958,
95), and surrendered to Macnaghten on November 3. Afghan, British,
and other historians still question why. The answer probably rests in
the tribalism of Afghan cultural patterns. Dost Mohammad Khan felt
political dissensions in Kohistan, even though he won a military victory.
Incidentally, the Kohistani had thrown their support to Shah Shuja as
the British approached Kabul in 1839 (Yapp, 1962, 515). Tired,
dispirited, mistrustful of allies who could be bought off with gold or
promises of power and all of whom desired local autonomy, Dost
Mohammad Khan, who wanted Afghan unity above all else, probably
decided the struggle not worthwhile, and as he could not find peace
for his unfortunate land, he attempted to find peace for himself.

Macnaghten received the former Amir with great honor, and Dost
Mohammad Khan impressed all the British officers with his intelligence
and personality; most of them compared Shah Shuja unfavorably with
the Dost in their accounts. Shah Shuja wished to execute Dost
Mohammad Khan, but Macnaghten had promised the Dost safe conduct
to India, and to India he went with a British escort.

Dost Mohammad departed Kabul on November 12, 1840, and two
months later Macnaghten penned the following words (Kaye, 1874,
II:98) to Auckland, which have relevance far beyond their immediate
intent:

> I trust that the Dost will be treated with liberality. His case has
> been compared to that of Shah Shoojah; and I have seen it argued
> that he should not be treated more handsomely than His Majesty
> was; but surely the cases are not parallel. The Shah had no claim
> upon us. We had no hand in depriving him of his kingdom,
> whereas we ejected the Dost, who never offended us, in support
> of our policy, of which he was the victim.

The stage set, the actors must be introduced. Macnaghten, already
appointed Governor of Bombay (one of the prime political plums in
British India), wanted to leave Afghanistan in peace and tranquillity.
Therefore, his reports continued to sound optimistic, and, in spite of
massive evidence to the contrary, he wrote to a colleague on August

20, 1841, that "the country is perfectly quiet from Dan to Beersheba" (quoted in Kaye, 1874, II:130).

Sir Alexander Burnes, waiting (but not too patiently) to take over as British Resident to the Court of Kabul, proved to be an ambitious, ambivalent personality. He recognized the gravity of the rising problems in the Afghan area, and reputedly said to Mohan Lal "that the time had come for the British to leave the country" (quoted in Kaye, 1874, II:165). But Burnes really wanted Macnaghten to depart as quickly and quietly as possible, so that he (Burnes) could step into the Envoy's shoes and settle matters. Burnes, therefore, lent ambiguous support to Macnaghten's optimistic reports. He fancied himself a great diplomat, and even though the adulation received in London after his first Central Asian expedition affected his vanity, it seldom clouded his judgment. Unfortunately, Burnes would never have the chance to test his potential fully (Burnes, *Cabool,* 1843). History was short-changed by Burnes' death, and certainly no one can accept the unfavorable, spiteful evaluations of the man by the talented, though vindictive, Masson (1842, 1844) at face value (Norris, 1967, 25). (Masson, a deserter from the East India Company army, was long assumed to be an American, which he professed to be. See the Masson Papers, 631–657, unpublished, *Eur. Mss.,* Vol. II, Part II, India Office Library, London.)

Major General William Elphinstone, an infirm, elderly (sixty-plus) Queen's officer, replaced Sir Willoughby Cotton as Commander of the British army in Afghanistan in early 1841. The appointment was considered by many as a slap at "John Company" (East India Company) officers and men. Unsubstantiated rumors branded Company troops as unreliable. The man considered by General Sir Jasper Nicolls, Commander-in-Chief in India, as the most competent officer to command in Kabul was an argumentative, irascible, abrasive, though tactically superb Company officer, Major General William Nott, Commander at Qandahar (Kaye, 1874, II:103–04). Elphinstone, to the surprise of Lord Auckland (Norris, 1967, 338), accepted the appointment. Although beloved by his officers and men (except by everyone's arch-villain, Brigadier Shelton), Elphinstone, because of his senile condition, aggravated by constant attacks of gout, did contribute greatly to the ensuing tragedy.

Brigadier John Shelton, 44th Light Infantry, a stubborn man with paradoxical prejudices, second in command to Elphinstone, ineptly carried out his military assignments and arrogantly blamed others for their failure.

Brigadier Sir Robert Sale, 13th Light Infantry, a brave, vain soldier and harsh disciplinarian, continually fought in the forefront of his convict-ridden brigade, as attested by his multiple wounds. His wife, Lady Florentia Sale, an excellent female copy of her husband, would keep a classic journal, a primary source of the British disasters in Afghanistan (Sale, 1843).

Others would appear and fade, some would shine brightly. Brigadier William Dennie, Major General George Pollock, Major General William Nott, Major George Broadfoot, Major Eldred Pottinger, Brigadier T. Anquetil,[16] Captain J. Sturt (son-in-law of Lady Sale), and Captain Colin Mackenzie (Macrory, 1966, 164–65) all had roles to play, lives to spend, blood to let, glory to win.

The Afghans involved included the illustrious son of Dost Mohammad Khan, Mohammad Akbar Khan, and other leaders in the revolt against the English, such as Amanullah Khan Logari, Mohammad Shah Khan, Shamsuddin, Abdullah Khan Achakzai, and many others. (Rishtya, 1958; Yapp, 1962, 1963, 1964).

The British lived in Kabul in a little bit of England transplanted via India. Horse races, cricket, formal dinners, amateur theatricals, and dancing were common. Unfortunately for the social season, the Queen's 16th Lancers had returned to India with their excellent polo ponies, but the English consoled themselves with boating on Wazirabad Lake, "went shooting," and ice skated in the winter (Gleig, 1861, 69–70; Kaye, 1874, II:143).

Most of the British force lived inside a specially constructed cantonment near modern Sherpur, one of the least defensible parts of Kabul. Surrounded by hills, the rectangular mud walls (1,000 by 600 yards), no more than waist-high in several sections, offered little cover from artillery or sniper fire. The commissariat sat outside the cantonment, a masterpiece of military stupidity. The responsibility for the location of the cantonment has never been satisfactorily determined, but it makes little difference, for between Macnaghten's dreams of peace and contentment and an ineffectual upper military echelon, collective idiocy reigned.

The causes of the British disaster relate to several factors: the occupation of Afghan territory and fraternization with Afghan women by

---

[16] Anquetil relieved General Abraham Roberts, famous father of a famous son (Lord Roberts of Qandahar and Pretoria), as commander of Shah Shuja's Force. Roberts clearly saw the dangers threatening the British in Kabul and bluntly proclaimed his views to all who would listen. Because he threatened the peaceful façade constructed by Macnaghten (and relunctantly reenforced by Burnes), Roberts was recalled by Auckland.

foreign troops was resented by the population;[17] placing an unpopular Amir on the throne compounded the problem; the harsh acts of the British-supported segments of the population against their enemies; the removal or reduction of subsidies paid to the tribal chiefs, particularly the Ghilzai, who controlled the important communication route from Kabul to Jalalabad.

In October, 1841, Sale's brigade moved from Kabul to Jalalabad with the mission of clearing the passes and securing the communication and supply routes constantly harassed by the Ghilzai. Sale met vicious resistance all the way, and, although he reached Jalalabad, he could not call his mission a success.

At about the same time, Mohammad Akbar Khan, leading Afghan player in the drama unfolding, arrived in Bamiyan from Bokhara. Time and charismatic man met, and the tribes flocked to his banner. A leader needed, the Afghans had one. A cause without a leader withers on the vine of inaction, as does a leader without a meaningful cause.[18]

Meanwhile in Kabul, anti-foreign elements, under such leaders as Abdullah Khan Achakzai, precipitated a violent demonstration which resulted in the murder of Sir Alexander Burnes, Lt. Charles Burnes (his brother), and several companions and retainers on November 2.

The British, seemingly more tribal than the Afghans during this period, expended more energy arguing than fighting. The first major argument concerned whether or not to remove the entire force to defensible Bala Hissar from the indefensible cantonment. Initially, barracks were constructed in Bala Hissar, but commandeered by Shah Shuja for his harem (Kaye, 1874, II:141). In addition, the Shah did not wish the public to think he depended on British bayonets for his personal protec-

---

[17] When soldiers of any nationality occupy foreign territory, fraternization occurs at all levels. British genes were generously pumped into willing Afghan females, and according to Kaye's prim Victorian phraseology, ". . . the inmate of the Mahomedan Sanana was not unwilling to visit the quarters of the Christian stranger . . . the temptations which are most difficult to withstand were not withstood by our English officers, the attraction of the women of Caubul they did not know how to resist. [That they must have paid for most of what they got is not mentioned—author's comment.] It is enough to state broadly this painful fact." (quoted by Macrory, 1966, 122), who adds in twentieth century Victorianese: "Regretfully, Alexander Burnes seems to have been one of the leaders in lechery." Fraser-Tytler, a more pragmatic, modern British historian, refers to the following proverb: "Necessity is the mother of invention and the father of the Eurasian" (Fraser-Tytler, 1967, 114).

[18] The life and death of Che Guevara offer a modern contrast: a successful Guevera in Cuba (1968a) *vs.* a failed Guevera in Bolivia (1968b).

tion, so he opposed proposals to station foreign troops at Bala Hissar. Later—too late—he changed his mind.

For inexplicable reasons, the British themselves decided to remain in the cantonment, thus dooming themselves in "the sheep-folds on the plain," as Kaye (1874, II:142) called it. Political arguments (e.g., "We will look weak if we leave the cantonment.") prevailed. Pride and inertia defeated logic, and not enough might existed to make it right.

Macnaghten at last faced up to the situation, but in response tried to bribe tribal leaders to desert the "rebels," who had elected Nawab Mohammad Zaman Khan, a cousin of Dost Mohammad, as leader. Some leaders accepted money, but few deserted the anti-foreign cause. Macnaghten used Burnes' excellent *munshi* (secretary), Mohan Lal, as go-between. So desperate did the British become that Lt. John Conolly (probably with Macnaghten's knowledge and possibly shuddering consent) wrote to Mohan Lal and encouraged him to offer 10,000 (reportedly increased to 15,000) rupees for each rebel leader's head (Kaye, 1874, II:202–03).

While the officers bickered and Macnaghten dickered, two beleaguered British outposts in Kabul bloodily and agonizingly fell. The Kohistani also decimated the Fourth Gurkha Regiment at Charikar, and only Major Pottinger (the hero of Herat, and political agent at Charikar) and Lt. Haughton survived among the officers, the latter loosing a hand (Haughton, 1879).

By December, the British arguments simmered down from *whether* to negotiate to *how* to negotiate. Food, water, medical supplies, and courage dwindled. Winter arrived early, but even before the first snowfall on December 18, Macnaghten sent a draft treaty to the Afghan chiefs on December 11. Signed on December 13, the treaty guaranteed the British free passage to Peshawar, in reality a retreat of the British forces from Afghanistan.

Macnaghten, ever the politician, did not give up hope for a miracle and tried to bribe several of the chiefs, not, however, without honest British twinges of conscience. Macnaghten himself, however, admitted to his lack of success in a letter to Captain Macgregor: "I have been striving in vain to sow 'nifak' [dissension] among the rebels and it is perfectly wonderful how they hang together" (L/P&S/5: Enclosures to Secret Letters received from India. Vol. 82, 9 Jan. 1842, No. 9. India Office Records, London).

Mohammad Akbar Khan, now in Kabul and accepted military leader (though Nawab Mohammad Zaman Khan remained nominal "rebel" Amir), led poor Macnaghten to the depths of duplicity. The wretched man seized on the proposals from Mohammad Akbar Khan which would permit the British to remain in Kabul until spring, and then withdraw voluntarily, in return for four lakhs rupees annuity and thirty lakhs bonus. In addition, Shah Shuja would remain king, but Akbar Khan would be *wazir* (principal adviser).

Understandably desperate and strained by the awesome responsibility thrust upon him, Macnaghten accepted and signed a Persian document which agreed to Akbar's terms. Akbar Khan showed the document to the other Afghan chiefs to expose Macnaghten's two-faced policy. Several of the "rebel" leaders admitted to receiving proposals from Macnaghten to betray Akbar Khan. Now, all united in a plan to seize Macnaghten and hold him as a hostage until the British implemented the December 13 treaty, which called for the restoration of Dost Mohammad Khan on the throne in Kabul.

At the conference between the British and the Afghan Sardars on December 23, Macnaghten found the peace he had sought for two months. His misjudgments came to fruition. He was murdered by the Afghans as he struggled to escape. Captain Trevor, one of his companions, died with him, and Captains Colin Mackenzie, and George Lawrence were taken prisoner. Most British contemporary sources agree that Akbar Khan killed Macnaghten, but even Kaye believes the killing occurred in a fit of passion as Macnaghten resisted, and was not premeditated by the Afghans (Kaye, 1874, II:315). A letter in the India Office Library, however, indicates that Akbar Khan may not have been the actual slayer. The letter, written from Agra on February 19, 1842, by T. C. Robertson to "The Honourable the Secret Committee of the Honourable the Court of Directors" (East India Company, London) states in paragraph two (L/P&S/5: Enclosures to Secret Letters received from India. Vol. 83. Letters from Agra, 19 Feb. 1842. India Office Records, London):

> Captain Mackeson appears to give little weight to the circumstances related by Captain Lawrence, the late secretary to the British Envoy, but I confess that the perusal of this correspondence has created a doubt in my mind as to the participation by Mahumud Akbar Khan in the murder of Sir W. Macnaghten.

The correspondence referred to by Robertson is a letter written from Peshawar by Captain Frederick Mackeson (former Political Agent at Jalalabad) addressed to G. R. Clerk at Ambala, which bluntly stated that Mohammad Akbar killed Macnaghten and later boasted of the deed. In a marginal comment on the letter, H. M. Lawrence noted that no proof existed to back up the allegation.

In addition, *The Illustrated London News,* (Vol. I, No. 1, p. 5, May 14, 1842) states that Burnes and Macnaghten were killed by "Afghan religious fanatics" and not by Akbar Khan.

Soon the death of Macnaghten and Burnes would fade to insignificance, however, as the remaining 16,500 people in the cantonment met their trials.

Major Eldred Pottinger, previously incapacitated by a wound received at Charikar, comes again to the center front of the stage. He took over the desperate negotiations with the Afghan Sardars, who, after the murder of Macnaghten, seemed rather regretful and wanted to wash their hands of the British as soon as possible. A new treaty (Kaye, 1874, II:438–40), signed on January 1, 1842 (over Pottinger's vigorous objection, but approved by the British military), was substantially the same as the earlier Macnaghten treaty.

Mohammad Akbar Khan and Nawab Zaman Khan tried to convince the British to wait until stores and an Afghan escort could be assembled to guarantee safe escort, but General Elphinstone, influenced by Brigadier Shelton and against the advice of Major Pottinger, decided to leave immediately for Jalalabad. The Ghilzai Pushtun and their allies, fired up against the *farangi,* refused to listen to pleas from the Durrani Sardar Mohammad Akbar to permit the British to pass through their country unmolested as stipulated in the January 1, 1842, treaty.[19]

The retreat began on January 6, 1842, as the unillustrious garrison marched to its "signal·catastrophe," after sixty-five days of siege at Kabul.

Told and retold by participants and others (Eyre, 1843, 1879; Forbes, 1892; Macrory, 1966; Sale, 1843), the horror and heroism, the freezing weather and hot fights, the panic and the price, and history and folklore tend to blend (L. Dupree, 1967c). A bare outline cannot adequately express the horror, nor the details flesh out the bones of the disaster.

Fate and history combined to immortalize a lowly assistant surgeon

[19] Some British sources, however, insist that Mohammad Akbar was overheard to yell at Khurd Kabul: "Slay them!" in Pashto, although in Persian he called out to stop the firing (Letter from Mackenzie to Pottinger, quoted in Forbes, 1892, 113). But this appears inconsistent with the bulk of the evidence. He simply had no authority over the Ghilzai, who resented the dominant position of the Durrani (Kaye, 1874, II:383.440–42).

of the East India Company. Dr. William Brydon was the only European to reach Jalalabad of the 16,500 forces (a total of 4,500 fighting men, 690 European, 2840 Indian Sepoy Infantry, 970 Sepoy Cavalry; the remaining 12,000 were families and camp-followers). Of course, a few Sepoys of the Company's Indian Army and about twenty Afghans of Shah Shuja's loyal forces reached Jalalabad (Orr to his mother, a letter dated June 21, 1842, India Office Library, London), but few European historians mention these survivors. Most accounts simply refer to Dr. Brydon as the "sole survivor," as depicted in the famous painting by Lady Butler.[20] Some also forget that all the British did not die in the retreat. Of the officers, thirty-five survived as prisoners and were rescued; of the "other ranks," fifty-one captured during the fighting lived to fight another day. In addition, two civilians, twelve wives and twenty-two children were among the European prisoners released, and Major General George Pollock found about 2,000 Sepoys and camp-followers, many crippled from frostbite, begging in the streets of Kabul when he returned in September 1842, with his avenging army. Most of these were taken back to India.

But Dr. Brydon was the only European to survive the entire length of this mid-nineteenth century death march,[21] and his account is obviously of great importance to historians. To my knowledge, however, his original report, forwarded by Brigadier Robert Sale, Commander of the "Illustrious Garrison"[22] at Jalalabad, to the Court of Directors of the East India Company in January, 1842, has been lost, misplaced, stolen, or destroyed. However, while examining the records of the First Anglo-Afghan War in the India Office Library-India Office Files during the summer of 1964, I found a copy of Dr. Brydon's report in Brigadier Sale's Brigade Book. The copy, in Brydon's handwriting, is signed by Brydon and countersigned by Captain H. Wade, acting Brigade Major (Home Misc. Series, Vol. 544. India Office Records, London).

Sale, a pompous and at times even a pathetic figure, jealously guarded his Brigade Book until he was killed during a battle against the Sikhs at Mudki (Punjab) in December 1845. As a result many valuable orig-

[20] For example: "Only one, Dr. Brydon, got through to Jalalabad to tell the tale to Sale's brigade" (Fraser-Tytler, 1967, 118) and " . . . (only one Englishman, a Dr. Brydon, survived)." (Gregorian, 1969, 101).

[21] Other interesting survivors' accounts are those of Sgt.-Major Lissant (1928) and Sita Ram (Lund, ed., 1970). Also see Diskalkar, (1933).

[22] The phrase "Illustrious Garrison" was coined by Lord Ellenborough in an "Order of the Day" to all troops, written on April 21, 1842, after the Jalalabad garrison had defeated Mohammad Akbar Khan in the field.

inal documents concerning the defense of Jalalabad from November 1841 to April 1842 remained unavailable to scholars for years. A transcript of the report appears below. (See L. and N. Dupree, 1967, for a photo facsimile; also see L. Dupree 1967c and Map 15B.)

/Copy/

Jelalabad January 19th 1842

Sir,

I have the honour to forward for the information of the Major General Commanding the following brief summary of the leading events, which took place between the 6th and 19th inst.

It had been announced to the troops on the 5th of January that the arrangement had been completed for our retreat to Hindoostan. Lieut. Evans of H.M. 44th Foot was left in command of such of the sick and wounded, as were unable to march, with Asst. Surgeons Berwick and Campbell in medical charge. Captains Drummond and Welsh with Lieutenants Warburton,[23] Webb, Airey and J. Conolly were placed as hostages in the hands of Muhomed Zeman Khan. The hospital was established in Zeman Shah's fort. The hostages remained with the new King.

We marched from Cantonments about 9 A.M. on the 6th inst. Brigadier Anquetil with the 5th N.I. [Native Infantry] 100 Sappers, and the guns of the mountain train formed the advanced guard. Next came the main body under Brigadier Shelton, followed by the baggage, in rear of which was the 6th Lt. Inf. S.S.F. [Light Infantry, Shah Shuja Force], and lastly the rearguard composed of the 5th L. [Light] Cavalry, 54th N.I., the remainder of the Sappers, and two H.A. [Horse Artillery] guns. All the cannons excepting those of the H.A. and M.T. [Mountain Train] were left in the cantonment together with a large quantity of Magazine stores. The rearguard was not able to start until dusk. No sooner did they move out than they were saluted with a volley from the ramparts, which killed Lieut. Hardyman 5th L.C. [Light Cavalry]. Great quantities of public and private property was carried off between the cantonment, and the Siah-Sung, at which place the two guns were abandoned, and it was seen that the cantonments were in flames. The rearguard arrived at its ground across the Loghur river [at Begrami] about midnight. Though this march was not more

---

[23] Warburton of the Bengal Artillery married a niece of Dost Mohammad. Their son later became famous as Col. Sir Robert Warburton, active among the Pushtun tribes from 1879–98.

than five miles a great number of women and children perished
in the snow, which lay about six inches deep.

We marched in the morning of the 7th to Bootkhak, a distance
of about five miles. The whole road from Cabool at this time being
one dense mass of people. In this march as in the former, the loss
of property was immense, and towards the end of it there was some
sharp fighting, in which Captain Shaw of the 54th N.I. had his
thigh fractured by a shot. The guns and mules of the mountain
train were carried off by the enemy, and either two or three of
the H.A. guns spiked, and abandoned. On the following day, the
8th, we effected the Passage of the Khurd Kabul Pass, with heavy
loss. The heights were in possession of the Enemy who poured
down an incessant fire upon our Column. Lt. Sturt of the Engineers
was killed by a shot in the Groin. Capt. Troup was wounded and
Capt. Anderson's eldest child[24] was missing when we arrived at
our Ground at Khurd Kabul.

The next day the 9th, all the Baggage, which remained to us
was loaded and off the ground, by about 9 A.M. and had proceeded
some distance, when it was recalled and a halt ordered, which owing to the intense cold at this elevated spot, proved exceedingly
destructive to the Sepoys and Camp followers. At this place, the
Married Officers with the Wives, and families, and also the
wounded, were delivered over to Muhamed Akbar for safe convoy
to Jelalabad, much difficulty on the road being expected for the
troops.

On the Morning of the 10th we resumed our march near the
Huft Kotul toward Tezeen. So terrible had been the effects of the
cold and exposure upon the Sepoys, that they were totally unable
to resist the Attacks of the Enemy who pressed hard upon our
flanks and rear; and on arriving at Tezeen, towards Evening, a
mere handful remained, of all the Native Regiments, which had
left Cabool. We halted a few hours at Tezeen and found that Major
Swayne, Captain Miles, Lts. Deas, Alexander, and Warren of the
5th N.I., Lt. St. George of the 57th N.I., Major Ewart 54th N.I.
and Drs. Duff, Macgrath, Bryce and Cardew were killed or missing
and that 3 European women[25] and one or two soldiers of the 44th

---

[24] Four-year-old Mary Anderson was returned to her parents on May 10,
1842. She had been well cared for by the family of Zaman Khan (Macrory,
1966, 260).

[25] Mrs. Bourke, Mrs. Stoker, and Mrs. Cunningham, all soldiers' wives, were
taken prisoner. Mrs. Stoker joined the other prisoners, but died before the rescue.
The other two disappeared into Afghan huts.

had been carried off by the Enemy. After a rest for a few hours and when it had become quite dark, our diminished party again moved on, leaving the last of the Horse Artillery Guns on this ground. We marched all night and arrived in the Morning of the 11th at Kutter Sung where from the nature of the ground, it was not deemed advisable to halt more than an hour or two for necessary rest. During all this march, we had been fired upon by the Enemy from the heights; and as we moved on to Jugdulluk, they pressed still harder upon us, and Lt. Fortye H.M. 44th was killed close to our ground. Shortly after arriving at Jugdulluk Genl. Elphinstone, Brig. Shelton and Capt. Johnson, went over to Muhamed Akbar, as hostages for our Troops, evacuating Jellalabad. We halted here the next Morning /the 12th/ but were greatly annoyed by the constant fire of the Enemy, who had possession of all the surrounding Hills. In the course of the day, Capt. Skinner of the Commissariat was killed and Major Thain, Capts. Grant, Marshall, Hay and Hamilton and Lt. Macartney wounded. Soon after dark orders were given for an immediate March, owing I believe to the receipt of a note from Genl. Elphinstone, telling us to push on at all hazards as treachery was intended.

This move was so unexpected that we found the Abbattis, and the other impediments which had been thrown across the Jugdulluk Pass, undefended by the Enemy, who nevertheless pressed hard upon our rear, and cut up great numbers. The confusion became terrible, all discipline was at an end, and the shouts of "Halt halt" Keep back the Cavalry, were incessant. Just after getting clear of the Pass—I with great difficulty made my way, to the front, where I came upon a large body of Men and officers, who finding it was perfectly useless to remain with Troops in such a state, and gone ahead, to form a kind of advance Guard.[26] But as we moved

[26] In other words, Brydon and other officers deserted those on foot: "Upwards to forty others succeeded in pushing through, about twelve of whom, being pretty well mounted, rode on ahead of the rest with the few remaining cavalry, intending to make the best of their way to Jelalabad" (Eyre, 1843, 230). "The infantry had at last managed to tear a gap in the holly barricades; they were ridden over by mounted officers and men, rushing for the gap, and in their fury retaliated by firing on their own side" (Macrory, 1966, 229). Even the coldly factual account of Sgt.-Major Lissant mentions the incident: "The men in front then said the officers seem to care for themselves, 'Let them push on if they like, we will halt till our commrades in the rear come up'" (Lissant, 1928, 149).

I collected folktales along the retreat route which described similar scenes from the Afghan view (L. Dupree, 1967c).

steadily on, whilst they halted every second, by the time, this day dawned, we had left the Main Body far in our rear. Our Party gradually diminished as we proceeded, 'till on arriving at Fut-tehebad it was reduced to Captains Bellew, Hopkins and Collyer, Lts. Bird, Steer and Gray, Dr. Harpur, Sargt. Frill and about five other Europeans. Capt. Bellew, Lts. Bird and Gray, and the Euro-peans were cut down near Futtehebad whilst Capts. Hopkins and Collyer and Dr. Harpur being well mounted, soon left Lt. Steer and myself far behind. About 3 miles from this place, Lt. Steer told me that he would hide 'till night and left the road to do so. I proceeded ahead and reached this with great difficulty about 1 P.M. on the 13th Inst.

Lt. H. Wade
M. B. (Brigade Major)

I have etc.
Dr. Wm. Brydon[27]
Asst. Surgeon

Retribution slowly, but irrevocably, came. In the heyday of imperial-ism (Fieldhouse, 1966), the British set a beautiful pattern of defeat and then crowning success, except, of course, in the case of the Ameri-can Revolution.

New winds blew from the West. The Whigs had sent Lord Auckland to India, but now the Conservatives came to power. They wanted to get out, but with style and honor. Lord Ellenborough relieved Lord Auckland as Governor-General on February 28, 1842, and restored the policy of folly with one of pomp. Lord Auckland, who had never seen the harsh beauty of Afghanistan, turned his back on the blood and gore in that same February. Winter still held the flesh on the bodies piled high at Gandamak, where, in January, the 44th Foot and an assortment of survivors from miscellaneous outfits made a gallant last stand. Only six or seven badly wounded men, unable to fight, were taken prisoner.

Meanwhile, contrapuntal and disharmonic sounds rang through the Afghan hills. General Nott dallied in Qandahar, occasionally tilting with the Afghans, but usually sulking at home. A bright lining appeared at Jalalabad. Sale and his brigade girded for a siege, although Sale and

---

[27] Dr. Brydon did not die in Jalalabad, but returned to Kabul with Pollock's avenging army. He had another narrow escape at Tezeen, when a six-pound shot from an Afghan gun shattered his *dooly,* without injuring him (Greenwood, 1844, 222). Brydon rose steadily in the service of the East India Company, survived the seige of Lucknow during the 1857–58 War for Indian Independence and retired in November 1859, as Surgeon William Brydon, C. B. (Commander of the Bath).

his staff, in a Council of War held on January 26, favored evacuation to India. The logic of his argument: Shah Shuja had ordered them to leave (Kaye, 1874, II:57). Major George Broadfoot, a bold type, opposed retreat. His only support came from Captain C. Oldfield of the Staff, and Captain Henry Havelock, a supernumerary who had no vote. All talk of retreat ended on February 13, however, when word was received that the Government of India had not deserted them.

Throughout this period, Broadfoot and his Sappers strengthened the defenses. Little real fighting occurred. Actually only two engagements of note took place throughout the entire siege. Most of the time the garrison simply waited, foraged the countryside, or attempted to improve the defenses.

Probably, the Afghans contributed more to the defense of Jalalabad than the British inside the fort. Almost immediately after the defeat of the final remnants of the Kabul garrison at Gandamak, the illusion of unity loosened and finally broke down. Mohammad Akbar Khan could not hold together the exultant Ghilzai and other Pushtun elements, and, singing improvised songs of the improvised victory, many tribesmen returned home.

Allah struck the most important blow for the Afghans on February 19, when, in a few moments, an earthquake leveled or damaged much of the three months' work on the walls and other fortifications, but the ever efficient and energetic Broadfoot supervised immediate repairs.

While the "Illustrious Garrison" waited for relief and the Governor-General wrestled with how to evacuate Afghanistan via Kabul from Qandahar and Jalalabad, Shah Shuja played out his hand. Surprisingly, he remained as Amir after the British left Kabul, and many Afghans in the anti-Akbar factions hoped he would provide leadership, but the old man had not ruled for thirty years, and the British made him their puppet on his return. Fearing the worst, he continued to correspond with the British, but after repeated appeals from Mohammad Akbar Khan (who planned to replace Shuja later with his father Dost Mohammad) and Nawab Mohammad Khan for unity, he agreed to lead an Afghan force against Jalalabad.

On April 5, however, the luckless Shah met his fate at the hands of assassins, despite guarantees of safety from Nawab Mohammad Khan. Unfortunately, the killer was a son of the Nawab, who in a typical Afghan gesture of honor refused to permit his son to visit home again, and forbade the mention of his name in his (the Nawab's) presence (Kaye, 1874, III:110–11).

The assassination of Shah Shuja further contributed to the breakdown of Afghan unity in and out of Kabul.

Elements of the Ghilzai meanwhile held the British troops at Qandahar, commanded by Major General Nott (political officer at Qandahar was Major Henry Rawlinson) under loose siege. The fighting around Qandahar became particularly vicious. In November, 1841, *ghazi* (warriors dedicated to fight to the death) wiped out a detachment of one hundred thirty men near Ghazni. On January 12, Nott defeated the Ghilzai and "slaughtered every man, woman and child" within the village of Killah-Chuk (Kaye, 1874, III:138).

Nott refused to obey a loosely-constructed order (dated February 21) from General Elphinstone and Major Pottinger to evacuate Qandahar and Kalat-i-Ghilzai, and move to Quetta. Instead, General Nott prepared to hold out in Qandahar and fight the Afghans on any terms they chose. Rawlinson carried out extensive measures to guarantee the security of the garrison, and between March 3 and 6 forcibly removed most of the Qandaharis from the city, a total of about 6,000 people, but "every exertion was made to render the measure as little oppressive as possible; but the expulsion of so many citizens from their houses could not be altogether free from cruelty and injustice" (Kaye, 1874, III:150).

Ghazni and Kalat-i-Ghilzai, both garrisoned by the British, came under siege with two distinctly different results. Ghazni, commanded by Lt. Col. T. Palmer, surrendered on March 10. Kalat-i-Ghilzai, under Captain J. H. Craigie, held out until relieved in May by a column from Qandahar.

On March 31, the army of Major General George Pollock forced the Khyber Pass for the first time in history. (Earlier armies had paid tribute or skirted the pass through the Kabul River Valley). An attempt of Wild's Brigade to move through the Pass had failed in January. Pollock's force reached Jalalabad on April 16, greeted by the regimental band of the Somerset Light Infantry (13th Foot) playing "Oh, but ye've been lang o'coming" (Gleig, 1861, 165).

The arrival of Pollock's army further exposed the myth of Afghan unity as tribal leader after tribal leader led his levy home. Fighting broke out between feuding groups. In addition, an Afghan with a personal grudge made an unsuccessful attempt to assassinate Akbar Khan outside Jalalabad.

Meanwhile, in Kabul, the internal struggle for power continued. Fath Jang (second son of the Saddozai ex-Shah, Shuja), supported by

395

Amanullah Khan Logari and the Popalzai, had to compete for power with the Barakzai, led by Nawab Zaman Khan and Mohammad Akbar Khan. Logari originally supported Dost Mohammad, shifted to Shuja as the British arrived, and then led the "rebels" in the revolt against the British, all before supporting Fath Jang; these were moves not untypical of Afghan political maneuvers in the nineteenth century.

Nawab Zaman Khan still held the British prisoners in his power, but the British would only bargain for an exchange of prisoners and refused to get too involved in the struggle for power in Kabul (Norris, 1967, 410). Akbar Khan emerged as the real winner. He defeated the forces of Zaman Khan, and then purchased the British prisoners from the powerful religious leader, Mir Hajji, who had gained their custody from Zaman Khan after the death of Shah Shuja (Kaye, 1874, III:278–79).

On June 29, Akbar established Fath Jang as Amir with himself as *wazir,* the actual power remaining in Akbar's hands, but not for long. Fission continued to dominate the Afghan political scene, and as Generals Pollock and Nott prepared to withdraw from Afghanistan via Kabul under Lord Ellenborough's ambiguous orders,[28] civil war raged in Kabul.

Major General Pollock left Jalalabad on August 20 with 8,000 troops. He met and defeated the Ghilzai at Jugdalak on September 8. Akbar Khan's army, rent with desertions resulting from the tribal infighting for power in Kabul, met the same fate on September 13 at Tezeen. Pollock's army encountered little resistance from Tezeen to Kabul, but the skeletons of Elphinstone's defeated force lined the route, mute evidence of the winter agony (Greenwood, 1844, 232). The Europeans and Indians extracted a heavy vengeance in blood and property from the people in the area. Armies in the field still demand an eye for an eye, death for death; the innocent die with the guilty on both sides. Pollock camped his army on the plains east of Kabul on September 18, 1842.

Nott arrived two days later, unhappy to have lost the honor of being first. He had fought several hard engagements before leaving from Qandahar on August 7 with an army of 6,000 men. In May, Nott's

---

[28] Though they were not so ambiguous as Kaye (1874, III:289) implies. Ellenborough knew that Pollock could move to Kabul and return to India, but the route from Qandahar to Kabul was not only longer but more hazardous, especially in summer. The Governor-General, therefore, simply left· the decision to the man on the spot, General Nott (Norris, 1967, 406–07).

forces had sallied forth to engage the Durrani tribesmen led by Aktur Khan, and witnessed a scene not uncommon in Afghan history: a woman (widow of Akram Khan, executed earlier by the British) riding her husband's horse, waving his standard, and exhorting the men to fight on to victory—in vain, for Nott's superbly disciplined veterans and superior firepower won the day.

The brigade passed through Kalat-i-Ghilzai. The Ghilzai opposed Nott's advance near Moqor, where a major four-day (August 28 to 31) battle was fought. Again, British discipline prevailed, and the tribesmen under Shamsuddin and Sultan Jan fell back on Ghazni. Another brief encounter and the road to Kabul through Wardak lay open.

Nott paused briefly in Ghazni to perform a propaganda task for the ebullient, flamboyant Ellenborough. He removed the wooden doors from the tomb of Mahmud, the great Ghaznavid emperor. Legend identified the doors as the "Gates of Somnath," brought to Ghazni by Mahmud from one of his many raids to India. The tomb "gates," however, were not sandalwood (nor were the real Somnath Gates), and had actually been carved long *after* Mahmud's death. Ellenborough, however, in a later masterful piece of poetic justice, used these false ·symbols to celebrate a hollow victory.

In Kabul, General Pollock (another Queen's officer) outranked General Nott (a "John Company" officer), who remained; Achilles-like, in his tent sulking until General Pollock (ever the Queen's gentleman) visited him. The two never did agree on policy or whom to back among the vying Afghans, but Ellenborough's order specifically precluded British support of anyone at this time.

Tugs of war shifted the British prisoners from Budeabad (40 miles from Jalalabad) to Kabul and to Bamiyan after the defeat of Akbar Khan. Old General Elphinstone finally succumbed to his frailties (including rampant dysentery) at Budeabad. His body may lie in an unmarked grave in or near the modern Afghan army fort at Jalalabad. Under the circumstances, however, the prisoners had been well treated, and most gave testimony concerning the kindness of both Akbar Khan and Mohammad Shah Khan, their chief jailer, although Lady Sale does accuse Mohammad Shah of plundering the private gear of the prisoners just before their removal from Budeabad. The reasons for the "looting," though obviously not justified in the eyes of the looted, are certainly understandable. Some may think it surprising that the "wild and savage keepers" (Sale, 1843, 407–08; Kaye, 1874, III:229) waited so long to plunder the rich camel chests of the prisoners. Moving a large body of prisoners rapidly from one place to another required that all unnecessary accoutrements be left behind, so the jailers relieved the prisoners of such excess baggage as richly embroidered shawls, jewelry, and silverware, sending these items to their own homes.

The chief jailer, Saleh Mohammad, of the prisoners at Bamiyan, hearing of the arrival of the British armies in Kabul, offered to free the prisoners if they would agree to pay him a ranson of 20,000 rupees plus a monthly sum of 1,000 for life, as well as guarantee him an appointment as a regimental commander in the British Indian Army. The prisoners agreed to the terms (never fulfilled) and departed Bamiyan. A rescue party of 600 Qizilbash cavalry, led by Captain Richmond Shakespear, met them near Wardak on September 17.

The retreat avenged on the field of battle, the prisoners rescued, there remained only the collective punishment of the Afghans who participated in the revolts against the British army of occupation. Parts of Istalif and Charikar were destroyed in late September and early October for their roles in the uprisings, but Pollock added the final civilized touch when he ordered the destruction of the great bazaar in Kabul, the area where the mutilated body of Sir William Macnaghten and possibly that of Sir Alexander Burnes had been exhibited.[29] Pollock, apparently sincerely, tried to limit the destruction and ordered that no explosives or fire be used and instructed the engineer in charge to utilize only sapper tools. The engineer, Attock, found the sturdy construction of the bazaar made this impossible, and when he began blasting, the troops and camp-followers poured into Kabul (in spite of orders to remain outside), looting and killing. By October 10, the physical damage, never to be psychologically erased, was done. On October 12, Pollock's and Nott's armies departed Kabul, Fath Jang in tow and his younger brother, Shahpur, seated uncomfortably on the throne.

Shahpur did not hold his seat long, for Akbar returned with a strong force and drove him into exile with the rest of Shah Shuja's family. Akbar Khan waited for his father's return.

Lord Ellenborough, meanwhile, energetically threw himself into his production of the Ferozepore "follies" to be held from December 12 to 23 in honor of the victorious returning army. He personally supervised the painting of the elephant trunks and designed a gallows-like arch under which the Illustrious Garrison marched.

[29] Kaye (1874, II:317) and Macrory (1966, 265) say Macnaghten; Forbes (1892, 155) says both.

Earlier, he gave affront to all India, regardless of race or creed, caste or color, by issuing two proclamations (Kaye, 1874, III:380–81) on November 16 which included the following:

From the Governor-General to all the Princes and Chiefs, and People of India.

My brothers and my friends, our victorious army bears the gates of the temple of Somnauth in triumph from Afghanistan, and the despoiled tomb of Sultan Mahmud looks upon the ruins of Ghuznee The insult of 800 years is at last avenged. The gates of the temple of Somnauth, so long the memorial of your humiliation, are become the proudest record of your national glory, the proof of your superiority in arms over the nations beyond the Indus.

. . . May that good Providence, which has hitherto so manifestly protected me, still extend to me its favour, that I may so use the power now entrusted to my hands, as to advance your prosperity and secure your happiness, by placing the union of our two countries upon foundations which may render it eternal.

Ellenborough

The "Somnauth Gates" were stored in a warehouse at Agra, to collect dust (Kaye, 1874, III:397).

The realistic results of the First Anglo-Afghan War can be stated simply: after four years of disaster, both in honor, material, and personnel, the British left Afghanistan as they found it, in tribal chaos and with Dost Mohammad Khan returned to the throne of Kabul.

Several contemporary British comments give fitting epitaphs to this abortive experiment in imperialism. Even before the war began, Lord Auckland, a chief villain, had written (Kaye, 1874, I:316) to Sir Charles Metcalfe (temporary Governor-General of India from March 1835 to March 1836):

You are quite right in believing that I have not a thought of interference between the Afghans and the Sikhs. I should not be sorry to see strong, independent, and commercial powers established in Afghanistan; but short of Persian or Russian occupation, the present state is as unsatisfactory as possible, with national, family and religious feuds so inveterate as almost to make one party ready to join any invader against another. It is out of the question that we can ever gain direct power or influence amongst them.

399

If only Auckland had kept his original estimate of the situation!

Kaye, carried away with Victorian rhetoric, ends his classic work (III:402) with:

> The calamity of 1842 . . . was, in principle and in act, an unrighteous usurpation, and the curse of God was on it from the first. Our successes at the outset were a part of the curse. They lapped us in false security, and deluded us to our overthrow. This is the great lesson to be learnt from the contemplation of all the circumstances of the Afghan War—"The Lord God of recompenses shall surely requite."

However, Colonel Sutherland, a leading military analyst of the period, said: "It is a comfort to be able to look a native in the face again with confidence. Now all is right. How easily achieved! And we stand on surer ground now in all quarters than we ever did in any former period of our Indian history" (quoted in Macrory, 1966, 275). And then came 1857 and the Indian Mutiny.

No modern liberal historian could be as harsh as a contemporary British analysis (Extract from Report of the East India Committee on the Causes and Consequences of the First Afghan War, written before its conclusion, quoted in Hanna, 1899, I:1) of the 1838–42 Afghan adventure:

> This war of robbery is waged by the English Government through the intervention of the Government of India (without the knowledge of England, or of Parliament and the Court of Directors); thereby evading the check placed by the Constitution on the exercise of the prerogative of the Crown in declaring war. It presents, therefore, a new crime in the annals of nations—*a secret war!* It has been made by a people without their knowledge, against another people who had committed no offence.
>
> Effects on India.—The exhaustion of her flourishing treasury; complete stop to internal improvement; loss of the lives of fifteen thousand men (loss of camp-followers not known); destruction of fifty thousand camels; abstraction of her circulating medium of the country; loss of at least £13,000,000 [now estimated from £17,000,000 to £20,000,000]; permanent increase of the charges on India of £5,500,000; paralyzation of commerce; diminution of the means of culture, of transport and of revenue; chilling the

affections of the native army, and the disposition to enlist; loss of England's character for fair-dealing; loss of her character of success; the Mussulman population is rendered hostile; causes of rebellion developed by the pressure of taxes and the withdrawal of troops; and finally, the other political party in England is committed to the continuation of such deeds, after they are recognised by the people of those islands to be criminal, and after they had brought upon our heads disaster and retribution.

Dost Mohammad Khan Dreams of Unity: 1843–63

Dost Mohammad Khan followed two policies throughout his second reign: friendship with the British and attempts to unify his country. His arrival in Kabul found his former kingdom in great disorder. In addition, Akbar Khan, appointed *wazir* by his father, proved as politically ambitious as he was militarily able. The Dost wanted to establish internal unity; young Akbar wanted to reestablish the empire of Ahmad Shah Durrani. The son may have deposed the father if Allah had not intervened. Akbar Khan, hero of the First Anglo-Afghan War, died in 1845 at the age of twenty-nine.

From 1843 to 1855, Afghan-British relations remained moribund as the British busily gobbled up large portions of India, and Dost Mohammad reconquered Mazar-i-Sharif, Khulm, Kunduz, Qataghan, Badakhshan and Qandahar (controlled by one of his Qandahari brothers, Kohendel Khan, who died in 1855). In the interim, however, the Sikh Empire crumbled and the British gained control of the Punjab after two wars (1845–46; 1848–49). Dost Mohammad occupied Peshawar after the Sikhs abandoned it, and sent a small force to observe the fighting during the Second Anglo-Sikh War. The Sikhs defeated, the Dost withdrew from Peshawar to Kabul, in essence, though not in fact, relinquishing his claim to Peshawar, an act which still plagues Afghan policies.

Dost Mohammad's great dream of Afghan unity also embraced Herat, but the independent rulers of Herat resisted all his overtures and constantly looked to Persia for support. The British, disturbed over Persian designs on Herat and the Asian implications of the Crimean War (1853–56), sought a treaty of friendship with Dost Mohammad. The Treaty of Peshawar (March 30, 1855) signed by Sir John Lawrence (Chief Commissioner of the Punjab) and Ghulam Haider (heir apparent to Dost Mohammad) emphasized three points, all favoring the

British version of the *status quo* and offering little in return as Dost Mohammad Khan and his successors would soon discover. The three points were mutual peace and friendship; respect for each other's territorial integrity; the friends and enemies of one to be friends and enemies of the other.

The Persians occupied Herat in October 1856, with the consent of the ruling prince, Mohammad Yusuf (grandson of Zaman Shah). This act precipitated a three-month war with England. Persia evacuated Herat and agreed to abandon all claims to the area. As the Persian war began, John Lawrence and Herbert Edwardes invited Amir Dost Mohammad to Peshawar, and signed a supplementary treaty with him on January 25, 1857, under which the Afghan Amir received one lakh rupees (£10,000) per month during the war in order to maintain an army capable of resisting aggression from the west and north. Once again, presumably forgetting the years between 1838 and 1842, the British attempted to force Dost Mohammad to accept British officers in Kabul, Qandahar, and Balkh to supervise the proper expenditures of the money. With much misgiving, the Dost finally permitted Major H. B. Lumsden of the Guides to proceed to Qandahar, where he remained inactively engaged, but actively sweating during the Mutiny, which broke out in May 1857.

The War for Indian Independence (or the Indian Mutiny) put the sincerity of Dost Mohammad Khan's friendship with the British to its severest test. Many of his advisers wanted him to swoop down from the Afghan hills and support their revolting brethren in India. If Dost Mohammad had listened to their advice, the history of the Indian War for Independence might have been quite different, but the Dost, well aware of the ultimate resources and power of the British, more than once declared that he intended to maintain his pledge of non-interference (Fraser-Tytler, 1967, 125). As we shall see, the same could not be said for the British.

During the Mutiny, Sir John Lawrence contemplated recognizing the suzerainty of Dost Mohammad over Peshawar and the frontier zones to the Indus to encourage Afghan neutrality. As it became obvious the Dost planned no overt moves against the hard-pressed British, Sir John did not push this policy—or even notify the Afghans of the proposal. Afghan historians castigate Dost Mohammad Khan for not taking a more aggressive policy during the Indian revolt.

Dost Mohammad reached the peak of his ambitions with the conquest of Herat in May 1863, but he died in June, as though Allah had permitted him to glimpse his goal, and then, Moses-like, he died in sight of the Promised Land.

A fitting epitaph to Dost Mohammad is found in the Afghan saying, still popular: "Is Dost Mohammad dead that there is now no justice in the land?" (Fraser-Tytler, 1967, 127).

Civil Wars Again and the Second British Invasion: 1863–80

In the nineteenth century, several Amirs ruled twice in Kabul: Shah Mahmud (1800–03; 1809–18, and then in Herat until 1829); Shah Shuja (1803–09; 1839–42); Dost Mohammad (1826–39, although civil war kept him from declaring himself Amir-ul-Muminin until 1836; 1842–63); Sher Ali Khan (1863–66; 1868–79, although he never gave up his title of Amir, even when ousted from Kabul).

Dost Mohammad's three favorite sons (Akbar Khan, Ghulam Haider, Akram Khan) preceeded him to Paradise,[30] so he reached down among his younger sons to pluck Sher Ali Khan (born 1823) as his successor. Among others, the oldest two surviving sons, Afzal Khan (born 1811) and Azam Khan (born 1818), refused to accept the rule of their younger half brother, and the patchwork fusion of Dost Mohammad Khan disappeared in the fratricidal fission which followed. For six years, bloody civil war raged, and Sher Ali Khan first fought Azam Khan in Kurram. The defeated Azam fled to India but later returned. At Bajgah, Sher Ali overwhelmed the forces of Afzal Khan, who then accepted the young Amir. Defeated at Takht-i-Pul, Afzal's son, Abdur Rahman Khan, fled to Bokhara, and, in retaliation, Sher Ali imprisoned the father in the summer of 1864 (*Gazetteer of Afghanistan,* Part II (1811–67), 1907, xviii). At Kalat-i-Ghilzai, Sher Ali overcame the combined armies of two of his full brothers, Mohammad Amin (born 1829; Governor of Qandahar) and Mohammad Sharif (born 1830; Governor of Farah and Girishk).

While Sher Ali grieved over the loss of his eldest son, Mohammad Ali, slain in the battle of Kalat-i-Ghilzai, Abdur Rahman returned and raised an army. With his uncle, Azam, Abdur Rahman defeated Sher Ali three times in the field, entered Kabul, and in May, 1866, placed his father on the throne.

Azam Khan succeeded Afzal Khan, who died on October 7, 1867. Abdur Rahman, alienated by his uncle, left Kabul for Mazar-i-Sharif.

---

[30] Rumors still exist in Afghanistan that the Amir, fearful of his son's ambitions and popularity, poisoned Akbar "at the instigation of a foreign power" (Rishtya, 1958, 137).

Sher Ali Khan struck at Qandahar and Kabul with the aid of a vigorous son, Yaqub Khan, and became Amir of Kabul once again, in January, 1869.

Meanwhile, north of Afghanistan, the Tsarist Russians began to move straight into Central Asia. They interpreted the British invasion of Afghanistan (1839–42) as a direct threat to their interests.[31] With time out for the Crimean War and several minor scrapes with Persia and Turkey, the Russians slowly penetrated the independent Central Asian Khanates. The line established in 1864 (Map 15A) was neither "fixed" nor "permanent," although Prince Gorchakov, Russian Imperial Chancellor, issued a memorandum to that effect at St. Petersburg on November 21, 1864 (Fraser-Tytler, 1967, 321). The Russians continued to conquer and occupy the Asian khanates, or reduced them to political and economic vassalage through treaties and the control of trade. The British, busily consolidating their gains in India, looked nervously again toward Afghanistan. In 1869, the Khan of Bokhara became a Tsarist vassal. Therefore, only one year after Sher Ali returned to power in Kabul, Russian influence reached the banks of the Amu Darya. A paper written by Sir Henry Rawlinson in July 1868, and at first rejected, would, ten years later, become the cornerstone for the British "Forward Policy" in Asia. The main points of the paper were: occupy Quetta; gain control of the Afghan area by subsidizing the Amir in Kabul; establish a permanent British Mission in Kabul to keep the Russians out (Ghose, 1960, 10).

The Governor-General and Viceroy of India, Lord Mayo, who had replaced Lord Lawrence in January, 1869, invited Amir Sher Ali to a conference at Ambala in March to discuss problems of mutual interest. The conference, held in colorful spasms of oriental splendor, and attended by most princely rulers under British suzerainty, initially pleased the Kabul Amir, who desired three things of the British: a guarantee of his boundaries against Russian advances; the recognition of his descendants as the legitimate Amirs of Kabul; the recognition of his favorite son, Abdullah Jan, as immediate successor to the throne.

---

[31] Britain's response to Russia's moves in Central Asia resemble the Monroe Doctrine, in that the British attempted to extend their *influence* into an area where their *control* did not exist (Habberton, 1937, 83). In essence, the British, in their two nineteenth-century wars in Central Asia were fighting the Russians, but it was the Afghans, in reality, who suffered. Similarly, the Americans in Vietnam in the 1960s fought, in essence, the Russians and the Chinese under the generic term "Communist aggression," but the Vietnamese, in reality, were the ones who suffered.

Lord Lawrence could only give assurances of friendship, assistance, and non-interference in Afghan internal affairs, and further did not insist on British officials' being stationed in the territories of the Amir, as demanded in the Treaty of 1855 and the Supplement of 1857.

Sher Ali returned to Kabul and energetically began a series of far-reaching reforms. He created a national army, instituted a system for collecting land revenues in cash (previously one half in kind, one half cash), founded a Council of Elders to advise him on affairs of state, began a postal system, and published the first newspaper in Afghanistan, named *Shams-i-Nahar* (*Morning Sun*), in 1873 (Ahang, 1968a, 72). Recurring civil wars and Anglo-Russian imperialist competition aborted these imaginative efforts.

Mohammad Yaqub Khan, eldest son of Amir Sher Ali, broke with his father over the appointment of Abdullah Jan as heir apparent. In 1870, Yaqub fled to Persia via Ghazni, Qandahar, Girishk, and Sistan, accompanied by his younger full brother, Mohammad Ayub Khan, later hero of the Second Anglo-Afghan War.

Yaqub successfully conquered Herat from Persia in May, 1871, and, reconciled with his father, became governor of that province. In 1873, a royal *farman* officially named Abdullah Jan heir to the throne. Sher Ali, still suspicious, threw Yaqub in prison after guaranteeing him safe conduct to Kabul in 1874. Yaqub Khan spent most of his life incarcerated at his father's command. Ayub Khan, in Herat, failed to raise a revolt to free his older brother and fled to Persia.

External events now begin to shape Afghan destiny. Since the early 1850s the British had vacillated between two extreme policies, and ended by adopting neither. The two policies were to occupy Herat and Kabul, i.e., to annex the Afghan area into the British Indian Empire, or to retreat to the Indus River and leave Afghanistan strictly alone. This indecision resulted in another quasi-disastrous expedition, the Second Anglo-Afghan War (1878–80). Misunderstandings and mis-interpretations again played great roles in the development of this conflict.

The Anglo-Russian Agreement of October 1872, contributed to the problem, because the "present positions of the Afghan Amir" were never properly defined. Both the British and Russians at least tacitly agreed that the Amir's territories would be up to the Amu Darya (Oxus) and down to Khoja Saleh. The Russians eventually yielded to Badakhshan and Wakhan's being a part of the Amir's possessions in February 1873.

While the Afghans engaged in their fratricidal wars, the Persians occupied Sistan. The British offered to mediate in this territorial dispute, and both the Afghans and the Persians protested the unfairness of the resulting Goldsmid Award of October 1872.

As long as Lord Mayo, personal friend of Sher Ali and Viceroy of India, lived, the Afghan Amir had faith in his face-to-face assurances of British friendship and non-aggression. Even Lord Northbrook, Viceroy after Lord Mayo's assassination in 1872, remained sympathetic to Sher Ali's plight.

With Russian armies steadily approaching his borders, Sher Ali, in 1873, asked for a definite British commitment to aid Afghanistan if it had to fight the Russians. In July, an Afghan delegation led by Sayyid Nur Mohammad Shah met with British representatives at Simla. The British advised the Afghans to relax, because the Russians had agreed to honor the Amu Darya as the northern Afghan boundary, and all the areas to the south (including Balkh, Andkhui, Maimana, and Herat) would remain outside the Russian sphere of influence. Such hedgings did not encourage Sher Ali, and the events immediately following completely overwhelmed him. From the Simla Conference on, Anglo-Afghan relations became strained.

In 1874, Benjamin Disraeli (later Earl Beaconsfield) became prime minister of Great Britain, and the policy of non-intervention in the internal affairs of Afghanistan ended. The "masterly inactivity" of the previous decade shifted to the Forward Policy. The Secretary of State for India, Lord Salisbury, ordered Lord Northbrook to demand that Sher Ali accept a British mission in Herat, in order to observe and report on Russian movements in Central Asia. Similar missions already existed in Persia, and the Viceroy saw no reason for further antagonizing Sher Ali. In protest, the liberal Lord Northbrook resigned in November, 1875.

Disraeli appointed Lord Lytton as Viceroy to India in 1876. In the meantime, the Russian government sent a Muslin agent as its representative to the court of the Afghan Amir in 1875. An Indian Muslim had represented Britain in Kabul since the second reign of Dost Mohammad.

The occupation of Quetta and its conversion into a military base in 1876 heralded the advent of the new Forward Policy in Central Asia. Such rapid shifts in policy confused Sher Ali and he greeted these new British overtures with suspicion. Again the British demanded that Sher Ali accept a European-staffed mission in Kabul. The Amir refused, and stated that, if he accepted, the Russians might want reciprocal rights. The Viceroy, Lord Lytton, argued that the Russians had precluded such a request when they agreed, in 1873, that Afghanistan lay outside their zone of interest. Sher Ali countered by transmitting to the Viceroy a letter sent to him by General Kaufmann, Russian military commander of Central Asia. The letter contained veiled threats and intimated possible further penetrations toward Afghanistan. London immediately protested to St. Petersburg, but letters from Kaufmann continued to plague the Amir.

At the request of the British, an Afghan delegation, again led by the venerable Sayyid Nur Mohammad Khan, met at Peshawar in January 1877, with a British mission led by Sir Lewis Pelly. The Sayyid died in March, and Lord Lytton ended the conference, although Sher Ali had already dispatched a new envoy from Kabul. The Afghans, however, had made no concessions about European representation in Kabul.

Lord Lytton ordered his Indian Muslim representative, Ata Mohammad Khan, not to return to Kabul, for the Viceroy still insisted on the presence of an Englishman in the Amir's capital. A British envoy, in the mind of the Viceroy, would become an adviser, not simply a resident representative. The British, however, offered nothing substantial in return for their demand. An initial money gift to the Amir would be followed by a shaky stipend, and Lytton deemed it "inconvenient to commit his government to any permanent pecuniary obligations." The British tentatively agreed to accept Abdullah Jan as heir apparent, but backed away from any guarantees by stating this "did not imply or necessitate any intervention in the internal affairs of state." Even on the issue of assistance in the event of foreign (i.e., Russian) aggression on the territories of the Amir, the Government of British India hedged, and reserved the "freedom of judgment as to the character of circumstances involving the obligation of material support" (Forbes, 1892, 163).

The Russian-British rivalry in Asia shifted westward. The summer of 1877 witnessed another war between Russia and Turkey, with the Dardanelles at stake. Britain moved troops to Malta. When a Russian army threatened the Dardanelles, Britain sent its fleet through the Bosphorous, and British and Russian troops and ships eyed each other at battle stations for six months.

In July 1878, the Congress of Berlin ended the crisis and the Russians left Turkey, never again to threaten the Dardanelles. The diplomatic defeat rankled the Tsar and his advisors. Thwarted in Europe, they sought to recoup national honor by another movement in Central Asia (Singhal, 1963, 33). Kokand had fallen in 1875–76, and now advance parties pushed toward Khiva and Merv. During this period, the Ottoman Turks pressured the Amir in Kabul to join an anti-Russian alliance. Sher Ali, maintaining his neutral position, refused.

Then occurred the event which precipitated the Second Anglo-Afghan War. The Russians, without receiving permission from Sher Ali, sent a diplomatic mission under General Stolietov from Samarkand to Kabul in the summer of 1878. Amir Sher Ali Khan tried to stop the mission, but was too late. Stolietov reached Kabul on July 22, a day after the signing of the Treaty of Berlin. The Russian move obviously was related to the British Forward Policy in India, and to Britain's successful maneuvers in Europe (Mohd. Ali, 1959, 86).

On August 14, 1878, the Viceroy demanded the Amir accept a British mission, to counter the Russian mission. While the Amir vacillated, Abdullah Jan, his favorite son and the heir apparent, died on August 17, 1878. The Amir went into the traditional lengthy mourning and requested that the British wait until its completion. The British refused and, with little understanding and no sensitivity, accused the Amir of procrastination.

Major Louis Cavagnari moved to Ali Masjid, where the Afghan commanding officer, Major Faiz Mohammad Khan, courteously refused permission for the British Mission, led by Sir Neville Chamberlain, to proceed to Kabul. The British considered this a glaring national insult and delivered an ultimatum to Sher Ali, demanding a satisfactory explanation for the action by November 20.

Sher Ali Khan's reply of October 19 concerning the "insult" was not considered satisfactory, and on November 21, 1878, British troops crossed into the Amir's territory in a three-pronged attack: General Frederick Roberts moved through the Kurram; General Sir Sam Browne (inventor of the famous "Sam Browne" military belt) moved through the Khyber toward Jalalabad; General Donald Stewart moved from Quetta against Qandahar. Actually, General M. A. S. Biddulph commanded the Quetta force, but he came under the overall command of General Stewart, leader of the Multan Division.

Misunderstanding followed misunderstanding. St. Petersburg assured London that the Russian mission would be withdrawn, since war no longer threatened their two countries in Europe. Sher Ali, having earlier signed a defensive alliance with Russia in desperation, appealed for aid when the British invaded Afghanistan. General Kaufmann refused, tactfully emphasizing the impossibility of transporting troops and material across the Hindu Kush in winter. Sher Ali journeyed to Mazar-i-Sharif, determined to plead his cause in person to the Tsar. Across the Amu Darya, however, the Russians continually blocked his attempts to reach St. Petersburg, arguing that he should make his peace with Britain. Sher Ali, broken in spirit, became ill. He died near Balkh on February 21, 1879, while the Russians and the rest of the world watched the folly of the Second Anglo-Afghan War.

Yaqub Khan, previously released from jail and serving as Regent in Kabul during his father's absence, became Amir. The British armies of invasion had meanwhile occupied the Peiwar Kotal in the Kurram area, as well as Jalalabad and Qandahar, by the middle of January 1879. In order to prevent further British advances, Yaqub (under pressure) signed the Treaty of Gandamak on May 26, 1879, which the Afghans still consider the most disgraceful agreement ever signed by an amir. In all fairness, however, it must be stated that, at this time, little unity existed among the tribal leaders, and resistance against the British was unorganized and sporadic.

The main points of the Treaty of Gandamak were that the British would control Afghanistan's foreign affairs; that English-born representatives would reside in Kabul and other areas, under the protection of the Afghans; that the Amir ceded Kurram, Pishin, and Sibi to the British, and agreed to the extension of British control to Khyber and Michni Passes; that, in return for these concessions, the Amir would receive £60,000 per year and loose guarantees for assistance in the event of foreign aggression.

Sir Louis Cavagnari arrived in Kabul in July 1879 (with a small escort), to serve as the British Resident. On September 3, the pattern of the First Anglo-Afghan War repeated itself, and Cavagnari was killed by mutinous Afghan soldiers (who had been paid neither by the Afghans nor by the British) and elements of the Kabul population opposed to the presence of the British contingent.

General Roberts moved from Kurram, fighting a number of successful engagements against the troops of the Amir. He reached Kabul on October 12, 1879, and, on the same day, Yaqub Khan abdicated the throne. He went to India, where he died in exile in 1923.

For all practical purposes General Roberts became Amir in Kabul. He ruled with an iron hand and instituted a reign of terror remembered to this day. But the Afghans once again did not take lightly the occupation of their country by foreigners. Under the leadership of Mushk-i-

Alam Akhundzadah (an Andar Ghilzai; elderly, firey, religious leader of the Ghilzai), Mohammad Jan (Wardak), 'Ismatullah Allah (Jabar Khel Ghilzai), Mir Bacha Khan (Tajik) and others, a large Afghan *lashkar* (tribal army) moved on Kabul. General Roberts was driven from the field in December, and the British found themselves besieged in the newly constructed Sherpur cantonment, originally begun by Amir Sher Ali.

Two factors prevented a repetition of the 1841–42 debacle: the generalship of Roberts and the quality of his subordinates, who undertook constant, vigorous sorties beyond the cantonment to keep the besiegers off guard, and the inability (once again) of the tribal khans to maintain a sustained, unified front, so the Afghan forces, like the snow, slowly melted away as spring approached (*Abridged Official Account of the Second Anglo-Afghan War,* 1908). The *lashkar* and its leaders moved to Ghazni, which became the center of the anti-foreign resistance, and the movement became known as the "Ghazni" or "National Party."

In early February, 1880, Sardar Abdur Rahman Khan, a nephew of Amir Sher Ali Khan, crossed the Amu Darya with about one hundred followers. Following an abortive revolt against his uncle, Abdur Rahman spent twelve years exiled in Samarkand and Tashkent, where General Kaufmann, Russian Governor, had given the talented prince a rich allotment. At first hesitant, the northern khans and begs (except Maimana) joined Abdur Rahman's cause and he headed toward Kabul. On July 20, at Charikar, Abdur Rahman proclaimed himself Amir and the modern era of Afghanistan began.

The British had decided to support Abdur Rahman's claim to the throne of Kabul. At first glance, the move appears to have been a delicate gamble, for Abdur Rahman rode into Kabul wearing a Russian uniform and with reported Russian promises of 2,000 breech-loading rifles, 20,000 rounds of amunition, equipment for 100 cavalrymen and a 100-man personal bodyguard, plus 35,000 rubles (Hamilton, 1906, 356). The British, however, reasoned that Abdur Rahman, like the Afghan Amirs before him, would be neither pro-Russian nor pro-British, but militantly pro-Afghan.

But some months would follow before the British left Afghanistan, and they would suffer another disastrous defeat at the hands of the Afghans. On July 27, 1880, Mohammad Ayub Khan, fifth son of Amir Sher Ali, decisively defeated a British force under Brigadier G. R. S. Burrows in open battle at Maiwand, near Qandahar. Of the 2,476 British and Indian soldiers engaged in the fighting, 971 were killed in action,

168 wounded.[32] In addition, the Afghans slaughtered 331 camp-followers and wounded seven; 210 horses were killed and 68 wounded (*Abridged Official Account of the Second Anglo-Afghan War,* 1908, 526). At-the battle of Maiwand a legendary Pushtun heroine, Malalai, used her veil as a standard, and encouraged the warriors by shouting the following couplet (*landay*) in Pashto (Shpoon, 1968, 48):

Young love, if you do not fall in the battle of Maiwand,
By God, someone is saving you as a token of shame.

This disastrous defeat of British arms in Asia could not go unchallenged, so Lt. General Sir Frederick Roberts gathered a force of 9,987 men (2,836 European; 7,151 Indians), 7,000 camp-followers, 190 staff officers' horses, 1,779 cavalry horses, 450 artillery mules, and 8,167 transport animals: 1,589 *yabus* (Afghan ponies), 4,511 mules, 1,149 ponies, 912 donkeys, and 6 camels with hospital supplies (*Abridged Account of the Second Anglo-Afghan War,* 1908, 554–57). Roberts took no wheeled artillery and few camels, sacrificing firepower for speed.

The Kabul-to-Qandahar Field Force marched the 334 miles in the hot summer days between August 11 and August 31, with only one day's halt, a remarkable military feat, even without opposition. The opposition, however, waited outside Qandahar, and on September 1, 1880,

[32] One of the "wounded" was Dr. John H. Watson, M.D. (A. Doyle, 1930). At their first meeting Sherlock Holmes says to Watson: "You have been in Afghanistan, I perceive." Later, Holmes explains to Watson, who accuses the detective of having known beforehand: "Nothing of the sort, I *knew* you came from Afghanistan. From long habit the train of thoughts ran so swiftly through my mind that I arrived at the conclusion without being conscious of intermediate steps. There were such steps, however. The train of reasoning ran, 'Here is a gentleman of a medical type, but with the air of a military man. Clearly an army doctor, then. He has just come from the tropics, for his face is dark, and that is not the natural tint of his skin, for his wrists are fair. He has undergone hardship and sickness, as his haggard face says clearly. His left arm has been injured. He holds it in a stiff and unnatural manner. Where in the tropics could an English army doctor have seen much hardship and got his arm wounded? Clearly in Afghanistan.' The whole train of thought did not occupy a second. I then remarked that you came from Afghanistan, and you were astonished."
Several years ago, the Baker Street Irregulars asked the Afghan government for permission to put up a monument to Dr. Watson on the Maiwand battleground. No official decision has been made, but the embarrassed Afghans simply do not understand why the club wishes to put up a monument to a man who never existed on a battlefield where the Afghans decisively defeated the British!

411

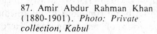

86. Amir Sher Ali Khan (1863-66; 1868-79) with several sons and advisers: (Dilkes, 1969, incorrectly identifies this photo as of Amir Abdur Rahman Khan). *Photo: Private collection, Kabul*

87. Amir Abdur Rahman Khan (1880-1901). *Photo: Private collection, Kabul*

without waiting for a rest, Roberts sallied forth to meet Ayub Khan. The British won a decisive victory, and Ayub Khan returned to Herat.

For his services in the Second Anglo-Afghan War, Roberts became Lord Roberts of Qandahar (Roberts, 1911).

In the meantime, however, the political pendulum swung once again in England. The Conservative Party of Disraeli went down in defeat before the Liberals of Gladstone in April 1880, and the new Prime Minister replaced Lord Lytton and appointed Lord Ripon as Viceroy of India.[33] Over the protests of many military men and civilians (Lord Napier of Magdala, Sir Henry Rawlinson, General Sir Frederick Roberts, and General Sir Donald Stewart, Roberts' commanding officer in Kabul), the British withdrew from Qandahar in April, 1881. (The force in Kabul under Sir Donald Stewart had left the country nine months earlier, in August, 1880). Other Englishmen, just as notable (such as Lord Lawrence, General Charles "Chinese" Gordon, Lord Wolseley), supported the move, for now a neutral—if not very friendly—Amir, Abdur Rahman Khan, sat on the throne in Kabul (Forbes, 1892, 325–26).

---

[33] For a list of successive Viceroys in British India see Majumdar, et al., 1961, 1042–43.

PART IV. THE PRESENT

"How can a small Power like Afghanistan, which is like a goat between these lions [Britain and Tsarist Russia], or a grain of wheat between two strong millstones of the grinding mill, stand in the midway of the stones without being ground to dust?" (Abdur Rahman Khan, 1900, II, 280).

The recent history of Afghanistan reveals the story of a piece of real estate trying to become a nation-state, its external patterns uncontrollably linked with those of the two great imperialist powers in the region. More important than the drawing of boundaries was Afghanistan's internal integration, hampered by a plethora of independent and semi-independent ethnic and linguistic units.

Therefore, Afghanistan discovered that the most important elements in the creation of a national consciousness are the attitudes of the people, for a nation-state must evolve as a state of mind as well as a geographic entity. The essence of the modern nation-state involves a reciprocal set of recognizable, definable, functioning rights and obligations between the government and the governed. All twentieth-century nations, including Afghanistan and the United States, still strive, in varying ways, to achieve this ideal, although in Afghanistan, as in most of the developing world, many social, political, and economic rights and obligations occur within kinship-oriented, not government-oriented, institutions.

415

CHAPTER 18

Amir Abdur Rahman Khan

AND THE BEGINNINGS OF MODERN
AFGHANISTAN 1880–1901[1]

INITIALLY, Abdur Rahman controlled only Kabul and surrounding territories, but, before his death in 1901, he had spread his influence—if not actual control—throughout most of what we recognize as modern Afghanistan. I call this process "internal imperialism." If, however, Abdur Rahman had been born a hundred years earlier, this charismatic leader would probably have followed the patterns of previous Central Asian emperors, and expanded as far as force and intrigue could carry his empire. But the Russians blocked him to the north and northeast, the British to the south and southeast, and the British and the Russians guaranteed Persia protection from Afghan invasion, at least tacitly and unwritten. So Abdur Rahman Khan funneled his many talents into the creation of a nation-state; i.e., the process of internal imperialism.

Born in Kabul in 1844, Abdur Rahman Khan spent most of his youth in Balkh with his father, Mohammad Afzal Khan. Abdur Rahman learned conventional warfare tactics from the Anglo-Indian soldier of fortune, William Campbell.[2] The young prince learned his lessons well,

---

[1] For a fascinating account of the life and times of Abdur Rahman Khan, see his autobiography: Sultan Mahomed Khan (ed.) (1900); or Abdur Rahman Khan (1904). I am greatly indebted to M. Hasan Kakar for permitting me to read his excellent M. Phil. thesis on this period (Kakar, 1968). Kakar (pp. 279–80), in commenting on the autobiography of Abdur Rahman Khan, says only the first eleven chapters were written by the Amir. Also see Gregorian (1969), who covers the period 1880–1946. Reisner (1954) offers an excellent Marxist interpretation of Afghan history.

[2] Campbell first appears as an officer in the Sikh forces of Ranjit Singh; then, fired by Ranjit, he served gallantly under the banner of exiled Shah Shuja. Badly wounded in the battle of Qandahar, 1834, when Shah Shuja unsuccessfully attempted to regain his throne, Campbell impressed Dost Mohammad, who made the adventurer virtual Commander-in-Chief of the Afghan army. Campbell embraced Islam, taking the name of General Sher Mohammad Khan. When the British returned Shah Shuja to the throne in 1839, Campbell once again shifted his loyalty to Shuja. The resilient Anglo-Indian remained as an Afghan general after Dost Mohammad returned to Kabul, and died peacefully in Mazar-i-Sharif in 1866 (Grey and Garrett, 1929, 224–31).

and early proved himself as a soldier, successfully commanding his father's forces in the field to suppress revolts in Qataghan and Badakhshan.

Abdur Rahman's troubles began early, and lasted throughout most of his reign. Political fission was the order of the day, and he spent most of his time and energy trying to penetrate and pacify zones of relative inaccessibility. At first most tribal leaders continued to maintain independence from Kabul's rule, so the Amir initiated his policy of internal imperialism.

The first threat to Abdur Rahman's power came from his cousin, Mohammad Ayub Khan, hero of the Second Anglo-Afghan War. Ayub Khan moved from Herat in July, 1881, and he defeated the forces of the Amir, commanded by Ghulam Haider Charkhi, at Karez-i-Atta near Girishk on July 20. For a time it seemed that the new Amir would become the ex-Amir, replaced by Ayub Khan.

But Abdur Rahman had not forgotten the lessons learned from Campbell. He took to the field personally and defeated his cousin on September 22. Ayub Khan retreated to Herat and found himself cut off from the city by two of Abdur Rahman's generals, Abdul Quddus Khan and Anbia Khan Taimani.

Ayub Khan's forces fissioned and melted away. He fled to Persia, but could gain no support for his cause. Discouraged, the Victor of Maiwand traveled to India in 1888, accepted the usual British pension for indigent Afghan Sardars, and died at Lahore in April 1914.

Wholesale executions and deportations usually followed the suppression of each rebellion, or the conquest of such independent areas as the Uzbak Khanates, the Turkoman who supported Mohammad 'Ishaq Khan,[3] the Hazarajat, and, to a lesser extent, Kafiristan. The following list includes all the major (and some minor) campaigns of Abdur Rahman:

Tribal Group, Region, or Leader	*Date*
Ayub Khan and followers	1881
Laghman	1881
Taraki Ghilzai	1881–82
Kunar	1882

[3] Son of Mohammad Azam Khan (and therefore first cousin of Abdur Rahman), by an Armenian wife. Abdur Rahman made him Governor of Turkestan in 1880. 'Ishaq Khan revolted in 1888, and declared himself Amir. Defeated, he was exiled to Bokhara.

Tribal Group, Region, or Leader	Date
Wali of Maimana	1882
Mir of Shighnan and Roashan (NE Badakhshan)	1882
Shinwari Pushtun	1882–92
Mangal-Zurmat Pushtun	1883–84
Wali of Maimana (submitted without fighting)	1884
Laghman	1885–86
Ghilzai Pushtun*	1886–88
Mohammad 'Ishaq Khan	1888
Safi Pushtun of Kunar	1888–96
Badakhshan	1889
Khan of Asmar	1890
Hazarajat	1891–93
Kafiristan	1895–96

* The Ghilzai revolt once again polarized the Durrani-Ghilzai rivalry, with the Durrani becoming the pampered tribe of the royal family. In the earlier fight with Ayub Khan, the Durrani and Ghilzai had split into pro- and anti-Abdur Rahman groups.

Abdur Rahman himself described his task as one of putting "in order all those hundreds of petty chiefs, plunderers, robbers and cut-throats. . . . This necessitated breaking down the feudal[4] and tribal system and substituting one grand community under one law and one rule" (quoted in Wilber, 1962, 19).

Forced migrations helped break the traditional power of the tribal kingdoms. In the late 1880s and early 1890s, Abdur Rahman shifted thousands of Ghilzai Pushtun (his major enemies) and others from southern and south-central Afghanistan to north of the Hindu Kush, where their descendants still dwell. By moving large numbers of his enemies, Abdur Rahman accomplished two immediate aims: he re-moved dissidents from areas which they might again infect with the germs of revolt, and he created a force loyal to himself, for, although the Ghilzai (Pushtun) might be anti-Durrani (Pushtun) while living in their own territorial tribal zones, they were pro-Pushtun in the northern non-Pushtun (Tajik, Uzbak, Hazara, Turkoman) areas. Also, in an at-tempt to mollify the non-Pushtun elements, Abdur Rahman abolished the *sarmardeh*, a tax imposed on non-Pushtun peoples by Amir Sher Ali Khan (Kakar, 1968, 92).

As he conquered his country, Abdur Rahman Khan instituted several

[4] For a discussion of "feudal" concepts, see L. Dupree, 1957.

innovations in governing Afghanistan. Unlike prior rulers, he kept his sons in Kabul and appointed loyal followers as provincial governors, whom he gave a free hand so long as they sent the required taxes and conscripts to Kabul. An internal spy system, as old as the Achaemenid "eyes and ears of the king," helped keep the modern satraps honest, for justice under Abdur Rahman was swift and harsh.

The provincial governors contributed greatly to the breakdown of the territorial tribal system. The villagers and tribesmen, unused to recognizing any but tribal law, knew little about the initial actions of the central government. For them, the provincial government tended to take the place of the tribal nation. The new provincial boundaries, drawn by Abdur Rahman, and the old tribal areas seldom coincided, however. Many tribes were split and divided between two and more provinces or subprovinces. Any signs of discontent were immediately put down. The provincial army, under the command of the provincial governor (usually a military man), enforced the governor's dictums and the Amir's *farman*. Thus, at least administratively, the provinces became quasi-independent units, partly, though not adequately, taking the place of the independent tribal nations.

Although the governors had the right and obligation to collect taxes, they did not own the land. In south-central and southwestern Afghanistan, however, the right to collect taxes sometimes became confused, either consciously or sub-consciously, with bona fide ownership of land. Land was sold and resold by government officials without any regard to the traditional joint ownership of village lands by the clan or lineage. The army was on hand to seal such transactions, if necessary. In this situation, obviously something had to give, and the tribal and clan organization began to disintegrate.

When Abdur Rahman Khan came to the throne in Kabul, ten clerks under the guidance of one official handled all the central government administration. Using the military branch or bureau as a watchdog, Abdur Rahman developed a civil administration which continues in modified form to the present day (McChesney, 1968). He instituted a Board of Treasury, Board of Trade, Bureau of Justice and Police, the Office of Records, Office of Public Works, Office of Posts and Communications, Department of Education, Department of Medicine, all of which can be roughly equated to modern cabinet departments or ministries.

Although fundamentally an autocrat, Abdur Rahman Khan did create a Supreme Council, similar to the modern cabinet. The Council had no prime minister, and no authority; it could only advise. The Council included the following: a gentleman known as the *'Ishik Aghasi* (The Lord Chamberlain, also called *Shahghasi*); Lord of the Seals; the Chief Secretary and other secretaries appointed by Abdur Rahman Khan; the officers of the Royal Bodyguard; the Treasurer of the private treasury of the Amir; the Secretary of State for War; the Secretaries of State for the four major areas of the country; the Postmaster General; the Commander-in-Chief of the Armed Forces; Master of the Horse; the *Kotwal* (equivalent to Minister of the Interior); Accountant General; Groom of the Bedchamber; Superintendent of the Magazine; Heads of the Board of Trade and the Board of Education (Hamilton, 1906, 273–74; Kakar, 1968, 99).

The Amir also appointed a General Assembly (*Loya Jirgah*) which included three groups of Afghan citizens: certain Sardars (princes) of the royal family; important khans or *khawanin-i-mulki,* in the rural power elite, from different parts of the country; the religious leaders, from whom, however, he brooked no opposition. At times, Abdur Rahman invited influential members of the General Assembly to attend Council meetings.

But the ultimate source of the Amir's power, his institution for control and implementation, was the army.

While the Amir busily pacified the interior of his country, attempting to create a nation-state, foreign powers drew his external boundaries, with or without his consent; which Singhal calls "demarcation without representation" (1963, 107).

An early major boundary dispute, the Panjdeh crisis of 1885, cost Abdur Rahman several thousand square miles north of Herat, and brought Tsarist Russia and Great Britain to the brink of war. A Brigadier General wrote a book describing in detail how it would be fought (Rodenbough, 1885). German observers also predicted war (Roskoschny, 1885).

Earlier Russian advances in Central Asia precipitated the crisis. In 1876, the Khanate of Kokand fell to the Russians; in 1879 the Tekke Turkoman defeated a Tsarist expedition; but in 1881 the Tekke Turkoman fell before superior Russian forces.

Early in 1884, after seven years of difficult warfare, Tsarist armies completed their conquest of the Turkoman with the submission of the Merv Oasis, once a part of Persia, and British politicians developed what some wags of the day called "Mervousness." Now the lines were drawn. The British had physically withdrawn from Afghanistan, but re-

421

tained control of Afghan foreign affairs. They also subsidized Abdur Rahman as he extended and consolidated his kingdom. The next Russian advance to the south would infringe on territory claimed by the Amir.

Summit conferences were rare seventy-five years ago, but numerous boundary commissions flitted from continent to continent, attempting to settle problems. These commissions had one thing in common: a genius for drawing a boundary in the wrong place, and we still live with the results of their decisions. The British (as representatives of the Afghan Amir) and the Russians established permanent boundaries between Afghanistan and Russian Central Asia. The British were interested in the rights of the Afghans; the Russians wanted the issue settled on an ethnographic basis before a mission arrived, e.g., all Turkoman should be incorporated into the Tsarist Empire.

Such a scheme would have placed the Panjdeh Oasis, (southeast of Merv), also claimed by Afghanistan, under Russian domination. The Tekke Turkoman of Panjdeh paid occasional tribute to the ruler of Herat, so legally the Afghans had at least a tenuous claim to the area. Legality, however, little intruded into the events which followed.

Slowly, the Russians under Colonel Alikhanoff pushed to within shooting-distance of the Afghan outposts in the Panjdeh. Colonel Alikhanoff wrote a vile letter to his Afghan counterpart, General Ghausuddin Khan, calling him a liar and a coward, and using other terms anathema to the Afghans. Ghausuddin answered in kind, referring to Alikhanoff as a thief trying to steal land which rightfully belonged to the Afghans. On the spot, the British Boundary Commissioner, Sir Peter Lumsden, became worried and communicated his fears to Whitehall. Britain informed Russia that an attack on the Panjdeh area would be regarded as a threat to Britain (implying that nothing would be done, however). Concerning Herat, the wording differed: if Russia attacked, or even approached, Herat, Her Majesty's Government would consider this a direct declaration of war (Ghose, 1960, 199).

On March 30, 1885, the Panjdeh Incident occurred. Russian troops moved towards the Afghans in battle order; the Afghan commander shifted his men across the Murghab River to meet the threat. No one knows who fired first, but a battle took place, and although the Afghans fought bravely, according to both British and Russian observers, they were overwhelmed in the end and forced to retreat. The Russians occupied the Panjdeh Oasis (Yate, 1887, 311–60). Amir Abdur Rahman Khan heard of the "Panjdeh Incident" while visiting the Viceroy, Lord

Dufferin, in Rawalpindi. He chided the Viceroy for the lack of British armed assistance in Afghanistan's time of need.

But around the world, the newspapers played up the coming war between Britain and Russia, although by this time, Abdur Rahman Khan had no faith in British promises. Editorials in Russia encouraged the Tsarist armies to seize Herat as the first step to reaching the Indian Ocean. The British army sent two engineers to assist the Afghans in the defense of Herat. Troop reserves were called up in both countries. Leaders on both sides, however, realized that war could not be limited to Afghanistan; another European blood bath seemed in the making. Both Russia and Britain, disregarding the legal and moral issues involved and the wishes of the Afghan Amir, sought peaceful solutions.

The Russians had gained territory they wanted; the British hoped to stop them there. The Russians, then as now, were able bluffers, able negotiators; they knew exactly how far they could press the British and did so. Next came the battle of the conferences, to determine where a permanent boundary should be established. Russia agreed to give up Zulfiqar, the point of farthest advance, but kept the Panjdeh. The proposed line ran from Zulfiqar on the Hari Rud to Khoja Saleh on the Amu Darya. The British agreed, and the Afghan Amir had no choice in the matter. Actually, Abdur Rahman personally did not consider Panjdeh as important as Zulfiqar, Maruchak, and Gulran (Ghose, 1960, 198).

So a compromise, reached at the expense of Afghan territory and British integrity, averted a major war. However, when a joint commission tried to lay out the boundary on the spot, a comic opera scene occurred. Previously, the Russians had known little about the rich agricultural lands of north Afghanistan. Their commission immediately tried to take advantage of an earlier cartographic mistake by Sir Alexander Burnes in order to gain control of the Turkestan Plains *south* of the Amu Darya. Burnes, in his report on his famous journey to Bokhara, stated that the Amir's jurisdiction reached to "Khojah Salih" or "Haji Salih," the point at which he crossed the Amu Darya (Burnes, 1835, III:113). The British-Russian agreement of 1873 used Burnes' data to establish the boundary between the Khanate of Bokhara and north Afghanistan. Later, the Bokharan and Afghan Amirs mutually established a frontier which coincided exactly with the Russian-British version.

The Joint Boundary Commission of 1886 located several "Khojah Salih," including a river ford, a ferry point, several villages, and a border port. Although the correct Khoja Saleh had been known for years by both Afghans and Bokharans, the Russian commission used the muddiness of the 1873 agreement to break off negotiations in September 1886. The British held firm, however, and finally the Russians accepted the 1873 boundary along the Amu Darya. The Afghans paid the price for the settlement; they relinquished more land in the Panjdeh area.

Many observers thought the boundary completely untenable—among them the chief of the British Boundary Commission, Sir West Ridgeway, after whom the Ridgeway Line of 1887 was named—and that the Russians would eventually absorb all of Afghanistan north of the Hindu Kush, forcing the British to occupy the south. For several years after 1887, sabers rattled along the northern frontier, and in 1889 the British had to repeat that any Russian move toward Herat would be treated as a declaration of war.

By 1891 the scene shifted to the northeastern boundary as the Russians attempted to explore and annex the Wakhan area. This would, in effect, outflank the northwestern boundary and give Russia a common boundary with British India. Considering themselves seriously threatened, the British reacted vigorously, and forced Russia to negotiate. Amir Abdur Rahman, with the British still in control of his foreign policy, resumed his role as bystander. Britain and Russia agreed to give Russia all the land north of the Amu Darya and Afghanistan all land south of the Amu Darya. Also, the British forced Afghanistan to accept control of the Wakhan, a rugged area still incompletely mapped. Abdur Rahman objected to the gift, exclaiming he had enough problems with his own people and did not wish to be held responsible for the Kirghiz bandits in the Wakhan and Pamir. Because of the Wakhan-Pamir award to the Afghans, however, at no point did British India touch Tsarist Russia.

Another Joint Boundary Commission fixed the extreme northeast boundary in 1895–96. At its easternmost point the boundary moves through a rough mass of perpetual glaciers to touch China. (In 1964, the Afghans and Chinese actually demarcated this boundary on the ground for the first time.)

By 1896, therefore, the northern boundaries of Afghanistan were fixed, except for an amazing oversight. No one bothered to define the boundary along the Amu Darya itself. This led to several disputes, none serious, until by mutual agreement in 1946 the *thalweg* (mid-channel of the river) became the official border between the Soviet Union and Afghanistan.

By far the most important boundary from the Afghan point of view was the Durand Line of 1893, a classic example of an artificial political boundary cutting through a culture area (L. Dupree, 1961b). Why and how did it come into being?

The British in India, happy at creating a no-man's-land between themselves and Tsarist ambitions, faced other problems. The Pushtun tribes, almost genetically expert at guerrilla warfare after centuries of resisting all comers and fighting among themselves when no comers were available, plagued attempts to extend *Pax Britannica* into their mountain homeland. Many raids into the Indus Valley plains (supposedly protected by the British Indian Army) originated outside the range of effective punitive action. As early as 1877, the British began their consolidation of a forward wall of protective outposts by outright bludgeoning of local Pushtun rulers. In 1877 they simply informed Amir Sher Ali that he had no claims on Dir, Swat, Chitral, and Bajaur.

In 1879, the British forced the Amir Yaqub, son of Sher Ali, to sign the Treaty of Gandamak (which the Afghans call the "Condemned Treaty"), under which "the British Government will retain in its own hands control of the Khaiber Pass and Michni Pass . . . and of all relations with the independent tribes, territory directly connected with the passes" (Aitchison, 1933, 242). Therefore, the treaty ceded large tracts of land in the districts of Loralai, Zhob, Pishin, Quetta, and Nushki, presumably giving legal justification for as much as the British could occupy and hold.

Troubled by annual incursions by the tribes, the British attempted to push the Forward Policy once more under Lord Landsdowne, who became Viceroy in December 1888. The British appreciably increased the size of the British Indian Army and constructed strategic cantonments (or expanded those already existing) at Rawalpindi, Attock, and Quetta. Railroads wriggled through the mountains to Chaman. Abdur Rahman resented British encroachments in the Pushtun tribal areas, which nominally looked to Kabul for supra-tribal guidance. He viewed both Russia and Britain with apprehension (as indicated by the quote which introduces this section of our book).

In his illuminating autobiography (1900), Abdur Rahman repeatedly states he never considered any Pushtun areas as permanently ceded to the British (also Kakar, 1968, 145).

In 1892, Abdur Rahman attempted to establish direct contact with the British Government in London, for he felt that he could not possibly receive fair treatment from the British Indian Government. Because of

British pressures, however, the Amir agreed to receive a mission under Sir Mortimer Durand, Indian Foreign Secretary, in 1893. To delineate once and for all British and Afghan responsibilities in the Pushtun area, the Durand Mission journeyed to Kabul in September. Beset by continuing tribal revolts in the Pushtun area and worried by British road- and railway-construction which pointed toward Qandahar and Kabul, "pushing like a knife into my vitals" (Abdur Rahman, 1900, II:159), Abdur Rahman at first seemed to welcome the proposed divisions.

Before Durand left Kabul on November 14, 1893, both sides agreed on a boundary from "Chitral and Baroghil Pass up to Peshawar, and thence up to Koh-i-Malik Siyah in this way that Wakhan, Kafiristan, Asmar, Mohmand of Lalpura, and one portion of Waziristan [i.e., Birmal] came under my rule, and I renounce my claims for the railway station of New Chaman, Chagai, the rest of Waziri, Biland Khel, Kurram, Afridi, Bajaur, Swat, Buner, Dir, Chilas and Chitral" (Abdur Rahman, 1900, II:160).

The last phrase tends to confirm Afghan acceptance of the Treaty of Gandamak, no matter how distasteful it may have been. One might suppose from reading his words that the Afghan Amir found the 1893 Agreement satisfactory, but further examination of his autobiography and his papers indicates his opposition to the Durand Line as a *permanent* boundary. He insisted the "boundary" delineated zones of responsibility, and did not draw an international boundary. In addition, Kakar (1968, 145) presents convincing evidence that the Amir *did not* actually write the "I renounce my claims" sentence. Even Durand did not anticipate annexation: "Durand . . . did not propose to move forward the administrative border of India, but merely pushed for *political control* [italics mine]" (Sykes, 1926, 219).

Numerous British writers, such as Barton (1939) and Holdich (1901, 1910), have commented on the Amir's antagonism to the Durand Line and the lengths to which Durand went in order to get Abdur Rahman's signature on the 1893 agreement. For example, the Amir's subsidy from the British jumped from 1.2 to 1.8 million rupees, plus increased arms and ammunition quotas, and Durand found it necessary to aim several veiled threats at the Amir.

The last paragraph in the final agreement of November 12, 1893, is vague and inconclusive (Caroe, 1965, 463):

Article 1, Paragraph 2: The Government of India will at no time exercise interference in the territories lying beyond this line on the side of Afghanistan and His Highness the Amir will at no time exercise interference in the territory lying beyond this line on the side of India.

Another quote by Caroe (1965, 382) is interesting:

It is true that the agreement did not describe the line as a boundary of India, but as the frontier of the Amir's dominions and the line beyond which neither side would exercise interference. This was because the British Government did not intend to absorb the tribes into their administrative system, only to extend their own, and exclude the Amir's, authority in the territory east and south of the line. In the international aspect this was of no account, for the Amir had renounced sovereignty beyond this line.

The Amir might question: voluntarily? At what point does coercion cease to be legal?

Other British administrators, however, contend the Durand Line was never meant to be an international boundary: "The Durand Agreement was an agreement to define the respective spheres of influence of the British Government and the Amir" (L/P & S/7: Letter from Elgin to Hamilton: Political and Secret letters and enclosures received from India. Vol. 85, Foreign Dept. Letter No. 77, 1896. India Office Records, London). Many Englishmen later serving in the frontier also considered the Durand Line and the boundary (administrative border) between the Tribal Agencies and Settled Districts of the North-West Frontier Province as simply delineating zones of influence and responsibility, e.g., " . . . the tribes between the administrative border and the Durand Line were a buffer to a buffer, and the line had none of the rigidity of other international frontiers" (Elliott, 1963, 53); also see Poullada (1969a, 22) and L. Dupree (1961b) for similar quotes from British sources.

The Kabul negotiations were peaceful, however, compared to the experiences of the commissions[5] assigned to fix the boundary in the field. Antagonism greeted the British Commissions in most areas, and tribesmen (particularly in Waziristan) several times attacked the group. Local mullah, some probably in the pay of Kabul, spread the word that the *farangi* planned to annex and occupy Pushtun lands on both sides of

---

[5] Special commissions demarcated the various segments of the Durand Line. For an excellent, detailed discussion on the legality of the Durand Line, see Poullada, 1969a.

the line. Occasionally the commissions treated their jobs as pleasant hunting trips. When a village could not decide on which side of the Line it wished to fall, the British Commissioners shouldered their Wesley-Richards bird-guns and "went shooting," asking that the villagers please make up their minds before they returned. In several instances split village loyalties resulted in placing parts of villages on separate sides of the Line. In addition, sometimes the fields of a village lay on the British side, the village itself on the Afghan side. British interest appeared to be more concerned with the topography rather than the decisions of the people.

The Durand Line, designed to bring stability to the frontier regions, failed. In reality, it little resembled the line agreed to by Durand and, the Amir (Hamilton, 1910, 413), and the Durand Line proved politically, geographically, and strategically untenable. British and Indian troops fought many bloody engagements with the fiercely independent border mountaineers. Much of the fighting was the direct result of British attempts to demarcate the hated Durand Line (Churchill, 1916; Davies, 1932; Elliott, 1968; Hutchinson, 1898; G. Robertson, 1898; W. Robertson, 1898; Swinson, 1967; Younghusband, 1895) or control the tribes near the Line.

Abdur Rahman's reign was not only characterized by external boundary-drawing and internal imperialism, but early attempts at modernization (McChesney, 1968). He hired many foreigners to assist in technological development, including Dr. John Gray (1895), an English physician; Messrs. Pyne, Stewart, and Myddleton, English engineers; Munshi Abdur Razaq, an Indian printer from Delhi; M. Jérome, a French engineer; Arthur Collins, an English mining engineer, who introduced relatively modern methods of mining copper, lead, and other metals; Captain C. L. Griesbach (1887), an English geologist; Miss Lillias Hamilton, English lady doctor to the Amir; Mrs. Kate Daly, English medical advisor to the harem (Hamilton, 1910, 389–99).

Workshops and small factories, furnished with European machinery, manufactured leather goods (mainly boots), soap, and candles for the harem. A mint produced 8–10,000 rupees a day.

Gout troubled Abdur Rahman during the last decade of his life, and he died on October 1, 1901. A rare event in Afghan history occurred, and Habibullah, Abdur Rahman's eldest son and close confidant, succeeded to the throne without the usual fratricidal fighting, in spite of the fact that Abdur Rahman had many wives, concubines, and children. He had wisely kept his sons in Kabul and had not made them provincial governors. Apparently, few (if any) of his other sons had political ambitions. The new provincial system had succeeded. In addition, Abdur Rahman Khan's policy of either killing or exiling all his enemies (real and potential) and the forced migration of dissidents inside the country, also succeeded. Another coercive policy initiated by Abdur Rahman remained a repressive coercive force in Afghanistan until the promulgation of the 1964 constitution: Afghans were denied the right of free travel inside and outside of the country without the express consent of the government.

CHAPTER 19

Habibullah

MARKING TIME, 1901–19

PALACE, rather than tribal, intrigue beset Habibullah. Although he was the oldest son of Abdur Rahman Khan, Habibullah (born 1872) was the child of a Wakhi slave girl, Guriz, also the mother of Nasrullah (born 1874). The most royal wife, however, strong-willed Bibi Halima, paternal granddaughter of Dost Mohammad Khan, intrigued to have her son, Mohammad Omar Jan (born 1889), placed on the throne. The activities of Bibi Halima forced Habibullah to place her son under constant surveillance. Habibullah himself had four wives, about thirty-five concubines, and approximately fifty offspring. Nasrullah Khan failed to obtain the support of many tribal leaders for the new Amir, but the army, founded by Abdur Rahman Khan, remained the base of power for Habibullah (Poullada, 1969, 106).

The religious leaders had been surpressed by Abdur Rahman Khan. He took over most *waqf* (religious endowments) and put the various brotherhoods on the government payroll (L. Dupree, 1966, 270). Abdur Rahman brooked no opposition from the religious leaders. Under Habibullah, however, the religious leaders (backed by Nasrullah) regained much political power and influenced many of Habibullah's decisions. A parallel rise in modernist thinking, however, led by Mahmud Beg Tarzi, greatly affected Afghanistan in the second decade of the twentieth century.

British and Russian power-plays dominated Habibullah's foreign affairs, along with the disputed drawing of the Persian–Afghan boundary in 1905. As had his predecessors, Habibullah notified the British Viceroy, Lord Curzon (who had succeeded Lord Elgin in January 1889), of his accession to the throne, but Curzon, a great Forward Policy advocate, wanted to extract concessions from Habibullah before recognizing him as Amir. The early 1900s saw the British once again in close competition with Tsarist Russia in Asia. Worldwide imperialist fever swept the West. Bismarck performed a miracle of fusion by uniting the disparate German principalities, and, a latecomer to imperialism,

Germany frantically sought colonies in Afro-Asia in order to gain international imperialist respectability. The Americans, not to be outdone, acquired territories in the Caribbean and the Pacific from Spain. The Ottoman Empire, long the "Sick Man of Europe," continued its headlong dash toward total collapse.

The British pushed outposts into tribal territories from Chitral to Baluchistan, recruited and trained local levies, paid high subsidies to some tribes, fought others, and built rail lines to Dargai, Thal (terminus of Afghan lumber trade), and Jamrud (entrance of the Khyber, where the old fort today squats like a battleship pointing toward the rough seas beyond).

In 1901, the British separated the Cis-Indus region of the Pushtun from the body politic of the Punjab to form a new province: the North–West Frontier Province (Dichter, 1967). Tribal raids increased rather than diminished as the British moved forward. In 1907, 56 raids were recorded in the Settled Districts of the North–West Frontier, 99 in 1908, 159 in 1909 (Davies, 1932).

Lord Curzon informed Habibullah that the British treaty with Abdur Rahman had been a personal document and, therefore, a new one must be considered. The Curzon note constituted a grave insult to Habibullah and Afghanistan, for the British always insisted that successive regimes in Kabul inherit treaty obligations. In attempts to coerce Habibullah, the British prevented arms supplies ordered by the Amir from passing in transit through British India. Curzon invited Habibullah to come to India for consultations. Habibullah, well within his rights, refused and insisted a country-to-country treaty does not need revision unless both parties desire changes. Lord Curzon, undeterred, asked Habibullah again in June 1904, and again received a negative reply. Curzon, one of the great White Man's burdens, pushed for war, and spread the rumor that Habibullah was considering an Afghan–Russian alliance. Luckily, calmer and more senior heads prevailed in London, and Curzon relaxed.

To the north, the Russians pushed their railheads to within easy striking-distance of Afghanistan. Thwarted in Tibet by the British, and by the Japanese in the Far East (Russo-Japanese War of 1904–05), the Russians might have won favor with the Afghans if Curzon had been permitted to continue his shortsighted policies.

While Curzon ranted in London, having been recalled for consultation, Habibullah made a shrewd move. Since the British wanted to talk over a new, personal treaty with him, he saw no reason to honor the existing treaty. He decided to try to open diplomatic intercourse with the outside world without consulting the British Indian Government. Among the countries he proposed to contact were the United Kingdom, Russia, Japan, Turkey, Germany, Persia, China, Egypt, and the U.S.A. An outraged Curzon demanded an, invasion. Again, saner heads prevailed, and a mission under Sir Lewis Dane, dispatched by the acting Viceroy, Lord Ampthill, conducted formal negotiations with Habibullah from December 1904, to March 1905.

The British demands were rigid (extend British railheads to Kabul and Qandahar; connect the Afghan telecommunications networks with those of India; restrict arms importation through India to Afghanistan), but Habibullah's opposition proved just as rigid. He gave the British a take-it-or-leave-it draft, based on the prior Anglo-Afghan treaty of his father, and insisted upon being addressed as "Your Majesty" and acknowledged as "independent ruler of Afghanistan and its dependencies." The British relented and the new agreement was signed on March 21, 1905. Curzon resigned in August 1905, amid cheering in London, Delhi, and Kabul, and was succeeded by Lord Minto, co-author of the liberal Minto-Morley Reforms (Government of India Act of 1909), a great step toward Indian self-government.

Another artificial boundary remained to be drawn. Neither the Persians nor the Afghans were satisfied with the Sistan boundary drawn by Sir Frederic Goldsmid's Commission in 1872. In 1902, the British, at the request of the Persians and with the acquiescence of the Afghans, agreed to draw a more precise boundary to replace the vague Goldsmid Award. Colonel A. H. McMahon led the British commission (Hamilton, 1906, 211–41). In spite of continued pressure from German and Russian diplomatic missions in Tehran and the intrigues of the Russian Consul at Nasratabad, M. Miller, the Boundary Commission completed its demarcation work in April 1904. With continued reservations, both Persians and Afghans accepted the boundary in September 1904; it was essentially the same as that of Goldsmid, which followed the course of the Hilmand, a shifting, relatively unpredictable stream. A second phase of the mission's work, the equitable distribution of the Hilmand waters, met with less success.

Habibullah immediately accepted the decisions reached in May 1905, and the local population reportedly supported the results. The Persians, on the other hand, have never accepted the 1905 distribution decision, and officially notified the British Government of its non-acceptance on February 26, 1906. The festering sore remains, now fortunately encrusted with diplomatic tact.

Habibullah visited British India from January 2 to March 7, 1907, as a guest of Lord Minto, and was received with all the pomp and circumstance befitting royalty. He gained a healthy respect for British power during the largely ceremonial visit, but still had the courage to refuse to be a party to the Anglo–Russian Convention of 1907, which, importantly, laid the groundwork for future Afghan neutrality.

Until the Russo–Japanese War of 1904–05 and the subsequent Russo–British alliance against Germany, the Russians continued their efforts to penetrate Afghanistan politically and economically, but not militarily. Russian activities in eastern Persia, particularly Sistan, and British attempts to gain a foothold in Tibet finally forced the two great European powers to break up the region into formal spheres of influence. After eighteen months of negotiations, the 1907 Convention was signed in St. Petersburg, with the following important provisions:

1. Persia was divided into two zones of influence: Russian in the north and British in the east and south, thus protecting the western frontier of Afghanistan from Russian penetration; in addition, both sides agreed to the other's right to occupy its zone of influence if threatened by a third party.[1]

2. Russia and Britain recognized Chinese control of Tibet and agreed not to interfere in this area.[2]

3. Russia agreed that Afghanistan was outside her sphere of influence and agreed to confer directly with the British on matters relating to Russian-Afghan relations.

4. Britain was not to occupy or annex any part of Afghanistan, nor to interfere in any way in the internal affairs of that country.

A final article stated that the Amir of Afghanistan must agree to the Convention in order to make it legal and binding. Habibullah, however, immediately declared the Convention illegal, for the Afghans had had no voice in the deliberations. The Amir wanted the British to join him in an attack on Russian Turkestan to recover lands lost to Russia in the 1880s. The defeat of Tsarist Russia by Japan probably made him think his scheme would succeed. The British refused his request. With

[1] The British and Russians used this provision to invade and occupy Iran during World War II (Skrine, 1962).
[2] The People's Republic of China referred to this provision after the invasion of Tibet in 1950, even though the last Chinese mission had been expelled from Lhasa in 1912 (Fisher, Rose, and Huttenback, 1963, 81).

433

typical Afghan independence, Habibullah then rejected the Anglo–Russian Convention of 1907. Both Russia and Britain ignored his objections and declared the Convention legal. Thus, in 1907, both European powers heaved diplomatic sighs of relief, believing that political stability had at last arrived in Central Asia. World War I and one of the more unstable periods in history quickly followed.[3]

In spite of the Amir's resistance to coercion from external sources, he refused to bow to internal pressures to enter World War I on the side of the Central Powers. The forces for war became particularly vociferous after Turkey entered the conflict and Sultan Abdul Hamid, nominal Caliph of the Muslim world, called for a *jihad* (holy war) against the infidel Allies. Propaganda pictured the German Kaiser in Arab dress and the Turkish press referred to him as "Hajji Wilhelm."

Habibullah kept his hawks leashed. He insisted a call for a *jihad* was invalid unless proclaimed inside Afghanistan by Afghan religious leaders. However, the Afghan Amir reportedly wrote a letter to Enver Pasha, Young Turk Minister of War, asking if he should attack British India or Tsarist Central Asia in support of the Ottoman cause (Adamec, 1967, 83).

Probably all Habibullah's negotiations with the Central Powers during World War I simply reflected the usual Afghan game of positive neutrality, waiting to see which side would win, and being prepared for either eventuality. His position, therefore, became embarrassing with the arrival in September 1915, in Kabul of a Turco-German mission. Negotiations were complicated because the mission actually had *two* leaders. Captain Oskar von Niedermeyer and Lieutenant Werner Otto von Hentig, with Kazim Bey as representative of the Ottoman Turks (von Hentig, 1963; von Niedermeyer, 1942).

By judicious procrastination, Habibullah forced the mission to agree to a ludicrous treaty, under which the Germans agreed to give the Afghans 100,000 rifles, 300 cannon, and £20 million in gold. The mission's immediate goal, an Afghan attack, in concert with tribal elements in British India, collapsed. Habibullah hinted he would attack India— but only after the victorious German and Turk armies entered Afghanistan to lead the assault (Adamec, 1967, 94).

In addition, Habibullah initiated correspondence with the British in India, indicating that in exchange for his holding the Central Powers at bay, he would like the British to relinquish their control of Afghani-

[3] For an excellent, detailed study of early twentieth-century Afghanistan, see Adamec, 1967.

stan's foreign affairs. The anti-British clique in his court demanded more action (i.e., a *jihad*) and less letter-writing.

The second, more far reaching, goal of the Turco-German mission succeeded, however. Included in the mission were two well-known Indian nationalists and revolutionaries, Maulana Barakatullah and Raja Mahendra Pratap. Under their guidance, elaborate plans evolved to coordinate uprisings inside British India in late 1916, simultaneously with revolts by the Muslims of Tsarist Central Asia, which would liberate thousands of German prisoners of war in the Tashkent area (Pratap, 1925). The Afghan army would then march into India, and Habibullah would become Emperor of another Durrani Empire stretching from the Amu Darya to the Indian Ocean. The scheme failed to impress the shrewd Habibullah, although supported by the anti-British elements in his court.

The bubble predictably burst, for the British, with their efficient intelligence system, uncovered the plot in India and arrested most of the ringleaders. Some tribal fighting did occur. The Hajji of Turangzai, Abdul Wahid, a traditional worry in the precarious British position along the frontier, launched an unsuccessful series of attacks on Peshawar in 1917. An earlier attack by the Hajji in 1915 had also failed.

The Germans departed Kabul with their meaningless treaty in May 1916.

The peace ending World War I brought death to Habibullah. He was murdered by unknown assailants on February 20, 1919, while on a hunting trip near Tigiri. Rumor connected many with the murder plot. The Russians accused the British of employing an assassin named Mustafa Saghir (the British, along with Genghis Khan, are usually blamed for all the ills of Afghanistan). Eventually, the Afghans officially accepted this version, but not before Amanullah had executed a convenient scapegoat, Col. Shah Ali Reza Khan, for the murder, and sentenced Nasrullah to life imprisonment in April 1919 (Adamec, 1967, 109). An Herati sergeant, Ghulam Rasul, a giant of a man, locally referred to as "the wolf," was also executed. Saghir, arrested in Turkey and accused of complicity in a plot (again British?) to assassinate Mustafa Kemal Ataturk, confessed to the murder of Habibullah and other crimes while on trial in Ankara in 1922. Mustafa Saghir was hanged, in spite of attempts by the British to save him. Even King George V sent a message to Ataturk, asking for clemency.

Others, however, have linked the assumed anti-British clique in

88. Amir Habibullah (1901-19) and some of his wives and consorts in European dress. *Photo: Private collection, Kabul*

89. King Amanullah (1919-29) on his European tour (December, 1927-July, 1928), at state dinner with President Paul von Hindenburg in Berlin. Amanullah is second from left; Queen Soraya is on far right. *Photo: Private collection, Kabul*

436

Habibullah's court with the murder. No definite proof exists for these accusations. Among others, the following in varying combinations have been mentioned in connection with the plot: Nasrullah Khan, Amanullah Khan, Mahmud Beg Tarzi, Shuja Dawla (possibly the triggerman), Mohammad Nadir Khan and other members of the Musahiban family (i.e., Shah Wali Khan, Ahmad Shah, and Mohammad Ali). The mystery may ultimately be solved, but who did the deed is really academic. The deed done, Amanullah Khan, third son of Habibullah, seized the throne and, advised by his father-in-law, Mahmud Beg Tarzi (a gentle man, whose nature revolted at violence), plunged his nation into a decade of development, which ended in debacle.

Mahmud Beg Tarzi (1865–1933) is one of the more important, though neglected, early-twentieth century Asian nationalists. Whether or not Amanullah would have undertaken his extensive *mashruta* (constitutional reforms) [4] if Mahmud Tarzi had not had such a great influence on him remains a question, but one can not discuss the decade of Amanullah without a discussion of Mahmud Tarzi. [5] In the words of an Indian visitor to Amanullah's Afghanistan, "He [King Amanullah] married the daughter of a journalist who edited *Seraj-ul-Akhbar,* Mahmud Tarzi, a personality without parallel at home. He had ample share in the making of modern Afghanistan. He was for many years in foreign countries. The young King was greatly influenced by his father-in-law. To this Mahmud Beg Tarzi is partly due the credit of initiating the modernization of Afghanistan" (Katrak, 1929, xiii).

Tarzi was born on the move and remained in that state the rest of his life. His birth took place in Ghazni as his family traveled from Kabul to Qandahar in a time of unrest. His education proceeded along classical Muslim lines. He studied the Arabic and Persian languages and literatures, and poetry and philosophy particularly fascinated him. He spoke and wrote Pashto, Urdu, Turkish, and French, as well as Arabic and Persian. His father, Ghulam Mohammad Tarzi, well-known poet, broke with Abdur Rahman Khan over the Amir's strictness and brutality toward his enemies. Other tribal leaders (about fifteen in number) also opposed these harsh policies (as well as being threats to the Amir's power) and they and their families were banished by the Amir.

[4] Actually, Amanullah and other young Afghans belonged to a secret *Mashruta* (Constitutional) group, which met to discuss ways and means of modernizing Afghanistan. The party disappeared after Amanullah seized power.

[5] However, recent studies have begun to reintroduce Tarzi to scholars; e.g., Ahang, 1969b; L. Dupree (*AUFS Reports,* LD-1-64); de Dianous (1964); Gregorian (1967).

Mahmud Tarzi was sixteen years old when the exile began. His family moved to Damascus, where he worked in the Secretariat of the Syrian Province of the Ottoman Empire rather than simply exist as a guest of the government. His first wife, an Afghan, died in Damascus in 1884. In 1892 he married a beautiful Syrian lady, and the union resulted in twenty children; nine still survive. (Soraya, Amanullah's queen, died in 1968. Her body was returned to Afghanistan and is buried next to her husband and his father, Habibullah, in Jalalabad.)

Family life engaged only a part of his time, however. He savored the intellectual atmosphere of Damascus, and argued ideals, dreams, and *Realpolitik* with incubating Young Turks who eventually overthrew Sultan Abdul Hamid and shaped modern Turkey. He met and impressed the worldly wise exponent of Pan Islamism, Jamal ad-Din al-Afghani.

Young Mahmud Tarzi wrote his first book (*Travel in Three Continents*) in 1890, after a tour of Syria (Asia), Egypt (Africa), Turkey and France (Europe) with his father. Ostensibly a travelogue, the book nevertheless has one section which revels in political satire, a genre in which Tarzi excelled. In this section, a young Turkish liberal in Constantinople argues his way through the various Ottoman ministries. Everything the dissident young Tarzi wanted to say about Afghanistan he said through the lips of the Young Turk. The real-life Young Turks were delighted at the unpublished manuscript, and passed it from hand to hand. When published twenty-five years later (1915) in Afghanistan, the book was recognized by most Afghan liberals as a plea for more social justice in all Islamic countries.

His father's death in 1901 preceeded that of Amir Abdur Rahman by a few months, so Mahmud Tarzi, as head of the family, requested and received permission to visit Kabul to give condolences and congratulations to Habibullah. While there, he fascinated the new Amir with his ideas of reform, and accepted an invitation to return permanently to Afghanistan. The Tarzi family came back to Kabul in 1903 after twenty-two years of exile.

Under the direct influence of Mahmud Tarzi, Habibullah began several processes of Afghan modernization which continue today. The Amir (called *Seraj-ul-Mellat-wa-ad-din:* Light of the Nation and Religion), however, became more enamoured with mechanical gadgetry than with the social, political, and economic mechanics of change. He loved cars, so he began to improve the road from Kabul to the Durand Line. He also imported cameras, and photography became one of his principal hobbies. Many of his photographs still exist in private collections. An American engineer, A. C. Jewett, built the first power station in Afghanistan, so that Habibullah's palace and other buildings in Kabul might have electric light (Bell, 1948). Jewett's old G.E. generators at Jabul us-Seraj still serve as auxiliaries to the new German-constructed power station.[6]

Habibullah first appointed Mahmud Tarzi Chief of the Bureau of Translation, where his primary task was to translate Turkish editions of Jules Verne's novels into Persian so that Habibullah, an avid Verne fan, could read them. Several of these were later published in Kabul for public sale. Unofficially, however, Tarzi became one of Habibullah's most trusted advisers, a position of great power.

In 1911, Tarzi began his most ambitious project and, in many ways, his most enduring monument, the bi-monthly nationalist newspaper, *Seraj-ul-Akhbar* (*The Light*—or *Torch*—*of the News*). Tarzi lithographed the paper the first year. Then printing machines arrived from France and Turkey, and he produced a newspaper technically equal to many current Afghan newspapers.

Habibullah permitted Tarzi to publish *Seraj-ul-Akhbar* in order to needle the British Government of India because of its subtle attacks on him, but *Seraj-ul Akhbar* developed into a true political newspaper, revolutionary in implication if not in fact. Tarzi constantly attacked both European imperialism and resistance to change by orthodox Muslim religious leaders. He contested the prevalent belief that Muslims could learn nothing from the West. His pleas for independence from European political domination struck responsive cords in India and in Russian-controlled Central Asia. The Indian nationalist press often quoted Tarzi, much to the embarrassment of British officialdom which several times banned *Seraj-ul-Akhbar* in India.

Tarzi, along with most Asians, rejoiced at the defeat of the Russians in the Russo-Japanese War. He also translated the official account of the war by the Turkish general staff into Persian.

Embodied in his attacks on European imperialism was criticism of unprogressive Afghan internal policies and lack of national unity. The tiny class of Afghan intellectuals widely quoted Tarzi's poems. In one poem, a courtier complains: "Time and science are changing the world,

---

[6] Other foreigners serving Habibullah included Mr. Finlayson (architect and bridge-builder who also laid out a golf course near Kabul); Major Cleveland (physician to the Amir); Mr. Thornton (manager of leather factory); Mrs. Brown (physician to the harem); Mr. Donovan (ordnance specialist); and the German Herr Fleischer (ordnance specialist from Krupp).

and many nations suffer from impatience. Enough of quail shooting! Now we need to work!" This was a pointed reference to Habibullah's love of hunting (the Amir often included Mahmud Tarzi in his hunting-parties). But Tarzi, an introspective man of letters, hated "shooting, camels, horses, and camps" (L. Dupree, *AUFS Reports,* LD-1-64, 27).

Tarzi would begin some editorials with flowery praise to Habibullah, then quickly switch to general criticisms which, by implication, included the Amir. In one editorial he stated that "the Amir is the only supporter of modern education and science in Afghanistan," and then went on to belabor the fact that "no modern education and science exist in my unfortunate country!"

The seven and a half years (1911–19) of the publication of *Seraj-ul-Akhbar* were years of increased strain between the Amir and Mahmud Tarzi. Finally, Tarzi refused to leave his compound for formal functions. He composed his newspapers in an office adjoining his house. The printer came and went with proofs. Several times Habibullah threatened (never seriously, however) to kill Tarzi if he continued to harp on internal reforms, threats which the editor ignored. The Amir, however, always relented, for *Seraj-ul-Akhbar's* editorials demanded "complete independence from England," a line which evoked praise from other Asian nationalists, and pleased Habibullah. Another pet project of Tarzi's, *Seraj-ul-Atfal* (*Light of the Children*), a children's journal, came out in six issues in 1918.

In 1919, Tarzi turned the editorship of the paper over to a younger colleague, Abdul Hadi Dawi (now President of the Upper House of Parliament), who later changed the name of the paper to *Aman-i-Afghan* (*Afghan Peace*). The new paper would become the *official* organ of the Amir Amanullah, but *Seraj-ul-Akhbar* under Tarzi remained *free* to the end.[7] The ideas planted in its pages may still be studied, savored, and admired. When asked why he gave up *Seraj-ul-Akhbar* Tarzi would reply: "I had achieved my goal. Afghan independence of British control was near."

Before 1919 ended, Habibullah in death had gained what the British refused him in February: the right of Afghanistan to conduct its own foreign affairs.

---

[7] Three other free newspapers were published during the Amanullah period: *Anis*, begun in 1927, ceased as a free paper in 1931, then emerged as a government paper and is still published; *Nasim-i-Sahar* and *Nawruz*, both of which ceased publication after a few issues.

CHAPTER 20

King Amanullah

INDEPENDENCE, AND REFORMS
TWENTY YEARS TOO SOON, 1919–29

WHEN Mahmud Beg Tarzi first met Amanullah after the assassination of Habibullah, the two men embraced and Tarzi said, "Do not cry, now is the time for action" (L. Dupree, *AUFS Reports,* LD-64-8). During his father's absence on hunting trips, Amanullah often served as Regent, as well as being Commander-in-Chief of the army. He seized the *Arg* (a combination royal residence, fort, and treasury), traditional seat of power, and enlisted the army's support with promises of improved pay and conditions.

Meanwhile, Nasrullah, brother of Habibullah and his companion on the fateful hunting-trip, proclaimed himself Amir in Jalalabad, winning the support of most of Habibullah's other sons. Many courtiers and other government officials spent at least a part of the winter in the warmer climate of Jalalabad, a custom still practiced by those who can afford it.

The army revolted against Nasrullah and brought him and his supporters to Kabul in chains. When his uncle and brothers appeared in Kabul, Amanullah threw them into the *Arg* dungeons. Nasrullah presumably died there in 1921. After swearing fealty (*bay'a*) to Amanullah, the other brothers, including the eldest, Inayatullah (also a son-in-law of Mahmud Tarzi and later destined to rule for three days in 1929), were released. Two other sons of Habibullah, Hayatullah Khan and Abdul Majid, were killed during the reign of Habibullah Ghazi (Bacha Saqqao) in 1929. Amanullah released twenty others (including Nadir Khan and Shah Wali Khan), declaring them innocent of complicity in the assassination.

The new Amir immediately launched a series of reforms. Before 1919 royal whim often settled administrative matters and legal decisions. All Afghan subjects were entitled by custom to come before a royal durbar to present their cases. The Amir Habibullah, his brother Nasrullah, and Habibullah's three eldest sons all held such durbars, and the inconsistencies in their decisions can easily be imagined. If a petition failed in one court, a man had recourse to the other four. Sometimes, after winning his case in one court, a man would find himself dragged before one of the other royal personages and the previous decision reversed. The most minor royal decision often became a *farman* (proclamation). Each of the five had private prisons and personal bodyguards to help enforce his authority. Amanullah hoped to unify the entire system, and he permitted Tarzi to implement one of his pet governmental reforms, a cabinet of ministers using the Ottoman version as a model. Tarzi himself became the first Minister of Foreign Affairs. Sardar Abdul Quddus Khan was appointed Prime Minister.

The jailing of Nasrullah initially resulted in a swell of conservative opinion against Amanullah. By early spring, however, Amanullah had consolidated his power in the major urban centers, and most tribal leaders recognized him as Amir. From this position of strength, combined with reports which indicated British weakness along the frontier and growing unrest throughout India (O'Dwyer, 1925), Amanullah, at the urging of Mahmud Tarzi, General Mohammad Nadir Khan, and others, launched the month-long, Third Anglo-Afghan War of May 1919.

When Amanullah declared war at a mass meeting at the Idgah Mosque in Kabul, the crowd shouted enthusiastically, *"Ya margh ya istiqlal!"* (Death or Freedom!).

At first, Afghan troops were victorious against the startled British. A column under General Mohammad Nadir Khan (destined to be king from 1929–33) marched as far as Thal in Parachinar. Another column, under the Commander-in-Chief of the Afghan army, General Saleh Mohammad Khan, moved past Dakka in the direction of the Khyber Pass, but the British drove him back and occupied Dakka. A third group, under Sardar Abdul Quddus Khan, remained at Qandahar.

Many Pushtun in the paramilitary Frontier Scouts deserted the British to fight with the Afghans, and they were joined by many tribesmen from both sides of the Durand Line. Afghan confidence in a military victory, however, disappeared quickly with the appearance of a new weapon. The British escalated the war and Royal Air Force pilots, intrepidly flying World War I aircraft over the high mountains of eastern Afghanistan dropped bombs on Kabul and Jalalabad. Almost simultaneously, both sides initiated peace moves. The British, sick of years of bloodletting on several fronts during World War I, well remembered the difficulties of land campaigning in Afghanistan (Molesworth, 1962).

In addition, the British troops in India wished to return home, and some units actually refused to march to the Frontier.

The prompt cessation of hostilities no doubt saved Amanullah's throne for, when the bombs began to fall, the Amir found some of those who had been enthusiastically war-mongering a month before just as vigorously accusing him and Mahmud Tarzi of starting an unnecessary war.

The war at a standstill, the Afghans proceeded to win their victories at the conference table, first at Rawalpindi and then at Mussoorie. At first, however, things seemed to go wrong. The chief Afghan delegate at Rawalpindi, Ali Ahmad Khan (a cousin of Amanullah), appears to have been outsmarted by the British negotiators, headed by Sir Hamilton Grant. The original purpose of the Rawalpindi talks had been to establish a six-month armistice and lay the groundwork for a peace conference. Instead, the British largely dictated the "Treaty of Rawalpindi" (signed in August, 1919), which ambiguously left Afghanistan free to conduct its own foreign affairs (Adamec, 1967, 183).

Immediately after the signing of the Treaty of Rawalpindi, however, an Afghan mission headed by General Mohammad Wali Khan (a Tajik) departed Kabul. They arrived at Moscow in October, 1919, to explain the new Afghan independent posture in foreign affairs. A Bolshevik representative, Michael Bravin (or K. Bravin, according to Adamec, 1967, 144), had already arrived in Kabul (September, 1919) and entered into negotiations with Amanullah concerning the status of the Panjdeh territory. Bravin also attempted to get the Afghans involved in the civil war in Central Asia on the side of the Bolsheviks, in return for guaranteed Russian assistance against the British. The arrival of the Russian mission began a Soviet-Afghan relationship which continues to the present.

The Bolsheviksi, in reality, did not wish to get involved with the British in Central Asia, aside from watching the small British detachments, such as the Dunsterforce (Dunsterville, 1920) in northwestern Iran and the Malleson Force in northeastern Iran (Malleson, 1922).[1] Bravin preferred simply to talk, rather than act and assist the Afghans. The Afghans, for their part, did not wish to get too intimately involved with the Bolsheviks and were genuinely disturbed over Russian activities to the north. The Russians were beginning to shape up as the destroyers

---

[1] Also see Alekseyev (1963) for a Soviet view of these activities. Another good source in English is Kapur, 1966.

of the Central Asian Muslim Khanates, in spite of initial guarantees of freedom.

In addition, the Afghans slowly penetrated the lost areas of Panjdeh and Merv, only to be forced out without any fighting, however, when the Red armies, freed from fighting in southern Russia, appeared on the scene in Central Asia to help smash the rebellious Muslim population.

Mahmud Tarzi himself led the Afghan delegation to Mussoorie for the next stage in the British-Afghan negotiations. The conference lasted from April 17 to July 18, 1920, and broke up without a satisfactory treaty being signed. The negotiators traveled by train from Jamrud, at the entrance of the Tribal Territories along the Khyber Pass road, after lunching at Landi Kotal with Sir Francis Humphrys, who will appear again as British Minister to Kabul during the crucial happenings in the late 1920s. The Afghan delegates' train rushed through the urban centers, watering and refueling at lonely by-stations. The British took these precautions because they feared repetitions of the anti-imperialist riots which swept India at the end of World War I, when it became obvious that the "self-determination of nations" applied only to the smaller European ethnic and geographic units. Also, Mahendra Pratap, an Indian member of the Turco-German World War I mission, had remained behind in Afghanistan, and after a short trip to Russia, formed a "Provisional Government of India" in Kabul, with himself as president and Maulana Barakatullah acting as prime minister. This "Provisional Government" directed an active propaganda campaign against the British in India and sent across agents and supplies to carry on limited guerrilla warfare. All during the Rawalpindi and Mussoorie negotiations, tribal incursions into British India plagued the peace of the frontier region.

Advance word of Tarzi's train's passage through Lahore, however, brought hundreds of cheering Indian nationalists to the platform as it went by. The political and financial settlements at Mussoorie ran smoothly at first. The British once again recognized the Afghan right to conduct their foreign affairs, which, incidentally, they had already begun, since they had entered into extensive initial talks with the Bolshevik Mission to Kabul, and sent their own mission under Mohammad Wali Khan to Moscow. The major difficulty developed over the rights of the Pushtun on the Indian side of the Durand Line, especially those who had fought against the British in the Third Anglo-Afghan War. The Afghans wanted a loose suzerainty over the Pushtun on both sides of the Durand Line. The British, not unnaturally, refused, referring to the 1893 Durand Line agreement, which delineated, at the very minimum, zones of respective responsibility. After four months of impasse, primarily on this issue, the conference broke up, with talks scheduled to resume later in Kabul.

A most unusual confrontation took place daily at the Mussoorie conference. Nawwab Sahibzada Abdul Kayyum Khan (a Muslim Pushtun from Peshawar and a member of the British delegation) defended British policy, and Diwan Naranjan Das (an Afghan Hindu) defended Afghan policy. During the conference the Muslim celebration of *'Id-i-Qurban* occurred, and the British, fearing a riot in the volatile city of Dera Dun, refused the request of the Afghan delegates to be allowed to go there. Eventually, however, the British relented and Naranjan accompanied his Muslim colleagues to the mosque. Then the party visited the famous Hardwar Hindu temple of Dera Dun to symbolize the ethnic unity which theoretically existed in Afghanistan. All along the route people kissed the cars of the Afghan delegates and shouted independence slogans, but no riots developed.

Sir Henry Dobbs led the British delegation to Kabul (he had also headed the British Mission at Mussoorie) in January 1921, and Mahmud Tarzi again headed the Afghan negotiators, assisted mainly by General Mohammad Nadir Khan and his brother, General Shah Wali Khan. Several times the British delegates threatened to leave Kabul for Peshawar, and, according to Afghan sources, Amanullah and Mahmud Tarzi called their bluff and sent for their baggage. The British version differs, stating that the Afghans reopened negotiations after the British delegation prepared to leave (Fraser-Tytler, 1967, 198–200).

While British and Afghan negotiators continued to play diplomatic cat-and-mouse, the Russians and the Afghans ratified a Treaty of Friendship, the first international agreement signed by the Afghans with any other nation since declaring independence in 1919. The Russians signed the Treaty on May 26, 1921, and the Afghans announced ratification on August 13, 1921 (for text, see Adamec, 1967, 188–91).

On November 22, 1921, after eleven months of haggling, the British and Afghans signed a treaty, but the Afghan Amir insisted the document merely reestablished "neighborly relations" (Adamec, 1967, 165).

During the treaty negotiations, an Afghan mission, again led by Mohammad Wali Khan (the Tajik) visited Germany, Italy, the United Kingdom, and the United States, in order to establish normal diplomatic

445

relations with the rest of the world. Treaties quickly developed with Turkey, France, and Italy. Lord Curzon, an old enemy of the Afghans, became Secretary of State for Foreign Affairs in 1919, and continued to alienate Afghan attempts to make friends in Britain. He officially protested Afghan efforts to establish independent foreign relations without going through Delhi. In August 1921, before the signing of the Anglo-Afghan Treaty of 1921, Curzon, although he granted an interview to Mohammad Wali Khan, refused to discuss the negotiations going on between the Government of British India and Afghanistan, or to grant a request for an interview with King George V. Such a request, said Curzon, should be referred to the India Office. In addition, Curzon adamantly insisted that Afghanistan still lay "within the British sphere of political influence" (Adamec, 1967, 163).

But the Afghans, under the energetic Amanullah and shrewd Mahmud Tarzi, ignored British pronouncements as they rapidly signed treaties of friendship and established consular relations with other nations. So no matter what the British planned for Afghanistan's future, the Afghans themselves had already seized their future and become independent of overt British policy.

The looseness of the 1921 treaty satisfied few, for the question of the Pushtun tribes in British India remained, and ambiguous statements in the treaty made the Afghans again demand clarification. The British representative, Sir Henry Dobbs, sent a supplementary letter to Mahmud Tarzi which became a part of the Anglo-Afghan Treaty of 1921 and included the proposition: "As the conditions of the frontier tribes of the two governments are of interest to the Government of Afghanistan I inform you that the British Government entertains feelings of goodwill toward all the frontier tribes and has every intention of treating them generously, providing they abstain from outrages against the inhabitants of India. I hope this letter will cause you satisfaction" (quoted in Caroe, 1965, 465, and Pazhwak, 1953, 86).

Mahmud Tarzi, physically and mentally exhausted after two years of negotiations, as well as guiding the Afghan Cabinet of Ministers, asked to be relieved of his official responsibilities in 1922, and to be sent to Paris as Minister to France. Amanullah granted the request. Instead of taking a rest, however, Tarzi worked hard for further cultural relations with France, a country which has played a major role in the development of the current crop of Afghan intellectuals.

In September 1922, the French and the Afghans signed a protocol which created the Délégation Archéologique Française en Afghanistan (see below, Appendix F), a group which has done yeoman work in practically all periods of Afghan archaeology. (In 1952, the Afghans renewed this protocol for another thirty years). Istiqlal Lycée, a French-language high school staffed by French professors, founded in 1923, still functions, and from 1922 on, many Afghan students have attended universities in France under scholarships given by the Afghan and French governments. (The present Afghan King received much of his advanced education in France.)

During Amanullah's reign, two other foreign-language high schools were instituted in Kabul: Nejat College (German) in 1924 and Ghazi College (English) in 1928. In 1923, Amanullah made Habibiya College (founded by his father in 1903 and modeled after Aligarh College in India) the fourth foreign-language high school in Kabul, with English the medium of instruction in some higher classes.

While in Paris, Tarzi became the center of another controversy with Great Britain. He purchased French arms and ammunition for the Afghan army, and the British held up the shipment at Bombay. Tarzi claimed the stoppage violated the 1921 Treaty, as well as the natural right of a landlocked country to in-transit facilities and enlisted the aid of his friend, Raymond Poincaré, who sent the editor of *Le Matin* to get the Afghan side of the story from Tarzi. The resulting front-page publicity caused the British reluctantly to let the shipment go through, though they still feared the arms would be used to stir up trouble among the Pushtun on the Indian side of the frontier.

Trouble brewed outside Afghanistan as the post-World War I situation rapidly deteriorated in the Middle East. The Greeks attacked Turkey, which still officially held the standard of the Khalifate, and the attack was bitterly denounced throughout the Muslim world. In India, pro-independence riots and demonstrations were common, and among the Muslim community the Khalifate Party[2] gathered momentum and, in June 1920, several thousand Punjabi and other Indian Muslims moved to Afghanistan (the Hijrat Movement) to settle down. They had sold their lands (usually to Hindus or Sikhs) and the idealistic Amanullah initially greeted these people enthusiastically. It soon became obvious, however, that Afghanistan's limited resources simply could not support the thousands, and they ultimately returned to British India. Both

[2] A movement which encouraged Muslims to move from non-Muslim countries to Muslim nations. Amanullah actually toyed with the idea of declaring Afghanistan the seat of the Khalifate, particularly as it appeared that Turkey had collapsed as a leader in the Muslim world.

447

the Afghan and Indian Muslims blame the British for permitting this migration to take place.

Other troubles plagued the Afghans from the north as the Russians reconquered the Tsarist Central Asian empire. Muslim freedom fighters (called *basmachi,* "bandits," by the Russians) resisted and the 1920s witnessed repeated revolts in Turkestan. Although Amanullah sympathized with the *basmachi,* he could offer little material support. However, individuals and groups of volunteers from British India and Afghanistan crossed the Afghan-Russian border to fight with the *basmachi.*

In 1922, Amanullah sent his best troops to his northern frontier to await developments, and secretly corresponded with the former Young Turk, Enver Pasha, who, ousted from Turkey after World War I, tried to spread Pan-Turanism through Central Asia, attempting to form a Turkic-speaking state out of the confusion.

Enver Pasha was killed in August, 1922, while fighting the Bolsheviks, and the main force of the *basmachi* melted away to form guerrilla bands, some of which continued to fight against the Soviets well into the 1930s.

The Russians demanded the withdrawal of the Afghan forces from the border zones, and asked for and received a declaration of non-interference from Amanullah, who had met with General Mohammad Nadir Khan (whom Amanullah had sent north earlier) at Khawak Pass to discuss the situation. Nadir Khan failed to convince Amanullah that the Afghans should take a wait-and-see position on the Central Asian revolts. The Khanate of Bokhara fell and Amir Sayyid 'Alim Khan fled to Kabul in 1921 where he died in exile in 1956, the last Manguit Uzbak ruler of Bokhara.

A small border incident occurred in 1925 when Soviet troops occupied Urta Tagail (Yangi Qala), a small island in the Amu Darya. Afghanistan protested and the Soviets agreed to submit the issue to a joint commission, which subsequently awarded the island to Afghanistan. The Amu Darya had shifted its course slightly and the island, formerly north of the main stream, now fell south of the main channel. The peaceful settlement of this dispute and the U.S.S.R.'s ready acceptance of the commission's decision resulted in a subsequent Treaty of Non-Aggression and Neutrality between Afghanistan and the Soviet Union in 1926, and an agreement which established an air service between Tashkent and Kabul.

Internally, the Afghan political climate clouded. A revolt broke out

448

in the eastern mountainous regions of Khost. Let by Abdullah, the *Mullah-i-Lang* (or *Pir-i-Lang*), and his more vigorous assistant, the Mullah Abdul Rashid, the rebellion lasted from March 1924, to January 1925. The local Afghan press referred to the two leaders in the following rhyming manner: *Mullah-i-Lang, wa rafiq-i-dalang* ("inflexible friend").

The British role in the revolt is not clear, but Amanullah's outspoken anti-British attitude and his acceptance of Soviet technicians made him a prime target for overthrow by the British. In addition, it is always easy to stir up the truculent Mangal Pushtun tribesmen of Khost.

The revolt began in the name of religion against Amanullah's initial reforms and modernization programs, and it might have succeeded had not a dynastic factor been injected into the fray. Abdul Karim, a natural son of the former Amir, Yaqub Khan (who ruled for a few months in 1879 and then accepted exile in India), tried to assume leadership of the rebel tribes. Even the rebels were reluctant to accept him and the tide shifted in favor of Amanullah. The *Mullah-i-Lang* was brought to Kabul and executed, and Abdul Karim fled back across the border into India, from which the British exiled him for violating asylum. Later, Karim was killed in Burma, possibly by an Afghan agent. A blood feud in Afghanistan usually ends in blood—and more blood.

Another factor, one sometimes forgotten by the Afghans, helped turn the revolt in Amanullah's favor. The British sold the Amir two World War I aircraft which were flown by German mercenaries. These had a salutatory effect on tribal forces when they appeared on the scene, bombing and strafing the rebels.

Fights between rival Pushtun groups frequently occurred in the 1920s, with the British blaming the Afghans for stirring up the trouble, and vice versa. But in the frontier area trouble does not need to be stirred up; it is constantly whirling in the air waiting to light.

The end of the *Mullah-i-Lang's* revolt did not end opposition to Amanullah's modernization schemes. Two factions gyrated around the court, one led by the liberal Tajik, Mohammad Wali Khan, chief of Tarzi's overseas missions to Russia, the United States, and Europe, the other by the more conservative General Mohammad Nadir Khan and his five brothers. All of them, in order of age, were Mohammad Nadir Khan, Mohammad Aziz Khan, Mohammad Hashim Khan, Shah Wali, Shah Mahmud, Mohammad Ali Khan. General Nadir Khan realized the strength of the tribes and recognized their violent opposition to change, as well as the depth of the influence of anti-Amanullah religious leaders.

For this reason, if no other, he opposed the drastic reductions in the strength of the army proposed by the Amir.

Amanullah's solution to the criticisms he received was a general shake-up in the cabinet of ministers which sent General Mohammad Nadir Khan (who had been Minister of War and Commander-in-Chief of the Afghan army) to Paris as Minister. Mohammad Ali Khan became Minister of War. Mahmud Tarzi returned to Kabul and took back his old job as Minister of Foreign Affairs, replacing Mohammad Wali Khan (the Tajik) in 1924.

Increasingly, Amanullah refused to listen to the advice of his Foreign Minister, and as a result Mahmud Tarzi resigned in mid-1925. Officially, Amanullah did not accept the resignation until 1927, when Tarzi went to Switzerland for medical treatment. Tarzi returned just before Amanullah embarked in December 1927 on his fabled European tour, which would turn Afghanistan into a three-ring circus. Tarzi advised against the trip, for even he sensed the rising opposition to the high-handed but well-intended tactics of the King: Amanullah had changed his title from Amir to *Padshah,* or King, in 1923.

The European tour did produce results, for, as a result of the trip, diplomatic treaties were concluded with Finland, Latvia, Liberia, Poland, Switzerland, Egypt, and Japan, among others.[3]

The fairy-tale aspects of King Amanullah's tour, which lasted until July 1928, turned his royal head. With great style he visited India, Egypt, Turkey, and Persia as well as the major European capitals, Rome, Pairs, Brussels, Bern, Berlin, London, Warsaw, and Moscow. The crowned heads of Europe spared no efforts, because Amanullah's visit was the first extensive post-World War I royal tour. All Europe curiously followed the exploits of this visitor from another world. But Amanullah felt melancholy in London, where he told a confidant that he believed the British still wished to have him out of the way.

While Europe feted Amanullah, conservative forces at home, purportedly aided by the British, began a campaign condemning his personal life and his modernization programs as anti-Islamic. Unknown hands distributed photographs of Queen Soraya (Mahmud Tarzi's daughter) unveiled at European receptions. Rumors flew that the King planned to bring back from Europe machines to make soap out of corpses. The King, so the country was told, "had turned against Allah and Islam!" (L. Dupree, *AUFS Reports,* LD-1-64, 13).

[3] Previously, diplomatic relations had been established with Russia (1919), Iran (1921), Britain (1922), Turkey (1922), Italy (1922), and France (1923).

Amanullah returned to Afghanistan determined to modernize his country along the lines of the Turkey of Mustafa Kemal Ataturk. Even the U.S.S.R. of Stalin inspired him, and the Soviets offered more aid. Ataturk warned Amanullah not to start large-scale social and political reforms until he had a strong, well-trained army, and promised to send some of his best officers to train the Afghans. Amanullah, however, always underestimated the relationship of force to drastic reform, and announced elaborate programs immediately upon his return. The Turkish officers arrived, too late to do anything but observe the debacle which followed.

Mahmud Beg Tarzi preached reform all his life, but always recommended a good foundation. He advised the reorganization of government administration with the help of Ataturk's Turks. He wanted the King to raise the salaries of civil servants in order to fight bribery, and he agreed with Ataturk on the importance of a strong army to combat regional fractionalization and conservative elements opposing reform. In foreign policy, Tarzi suggested a balance: bring in the British to aid as well as the Russians.

Contrary to popular belief, Soviet aid to Afghanistan did not begin in 1950, but with several subsidies, in 1919. The Soviet Union sent Amanullah a gift of thirteen airplanes, plus pilots, mechanics, transportation specialists, and telegraph operators. Before 1928, the U.S.S.R. established an air route from Moscow to Kabul via Tashkent.[4] In 1924–1925, the Russians laid telephone lines between Herat-Qandahar and Kabul-Mazar-i-Sharif. The British offered to complete a good road from Peshawar to Kabul via the Tang-i-Gharu (finally built after World War II with American assistance).

Amanullah demanded cash to build the road, but the British refused. His annual verbal attacks on Great Britain during *Jeshn* (Afghanistan's national independence holidays), with the British Minister present, embarrassed many Afghans as well as the diplomatic corps. Amanullah scorned the advice of Tarzi and others, and the British, snubbed, worried more and more about Russian penetration. During this period, the British maintained consulates in Jalalabad and Qandahar; the Russians at Mazar-i-Sharif and Herat.

Before the end came, Amanullah surrounded himself with "yes men"

[4] Earlier, the German Junker firm obtained exclusive rights to establish and maintain an airline from Germany via Turkey and Iran, with an eventual extension to China. The original agreement stipulated that the planes would touch neither British nor Russian soil, thus freeing Afghanistan from dependence, on its northern and southern neighbors for air communication (Adamec, 1969).

451

and rushed headlong into his disorganized plans to change Afghanistan from a collection of ethnic groups and tribes into the outward appearance of modern nationhood. He began the construction of a new capital, six miles from Kabul, to be called Dar'ul Aman, which included a new palace overlooking the Kabul Valley and a parliament building. The palace now sits in semi-ruins and serves as a military headquarters. Until a fire gutted the parliament building in the winter of 1969, it housed the Ministry of Public Works. The old municipality building is now the Kabul Museum. German engineers constructed a narrow-gauge railroad (the only rail line ever constructed inside Afghanistan) which ran two or three times daily with open wagonettes between Kabul and Dar'ul Aman. Today the wagonettes and small engine rust quietly in the sheds near the old parliament building, reminders of idealism gone wild.

Amanullah struck at the roots of conservative Islam by removing the veil from the women, by opening co-educational schools, and by attempting to force all Afghans in Kabul to wear Western clothing. Second-hand-clothes dealers charged tribesmen exhorbitant prices for clothing to wear inside Kabul. The King also instituted a program for the education of the nomads, and actually sent a limited number of teachers to travel with some of the larger groups.

As the reform programs increased in momentum, resentment grew among the conservative religious leaders, the tribes, and dissident members of the royal family. Mahmud Tarzi aptly commented: "Amanullah has built a beautiful monument without a foundation. Take out one brick and it will tumble down."

Shinwari Pushtun tribesmen removed the brick in November 1928, when they burned down the King's palace and the British Consulate in Jalalabad. The revolt quickly spread, and a tribal army moved on Kabul, picking up adherents as it traveled. After much hesitation, Amanullah sent the regular army to meet the tribal *lashkar,* whereupon most of the regular troops deserted to join the rebels. Kabul lay open to invasion, which, however, came from an unexpected direction—the north. Habibullah (called Bacha Saqqao, "Son of a Water-carrier"), a non-literate Tajik who controlled Kohistan, entered Kabul, deposed Amanullah, and ruled Afghanistan for nine bloody months (Habibullah, n.d.)

Amanullah's "monument" collapsed with cruel swiftness. "If only," lamented Mahmud Tarzi, "he had waited for two years and built up the army as Ataturk suggested, what might he have done?" (L. Dupree, *AUFS Reports,* LD-1-64,15).

With a tribal army advancing from the east and the forces of the Tajik leader entering Kabul from the north, Amanullah had no choice but flight. He sped to Qandahar in his Rolls-Royce, accompanied by Mahmud Beg Tarzi, Ghulam Sadiq (whom Amanullah sent to Moscow from Qandahar, after it became obvious the British would not assist him in his attempts to retake the throne), Abdul Aziz Barakzai (Minister of War), and Abdul Ahad Wardak (Minister of the Interior, and father of the present president of the *Wolesi Jirgah*).

Amanullah abdicated in favor of his oldest brother, Inayatullah (married to Mahmud Tarzi's oldest daughter, Khaireah), who ruled for three days before Bacha Saqqao shunted him aside. King Inayatullah and his family flew to India in one of the British airplanes which evacuated most foreigners from Kabul.[5]

Amanullah hoped to gather loyal tribesmen around him and regain the throne. Tarzi opposed the move, believing the British would resist the deposed King's efforts (Tarzi had become convinced of a major British role in the overthrow of Amanullah). He insisted the only hope for the restoration of Amanullah lay in the north, where the British could not interfere and the Russians might prove sympathetic. It is doubtful, however, whether the bulk of the Uzbak, Turkoman, and Tajik of the north would have supported the Pushtun ex-King, in spite of the later initial successes of Ghulam Nabi Charkhi.

In any event, Amanullah stubbornly marched toward Kabul with an ill-equipped, badly disciplined force, and invested a small Saqqaoist unit in Ghazni. A Ghilzai tribal army easily defeated Amanullah and lifted the siege. The Hazrat of Shor Bazaar, a leading Afghan religious leader, had helped gather the *lashkar* sent to Ghazni, and in addition, dispatched to eastern Afghanistan another column which would later assist Nadir Khan in the overthrow of Bacha Saqqao. (See *Habib-ul-Islam, Friend of Islam,* May 23, 1929, for a reproduction of a letter from the Hazrat to Bacha Saqqao which announces the movement of the two armies, although no mention is made of the use to which the latter column could be put.)

Prior to Amanullah's departure for Ghazni a Junker four-seater aircraft appeared in the skies over Qandahar. It landed and out stepped

---

[5] For details on the airlift see *East India (Military) Report on the Air Operations in Afghanistan Between December 12, 1928, and February 25, 1929.* H.M. Stationery Office, London, 1929. An American woman, a Mrs. Isaacson, was listed in the tables as being evacuated, but I have been unable to discover anything else about her.

a Persian colonel bringing Reza Shah's condolences and offer of asylum to Amanullah. The aircraft also brought a reporter from the Paris edition of the *Chicago Tribune,* Larry Rue, who had chartered the plane and flown in from Tehran in hopes of an exclusive interview with Amanullah. Rue got his interview and also became involved in the flight of the royal family when he agreed to fly Mahmud Tarzi, his wife, and a pregnant sister of Amanullah's to Herat so they could cross into Persia.

Amanullah and his entourage crossed into India and went to Bombay where they took a ship to Italy. Victor Emmanuel reluctantly gave hospitality to his "cousin," Amanullah, who had been decorated with the Collar of the Annunciation during his European tour by the Italian king. The Collar carried with it the title "Cousin of the King."

A week before the Tarzis' arrival in Herat, a series of Sunni-Shi'a riots occurred. An inter-army fight resulted during which the pro-Amanullah governor was killed. Although Bacha Saqqao had little influence in the Herat area, the incident graphically answered the question of how much support Amanullah could have expected from the north.

Friends hid Tarzi, and several days later an aircraft sent by the Afghan embassy in Tehran flew him out before the rebels found him. His wife had returned to Qandahar before the governor was killed and left with Amanullah's entourage for India.

A tired Mahmud Tarzi rested for ten months at the pleasant resort of Shimran outside Tehran. Several plots to restore Amanullah bubbled in Tehran and would have boiled if Tarzi had supported them, but as he refused to participate, the intrigues cooled. He quoted the great Persian poet Hafiz, to explain his inaction: "We have not come here in pomp and show; we have taken refuge in this place from unfortunate events."

Mahmud Tarzi arrived in Turkey in October 1929, and lived the few remaining years of his life in Constantinople. He spent the first year of his final exile in meditation and bursts of poetry. He would travel for hours on the tram, notebook in hand, recording impressions of peoples and palces. The Bosphorus often beckoned, and he sailed to the islands in search of new impressions. He liked to sit in cafés and watch the people. He seldom participated in discussions and refused to read newspapers. Feeling he had failed in the realm of action, Mahmud Tarzi returned to his first loves, introspection and poetry. As did many Asian nationalists, such as Gandhi and Tagore, he became disillusioned with the ability of the West to integrate its values with Asian cultures and

90. King Inayatullah (reigned for three days in January, 1929) about to take a flight in a Russian airplane, a gift of the Soviet Union to the Afghan government, in Kabul, 1925. *Photo: Private collection, Kabul*

91. Habibullah Ghazi (also called Bacha Saqqao), Tajik adventurer who ruled Afghanistan for nine months (January-October) in 1929. *Photo: Private collection, Kabul*

extolled the village life. He died in exile of cancer of the liver in November 1933, and lies buried on a hill overlooking the Bosphorus. Today, Turkish scholars and students often visit his tomb, which may some day become a shrine. Although basically not a man of action, Mahmud Tarzi did help create the modern Afghan system of cabinet of ministers, and he led the fight for the international recognition of Afghanistan after the 1919 Third Anglo-Afghan War.

Some Afghans accuse Mahmud Tarzi of political opportunism. He convinced Habibullah of his usefulness, and married two of his daughters to sons of Habibullah. A third daughter married another son while in Turkish exile. Tarzi, always independent, however, broke with Habibullah over Afghan participation on the side of the Central Powers in World War I, the rate of educational reform, and other matters relating to modernization.

After Habibullah's assassination, Mahmud Tarzi supported Amanullah against the other candidates for the throne. This also seems opportunistic, especially since one of his daughters was married to Amanullah, but we must remember that his oldest daughter had married Inayatullah, another brother in the running for the Amirship. Tarzi also broke with Amanullah over reform procedures, but in the end refused to support other claimants against Amanullah, and remained in bitter exile for his few remaining years. Still, Tarzi can probably be accused of the normal political opportunism which drives a man to achieve his goals. Tarzi had two: to make Afghanistan's foreign relations independent of the restraining hand of Great Britain, and social reforms solidly built. His personal loyalty to the family of Amanullah seems unquestioned.

Mahmud Tarzi will be most remembered in the realm of political and social ideas as the Afghans look for heros in their march to modernization. Long ago he recommended a step recently taken by the new 1964 constitution of King Mohammad Zahir Shah: the separation of government administration from the royal family. He also proposed a party system, an elected Parliament, and an annual *Loya Jirgah*.

In his newspaper, *Seraj-ul-Akhbar,* and other writings, Tarzi continually asked the question: " *'Ilm chist?*" ("What is knowledge?"). He wrote that simply teaching in the name of Islam is not knowledge, that modern technology, natural science, and social science must be included: "Once Europe existed in a Dark Age and Islam carried the torch of learning. Now we Muslims live in a Dark Age." He wrote also: "If Islam is worthwhile, it is worthy of challenge." (L. Dupree, *AUFS Reports,* LD-1-64, 20).

Mahmud Tarzi lived partly in action, but mostly in thought. King Amanullah, a man of action, seized events and tried to twist them to his desires, regardless of whether time, place, and people were ripe for such moves. If Tarzi, the thinker, and Amanullah, the activist, could have pooled their intellectual resources—backed by a loyal, Turkish-trained army—Afghanistan might today be farther along the road of modernization, instead of just beginning.

CHAPTER 21

King Mohammad Nadir Shah

THE VIOLENT INTERLUDE AND
SLOW STEPS FORWARD, 1929–33

ALTHOUGH ill, General Mohammad Nadir Khan returned from self-imposed exile to overthrow Habibullah (Bacha Saqqao, who called himself *Khadim-i-din-i-rasululah*, "Servant of the Prophet's Religion"), whose reign lasted only nine months, from January to October 1929. Nadir Khan, former commander of Amanullah's army, had fought the military cutbacks of the young king. He was sent to Paris as ambassador in April 1924, and later retired to the Riviera ostensibly for his health, but also to protest Amanullah's rapid modernization programs.

Three of the Musahiban (lineage name) brothers (Nadir Khan, Hashim Khan, Shah Wali Khan) returned through British India, and the British established ground rules for the game to be played. An unstable Bacha Saqqao worried the British, as did the spectre of Amanullah's supporters, such as Ghulam Nabi Charkhi (son of Ghulam Haider Charkhi, a general under Abdur Rahman Khan), sitting across the Oxus with volunteers from the Soviet as well as the Afghan side, waiting to strike in support of the defeated king.

The British rules were quite simple. The brothers Musahiban could pass through the North–West Frontier Province and the Tribal Agencies. Once across the Durand Line, however, none of the belligerents could return to British India, or they would be interned.[1] The British prohibited the Musahiban brothers from collecting a *lashkar* (tribal army) along the way, but the brothers ignored the restraint and, on the whole, the British political agents of the Tribal Agencies did not interfere.

---

[1] An interesting sidelight of the period occurred when T. E. Lawrence (of Arabia fame) showed up at Miranshah R.A.F. installation near the frontier. Lawrence served as "Aircraftsman Shaw" on the duty roster, but he saw to it that everyone knew his true identity (Nutting, 1962, 223–24). Afghan and Russian sources accuse Lawrence of directing the campaigns against both Amanullah and Bacha Saqqao, but no evidence has ever been unearthed to support such allegations. Lawrence was merely sulking in his garrison, as a result of post-World War I British rebuffs to his Arab friends and to his own monumental ego.

Mohammad Hashim Khan, caught when driven back across the border, was interned in Quetta, while Nadir Khan and Shah Wali Khan, dishearteningly unsuccessful at first, continued their efforts to overthrow Bacha Saqqao. The three brothers originally arrived in Peshawar on February 25, 1929 (Fletcher, 1965, 220), and crossed the border on March 8, arriving at Matun in Khost, where, during the Third Anglo–Afghan War, Nadir Khan had launched his attacks on British India (Mohd. Ali, 1959, 163).

A younger brother, Shah Mahmud, caught in Kabul by the Saqqaoist coup and appointed provincial governor in Gardez by the Tajik Amir, joined his brothers after being sent by Habibullah to bargain with Nadir Khan.

Twice Nadir Khan moved toward Kabul and twice withdrew, the army being led both times by Shah Mahmud. Recurring blood-feuds in his ranks, combined with the successful defense of Habibullah, caused the breakup of Nadir Khan's armies. Patiently, Nadir Khan collected a third army of Mangal, Jaji, Jadran, Ahmadzai, and Tota Khel Waziri, as well as Darwesh Khel Waziri from the British side of the Durand Line.

During this period the cyclostyled newspaper *Islah* (*Reformation*) came into being as an underground sheet, smuggled into Kabul and distributed among the population in support of the Musahiban brothers. *Islah* is still published in Kabul as an official government newspaper.

Led by Shah Wali, the army made a surprise march through the Dobandi Pass and caught the Saqqaoist forces by surprise, defeated them, and occupied Kabul on October 10, 1929. Bacha Saqqao fled to Kohistan. He surrendered a few days later and, in spite of promises of reprieve, was publically executed along with seventeen of his lieutenants on November 3 by a firing squad at the insistence of the tribal leaders of Nadir Khan's army.

Many of Amanullah's supporters believed that Nadir Khan would bring the deposed King back to Kabul. Nadir Khan had intimated as much. In addition, he constantly refused to proclaim himself king before he arrived at Kabul on October 16. However, on October 17, a *jirgah* of the tribal army clamored for Nadir Khan to be king, and he bowed to its will, and became Mohammad Nadir Shah, King of Afghanistan. The same tribal army looted government buildings and the houses of wealthy people in Kabul because the treasury was empty. Missing items still show up in the Kabul bazaar, and customs officials constantly check for national treasures as foreigners attempt to take them from the country.

Nadir Shah called a *Loya Jirgah* to legitimize his accession to the throne, and the Great Council proclaimed him King in September 1930 (Fraser-Tytler, 1967, 227).

The reform attempts of Amanullah quickly dissipated, for the new King correctly judged the tenor of the times. He abolished reforms by *farman,* women returned to the *chadri* and purdah (*pardah*), religious leaders (such as Fazl Omar Mujadidi and his successor to the title, Mohammad Saddiq, Hazrat of Shor Bazaar, and Sher Agha Naguib of Jalalabad) assumed stronger power, internal security increased, conditions improved in the army, and a military college was built on the ruins of the Bala Hissar. The army remained relatively weak, however, and conservative tribal and religious leaders were one of the foundations of power in Afghanistan from 1929 to 1953, when the army finally came into its own.

Not all Afghans supported Nadir Shah as strongly as did the tribal Pushtun, and in May 1930, the Shinwari revolted in favor of Amanullah, but Nadir Shah bought off the khans. Although the Shinwari actually began the 1929 revolt, they were not so much anti-Amanullah as against the local tax-collectors at Jalalabad. Later the Ghilzai southwest of Kabul also struck at Nadir Shah.

The Kohistani Tajik, led by Purdel, revolted in July 1930, and Nadir Shah once again called on the Pushtun tribesmen from along the frontiers with British India to deliver the *coup de grâce* with a brutality still shuddered at in Kohistan. Purdel was killed in the fighting.

With the rise of Mohammad Nadir Shah to the throne of Afghanistan, the Russians lost the favored position they had partly developed under Amanullah. Before the signing of a new Treaty of Neutrality and Non-Aggression in June 1931, the activities of a famous *basmachi* leader, Ibrahim Beg, a Lakai Uzbak, threatened to disrupt peaceful relations between the two countries. While Nadir Shah and his brothers were busy pacifying south Afghanistan, Ibrahim Beg waged a guerrilla war against the Soviets, using hit-and-run tactics, always falling back to sanctuary across the Afghan border. In June 1930, the exasperated Soviet army crossed the Amu Darya and followed Ibrahim Beg for about forty miles, "in hot pursuit." The troops failed to capture the *basmachi* leader, but succeeded in stunning the Afghans by this frontier violation. Further revolts in Kohistan delayed Afghan action against Ibrahim Beg. In December,[2] the King's brother, Sardar Shah Mahmud, led a force across the snow-covered Hindu Kush by way of the Khawak Pass. Ibrahim Beg, driven across the border by Shah Mahmud, was captured and executed in April 1931, by the Soviets (Fraser-Tytler, 1967, 230).

By late 1931 most of Afghanistan south of the Hindu Kush had been pacified, the last adherents of Bacha Saqqao at Herat defeated, and the truculent Uzbak and Turkoman calmed down by Shah Mahmud.

The military campaigns of the north impressed Nadir Shah with the necessity of an improved network of roads and communications, so he employed (in reality working under a system of corvée) thousands of men in constructing a road through the Shibar Pass to Afghan Turkestan (the road was completed just before Nadir Shah's death), the main north-south route until the opening of the Salang Tunnel in 1964.

To secure peace along the frontier, Nadir Shah abandoned the active needling carried on by prior Amirs and, in return, received 10,000 rifles, 5 million cartridges and £170,000 from the British, the only external aid he ever received. He put the aid to good use primarily road-building, education, and subjugating the tribes in both north and south (Fletcher, 1966, 232). Even though his government publicly acknowledged the gift, many in Afghanistan believed (most unfairly, in my opinion) acceptance indicated a pro-British bias.

In order to create at least a semblance of stability inside Afghanistan, Nadir Shah also produced a constitution, modeled on Amanullah's 1923 constitution, but more conservatively oriented as a sop to the religious leaders.

Constitutional Development to 1931

Amir Abdur Rahman had left the following written legacy (Abdur Rahman Khan, 1900, II: 178–90; MacMunn, 1929, 247–49) to Afghanistan:

> The first and most important advice that I can give my successors and people to make Afghanistan into a great kingdom is to impress upon their minds the value of *unity;* unity, and unity alone, can make it into a great power. All the royal family, nobility, and people must have one mind, one interest, and one opinion to safeguard their homes. . . . I have arranged matters during my lifetime in

[2] Grassmuck, et al. (1969, 272) say Shah Mahmud went north in September 1931.

such a way, that all the members of my family and the Afghan people acknowledged the supremacy of my eldest son. . . . The foundation stone of a Constitutional Government has been laid by me; though the machinery of a Representative Government has not taken any practical shape as yet. It is necessary that every ruler observe and consider the various modes of Government adopted in various countries, not jump at conclusions in a hurry. . . . There are three kinds of representatives who assemble in my court. . . . These three classes are called *Sirdars* [the aristocracy], *Khawanin Mulki* [Commons or representatives of the people, usually tribal leaders loyal to the crown], and Mullahs [ecclesiastical heads and church representatives]. . . . This constitutional body has not yet attained the ability nor the education to qualify it for being entrusted with authority of any importance for giving sanction to Bills or Acts of the Government. But in time perhaps they will have such authority. . . . I must strongly urge my sons and successors never to make themselves puppets in the hands of these representatives of constitutional Government. . . . My sons and successors should not try to introduce reforms of any kind in such a hurry as to set the people against their ruler, and they must bear in mind that in establishing a Constitutional Government, introducing more lenient laws, and modelling education upon the system of Western universities, they must adopt all these gradually as the people become accustomed to the idea of modern innovations.

As should be obvious, Abdur Rahman Khan rarely asked for advice from his three consultive bodies. He did, however, occasionally consult his loosely-formed Cabinet of Ministers.

Abdur Rahman's son and successor, Habibullah, followed his father's advice and consultative procedures, but gave freer rein to the religious leaders.

Amanullah's reforms included the writing of a constitution modeled on the Iranian constitution of 1906 and the Turkish administrative codes of Mustafa Kemal Ataturk. The 1923 Afghan constitution, originally published in Pashto, theoretically established an appointive Council of State (Cabinet), and several partly elective consultative bodies. By 1924, however, pressure from conservative advisers, religious and tribal leaders, coincident with the Mangal revolt, forced Amanullah to call a *Loya Jirgah* which made minor amendments to the seventy-three articles of the constitution (e.g., give the religious judges, *qazi,* more discretion in making judicial decisions), but left the liberalized administrative code (*Nizamnameh*) untouched (Poullada, 1969b). The 1923 constitution also called for a hereditary, absolute monarchy.

After his extended trip to Europe, King Amanullah had intensified his efforts at modernization. He announced a new series of reforms in late August 1928, before a *Loya Jirgah* of about a thousand of Afghanistan's most influential tribal, ethnic, and religious leaders. The reforms included a nominated Upper House, an elected Lower House of 150 legislators, abolition of the *Loya Jirgah* concept, creation of a Western-style cabinet and constitutional monarchy, the separation of Church and state, the emancipation of women, enforced monogamy, and compulsory education for all Afghans. The *Loya Jirgah* rejected most of the proposals, so two months later, Amanullah convened a smaller *jirgah* of about one hundred loyal followers (mainly government officials and some leading citizens of Kabul) to approve the items not passed. Amanullah dramatically removed the veil from his wife to symbolize the voluntary abolition of purdah and announced himself a "revolutionary king."

The 1928 proposals were never implemented, however, for anti-Amanullah elements, both inside and outside Afghanistan, combined to overthrow the King.

In September 1930, General Nadir Khan summoned a *Loya Jirgah* of 286 notables. The assembly confirmed him as King of Afghanistan, announced support of his November 1929 proclamation (which renounced Amanullah's reform programs), and promised to move Afghanistan back into the mainstream of the Hanafi Shari'a of Sunni Islam. Even before the *Loya Jirgah,* Nadir Shah had appointed a ten-man cabinet mainly from among his kinsmen; and at the instance of the newly-proclaimed King, the assembly made another attempt at parliamentary procedure. The body selected (with the King's approval) 105 of its members to form a National Council, which would serve as a consultive body to the King, but which would also pass on legislation proposed by the throne. In reality, the National Council simply rubber-stamped Cabinet proposals. The major contradiction in the 1931 Constitution was that, although the government was declared to be responsible to the Parliament, members of Parliament had to swear loyalty to the government.

Nadir Shah slowly moved ahead with modernization programs, but these were cut short by his assassination in November 1933. During his short reign, however, he promulgated a new constitution, which, technically, became effective in October 1931, after approval by the National Council.

The 1931 Constitution in Theory and Practice[3]

The 1931 Constitution embodied a hodgepodge of unworkable elements. Extracted from the Turkish, Iranian, and French constitutions and the 1923 Constitution of Amanullah, plus many aspects of the Hanafi *Shari'a* of Sunni Islam and local custom (*'adat*), several of these last contradictory to the *Shari'a*. Many of the Constitution's 110 articles and 16 parts seemed to have been borrowed at random from the various sources.

The ideals of Afghan society are more or less expressed in the 1931 Constitution, but the government never implemented the proscribed constitutional monarchy within the parliamentary system. The institutions created by the document appeared to allocate authority to various government offices, but, in reality, power centered in the monarchy and the royal family, creating a veritable oligarchy (L. Dupree, 1963b). Therefore, the Constitution created the illusion of popular participation without proper enforcement provisions.

The 1931 Constitution only partly suited the Afghan character and social system, which can be generally described as tribal, authoritarian, patrilineal, and patriarchal. Mohammad Nadir Shah permitted the religious leaders much more freedom than they enjoyed under Amir Abdur Rahman (who had sought to destroy their political power and wealth), Habibullah (who had tolerated them), or Amanullah (who had sincerely tried to create a secular state). As a consequence, Islam pervades the 1931 Constitution. The following words were its preamble: "In the name of Allah, the Most Merciful . . ."

Section I (Articles 1–4) bluntly stated that the official religion of Afghanistan would be the Hanafi *Shari'a* of Sunni Islam and specified that the king must be Hanafi Muslim (Article I). In effect, this loosely-worded article not only excluded the various *Shari'a* of Shi'a Islam, but also the other *Shari'a* of Sunni Islam. The same article said that " . . . followers of other religions such as Hindus or Jews residing in Afghanistan also enjoy protection provided they do not violate the ordinary rules of conduct and propriety," the "ordinary rules of conduct

---

[3] For a detailed discussion of constitutional development in Afghanistan and Pakistan see *AUFS Reports,* vol. IX, South Asia Series, 1965.

and propriety" being undefined. Most members of Afghan minority groups (particularly Shi'a Muslims) can cite many specific examples of discrimination in Afghan government offices and courts in spite of the "guarantees" in the 1931 Constitution.

Shi'a Islam, however, permits *taqiya* (to deny that one is Shi'a to save life or property or to prevent unpleasant situations from arising, so long as one remains pure in belief), and some Shi'a Afghans, mainly Qizilbash, claim to be Sunni Tajik (another ethnic group) in order to obtain and hold government jobs. Several extremely important Afghan administrators and statesmen fit into this category.

Section II ("Rights of the King," Articles 5–8) gave fulsome praise to "His Majesty Mohammad Nadir Shah Ghazi in obtaining the independence and the deliverance of the land of Afghanistan. . . . The Afghan nation in general has recognized His Majesty as a fit and worthy king of his country and has accepted him with the greatest esteem and respect." Because of Nadir Shah's services, Article 5 said, "the noble Afghan nation . . . agrees that the Crown of Afghanistan will be transferred to the family of the king . . . and that succession to the throne will be in accordance with the selection of His Majesty and the people of Afghanistan." In other words, Article 5 eliminated Amanullah and his heirs from the kingship, but very loosely established the succession in the "family" of Mohammad Nadir Shah. Some Afghan legal scholars interpreted "family" to mean eldest son or brother, but just as many disagreed and included collateral relatives as well. After the death of Nadir Shah a new amendment technically eliminated his brothers from contention for the throne.

Political succession in the Islamic world has always been dependent on the "Will of Allah." A Muslim ruler, to be Caliph, Amir, King, or President, rules with the divine *sanction* of Allah, not the divine *right* which justified European monarchies for centuries. If a Muslim ruler violates Islam or displeases Allah, sanction is removed. Every time a Muslim government, in medieval or modern dress, changes hands or heads, either through legitimate or illegitimate means, the new ruler proclaims in his first public utterance, "By the Will of Allah, I am now king [or president, premier, etc.]."

Article 6 gave the oath the king must take before the National Assembly on his accession to the throne, which includes the phrase "So help me God through the blessings of the spiritual force of the blessed saints (the approval of God be upon them)."

The reference to "saints" worried some Islamic purists, because they consider only Allah divine, and sainthood always confers a bit of divinity

465

on the recipient. In spite of occasional injunctions against the cults of saints by various *'ulama* (learned religious bodies in different Muslim nations), such cults thrive throughout the Islamic world.

Article 7 specified that the king's name would be mentioned in Friday sermons and "the coin of the realm will bear his name." The article specifically omitted mention that the king's picture should be on the coinage, because most religious leaders would have interpreted this as anti-Islamic; i.e., the king competing with Allah, for many ultra-conservative Muslims believe that human forms should never be represented in art. In recent years (beginning during the prime ministership of Hashim Khan), the present king has appeared on Afghan paper money, coins, and stamps.

Section III (Articles 9–26) spelled out the idealistic "General Rights of Afghan Subjects." Until recently, these rights were more violated than perpetuated. Article 10 negated the other articles which prohibited imprisonment without due process of law (Article 11), slavery (Article 11), search of personal property without an "order under *Shari'a* law or the law of the land" (Article 16), confiscation of properties "with the exception of that belonging to persons . . . making propaganda or intrigue against the Afghan government" (Article 17), forced labor (Article 18), and so forth. Article 10, however, had already stated, "All Afghan subjects, *although required to observe the injunctions and prohibitions of their Government in religious and political matters* [italics added], are free to enjoy all their legal rights." (The phrase seemed to imply: "Just try and enjoy them!")

Section III also established other ideals still not fully achieved, but constantly sought: compulsory primary education (Article 20), appeal of court decisions all the way up to the king (Article 24), and the right to publish newspapers and periodicals as belonging "to the Afghan government and subjects," implying a nominal freedom of the press (Article 23).

All persons, according to Article 9, having Afghan citizenship are equal. Women were not specifically mentioned, so presumably they shared in all the rights mentioned in Section III. During the tenure of the 1931 Constitution, however, all persons were not given equal treatment before the law, and women held a decidedly inferior position in Afghan society.

The remainder of the Section recognized the theory of parliamentarianism, and accepted tribal traditions without yielding royal control. Such an arrangement fitted nicely into classical Islamic political theory.

Sura 42 of the *Qor'an* discusses counsel or consultation: "That which Allah hath is better and more lasting for those . . . whose affairs are matters of counsel"; therefore, a ruler should have advisers.

Section IV (Articles 27–39), Section V (Articles 40–56), Section VI (Articles 57–66), and Section VII (Articles 67–70) established the mechanism to create a bicameral parliament and defined its duties and interrelationships. The *Majlis-i-Shura-yi-Melli* (National Assembly, or Lower House) was to be elected for three-year terms, meet regularly, with fifty percent attendance constituting a quorum, and bills to be passed by a simple majority vote of those present. When the National Assembly was not in session, the king issued royal *farman* (decrees) in the name of the government; but, in theory, it was necessary for the National Assembly to approve after reconvening.

Articles 38 (members of parliament could freely express opposition to government policies) and 39 (all parliamentary debates were to be open to press and public) probably represented the most important ideals expressed in Section IV, but, as the government tightly controlled the press and the selection of National Assembly members, these two articles remained emasculated for the life of the Constitution.

Articles 52 and 53 negated Articles 38 and 39, for they permitted the president of the National Assembly (elected by its members), ten National Assemblymen, or a cabinet minister to call secret sessions "in case of need." In addition, the president could call meetings which barred any members of the National Assembly he so chose. The outcome of such secret meetings had to be officially announced *only* if the group reached a decision (Article 52). If a minister called a meeting, however, disclosure of the results rested with the discretion of the minister (Article 53).

The duties of the National Assembly included the right to initiate and pass laws (Articles 41, 44), to interrogate ministers (Article 61), examine and approve the national budget (Article 43), and to sanction internal and foreign concessions (Article 45), contracts (Article 46), loans (Article 47), and control public works (Article 48). Although the National Assembly could initiate laws, it seldom did, and the various ministries took the lead in proposing laws relating to their respective spheres, as provided for in the Constitution (Article 51). The National Assembly normally rubber-stamped all ministry proposals.

Section VII (Articles 67–70) dealt with the *Majlis-i-A'yan* (Upper House), sometimes translated as Senate or House of Nobles, a body of twenty or more (later limited to forty-five) "experienced and farsighted persons" (Article 67) appointed by the king. The Upper House served primarily as a consultive body, but bills were supposed to be passed by both houses (Article 68). However, a bill passed by the Lower House while the Upper House was in recess became law immediately after being signed by the king (Article 69).

Under Section VIII (Articles 71–72) each provincial center would have a "Provincial Advisory Committee," theoretically elected, but generally appointed by government officials from among loyal local supporters of government policy.

The "Rights of Civil Servants" (who are still woefully underpaid and prone to accept graft as a means of supplementing their meager incomes in spite of recent substantial pay raises) were defined in Section X (Articles 84–86). Civil servants were enjoined to obey superiors (Article 85), to observe proper regulations in the daily performance of their duties (Article 86), and encouraged to inform on their superiors if they noted any irregularities (Article 85).

From the point of view of the development of a modern state, Section XI ("Courts," Articles 87–94) and Section XII ("Supreme Court," or *Dewan-i-Ali,* Articles 95–96) represented the weakest links with the present. Fundamentally, Section XI established in principle that all legal battles would be within the framework of the Hanafi *Shari'a* of Sunni Islam, but confused the issue by stating in Article 94: "The classification and powers of courts have been laid down in the Fundamental Organization Law," a secular document. Therefore, two separate and often contradictory legal systems, one religious (headed by *qazi,* religious judges), the other semisecular (operating under the supervision of provincial governors and their assistants), attempted to function side by side. Probably the only consistent thing about the final results was inconsistency.

The secular law tried to ameliorate some of the harsher, eye-for-an-eye, tooth-for-a-tooth aspects of legalistic Islam. Often, however, a criminal would request a judgment from a *qazi* in preference to a civil decision. In one 1951 case with which I am familiar, a secular court sentenced a thief to ten years in Kabul's Deh Mazang prison. The thief then pleaded for judgment from a *qazi,* which meant he would have his right hand cut off. He preferred this to a decade of living in the unhealthy atmosphere of Deh Mazang, tantamount to a death sentence to the free spirit of an Afghan. In the early 1940s, modern science entered the scene. Previously, a man's hand had been cut off with a sword or an axe. However, a judgment decreed that although a man's hand could be removed, not one inch of wrist must be damaged. So thieves had their hands cut off under local anesthesia by Afghan surgeons. These practices are now rare, and have been rapidly giving way to more secular punishments, particularly since the accession of King Mohammad Zahir.

The "Administration of Provinces" (Section XIV, Articles 102–05) invited each ministry to send its own representatives to the provinces (Article 103), and insisted on the formation of municpal councils, according to a separate law (Municipal Law of 1947) designed to institute elected bodies in towns with populations over 18,000. An important article (Article 104) gave the government power to put down "signs of unrest and rebellion, tending to the disturbance of public peace."

Two miscellaneous articles comprised Section XVI. Article 109 guaranteed the privacy of the mails. Sometimes even foreigners received packages and magazines with the corners not too casually torn open by postal clerks who fingered inside looking for money, loose objects, and subversive literature. Article 110 instructed civil servants to get all orders given them by the king and prime minister in writing.

Another interesting inconsistency occurred at the end of the 1931 Constitution. Although no provision was made for amendments, in fact three amendments and one amendment to an amendment exist. Traditionally, however, a specially convened *Loya Jirgah* would be needed to legitimate amendments. According to Donald N. Wilber (1962, 158), "Presumably the courts could speculate and the National Council debate on any issue, but the Crown would decide, or in very important cases submit the matter to a Loya Jirgeh."

Amendment 1 prohibited Foreign Ministry officials, military officers, and Afghan students on government scholarships abroad from marrying foreigners, a rule frequently broken. Amendment 2 forbade foreign subjects to own land in Afghanistan, but it permitted foreign legations to exist in accordance with bilateral agreements. A sub-amendment to Amendment 2 further complicated matters by stating: "Foreign subjects in Afghanistan have no *right* [my italics] to own property," implying that the possibility might exist, but the means remain undefined. Amendment 3 was an Amendment to Article 51 (which required ministries to initiate laws relating to their respective spheres), and required each minister to present proposed laws to the Council of Ministers for study and approval before forwarding the bill to the Upper and Lower

92. King Mohammad Nadir (1929-33), successful field commander on the Thal-Kurram front during the Third Anglo-Afghan War, 1919. Nadir Shah is in the center, wearing glasses. *Photo: Private collection, Kabul*

93. King Mohammad Zahir (1933-present) and others; front row, right to left: Field-Marshal Sardar Shah Wali Khan (uncle of the King); Her Majesty, Queen Homaira; His Majesty the King; General Khan Mohammad Khan, Minister of Defense; Brigadier Abdul Wali Khan, Commander of Central Forces, Kabul, son of Marshal Shah Wali Khan, and first cousin and son-in-law of the King. *Photo: Ministry of Information and Culture, Royal Government of Afghanistan*

Houses, both of which technically had to pass the bill before it went to the king for signature.

The 1931 Constitution, in essence, established the kingship in the line of Mohammad Nadir Shah, created a facade of parliamentary government while leaving control in the hands of the royal family, kept the judiciary primarily under the religious leaders, created a semi-socialist economic framework with the principle of free enterprise accepted, and guaranteed theoretical individual equality. Therefore, in the legalistic sense, pre-1964 Afghanistan was governed by the following types of laws: Hanafi *Shari'a* of Sunni Islam as interpreted by religious leaders; royal *farman* (decrees); laws passed by Parliament, usually first proposed by the ministries; ministerial decrees (*ta'limat-namah*) relating to the operation of individual ministries; and the Constitution (*qanun-i-asasi,* Fundamental Principles), seldom implemented but often invoked to justify inconsistent policies.

A Laissez-Faire Economy Develops

The Afghan economy received great impetus in the 1930s under the guidance and leadership of three entrepreneurs: Abdul Majid Zabuli from Herat, Loe Sher Khan Nashir Ghilzai (Kharoti) from Qarabagh, Ghazni, and Abdul Aziz Londoni (whose forebears came from Kashmir to Afghanistan during the eighteenth century).

The rise of Abdul Aziz Londoni is typical of the three men. His father began an import-export business based on fox furs and *pustin* (embroidered Afghan sheepskin coats), which he sent to British India in exchange for tea, spices, and cotton cloth, in turn sold through his bazaar shop outlets.

The fur and skin business virtually collapsed before the end of World War I, and Abdul Aziz traded all his furniture and household goods for Afghan carpets. He took these to Tashkent and Bokhara in Tsarist Central Asia and exchanged them for *qarakul* skins, an investment which most Afghan merchants thought mad. Abdul Aziz paid the exchange value of Rs. 1 per skin, and when he transported these *qarakul* skins to Peshawar, he received, to his amazement, Rs. 6 per skin. He purchased and shipped tea to Afghanistan with his profits, and thus began the Afghan *qarakul* industry which today brings in the bulk of Afghanistan's hard currency, mainly dollars and pounds sterling.

Abdul Aziz went to England in 1922 and introduced *qarakul* skins to the London market, which until World War II took almost all the skins the Afghans could supply. After his successful appearance on the British economic scene, he became known as Abdul Aziz Londoni, a name which stuck with him the rest of his life.

Londoni returned to Afghanistan through Moscow. The Communists now ruled Russia, but from the very beginning, Communist Russia and Afghanistan developed reasonably friendly relations. In addition, a major portion of the pre-World War I trade had been with the Central Asian states to the north of Afghanistan (Hamilton, 1906). During his 1925 visit to Tashkent, Londoni found the new Soviet state hungry for cotton, which had been the mainstay of the economy of pre-World War I Uzbakistan and had been almost completely disrupted by the Russian Revolution and by the nationalist revolts of the *basmachi*. Londoni knew little about cotton, but he did know that the ecological factors across the Amu Darya in Afghanistan were similar to those in Uzbakistan, so he made a deal with the Soviets to supply all the raw cotton he could buy in Afghanistan, with payments to be made half in gold, and half in cotton cloth. In eight months' time, he fulfilled his end of the bargain. The Russians paid promptly and extended his contract. They also took a cue from Londoni and flooded the markets of Western Europe with *qarakul,* but by that time Londoni had seen a vision of "White Gold" in north Afghanistan. Although his *qarakul* business continued to flourish for several years, he transferred most of his money into cotton.

In Moscow, Londoni met another business pioneer, Abdul Majid Zabuli, who at that time (1925) was primarily exporting wool to Russia. The two founded a partnership which greatly benefited Afghanistan as a whole as well as individual investors in their enterprises.

Zabuli, a pragmatist, became a capitalistic man of action, his great achievement being the *Sherkat-i-Sahami-yi-Afghan* (now known as the Bank-i-Melli), which first began as a stock company in 1932 and later became an investment bank. He opened the bank in 1934 with 120 million afghanis (the afghani replaced the rupee as exchange medium after 1925. The metric system was introduced at the same time, but few use it, even today). The Bank-i-Melli served as a center for capital accumulation, and investments flowed from the bank to northern Afghanistan and contributed greatly to the creation of almost all pre-World War II industrial development at Pul-i-Khumri, Kunduz, and Kabul.

The bank developed by Zabuli came under the government monopoly system (*sherkat*) which still permeates much of Afghanistan's economic structure; that is the government controls 40 to 45% of stock in a company—although seldom investing that percentage of capital—whereas the private sector has 55 to 60% of the stock. The *sherkat,* or monopoly system, came into being in order to control production, guarantee investment capital and profits to investors, as well as to provide the government with an easy source of extracted income.

Although a certain percentage of the profits stayed outside Afghanistan, or was spent on luxury imports, the *sherkat,* particularly the Bank-i-Melli, did contribute greatly to the beginning of industrialization in Afghanistan. Since many members of the royal family held large blocks in stock in various *sherkat,* government cooperation helped sustain high profits to stockholders.

Although few Afghans believed in cotton as an investment,[4] Zabuli and the Bank-i-Melli agreed to underwrite part of the cost in order to open up new lands for cotton and build a ginning-plant and pressing-mill in Kunduz. Londoni later brought machinery from the U.S.S.R., the United Kingdom, and Germany, and increased the activities of the Cotton Company of Kunduz to include seed pressings, soap, and ceramics, as well as the ginning and pressing of raw cotton. Londoni's paternalistic social conscience drove him to build adequate housing and hospital facilities for his workers, and he also expanded his ginning operations to six other towns in north Afghanistan. The housing, hospitals, and schools were little improved over the years, although profits continued to climb. Investors benefited, but the Bank-i-Melli, which controlled policy, choose not to put money back into the welfare of the workers. The Bank, however, expanded plant facilities, not only in the Kunduz area but also at Pul-i-Khumri in central Afghanistan.

Before he died in 1940, Londoni witnessed the realization of his dream. He had been instrumental in cleaning out the Kunduz and Pul-i-Khumri areas of Afghanistan—and of the former it had been said, "Go to Kunduz, and die," because the area literally swam in malarial swamps. Londoni first purchased 1,000 acres of land at about $1 an acre and moved farmers on to the land with liberal contract terms to raise cotton. Later, he expanded the holdings of the Cotton Company and encouraged other groups of Afghans to participate. Many had no choice, because, in 1929 and 1930, the new King of Afghanistan, Nadir Shah, forcefully encouraged many well-to-do landholders and merchants to buy cheap land in the north in order to replenish a treasury exhausted by a year of civil war, looting, and corruption. The new settlers drained

---

[4] For example, a younger brother of Londoni, Abdul Ahad Hamidi, invested in a department store, also an innovation in Kabul during the 1930s.

the swamps, and the north developed through the joint process of persuasion and coercion.

The man who took over as President of the Cotton Company of Kunduz had shared Londoni's dream from the beginning. Sher Khan Nashir, Governor of Qataghan when Londoni came north with his plans and his deeds to the untenable lands, could have smashed or impeded Londoni's dreams, but instead he assisted with all the resources at his command, including forced labor.

The pioneering free enterprise system developed by Londoni, Zabuli, and Khan Nashir continued until 1953, and the rise to power of General Mohammad Daoud Khan, Minister of War and first cousin of the King. The Kunduz Cotton Company and other free enterprise activities came under stricter government supervision, for the new regime emphasized the public over the private sector in the economic sphere.

A King Dies Violently

Schools, closed during the 1928–29 fighting, were reopened by Nadir Shah. The rebirth of education indirectly caused the death of Nadir Shah and one of his brothers, Mohammad Aziz, Minister to Berlin. Both events, however, directly related to a blood-feud between the ruling family and the powerful Charkhi family, supporters of Amanullah.

Three brothers formed the nucleus of power in the Charkhi family: Ghulam Sadiq, Ghulam Nabi, and Ghulam Ghilani. Ghulam Haider Khan, their father, had been one of Amir Abdur Rahman's favorite generals. Ghulam Nabi, Ambassador to Moscow at the time of Saqqaoist War, came down from the north, reputedly with Russian arms and tacit support. After Amanullah's precipitous flight, Ghulam Nabi, disgusted, but still pro-Amanullah, returned to Russia.

Both Nadir Shah and the Charkhi brothers appeared to desire reconciliation, but royal rivalries often preclude cementing alliances. The supporters of Amanullah and the Charkhi family continued to agitate among the eastern Pushtun tribes, creating small wars against the Musahiban ruler in Kabul. In spite of this, Nadir Shah invited the Charkhis to return to Afghanistan, and Ghulam Sadiq, former Foreign Minister and Minister to Berlin, appeared in Kabul on July 21, 1932, to swear fealty to the King, who, soon afterward, reappointed him Minister to Germany.

In October 1932, Nadir Shah received Ghulam Nabi Charkhi (who had returned from Ankara, where he served as Nadir Shah's ambassador) at Dilkusha Palace in the presence of Afghan notables and foreign diplomats. One of those present, Fraser-Tytler, describes the meeting (1967, 239): "We who watched felt the tension of the moment, noted the unruffled courtesy of the King's greeting, and will never forget the look of hatred and malice on Ghulam Nabi's evil, crafty face as Nadir Shah turned away after a few brief words."

A revolt in the Jadran Pushtun country coincided with Ghulam Nabi's return to Kabul. The Afghan Government claimed to possess conclusive proof of Ghulam Nabi's collusion in the uprising. In a subsequent interview on November 8, Nadir Shah formally charged Ghulam Nabi with high treason. The Charkhi firebrand verbally attacked the King in public, and an enraged Nadir Shah ordered Ghulam Nabi executed on the spot. Other members of the Charkhi family were rounded up and arrested.

The scene shifts to Berlin, where Mohammad Aziz, the elder Musahiban brother, and father of Mohammad Daoud (later prime minister), had replaced Ghulam Sadiq Charkhi as Afghan Ambassador to Germany. On June 6, 1933, he was shot to death by a young Afghan student named Sayyid Kemal. The assassin accused the Nadir Shah regime of being pro-British, but in Kabul most observers preferred to link the murder with the Musahiban-Charkhi feud (Adamec, 1969, 242). Many in Afghanistan also believed this charge, for the new King had received foreign assistance from the British alone, and the ease with which the brothers Musahiban operated in the frontier region in 1929 caused eyebrows to rise in suspicion. In addition, the government in Kabul failed to give active support to the growing anti-British activities along the frontier.

An Afghan teacher at Nejat school, Mohammad Azim, continued the blood bath on September 7, 1933, when he entered the British Embassy in Kabul and killed the first three persons to cross his path: an Englishman, an Indian, and an Afghan. Azim confessed he hoped to kill the British Minister, force the British to interfere in Afghanistan's internal affairs once again, and overthrow Nadir Shah. An imprisoned Charkhi (Ghulam Ghilani), Mohammad Wali Khan the Tajik, and four other prisoners were executed for assumed complicity in the legation attack. These final executions destroyed the last of Amanullah's major supporters inside Afghanistan.

The final act of violence occurred on November 8, 1933, exactly one year after the execution of Ghulam Nabi Charkhi. At a presentation of awards inside the palace grounds, Abdul Khaliq, either the natural

(Fraser-Tytler, 1967, 241) or adopted (Fletcher, 1966, 234)—or both—sixteen-year-old son of Ghulam Nabi, shot and killed Nadir Shah. Actually, Abdul Khaliq may have been simply the son of one of Ghulam Nabi Charkhi's favorite retainers. The official version in *Islah* accused Ghulam Sadiq, the surviving Charkhi brother (in exile in Germany), as instigator, and declared that he had been able to manipulate the assassination because of an illicit love affair between Abdul Khaliq and the wife of Ghulam Sadiq (Adamec, 1969, 243), although the relevance of such a connection escapes me. In addition, it should be pointed out that Abdul Khaliq would have been 11 years old when the affair reputedly began.

Whatever the reasons (and the Musahiban-Charkhi blood-feud was probably the key factor), German prestige certainly suffered: " . . . all the murderers had attended German schools. Sayyid Kemal had been a member of the first group of students sent to Germany in 1922. He stayed until 1928, then returned to Afghanistan, leaving again during the civil war in 1929. Muhammad Azim was a teacher of German who had studied in Germany after graduating from the German high school" (Adamec, 1969, 243). Abdul Khaliq was an eighth-grade student in the German high school when he committed the murder.

A classic situation presented itself. Its ingredients were a king assassinated, one brother (Mohammad Hashim) outside the capital on tour of the northern provinces, a younger brother (Shah Mahmud) in Kabul and in command of the army, and a young, inexperienced, highly vulnerable nineteen-year-old French-educated (Lycée Janson de Sailly, Lycée Michelet, College de Montpellier) crown prince. Logically and in keeping with the pattern of Afghan illegitimate succession, Shah Mahmud should have seized power, proclaimed himself king, incarcerated his nephew, Mohammad Zahir, and perhaps fought with his brothers for the throne. What actually happened changed the character of the modern Afghan monarchy, and set Afghanistan on the evolutionary political path it still follows.

Family solidarity and dynastic survival overrode any personal ambitions the uncles may have had, and the Crown Prince became King Mohammad Zahir Shah, *Almutawakil-Alalah* ("He Who Puts His Faith in Allah"), in the late afternoon of November 8, 1933.

CHAPTER 22

The Avuncular Period

1933–53

KING Mohammad Zahir Shah reigned but did not rule for twenty years. His uncles, as befitted Islamic cultural patterns, ruled. When a young man's father dies (or is killed), his paternal uncle or uncles replace his father in the culturally defined father-son rights and obligations. So rule by the uncles was most logical, and gave the King time to study his nation, his role, and his responsibilities, and to assess his political future.

Nadir Shah early began to groom Mohammad Zahir for the monarchy. When the eighteen-year-old Crown Prince completed his course at the Military College in Kabul, his father appointed him Minister of War and Minister of Education, those two complimentary institutions.

Only three of the Musahiban brothers still lived in 1933: Mohammad Hashim, Shah Wali, and Shah Mahmud. Mohammad Hashim served as prime minister from 1933 to 1946, when the youngest brother, Shah Mahmud, took over. (In reality, Hashim Khan became prime minister, or chief adviser, to King Nadir Shah in 1929.) Shah Wali, *Fateh-i-Kabul* ("Conqueror of Kabul" during the Bacha Saqqao war), never actually sought formal power, and represented Afghanistan as Minister to England and France (1930–47), and Ambassador to Pakistan for about a year after the 1947 Partition of India. However, his advice was always sought on matters of family and national importance. Today he remains one of the King's most influential confidants.

Time and tribes stood still for months following the accession of the young King. No fratricidal wars occurred, and Amanullah's followers, disorganized and discouraged after the execution of Abdul Khaliq and seventeen others and the arrest of hundreds, could not unite to take advantage of the opportunity presented them. On the international scene, Afghanistan greatly expanded its relations during the 1930s. It joined the League of Nations in 1934, only to be disillusioned, along with most other nations, when the League, led by Britain, failed to deal effectively with the Italian invasion of Ethiopia in 1935–36. In the same year (1934), the United States formally extended recognition to Afghanistan.

The first official treaty of friendship with the United States took place in 1936, when the American chargé d'affaires in Tehran visited Afghanistan to sign the agreement. An earlier American diplomat, Cornelius H. van Engert, visited Afghanistan in 1924, after initial attempts by Amanullah in 1922 to establish diplomatic relations with the United States (Engert, 1924). Engert became the first American Minister to reside in Kabul when official missions were finally exchanged in 1942 and 1943. Abdul Hussain Aziz became the first Afghan Minister in Washington. In 1948 the two countries exchanged Ambassadors: Ely E. Palmer and Sardar Mohammad Naim Khan, brother of Daoud Khan and first cousin of the King.

During the 1930s the Afghans cast around for foreign assistance, dormant since Nadir Shah accepted British aid in 1931. Although both Russia and Britain were willing to provide aid, Hashim Khan well remembered the fate of Amanullah's flirtation with the Soviets, and in the 1936 Russo–Afghan barter agreements still refused the Russians permission to establish trade missions inside Afghanistan. By 1935, therefore, the Afghans had agreed to accept assistance from the three countries they thought would cause the least disruption on the local scene: Germany (with little colonial past in Asia and Nazism rising under Hitler); Italy (following Mussolini down the Berlin–Rome Axis trail); and Japan (later founder of the Greater Asian Co-Prosperity Sphere).

In 1935, a German scientific-cum-intelligence mission researched in Nuristan, and left behind some superb preliminary statements. The bulk of the research, however, died with the scientists in the holocaust of World War II.[1] To my knowledge, only one, a dentist, survives in Hamburg.

Germans gradually became the most important influential foreign group in Afghanistan prior to World War II. In addition, a group of students went to Japan in February 1936, primarily to study mining. Some returned through Siberia during World War II, and several high Afghan officials still speak fluent Japanese.

Lufthansa planned an air route from Berlin to China through Afghanistan, an aerial *Drang nach Osten*. A reasonably regular weekly service between Berlin and Kabul was established in 1937. Siemens

[1] For invaluable reports on the Nuristan expedition see Scheibe (1937) and Lentz (1937).

Company established commercial ties with Afghanistan, picked up the broken threads again after World War II, and remains one of the larger foreign companies with offices in Kabul, and actually won bids for several post-World War II American projects. The Germans also began to explore the mineral resources of Paktya in 1937.

An important step in the regional sense took place on July 8, 1937, when Afghanistan, Turkey, and Iran signed a Treaty of Non-Aggression and Friendship at Sa'adabad, Iran. Never really implemented because of World War II, the treaty did lay the groundwork for the Regional Cooperation for Development (R.C.D.), a loose, economic entente between Turkey, Iran, and Pakistan growing out of the decaying bones of the Central Treaty Organization (C.E.N.T.O.) (L. Dupree, 1968d).

The Americans, slowly emerging from their isolationist cocoon, were not completely idle. Afghanistan granted the Inland Exploration Company of New York a twenty-five-year-oil concession, but after initial surveys (Fox, 1943), the Americans gave up their rights in 1939. War loomed over everyone's horizon.

Economically, Da Afghanistan Bank (State Bank of Afghanistan) was incorporated in 1938, in competition with the free enterprise Bank-i-Melli, and opened overseas branch offices in British India, Munich, and London. The new bank also controlled the Afghan–American Trading Corporation of New York. Several German, Italian, and Japanese companies responded, and still maintain Kabul branches.

Neither German, Italian, nor Japanese work proved of any material consequence. Lacking in understanding of local materials (national resources and people), they constructed collapsible small dams and bridges which washed away at the first big spring floods. A hydro-power station in Wardak, however, still functions.

Attitudinally, the Germans injected a new bit of racist folklore into the Afghan mainstream. Until convinced by German propagandists they were the original Aryans (contrasted to "honorary Aryans" like the Japanese), many Afghans sought their origin in the legend of the lost, wandering tribe of the ancient Beni Israel.

Small frontier wars plagued both the British and the Afghans in the late 1930s. The most serious threat to the Afghans was the so-called Shami Pir revolt, led by an Iraqi kinsman of Queen Soraya, Sayyid Mohammad Sa'adi (Fletcher, 1965, 239). On January 15, 1939, the Shami Pir ("Syrian Saint") declared Amanullah to be the true king of Afghanistan, and several tribes, among them the Waziri and Sulaiman Khel Ghilzai, attacked Matun in Khost. The assault failed, and the British, having enough trouble with home-grown Pushtun agitators, bribed the Shami Pir (£20,000) to take the trip back to Baghdad.

On the British side, various sections of the Waziri, usually led by Hajji Mirza Ali Khan, the Fakir of Ipi, forced the British into action several times before World War II. Hajji Mirza Ali Khan, who died in 1959, continued to be a thorn in the side of the Pakistanis from the 1947 Partition of India until his death.

At one time the British army had three divisions in the field against the Faqir's irregulars. The North–West Frontier Province and the Tribal Agencies served as an excellent training ground for British officers and troops between major European wars (Elliott, 1968; Masters, 1956; Pettigrew, n.d.; Skeen, 1943; Swinson, 1967), and until the airplane became a factor, both sides engaged in annual (i.e., off-agricultural, off-herding season) *gusht* (patrols or fights). The airplane, a most un-cricket like instrument in tribal guerrilla warfare, changed the essence of the game. The tribesmen continued to raid the plains in spite of the fact that their villages were bombed in retaliation. The British, however, usually dropped leaflets (although few Pushtun could read them) before bombing a village. During the incursions, the tribesmen stole cattle, horses, sheep, women, and other livestock.

World War II brought an abrupt slow-down to economic development in Afghanistan, and the King, on August 17, 1940, issued a *farman* proclaiming a continued policy of neutrality. Many literate Afghans, however, covertly cheered for the Nazis, particularly since Germany, at one time or another, had fought against both Britain and Russia.

Afghanistan's neutrality was sore strained in late 1941 when the British and Russians on October 9 and 11 demanded the Afghans expel all non-diplomatic Axis personnel, some of whom had been causing trouble and casualties along the frontier. The German Ambassador to Afghanistan at this time was Hans Pilger, but the German Foreign Office proposed that the Afghans accept Otto von Hentig, co-leader of the World War I German Mission to Afghanistan. Allied pressure and the German invasion of Russia precluded Afghan acceptance of the appointment (Adamec, 1969, 252).

German agents also worked in the Zagros Mountain area of Iran (Schulze-Holthus, 1954; Skrine, 1962) and others helped precipitate the pro-German "Golden Square" revolt of Rashid Ali el-Gilani in Iran in early 1941. The brilliant forced march of Glubb Pasha's (Sir John

Bagot Glubb) Arab Legion from Transjordan (Glubb, 1948) and other British maneuvers finally brought down the Rashid Ali regime.

Prime Minister Mohammad Hashim Khan and his confidants did not doubt for one moment that a Russo–British force would invade Afghanistan if the Afghans refused the Allied demands. They had the example of Iran as a guideline. On July 1, 1941, Sir Reader Bullard, British Ambassador in Tehran, requested that the Persians expel four-fifths of the Germans from Iran, after delivering proof to the Persian prime minister of the disruptive activities of Axis personnel. On August 17, the British and Soviet ambassadors presented a joint note to the Iranians, and demanded that all Germans (except the few needed to operate the German Embassy) be expelled. The Iranian government vacillated. Therefore, in the early light of August 25, 1941, Britain and Russia jointly invaded Iran. The British smashed the pitiful but gallant resistance of the Iranian Navy in the Persian Gulf. The Russian bear swung roughshod over the pitiful but ungallant Iranian army in Azerbaijan. Only the Shahsavan (traditional "Protectors of the Shah") offered any semblance of resistance (Skrine, 1962, 77–79).

Iran, an invaded and conquered nation (necessarily so according to Allied strategy: to protect Iranian oil for the Allies, and to open a southern supply route to beleaguered Russia), did not declare war on the Axis until September 9, 1943, when it appeared obvious to everyone that the Axis powers would lose the war.

The Afghan prime minister, Mohammad Hashim, even with the invasion of Iran fresh in the news, considered the Russo-British ultimatum an insult to traditional Afghan hospitality and neutrality, an affront to the Muslim custom of sanctuary, and a slap at the growing national integrity of a small nation. Many Afghans wanted to reject the note, and, if necessary, fight. But the wily Afghans usually come up with a better way, and they did. The Afghans ordered *all* non-diplomatic citizens of belligerent nations to leave, but naturally the Axis lost the battle of the numbers, although a few still wandered about and attempted to stir up trouble. Of the 180 Germans in Afghanistan, only 10 remained behind to assist Hans Pilger in the legation (Adamec, 1969, 252–53). The British agreed to permit the deported personnel free passage through India, and eventually most of the Germans, Italians, and Japanese reached home. But several known agitators were interned in India, and the Afghans denounced this alleged breach of international decorum.

The compromise reached, the King called a *Loya Jirgah* of all the tribal and religious leaders, the notable of Afghanistan, to consider what should be done in the future. The *Loya Jirgah* decided to resist any further interference from either side with armed force.

Even after the non-diplomats left, Afghanistan remained the Switzerland of Asia, where spies swapped lies and information and played cat-and-mouse with counter-agents and counter-counter-agents.

The war ended. The combatants licked their wounds, some with whines and whimpers, others with hip-hip-hoorays, others with awe at what man had wrought. The Afghans counted their dollars and pounds sterling, for during the war they had been able to buy little but sell all. The Allied armies in India needed all the foodstuffs Afghanistan could supply, and, even before the war ended, New York happily replaced London as the chief purchaser of *qarakul* skins. Very shortly, the United States would become intimately involved with the future of Afghanistan, as the new government of Shah Mahmud (1946–53) pushed ambitious plans to develop the Hilmand Valley.

The Hilmand Valley Project, Phase I: 1946–53[2]

The longest river in Afghanistan, the Hilmand, joins its major tributary, the Arghandab, at Qala Bist, about 350 miles from its source high in the Hindu Kush, and continues to the Sistan Basin, another 250 miles. Seasonal flow varies greatly, but the river is usually perennial. The problem, however, is not lack of water but adequate control. Control probably did exist in the historic past, as attested by miles of silted canals, hundreds of mounds, and deserted towns and large cities in southwestern Afghanistan and southeastern Iran. The dream of making deserts bloom again continually thrives in the mind of man, but seldom in the deserts, and, in fact, Sistan may possibly have never supported the large population envisioned by planners.

Previous modern attempts to rejuvenate the Hilmand Valley occurred long before the Americans reinvented foreign aid. The Afghans themselves constructed the first new functional canal between 1910 and 1914. The Germans gave some technical assistance in the early 1930s, and the Japanese (1937–41) helped dig nine miles of canals at Boghra. From 1941 to 1946, a Cornell-educated Afghan engineer, Dr. S. W. Shah, pushed ahead another 16 miles of canals.

[2] Also see Michel (1959).

Negotiations between the Afghan Government and Morrison-Knudsen began in late 1945, and resulted in the formation of Morrison-Knudsen Afghanistan Inc. (M.K.A.), with its headquarters in San Francisco. After a preliminary survey M.K.A. made several estimates: an initial $10.7 million would be needed for all surveys and roads necessary to begin the construction of two dams and an extensive canal system; the total cost would be $63.7 million, including $53.7 million in foreign exchange. The canal system would include intakes, waterways, laterals, and sublaterals.

Human problems at all levels, from peasant resistance to bureaucratic folderol, beset the Hilmand Valley project from its conception. Neither the Afghan government nor the American engineering company understood the monumental problems of enfolding an entire region in the embrace of a single project. The Hilmand watershed drains forty percent of Afghanistan's land area, directly affecting between two and three million people, or about one fifth of the entire population.

A major technological change usually involves an almost total ecological change. Given the ingredients of the non-literate, peasant-tribal, inward-looking society described earlier (above, Part II), the human problems appear as monumental as the magnificent engineering edifices left on the landscape; but, without consideration of the human factor, great dams simply make great ruins.[3]

From the beginning, misunderstandings arose concerning areas of responsibility and capability of the two parties. In order to save foreign exchange, the Afghans agreed to undertake some extremely important aspects of the total project (e.g., to construct feeders and ditches in order to drain the canals properly). The Afghan government also talked M.K.A. out of several extensive surveys (e.g., soil and ground-water surveys in certain areas), which later proved to be critical mistakes. M.K.A. engineers in the field reluctantly accepted the cuts forced on them by company policy.

In addition, the few Afghan engineers were constantly used as administrators, so the Afghans were never able to fulfill their engineering obligations. The Americans, for their part, did not understand Afghan cultural patterns. M.K.A. moved along with its end of the project, at first not realizing that the Afghans could not complete their commitments, nor would their pride permit them to admit it.

[3] With apologies to Maxwell Anderson (n.d.):
"Nothing is made by man
but makes, in the end, good ruins." (*High Tor*, p. 142)

By 1949, costs had mushroomed, as they have a habit of doing, especially when projects sit halfway around the world. *All* equipment had to be shipped from the United States and then sent by rail or truck in-transit through a semi-hostile Pakistan, which often bureaucratically hindered shipments to Afghanistan in retaliation for Afghan agitation over the "Pushtunistan" problem.

The Afghan foreign exchange surplus rapidly flowed down the Hilmand into the pockets of Morrison-Knudsen ($20 million by September 1949), and Abdul Majid Zabuli (Minister of National Economy) asked the Export-Import Bank for a $55-million loan. Initially, Export-Import refused until the Afghans formulated a Hilmand Valley Authority (H.V.A., modeled on the Tennessee Valley Authority) to integrate the project, but finally approved a $21-million loan in November 1949. The Export-Import Bank eliminated the incentive bonuses M.K.A. had previously received, so the company apparently slowed down its pace from April 1950 to March 1951. Then when it became obvious that additional money would be needed, the project was completed quickly. M.K.A. took several short cuts and rushed toward completion of the two dams and the Boghra Canal system (completed in 1951), but dropped some projects and curtailed others, among them intensive ground-water surveys, certain road pavings, and hydroelectric projects.

In 1951, at last embarrassed to action, the Afghan Government asked M.K.A. to take over its engineering obligations, which would require additional funding. In an attempt to unify the efforts, the Afghans finally created the Hilmand Valley Authority (H.V.A.) in July 1952, with overall responsibility for implementation. The president of H.V.A. was given cabinet status.

M.K.A., ahead of schedule, finished the 145-foot-high Arghandab Dam (18 miles above Qandahar), which is 1,740 feet long and has a storage capacity of 388,000 acre-feet of water.[4] In April 1953, the Kajaki Dam (45 miles above Girishk on the Hilmand River), 300 feet high and 887 feet long with a 32-mile-long reservoir and a capacity of 1,495,000 acre-feet of water, was inaugurated with proper ceremonies.

Much, however, remained to be done. Deep drains had to be dug, canals needed lining to prevent seepage, and maintenance (particularly periodic dragging with chains to clear the canals of algae) had to be performed. Aside from the human problems, the technical problems

[4] An acre-foot of water is one acre of water, one foot deep.

proved to be more formidable than M.K.A. had anticipated. Only 170,000 acres received adequate water, and most of these were already being farmed.

Point IV (the Technical Cooperation Administration) sent two extension advisors to the project in December 1952. (The first Point IV agreement had been signed on February 9, 1951.) Since then, fairly or unfairly, the Hilmand Valley and United States prestige have been entertwined in the minds of many observers.

In June 1953, the Afghans and T.C.A. signed their initial project agreement, and in November the Export-Import Bank issued another $18.5-million loan. H.V.A. had asked for $36 million for drains, and power and land development in the Hilmand Valley, as well as money to pave the streets of Kabul. The project would move slowly ahead, but Afghan development would mushroom under Sardar Mohammad Daoud Khan, who became prime minister in September 1953, and gave Afghanistan a dynamism not seen since the abortive modernization efforts of Amanullah.

"Pushtunistan": 1946–53

Several times before the 1947 Partition of India, Afghan governments in power reaffirmed their treaty obligations with the British. Habibullah, not without personal misgivings and outside threats, signed the Anglo–Afghan pact of 1905, which stipulated: "His said Majesty does hereby agree to this that in the principles and in the matters of subsidiary importance of the engagements which His Highness my late father [Abdur Rahman] concluded and acted upon with the Exalted British Government, I also have acted, am acting, and will act upon the same agreements and compacts, and I will not contravene them in any dealing" (Caroe, 1965, 464).

The first mention of the Durand Line as a "frontier" occurs in the 1919 Treaty of Rawalpindi, signed at the conclusion of the Third Anglo–Afghan War. Paragraph 5 states: "The Afghan government accepts the Indo–Afghan frontiers accepted by the late Amir" (Caroe, 1965, 464). The "late Amir" was Habibullah; his son, Amanullah, signed the 1919 treaty. (An avowed Afghan purpose in the Third Anglo–Afghan War was to secure independence for the Pushtun in British India [D. Franck, 1952, 54].) The 1919 treaty also slightly adjusted the Durand Line in the Khyber area.

Two paragraphs of the subsequent Anglo–Afghan Treaty of 1921 refer to the Durand Line. Paragraph 2 reads: "The two high contracting parties having mutually satisfied themselves regarding the good will of the other and especially regarding their benevolent intentions towards the tribes residing close to their respective boundaries, hereby undertake each to inform the other in future of any military operations which may appear necessary for the maintenance of order among frontier tribes residing within their respective spheres before the commencement of such operations" (Aitchison, 1933, 293). Article XIV in the treaty provides that the treaty "shall remain in force for three years" and "in case neither of the high contracting parties should have notified twelve months before the expiration of the said three years the intention to terminate it, it shall remain binding until the expiration of one year from that date on which either of the high contracting parties shall have denounced it" (Aitchison, 1933, 293).

The Afghans questioned the responsibilities of both governments toward the Pushtun areas, and asked that Afghan interests there be recognized. A supplementary 1921 letter from the British representatives to the Afghan Foreign Minister continued the vagueness which has plagued the vague mountainous frontier (see above, pp. 425–29).

Immediately after his accession to the throne, King Mohammad Nadir Shah reaffirmed "the validity of the Treaty concluded at Kabul on November 22, 1921" (Caroe, 1965, 465).

Events in the Pushtun region on the British side of the Durand Line affected the rise of the "Pushtunistan" issue. The formation of the North–West Frontier Province in 1901 separated the Pushtun country from the Province of Punjab, and divided the area into the Settled Districts and the Tribal Agencies, sowing the seeds of independence movements among the British Indian Pushtun. The five Tribal Agencies (Malakand, Khyber, Kurram, North Waziristan, South Waziristan) did not come under the administrative aegis of the North–West Frontier Province, but each had a British Political Agent, responsible only to the Government of India in Delhi. The local khans continued local control.

The Montagu-Chelmsford Reforms of 1919, which launched the rest of India on an experiment in provincial democracy, did not affect the Pushtun country. The dynamic, dogmatic, conservative Sir George Roos-Keppel ruled the North–West Frontier Province from 1908 to 1919, and convinced the British Raj that the Pushtun had no use for the formal legislative mechanisms provided in the Reforms. He insisted the Pushtun *jirgah* system was democracy in action. Simultaneously he created Islamia College, which rapidly grew into the modern University of Peshawar, threatening tribal traditions but leaving nothing to replace them.

The opinions of Roos-Keppel prevailed, although the Frontier Inquiry Committee of 1922 recommended a provincial legislature for the North–West Frontier Province. The Simon Commission (Royal Stationary Commission of 1928–30), after consultation with many North–West Frontier Pushtun and their khans at Peshawar, had even more drastic recommendations. The khans reputedly reported: "The contiguity of the province with independent territory and Afghanistan, the free intercourse between the people on both sides of the borderline, the simplicity of their ideals, customs, and mode of life, and especially their descent from the common stock, strongly distinguish the people of our province from those of the rest of India" (Pazhwak, 1953, 95–96).

Pertinent quotes from the Simon Commission Report include: "The situation of the province and its intimate relation with the problem of Indian advance are such that special arrangements are required," and "British India stops at the boundary of the administered area." The boundary referred to is between the Tribal Agencies and Settled Districts of former British India.

Denied the right to develop constitutionally with the rest of India, the Pushtun intelligentsia of the North–West Frontier Province cooperated with the Hindu-controlled Congress Party, and actively participated in the Civil Disobedience Movement of the 1930s. The official Frontier Congress and its attendant movement *Khuda-yi-Khidmatgaran* (Servants of God, or "Red Shirts," so-called because of the color of their clothing), organized chiefly by Dr. Khan Sahib and his younger brother, Khan Abdul Ghaffar Khan, merged as powerful political forces (Tendulkar, 1967). In the Tribal Agencies, the Faqir of Ipi and Hajji Turangzai led *lashgar* (or *lashkar,* tribal raiding parties) to the plains from the mountains and forced the British to send annual punitive expeditions to the frontier region.

The Frontier Congress organized the North–West Frontier Province so effectively that in 1932 the British Indian Government replaced the Chief Commissioner of the province with a Provincial Governor, and allotted all the rights and obligations of provincial self-government to the Settled Districts. The 1935 Government of India Act included the North–West Frontier Province, and increased participation in self-government resulted.

487

The 1893–1939 patterns in the Pushtun areas of Afghanistan and British India can be outlined as follows: Afghanistan: intra-tribal wars and attempts at pacification by the central government; forced migration of several dissident Pushtun groups to north Afghanistan; few attempts at development of socio-economic-political institutions; British India: separation of Pushtun region from Punjab Province to form North–West Frontier Province; Settled Districts at first ignored in legislative reforms, then placed in mainstream of political life in 1932; independent tribes in Tribal Agencies maintained independence, provided for by treaties with British Indian Government; raids forced British to keep large outposts in tribal areas and participate in periodic fights.

When it became obvious during World War II that the Indian subcontinent would become independent shortly after the defeat of the Axis powers, the Afghan Government in 1944 reminded the Government of British India in a letter of its interest in the fate of the Pushtun on the Indian side of the Durand Line. The British observed that since, in their opinion, the Durand Line was an international boundary, it should not concern the Afghans. Lord Louis Mountbatten, last British Viceroy in India, did concede vaguely: "Agreements with the tribes on the North–West Frontier of India will have to be negotiated with the appropriate successor authority."[5]

Mountbatten's statement encouraged the Afghans, but in June 1947, the Congress Party-controlled cabinet of the North–West Frontier Province voted to go with India in the Partition. Several Pushtun and Indian friends of mine have indicated that Gandhi and Nehru promised the Khan brothers autonomy in the North–West Frontier Province if they would support the Congress Party's efforts to keep the Indian subcontinent together. When Pakistan's birth could not be aborted, however, the "Red Shirts" and their leaders opted for either independence or at least autonomy within Pakistan.

Meanwhile, the Afghan Ambassador in New Delhi, Najib Ullah Khan (later Ambassador to the United States and a visiting professor at Princeton University and Farleigh Dickinson University; he died in the United States in 1965), continued to press the Government of India concerning Afghan interests in the Pushtun in British India.

The N.W.F.P. Congress Party cabinet vote to join India displeased many Pushtun in the Settled Districts, with an over 90% Muslim population. Few Pushtun would agree to Hindu domination under any cir-

[5] Paragraph 17 of the Partition Agreement, made public on June 3, 1947, by Mountbatten.

cumstances. In a British-sponsored referendum, held in July, the N.W.F.P. voted to join Pakistan. The referendum offered the Settled Districts the choice of joining India or joining Pakistan, in keeping with the Partition Agreement referring to British-administered provinces. The 500-odd Native or Princely States, however, had three alternatives: join India; join Pakistan; remain independent for a specified period until a decision could be made whether to join India or Pakistan. Presumably, the waiting period would be used to ascertain the desires of the princes' subjects. Several (such as Kashmir, Hyderabad, and Kalat), tried independence for varying periods of time; none succeeded for very long (Wilcox, 1963).

The Khan brothers initially advocated independence for the Pushtun areas of northwest India, a claim which Afghanistan officially supported. Both the Khan brothers and the Afghan government declared the proposed boycott of the British referendum successful, although some observers disagreed, including a close friend of the Khan brothers, Maulana Abul Kalam Azad (Azad, 1960). In view of the following election results, the boycott seems to have been only partly successful:[6]

1946 Provincial Elections	*1947 Referendum*
% of eligible voters who voted:	% of eligible voters who voted:
68%	55.5%
	Of those voting: for India, .5%
	for Pakistan, 55%

The British sponsored *jirgah* in the five Tribal Agencies and all the tribal groups agreed to go with Pakistan. The Afghans, however, objected to the procedures. The only choice presented was to join Pakistan or join India. The Afghans, supported by the Indians, challenged the validity of the Durand Line as an international boundary, and insisted the Tribal Agencies should have been equated with the Princely States and permitted to select at least initial independence if they so desired. An independent "Pushtunistan," which may or may not have joined Afghanistan later, would have been created. After all, argued the Afghans, the tribes had separate agreements with the British Government, and therefore functioned as independent nations, with relations regulated by the Ministry of States and Frontier Regions of the central government in Delhi.

To the surprise of many, Pakistan, though anemic, survived. In the

---

[6] Figures from *The "Pukhtunistan" Stunt* (1956), an official Pakistani publication, Azad (1960), and Pazhwak (1953).

early period of Pakistani struggles to exist (1947–50), a shift in anti-Pakistani activities occurred. Although most Pakistani Pushtun accepted Pakistani sovereignty, a few, mainly in the Peshawar area, still insisted on either outright independence or regional autonomy. To counter any tribal uprisings and to gain the confidence of the tribes, Pakistan, in December 1947, withdrew all its regular army units from the tribal area under the leadership of Brigadier Mohammad Ayub Khan, later Field Marshal and President (1958–69). Only five battalions of the locally recruited Frontier Corps remained behind to maintain order. The British usually kept about forty-eight battalions along the frontier.

Pakistan permitted the tribal groups to maintain virtual autonomy, even after the One Unit Plan of 1955 made all West Pakistan (*except* the Tribal Agencies) a single province. The Tribal Agencies remain intact, with Pakistani Political Agents now being directly responsible to the central government's Ministry of States and Frontier Regions, not the provincial government of the N.W.F.P. In addition, the Pakistanis created a sixth Tribal Agency among the Mohmand Pushtun to handle the peculiar problems of that truculent area. Amnesty was declared for all warriors involved in anti-government raids (particularly prevalent in Waziristan in October 1947) prior to 1948. Thus the Pushtun most directly affected by the Afghan claims for an independent "Pushtunistan" enjoyed a greater degree of freedom than they had had under British rule. The Settled Districts of the old North–West Frontier Province became a part of the province of West Pakistan in 1955.[7]

Some observers believe that if Pakistan had been as certain as it claimed that its Pushtun (except those mentioned above and possibly a few others) would vote to remain Pakistani, it might be logical for Pakistan to consider a plebiscite in its own self-interest. If the plebiscite went in Pakistan's favor, two important results could be achieved: Pakistan's demand for a plebiscite in Kashmir would be strengthened in international circles; Pakistan and Afghanistan could resume normal relations. To hold a fair, impartial plebiscite presented many legal and administrative problems, but the United Nations was already becoming experienced in such operations. As long as neither side was willing to accept a compromise, however, a plebiscite remained impossible. In addition, the Government of Pakistan could never be really certain how the tribal Pushtun would vote.

[7] On July 1, 1970, the Province of West Pakistan ceased to exist, and the Pakistani government reinstituted the old provinces of Punjab, Sind, Baluchistan, and the North-West Frontier Province.

490

A silent war developed alongside the loud propaganda war. Afghan transit trade through Pakistan became a battleground. Beginning in 1947, the Pakistanis subjected Afghan in-transit goods to delays, resulting in high demurrage charges. They limited the number of railway cars transporting goods north from Karachi and refused the Afghans permission to re-export goods. Often items in transit never reached Afghanistan, and were pilfered or damaged en route. Pakistan's growing pains after Partition's upheavals obviously caused some of these inconveniences, however.

As Pakistan continued to exist, India began to lose interest in the "Pushtunistan" issue. In the early 1950s, India withdrew its unofficial backing of the "Pushtunistan" claims of Afghanistan, thereby leaving the Afghans to cope with the issue alone. In 1949 and 1950 I met several Indian Congress Party representatives in southeastern Afghanistan. They claimed to be supporters of "Pushtunistan."[8] Some observers hold the Indians responsible for the growth of the concept of "Pushtunistan" from the old N.W.F.P. and the Tribal Agencies all the way down through Kalat, Baluchistan, and the Makran Coast to the Arabian Sea, leaving West Pakistan only the narrow corridor of the Indus River system. This obviously irredentist move alientated many sympathetic with the original plebiscite demands of the Afghans.

The Afghans had earlier antagonized Pakistan when Pakistan applied for membership in the United Nations in September 1947. Afghanistan cast the only negative vote, stating that as long as the "Pushtunistan" problem remained unsolved, Pakistan should not join the brotherhood of peaceful nations in the United Nations. Later in the year the Afghans withdrew their negative vote and indicated their willingness to discuss "Pushtunistan" with Pakistan through normal diplomatic channels.

The two countries exchanged ambassadors in February 1948, but both (particularly Afghanistan) continued to wage fierce propaganda duels. To counter, the Pakistanis opened a Radio Free Afghanistan at Quetta in 1949. A half brother of Amanullah, Mohammad Amin, tried to calm down the tribes, several of whom at least tacitly supported the exhortations of the Faqir of Ipi.

Slowly, however, the Pakistani Central Government is permitting provincial administration to infiltrate the Tribal Agencies, particularly in the zones of relative accessibility. Often, the tribes themselves demand more education, hospitals, roads, and social welfare activities. As these expand, the tribes may possibly become more and more inte-

[8] Also see Sinha (1961), back cover.

491

grated into Pakistani political and economic life. Economic developments on the fringes of the tribal zones, such as the great Warsak Dam outside Peshawar, proceed rapidly to diversify the economic base of the northwest region of modern Pakistan.

Pakistan continues subsidies to the tribal areas and in some cases has increased them. These subsidies are more in the form of handouts to *khassadars* (local levies) and workmen. However, some troubles have occurred, and as the Pakistanis attempt to push roads into certain areas, the tribes sometimes strike back. In February 1967, for example, the Marri Baluch unsuccessfully resisted the Pakistan Government's attempts to build a road through their territory. In the north, the Mohmand successfully opposed road-building late in the 1950s and early 1960s.

The suppression of pro-"Pushtunistan" press organs, and the arrest of Pushtun independence leaders (some reportedly executed) by Pakistan, alienated some moderates. Also, occasional Pakistan Air Force strikes to quell expected or actual uprisings along the frontier fostered or created enmity in the Tribal Agencies. On June 12, 1949, during one of these attacks, a Pakistani aircraft (inadvertently, according to the Pakistanis; deliberately, according to the Afghans) bombed the village of Moghulgai, 2,100 yards inside the Afghan border. The Pakistanis ultimately offered to pay but continued to deny intentional bombing. The Afghans, however, refused payment, preferring to keep the matter open. As a result, however, the Afghan Government convened a *Loya Jirgah* (which included the National Assembly) in Kabul, which, on July 26, voted national support for the "Pushtunistan" issue and officially declared the 1893 Durand Agreement, the Anglo–Afghan Pact of 1905, the Treaty of Rawalpindi of 1919, the Anglo–Afghan Treaty of 1921, and any other treaties which referred to the status of the Pushtun, to be illegal and dead. In addition, on August 12, 1949, a large segment of the Afridi Pushtun met at Tirah Bagh on the Pakistan side of the Durand Line to establish a "Pushtunistan" Assembly. A larger assembly at Razmak elected the Faqir of Ipi as President of "Pushtunistan." He already served as Chairman of the Provisional Assembly of Independent "Pushtunistan" (Central Section).

Tension continued to intensify, as three Afghan *lashkar* columns, one led by the Pushtun leader Wali Khan Afridi[9], crossed the Durand Line

[9] Wali Khan, a malik of the Kuki Khel Afridi, made his peace with the Pakistan Government and returned home in 1959. Not the same man as Khan Abdul Ghaffar Khan's son, Wali Khan, now a major political leader in Pakistan.

in 1950 and 1951 with the avowed intention of planting "Pushtunistan" flags on the Indus River. Pakistan protested, and the first "blockade" of Afghan in-transit goods occurred. The Afghan Government denied any connection with the irregulars, merely stating they were "freedom fighters" trying to free their Pushtun brothers from the "imperialistic yoke" of Pakistan.

Three times the United States indicated it would mediate on the problem of "Pushtunistan," but neither side would agree for one reason or another. Later, Egypt and Turkey were also (unsuccessfully) suggested as possible mediators between the two antagonists.

The 1950–51 tribal incursions adversely affected the two countries' relations, and their respective ambassadors departed, leaving chargés d'affaires in charge of the embassies. Patient Pakistani initiative finally resulted in another exchange of ambassadors in March 1952.

Another incident could have very well exploded the relationships between Afghanistan and Pakistan into a general conflagration: Pakistan's Prime Minister Liaquat Ali Khan was assassinated in October 1951. His assassin was an Afghan living in exile in Pakistan, and some Pakistanis believe the Afghan Government had something to do with the assassination, but the Pakistani Government officially accepted Afghan denials. The murder, however, probably still plagues certain Pakistani consciences.

In retaliation for the tribal incursions, Pakistan stopped Afghan petroleum imports for about three months in 1950, officially because Afghan trucks did not conform to Pakistani safety regulations. The gasoline supply in Afghanistan had always been precarious and rationed in those days.

Frustrated by the "Pushtunistan" stalemate, increasing United States aid to Pakistan, and the apparent American lack of interest in its problems, Afghanistan turned north and listened to Soviet overtures. In July 1950, Afghanistan and the U.S.S.R. signed a four-year barter agreement under which the Soviets agreed to export petroleum products, cotton cloth, sugar, and other important commodities in return for Afghan wool and raw cotton. The Soviets offered a much higher exchange rate than any capitalist country could afford. This agreement made the Afghans partly dependent on the Soviets for many items formerly imported exclusively from the West.

The 1950 agreement went beyond barter (P. Franck, 1960). The Soviets offered to construct several large gasoline-storage tanks, and to take over the oil exploration of north Afghanistan from a Swedish com-

493

pany. The U.S.S.R. also agreed to permit Afghan goods free transit through Soviet territory.

Disturbed by the Afghan–Russian deals, the Pakistanis relaxed the "blockade" (actually never a blockade; "slow-down" would be more accurate, and very easy to accomplish because of the Pakistani adaptation of the British imbued law-and-order bureaucratic system), but the swing to the north, with its immediate economic benefits, continued.

By 1952, Afghan–Soviet trade had doubled, and the Soviets established a trade office in Kabul, something never permitted by previous Afghan foreign-policy makers. The Russians exported enough gasoline to make rationing unnecessary. Tashkent cotton cloth competed successfully with more expensive Indian and Japanese textiles. Russian cement satisfied Afghanistan's needs; previously it had depended upon Pakistani, Indian, or European cement, very expensive items to transport. Soviet technicians (including oil geologists, seismic engineers, veterinarians, and agricultural specialists) entered Afghanistan, though not in great numbers. Oil surveying teams increased appreciably after the 1957 visit of King Mohammad Zahir Shah to Moscow, at which time the Soviets contributed another $15 million for oil exploration in north Afghanistan. The early-bird technicians in 1952 primarily did surveys, some equipped the Kunduz cotton-cleaning plant, while others supervised the construction of 625 miles of improved and new telephone-telegraph lines.

Between 1950 and 1955, Afghan transit trade through Pakistan actually *increased* annually, but trade with the Soviet Union mushroomed. (See Charts 27 and 28).

The Liberal Parliament: A Democratic Experiment Fails, 1949–52

The post-World War II period produced an interesting experiment in democracy. Shah Mahmud, another uncle of the King, replaced his brother, Mohammad Hashim (who died on October 26, 1953), as prime minister in 1946 and, encouraged by Western-educated young Afghans, made modest attempts to bring about free elections, at least relative to past elections. The resulting "Liberal Parliament" of 1949 had a hard core of 40 to 50 (of the total 120) reform-minded members who took their roles as parliamentarians seriously. They questioned individual ministers about budgetary matters, and in a nation where corruption often serves as a major path to riches and power, such investigations can deeply upset entrenched patterns. Several ministers refused to reply to inquiries, and stated that, although the National Parliament had the right to question the national budget as prepared by the Ministry of Finance (Article 43 of the 1931 Constitution), it had no jurisdiction over the budgets of individual ministries, using Articles 55 and 61 to justify their positions. These two articles taken together permitted a minister to ignore any parliamentary rejection of a bill he had introduced. In addition, Section IX (Articles 73–83) elaborated the "Duties and Rights of Ministers," gave cabinet ministers almost unlimited power, and freed the king of any responsibility for ministerial actions (i.e., mistakes). Article 76, however, theoretically made ministers "responsible to the National Assembly as regards the policy of the government in general and of the ministry under their charge in particular," further confusing the situation.

The "Liberal Parliament" passed laws permitting freedom of the press. Overnight several newspapers sprung up, all in opposition to the ruling regime. The three most important were *Watan* (*Homeland*), *Angar* (*Burning Embers*), and *Nida'-yi-Khalq* (*Voice of the People*). *Watan,* a biweekly published in Persian, was edited by Mir Ghulam Mohammad Ghubar, assisted by Abdul Hai Aziz (later to become Minister of Planning in the 1960s) and Mir Mohammad Siddiq Farhang (formerly Deputy Minister of Planning and a parliamentary leader in the *Wolesi Jirgah* from 1965 to 1969). *Angar,* a Persian and Pashto biweekly, was published by Faiz Mohammad Angar, a noted Qandahari "Pushtunistan" advocate. *Nida'-yi-Khalq,* a biweekly Persian publication, generally supported the government's foreign policies but demanded more genuine neutrality and increased freedom of the press, though it accepted the necessity of the monarchy at this time. All three papers had circulations of approximately 1,500.

Conservative religious leaders and their supporters in government received the brunt of the attacks in the free press. The editors and their staffs demanded that elections be genuinely free, that the government be responsible to Parliament. A National Democratic Party was founded with the dissidents as its nucleus.

"Letters to the Editor" became very popular institutions in these new papers, even though letter writers sometimes were arrested for violent anti-government or anti-clerical criticisms. One such correspondent, Mohammad Ghulam Hassan Safi (an influential Safi Pushtun from the Laghman area and currently Ambassador to Indonesia), criticized the construction of a shrine outside Jalalabad which would house a hair of the Prophet Mohammad. Safi considered the project "superstitious, wasteful idiocy," when most Afghan children were still illiterate and their "living conditions practically impossible."

The three newspapers were published in 1951 and 1952, and then banned; but old copies can still be purchased surreptitiously in the bazaar. An Afghan associated with one of the newspapers told me at the time of first publication: "When we finished the writing and printing, dawn approached. We had worked all night on the first issue without realizing it. I walked home in the early morning chill and watched the moon go down and the sun rise. I felt the sign good. We did have a new day coming in Afghanistan."

Under the free-swinging impetus from Parliament, other groups began to react, especially the Kabul University students, who formed a student union. This small group (no more than twenty or thirty) debated everything from communism and atheism to the role of religion in a Muslim state. Several European and American teachers in Kabul's high schools encouraged these discussions and some actually participated.[10]

The Afghan government at first chose to ignore the movement. Then, realizing that the rising strength of the vocal opposition might become a menace to the *status quo,* the government attempted to form a pro-government political party. This move failed, for even the civil servants encouraged to join the party showed a monumental lack of interest in its function, and many secretly sympathized with the "liberals."

But initial rebuffs to their constructive demands for extended freedom of speech and the press, parliamentary checks and balances, formation of political parties, scrutiny of ministerial budgets by parliamentary committees, and the rest caused the "liberals" to adopt a more virulent tone. During this period of frustration the "liberal" political brotherhood, *Wikh-i-Zalmaiyan* ("Awakened Youth," or *Wish-i-Zalmaiyan,* in the soft Qandahari Pashto dialect where the movement began), founded in 1947, prepared to go undergound if the need should arise. The free press published more and more articles personally attacking members of the ruling clique. More and more pieces pointed to religious fanaticism as the major institution holding back Afghan progress. Although partly true, jibes at powerful religious leaders drove many fence-sitters away from the "liberal" camp. Students wrote and acted plays that insulted the royal family and Islam. Some speeches approached obscenity in the facile *double entendre* of Farsi. In 1951 the government ordered the dissolution of the student union and several

---

[10] At the time of the "liberal parliament" about 14 Americans (later including four women) taught in Kabul (Klass, 1964).

student leaders (accompanied by two army officers) fled to Pakistan, unfortunately killing a border guard on the way.

Before the 1952 parliamentary elections, the government took further steps to smash the "liberals": it closed down all non-government newspapers, arrested about twenty-five of the "liberal" leaders, thereby ending the *Wish-i-Zalmaiyan* as an effective political organ. The Afghan jails where the liberals were held are not designed for rehabilitation but for punishment. After a bit of soul-seaching and various types of coercion, about half of those jailed agreed to cease their anti-government activities. Several subsequently gained high positions in the Daoud (1953–63) government. Others remained in prison and died there. Those still alive were released by the King in 1963 at the beginning of his reform movements.

When Afghanistan achieves a democratic form of government, such "liberals" as Dr. Abdur Rahman Mahmudi, who died three months after his release from prison, and Mir Ghulam Mohammad Ghubar, who today lives in political retirement, will probably be resurrected as martyrs.

So the new day did not dawn. The "liberal parliament" failed because of several factors: opposition was directed against an established independent regime, not against a colonial oppressor; to many, in and out of government, a freer society would have meant less graft; the central government maintained tight control of the civil service, which did not participate widely in the "liberal" movement for fear of retaliation; the massive illiteracy prevented the "liberal" press from having an impact outside its own circle; personal attacks on the royal family and religious leaders antagonized many fence-sitters; the government refused to believe that the "liberals" merely wanted to liberalize the existing government, and looked on all opposition as preparation for overthrow, a feeling common among most power elites in Afro–Asia.

The great experience in development and democracy had either failed or slowed down by 1953. The Hilmand Valley Project floundered in the salty soils of the south, and the "liberal parliament" had frightened Shah Mahmud and the royal family, many of whom remembered the terror of 1929. For the first time since the return of Nadir Shah, a serious intrafamily, generation-gap, crisis occurred. Younger members of the royal family challenged the king's surviving uncles, Shah Mahmud (who died in 1959) and the still surviving (and active) Marshal Shah Wali. The leaders of the "Young Afghan" revolt were two brothers, sons of Sardar Mohammad Aziz (assassinated in Berlin in June 1933), and, therefore, first cousins of the king: General Sardar Mohammad Daoud Khan and his younger brother, Sardar Mohammad Naim Khan (Foreign Minister, formerly ambassador to France, the United Kingdom, and the United States). Contemporaries, King Mohammad Zahir Shah (born 1914) and Daoud Khan (born 1912) had been classmates at the Afghan Military College.

After the death of their fathers, Zahir Shah, Daoud Khan, and Naim Khan came under the tutelege of their bachelor uncle, Hashim Khan, who taught the boys the harsh facts of Afghan political life. All three, especially Daoud Khan, learned their lessons well.

The change, surprisingly sudden to some foreign observers, came with the knowledge and approval of the royal family, and the consensus of the majority of its members on September 20, 1953. Unlike most Middle Eastern palace revolts, no bloodshed occurred although the new prime minister did arrest some of his more outspoken critics. Daoud Khan, at the time of the coup, was Commander of the Central Forces (*Quwar-i-Markazi,* in Dari; *Da Markazi Quwar,* in Pashto) in Kabul, an important position for anyone wishing to seize and hold power in Afghanistan. He had earlier resigned as Minister of the Interior because of policy differences with his uncle. The transition of power went smoothly at all levels.

The development programs begun under Shah Mahmud continued but emphasis shifted and accelerated in all institutions of Afghan society.

CHAPTER 23

The Decade of Daoud

1953–63

SEVERAL factors encouraged the forty-three-year-old Daoud Khan
to become prime minister. A simple desire for power cannot be minimized as possibly one of his motives, but power within the precedents
established by his uncles in 1933: with a general consensus of the royal
family and without bloodshed. Many literate Afghans hoped for the release of the remaining political prisoners and a vigorous implementation
of social reforms. They were disappointed, for the Prime Minister preferred to move ahead with slow, but steady progress. Although he did
release some political prisoners who promised not to participate in active oposition against the regime, Daoud Khan crushed opposition as
it rose, and made no pretense of returning to the days of the "liberal
parliament."

Daoud Khan attacked the four major, interrelated problems which
had led him to seize power: the sluggishness of the Hilmand Valley
Project; the apparent tendency of Shah Mahmud's government to lean
more and more toward the West politically as well as economically, in
spite of traditional Afghan neutrality; softness toward the "Pushtunistan" problem with Pakistan; slowness in pushing social and economic reforms.

The H.V. A., Phase II: 1953–63

The Daoud regime, disturbed by reports of maladministration, graft,
and corruption in the Hilmand Valley, shook up the administration.
Some of the accused Afghans in turn accused the Americans of aiding
and abetting any existing tendencies toward graft. At the minimum,
most American engineers, though dedicated, failed to realize the great
changes which would result because of the massive contracts. As individuals, the American technicians, easily made friends and gained the
respect and genuine affection of the men working with them, and trained
a generation of Afghan mechanics and truck drivers, many of whom
now operate machine shops or own trucks, so, indirectly, M.K.A. ap-

preciably helped create a new working class of specialists to meet the needs of the twentieth century.

In addition, tourists visiting Kabul will probably eat in either the Ministry of Finance operated Khyber Restaurant in "Pushtunistan" Square, or Bagh-i-Bala, just outside Kabul, where they will dine on good construction-camp food, for the chef-manager learned his trade from M.K. American cooks.

The inward-looking society defined earlier militates against change, and any major shifts in the ecological patterns tend unfavorably to tilt centuries-old, functioning cultural practices. Someone involved in the Hilmand Valley Project, therefore, should have considered the human factor in exact detail. The American government has had enough troubles with its Tennessee Valley Project, even though the American society is largely outward-looking and literate. Rural communities, regardless of culture and percentage of literacy, still remain one of the more conservative socio-economic groups in any society. The Tennessee Valley Authority, in spite of over thirty-five years of almost universally accepted success, still has problems of communications with the public, and the government (national, state, and local), as well as its local beneficiaries (Egerton, 1967).

From the beginning of the Hilmand Project, both Americans and Afghans, by ignorance and not design, virtually ignored the human problems. Between 1949 and 1951, I asked many American M.K.A. technicians and administrators who would be responsible for preparing the villagers for the new influx of water, which, theoretically, would permit two grain crops per year and greatly increase the production of vegetables in the summer. Replies varied from "Who cares?" to "That is properly the business of the Afghan government."

My feelings are otherwise, however. If an outside force institutes major internal changes in cultural and natural ecological patterns, moral responsibility for later effects should rest as heavily on the construction companies as on government planners. At least one feasibility survey (and no project can possibly begin without a plethora of feasibility surveys) should involve human engineering to help the technicians and implementers from making avoidable culturally-oriented mistakes during construction and after completion, i.e., make the blows of change fall the lightest on the most people, a process of undermining and rebuilding cultural patterns at the strongest and weakest links. Including human engineers (anthropologists, rural sociologists, agricultural economists) on project teams would not be expensive when compared to the cost of technical engineers, and competent advice could save much money and years of agony.

But in 1949, when I asked my first questions, neo-colonial U.S. operations were relatively new, and the idea that "all the people need are the benefits of our know-how, and they will thrive" prevailed. The non-literate was as little understood as the motives which led the United States to a position of world power. Accidents of history continued to force American and Soviet "know-how" on an unsuspecting, underdeveloped world.

Two major groups of Afghans would be directly affected by H.V.A.: the "old villagers," who had lived along the river system for generations, and the "new villagers," who would farm the reclaimed land. Afghan government officials answered my several questions with the same hazy misunderstanding which permeated the thinking of American technicians.

"How," I asked, "will the old villagers be prepared to use the extra, off-season water? Who will tell them?" At the time I asked this question I had been studying a village within twenty miles of the gigantic Arghandab dam then under construction, and the people in the village had never even heard of the project, a common phenomenon up and down the Hilmand and Arghandab rivers. Even those who knew could not conceive of its magnitude. To them *band* (dam) meant a knee- or hip-high pile of mud to block off their small village *juy* (canals) when watering their fields.

I was told by Afghan officials: "These people are farmers. They known how to handle water. They have been doing it for centuries." Few literate Afghans, particularly government officials, really understand their peasant villagers or tribal nomads. Few know the functions of the *mirab*, the watermaster, the complexities of water-sharing in rural Afghanistan, or the tight, traditional discipline which must be maintained to control the seasonally predictable (within certain limits, of course) water supply. In addition, considerable readjustments follow the occasional unseasonal disastrous floods. The dams should establish a regularity heretofore unknown, and give the peasant farmer better control over his productivity. But, to quote the late Kirk Bryan, my old geology professor at Harvard, "Forget annual averages. It's those unusual years that cause havoc and really effect the lives of the people."

In any event, the dedication of the dams took place in the mid-1950s, with crowds of important Afghan and American government and M.K.A. officials present, but not a peasant farmer in sight.

501

The appearance of x number of acre-feet of water during the off-agri-cultural season for the use of the farmers was met at first with incredulity, and then delight: a gift from Allah had arrived. But the *mirab* and the villagers could not control the water, which flooded the village fields. In 1969, many fields still suffer from waterlogging, and production, instead of being increased, has dropped fifty percent and even more in some areas. To many, the dams remain as remote as ever. The following chart gives a rough estimate of what happened in the area (Stevens and Tarzi, 1965, 29):

District	% of yield in 1955
Arghandab	74
Dand (ov = old village)	120 (highly suspect)
Panjwai-Maiwand (ov)	111 (highly suspect)
Nad-i-Ali (nv = new village)	22
Marja (nv)	51
Shamalan (ov)	58
Darweshan (ov)	37

The crop yields for new villages are percentages of first year's yield.

Other reasons for the decline in the old villages include inadequate distributional control of water; silt formerly spread over land now being trapped behind dams (currently a *technical* problem as the reservoirs continue to silt up); higher water table resulting in proliferation of weeds, which cultivators failed to destroy; farmers failing to follow cropping advice of agricultural specialists.

"Where will the new settlers come from?" I next asked. The answer was: "The nomads. We will settle our nomads. All we have to do is offer them land, and they will settle down. The only reason they still wander, poor and unfortunate, is because they have no land, but they all desire it." (Show me a nomad who wants to settle down, and I'll show you a man who is psychologically ill. No one seemed to remember the unsuccessful attempts of Reza Shah Pahlavi to "settle down" the Zagros nomads in Iran during the 1930s, or the bloody difficulties the Soviets had in Central Asia.)

Settlers were and still are selected by the Ministry of the Interior after careful security checks, and the Ministry decides whether the people will go to the south or to the north. Among other areas, several very successful resettlement programs have been undertaken near Kunduz and Balkh.

The site chosen for the first experiment in 1954 could not have been more ineptly selected, nor the plan implemented more inefficiently. The fruits of the seeds of bad planning by both the Americans and Afghans led to misunderstandings which bloomed, though the desert did not. But, we must remember, it was the first experiment of this sort in Afghanistan and the lessons learned should have been applied to later schemes.

Nad-i-Ali, located ten miles from Lashkar Gah (then called Bost, but in 1967 changed back to Lashkar Gah), was selected as the site for the first new villages, seven in all, to be referred to by the letters A through F, with the seventh named Chah Mirza. The sixth village was never occupied. The land, improperly surveyed for soil and water feasibility, was finally discovered to have an impermeable substratum of impenetrable boulder conglomerate, sitting from four feet to a few inches below the surface. Once plowed, topsoil either washed away or quickly became encrusted with percolating, evaporated salts.

To the already constructed villages (with a centralized mosque-bazaar area) came an initial 3,000 Pushtun families (about 1,200 nomadic) as well as a few Farsiwan, Bokhari Uzbak (originally from the U.S.S.R.), Hazara, and groups calling themselves "Arab."[1] The number "3,000 families" was the unofficial figure available in 1959. Stevens and Tarzi (1965, 35) say that 1,300 were in the first group, and Michel (1959, 174) gives the figure as 1,238, with another 100 to 150 families in the valley waiting for land to become available. The actual figure may be, according to my estimates, about 2,500 families, with about 500 Baluch families of poachers living on the fringes.

Each new villager received (Stevens and Tarzi, 1965, 50):

30 *jerib* (*jerib* = ½ acre) of land @ 250 afghani per jerib	7,500
material for house	5,000
ox	2,000
farm implements	300
wheat, seed, and food	1,000
cash	2,000
	17,800 afghani

[1] Many of the nomadic families came under protest and virtually with military escorts. At least twenty separate Pushtun tribal units were represented, including: Sulaiman Khel Ghilzai, Kharoti Ghilzai, Taraki Ghilzai, Achakzai Durrani, Daftani, Kakar, Matai Afridi, Khugiani, Wardak. Each group lived in separate village wards.

The new farmers would pay for the wheat after the first harvest, the balance, 16,800 afghanis, to be paid in equal amounts over a twenty-year period, at no interest. Title to the land would be given to the farmer when the debt was finally paid. Few payments have been made, even now, because of a continued drop in production in the first new villages.

The complications intensified. Nomads of mixed ethnic groups had moved onto land unsuitable for farming. The alloted plots proved to be too small to support a family, and the houses were too far away from the fields, often up to four kilometers. The new villagers, most with no prior farming experience, made serious attempts to work the land. Ethnocentrism developed, and most Uzbak left before 1955; the various Pushtun and non-Pushtun groups remained generally aloof from one another, and residential disunity quickly manifested itself. Within two years, about one-half had left Nad-i-Ali; in 1965 only 1,118 families lived in the area, many of whom, mainly landless peasant farmers from eastern Afghanistan, were replacements for the deserters. (Stevens and Tarzi, 1965, 35). Only about thirty percent of the original nomads lived in Nad-i-Ali in 1960.[2]

When the Hilmand Valley Authority began to settle the second area, Marja, in 1957, the lessons were obvious. Since the Nad-i-Ali new villagers had complained about housing and the distance from house to field, Afghan planners laid out Marja with a maximum walk of one kilometer to any field. Thirteen villages existed in 1966, embracing 730 families, but eventually the number at Marja should increase to 2,500 in a total of 66 villages.

The original 600 Marja families moved onto good, adequately surveyed land, and lived in tents while they built their own homes, supervised by Hilmand Valley Authority experts. Some individuality was permitted, but the new settlers had to conform to a house-type designed by the Afghan architects which suited the geographic situation. Marja villages average 30 to 40 families, and a total of 55,000 *jerib* have been put under cultivation.

The major ethnic units at Marja include the following Pushtun: Suleiman Khel Ghilzai, Hotaki Ghilzai, Achakzai Durrani, Barakzai Durrani, Matai Afridi, Daftani, Kakar, Khugiani, Safi, and Wardak. Other ethnic groups included "Arab" and Farsiwan (list adapted from Stevens and

---

[2] An interesting development has been that about one-third of the nomads who departed had reapplied for land by 1965. These were the more impoverished groups, not *maldar* (owners of large flocks of sheep and goats).

Tarzi, 1965, 34). Because of the intra-village trouble which developed at the integrated villages of Nad-i-Ali, the distinct units were permitted to settle in single villages.

Two other areas, Shamalan and Darweshan, farther south down the Hilmand, received small numbers of new villages. Both regions have about 136,000 *jerib* of potentially cultivable land, but government disputes with large and small landowners over ownership and water control inhibit further development.

Land had been classified in a series of qualitative gradients, I to IV, with IV being the least fertile. A man with all Class I land received less than those in the Class IV classification.

Outside Marja and Nad-i-Ali, old settlers dominate and new antagonisms have grown between the old and new settlers, particularly over water rights.

Everyone seemed to criticize the Hilmand Valley Authority, but no one did much about it. A talented Afghan team, hamstrung by lack of funds and central government apathy, at times even antagonism, toward the project did what it could with available resources. Occasional floods, especially drastic in 1957 and 1959, continued to complicate the situation. The 1959 flood occurred partly because Kabul did not permit the reservoir at Kajaki to be kept at a specified level, again a breakdown in communications and understanding between the central government and the local officials. Proper drainage remains a problem all over the valley. Few Afghan peasants seem to understand that water which flows into fields must flow out, even though deep drainage ditches obviously take some land out of cultivation.

Dissatisfaction with the project prompted the American embassy in Kabul to recommend an independent, impartial survey be undertaken to make specific proposals for successful development of the Hilmand Valley. The Tudor Engineering Company (a consulting firm) received a contract from I.C.A. to undertake the task, but the survey was to stop at Khairabad, southernmost village within the M.K.A. construction effort. The Afghans objected, believing the entire Hilmand Valley should be considered an entity for development.

Although the Afghans did not know it at the time, the Tudor Company was simply a temporary affiliate of M.K.A., both with offices at 74 Montgomery St., San Francisco, California. Some may argue about the ethics of this arrangement, but, in another sense, M.K.A., with ten years of experience, including the construction of two dams, miles of

505

irrigation canals, and an hydroelectric system at Girishk, could possibly put its experience to good use in future programs, and the team appointed to evaluate the H.V.A. did come from outside M.K.A.

The Tudor Report, published in November 1956, criticized many aspects of the Hilmand Valley, placing an unproportionately unfair amount of blame on the Afghans, who rejected much of the report as inadequate and refused to accept M.K.A. as contractor to implement certain Tudor Report recommendations. I.C.A. dithered with ineffectual technical assistance (sometimes not because of the quality of American technicians but primarily because of I.C.A. paper-shuffling) until Henry Byroade became American Ambassador to Afghanistan in January 1959. He helped get the loan of a team of United States Bureau of Reclamation technical advisers, some from the Columbia River Basin, which had many problems similar to those in the Hilmand Valley. In February 1960, an agreement between the American and Afghan governments concerning the use of Bureau of Reclamation personnel was signed.

M.K.A.'s contractual agreements in the Hilmand Valley were terminated in 1959. The new arrangement would be for I.C.A. American technicians and third-country nationals (I.C.A.-financed) to serve as advisers while the Afghans themselves utilized the newly formed Afghan Construction Unit (A.C.U.) to undertake the construction and, particularly, the maintenance required along the primary canals, which were already clogged with algae and weeds. A.C.U. inherited most of M.K.A.'s heavy equipment and facilities.

By mid-1961, the Bureau of Reclamation team and their Afghan colleagues were busily at work, and before Byroade left Kabul in 1962, several programs moved ahead under Afghan leadership, provided primarily by Dr. Abdul Wakil and Dr. Abdul Kayeum: surface water investigation; agricultural extension; irrigation and drainage; livestock and poultry; reforestation; horticulture; fertilizer; crop rotation; agricultural research; plant protection; agricultural credit research; public health and sanitation. M.E.D.I.C.O. had been active and had helped create one of the more modern hospitals in the Middle East at Lashkar Gah, with major problems existing, however, for there were no auxiliary mechanisms for the air conditioning and electrical systems, a situation which could be disastrous in an operating-room emergency.

Much of all this remains in the planning stage, and plans do not necessarily mean implementation. Although many willing hands tried to step up the pace, the pace would not respond. American-style bureaucracy, the Afghan inward-looking society, and lack of decision-making all impeded implementation. Traditionally suspicious, peasants (both new and old villagers) subtly resisted change in the Hilmand Valley. Technological monuments can be easily constructed, but the attitudes necessary to operate, maintain, and repair them develop slowly. Too many decisions went unmade, too many farmers unsettled, so the desert did not bloom and the bread basket remained relatively empty as Afghanistan approached the end of the decade of Daoud.

A Shift to Étatism and the Big Gamble[3]

Dissatisfied with the development pace, excessive profits taken by various *sherkat,* and the failure of the former government to obtain additional loans from the Export-Import Bank for extensive, long-range development, the Daoud regime pushed large-scale étatism, or state planned and -guided economic development. General Abdul Malik (former Quartermaster of the Army), new Minister of Finance and National Economy, probably greatly influenced Daoud in this decision. General Malik had studied in Turkey and was impressed with the Turkish planned economy. But to implement these programs Afghanistan needed an infrastructure (roads, airports, river ports, an improved telecommunications network), outside capital, and technical assistance.

Early in his regime, Daoud Khan moved toward closer relations with the U.S.S.R. in order to rebalance Afghanistan's non-alignment. Rewards for his efforts also came early. In January 1954, the Soviet Union loaned the Afghans $3.5 million to assist in the construction of two silos and bakeries, one each at Kabul and Pul-i-Khumri.

Then, the exchange of Pakistan–Afghan riots in 1955 over the "Pushtunistan issue" occurred and Pakistan again closed the border, this time for five months. The Afghans asked the Americans for assistance in creating a new transit route through Iran to the port of Chahbahar on the Persian Gulf, but both Iran and the United States pronounced the idea economically impractical, since 3,600 miles of new roads (mainly in Iran) plus additional port facilities would have had to be constructed.

The Afghans then requested that the Russians renew the 1950 transit agreement, and, on June 21, the Soviets agreed to a five-year extension. On August 27, 1955, a new Afghan–Russian barter protocol on com-

[3] For a Russian version of this period, see Akhramovich (1966, 1967). Also, L. Dupree (1964a), Gurevich (1962), Pikulin (1961), Polyak (1964).

modity exchange guaranteed petroleum imports, building materials (especially cement), and rolled ferrous metals, in exchange for Afghan wool, raw cotton, and hides.

In December 1955, Bulganin and Khrushchev stopped in Kabul after their semi-triumphant tour of India. The Kremlin's "traveling salesmen" wanted to keep Afghanistan from joining the Baghdad Pact Military Alliance, which, incidentally, Afghanistan never seriously considered doing at the expense of its traditional non-alignment policies. On December 15, 1955, Premier Bulganin drove a further wedge between Afghanistan and Pakistan. He announced that the Soviet Union supported Afghanistan's demands for an impartial plebiscite in the Pushtun areas of Pakistan; thus he destroyed the Western powers' hope to lure Afghanistan into a mutual defense agreement. The Soviet Union has yet to back Afghanistan in the United Nations on the "Pushtunistan" issue, however.

On December 18, 1955, Moscow newspapers announced the Soviet Union had granted a $100-million, long-term development loan to be used for projects jointly determined by U.S.S.R.–Afghan survey teams. The Soviets had agreed to make a joint official announcement with the Afghans on December 19, but Tass correspondents relayed the news to Moscow a day early over a special transmitter used on the Bulganin–Khrushchev junket. The breaking of the release date angered non-Soviet newsmen, including Afghans, in Kabul. Prime Minister Daoud expressed his regret over the incident at a press conference held the same day. He also declared that Afghanistan was free to look around in the world market to spend the loan. In practice, however, all contracts went to the Soviet bloc, mainly because in those countries political considerations were paramount and, therefore, they could underbid Western competitors. At the same time Prime Minister Daoud announced a ten-year extension of the 1931 Soviet–Afghan Treaty of Neutrality and Non-Aggression.

The official agreement, signed on January 28, 1956, stipulated the loan would be repaid in barter goods at 2% interest over a 30-year-period in 22 equal installments. In March 1956, the Soviet–Afghan survey team announced several selected projects: two hydroelectric plants (Pul-i-Khumri, Naghlu); three automotive maintenance-repair shops (Jangalak, already in existence would be improved and expanded; Herat; Pul-i-Khumri); a road from Qizil Qala (also called Imam Sahib and now renamed Sher Khan Bandar) to Kabul, including the three-kilometer-long Salang Tunnel; an airport at Begram and improvements to the Kabul airport; three irrigation dams with canal systems (Pul-i-Khumri, Jalalabad, Naghlu); a materials-testing laboratory at Kabul; a fertilizer factory; improvement to port facilities at Qizil Qala; the Alchin bridge north of Kunduz.

Also in March 1956, on the basis of recommendations primarily from Soviet advisers, the Afghans launched their first Five Year Plan (March 1956 to September 1961). To be respectable, a developing nation must have Five Year Plans and a colonial past. Although never a colony, Afghanistan certainly has a colonial past, and is essentially a creature of nineteenth-century European imperialism and colonialism in Central Asia.

The Ministry of National Economy split into two distinct ministries (The Ministry of Commerce and the Ministry of Planning), in order to avoid confusion and duplication in planning and implementation. The First Five Year Plan, overly ambitious and with no legitimate statistical base, established the lines of approach still followed by the Afghan government, however.

As usual, increased U.S. aid followed Russian aid, and steadily grew as Daoud Khan's big gamble gathered momentum. (For chronology, see Grassmuck, et al., 1969, 281–328.)

Afghanistan's great leap forward coincided with several important interlocking developments on the world scene, related primarily to U.S.–Russian relations in Mr. Churchill's aptly named Cold War, without which developing nations would have received much less assistance than they did. The Cold War existed long before Eisenhower's election in 1952, and hot wars in China, Greece, Indo–China, and Korea (to mention but a few) gave indications that the post-World War II Stalinist expansionism was not merely a myth created by John Foster Dulles, Eisenhower's Secretary of State. The pactomania of Mr. Dulles, however, would almost encircle the Sino–Russian Communist world, so that viewing the scene from Mars after Stalin's death in 1953, it would have been difficult to determine who was the aggressor against whom.

The cry was "Contain Communism" and military pacts and alliances became the password. To be assured of substantial foreign aid, underdeveloped nations had to sign mutual security agreements with the United States and join military pacts against "Communist aggression" or have the Soviets actively support their military institutions. Most nations Dulles approached jumped on the American gravy train, but more from their own selfish national interests than to help prevent the spread of international Communism. In 1954–1955, Pakistan, for example, on the verge of economic and political collapse, became deeply involved in the American military web when it signed Mutual Security Agreements with the U.S.A., and became the link joining S.E.A.T.O. (Southeast Asia Treaty Organization) to the Baghdad Pact countries or "the Northern Tier" (Wilber, 1958b; Ramazani, 1966), later C.E.N.T.O. (Central Treaty Organization), when Iraq withdrew after the overthrow of the Hashemite Dynasty in 1958.

The Northern Tier was to include Turkey (the link with N.A.T.O.), Iraq, Iran, Afghanistan, Pakistan, and Great Britain with the United States as an *ex officio*—but paying—member. A thousand miles of neutral India, however, prevented the forging of a solid chain. The Indians may still consider themselves neutral in the Soviet–American Cold War confrontations but since the Sino–Indian Himalayan fighting of October 1962, they are certainly anti-Chinese. (Indeed, the Chinese claims in the Aksai Chin area of Ladakh may well be more legitimate than those of the Indians.[4])

Until the second Kashmir War of 1965, Pakistan received about one million dollars a day in foreign assistance of all types from the United States, and survived nicely, so well, in fact, that Pakistan now follows a foreign policy entirely independent of American desires. Theoretically, American foreign assistance (economic and military) was designed to help developing nations help themselves, to keep newly independent nations from "going Communist," to help them become functioning independent institutions in the society of nations, to assist in the creation of economic viability and political stability relative to the potential of each. Therefore, Pakistan's flirtation with the People's Republic of China may not be popular among American policy-makers, but they can congratulate themselves on the success of their original aid objectives.

The Afghans refused to participate in the Baghdad Pact, but asked the Americans once again for arms assistance to correct the upset "balance of power" in the region. "Why should America arm Pakistan?" government officials asked. "Who will the Pakistanis use the arms against? Surely not the Russians, since Pakistan and the Soviet Union have no common boundary." India had similar objections, and, in truth, Pakistan always considered India more an enemy than either the Soviet Union or the People's Republic of China.

The Daoud government officially stated the Americans refused to give Afghanistan military aid because the Afghans would not sign the re-

[4] Maxwell (1970).

510

quired Mutual Security Agreements or join the Baghdad Pact. The unofficial American version of Afghanistan's "reluctance" to join the Baghdad Pact differs somewhat. According to U.S. diplomats on the scene at the time, some in the Afghan military wanted to join the Pact, but demanded assurances that they would be defended by the U.S. if their acceptance of arms aid precipitated a Russian invasion or major subversive efforts inside Afghanistan. For strategic (Afghanistan is not all that important to the defense of the free world), logistical (how to defend Afghanistan given its geographic position), and pragmatic (few believed the Soviets capable of sending the Afghans massive military assistance) reasons, American military planners decided against giving such assurances. Some believe the Afghan government used the American rejection as a ploy to justify to the Afghan people the acceptance of Russian military assistance.

Both Afghans and Americans exhibited a sophistication seldom equalled in their post-World War II diplomatic history during the visit of the Richards (James P. Richards, President Eisenhower's Special Ambassador touring the Middle East to explain the Eisenhower Doctrine) Mission from March 31 to April 3, 1957. The Eisenhower Doctrine loosely guaranteed all the states of the Middle East American protection against Communist invasion. Neither the U.S. nor the Afghans, however, wanted Afghanistan to openly and publicly place itself under the American protective wing, and the resulting communique was a masterpiece in diplomatic doubletalk. No one could be sure whether the Afghans were to be included under the Eisenhower Doctrine, and so both sides could continue uncommitted.

In practice, however, the Afghans showed a neutral non-aligned face to the world. Perhaps the Farsi term, *bi-tarafi,* more aptly describes the situation: *bi-tarafi* simply means "without sides," i.e., without sides in the big-power Cold War confrontations, which occasionally threatened to errupt into a major war. What would the traditionally non-aligned Afghans gain by choosing sides? They remained neutral in two earlier world wars, and if necessary will remain neutral in World War III, for the Afghans realize that nuclear fallout will respect no national boundaries.

In reality, the so-called "neutral" nations have no monopoly on neutralism. The United States, for example, remains neutral on the "Pushtunistan" issue, for it wishes to retain the friendship of both Afghanistan and Pakistan. On the Kashmir problem, the United States attempts to straddle the razor blade of neutrality, trying to remain neutral without

511

becoming neuter. But neutrality on specific political issues does not mean ideological neutrality, and I maintain that a genuinely non-aligned nation during the Stalinist-Dulles era was, in fact, pro-Western, for classic Communist theory considered neutrality a temporary phase before a Communist takeover. My Soviet colleague, Akhramovich (1966), disagrees with my interpretation, but I find little altruism in either Soviet or American actions during this period.

Immediately after World War II, and as late as 1949, however, small groups of Soviet provocateurs crossed the border into Afghanistan. Soviet Uzbaks tried to proselytize Afghan Uzbak; Soviet Tajik, Afghan Tajik; Soviet Turkoman, Afghan Turkoman. The Afghan counterparts turned in their surprised Soviet-oriented fellow tribesmen to Afghan authorities. Afghan Uzbak, Tajik, and Turkoman are often either *basmachi* or sons of *basmachi*. Others know well the brutality of the 1930s collectivization programs in Russian Central Asia. In addition, the north Afghan ethnic groups did not want to give the dominant Pushtun an excuse to disturb further their relatively independent ways.

Some refugees (Uzbak, Kirghiz, Kazakh, Kara Kalpak) fled to Afghanistan and India from the U.S.S.R. during World War II, and the Soviets reinforced their border control mechanisms: watchtowers, overlapping searchlights, barbed wire, ploughed fields next to the border to reveal footprints; the only illegal border crossings today are usually a few lost sheep and goats near the western end of the Afghan–Russian frontier. Border officials on both sides quickly and amicably settle these small, insignificant incidents.

To counter aggressive American counters against Soviet aggression (real or imagined), the Soviets, to the surprise of many American policy-makers who thought the crippling effects of World War II on Russian manpower and economy precluded such an event, retaliated in kind. It began extensive foreign aid programs and offered arms assistance to whoever would take it. The Soviets entered the foreign assistance arena with the identical publicly avowed goals as the Americans: to help the people help themselves and to keep newly independent nations from falling into the hands of the capitalist and imperialist bloc. Of course, their real goal paralleled that of the Americans: to gain friends and influence governments in the name of foreign assistance. Foreign aid became an instrument of national policy and was continued in the national interest. The Soviets sometimes wielded the weapon more efficiently than the Americans, particularly in the decade between 1955 and 1965. Actually, the main theme of U.S. foreign policy since World

War II has apparently been a negative anti-Communism, or simply reactions to Soviet and Chinese moves.

Because of the American horror (often unreasoning) of Communism, developing nations merely had to hint that the Russians would do something if the Americans did not, and the Americans usually jumped into the breach. Sometimes, the reverse gambit worked on the Russians, and at times, they picked up projects rejected by the Americans.

For example, when the Afghans applied to the Export-Import Bank in 1953 for the Hilmand Valley loan, they inserted a request for a loan to pave Kabul's streets. The bank questioned the germaneness of the project to the Hilmand Valley and subsequently rejected the request. The Americans advised the Afghans to submit a separate proposal, but the Afghans seemed to consider the matter relatively unimportant, for foreign advisors had convinced the government that education and public health should have priority over most other projects. Anyone walking down the dusty (summer), muddy (spring, fall), or snow-filled streets of Kabul before the pavings would disagree. So would the truck drivers whose vehicles were literally shaken apart by the deep ruts in the swirls of dust or splatterings of mud.

The Soviets subsequently assisted in paving the streets. Only when foreign newsmen pointed to the paved streets as visible evidence of Soviet aid did the Soviets begin to publicize this achievement. Thus, with a small loan to cover heavy equipment, asphalt, and a few technicians, the Soviets gained many propaganda points with the Afghans. The truth, however, is that Afghans trained by the Soviets did most of the work, true of many projects for which the Soviets get full credit.

In 1956, however, the U.S. government knowingly took on one project which it realized could become a "white elephant": the Qandahar International Airport, which cost about $15 million ($10 million in grants and $5 million in loans), and officially opened in December, 1962. The idea for the airport originated with Col. Malsowski (I.C.A.O. adviser in Kabul), and the Afghans caught the dream of establishing a modern air center to function as Balkh had functioned as a caravan center in the past. In theory, the Qandahar airport would have been a refueling stop for piston aircraft on their way across the Middle East and South Asia. In addition, the airport would have relieved the crowded facilities at Karachi and shortened the Tehran–Delhi flight route by 900 kilometers. The introduction of the jet age smashed this dream before the completion of the project, and the magnificent facilities now sit, virtually unused, in the desert outside Qandahar. American assistance policy in the mid-1950s, however, dictated that no expense be spared to prevent Soviet-sponsored national airlines from being established in South Asia and the Middle East. So the U.S. accepted the Afghan overtures to build the Qandahar International Airport and develop Ariana Afghan Airlines (L. Dupree, *AUFS Reports,* Appendix H, LD-9-60).

In undertaking extensive 'projects in the underdeveloped world, Soviet experts took their cue from the success of the Marshall Plan in Europe. The Americans tore a page or two from Marx to implement the plan. They used simple economic aid to rejuvenate the smashed economy of Western Europe and therefore greatly reduced the possibility of a Communist takeover in the late 1940s and early 1950s. Soviet planners reasoned that if economic aid did the trick in Europe, why not in Afro–Asia, even Latin America? But—and this was a big but— the Soviets failed to consider adequately the human factor in the developing countries; i.e., the inward-looking, peasant-tribal society. They had forgotten (or suppressed knowledge of) the agonies of the Central Asian *basmachi* revolts of the 1920s, and the collectivization fiascos of the 1930s. The important difference was that Western Europe had developed all the skills and attitudes necessary for the perpetuation of a modern industrialized, pluralistic, outward-looking society, and, therefore, the creation of such a milieu was not necessary. The second World War smashed the economic institution, but not the socio-economic patterns. Only money and machines, not a whole new set of values, were needed to revitalize Western Europe. If the United States had not aided Europe, the Communists may have gained political control, but the society's values would not have changed, only shifted slightly, as occurred in the Soviet Union after the Tsarist downfall.

Soviet planners ignored the difficulties of changing a society (i.e., its values and attitudes) by economic means alone. Let us examine the Soviet experiment in some detail, for it has relevance far beyond its Afghan manifestations.

The "Economic Korea" Develops

In the words of Mr. Khrushchev (1959):

> You may like your neighbor or dislike him. You are not obliged to be friends with him. But you live side by side, and what can you do if neither you nor he has any desire to quit the old home and move to another town? All the more so in relations between

states. It would be unreasonable to assume that you can make it so hot for your undesirable neighbor that he will decide to move to Mars or Venus. And vice versa of course. . . . Peaceful coexistence can and should develop into peaceful competition for the purpose of satisfying man's needs in the best possible way. We say to the leaders of the capitalist states: Let us try out in practice whose system is better, let us compete without war. . . . We stand and always will stand for such competition as will help raise the well-being of the people to a higher level. . . . We believe that ultimately that system will be victorious on the globe which will offer the nations greater opportunities for improving their material and spiritual life. . . . But when we say in the competition between the two systems, the capitalist and the socialist, our system will win, this does not mean, of course, that we shall achieve victory by interferring in the internal affairs of capitalist countries. Our confidence in the victory of Communism is of a different kind. It is based on a knowledge of the laws governing the development of society.

A major article by a Soviet specialist declared: "Unlike the leading capitalist industrial powers, the U.S.S.R. gives extensive aid to other countries without imposing terms incompatible to their national interests and dignity. There are no military or political strings attached" (Rymalov, 1959).

In view of the flexibility of the Soviet approach—sometimes driving a hard bargain, sometimes seeking political advantage through ostensible generosity—the "no strings" claim is disingenuous. Nevertheless, nations seeking aid have often seemed to accept Soviet protestations of good faith while rejecting similar assurances from the United States. The times when the United States has extended aid purely in the interest of promoting economic health and political stability have gone relatively unheralded, while grants and loans linked to the American need for strong allies and for bases on foreign soil have been well publicized. The Soviets, relatively sophisticated in their approach to foreign aid and unencumbered by any demands from an electorate or a congress for an indentifiable *quid pro quo,* have demonstrated a good deal of finesse. They seem to understand that it is unnecessary to attach military and political strings, because (in the purest and impurest Marxian sense) economic penetration is the easiest and most logical way to influence all institutions in a society.

Fundamentally, the Soviets are correct in this assumption. A nation does not accept technology without ideology. A machine or a dam is the product of a culture, and even the method of manufacture (union shop, sweat shop, socialist shop) becomes important. Further, the way a nation markets its machines, the way people learn to operate the machines, and the way the machines are used (private farms, collective farms, state farms) cannot be ignored as the machines enter a second country. Machines and technology do not exist in separate vacuums. People serve as the action component, and the way they teach other people to use these tools becomes a part of the recipient culture's way of life. In a major sense, American programs in Afghanistan have been effective: just by being there, they have helped prevent the success of the pat, eminently feasible Soviet plan.

Probably the most important American programs in Afghanistan relate to education, and so nine-tenths of the American aid sits, iceberg-like, below the surface, invisible to the journalistic eye. English has become the major non-Afghan language, and language is a most essential cultural tool. It spreads ideology as well as technology simply by the way it expresses ideas, both concrete and abstract. The depth of the penetration of English can be gauged by the fact that all embassies must, by Afghan regulation, publish their daily news bulletins in their own languages or *in English*. The Afghans realize that such bulletins published in Persian or Pashto would be excellent propaganda vehicles. So the Russian, Chinese, and most other embassies publish their bulletins in English.

Some International Cooperation Administration (I.C.A.; later the Agency for International Development or A.I.D.) officials overseas attempted to persuade recipient nations that the U.S. has no intentions of interferring in internal affairs. Many Americans sincerely believe this, but such an attitude is naïve for it ignores the interrelations of institutions to a culture as a whole. A change in the religious, economic, social, or political institutions will affect all other institutions. The pouring of millions of dollars or rubles into a country must be recognized as "interference." the Soviets, with their "knowledge of laws governing the development of society," may or may not be far ahead of American policy-makers in conceptualizing the importance of foreign aid without visible strings attached, but they seem to have convinced much of the uncommitted world of the purity of their intentions. Rymalov admits (1959, 24) that Soviet aid for underdeveloped countries is "guided by the principles of proletarian internationalism," a further hint that doctrinaire Communists expected their system to spread globally.

Given such Soviet intentions, an important question arises: What is the significance of Soviet aid to Afghanistan, other than the obvious development benefits? The answer is rather involved, but focuses on a theme expressed in the words of Khrushchev above: peaceful competition with capitalist states in underdeveloped countries, and the ultimate victory of world Communism, i.e., peaceful economic competition (the means), world Communism (the end). Afghanistan was to be a testing ground.

The Soviets have often experimented with living laboratories to obtain data on the dynamics of social change (*Technical Research Reports,* 1952). In the late 1920s they systematically used the Volga Tatars as guinea pigs before collectivizing the predominately Muslim population of Central Asia. Three million Turkic-speaking, Sunni Muslim, Volga Tatars now live scattered from just east of Moscow to central Siberia. They were the most literate Muslim ethnic group. Extremely active pan-Turanists after World War I, the Volga Tatars hoped to participate in establishing an independent nation of all Turkic-speakers in the Middle East and Central Asia. Their dispersal into experimental collective farm situations accomplished political as well as "scientific" ends, therefore. Among other things, Soviet social scientists found the people accepted collectivization, forced migrations, and antireligious dogma with a minimum of friction if their mullahs were removed.

Other authors have discussed similar developments (especially the destruction of Islamic ritual obligations) in the five republics of Soviet Central Asia: Kazakhstan, Turkmenistan, Tajikistan, Uzbakistan, Kirghizistan (Bacon, 1966; Bennigsen and Lemercier-Quelquejay, 1967; Caroe, 1953; Pipes, 1955). The degree of change in any given Soviet area has been in direct proportion to Russian economic interest in that area.

Generally, the removal of indigenous Muslim religious leaders accelerated forced collectivization or industrialization. After Russification had taken root and religion had been successfully deemphasized, especially in its ritual in symbolic aspects, the Soviets often permitted Communist-sanitized Islam to exist. Communist theorists concluded political Communism can be made compatible with any form of religion through a shift in economic patterns and the removal of religiously oriented vested interest groups.

In the 1950s, the Soviets began testing the effects of financial aid on Asian and certain Latin American countries, and, according to numerous statements by Soviet leaders, expected to offer massive economic aid to underdeveloped Afro–Asian countries by the late 1960s. In Latin America the process started in 1958, when the Soviets lent Argentina 400 million rubles (about $100 million at the official exchange rate) at 2¼% interest to be paid over a 10-year period, first payment after three years. More important, on February 14, 1960, the Soviet First Deputy Premier, Anastas Mikoyan, and Dr. Fidel Castro signed an agreement under which the Soviet Union agreed to lend Cuba $100 million. Mr. Mikoyan further promised that the Soviets would install several sugar factories in Cuba, and offered to buy five million tons of Cuban sugar during the following five years. Initial Soviet loans to Ethiopia and Indonesia were also $100 million. I believe that it is not coincidence that the amount lent each of these countries is identical with that lent Afghanistan in 1955. The result of the Soviet experiment in Afghanistan was soon put to the test in many far-flung areas, and in one even less than one hundred miles from the American mainland.[5]

When Afghanistan first accepted Soviet aid, it became, in my opinion, a primary "guinea pig" in the Soviet plan to penetrate developing countries economically. Afghanistan suits all the conditions for such an experiment, and, in addition, has a common boundary with the U.S.S.R., facilitating commerce and communication.[6] Three other non-Communist countries border the Soviet Union: Iran, Turkey, and Finland. Afghanistan is underdeveloped and neutral. Iran and Turkey, though relatively underdeveloped, have been aligned with the West in military pacts. Finland, though staunch in its neutrality, has secured many economic benefits from the Soviet Union without becoming a Soviet satellite, a feat the Afghans hoped to emulate.

Several Afghan cultural and political factors are important to the Soviet experience. Afghanistan shares with other Afro–Asian and Latin American countries bitter memories of Western imperialist activities. Newly independent nations tend uncritically to embrace Soviet trade and aid; they have tasted Western imperialism but are comparatively unfamiliar with the Soviet brand.

Afghanistan is an artificial country, created out of tribal kingdoms as a buffer state by the British and Russians in the nineteenth century. The boundary commissions largely ignored cultural entities. Trouble gravitates to such unnatural frontiers, salient features on the twentieth-

[5] See Goldman (1967) for additional discussion and a good bibliography of Russian source material.

[6] For a Soviet rebuttal of this view, see Akhramovich (1966).

century political landscape: East–West Germany, North–South Korea, Laos–Cambodia–North Vietnam–South Vietnam, India–Pakistan–Kashmir, Israel and the Arab States, among others. Generations ago Europeans divided Afro–Asia and Latin America into zones of influences or colonies, often with little regard for ethnic or geographical realities. Latin America, nominally independent for over a century, still has occasional border flareups. The boundaries of free Africa are frequently unsettled, and tensions tend to increase as various tribal units attempt to gain regional autonomy or outright independence. These new states usually have several distinct ethnic or linguistic groups, just as has Afghanistan. The "Pushtunistan" question between Afghanistan and Pakistan was perfect for the Soviet experiment. With little effort, the Soviets could keep Afghanistan and Pakistan unbalanced and hostile. Other pertinent factors which exist both inside Afghanistan and in most other underdeveloped countries are delicately balanced, or potentially unbalanced, relations between the haves and have-nots; a growing middle class; a wide economic gap between the few educated and the masses of uneducated people; generally, a strong centralized power, often controlled by one man or an oligarchy; volatile student populations. Take varied ethnic groups, artificial political boundaries, and distinct socioeconomic classes, mix well, and the result is an excellent cocktail of intrigue.

Afghanistan is an Islamic country, a fact which is also significant. Most Afro–Asian nations have an Islamic tradition, or contain Muslim ethnic groups. Even Latin America is permeated with Hispano–Muslim culture, transplanted to the Western hemisphere after 500 years of miscegenation and social interpenetration in Spain.

A final and important point ought to be made here: the United States has economic commitments, government and private, in most of Afro–Asia and all of Latin America. Part of the Soviet experiment was probably to test U.S. reactions and see how far the United States would go to compete under pressure in uncommitted, underdeveloped countries.

For these reasons, I consider Afghanistan to have been an "economic Korea," and as time passed the stakes grew higher and higher.

Concurrently with Soviet grants and loans, other Communist bloc countries played increasing roles in Afghan development projects. Amazingly enough, in the late 1950s and early 1960s, many trade items from Czechoslovakia and Poland were transported by sea from the Polish ports of Gdynia, Gdansk (Danzig), and Szczecin (Stettin) to

Karachi, and reached Afghanistan in-transit through Pakistan instead of the Soviet Union. The Czechs have been the most active in Afghanistan, with the Poles a close second. In 1954 a Czech loan ($15 million at 3% interest to be paid over 8 years) was made to build cement plants, a glass factory, a coal briquette plant, and a food processing-and-preserving plant.

Two additional barter agreements were signed in 1954, and the Czechs agreed to exchange machinery, motor vehicles, and telecommunications equipment for cotton; and a 1958 extension agreed to include Czech building materials, glassware, ceramics, and the construction of a new telephone exchange. As a result of the 1954 negotiations, the Czechs also opened a trade office in Kabul. Later, in 1959, the Czechs loaned the Afghans an additional $15 million to be repaid in cotton, wool, oilseeds, dried fruits, and nuts.

Poland and Afghanistan signed a barter agreement in 1956 to exchange Afghan raw materials for machinery, tractors, cement, and consumer goods. Polish experts reorganized woolen mills in Qandahar and Kabul. In 1958 the Poles extended a $2 million credit to Afghanistan to permit the exchange of chemicals, textiles, and agricultural and industrial equipment for wool, cotton, hides, skins, and oilseeds. The exchange took place in 1959. In December 1959, the Poles opened a large trade office on "Pushtunistan Square," near the center of Kabul. As commercial activity increased, Bulgaria opened an economic trade office in Afghanistan. An extremely important protocol signed on June 26, 1958, called for joint Soviet–Afghan efforts in establishing a hydroelectric irrigation project on the Amu Darya. The project is being implemented. The rich loess grasslands of north Afghanistan are relatively unexploited although every year more Pushtun farmers move north from the barren southern mountains. North of the Amu Darya, the land is a sea of green with white caps—the cotton growing centers of Uzbakistan and Tajikistan S.S.R.s. The new reclamation projects shift more Afghan cotton to Tashkent mills and give the Soviets a larger surplus of cotton cloth to export to the other developing countries in Afro–Asia and Latin America.

The Soviets and Afghans signed several important economic agreements early in 1960. On January 19, they completed the ninth protocol for the exchange of goods between the two nations. These protocols are usually renewed each year. On the same day, the Afghan Ministry of Public Works signed a contract with Soviet Techno-Export (the state-controlled overseas construction company of the U.S.S.R.) for the

94. Sardar Mohammad Daoud
Khan, Prime Minister of
Afghanistan, 1953-63. *Photo:
Ministry of Information and
Culture, Royal Government of
Afghanistan*

.95. General view of the 1964 Constitutional *Loya Jirgah*, October, 1964. *Photo:
Jimmy Bedford*

521

construction of the Ningrahar irrigation project near Jalalabad. On January 20, 1960, the Afghan Ministry of Mines and Industries signed a contract with the Soviets to construct the Naghlu Dam and a hydroelectric plant on the Panjsher River. The planned power capacity of this project was 60,000 kilowatts. The Naghlu Dam, now completed, is about 350 feet high. Both these projects were financed from the original $100 million loan.

These activities indicated no let-up in Soviet participation in Afghan modernization schemes. Or, as a member of the Soviet oil exploration team told me in Tashkurghan in November 1959, "We are here for a long time. The Afghans need our help." He added, parenthetically, "Why don't you Americans go home? Afghanistan is our neighbor, not yours."

American policy relating to Afghanistan during the decade of Daoud, it seems to me, must be projected against the background of Afghan history, Soviet strategy toward world domination (assumed if not real) during this period, American reaction and sometimes overreaction to the experiments in economic penetration, and Afghanistan's maneuvers to maintain its identity despite pressures from both blocs. Three words consistently characterized Afghanistan's post-World War II position: non-alignment, independence, and development. The failure of one would weaken the other two.

The seeming inconsistencies in United States foreign policy, however, puzzled Afghans, as well as many Americans. Some Afghans cannot understand why the United States and the Soviet Union, staunch allies in World War II, became post-war antagonists so quickly. Conversely, the United States alignment with West Germany and Japan, former blood enemies, runs counter to the Afghan concept of loyalty. American policies with regard to Israel, the Arab States, Kashmir, and "Pushtunistan" also baffle the Afghans. Beyond all comprehension were the American frantic efforts to bring neutral nations into military regional pacts.

A National-Oriented Military Base of Power Evolves

Failing to obtain military assistance from the U.S.A. after several requests (1953–55), the Afghans took the next logical step. In August 1956, Afghanistan contracted for $25 million in arms (T34 tanks, M.I.G. 17s, Ilyushin-28 jet bombers, helicopters, small arms) from the U.S.S.R., Czechoslovakia, Poland, Hungary, and East Germany. In addition, the Soviets assisted in the construction or expansion of military airfields near Mazar-i-Sharif, Shindand, and Begram.

In view of the development of the Vietnam situation, the American reasons for not arming small nations like Afghanistan may appear outmoded, but American ideology at the time demanded that no weapons be given to any nation which might use them for aggressive purposes; the U.S. insisted that the weapons be used only to resist aggression. Nations which did not accept these stipulations were normally refused arms aid under standard mutual assistance agreements. Nations not aligned with military pacts questioned these conditions, however. They asked, "What is aggression? Who is to define it?" The Afghans often mentioned Algeria as a case in point. They, and the rest of the Muslim world, considered the French the aggressors; the French considered Algeria an internal problem, for, in fact, Algeria was a province of metropolitan France. In 1959, a French diplomat in Kabul was declared *persona non grata* when he personally stripped down posters advertising an anti-French film on Algeria and demanded that the manager of the cinema stop the film. With such publicity, the film became very popular in Afghan movie houses.

Afghans asked, "Who can guarantee that mutual security weapons, ammunition, planes, and bombs were not used against the Algerian nationalists?" The aggressor is difficult to pinpoint in a civil war or revolutionary context. When does resistance against an established regime constitute aggression? For example, if the Pakistani Pushtun should revolt, should United States-supplied equipment be used by their government against them? As a matter of fact, U.S. planes and weapons were used against Pushtun rebels in Pakistan in the 1960s, and Bangladesh in 1971.

The Soviets required no verbal or written pledges, because they realized such commitments are unnecessary; certain commitments are present when arms are delivered. Any new technological equipment, be it military or agricultural, brings along a dependence on the system which developed the machines. Military arms and equipment are followed by instructors and spare parts. Pilots and mechanics must be trained to fly and maintain aircraft; infantrymen must learn to break down and operate different small arms; tankers must learn the intricacies of their new equipment. In accepting Soviet arms, Afghanistan did not embrace Communism. If, however, Afghanistan becomes totally dependent on the U.S.S.R. for replacement items, spare parts, and military instructors, and if an anti-American coup occurs in the armed

523

forces, the inflexible American arms aid philosophy of the 1950s must accept a share of the responsibility.

Another important aspect of military aid must be considered: the attitudinal. Afghan acceptance of Soviet arms assistance brought anguished cries of surprise and protest from the American military establishment. A form of five-square thinking emerged from the Pentagon (and its Russian counterpart in Moscow) in the late 1940s and early 1950s, which, in essence, stated: when one nation arms another and partly trains its officer corps, the recipient nation "belongs" to the United States (or the U.S.S.R. as the case may be). In this view, hardware, spare parts, and tactics take on menacing, almost genetic, qualities.

For example, when the United Arab Republic, Iraq, Indonesia, Afghanistan, and others signed arms agreements with the Soviets, official Americans cried, "They're going Communist!" Even the State Department (particularly during the heyday of Senator Joseph McCarthy) became infected. A high-ranking American diplomat in Kabul reportedly told Prime Minister Daoud bluntly that Afghanistan would "go down the Communist drain in a few years."

However, no developing country accepting Soviet aid has "gone Communist" in the sense that international Communism (i.e., the U.S.S.R.) has gained total control. If anything, the nations listed in the preceeding paragraph are now less enthusiastic about the Soviets than when they were the exclusive playgrounds of the West.

Mr. Dulles properly defined the potential Stalinist threat in the late 1940s and early 1950s, but failed to understand that most of the non-Western world existed in a gray zone which sought self-identification, not alliances with either the Soviet or Western blocs.[7]

Many Western observers worried about the political orientation of Afghan officers trained in the U.S.S.R. and the fact that Soviet personnel served as advisers to Afghan military schools. The Afghan government, however, maintained its *bi-tarafi* ("without sides") pattern and dispatched some officers to the U.S.A. for training, a practice which continues today. Army officers attend the Infantry School, the Armor School, the Command and Staff Schools, and return to Afghanistan to use Russian small arms, tanks, and tactics. Afghan Air Force officers learn to fly U.S.A.F. jets and then return home to fly M.I.G.s. Afghan officers, trained in Russia and the U.S., often compare their experiences and find them reasonably similar. American and Russian military bases

[7] A readable antidote to the American overreaction to the Communist threat is O'Kearney (1958).

. 96. Arghandab (Dahla) Dam. U.S.-assisted project, part of the Hilmand-Arghandab Valley Authority. June, 1960

97. Modern Kabul, western sector. December, 1970

apparently resemble one another; so do the attitudes of the instructors and the instruction received. After all, only a limited number of ways exist to teach a rifle platoon to kill another rifle platoon, or to engage in air combat. Neither the U.S.A. nor the U.S.S.R. turned out to be the paradises painted by their respective propaganda, and attempts to proselytize and penetrate (I think that is the correct intelligence terminology) sound almost identical. In addition, Soviet and American ideals sound alike—day-to-day reality is often something else.

The end result of Soviet (and American) military training tends to make the military even more pro-Afghan (or pro-Egyptian, pro-Iraqi, pro-Pakistani, pro-Iranian, pro-Turkish) than pro-Soviet or pro-American. Therefore, the military institutions which the Soviets helped create in Afghanistan, Egypt, Iraq, and Syria, and which the Americans helped create in Pakistan, Iran, Turkey, and Jordan, are not deterrents to external invasion by major powers (U.S.S.R., U.S.A., China), but rather *internal security forces,* capable of squelching any revolts threatening the powers that be; or they are instruments to bring about coups, not necessarily bad, though each situation must be examined individually.

U.S.A.–U.S.S.R. Competition Becomes "Cooperation"

The Soviet-American competition which began during the decade of Daoud evolved into *de facto*—if not *de jure*—cooperation. The Afghans, Americans, and Russians all learned quite a bit about each other. The Afghans, as have many other developing nations, discovered that the Soviets are no more unreasoning, brainwashed automatons than some Americans. Both made human and technological mistakes. If it is any comfort to Americans, several high-placed Afghans have remarked to me: "Why, we found out that the Russians are just as stupid as the Americans!"

Several Soviet projects fell behind schedule because of inadequate surveys, e.g., oil exploration, Ningrahar Valley Project, Naghlu hydro-electric project. Others, such as the Kabul silo-bakery, began to function with less than unqualified success. Shortly after completion of the complex, a mob, led by several anti-Communist, ultra-conservative religious leaders, marched on the multistoried structure and broke out windows as high as thrown stones could reach. Few Afghans prefer the leavened bread of the silo-bakery to their traditional unleavened *nan.* A major consumer of the *nan-shuravi* ("Russian bread"), however, is the Afghan army, a fact which certainly does not make the Afghan G.I. pro-Soviet.

Many of the enlisted men (mostly conscripts) spend part of their meager pay to purchase Afghan *nan* in the ubiquitous bazaars which are near every military installation and cater to the varied tastes of the soldiers. Few outsiders know of Russian foreign assistance mistakes, however, for, unlike the Americans, the Soviets seldom flagellate themselves for their mistakes.

Many Afghans condemn Americans for living too well in Kabul, with a plethora of servants, high living-allowances, and a commissary which often stocks instant rice[8] in a country with some of the world's finest rice, and canned fruits and nuts in a country with some of the finest fresh fruits and nuts in the world. The same Afghans (particularly those educated in the West) comment unfavorably on the living conditions of Soviet technicians. The Soviets in Kabul often cram five or six families into a house where one American family would live. Afghans of all classes gape in amazement as Soviet technicians and their wives scramble to buy second-hand American clothing in the Kabul bazaar. In addition, few Russian technicians speak fluent Farsi or Pashto, nor do they mingle unrecognized in the Afghan population, in spite of myths spread to the contrary.[9]

In towns outside Kabul such as Herat, Mazar-i-Sharif, and Pul-i-Khumri, where Russians had major projects, their technicians lived as well as—if not better than—the Americans. Spacious hotel and apartment accommodations, lavish commissaries, private theaters, olympic-sized swimming pools today sit relatively unused and deteriorating, having been turned over to the Afghan government, which, incidentally, paid for these luxury constructions out of the Soviet loans. Many Soviet technicians genuinely felt disturbed when ordered home after a tour of duty. Like their American counterparts, they had never had it "so good."

The Soviet blue collar workers live more clannish lives and fraternize less with Afghans than do American technicians who, however, still live

---

[8] Incidentally, "Minute Rice" was actually invented by an Afghan, Ataullah Ozai-Durrani, who died in Englewood, Colorado, in 1964. In 1941 Mr. Ozai-Durrani walked into the offices of General Foods Corporation, set up a portable stove, and cooked a pot of rice in approximately sixty seconds. His discovery made Mr. Ozai-Durrani a millionaire.

[9] For the definitive "folklore" of Russian infallibility in aid, see Toynbee (1961, 188) and A. Wilson (1961). The latter attempted to pass himself off as Russian during a 1959 trip through north Afghanistan. I happened to pass through several Afghan towns in his wake, and Afghan hotel keepers and government administrators asked "Do you know some *diwanah-farangi* [crazy Englishman] claiming to be *shuravi* [Russian]?"

mainly in what I call the "covered wagon complex." As American settlers moved West in their covered wagons during the nineteenth century,
they drew their wagons in a circle at night and camped inside to protect
themselves from hostiles, although the hostiles happened to own the
land. In many overseas U.S. foreign aid outposts, the Americans live
in one section of a city in their own "covered wagon complex" to protect
themselves from the outside world. They daily drive to their offices and
return along the same route, much as nomads move from winter to summer grasslands and back again. Well insulated in the daytime, the
Americans nightly fortify themselves at parties and exchange tales about
how difficult their life is and how much good they could accomplish
if the locals would only let them. On the other hand, it is only fair to
say that the situation has slowly, but steadily, improved over the past
twenty years, and many official Americans have become intimately and
effectively involved with the Afghans, both professionally and socially.

In addition, Afghanistan has become one of the few countries in the
world where Americans and Soviets could mingle socially outside the
official party circuit. The focal point for social meetings among the international set has become the International Club (formed in the mid-
1950s), with its swimming pool, tennis courts, play area for children,
dining room, and bar. Membership includes representatives of all the
foreign communities except the Communist Chinese. Afghans are also
eligible for membership.

When common means of communication can be found, Russian and
American technicians who do break out of their own circles find how
surprisingly alike their opposites are in temperament and outlook. The
similarity between Russian and American types has not escaped psychologists, sociologists, and historians, who point to parallels in Russian
and American development, such as the Russian and American drives
to the Pacific, our frontier societies, and the treatment of native peoples
within our national boundaries (Pares, 1949, 15–32; Lobanov-Rostovsky, 1951).

The Soviets, because of their overseas experiences since World War
II, now believe (in my opinion) in peaceful coexistence, and their
planners possibly shudder with horror when they think of what might
have happened if the U.S.S.R. had secured control of the Middle East.
Multiply the Central Asian anti-Soviet *basmachi* revolts by one hundred
times in order to imagine the resulting chaos if the Soviets had gained
physical control in the post-World War II Middle East. In 1959, I remarked, half in jest, to several U.S. State Department officials, that,

if the United States really wanted to destroy the U.S.S.R., it should permit Russian to occupy the Middle East from Morocco to Afghanistan. Imagine trying to collectivize, and develop singlehandedly, the Arabs, Turks, Persians, Afghans, and Israelis!

The Afghans effectively ended the Russian–American competition in the early 1960s, when they agreed to have the Americans build a number of commercial airfields in north Afghanistan (near several Russian projects), and the Russians initiated a large-scale irrigation project in the Jalalabad area (near not only several American projects, but also the Pakistan border). The imperialistic concepts of "zones of influence" (i.e., U.S. south of the Hindu Kush; Russia north of the Hindu Kush) ceased to exist. The Afghans reasoned they had nothing to hide for the U-2 spy-flight pilots had probably tuned up their cameras over Afghanistan after leaving the U.S. Air Force microwave monitoring station outside Peshawar, Pakistan, on their way to fly over the U.S.S.R.[10]

At first shocked, both Americans and Russians finally accepted the fact that the Afghans had forced them into *de facto* cooperation, though neither would officially express it in this manner.

In fact, both sides seem to be exceedingly uncomfortable when independent observers mention the process. However, a few examples will illustrate the pattern as it developed. The Soviets assisted the Afghans in building roads from the north, the U.S. from the south. These roads join together at given points. The U.S.S.R. aerially photographed and mapped the northern one-third of Afghanistan; the Americans the southern two-thirds. The two mapping projects overlapped, and American–Soviet teams established mutually recognizable benchmarks and checkpoints on the ground. The Soviets helped construct the landing strips and buildings for the new International Airport at Kabul; the Americans installed the electrical and communications equipment. Many conferences between the two nations' technicians meshed the construction details.

Czech engineers advised the Afghans on coal mining operations near Pul-i-Khumri. North of Pul-i-Khumri, in the Darra-yi-Suf area, near where the Russians drill for oil, American mining engineers until recently advised the Afghans in another coal mining operation. American pumps fill the tanks of Soviet-bloc and American trucks with Russian gasoline. Outside Jalalabad is a military airport, filled with Afghan-owned Soviet aircraft, although the Americans originally built the air-

[10] President Dwight Eisenhower formally announced termination of these flights in 1960.

port for civilian purposes. At the Ministry of Planning, Afghan planners, United Nations planners, Soviet planners, and U.S. planners (from Robert Nathan Associates, an international development consulting firm in Washington, D.C.) sit in on conferences at the ministry and spend one another's money in overall projects. As I write, the People's Republic of China is considering sending a planning specialist to the ministry. None of these joint endeavors came about voluntarily, and most of them occasioned bitter arguments between participants, but the practical result has been American–Russian cooperation in Afghanistan.

Thus, the United States and the U.S.S.R. began their overseas economic and military assistance programs with the same ultimate, national goals: to gain friends or allies and to counter each other's moves. In Afghanistan, the result has been, with the Afghans serving as the catalyst, *de facto* cooperation. But since the West and the Soviet Union are both interested in winning, the question of "Who's winning, the Americans or the Russians?" should be considered. In all honesty, one must answer, "Neither—the Afghans are winning." Perhaps that is as it should be.[11]

Socio-Political Reforms

One of the more important events in modern Afghan history occurred in 1959. With no prior public announcement or official proclamation, Prime Minister Mohammad Daoud, Foreign Minister and Deputy Prime Minister Mohammad Naim, other members of the royal family, the cabinet, and high-ranking army officers appeared on the reviewing stand with their wives and daughters on the second day of *Jeshn* (August 24–30 that year), the week-long celebration of independence from British control of Afghan foreign affairs after the Third Anglo–Afghan War (1919).[12] The women had exposed their faces for all to see.

---

[11] A much maligned, in my opinion, observer of the South Asian scene, Rudyard Kipling, writing of a similar pattern in the late nineteenth century, expressed it thus ("The Ballad of the King's Mercy"):

> Abdur Rahman, the Durani Chief,
>   of him is the story told.
> He has opened his mouth to the North
>   and the South, they have stuffed
>   his mouth with gold."

[12] Actually, the independence war took place in May, but the end of August is a slack agricultural season, when more people can celebrate the holidays. In addition, the Treaty of Rawalpindi which gave Afghanistan the right to conduct its foreign affairs was signed on August 8, 1919.

Just thirty years before, the government of King Amanullah fell because (among other reform attempts) he abolished purdah and the *chadri* and established coeducational schools in Kabul.

Purdah is the isolation of women from all men except their near relatives. Before 1959, all women past puberty in Kabul and other major urban centers wore the *chadri* (veil) outside the family compound. For centuries the custom of purdah was justified by an assumed religious sanction. A careful examination of the *Qor'an*, the *Hadith* (*Sayings of the Prophet*), and the Hanafi *Shari'a* of Sunni Islam (the religious law practiced in Afghanistan), reveals no definite, unqualified requirement for purdah and the veil. Early Islam did not consider women inferior, and they played important, active roles in political as well as social and economic matters. The basically nomadic Arabs began to adopt the customs from the urbanized, property-conscious Byzantine (Anatolian) Christian Empire and Sasanian (Persian) Zoroastrian Empire which fell before their military might in the seventh century A.D. (Baynes, 1952; Penzer, 1936).

Village and nomadic women in the Muslim world have seldom kept purdah or worn a veil. Hard work in the fields and camps prevents such frills, again emphasizing the urban, property-oriented concept of the custom.

The present social reforms and modernization programs in Afghanistan strike at many key customs which have worn a mantle of religious sanction, although, in reality, no formalized religious justification may exist. Prime Minister Daoud operated within this framework in his reform efforts. His chief legal advisers, trained religious leaders with Western legal educations as well, carefully examined each modernization step to insure against violation of Muslim law. The Prime Minister then instituted the program without the issuance of a *farman* by the King, and presented the country with a *fait accompli*. The young legal advisers of Mohammad Daoud Khan (including one of the "Fathers" of the 1964 Constitution, Mohammad Moosa Shafiq Kamawi; the other two drafters are Mir Mohammad Siddiq Farhang and Samad Hamed) had been educated first in Afghanistan at the Faculty of Theology, and then sent to al-Azar, the fountainhead of Muslim learning outside Cairo. The young men took their final secular legal training at such disparate places as Switzerland (Germanic law), France (Napoleonic law), and Columbia University Law School.

Having determined that purdah and the veil could not be absolutely, unqualifiedly justified in Islamic law, the Prime Minister and his advisers acted dramatically but unofficially. During the 1959 *Jeshn* holidays, when the wives and daughters of those high officials on the reviewing stands appeared with their faces bared, the large crowd of spectators stared in stunned disbelief.

Earlier efforts, however, had paved the way for this bold move. Afghan women accompanying their husbands to overseas posts never wore the *chadri* outside Afghanistan, and, one or two years before 1959, Radio Afghanistan tested female singers and announcers. The initial flurry of protests soon died down and several women began to work permanently on the Radio Afghanistan staff. In 1957, a delegation of Afghan women attended a conference of Asian women in Ceylon, the first Afghan group to do so. In 1958, the Afghan government sent a woman delegate to the United Nations.

Several tests were conducted just prior to the 1959 *Jeshn* celebrations, mainly under the supervision of Said Mohammad Qassim Rishtya, the president of the Press Department. Some four months before *Jeshn* the government sent about a dozen women to work as receptionists and hostesses for Ariana Afghan Airlines. Obviously, they could not wear the *chadri* in such work. However, the public readily accepted them. Two months before *Jeshn* a class of girls finishing the sixth grade were asked if they wanted to work in the Kabul China (pottery) Factory. Forty girls volunteered and all obtained letters of consent from their parents. They worked alongside men, and only mild protests arose. Unveiled operators were also employed by the telephone exchange before August 25, 1959. Admittedly, none of the above experiments received wide publicity.

After the great public unveiling, however, the inevitable happened. A delegation of religious leaders requested and received an audience with the Prime Minister. The mullahs accused him of being anti-Islamic for permitting atheistic Communist and Christian Westerners to pervert the nation. The Prime Minister informed the delegation that if they could find incontrovertible justification for purdah and the veil in Islamic Law, he would be the first to return his wife and daughter to purdah. This sporting proposition did not appeal to the religious leaders, several of whom were illiterate folk mullah. Mere logic cannot destroy over night the aura of religious sanction hanging over a custom for longer than anyone can remember, as witness the cries of some crossroads preachers (Christian folk mullahs) in the southern U.S.A. who insist the Bible condones racial segregation as the will of God.

Immediately after leaving the Prime Minister's office the religious leaders began to preach against the regime. Sardar Daoud's efficient secret police arrested and jailed about fifty of the ringleaders. No popular revolts followed the arrests, as had been predicted by a few Afghans and many foreigners. The government did not fall, but rather became stronger. The arrested mullahs were charged on two counts, treason (advocating the overthrow of the government) and heresy. Within the context of traditional Muslim political theory, the charge is irrefutable, for the concept of "divine sanction" made the mullahs guilty of both treason and heresy. Unlike the medieval Christian kings of Western Europe, Muslim rulers rule because of "divine sanction," not "divine right," and sanction can therefore be withdrawn any time the ruler violates the laws of Islam or goes against the will of Allah. In attacking the state and failing to destroy it, the mullahs actually attached Islam as well as the Afghan state. (See also above, p. 465.)

Government spokesmen informed the imprisoned religious leaders that removal of the veil was voluntary, which was only partly true for the government did force officials to attend public functions with unveiled wives in order to set examples for the masses. For the bulk of the population, however, unveiling remains an elective act, and many women still wear the *chadri,* either by their own or by their husband's (or some other male relative's) choice.

The weight of this logic (plus the fact that Afghan jails are designed to punish, not rehabilitate) convinced the mullahs of the error of their ways, so the Prime Minister ordered their release after about a week of incarceration.

Not all religious leaders accepted the voluntary abolition of the veil and other reforms, however, because each intrusion into their customary power erodes their secular influence. They oppose secular education, for in the past they have controlled the educational institution; they call land reform anti-Islamic, for they own large tracts of land in the name of *waqf* (religious endowments); they oppose a constitutionally-separated Church and state, for such a move diminishes their temporal power.

The voluntary abolition of purdah was not only a great social and political reform, but it was also economic, for it increased the potential labor force by fifty percent. Today it is impossible to go into a government office or many private offices in Afghanistan without seeing women behind typewriters, or, in rare cases, actually working in administrative positions.

The religious leaders have had to accept other somewhat unhealthy, emerging patterns. For example, when I first traveled to Afghanistan in 1949, most mullahs decried smoking as an anti-Islamic evil. In 1959, some of the same mullahs told me they accepted smoking unless the believer inhaled, thus contaminating himself.

The next threat to the power of the central government occurred in the Khost area of Paktya, where tribal feuds still loom large in the cultural patterns. The government had been slowly pushing roads through the Paktya area, a move resented by the tribes. They considered these moves an infringement on special rights of non-intervention given to them by King Mohammad Nadir Shah for their participation in the overthrow of the Bacha Saqqao regime in 1929 and subsequent assistance in putting down revolts in the north.

The initial fighting in September 1959 broke out over the ownership of trees, however. Paktya is one of the few extensively wooded areas in Afghanistan and important to the lumber export trade to Pakistan via Parachinar and Thal. Elements of the Mangal and Zadran (Jadran) Pushtun (traditional blood enemies) fought over the ownership of a few stands of Asian conifers. Tribal fighting easily escalates, and within a week other Mangal and Zadran elements became involved. An Afghan army officer, hearing of the outbreak, decided to stop the fighting and therefore gain renown as a peacemaker. He tied a *Qor'an* on his head (traditional way to identify a neutral seeking to parley), and rode his horse into a valley between two war parties. From a distance it is difficult to differentiate friend from foe in a forest zone, or an Afghan officer with a *Qor'an* tied on his head from an Afghan officer *without* a *Qor'an* tied to his head. A Mangal put a bullet through the officer's head, killing him instantly.

When the Mangal discovered what had happened, between three and four thousand fled Afghanistan in early November, crossing the Durand Line. Pakistan, smarting over Afghan agitation on the Pakistan side of the Durand Line over the "Pushtunistan" issue, tried to score propaganda points, as can be seen from the following press release (now defunct *Civil and Military Gazette,* Lahore, Jan. 1, 1960), reportedly a statement by Habibullah, a leading Mangal khan, who accused the Kabul government of being pro-Russian and anti-Muslim:

I have come here from the snowbound area of Kurram Agency [he was speaking in Peshawar] to appeal to the conscience of the justice-loving nations of the world to focus their attentions on the atrocities perpetrated by the Afghan Government on Pathan tribes-men in its own country.

No one in his senses would ever leave his hearth and home in this biting, cold winter and seek asylum in another country, unless he had been pressed to a degree beyond human endurance.

We have committed no wrong and have all along been loyal to our government. The exodus of about 4,000 Mangals from their homeland, in whose liberation from the Bacha Saqqao rule they had played a prominent part, is a matter which deserves serious consideration by all those who believe in fundamental human rights.

My countrymen in Afghanistan as well as our co-religionists in Pakistan probably know that the late king, King Mohammad Nadir Shah, had through a royal proclamation granted us certain concessions, which the present regime in Kabul has decided to withdraw for no fault of ours.

The crux of the matter is that the Afghan Government has taken strong exception to our objection to the growing Russian influence in Afghanistan which has brought the country into the iron grip of communists, who are preaching their atheistic creed under one garb or another. As true Muslims, we cannot silently watch the spread of communist ideology in the land of the iconoclasts Mahmud Ghaznavi and Sayyid Jamaluddin Afghani.

I, therefore, appeal to all nations of the world to take note of this deliberate interference in the affairs of one country by another and would also request the United Nations to send some neutral observers to study the situation on the spot.

One can only wonder which member of the Pakistan Tribal Affairs Department wrote this statement.

The Afghan army moved into the Mangal and Zadran area after the incident and completed several important roads, but did not interfere in the normal migration patterns of the Paktya Pushtun. In the spring of 1960, Prime Minister Daoud let it be known that general amnesty would be granted to all those Mangal who returned. Most did, to the relief of the Pakistanis, for they had become increasingly nervous at having 3,000 to 4,000 potentially dangerous Mangal in the Kurram Agency. Actually, many of the Mangal would have normally returned during the spring at the end of their migratory lumber-trading expeditions, which would have taken place early in the fall, if fighting had not developed. In general, however, no more than a few hundred of the Mangal make the annual trek into Pakistan to sell lumber.

But what really impressed the Paktya tribes was the rapidity (compared with the past) with which the newly mechanized Afghan army sped to the scene of the tribal fighting.

Flushed with success, Daoud and his regime continued the offensive against the political power of the religious and tribal leaders. The next major test came at Qandahar, one of the more conservative religious areas, where landowners had been exempt from the ridiculously low land tax (about 1 afghani per half acre) since the time of Ahmad Shah Durrani, who centered his empire at Qandahar. Subsequent Afghan rulers (including Amanullah) attempted to collect land taxes from the Qandahari, but the landlords and their *arbab* (representatives) developed an easy counter to the government's feeble efforts. In addition, some of the large landholdings were technically religious endowments.

Each year, about December, the governor of Qandahar notified the landowners of their delinquent taxes. Each year the landowners (or their *arbab*) gathered in and about the governor's compound, listened to the governor's complaints, and then marched en masse to the nearby mosque compound, Masjid-i-Jami-Kherqa-Mobarak, which traditionally contains a fragment of the cloak of the Prophet Mohammad.

Declaring *bast* (sanctuary, a custom which still permits a Muslim to remain in a holy place—or other area designated *bast*—unmolested by government authority), the landowners and *arbab* settled down for a few hours (or a few days at the most) until the exasperated governor gave up. These annual tableaux offered a welcome break in the beginning of winter before January's maxima swept in. All—except the governor—seemed to enjoy these exercises of will and tradition.

Tranquillity was the price of no taxation, but Daoud Khan determined to change the situation, so the governor of Qandahar received orders to collect not only the land taxes with no more pantomimes, but to levy an increased income tax on urban shopkeepers as well. So, on December 21, 1959, the usual landlords and *arbab* listened to the usual government ultimatum: pay taxes or else. They had heard the same admonition before and left to take *bast* in the Masjid-i-Kherqa compound. But another ingredient had been added: blocking their line of march between the Governor's compound and the mosque were armed police.

Stunned at the turn of events, the crowd moved away from the mosque road. *Bast* would not be declared this year. Quickly, several

536

ultra-conservative religious leaders and landlords whipped up the *pay-i-luch* ("barefoot boys"; similar groups in Kabul are called *sher-bacha,* "lion boys") of the Qandahari bazaar, who have a reputation for troublemaking. What began as a traditional refusal to pay taxes rapidly grew into an anti-government riot. Obvious manifestations of modernization were attacked, including the local cinema. The rioters later regretted this, for they did enjoy those Indian movies. They also damaged a girls' school, several government buildings, and entered the women's public bath (*hamam*).

At this point, the government in Kabul dismissed the civilian governor, appointed General Khan Mohammad Khan, the provincial military commander (now Minister of Defense), as governor, and ordered him to use the army to assist the police. Several times the troops had to fire on the rioters. Probably three were killed and eight injured. By the afternoon of the next day, however, calm prevailed. Helmeted soldiers with machine guns, backed by tanks, had a salutary effect on the Qandaharis.

Although the rioters marched past the district occupied by the American A.I.D. and contracting company families, they made no attempt to demonstrate against the Americans, a strange phenomenon in Asian demonstration techniques. One American, however, making the rounds to warn others to stay inside their compounds, was knifed as he inadvertently stumbled into part of the mob. He was not seriously injured, and, helped by sympathetic, apologetic Afghans, escaped and was immediately evacuated. The A.I.D. mission in Qandahar maintained constant radio contact with A.I.D. in Kabul, and at no time were the American personnel in actual danger. However, the mob overturned and burned an air-conditioned, fuchsia-colored Cadillac owned by an American A.I.D. official. As an obvious symbol of modernization, it made an attractive target.

The Qandahar riots of December 1959, offer great contrast to the Safi revolt (near Jalalabad) in 1947–1949, in which the Safi Pushtun defeated several Afghan army units in the field, *before* Kabul even knew a revolt had occurred. Fighting also developed between the Safi and their Nuristani neighbors. General Mohammad Daoud Khan successfully put down the revolt, however, which resulted in the last large-scale forced migration in modern Afghan history. Many leaders of the Safi revolt were scattered in extended family units across north Afghanistan.

Although the new roads, extended telecommunications, and quick action by the improved army prevented the Qandahar riot from turning into a full-scale revolt, as yet few Qandaharis pay full land taxes.

"Pushtunistan": The Border Closes, 1961–63

The problem of "Pushtunistan" continued to dominate Afghan foreign policy. The Pakistanis, now with strong allies and growing military capacity, tended to consider the issue non-existent or unimportant. But "Pushtunistan" and Kashmir, two legacies of the British period, did exist. Both involved the principle of the self-determination of peoples, once thought a panacea for international tensions, now a violent spectre in many areas. Both concerned Pakistan.

Pakistan's internal and external political troubles intensified after March 1955, when it announced the One Unit Plan, which created the single province of West Pakistan. Previously, West Pakistan consisted of several provinces,[13] whereas the East Wing, with a larger population, had always been a single province for administrative and legislative purposes. Since representation in the Constituent Assembly was equal by province, for example, West Pakistan's members greatly outnumbered their East Pakistani counterparts. The One Unit Plan was designed to help end such disparity between East and West, which ultimately, however, led to the creation of independent Bangladesh in 1971.

Prime Minister Daoud protested the One Unit Plan. So did many of the Pakistani Pushtun tribal leaders, for, although the Tribal Agencies were not included in the Province of West Pakistan, the khans feared the move was simply a first step toward eventual integration. Intense propaganda campaigns precipitated violent demonstrations on both sides of the Durand Line. In late March, a Kabul mob tore down the Pakistani flag from the Pakistani embassy, and other mobs ransacked the Pakistani consulates at Qandahar and Jalalabad. The Afghan consulate in Peshawar was attacked in retaliation.

Afghanistan mobilized its reserves and prepared for war, and both nations recalled their citizens, but before any fighting took place the two antagonists agreed to submit the incidents to an international commission consisting of Egypt, Iran, Iraq, Saudi Arabia, and Turkey. The Americans had offered three times to act as mediators. The Afghans indicated mild interest, but the Pakistanis ignored the gestures.

[13] West Pakistan consisted of three Governor's provinces (Punjab, Sind, North-West Frontier Province), plus the princely states of Bahawalpur, Khaipur, the Baluchistan States Union, and the Tribal Agencies.

Meetings of the commission produced no definite results but in separate reports the Saudis and the Egyptians blamed the Afghans for their intransigence and, therefore, for the failure of the arbitration commission. At the height of the tension the Afghan government called a 360-man *Loya Jirgah* to reconsider the "Pushtunistan" issue. The *Loya Jirgah* once again unanimously supported the government's stand in demanding a plebiscite in the Pushtun areas of Pakistan.

Reason finally prevailed, and in September 1955, official flag-raising ceremonies at the embassy and consulates seemed to put the issue to rest, at least temporarily.

At last disturbed by the frontier problem, Pakistan stepped up its anti-"Pushtunistan" propaganda on both sides of the Durand Line. Over Radio Peshawar the Pakistanis broadcast in Pashto to the Afghan side of the Durand Line, demanding to know whether or not the Pushtun in Afghanistan would be able to vote to join an independent "Pushtunistan," as the Afghans demanded the Pushtun in the Tribal Agencies and former Settled Districts be given the right to do. This became one of the major Pakistani counter-propaganda lines until the 1963 re-establishment of diplomatic relations.

Prime Minister Daoud had long been an enthusiastic supporter of "Pushtunistan," and, on the basis of false intelligence reports concerning the implications of local tribal fights, twice sent several thousand Afghan troops to the Bajaur area. Afghan irregulars and army troops dressed as tribesmen entered the Bajaur in late September 1960, but were driven back by the Bajauri Pushtun themselves, who, although they often fight each other, resent intrusions from the outside, be they from the Pakistani or the Afghan area.

A larger attack by Afghan regular troops (again dressed as tribesmen) occurred in May 1961, after the Nawwab of Dir, and his son, the Khan of Jandol, convinced the Afghans to assist them in their fight with the Khan of Khar. Before the Afghan *lashkar* moved across the border, they were addressed by their officers, who confidently (according to Pakistani sources) told them they would all meet in Malakand.

The Afghans moved rapidly toward Shahi, Miskanai (capital of the Khan of Jandol), and Sangpura. This time the tribesmen, plus the newly-formed Bajaur Scouts (a paramilitary unit locally recruited, but officered by regular Pakistani officers seconded for duty with the Frontier Corps), met the Afghans, who fought well at night, but were vulnerable to daylight attacks by American-built, Pakistani-piloted F-86 jet fighter-bombers. The Pakistani Air Force also claimed to have destroyed a major ammunition dump at Balmalai on the Pakistan side of the Durand Line. The Pakistanis accused a "Pushtunistan" nationalist, Fazl Akbar (alias Pacha Gul) of creating the dump and distributing about 170 million afghanis worth of arms, ammunition, transistor radios, and watches to Pakistani Pushtun in attempts to gain their support.

Even the Pakistanis, however, underestimated the fierce pride and love of independence which sits like a monument in the hills along the Durand Line. Elements of the First Punjab Regiment were moved by rail to Dargai and then across the West Pakistani provincial line (or boundary) into the Malakand Tribal Agency. Although the Bajauri accepted the locally-recruited Scouts in their midst, they violently objected to the presence of the regular Pakistan army. During the first night, sniping and an ambush caused several casualties among the Punjabis, and the Pakistani government prudently withdrew the unit. It had become obvious that the Bajaur Scouts and the local tribesmen (in combination with Pakistani Air Force attacks by day) would successfully defeat the *lashkar* and drive it from the area. The Khan of Jandol, Pakistani loser in the affair, now lives in Lahore and receives a monthly pension of about 3,000 Rs. from the government of Pakistan.

According to Pakistani sources, a small-scale (about 500 Afghans) attack in the fall of 1961 in the same area degenerated and resulted in the dismissal of the ranking Afghans responsible. The assault turned out to be an entirely local affair, probably undertaken without the knowledge of the central government in Kabul.

Small bands of Pakistani Pushtun, however, encouraged and armed by the Afghans, launched attacks on Scout units, sniped at outposts and pickets, and attempted to blow up bridges. Afghan and Pakistani radio and press propaganda, though often vitriolic, seldom sustains the pitch it reached from 1961 to 1963. Taking their cue from the war of words, young warrior Pushtun along the frontier enjoyed themselves as they had not since the departure of the British. Every day newspapers of both countries printed lengthy articles on the desultory fighting, defections, and tribal *jirgah* announcing support of one side or the other. In the Afghan and Pakistani word-skirmishes the Pakistani press often referred to the "Democratic Party of Afghanistan," a shadow organization at best, as "underground freedom fighters" opposing the Daoud regime. Afghanistan always referred to the Pakistani Pushtun area as "occupied" or "independent Pushtunistan," and divided the "country" into three provinces: "Northern, Central, and Southern Occupied Independent Pushtunistan."

During the peak period of intense anti-Pakistani propaganda, I kept casualty figures for eighteen months, and a minimum of a battalion of Pakistani soldiers were reported killed in action. A day seldom passed without an attack being reported. The Afghan reports were obviously exaggerated, but some casualties did occur, as admitted in published, official statements of the Pakistan government.

I visited the Bajaur area shortly after the 1961 fighting, and examined much Russian equipment allegedly seized from the Afghan *lashkar*. I was also permitted to talk to Afghan "refugees" who had fled from the "deviltry of the Daoud regime," and to several Afghan soldiers captured during the fighting. All confirmed that young Pakistani Pushtun constantly slipped into Afghanistan for weapons, ammunition, and grenades. The Afghans could never be certain the bullets or grenades would be fired against Pakistani or Afghan soldiers, or used in local tribal feuds with no relationship to the overall "Pushtunistan" issue. However, the Afghans paid a specified bounty for each empty cartridge and pulled grenade pin brought back to the Afghan side with claims of kills or attacks on Pakistani outposts. Often, the warriors would bring old unusable cartridge casings for new bullets, or replace the grenade pin with a homemade substitute, thus saving the grenade for later use. The situation developed into a great game, practiced by the Pushtun on both sides of the Durand Line. They indiscriminately accepted arms and money from both the Afghans and the Pakistanis, using these material gains in any way they desired.

The October, 1958, seizure of power in Pakistan by General Mohammad Ayub Khan, himself a Spin Tarin Pushtun from the Hazara District, probably contributed to the downward plunge of relations between the two countries over "Pushtunistan." Ayub Khan took firm control of a government floundering toward anarchy. He brought economic stability and consolidated power to the center, with the support of the army, to stiffen the backbone of the nation. Internal progress seemed to make Pakistan restless, and President Ayub tackled foreign policy with a bold, aggressive approach.

In spite of its renascent vigor, however, Pakistan interpreted with some alarm the post-election announcements of President Kennedy and his advisers on Asia, which seemed to indicate that neutral India would hold a favored place in the policies of the new administration. Pakistan, militarily allied with the United States, felt slighted in both the economic and political arenas. President Ayub, concerned over developments, made a state visit to the United States in July 1961, instead of November as originally planned.

It is my opinion that President Ayub and his forceful Minister of Foreign Affairs, Mansoor Qadir, planned their moves very carefully, being guided by the thesis that most so-called neutral Afro–Asian countries now had sufficient practical experience with the Soviet bloc, so that if forced to make a political or economic decision based on strict national interest, they would line up with the Western camp. Therefore, the West could exert pressures on certain neutral nations to bring about peaceful solutions of potential threats to peace, e.g., the Kashmir problem. If, the Pakistanis may have reasoned, the United States should threaten to withdraw a sizeable portion of the loans, grants, and technical assistance programs projected for India, an aging and perhaps mellowing Mr. Nehru, watching the Communist Chinese moving unchecked into more than 50,000 square miles of territory the Indians claimed in Ladakh, would demur but, after thinking it over, would agree to a U.N.-sponsored plebiscite in Kashmir to keep from becoming economically more dependent on the Soviet bloc.

As one step in his strategy, Ayub had hinted at a reappraisal of Pakistani foreign policy, and neutralism became a favorite topic of conversation in Pakistan. Later, in July 1961, Pakistan signed an oil exploration agreement with the U.S.S.R., the first step along the road to establishing a community of interests with Afro–Asian neutralism. So Washington knew before Ayub's arrival that he would push a hard bargain.

Ayub Khan, pleased with the official reception and widespread press, radio, and television coverage, pressed his arguments articulately in private conversations with American officials. Much of what he wanted he got: a chance to state his case to the Kennedy administration; a sympathetic hearing for such problems as the spreading salinity and waterlogging in the Punjab; and reassurances of American friendship for Pakistan. However, he made no headway at all on his pet project: to have the United States force India to agree to a Kashmir plebiscite. President Ayub may have felt all the more disappointed about this because his blunt major address to the joint session of Congress on July 12 helped sway doubtful legislators toward a more favorable reception of President Kennedy's bold five-year approach to foreign assistance programs.

President Ayub returned to Pakistan in late July with his primary aim thwarted. Soon after his return a new crisis with Afghanistan over the "Pushtunistan" issue and the transit trade began. Possibly, Pakistani officials planned their moves before President Ayub's visit to the United States, to be put into effect if he failed to get unqualified support on the Kashmir question. Unless this is true, a crisis over "Pushtunistan" at that time makes no sense. Some observers, however, feel that Ayub needed external issues to divert attention from growing internal dissatisfaction with his autocratic regime.

In broad outline the Pakistani plan to make itself felt and heard militarily and diplomatically in South Asia involved moves to bring about a closing of the Afghan–Pakistani consulates, which would cause a break in diplomatic relations and effectively close the border. Deprived of channels for the movement of goods except through the Soviet Union, the Afghans would have to agree to a settlement of the "Pushtunistan question," or at least unofficially return to the *status quo ante* and cease incitement of Pakistani Pushtun tribes.

If such were the planning behind Pakistan's maneuvers in the summer and fall of 1961, a succesful outcome would have provided Ayub Khan with diplomatic ammunition to argue that the United States institute a policy of economic pressure on neutrals, specifically aimed at having the Kennedy administration force a resolution of the Kashmir dispute.

The uneasy relations between Afghanistan and Pakistan had been marked for years by ritual harassment of consular establishments, and the Pakistanis chose this as their weapon. Pakistan closed its consulates in Afghanistan on August 23 (during *Jeshn*) and simultaneously requested that the Afghans close their consulates and trade agencies in Quetta, Peshawar, and Parachinar. The Pakistanis charged that the Afghans had interfered in the internal affairs of Pakistan by stirring up resentment against the Rawalpindi government by pushing the "Pushtunistan" issue. On August 30, the Afghans reacted by giving the Pakistanis one week to rescind their action or suffer a break in diplomatic relations. The Pakistanis ignored the ultimatum, and on September 6 relations between the two countries were broken. Some weeks later the Pakistanis issued a White Paper listing its grievances over the mistreatment of Pakistani consulate personnel: Afghan servants would not work in Pakistani consulates; inordinately high rents had been charged; purchasing food in the bazaar had been difficult; Afghan intelligence officers kept consular personnel under constant surveillance;

Afghan officials continually rained insults on Pakistani diplomats; on occasion, exit permits had been refused to consular officers.

Many amusing incidents occurred relating to the embassy closures following the break, and gave rise to multitudinous rumors in a land where rumors breed like *Drosophila*. On the night of September 6, a multi-engined aircraft droned over Kabul several times, shaking the jumpy foreign community. Some said, "The Russians are sending a special economic envoy to advise the Afghans on in-transit difficulties." Another set of voices cried, "No! Not an envoy, but a field marshal to direct the Afghan army in the war with Pakistan." And even: "The Russians are dropping paratroopers!" Actually the plane contained most of the Afghan embassy staff from Karachi. Unable to land at Kabul because landing-lights were not available at the time, the plane then flew to the military airport at Begram, forty miles north of Kabul.

Other rumors spread, though none materialized: Germany had agreed to have Lufthansa fly into Afghanistan all materials necessary for the completion of West German projects; all United States projects would close down, and 150 exit visas had already been issued to American technicians in Kabul; all United States personnel in south Afghanistan had departed Qandahar for Pakistan; a M.A.T.S. (U.S.A.F. Military Air Transport Service) airlift had been planned to bring in road equipment from Amritsar (India) to build the American-contracted Kabul-to-Qandahar road.

Another series of events emphasized the nineteenth-century atmosphere pervading the situation. The Pakistanis requested that the United Kingdom handle its interests in Kabul. The Afghans refused, an event almost unique in diplomatic history. On September 23, the Afghans accepted the embassy of Saudi Arabia as caretaker of Pakistani interests; the United Arab Republic represented Afghanistan in Rawalpindi and Karachi.

Many literate Afghans believed the British to be the ultimate culprit, and the Afghan press repeated this accusation with relish. One influential Afghan told me at the time: "Ayub Khan got his orders in London on his way to Washington." Another Afghan intellectual accused the United States of blindly following British policy: "The British are using America to reassert themselves in Asia. America is still a British colony whether it chooses to believe it or not."

The closing of the Afghan–Pakistan border surprised many observers, who believed the Afghans would relent at the last minute. Logically, as everyone knew, the border closure would adversely affect the now booming American assistance programs, threaten Afghan merchants and fruit growers with loss of 1961's fruit crop, and possibly deliver the whole trade of the country into Soviet channels. But pride overrode practicality, as it often does in international affairs.

American government officials in Kabul pleaded with the Afghans not to close the border. The Afghans maintained they had no choice. An official said, "We cannot issue the proper papers or maintain proper control over the import of goods after the closing of our trade missions. We always have trouble with willful damage and pilfering on the Pakistan side. Electrical equipment is often damaged, and wires cut on radios, refrigerators, and the like. Now we can't check on anything."

The fact that the Afghans could not prevent such damage *with* trade agencies in Pakistan seems to indicate that goods could still come through, probably in the same condition, *without* trade agencies. The Afghans had no equivalent trade agencies in the Soviet Union, so their true necessity escaped many observers. Pakistan announced that it would honor its international obligations to keep the Afghan in-transit goods flowing. Thus, in the eyes of world legal and public opinion, Pakistan put the onus of the diplomatic break squarely on the Afghans. A wiser course, in the opinion of many foreigners and Afghans, would have been for Afghanistan to have maintained relations, however strained, and permitted in-transit items to cross the Durand Line.

All these developments pleased the Soviet long-range planners. Their economic penetration experiment could not have received a greater boost. On September 16, just ten days after the border closed, the Afghan foreign minister, Sardar Mohammad Naim, made a quick trip to Moscow, returning on September 21. The trip resulted in an airlift of the fruit crop and a new Afghan–Soviet agreement signed in November, which called for a major increase of transit facilities through the Soviet Union.

The first quasi-official statements on the closure came from unimpeachable sources. In an interview with a West German journalist, Prime Minister Mohammad Daoud replied in answer to a direct question: "The border will remain closed until the Pushtunistan issue is settled." On October 1, a *Times of India* correspondent quoted Foreign Minister Naim as saying: "If the Americans want to help, they will find a way like our other friends. The West Germans, the U.N.O., and others will send goods through the Russian transit route."

No imagination is necessary to visualize the effect on the American Congress and public if the United States government had shipped aid

545

equipment through the U.S.S.R. to support non-aligned Afghanistan in a quarrel with the American ally, Pakistan. In any event, the repercussions of the border closure extended far beyond the Durand Line and affected an intricate network of international relations, involving not only Afghanistan and Pakistan, but all countries which had trade or diplomatic relations with either or both.

From early October to early November about 13 Soviet aircraft took off each day from Kabul airport, airlifting 100 to 150 tons of grapes to the U.S.S.R.

At the onset of Afghanistan's self-imposed blockade, some foreign observers predicted the collapse of the Afghan economy if the fruit crop rotted along Afghan roads. The importance of fresh and dried fruit and nuts cannot be underestimated, because these two items account for the bulk of Afghan exports abroad. However, similar dire predictions of economic collapse followed Western boycotts of Iranian oil after Premier Mossadegh nationalized the Anglo–Iranian Oil Company in 1953, and after several western nations boycotted President Nasser's nationalized Suez Canal in 1956. These prognostications failed to consider that over ninety percent of the Iranian and Egyptian populations received little or no benefit from the economic gains of such formerly foreign-controlled enterprises as the A.I.O.C. of the Compagnie Maritime du Suez, and, often, the local governments proved to be as responsible as the companies for the improper utilization of realized profits. Most Middle Easterners depend on subsistence agriculture and animal husbandry for their livelihood and would live just as well without the oil, the canal, or the grape profits.

A small minority of Afghan fruit exporters and large landholders stood in most immediate danger of financial loss. Many in this class can easily survive one year's loss of grape revenue, however. The Pushtun tribal trucking companies, a group previously pampered by the Afghan government (because roads south to Pakistan lead through their territory), monopolize the transport of most trade items between Afghanistan and Pakistan, and probably suffered the greatest immediate loss of income. A little *bakhshish* in the right places enabled some trucks to continue crossing the border in spite of the closure. Only a few trucks operated in this manner, however, whereas in past peak seasons of fresh grape export, 100-plus trucks moved about 1,000 tons of grapes a day from Kabul to Peshawar. If a driver reached Peshawar in time for the grapes to catch the southbound 10 A.M. train, he received a fee of 500 Pakistani rupees (official rate 4.76 rupees to the U.S. dollar). Later arrivals got substantially less, depending on the state of the grapes.

Since I first visited Afghanistan in 1949, a new merchant and entrepreneur class has emerged to cater to the desires of foreigners and the small (but growing) Afghan middle class. Most merchants belong to minority ethnic groups, mainly Tajik, Qizilbash, and Uzbak, and the border closure affected them more than most other Afghan economic groups. Millions of dollars worth of goods ordered by the free enterprising businessman lay stalled in Pakistan. One grocer claimed to have goods worth $30,000 blocked in Peshawar alone. Luckily, Kabuli merchants keep large godowns full of products, so many rode out the crisis and raised prices fifty percent or more to meet the needs of the commissary-deprived foreign community. Some merchants flew in merchandise from Beirut.

In addition to the massive Soviet airlift of grapes to the north out of both Kabul and Qandahar, Ariana Afghan Airlines (Pan American owns 49% of the stock; the Royal Government of Afghanistan, 51%) instituted its own fruit airlift to India, traditionally Afghanistan's most important customer for its fresh and dried fruits and nuts. In spite of initial lukewarm official reaction and the usual graft, everyone involved—the grape growers, the exporters, and the airline—made a profit. About twelve export companies flew grapes to Amritsar on charter consignments, for which they paid an average of $2,850 air freight charges per trip for 7.5 tons of grapes. The exact profit an Afghan merchant averaged per trip remains unrecorded. Profits must have been considerable, however, because a charter allocation from Ariana which cost from 8 to 10,000 afghanis (40 afghanis to the U.S. dollar) could be resold in the bazaar to another grape merchant for 10,000 Indian rupees (one Indian rupee equaled about twenty-one cents U.S. officially).

In 1960, the average price in Amritsar for fresh grapes was 15 to 20 rupees per *sir* (pron. *seer;* one *sir* = 15 to 16 lb. in Kabul, but varies according to region). The price in 1961 rose to 65 rupees per *sir,* then leveled off at about 50. Therefore, an average planeload sold for about 52,125 Indian rupees.

In order to maintain its modest airlift, Ariana chartered additional aircraft (never less than two per day after October 10) from Indian and Lebanese airlines. On December 12, Ariana chartered three additional planes, bringing the total in service to five.

In contrast to the straightforward, profit-motivated venture by Ariana and its shippers, the Soviet airlift presented two distinct faces: political propaganda and strictly commercial enterprise. A few Afghans praised the Soviets for their humanitarianism and compared the grape airlift with the Berlin airlift. They said: "The human factors overwhelm any political and economic considerations. The airlift prevents bankruptcy from striking many Afghan farmers." Most observers thought this a gross exaggeration, but the Russian airplanes droning overhead created a favorable image of the Soviets for the average (mythical creature that he is) Kabuli or Qandahari.

Soviet–Afghan economic relations seldom follow smooth paths. Both sides think they are excellent horse-traders and each constantly tries to outsmart the other. The Soviets are in control, however, because they usually act as the bookkeeper in all transactions. When an item crosses the Afghan frontier from the U.S.S.R., the Soviets immediately telegraph Kabul and order the Afghans to debit the proper account. Accounting for goods moving in the opposite direction is more casual. Weeks and even months may pass before an Afghan export item crosses the Amu Darya and the Soviets acknowledge receipt.

Afghan merchants have told me that the Russians sometimes offered one price in Kabul but actually paid another, lower, price, after receipt of the goods. In these instances the Soviets insisted that the quality of the received items did not meet the agreed specifications, probably the truth.

Occasionally, during the early phase of the grape airlift, the Soviets refused to pay the agreed price for fresh grapes, claiming damage or low quality. In many cases their protests were justified. The Afghan–Soviet agreement also called for the grapes to be shipped in wooden crates, each containing two *sir*. Spot checks indicated many crates only contained 1.5 *sir*.

At first the Soviets did not seem to be interested in turning the airlift into a reciprocally beneficial economic enterprise. Their aircraft brought no marketable goods in exchange, but instead transported aviation gasoline to keep the planes flying. No one knew how the Soviets planned to dispose of the grapes, because the Soviet Central Asian Republics almost always produced bumper crops, and the Afghan variety sold in the U.S.S.R. could not be used in making wine. An apocryphal story maintained that the Soviets dumped the grapes into the Amu Darya (the river boundary between Afghanistan and the U.S.S.R.), and would have brought more if the river had not clogged up. Another version gave the Aral Sea as the dumping area.

Officially, the Russians sent many of the grapes to Siberian settlements, and as the unseasonally fresh grapes appeared in Moscow markets, long lines of consumers purchased the high-quality Afghan product. Others were exported to Eastern Europe and sold at high prices, thus making a sizeable capitalistic-type profit for the Soviets.

Most of the final loss of about $1 million was felt by the grape growers and exporters. The Afghan government itself made money on the airlift. The government paid the grower or seller 30 afghanis per *sir* for fresh grapes and sold them to the U.S.S.R. for $162 per metric ton (139 *sir* to the metric ton), bringing the government a profit of about $58 per metric ton.

All parties concerned realized that eventually, to regain economic flexibility, Afghanistan must reestablish trade routes to the south, and that economic flexibility must be maintained to prevent total Soviet control of Afghanistan's economic institutions, with attendant loss of political flexibility.

The United States found itself in the most difficult position of all nations involved in the crisis. Several levels must be considered. The first reaction among many Americans in Kabul was: "What happens to the commissary?" Afghan reaction to this type of American reaction pointed out a little mentioned but ever present sore spot: "Now maybe Americans will leave their isolated ghetto and act more like Americans do in the States." But the Americans were not alone in their misery, for the U.N. and British embassy commissaries also suffered shortages, especially of whiskey.

Some Americans and others converged on the bazaar to find, to their surprise, what other non-commissary foreigners had known all along. The bazaars of Kabul contained excellent canned goods from all over the world: Dutch chocolates and powdered milk; Danish hams, cheeses, and butter; Norwegian sardines; American pork and beans; Swiss ravioli; Italian pasta; Russian king crab; Japanese tuna; Tanganyikan corned beef; Malayan pineapples, to mention but a few. The unsurpassed local fresh fruits and vegetables astonished many. The American commissary began to buy the best grade of flour from the Kabul silo instead of importing flour from the United States.

The eighteen months before the border closure witnessed the rise of United States political and economic efforts to unprecedented heights of success, under the leadership of Ambassador Henry Byroade. President Eisenhower's visit to Kabul in December 1959, boosted American prestige, and many A.I.D. programs which had bogged down in logistical or administrative incompetence, or both, surged ahead. Now the border closure threatened to stall or terminate several important heavy engineering construction projects, including the long-delayed Kabul–Qandahar road, the Spin Baldak–Qandahar road, and improvements in the Hilmand Valley Project. Much of the heavy equipment collected dust in Pakistan: for example, about ten percent of the equipment for the Kabul–Qandahar road project crossed the border before the shutdown, while the other ninety percent waited in Pakistan for the border to reopen. Some aspects of educational aid (teaching, agricultural extension, etc.) continued, but the construction of Kabul University by a West German firm with American funds was curtailed. One American official at the time bitterly remarked: "The damned border closure wastes two years of solid preparation."

Obviously, the United States A.I.D. programs in Afghanistan had to be carefully reexamined in the light of the border situation, and the fate of each project determined by the feasibility of completion without excessive extra expenses. When United States officials confronted Afghan officials with this problem, the Afghans sometimes accused the Americans of trying to exert pressure on them to reopen the border by threatening to terminate A.I.D. programs. This Afghan attitude tended to anger those Americans who genuinely tried to find ways to help Afghanistan to continue its development, in spite of the difficulties posed by the Afghan unilateral closure of the border.

The Pakistani press waxed unenthusiastically about Mr. Kennedy's proposal to send an emissary to Pakistan and Afghanistan to discuss the possibilities of reestablishing diplomatic relations. President Ayub, on receipt of the Kennedy letter suggesting such a visit, gave an interview in which he said to an American reporter: "Are all countries prepared to be friendly to you? Whose friendship is of any worth to you? The time for a choice has come—in fact it came a long time ago. A great deal of hard, pragmatic thinking is required. The Russians have friends whom they back up to the hilt right or wrong" (*New York Times,* October 3, 1961). This certainly constituted a slap at President Kennedy, for the mediation offer had not yet been made public. President Ayub could probably see his Kashmir plebiscite via a "Pushtunistan" solution slipping through his political fingers.

Afghanistan, on the other hand, greeted the proposal in glowing terms, and the press lauded Mr. Livingston T. Merchant, U.S. Ambassador to Canada and President Kennedy's special envoy, with friendly front-page publicity. Merchants's mission, doomed from its inception because neither side would consider compromise, began in Karachi on October 19. It ended in Karachi on November 7. Both the Afghan and

Pakistani press carried verbatim statements of failure. Between October 19 and November 7 the peripatetic Mr. Merchant traveled from Karachi to Rawalpindi to Peshawar to Kabul to Karachi to Rawalpindi to Kabul to Karachi. During this period and effort, the Afghan press and radio repeated over and over that the Pakistanis had closed the border, and waited for the United States to apply pressure on President Ayub to permit its reopening. As I was told: "Field Marshal Ayub is *your* [American] responsibility."

On November 10, 1961, the Karachi Trust Port Authority instructed clearing agents for Afghan companies to remove uncleared goods from transit sheds. If not removed, the goods would be sold at auction. Afghan in-transit goods crowded Pakistani customs warehouses in Karachi, Peshawar, and Quetta, and over 400 loaded wagonette train cars stood idle. In addition, the Peshawar Chamber of Commerce complained to the Pakistani government about the adverse local economic effects of the border closing, and the Pakistani Ministry of Commerce in Rawalpindi became genuinely concerned and issued statistics to indicate how much the country was suffering.

American A.I.D. material to Afghanistan worth several million dollars sat immobile in Pakistan. Estimates indicated that about 23,000 tons sat in Karachi, Peshawar, Chaman, and Quetta. An American wheat gift of 8,000 tons rotted in Peshawar warehouses. Non-governmental American programs adversely affected include those of C.A.R.E. (its milk for school children program almost collapsed) and M.E.D.I.C.O. (just beginning to see results from its pioneer work). A warehouse fire in Peshawar destroyed most of M.E.D.I.C.O.'s drug supplies, about $75,000 worth, along with many other in-transit items. Several U.N. efforts, especially the malaria eradication program of W.H.O., were initially in danger, but the U.N. began to ship supplies through the Soviet Union.

Some Americans and Afghans often made wistful mention of an alternate in-transit route first proposed by the Afghans in 1950 during the Pakistani imposed slowdown of in-transit goods in retaliation for Afghan agitation among Pakistani Pushtun tribes. The route would have led through southwest Afghanistan to Zahidan in Iran, and then to the Persian port of Chahbahar. In spite of the length of the proposed route, and the difficulties of road construction and port improvement, such an alternative would have removed some of the pressure on the now overwhelmed port of Karachi and answered a pressing need for another major port between Khurramshahr in Iran and Karachi.

A new Iranian in-transit route did begin to function in the summer of 1962, however, and continued to improve. An Afghan trade delegation went to Tehran in March 1962, to conclude an agreement to purchase additional Iranian P.O.L. (petroleum-oil-lubricants). The P.O.L. would be primarily for the new international airport at Qandahar. The Afghan delegation signed a continuation of the one-year transit agreement originally agreed to in 1962. The in-transit route was used primarily by the United States Agency of International Development and certain Kabul merchants and the goods had to travel the long route by sea to Khurramshahr, by rail to Tehran and Mashhad, and then lorry to Herat and Kabul via Qandahar.

A year went by, and the border remained closed. The 1962–63 fresh fruit airlift to India, which Ariana Afghan Airlines operated primarily with charter aircraft, flew a much greater tonnage than in the 1961–62 lift: 1,500 tons in 1961–62, compared to 2,797 tons in 1962–63. (Incidentally, Ariana still flies out the best quality grapes to India each year.) The Soviet fresh fruit airlift also increased (from 7,250 tons in 1961–62 to about 11,000 tons in 1962–63), but the Soviets gave the Afghans less credit per ton this time. So, contrary to the situation in 1961–62, when the Afghans gained a $1,468,000 credit from the Soviet Union, only $1,430,000 resulted during the 1962–63 airlift for more tonnage. Unless the border opened before the next fruit crop went out in summer, 1963, the annual interest increase of the Afghan dollar debt to the Soviet Union would soon be more than the annual return on the fruit crop.

Neither Afghan economists nor the power elite missed the real significance of the trade situation which annually trapped an additional increment of total Afghan exports for the U.S.S.R. The cold economic facts, therefore, indicated that both Pakistan and Afghanistan should be eager to reestablish trade and diplomatic relations, but everything revolved about the single issue that had flavored Afghanistan's foreign policy since World War II: "Pushtunistan."

In the years following World War II, the Government of Pakistan periodically threatened to stop the nomadic movements, primarily by Pushtun tribesmen, between the two countries (see above, pp. 169–70, for details).

Pakistani attempts to close the border to nomads prior to 1961 usually related to the spread of hoof and mouth disease, which occasionally strikes local cattle. In 1961, however, the move was purely political. The Pakistani Government officially claimed, however, that the diplomatic break by Afghanistan had no relation to its decision to prevent nomadic movements across the border. Many of the nomads with whom I talked in the Jalalabad area, the Gardez area, and the Hazarajat in 1961 expressed little concern. They all believed the border would remain open and moved toward their annual objectives. The Pakistanis, however, stopped most of the nomads. Afghan authorities admitted that many had been turned back to seek alternate grazing lands in eastern and southern Afghanistan. Being a warrior people, not all the nomads accepted the closure peaceably, but attempted to infiltrate through difficult—but· unguarded—passes. Some fighting between Pakistani forces and nomads resulted and infected the Pakistani Pushtun, who at times joined their brothers from across the border in the fighting. In fact, the Pakistani efforts to stop nomadic bands from crossing the border gave "Pushtunistan" a regional and international respectability it had never before enjoyed.

Several Western journals (such as *Eastern World,* London, October, 1961, and the *New Republic,* Washington, October 30, 1961) published articles which dealt sympathetically with the Afghan point of view. The Afghan press gave such articles prominent display. For example, the leading article of the Pashto daily, *Heywad,* November 16, 1961, entitled "The Truth about Pushtunistan at last Emerges in Washington," discussed both the *Eastern World* and the *New Republic* pieces.

As the nomads arrived at frontier crossing-points, Pakistani officials demanded passports and visas as well as international health certificates. Of course the nomads had none and never have had. The Pakistanis, therefore, blamed the Afghan government, which refused to issue passports to nomads. The Afghan Government realized that if one nomad crossed the frontier with a valid Afghan passport and Pakistani visa, the "Pushtunistan" issue would be dead. The Pakistanis could then claim that the Afghans, because they issued passports to nomads, had accepted the Durand Line as an international boundary. The Pakistani Government, on its part, issues special "Red Passes" for travel through the tribal territory to Afghanistan, *not* Pakistani passports, which seemed to indicate that even the Pakistanis continued to respect the virtual independence of the Tribal Agencies in spite of official attempts to integrate some of these areas into the provincial government network.

The Afghan government played a waiting game and refused to support militarily the attempts of the nomads to cross the border, remembering well the dismal results of the 1960–61 fighting.

Before the border could be opened one (or both) of the two major personalities involved in the dispute would have to go, either Prime

Minister Mohammad Daoud Khan of Afghanistan, or Pakistani President Field Marshal Mohammad Ayub Khan, both Pushtun. In spite of the growing vocal opposition to certain of his policies, President Ayub appeared to be as strong as ever, although many observers felt it would be better if both Daoud and Ayub left the political scene.

The Afghan radio and press propaganda hit the Pakistanis hard, and often unfairly. At times, however, the Pakistanis unjustly tormented the Afghans. When the Daoud regime courageously encouraged Afghan women to come out of purdah and remove the veil in 1959, for example, the Pakistani news media ridiculed the move and reported many false horror stories about police ripping veils off women. True, the Afghan Government exerted pressure on certain recalcitrant high officials to have their wives set examples, but Pakistani propaganda on this issue listurbed the Afghans, especially since many high ranking Pakistani officials still keep their wives in purdah.

Daoud Steps Down

The impasse was broken with a dramatic Radio Afghanistan announcement on March 9, 1963:

> Sardar Mohammad Daoud, the Prime Minister of Afghanistan, after nine and one-half years discharging the heavy responsibilities of the office, submitted his resignation to His Majesty the King on March 3, which received royal acceptance. The King gratefully acknowledged the past services of the Prime Minister and requested Sardar Mohammad Daoud to continue to serve until the formation of a new government. His Excellency, Dr. Mohammad Yousuf, the Minister of Mines and Industries, has been asked to form a new government. At the time of his resignation, Sardar Mohammad Daoud presented His Majesty with several proposals for stabilizing the social conditions in the country and improving the administrative structure. After further study the new government is expected to incorporate these suggestions into future policies.

Thus the decade of Daoud ended—or at least dramatically paused. After thirty years of tutelage, King Mohammad Zahir Shah exhibited a strength few realized he possessed, but, because of his liberal inclina-

554

tions, he may never rule in the absolute sense. The change in govern-ment did not come as a surprise (except to certain members of the for-eign colony), for the King had slowly consolidated his power over the past few years and often acted as a moderating force on those Afghans who wanted to align their nation with either the Soviet Union or the West.

For ten years, Sardar Daoud ruled and consolidated his strength through the army and the police. During the decade of Daoud, however, a slow, accretionary broadening of the base of power developed. King Mohammad Zahir Shah, with a cousin and age peer as Prime Minister, took a more active role in decision-making, as did Sardar Mohammad Naim, Foreign Minister, Second Deputy Prime Minister, and brother of Sardar Daoud. In addition, Prime Minister Daoud reached outside the royal family and even outside the Pushtun ethnic group for cabinet ministers and advisers.[14] Decisions, although the Prime Minister had the final say (as does the American President on such things as foreign policy matters), were announced after theoretically open discussions, but few cabinet members chose to disagree with the dynamic, dogmatic Sardar Daoud. When the time came for the 1963 change, a large group of Afghan influentials, in and out of the royal family, became involved in the ultimate decision.

Besides, during the 1953–63 decade, the King made his presence known to the Afghan people. He traveled widely and mingled paternally with the population.[15] I have visited many remote villages in Afghanis-tan where the people speak fondly of a visit by the King. Before the King's appearance, some villagers believed that Habibullah (1901–19) or Amanullah (1919–29) still ruled the country.

More than anything else, I think the traditions of the Afghan *jirgah* (village or tribal council) carried Afghanistan safely over its post-1933 internal power crises. Few secret family plots affected Sardar Daoud while he was Prime Minister. The King, and others concerned, consulted him at each stage of the planning of the 1963 changeover, in keeping with the *jirgah* tradition.

The Afghan changeover on March 9, 1963, stands out as a civilized

[14] Mohammad Wali Khan, a Tajik, had served as Prime Minister and in other cabinet positions (as well as Regent) during the reign of King Amanullah, however.

[15] The laxity of Afghan police in protecting the King's person shocked the American Secret Service when President Eisenhower visited Kabul in December, 1959. Mobs of friendly Afghans swarmed all over the car in which the King and President Eisenhower traveled.

exception when compared with the recent bloody uprisings in the Middle East and other Afro–Asian areas. The shift in prime ministers, orderly and bloodless, was the result of a position of strength, not weakness, and a cold recognition and acceptance of the necessity for change.

Some may wonder why the usually volatile Afghans accepted the changeover so peacefully or, more important, why Sardar Daoud moved aside without an overt fight. His swansong proved to be a gentlemanly model of outgoing speechmanship. Few strong men in history voluntarily give up political power, especially if they have the means to continue their control, and Sardar Daoud had the means: the Afghan army and air force. Sardar Daoud, a professional soldier and a very active Minister of Interior before his tenure as prime minister, shaped the Afghan armed forces in his own image. He modernized (relative to its previous condition) the military institution with Russian assistance. He brought many non-Pushtun into the officer corps and promoted men loyal to his person to high positions. He improved pay and living conditions, still woefully inadequate for the bulk of enlisted men serving in the provinces, however; but in the capital, Kabul, the seat of power, army and air force personnel now live much better than before 1953. The armed forces proved their loyalty to Sardar Daoud several times when threats arose during the decade, during the Qandahar riots and the Mangal revolt of December 1959, for example. And yet, when the time for decision came, Sardar Daoud did not use the army to remain in power.

Why?

In my opinion, Sardar Daoud stepped down for the good of the nation, a most remarkable feat for a strong man in a developing society. He fully realized that his presence made normal relations with Pakistan difficult if not impossible. In addition, I think he actually thought he would be brought back to political power by means of the free elections he envisioned for Afghanistan eventually (L. Dupree, *AUFS Reports,* LD-3-59,3; LD-5-60,10).

Despite all the criticisms, internal and external, directed at Sardar Daoud and his policies, I feel he will be remembered as one of the truly great figures in modern Afghan history, along with Amir Abdur Rahman Khan (1880–1901), who began the consolidation of Afghanistan into a nation-state. Sardar Mohammad Daoud brought Afghanistan quickly, and at times brutally, into a program of modernization. In the short period of a decade, Afghanistan moved from relative inaction to relative action. The modernization cannot be stopped; only the direction and rate of the changes he instituted can be affected by subsequent governments.

The solid achievements of his regime are many: a reaffirmed nonaligned (*bi-tarafi*) policy brought in increased foreign aid, both from East and West, and greatly speeded up the construction of an Afghan economic infrastructure (roads, airfields, river ports, communication networks); the status and morale of the armed forces improved; educational opportunities increased manyfold; the ultra-conservative, anti-progressive religious elements lost much of their secular power; regional economic planning spurred additional development; the political base of power broadened, and each municipality election in Kabul became comparatively more democratic (L. Dupree, *AUFS Reports*, LD-7-63,12). He also raised the still woefully inadequate pay of civil servants.

Although most of Sardar Daoud's achievements relate to the economic establishment, probably his most important legacy was the voluntary removal of the veil from the women, a move which struck at the roots of ultra-conservative Islam and directed urban women toward the mainstream of Afghan life. Many Afghans accuse Sardar Daoud of neglecting social and political reforms and overemphasizing the economic development programs which put Afghanistan deeply in the red (economically, not politically). One influential Afghan said: "Sardar Daoud could see clearly the goals of his programs, but he wore blinders which kept him from seeing the side effects which would occur along the way."

Most of Sardar Daoud's shortcomings relate to his emotional attachment to the "Pushtunistan" issue and his violent temper, characteristic of many great men in history. The closure of the Pakistan–Afghanistan border by Sardar Daoud's government, justified in the eyes of proud Afghans, rates as a major mistake. This move seemingly pushed the reluctant Afghans closer to the Soviet camp, and many Westerners and Afghans continue to worry (sometimes overly so) about the Soviet penetration of Afghanistan.

Most of Daoud's advisers were afraid to oppose his wishes in the cabinet or at informal meetings. Because of this, many of his ideas went unchallenged or subordinates fed him false or slanted information: e.g., the fallacy that all segments of the Pakistani Pushtun population supported the "Pushtunistan" movement, when, in fact, only a few dissident groups did; the goals of the first Five Year Plan were far from fulfilled, yet the first reports to Sardar Daoud from his subordinates indicated completion or near completion.

Because of his personality and personal strength, Sardar Daoud remains a key figure in Afghan political affairs. His resignation, however, may well be remembered as his finest hour. He did not have to step down; the army would probably have supported him if he had given the word, but he chose to listen to the King and informal *jirgah* of family and advisers. The decade of Daoud may be over, but most of Sardar Daoud's policies live on. The world witnessed a strange, yet typically Afghan, performance in March 1963: a strong man stepped down from a position of strength for the good of the nation. The former Prime Minister can be seen even today as he walks alone near his home in Shahr-i-Naw, unescorted by guards, just as he used to take long drives with his driver only. Or he may be seen at Qargha Lake, a resort development for which he was largely responsible. The resort is used on every Afghan holiday by many in the Kabul population.

Sardar Daoud now rests and meditates, and occasionally talks politics with friends and members of his family. The King who reigned for thirty years now rules. The patience of King Mohammad Zahir Shah has been phenomenal, for seldom can one find kings or queens without the desire to rule, if it is within their capability. Quite probably the recent successes of the Shah of Iran inspired the Afghan King, just as Mustafa Ataturk influenced the unsuccessful modernizing efforts of the King Amanullah. But thirty-five years, two kings, and three prime ministers later, Afghanistan may prove ready for Amanullah's attempted reforms.

CHAPTER 24

The Constitutional Period Begins

1963–?

MARCH 10, 1963, came in sunny, bright, and clear. An unseasonable snow had fallen a few days before and the mountains shone like reflecting glass. All day people roamed the streets of Kabul and families walked about in a festive mood. Government offices remained open, but many civil servants left their desks to join the crowds briefly and then returned to their drudgery. Friends visited friends and discussion on the implications of Sardar Daoud's resignation raged far into the night. Some Afghans ostentatiously visited the homes of American and West German friends. Convinced that the West (i.e., C.I.A.) had somehow been behind it all (which, given the evidence at hand, I simply cannot believe) many opportunists wanted to curry favor. During the Daoud regime, few Afghans freely visited the homes of foreigners, most of which were kept under police surveillance, not only to check on visitors, but to protect the foreigners from theft and vandalism.

In many villages, illiterate peasants gathered around battery-powered transistor radios to hear the latest developments, and literates mobbed the newsstands in Kabul, established two years before, for copies of the government-controlled daily newspapers. No more than the normal complement of police roamed the city, and no signs of the army existed, no olive-drab trucks, no needlenosed tanks. Another quiet revolution, even quieter than the Pakistani revolution of October 1958 had occurred.

Most Afghans rejoiced at the King's announcement, but for many and varied reasons. The import-export fraternity and bazaar merchants looked forward to the reopening of the border and the reestablishment of normal trade relations to the south. The Afghanistan–Pakistan closure affected the in-transit shipments of U.S. A.I.D. items. Commercial smuggling, however, increased all along the frontier, and fantastic quantities of goods, including fresh fruits and vegetables from the Peshawar Valley, streamed into Kabul on camel and donkey, as well as in the false bottoms of trucks, all coming through the several unguarded or bribable passes which feed into Afghanistan. Entrepreneurs, businessmen with money to invest, hoped for an expansion of free enterprise activities.

The approximately 200,000 Afghan nomads who semiannually crossed and recrossed the frontier hoped they could once again follow their old migratory routes. This did not prove possible, however, and all have been integrated geographically inside Afghanistan, a painful, though necessary, process.

The Kabulis expected a drop in consumer prices after the border reopened. Prices since the 1961 closure had risen over one hundred percent on certain items, especially food.

Conservatives (especially religious leaders and their devout followers) predicted a return "to the principles of Islam," for Daoud Khan had always said, "Yes" to the Russians every time they mentioned an anti-Islamic reform. "Take the veil off the women," said the Russians. "Yes," said Daoud Khan. "Send the women to the offices and the factories," said the Russians. "Yes," said Daoud Khan. These religious conservatives probably became the most disappointed of all groups as the new government moved ahead with secular reforms.

The literate groups (mainly civil servants, students, and professional elements), however, sensed the speeding-up of social and political reforms, and in a burst of euphoria, talked excitedly about democratic processes and free elections.

The consensus was that Sardar Daoud had been good for the country, especially in economic development, but his usefulness ended when his stubbornness over the "Pushtunistan" issue closed the border.

Only three Afghan groups expressed immediate concern over Sardar Daoud's resignation: the violent "Pushtunistan" supporters; royal family members who had sinecures or who believed it a mistake to separate the family from ostensible government control; and those few army officers and intellectuals committed to the Soviet line. Many in these three groups had always been opportunists, however, and found it easy to switch alliances. Others, more sincere, have become a recognizable responsible opposition.

All Western diplomats rejoiced, especially the Americans and West Germans, because, they hoped, aid and commercial items would soon begin to reach Afghanistan via Pakistan. (For a period of eight weeks in 1963, beginning on January 29, the Afghans permitted the border to open so that American aid material piling up in Pakistan could enter the country. This special dispensation was given primarily as a friendly gesture to popular, departing Ambassador Henry Byroade, who had been replaced by John M. Steeves on January 24, 1963.)

The Iranians cheered the new developments in Afghanistan, because the Shah of Iran would probably claim some credit for bringing about a Pakistani–Afghan rapprochement should it occur, though some diplomats in Kabul believed that earlier Iranian efforts in this direction hindered more than helped. Naturally, Pakistan would be happy to reduce the tension along its vulnerable north-west frontier and to reestablish trade relations because both the government and private merchants suffered financially because of the border closure.

In the foreign camp, only the Soviet Union, its satellites, and the People's Republic of China did not initially welcome the change, and several high officials in the Soviet embassy were recalled to Moscow for consultations. They later returned. Some Soviet friends of long standing avoided Americans for several weeks, an attitude which changed after the Russians became convinced that the Daoud resignation was not the result of American interference. Mr. Khrushchev, along with other heads of states, sent congratulations to the new prime minister.

Dr. Mohammad Yousuf (Minister of Mines and Industries under Daoud), the new prime minister, searched for cabinet members. Many of those approached were understandably reluctant, especially since the new regime would represent a radical departure from the old system, for the King seriously meant to separate the royal family from the executive branch of government.

Dr. Yousuf finally announced his cabinet on March 13. Six members of the previous cabinet retained their positions, all but four of the total twelve had held previous cabinet posts; none could be considered members of the royal family; only four were Durrani (the tribe of the royal family); two were non-Pushtun (see Appendix G).

First and foremost, no arrests or executions occurred, and former Prime Minister Daoud received an abundance of laudatory comments conveyed by the government-controlled news media. Sardar Daoud's final message to the nation sounded very little like that of a man about to retire permanently. He paid tribute to the army, to the middle-range civil servants, and to the liberated women. He called for changes in the Constitution, an adequately enforced election law, and separation of the three branches of government. More important, his extremely mild statement on "Pushtunistan" surprised many: "At this time I offer my best feelings to our 'Pushtunistani' brethren and hope that the people of 'Pushtunistan' will succeed in the attainment of their sacred national aspirations." (L. Dupree, *AUFS Reports*, LD-7-63, 23.)

March 11 proved to be a day of great success for the outgoing Prime Minister. He talked to students and teachers, and made a special trip to the Womens' Institute where he received a tearful good-by and a handwritten copy of the *Qor'an*. Many of Kabul's non-literates heard about these meetings at second hand, or over the radio, and garbled reports of what Sardar Daoud said leaked all over town. On March 10, I had heard many in the bazaar referring to Sardar Daoud as a "bad man" and a "friend of the Russians." After his March 11 talks to students and women, these *same* detractors told me: "What a fine man Sardar Daoud is! He explained that we have to deal with the Russians because they are next door, very close [*besyar qarib*] to us, but our other friends are thousands of miles away. We must help ourselves, and even if we accept money and aid, we do not have to accept ideas. What a marvelous man Sardar Daoud is! He should have told us before that he would not allow the Communists to force us to forget Islam as they did in Central Asia. He is a fine man! He knows how to deal with the infidel!" Twenty-four hours can make a great deal of difference in the attitudes of the bazaars of the Middle East.[1]

On leaving office, Sardar Daoud articulated the reasons why he had acted as he did in a way clear enough for the non-literate urban worker to understand, no small achievement.

On the night of March 14, after the King had confirmed his cabinet, Prime Minister Yousuf delivered a radio speech to the nation outlining his government's policies, which largely resembled the policies of the previous regime. Dr. Yousuf paid high tribute to his predecessor and to the King, and then announced that a planned and guided economy would continue in most spheres, but "private enterprise will be further supported and encouraged in the framework of national economic policy." He emphasized the need for constitutional reforms and a more representative system of government. In foreign affairs he pledged to continue "the traditional policies of non-alignment and independence." His references to "Pushtunistan," like those of Sardar Daoud, were mild and non-inflammatory, and he obviously selected the Persian terms with care so as not to provoke the Pakistanis. In conclusion, he dealt in some detail with Afghanistan's relations with the Soviet Union, Iran, the Peo-

[1] Witness the 1953 turnabout in Tehran. The bazaar supported Mossadegh one day, the Shah the next (Avery, 1967, 438–39; Wise and Ross, 1965, 116, 121).

ple's Republic of China, the United States, India, Pakistan, West Germany, and the United Nations (L. Dupree, *AUFS Reports,* LD-7-63,24-27).

Everyone cheered Prime Minister Yousuf's first speech and waited expectantly for quick results, an unfortunate syndrome which affects developing nations. After centuries of virtual stagnation, many expect miracles over night, but miracles always bring pain to the mass of the people, while the slow, sure path usually brings frustrations to the literate minority.

From March 14 to March 28 a lull occurred—or rather, what appeared to be a lull to the public. In reality, the cabinet met time and again, discussing problems both in the general and in the specifiç sense. Was it possible for changes to be effectively introduced without revamping the whole administrative structure? How to abolish the stuffy law-and-order, government-by-signature bureaucracy which slowed down the simplest requests for action?

The interim government made several important announcements, however. On March 18, the Ministry of Finance announced fiscal reform with the afghani fixed internationally at forty-five to one U.S. dollar. A large grant ($5.6 million) from the International Monetary Fund helped in this adjustment. On March 20, the Ministry of Public Works announced that the Soviet Union and the United States had signed agreements to implement new road projects. On March 24, Ariana Afghan Airlines announced plans to purchase new aircraft in the United States and expand services. On March 26, the Ministry of Public Works announced that the United States would contribute another $1 million to complete construction of Kabul University. Although the new regime received credit for all this, negotiations on all had begun months previously, but such rapid-fire announcements did give the interim government a public boost.

While arguments raged over how to implement suggested reforms, intellectuals wondered if the Prime Minister would prove strong enough for the job. Action they wanted, and action now, and they knew a strong man was necessary to implement their desires. Afghan intellectuals, like many in the West, are quick to criticize inaction, until they themselves become involved in the action processes and see at first hand the complex problems and compromises involved in decision-implementing. Decision-making is always easier than decision-implementing.

The cabinet, quick to sense the growing discontent, made a series of announcements in late March and early April. On March 28, Dr.

Yousuf announced the formation of a committee to prepare a preliminary draft of constitutional changes. On the same day he held a press conference, attended by most members of the Ministry of Press and Information. Since the government controlled all news media in Afghanistan, many foreign observers ridiculed the press conference, but I feel that Dr. Yousuf and his press minister, Said Qassim Rishtya, wanted to prepare the ground for a non-controlled press within the next few months and the press conference served as a preliminary step. In addition, the daily *Anis* invited its readers to write letters on any topic for publication in a column called "Reminders." The unpublished letters probably revealed much more than those published. Several published letters were extremely critical, however. One letter, on April 2, took the municipal bus company sharply to task for its decision to charge school children for fares to and from school. Another letter, published on April 3, punched at the sanctity of Radio Afghanistan announcers: "Although I am not a newscaster, it is obvious to anyone that the announcers of Radio Kabul are substandard. Most of them make unnecessary pauses, emphasize the wrong word or phrases. In addition, I feel that the news readers have little confidence in what they are reading." This indirect slap at news censorship could not have been misread by many readers. Many letters discussed the meaning of "democracy," and related it to Afghanistan: most indicated preference for a "guided democracy led by benevolent leaders."

A long-awaited announcement came on March 31, when Dr. Yousuf ordered the Ministry of the Interior to appoint an investigating committee to report on prison conditions in Kabul and in the provinces. Anyone traveling extensively in Afghanistan in 1963 would have seen Afghan prisoners shackled in the most medieval conditions, would have witnessed the Afghan police, undereducated and underpaid (often simply draftees serving their two years national service), brutally beat prisoners into confession, for, as they would explain, "In Islamic law a man accused of a crime can be found guilty only if witnesses attest to the crime—or if he confesses." Bastinado (the beating of the soles of the feet), a most painful experience, was commonly employed. The penal concept of Afghanistan has always been to punish, not rehabilitate. A key sign of change occurred when the new government began to release political prisoners in early April.

On April 2, the Prime Minister announced the formation of a committee to coordinate activities in the development field. The committee included the Deputy Ministers of Commerce, Education, Finance, Planning, Public Health, Mines and Industries, plus the President of *Da*

Afghanistan Bank and the President of the Rural Development Department.

In theory, a man could resign from a government job whenever he chose, and anyone could obtain a passport, but implementation of these ideals had never been achieved. But the new regime promised prompt implementation. The prime minister also announced a twenty percent pay increase for government employees, thus taking a step in the right direction.

But to justify the resignation of Prime Minister Daoud, a new Pakistani–Afghan rapprochement had to be rapidly achieved. In the summer of 1962, the Shah of Iran had visited both countries and failed in his attempts at reconciliation. Now, however, both sides sent delegations to Tehran at the invitation of the Shah in late May 1963. On May 29, a communique was issued simultaneously from Tehran, Rawalpindi, and Kabul announcing the reestablishment of diplomatic and trade relations between Afghanistan and Pakistan. Both sides agreed to reopen embassies, and the Pakistanis reserved the right to reopen their consulates in Qandahar and Jalalabad when they thought it necessary; the Afghans opened their consulates and trade missions immediately. Both nations agreed to abide by the 1958 transit agreement. In addition, they agreed to approach all mutual problems in accordance with international law, and to continue "to create an atmosphere of good understanding, friendsihp, and mutual trust," an obvious allusion to hope-for Afghan moderation on the "Pushtunistan" issue.

The Afghan and Pakistani representatives praised the efforts of the Shah of Iran in the long negotiations, and the head of the Afghan delegation, Said Qassim Rishtya, Minister of Press and Information, stated that the development of a new in-transit route through Iran would continue.

Essentially, the Tehran agreement simply separated the political question of "Pushtunistan" from normal diplomatic and economic relations between Afghanistan and Pakistan.

Islam and the 1964 Constitution: Face-to-Face with the Twentieth Century

The most important achievement of the Interim Government was the promulgation of a new constitution, in my opinion, the finest in the Muslim world.

One of the King's first acts after the establishment of the Yousuf Cabinet was to appoint, on March 28, 1963, a constitutional committee of seven members to write a new liberalized constitution. (Actually, ex-Prime Minister Daoud had presented a draft constitution to the King when he resigned, and the committee used it as a working draft.) The committee included prominent Afghans from many walks of life: Sayyid Shamsuddin Majrooh (Minister of Justice), chairman; Said Qassim Rishtya (Minister of Press and Information); Dr. Mir Najmuddin Ansari (Adviser to Ministry of Education); Mohammad Moosa Shafiq (Director of Law Department, Ministry of Justice); Dr. Abdul Samad Hamed (Chief of Secondary Education, Ministry of Education); Hamidullah (Professor of Law and Political Science, Kabul University); Mir Mohammad Siddiq Farhang (Chief of Planning, Ministry of Mines and Industries). All these men were known to be reform-oriented, even though four (Majrooh, Rishtya, Shafiq, and Hamed) had held high positions in the Daoud government.

The Constitutional Committee held its first meeting on March 31, 1963, and the chairman appointed a subcommittee (Hamed, Hamidullah, Farhang, and Shafiq) to establish a reference library on constitutional law in the Ministry of Justice. The committee met almost daily over the next year, seeking opinions from Afghans of all occupational, ethnic, and social levels, as well as from many foreigners. A French constitutional expert came out to give advice, which gave rise to some good-natured joking from other Westerners: 'Afghanistan is seeking stability in government, so why choose a French adviser? Since 1789 France has had two monarchies, two empires, five republics, the Vichy interlude, and *fifteen* constitutions!"

Obviously, however, Afghan non-alignment could ill afford to ask officially for Russian or American advisers (although several were approached informally for comment), and Afghanistan's traditional—but fading—antagonism to Great Britain eliminated such renowned experts on constitutional law as Sir Ivor Jennings.

The committee completed its draft of the new Constitution in February 1964. King Mohammad Zahir then appointed a twenty-nine-person (including two women) Constitutional Advisory Commission to go over the draft carefully and make suggestions before calling a *Loya Jirgah* to approve. The twenty-nine members included a diversity of occupations, ethnic groups, and educational backgrounds, including several collateral members of the royal family, both liberal and conservative.

Two appointees, Professor Salahuddin Seljuki and Mir Ghulam Mohammad Ghubar, declined to serve because of ill health; both had been members of the 1949–52 liberal movement and the latter spent several

566

years in jail. Dr. Mohammad Asif Sohail (a former member of the Daoud cabinet and a known conservative) pleaded fatigue and personal reasons. But the other twenty-six members of the advisory commission, with Dr. Abdul Zahir (President of the National Assembly) as chairman, met with the seven-man constitutional committee from March 1 to May 1, 1964. The sessions were far from peaceful, with arguments centering around the role of the royal family and the extent to which it should be permitted to participate in political activities. The final result became the controversial Article 24.

The commission considered the draft of the new Constitution article by article in both Pashto and Persian, discussed possible changes, voted on the proposals (a simply majority could make alterations), and finally voted on each full article as revised.

Between the end of the deliberations of the commission and the convening of the *Loya Jirgah,* all Afghan press and radio media (entirely government-controlled) undertook the task of explaining the general concepts and specific points found in the Constitution. Since about ninety-five percent of the Afghans are still non-literate, broadcasts were obviously more important than newspapers and magazines in reaching the masses. The importance of the press should not be underestimated, however, because many literate Afghans continued to view the attempt to write a new Constitution with suspicion, or as simply another move to perpetuate the present regime with an improved façade of constitutionality. Thus it behooved those involved in the writing of the Constitution to demonstrate the sincerity of their efforts. The press campaign intensified as the time appointed for the *Loya Jirgah* approached.

The stage was set, the script written. Only the supporting cast remained to be selected, and the constitutional drama would unfold.

In the spring of 1964, King Mohammad Zahir Shah issued a *farman* which defined the composition of the constitutional *Loya Jirgah.* Each time a *Loya Jirgah* had met in the past, the reigning monarch decided who and how many should attend, usually packing the assembly with king's men. In order to give the 1964 *Loya Jirgah* the broadest possible representation, King Mohammad Zahir included the National Assembly, the Senate, the Cabinet, the Supreme Court, the Constitutional Committee, the Constitutional Advisory Commission, additional members to be elected from the provinces equal in number to the National Assembly, and, finally, members appointed at the King's discretion to insure adequate presentation of all points of view.

The government held indirect elections all over Afghanistan in mid-

August 1964. In Kabul, for example, a hundred Kabulis (ten from each of Kabul's ten wards) had been elected to represent the voters in the election of *Loya Jirgah* members. The hundred electors and the ten members of Kabul's Municipal Council met and elected two from among themselves as delegates to the *Loya Jirgah*. Technically, the same general procedure was followed throughout Afghanistan, but, as usual, government officials screened out potentially anti-government candidates, and many tribal units (especially in the Pushtun areas) selected members in an open *jirgah* (a village or tribal council). On the whole, however, delegates to the *Loya Jirgah* appeared to represent the full range of social, political, and religious opinion.

On August 30, the King appointed twenty-seven additional persons to the *Loya Jirgah,* including three retired generals, a group of well-known religious leaders, several professors (some of whom professed to be "Marxists" or leftists), government officials, and a free-enterprise banker. On the day the *Loya Jirgah* opened, His Majesty appointed three more religious leaders and four women: two principals of girls' schools, an archivist from the Foreign Ministry, and the publicity director of the Afghan Red Crescent (or Red Cross) Society.

Members elected or appointed to the *Loya Jirgah* totaled:

Elected members	176	
National Assembly (11th Session)	176	
Appointed by the King	34	(including 4 women)
Senate (an appointed body)	19	
Cabinet	14	
Supreme Court	5	
Constitutional Committee	7	
Constitutional Advisory Commission	24	(including 2 women)
	455	

Three *Loya Jirgah* members are included twice in this listing, so the total active membership was in fact 452. One of the women appointed by the King had a baby during the *Loya Jirgah,* so she was unable to participate in all sessions, which led to unofficial comments by several religious leaders on the superiority of men in legislative matters, though they granted the biological superiority of women.

A few days before the *Loya Jirgah* convened, the constitutional draft was published in Pashto, Persian, English, and French.

Delegates began to drift into Kabul several days before September 9. They came from the Pamir Mountains (the "Roof of the World" where Afghanistan touches Pakistan, the U.S.S.R., and China), the forested mountains of Nuristan, the Turkestan plains of the north, the rugged hills of Paktya in the east, the deserts of Baluchistan, and the central mountain core of Afghanistan, the Hazarajat. The men varied as much as the terrain: gray-bearded mullah with neatly tied white turbans and long, flowing robes; young men in natty Western clothes and rich *qarakul* hats; others reflecting the transitional period in which Afghans found themselves wore turbans, Western jackets and vests, Afghan shirts, pantaloons, and pointed Italian shoes. Distinctively embroidered turban caps identified various Uzbak, Tajik, Pushtun, and other ethnic groups; some wore sandals, some, boots.

Mongoloid Hazara, Uzbak, Turkoman, Kirghiz, and Aimaq mingled with Mediterranean-looking Pushtun, Tajik, Baluch, and there was a smattering of redheads and blonds with blue eyes, these mainly from Nuristan and its periphery. A babel of tongues was heard: Pashto, Persian, Baluchi, Hazaragi (a Persian dialect), and various Turkic and Nuristani dialects.

The government housed the out-of-town delegates in the compound of the Salamkhaneh, where the deliberations of the *Loya Jirgah* would take place. The delegates were also fed in the Salamkhaneh, not only for convenience but also for tighter government supervision and protection if (as some predicted) trouble broke out during the sessions. The Ministry of Communications offered the delegates free postal and telegraphic services inside the Salamkhaneh grounds, and the Ministry of Public Health provided free medical facilities. Administrative matters were the job of the Secretariat of the Constitutional Committee, originally appointed to handle administration and research for the committee. Some observers thought that the delegates might be isolated from the outside world by these kind attentions; but instead they wandered in and out of the Salamkhaneh, visiting and arguing with friends and relatives and inspecting the modern wonders of Kabul in the manner of convention-attenders anywhere in the world.

The rumor quotient (always high) in Kabul increased appreciably during the week preceding the first meeting of the *Loya Jirgah*. Most persistent rumors were of coups and counter-coups: the former supposedly to be instigated by members of the officer corps still loyal to ex-Prime Minister Sardar Mohammad Daoud, the latter supposedly to be the work of military elements loyal to the King. Genuine tension gripped the intelligentsia, and some openly predicted that Daoud and his followers would not permit the *Loya Jirgah* to convene.

Another rumor circulated that Daoud had requested permission to participate in the *Loya Jirgah* but that the King had refused. Furious, Daoud was said to have planned to make a dramatic appearance at the first session and be brought back to power by popular acclamation— which assumed that the mere presence of Daoud would panic the delegates into thinking he had seized power. Many foreigners, especially in the American colony, grew increasingly apprehensive as the time for the *Loya Jirgah* approached, and some announced that they planned to remain in the safety of their compounds on the opening day. However, a sizable number in the foreign community think they lead boring lives, and any excitement—real or imagined—is welcome.

In fact, September 9 went smoothly, as did the entire *Loya Jirgah.* Quite naturally, the government alerted the Central Forces in Kabul, which includes all army units from Kabul to the Pakistani frontier, and stationed enough troops in and near the Salamkhaneh to maintain order. Additional army units lined the road from Kabul to Paghman, a traditional summer resort where Daoud resided—a tribute to his power. As the days passed, however, the army withdrew most of the troops in and around Kabul, although maintaining an alert state. Cynics had insisted the presence of the troops would intimidate the delegates; but throughout the *Loya Jirgah,* from the first to the last, few delegates seemed cowed and arguments often became vitriolic.

Having found their assigned seats, the primly stiff delegates sat waiting for the King, talking in stage whispers while attendants passed among them with cigarettes, water, and tea. Several Western-educated members pulled reflectively on their pipes; religious leaders fingered their *tasbih* (prayer beads) and mumbled verses from the *Qor'an;* and a few old men with white beards slept. Electric fans whirred softly. The clothing, physical types, and dialectic chatter indicated that Central Asia, South Asia, the Middle East, and the Far East had met—a miniature United Nations, and with similar problems. The *jirgah* is typically a Pushtun custom, but most ethnic groups in Afghanistan have some kind of tribal, village, or regional council. A member of the secretariat read in Pashto the first formal instructions to the delegates: "The King will enter at 10 A.M., so all will rise," etc. I wondered how many in the *Loya Jirgah* understood Pashto, the language usually associated with Afghanistan.

Dr. Mohammad Yousuf, the Prime Minister, preceded the King by a few minutes and received a rousing acclamation. The King, wearing mufti, arrived at exactly 10 A.M., amid a wild standing ovation. A military band played the national anthem, and a religious leader (wearing Western clothes except for his white turban) recited briefly from the Qor'an.

The King rose to deliver his address, standing before a huge representation of the national seal of Afghanistan. In a calm, unhurried voice, the King delivered his ten-minute speech in Persian, a language of poetry rather than administration, of passion rather than logic. King Mohammad Zahir asked the delegates for their help and advice. He told them that Afghanistan was their country and that, with the help of Allah, both the country and its people would be better after the deliberations of the Loya Jirgah. His speech finished, the King departed, the applause of the delegates echoing in the Salamkhaneh. Mr. Mohammad Moosa Shafiq, chief of the secretariat and one of the major architects of the Constitution, then introduced retired General Ata Mohammad Tukhi from Mazar-i-Sharif in northern Afghanistan, the King's appointee as temporary vice-president of the Loya Jirgah. Throughout the sessions, Mr. Shafiq, American-educated and bilingual in Pashto and Persian as well as fluent in English, Arabic, and Urdu, proved indispensable to the proceedings.

General Tukhi, speaking in Persian, thanked the King for the honor and trust bestowed on him and then opened the floor for nominations to elect a permanent vice-president of the Loya Jirgah, the King being official president.

Professor Mohammad Asghar, the American-educated Mayor of Kabul and ex-president of Kabul University, nominated American-educated Dr. Abdul Zahir (the President of the National Assembly), who was conveniently seated in the front row. Two delegates (Professor Ghulam Sarwar Rahimi and Mohammad Ismail Mayar) gave brief seconding speeches, and a general acclamation for Dr. Zahir began to swell through the hall. Before General Tukhi could make it official, however, Mohammad Ibrahim, a religious leader and member of the prominent Mujadidi family, pushed forward to the microphone and delivered a short speech in the singsong style of the call to prayer, extolling the virtues of the King, "who has brought us to this day." He also catalogued a list of great Afghan historical figures from the past.

At 10:35 A.M. the Loya Jirgah unanimously proclaimed Dr. Zahir the vice-president and presiding officer. He strode to the president's desk, took the gavel from General Tukhi, called the session to order, appointed Moosa Shafiq to be Secretary to the Loya Jirgah, and introduced the Prime Minister, Dr. Mohammad Yousuf, who made a speech in Persian, lauding the Afghan nation and its rapid development. All through his speech the delegates listened politely, but without general interest. To all familiar with group behavior, the *Loya Jirgah* had become involved with the issues and was waiting for something to happen.

Moosa Shafiq read the Rules of Procedure in Pashto and Persian, and Dr. Zahir invited the delegates to consider each rule separately. The debating took place in either Persian or Pashto, as it did throughout the *Loya Jirgah*. Seldom did the Secretary bother—or, indeed, have time—to translate one into the other, and obviously some, though not many, of the delegates missed part of the discussions.

All but four of the rules passed unanimously. Many delegates argued that the five-minute maximum per delegate per article inhibited free discussion. With 128 articles and 452 delegates, however, the minimum time on each article, *if* every delegate chose to exercise his five minutes, worked out like this (not including procedural matters and voting): 452 delegates and 128 articles; five minutes per delegate per article; each article: 37.8 hours or 5.8 days, because the *Loya Jirgah* met for 6.5 hours each day; total for all 128 articles = 742.4 days, or more than two years! Ideally, only a few delegates would speak on each article. The *Loya Jirgah* did agree that after all who desired to do so had spoken about an article, anyone could be heard again.

Many members objected to the meeting time (Rule 9: daily hours, 9 A.M. to 12:30 P.M.; 2 P.M. to 5 P.M.). Some thought 8 A.M. a better starting time, and all the city folk shuddered; others suggested 9:30 A.M., at which the country people hooted in derision. None disagreed about the length of the lunch period, for time had been allotted for prayers. A woman delegate objected to the possibility of night meetings (Rule 9), at first pleading children as an excuse, and no one, even in Afghanistan, can argue against motherhood. She finally destroyed her own case, however, by stating that she had no car. Easily solved, said the presiding officer: "We will send a car for you."

The four disputed procedural rules were passed by majority vote, and the *Loya Jirgah* buckled down to the task of approving (and changing, where thought necessary) the 1964 Constitution, consisting (as published) of 11 titles and 128 articles, in 62 pages.[2]

---

[2] For a full text of the 1964 Constitution and brief commentary, see Wilber, 1965. In addition, for a detailed discussion of the day-by-day and article-by-article proceedings, see Vol. IX; South Asia Series, *AUFS Reports*, New York, 1965, articles by L. Dupree. Also, text of Constitution in Pashto, Dari, English, and French, published in 1964, by the Franklin Book Programs (Education Press), Kabul.

The titles of the Constitution are: I. The State; II. The King; III. The Basic Rights and Duties of the People (Fundamental Rights); IV. *Shura* (Parliament); V. The *Loya Jirgah* (Great National Council); VI. The Government; VII. The Judiciary; VIII. The Administration; IX. State of Emergency; X. Amendment; XI. Transitional Provisions.

From the initial discussion on the first article, it became obvious that this would never be a rubber-stamp *Loya Jirgah*. Most, though not all, of the fears of a docile, "stacked" assembly disappeared before the end of the first day. The rural delegates demonstrated their oratorical skills sharpened by years of practice in local *jirgah,* and flowery, effective, sustained imagery characterized many speeches. The Secretariat recorded the proceedings on tape, and when this became common knowledge after the *Loya Jirgah* ended, many believed that the tapes would be used to mark those opposing the passage of certain articles or encouraging amendments possibly unpopular with the King and the power elite. The tapes, however, have reportedly been placed in government archives for future study by scholars; but the possibilities of future repression cannot be ignored.

Another factor in the debates surprised some observers: the intensity with which the delegates defended individual rights. The framers of the Constitution thought the *chapanwalla* (delegates from outside Kabul, so-called because many wore the brightly striped, traditional overcoats called *chapan*) would strictly adhere to ethnic or tribal group loyalties at the expense of the rights of the individual.

The first day's argument convinced the *Loya Jirgah* that it should not expect an unanimous approval of the Constitution at the end of the deliberations. The members agreed to permit dissenters to put their opinions in writing. The 1964 *Loya Jirgah,* therefore, became the first literate *Loya Jirgah*. Previously, members had only a "yes" or "no" vote after thoroughly discussing the issues at hand.

Conservative religious leaders attending the *Wolesi Jirgah* were argued down point after point by the finely trained Afghan mullahcum-lawyers. In addition, the King held interviews with those conservatives who continued to fight various secular-oriented articles. A combination of flattery, cajolery, and partly veiled threats won over most recalcitrants. Some never wavered in their opposition, however.

The first day ended with the delegates tired, pleased, and in an anticipatory mood. The constitutional committee and the advisory commission had been surprised, but not displeased, with the vigor displayed in the debates on both major and minor points. All foresaw crucial struggles shaping up, but the constitutional committee preferred not to enter into the debates except to clarify technical points. Often the *chapanwalla* posed practical and personalized questions concerning the technical language, and these individualized queries sometimes grew into lengthy speeches as the *Loya Jirgah* moved along. At times, speakers ran over the allotted five minutes, and the presiding officer wisely permitted them free rein unless the speaker wandered too far afield. Although several microphones were conveniently scattered throughout the Salamkhaneh, most speakers preferred to stride to the front microphone and face the bulk of the audience.

On September 9, 1931, King Mohammad Nadir Shah had convened a National Assembly at the Salamkhaneh to give Afghanistan a constitution. Now his son, King Mohammad Zahir Shah, inaugurated a new attempt. On the night of September 9, 1964, a crescent moon, sign of good favor, shone over Kabul.

Let us examine a few of the more important articles of the 1964 Constitution, finally approved by the *Loya Jirgah* on September 19, after 11 days of intensive deliberation.

Articles 1 and 2 state that "Afghanistan is a constitutional monarchy; an independent, unitary and indivisible state;" and that "Islam is the sacred religion of Afghanistan." Unlike the 1931 Constitution which made the Hanafi Shari'a the state religion, the 1964 Constitution simply prescribes that the state shall conduct its religious ritual according to the Hanafi school (Article 1, Paragraph 3). The 1964 Constitution also guarantees freedom of worship to non-Muslims "within the limits determined by law, decency and public peace" (Article 2, Paragraph 2). The one non-Muslim *Loya Jirgah* member, a Hindu from Kabul, expressed satisfaction with this article, but hoped that laws concerning minority groups would keep the spirit of the Constitution.

The tightly-defined (when compared to the 1931 Constitution) royal succession (Articles 16–23) represents a great stride toward stability. Naturally, however, the possibility that a dissident faction of the royal family may at some time stage a coup cannot be completely disregarded. Article 16 attempts to eliminate potentially competing lineages from having legal access to the throne, and stipulates that the kingship "will be carried on in the House of His Majesty Mohammad Nadir Khan Ghazi (the Martyr), in accordance with the provisions of this Constitution."

The succession "on the King's abdication [discussed and defined in Article 17] or death" passes to his eldest son, or if the eldest son lacks the "qualifications set forth in this Constitution, the throne shall pass on to his second son, and so on" (Article 18). Much argument raged about the word "qualifications." Who decides? What are the necessary qualifications, other than that the king be an Afghan national and an Hanafi Muslim, as stipulated in Article 8? Various members of the constitutional committee tried to explain the intricacies of legal and psychological qualifications in terms of psychotic and anti-social behavior to the *chapanwalla*. The committee lamely admitted the dangers of leaving the word undefined, but decided that it would be even more dangerous to define it tightly in the Constitution. "Let us leave it to the common sense of the Afghan people," they urged.

Another objection (with the not too distant past in mind) arose: What if the second son kills or incapacitates the first? One delegate suggested an amendment which would deprive the second, or any other, son of the throne if he killed the crown prince. Some insisted that murder would always be covered under Islamic law, and others said that criminal law would obviously take care of the case. A few pointed out that an amendment such as this would make Afghanistan appear savage and ridiculous in the eyes of the rest of the world. If a murderer proclaimed himself king with the support of the army, however, he could possibly claim immunity under Paragraph 1 of Article 15: "The King is not accountable." The arguments could not be resolved, so the presiding officer appointed an *ad hoc* committee to study the matter and report back to the *Loya Jirgah*. (The committee later recommended that Article 18 be accepted as written, to which the *Loya Jirgah* agreed.)

If a king dies without a son or qualified heir, the throne goes to his eldest brother, or if the eldest brother' lacks the necessary "qualifications," to the second brother, etc. With no living qualified sons or brothers to succeed the king, a successor is to be elected from among the other "male lineal descendants of His Majesty Mohammad Nadir Shah the Martyr" by an electoral college consisting of the *Loya Jirgah* the cabinet, and the supreme court, to be convened by the prime minister within fifteen days of the king's death or, in the event of abdication, within seven days after the effective date. A majority vote of those present (plus the consent of the person chosen) elects a new king (Article 19). The Minister of the Royal Court serves as regent until the election.

To the surprise of many and the horror of some, a delegate asked why the throne should not go to the eldest daughter of the king if no qualified males exist. Another *chapanwalla* answered, "This is a wild idea, impractical to consider now," and there the matter ended. Still, the mere fact that the question arose indicated a sophistication many observers never thought possible. Eventually, the Afghans will probably amend or write a new Constitution to make it possible for a woman to suceed to the throne.

One of the key articles in the entire Constitution is Article 24, which was debated for more than two hours. The Article defines the royal family and describes its role:

1. The Royal House is composed of the sons, daughters, brothers, and sisters of the King and their husbands, wives, sons, and daughters; and the paternal uncles and the sons of the paternal uncles of the King.

2. In the official protocol of the state, the Royal House comes after the King and Queen.

3. The expenditure of the Royal House shall be fixed in the budget of the Royal Expenses.

4. Titles of nobility are exclusively confined to the Royal House and shall be assigned in accordance with the provisions of the law.

5. *Members of the Royal House shall not participate in political parties* [my italics], and shall not hold the following offices: Prime Minister or Minister; Member of Parliament; Justice of the Supreme Court.

6. Members of the Royal House shall maintain their status as members of the Royal House as long as they live.

Three basic amendments were proposed from the floor. The first would have extended the definition of the royal family to include maternal and paternal aunts of the king, their husbands, and children, and the maternal uncles of the king, their wives, and children. The *Loya Jirgah* defeated this proposal.

The second amendment relates to Paragraph 5, into which the *Loya Jirgah* incorporated a new introductory phrase (see the italicized portion above). More than ten members opposed the amendment, and many literate Afghans have given the provision additional thought. A nation with five percent literacy can ill afford to let any literate manpower remain idle, and intelligent political activity cannot exist without qualitatively literate leaders. Of course, members of the royal family may serve in the various ministries (even as deputy ministers), in the diplomatic corps, and in the military, so they will not be lost to government service; but many Afghans now consider it regrettable that this blanket rule eliminated certain talented, peripheral individuals in the royal family.

Actually, someone suggested that the amendment include "political activity" as well as "political parties," but legal experts on the constitutional committee explained the difficulties of defining "activity," which, if stretched sufficiently, could include discussions at cocktail parties.

The third amendment added Paragraph 6 to the Article, and covers the possibility that a commoner may marry into the royal family and then be divorced or be widowed. Such a person remains by definition a member of the royal house and therefore cannot participate in political parties.

On the night of September 10, several parties were given by Afghans to celebrate the passage of Article 24. Many believed that it would have rough going in the *Loya Jirgah,* because of Daoud Khan's continuing popularity among certain tribal and ethnic elements. With the relatively easy passage of Article 24, however, much of the tension went out of the *Loya Jirgah*—although many arguments lay ahead.

Under Title III, the Constitution lays down the fundamentals of social justice, equality before the law, personal liberty, protection of private property, freedom of thought and expression, the right to educational and health facilities, and the right to form political parties.

Long arguments ensued over words and phrases, many of which, such as "liberty and dignity of the human being" and "innocence is the original state," were new to Afghan jurisprudence. Some thought that the section was anti-Islamic; others thought that it was unnecessary; and still others wanted to use more precise definitions. Finally, the *Loya Jirgah* agreed to a significant change in Article 26, Paragraph 16 which originally read: "No Afghan shall be sentenced to banishment from Afghanistan." To banish a man from his tribe or nation cuts him off from an intricate system of economic, social, and political rights and obligations, and literally makes him an outcast. In addition, several older members of the *Loya Jirgah* remembered the forced migrations of the Abdur Rahman period (1880–1901), and even later, when whole segments of anti-government tribal groups were moved bodily from one point in the country to another. To prevent such collective punishment in the future, the *Loya Jirgah* added the following final phrase to Paragraph 16: " . . . or within its territory," in spite of the fact that the constitutional committee had thought this a purely legislative issue.

Article 27, a single line—"No Afghan accused of a crime can be extradited to a foreign state."—brought argumentation. The issue was not the essence of the article; discussion revolved about the meaning of the term "Afghan," which had been argued previously in the *Loya*

Jirgah and would be again. Several women delegates entered the fray for the first time. One insisted that "women" should be specifically mentioned, but finally withdrew her proposal after the constitutional committee assured her that the word "Afghan" embraced both sexes. The emphasis on the legal equality of women is one of the more important aspects of the 1964 Constitution.

In the legal terminology of the Constitution, "Afghan" refers to all citizens of Afghanistan, but to most citizens the word means the Pushtun ethnic group, which makes up probably less than fifty percent of the population. The minority groups, therefore, insisted on a definition which would, once and for all time, declare *all* native peoples, not only Pushtun, to be Afghan. No satisfactory definition could be reached, even after four hours of heated debate, so the presiding officer reminded the *Loya Jirgah* that a committee had been appointed on the first day to consider the problem. He then appointed two additional members from the floor to assist in the committee's deliberations and then closed off the debate. (The *ad hoc* committee suggested the following sentence be added to Article 1, Paragraph 3, "the word Afghan shall apply to each such individual." The *Loya Jirgah* approved the definition.)

Other arguments occurred over Paragraph 5 of Article 37, theoretically another extremely important section: "Forced labor even for the benefit of the state is not permissible. The prohibition of forced labor shall not be so construed as to effect the implementation of laws governing the organization of collective work for the public interest." This wording seems somewhat contradictory, and many delegates said so, protesting that the so-called "collective work for public interest" often actually means for the interests of government officials, and many examples of such abuses were passionately and eloquently presented. Paragraph 5 passed, but by a narrow margin, the closest vote of the entire *Loya Jirgah*. Few Afghans believed that the custom of "collective work for public interest" (i.e., forced labor) would immediately disappear, but the Ministry of the Interior has been vigorously attacking the problem, dismissing any official caught in such practices.

Article 63 gives the king the unqualified right to dissolve Parliament at any time and for any reason. Several questioned these far-reaching powers. One delegate asked: "Why not give His Majesty the power to adjourn Parliament for a period of time, but not to dissolve it?" Another asked why no time limit had been placed on the dissolution before a new Parliament must be convened. Most delegates, however, for various reasons, preferred not to question this Article and the king was left with

578

the ultimate power to dissolve Parliament if and when it was considered necessary.

Article 69, another extremely important article, brought on a long discussion of legal and philosophical points. This article reads: "Excepting the conditions for which specific provisions have been made in this Constitution, a law is a resolution passed by both Houses [of Parliament], and signed by the King. In the area where no such law exists, the provisions of the Hanafi jurisprudence of the *Shari'a* shall be considered as law."

Immediately after the reading of Article 69, several religious leaders demanded to know why the Hanafi *Shari'a* had been placed in a secondary position to secular laws. The secretary patiently explained (ironically, to his own father, a respected religious leader) that Article 64, Paragraph 2 ("There shall be no law repugnant to the basic principles of the sacred religion of Islam. . . .") covered repugnancy to Islam for all time. Only a few of the more traditionalist mullahs voted against Article 69, a great triumph for the new breed of liberal religious thinkers in Afghanistan.

The writers of the 1964 Afghan Constitution used Islam as a weapon against the traditionalists. The implacable attitude of former Prime Minister Sardar Mohammad Daoud toward the conservative religious leaders helped to smother potential opposition from these quarters during the constitutional *jirgah*. Prime Minister Daoud had not hesitated to use his military base of power to smash any opposition, secular or religious, to his modernization plans. Religious leaders at the *Loya Jirgah* remembered this, and for the most part limited their comments to technical points. They often made long, involved, clarifying statements, sometimes surprisingly objective in the modernist sense.

Islamic modernists in Afghanistan accept the principle that *ijtihad* (legal decision based on knowledge and reason) holds precedence over the hardening of the legal arteries which occurred in Islam about a thousand years ago, when *qiyas 'aqli* (logical deduction by analogy) and *qiyas shar'i* (legal deduction by analogy) made it possible for a Muslim judge to reach a verdict (opinion or *zann*) in a case (*qadiya*) without considering changed social conditions or legal decisions other than the analogs.

Multi-interpretation, however, represents an essential feature of Islam (Gibb, 1962, 3–46; also see Coulson, 1964), illustrated by the fact that each of the two major divisions (Sunni and Shi'a) is further subdivided into several *Shari'a*. Modernist Islamic thinkers in Afghanistan consider themselves the intellectual heirs of the ninth and tenth centuries A.D. Baghdadi scholars. They believe Islamic jurisprudence must operate at two levels: the basic dogma (the ideals or essence) *and* attendant laws and interpretations based on actual cases in order to translate the ideals into reality. To accomplish these goals, the writers of the Constitution also drafted laws to reorganize the country along completely secular lines. A National Center for Legislation in the Ministry of Justice continues to examine all existing laws to determine which ones are unconstitutional or un-Islamic.

Deliberations on Title VII ("The Judiciary") became lengthy and heated. Some may think it strange that so much time should be spent on a simple two-line introduction: "The Judiciary is an independent organ of the state and discharges its duties side by side with the legislative and executive organs." Previously, the judicial branch had been semi-religious and semi-secular, with the hundred-odd *qazi* (religious judges) often semi-trained, but each having the power of life and death in the small seal he always carried with him. The power of these personalized seals (each *qazi* had one especially designed for himself) can be illustrated by the following incident. In 1959, while touring north Afghanistan, I had long talks with several *qazi* in various towns. I asked one if he would place his seal in my notebook so I would have a sample for my records. He took out his seal and ink pad, moistened the seal with his breath and inked it, poised it over an empty page—and then stopped in mid-air. "I cannot," he said, "for if I place my seal in your book, the book becomes a legal document and whatever it says can be used in courts of law. Maybe you have written that I owe you 50,000 afghanis. If so, you could collect. No. I cannot do it." But he did permit me to copy the inscriptions on his seal, which consisted of his name, his position, the administrative area for which he was responsible, and verses from the *Qor'an*.

The debate on the judiciary in the *Loya Jirgah* followed three lines of reasoning. One group (of conservative religious leaders) defended the old system of administering justice under the *Shari'a* (code of Muslim law), while another group of religious leaders (the tame mullahs under the influence of the government) defended the new concept of an independent judiciary. The third group (the bulk of the *Loya Jirgah*) attacked the old system and its inequities, and pressured for a new system with additional guarantees for individual rights.

Over forty members gave speeches. The attacks on the *qazi* system became vicious, with most delegates flavoring their comments with personal reminiscences. Long applause followed the many recitations of judicial capriciousness and callousness, and tears flowed openly when a man told how he had lost his wife to another man who had successfully bribed a *qazi*. Still others told of the use of bastinado to obtain confessions. "The judiciary only wanted victims; every crime had to be solved!" cried a delegate. Case after case illustrated these inequities. No patterns existed, and it was clear that the harassed, poorly-paid *qazi* often did accept bribes and render dissimilar decisions in similar cases.

Theoretically, the *qazi* made decisions under the Hanafi *Shari'a*, but in the time of King Mohammad Nadir Shah (1929–33), law increasingly moved into the hands of provincial administrators. Law evolved along two convergent lines: *haq-ul-Allah* (Rights of the State and Religion) and *haq-ul-'abd* (Rights of the Individual). A case first went to a *qazi* who gave his judgement on the *haq-ul-Allah*. The local provincial council, including the governor and his staff, as well as the *qazi,* could change the decision in accordance with the growing body of secular law. Such procedures often confused the issue and undermined the prestige and power of the *qazi*. A *qazi,* for example, might sentence a thief to have his hand cut off, and the provincial council would overrule this punishment and send the offender to prison for ten years. After the promulgation of the 1964 Constitution, all legal decisions have been transferred (at least theoretically) to the *qazi,* but secular law has supremacy.

For their part, the *qazi* have been undertrained, overworked, and poorly-paid. The legal minds of Afghanistan have not come from the Western-oriented Faculty of Law and Political Science of Kabul University, but rather from the conservatively oriented (in the religious, legalistic sense) Faculty of Theology. The Faculty of Law and Political Science, which is the prestige faculty, previously produced candidates for the diplomatic service rather than the law. However, some of the faculty's graduates actually entered the Ministry of Justice for the first time in 1964: fifteen in jurisprudence, ten in commercial law.

The Ministry of Justice founded a training center in 1964 to help the *qazi* improve their foreign-language capabilities (Arabic, English, French), and to provide courses in the practical nature of the new secular laws. Clerks are also instructed in how to fill out the new legal forms and petitions. Many of the top *qazi* go abroad on in-training fellowships, established to enable them to adapt a secular outlook more easily. A dozen went to Australia for six months under the Colombo Plan and then on to London. Thirty traveled to the United Arab Republic for three months to observe secular court procedures in another Muslim country. Others toured the United Kingdom, West Germany, and the United States.

The founding of a bar association represented another advance. In 1965, only sixteen western-trained lawyers existed in Afghanistan and they all worked (at least part-time) for the Ministry of Justice.

A judicial law, designed to establish the institutions necessary to implement Article 97, was passed by the new parliament in October, 1965. The law technically separates the judiciary from the Ministry of Justice as specified in the Constitution, and attacks the chronic problems of the current system: the inadequate legal training of judges, the lack of adequate accommodations (fewer than 20 of the currently functioning 273 courts have adequate building facilities, and often the judge must use a mosque or rent a house), and the lack of competent clerical staffs. Another important innovation in the new law concerns the admissibility of police evidence. Previously, the courts could reject police reports on a case being tried, and usually for good reason, because Afghan police have been notorious for extracting confessions from those arrested for crimes. Provincial police sometimes kept suspects in jail for six months or longer, so that a man often served his time *before* being presented to a judge. The new law requires booking on a charge and a preliminary hearing within specified time limits. The Ministry of Justice has also instituted courses to acquaint police (a limited number in urban areas, however) with the new procedures of arrest and detention.

In the past (again theoretically, for in practice bribery and the relative influence of the accused played important roles in judicial decisions), a three-tiered court system existed. This consisted of the preliminary courts (which handled most cases) in the subprovinces; the appellate courts in the provincial capitals; and the supreme court in Kabul. Appeals could be made on two counts: legalistic (the substance of the case) and personal (the conduct and character of the presiding judge). In practice, appeals could be—and often have been—taken as high as the prime minister or even the king.

Afghan courts have long been under fire for corruption, nepotism, favoritism, and inconsistency in rendering judgments. With new laws, the Ministry of Justice hopes to establish effective procedures for inspection in order to take the necessary disciplinary action against corrupt judges and officials. To help counter corruption, salaries have been raised, the number of clerks (the ideal, of course, is that they be trained) increased, and additional courthouses constructed. The ideals behind these moves, however, may not be realized in the lifetime of the youngest signer of the 1964 Constitution.

It is probable that Dr. Zahir purposely let the debate on Title VII run its lengthy, provocative, emotionally violent course in order to show the conservative religious leaders the depth of the threats to their secular power. Again, and sadly, the *chapanwalla* often does not differentiate between Islam, the eternal religion, and its interpreters, the religious leaders. The hope remains that, as Afghanistan's very secularized Constitution begins to function, religious leaders will confine most of their activities to souls instead of minds. They can be expected, however, to continue to resist laws which cut into their vested interests (e.g., those concerning education, land tenure, the emancipation of women, etc.).

In my opinion, Article 102 is the most important in the 1964 Constitution: "The courts in the cases under their consideration shall apply the provisions of this Constitution and the laws of the state. Whenever no provision exists in this Constitution or the laws for a case under consideration, the courts shall, by following the basic principles of the Hanafi jurisprudence of the *Shari'a* of Islam and within the limitations set forth in this Constitution, render a decision that in their opinion secures justice in the best possible way."

It is noteworthy that Article 102 enjoins the courts to consider cases in the light of the "Constitution and the laws of the state," and mentions the Hanafi *Shari'a* as a last resort. In effect, Article 102 (with Article 69, which deals with legislation) makes Afghanistan essentially a secular state, even while paying lip-service to Islam throughout. The essence of Islam, however, permeates the whole Constitution, and the action component articles (the executive, legislative, and judiciary articles) embody secularization *without* divorcing them from the values expressed in Islam.

Predictably, conservative religious leaders rose to question the order of precedence in Article 102. Immediately, however, they sensed the electric tension brought about by and hostile to their questioning, and insisted that they had doubts about the wording merely and not the concept. The Article passed almost unanimously.

Many thought that the passage of Article 102 took the *Loya Jirgah* over its final emotional hurdle, but the arguments which followed during the remainder of discussion of Title VII proved this assumption false The reason, in my opinion, is that Article 102, as important as it is, deals with the *theoretical* basis of law, whereas the rest of Title VII defines the role of individuals implementing the law. In this sphere the *chapanwalla* had had extensive, often painful, experiences, and they continued to dwell on the specifics of the past and their relationship to the possible specifics of the future.

Article 103, in particular, worried many delegates. It states that crimes will be investigated by the attorney general. A new law elaborately and precisely defines the office of the attorney general. Investigations and fear of investigations play an integral part in the relationships among the Afghan government, its employees, and the Afghan people. Each ministry has an investigative branch to check on its internal affairs. The King's secretariat maintains a section to keep constant check on plots or rumors of plots against the royal house, and the secretariat of the Prime Minister has a similar branch to check on plots against the government. In the past, some of these special investigative branches, both in method and result, have smacked of the classic procedures of totalitarian secret police.

After the March 1963, change of government, the new council of ministers, encouraged by the King, had tried to soften the reality and image of the investigative branches, and Article 103 embodies these attempts in the Constitution. Questions from the floor included: "What will happen to the ministries' investigative sections?"; "Why not place the attorney general in the Ministry of Justice?"; "Why does the state need a public attorney?"; and "What will be the relationship between the Ministry of Justice and the attorney general?"

Under Article 103 (which eventually passed), the attorney general forms a part of the executive, presumably independent of the judiciary, whose members will not institute legal proceedings against individuals or groups, but serve as presiding officers at hearings and trials. The legal differentiation between crime (committed against the state or society in general) and tort (wrongful act which brings civil action between individuals or groups) will come later.

Under Article 126, the government was enjoined to prepare ordinances relating to "elections, basic organization of the state, the press, and judicial organization and jurisdiction . . . to prepare draft bills relating to political parties and Provincial Councils, and submit them to Parliament."

Many delegates insisted that political parties should be permitted to participate in the first parliamentary elections; but the constitutional committee argued that parties should evolve slowly during the tenure of the first elected parliament, that the important Political Parties Bill should be presented to parliament and not issued as an arbitrary ordinance without searching prior discussions. Other members of the *Loya Jirgah* argued against political parties, citing the troubles of many Afro–Asian countries. Twenty-seven delegates (mainly urban intellectuals) voted against Article 126, and the grumbling continues to the present day.

Article 127 called for the creation of a functioning supreme court on 22 *Mizan* 1346 (October 14, 1967). A paragraph added to the article by the *Loya Jirgah* gave the King the authority to "take necessary measures for securing the performance of the functions of the Supreme Court" until 1967. (King Mohammad Zahir Shah did appoint a supreme court—*Istra-Makhmeh*—on October 15, 1967, thus completing the formation of the governmental trinity; executive, legislative, judicial branches now function, theoretically, as equal and relatively separate partners.)

The final article (Article 128) passed quickly on the eleventh day of debate. It gave the interim government the responsibility of examining laws now in existence and determining if any are "repugnant to the provisions of this Constitution."

The end of the sessions came suddenly and surprised everyone. For a few moments, the stunned delegates hardly seemed able to decide what to do. History had been made, and no one quite wanted to end the euphoric feeling of participation.

Quickly, the vice-president and presiding officer of the *Loya Jirgah,* Dr. Abdul Zahir, and the secretary recovered. They asked the *ad hoc* committees appointed to consider four amendments to make their reports, which were all approved by the *Loya Jirgah.* With time still left Dr. Zahir decided to present a statement on "Pushtunistan" from the cabinet for the consideration of the *Loya Jirgah.* The statement proved much milder than the bellicose 1955 proclamation issued by a previous *Loya Jirgah,* but many observers wondered why the Afghan government chose this moment to call attention to the border problem and possibly irritate Pakistan, with whom relations had steadily improved since the 1963 resignation of Prime Minister Daoud. Of course, the resolution states the official Afghan view, but other reasons come to mind. Pressure from the vocal, though small, activist pro-"Pushtunistan" group obviously influenced the decision, and, in addition, all *Loya Jirgah* since World War II had passed resolutions on the problem. If the constitutional *Loya Jirgah* had failed to do so, the Pakistanis may have interpreted this as a lessening of Afghan interest in the area. Also, in the months following the *Loya Jirgah,* the Afghan government would be busily preparing ordinances and draft laws, holding an election, and doing nothing bold enough to cause criticism from the conservatives while hopefully being active enough to keep the liberals happy—a political tightrope act which would end with the convening of the new parliament in October 1965. Hints of dissatisfaction continually plagued the government, and if some of the energy of the nation could be diverted to an external problem (i.e., "Pushtunistan"), the possibility of calamitous internal dissension would possibly be diminished.

Between forty and fifty delegates wanted to speak on the "Pushtunistan" statement, but only a few reached the floor. The *Loya Jirgah* unanimously approved the resolution, and Prime Minister Yousuf then made a speech expressing thanks to the *Loya Jirgah* on behalf of the interim government, at the conclusion of which he asked for an endorsement (which he received unanimously) on a foreign policy statement, which said in part: "We confirm the policy outlined by the Prime Minister which is based on the traditional principles of non-alignment and free judgment in international affairs, non-involvement in military pacts, peace, peaceful coexistence on the basis of mutual respect and adherence to the United Nations Charter."

The *Loya Jirgah* unanimously approved a resolution thanking the King, the Prime Minister, the cabinet, the vice-president and secretary of the *Loya Jirgah,* the constitutional committee, and the advisory commission for their contributions to the success of the sessions. Dr. Abdul Zahir read a final statement of his own, and one from the King, both of which congratulated the *Loya Jirgah* on properly fulfilling its destiny. At 4:30 that afternoon, after a recitation from the *Qor'an,* the *Loya Jirgah* adjourned amid shouts, applause, hugs, and tears. Some delegates, however, failed to realize that they may have voted the traditional *Loya Jirgah* out of existence for Title V defined future *Loya Jirgah* as consisting of members of Parliament and the chairmen of the still-unelected twenty-eight provincial councils, thus legally eliminating the body as an organ appointed by the King and his advisers.

On the next morning (September 20) at 11 o'clock, the 452 delegates lined up to sign the Constitution before its submission to the King.

On October 1, 1964, King Mohammad Zahir Shah signed the Constitution, making it the law of the land, and issued the following *farman* in Dari (Persian) and Pashto:

We, Mohammad Zahir Shah, the King of Afghanistan, in the name of Almighty God, do herewith sign the new Constitution of Afghanistan, approved by the *Loya Jirgah* in its sessions in Kabul, beginning on the 18th and ending of the 28th of *Sonbula,* 1343.

We promulgate this new Constitution today throughout the entire state.

From today we declare the abrogation of the Constitution approved by the *Loya Jirgah* of 1309 prior to this day in force in the country and all amendments thereto.

Each member of the *Loya Jirgah* received a medal struck especially in honor of the occasion, and Afghanistan received a new Constitution.

First Elections and the New Shura

The 1964 Afghan Constitution provided for a bicameral parliament (*Shura*): a fully elective 216-member *Wolesi Jirgah* (Lower House, or House of the People) and an 84-member partly elective, partly appointive *Meshrano Jirgah* (Upper House, or House of Nobles). The King appoints 28 members to the *Meshrano Jirgah;* each of the twenty-eight provinces elect a member, and the not-yet realized twenty-eight provincial councils will also elect one member each.

Few Afghans would participate in the first elections held under the new Constitution. The bulk of the ninety-five percent non-literate Afghans living in villages and nomadic camps, knew little and cared less about the new Constitution and "New Democracy." Interest rose very high, on the other hand, among the intelligentsia in the major urban centers (Kabul Qandahar, Jalalabad, Mazar-i-Sharif, Herat, Kunduz), and many educated Afghans chafed at the slowness of the government, under commoner Dr. Mohammad Yousuf, in moving toward a "true" democracy. "The people won't wait," they said, but what they really meant was that *"We* [the intelligentsia out of power] won't wait. *We* want power to implement our own ideas and create an Afghanistan in our own image." What these dissident intellectuals (usually Western-trained) wanted was "instant democracy": take dry constitution, combine with fluid elections and stir, and *voilà,* "instant democracy"—without the agony of generations of development.

Several in this group of young—and not so young—intellectuals were avowed socialists, Marxists, or communists. All insist, however, that they want an Afghan brand of socialism, not Soviet or Chinese, and in most cases I believe this to be true. The Soviets and Chinese have so far been remarkably unsuccessful in penetrating the Afghan intelligentsia and the growing working class. The future, however, might provide a more fertile breeding ground if the Afghan government fails to live up to its announced goals and meets neither the articulated desires of the intelligentsia nor the underlying aspirations of the non-literate masses for economic betterment.

Another factor which would encourage Soviet or Chinese penetration would be the complete withdrawal of American interests in Afghanistan. Still another danger might lie in a military coup led by the Soviet-trained lieutenants and captains of today, when they reach (in about a decade) the frustrations of slow promotion as regimental or staff officers. No matter what a future Afghan government might do, opposition to any existing regime will increase as literacy increases, and ambitious men out of power try to achieve power, ideology take the hindmost.

The rising young men in Afghan government and political circles want (in addition to the continued opportunity to criticize openly) to participate in the decision-*making* as well as the decision-*implementing* processes. Prime Minister Daoud encouraged this idea, but many Afghan civil servants remembered that a few years before mistakes put an offender in jail, and few wanted to pioneer new ideas—or even implement old ones—without a direct order from the top.

Before and during the election, government-controlled broadcasts bombarded the populations through loudspeakers in city bazaars and transistor radios in teahouses and village huts, giving election news, discussing Afghan and foreign constitutions, and reading paid political announcements. Candidates had handbills and posters printed, bought press and radio (both government-controlled) space and time; the paraphernalia of Western elections proliferated in the cities.

Government officials, particularly the newly appointed twenty-eight provincial governors,[3] held meeting after meeting to acquaint the people with the forthcoming elections. From past experience, few Afghans believed the elections would be free. I heard a district governor speak in his town capital on every bazaar day in July and August, always trying to drive home the point that elections would be completely free and that each man in a voting booth would be alone with God to make his own decision. After listening politely, the local *rish-i-safidan* ("white beards," or "elders") would say: "We appreciate all the government is doing to give us a 'New Democracy,' and your speech was grand *but*

---

[3] A semi-serious joke passing about Kabul declared that the qualifications for provincial or subprovincial governor included a foreign degree and a foreign wife.

now please tell us who we should vote for, as all the governors have in the past." The exasperated governor continued to repeat his message of free elections, and, on the whole, the message got through. Most observers agree that the elections were as fair as any they had seen in Asia, or in some parts of Alabama—or in Cook County, Illinois.

One objection to the secret ballot is culturally oriented. In the *jirgah* system all voting is open, and participants raise their hands (or rifles) to vote on issues; but under the secret ballot, as many expressed it, "A man can talk one way in public and vote another in private."

Few non-literate Afghans wanted to help make the "New Democracy" work, and simply would not register to vote. Villagers and nomads consider a minimum of contact with government officials desirable. Some, however, do have the vague idea that government administrators can no longer use their official positions to extract money, goods, and free labor from them, and have begun to complain at every new government regulation in the name of the *democracy-yi-naw*. In relatively more isolated areas, local officials can still rule virtually as satraps, unhampered by the Constitution or higher authority. At other places, honest governors shocked and surprised tribal and village leaders by refusing to accept traditional *bakhshish* of livestock and grain. The gifts had been given in the past as insurance against any decisions the governor would have to make which concerned the leaders or their followers.

The Afghans elected representatives to the *Meshrano Jirgah* from August 26 to September 9, and to the *Wolesi Jirgah* from September 12 to 24. Staggered dates were necessary because of the lack of competent election personnel. Election committees usually consisted of local judges, teachers, and government clerks. At the end of the voting in each area, the committee sealed the ballot boxes in the presence of the candidates or their agents, and sent the boxes to the provincial capital for the vote count, which again took place in the presence of the candidates or their agents. The Ministry of the Interior, with overall responsibility for the elections, released the results on October 1, 1965, after a careful scrutiny of the successful candidates, which gave the government a last chance to weed out known subversives and others violently opposed to King Mohammad Zahir Shah's progressive programs.

The government tried to remain scrupulously aloof during the elections, although subtle pressure was brought to bear in certain key fights, such as in Laghman, where Dr. Abdul Zahir had resigned as Deputy Prime Minister to run against Ghulam Hassan Safi, who had resigned as Afghan envoy to Iraq. Safi is a fiery supporter of "Pushtunistan" which the Afghan government has played down since 1963. Although no evidence of direct government intervention exists, word got about that Laghman would benefit more if Dr. Zahir was elected. He was.

The results announced on October 1 startled no one, even though four women were elected, two from Kabul, one from Herat, and one from Qandahar. The reason why few eligibles voted was that, as we have seen, Afghans traditionally avoid contact with the government and government officials whenever possible. In Kabul, about 15,000 of the 40,119 eligibles voted, but results from Aq Kupruk, a subdistrict center in north Afghanistan, probably more closely reflected the national average: 3,000 of the 19,003 eligibles voted. Women, although enfranchised by the Constitution and the election law, voted only in the larger urban centers.

These first free Afghan elections were held in the absence of political parties, a development which still awaits the implementation of a Political Parties Act. Thus the campaigns centered around personalities rather than political party platforms. Nonetheless, the deputies who assembled to hear the King's inaugural speech on October 14 probably reflected the true power structure of Afghanistan better than any of the eleven previous parliaments "elected" since 1931.

Student Demonstrations Erupt

Untried in formal parliamentary procedures, but well-versed in *jirgah* in-fighting, many deputies came to Kabul skeptical of the government's decision about the *democracy-yi-naw,* but they soon took the idea of freedom firmly in hand and gave Dr. Zahir (elected President of the *Wolesi Jirgah* on October 12) a difficult time as he attempted to maintain order.

The *Wolesi Jirgah* immediately split into approximately six groups: a conservative, go-slow element, headed by the traditional religious leaders (led by the influential Mujadidi family), who, previously regionally oriented, now had a *national* platform from which they could express their views; a laissez-faire-economy group, favoring free enterprise, at least tacitly supported by Abdul Majid Zabuli, the dynamic, able, founder of the Bank-i-Melli, and the nation's foremost financial entrepreneur and industrialist; the *Wahdat-i-Melli* (an informal "National Party" led by Khalilullah Khalili, one of Afghanistan's most famous poets and a close confidant of the King), a group presumed to be in the center and oriented toward the King's progressive policies;

a small group of articulate liberals, led by Mir Mohammad Siddiq Farhang, favoring the public sector in development, though not at the expense of private enterprise; and finally, a minute but vocal group on the far left, dominated by Babrak Karmal and Dr. Anahita (a woman deputy from Kabul), which professed a local brand of political Marxism. Another group of Afghan (Pushtun) super-nationalists, led by Ghulam Mohammad Farhad, grew in numbers. Few deputies understood the responsibilities and obligations related to the democratic system, and so, with probably a minimum of (or no) outside influence, the events which followed developed into tragedy.

Dr. Mohammad Yousuf presented the report of the interim government to King Mohammad Zahir Shah on October 14 (*Afghanistan . . . Interim Government*, 1966), and was asked to form a new government. No man, however, in feud-ridden Afghanistan, with its tribal codes of reciprocity and sensitivity to insult, is without enemies, and, after many years of government service, Dr. Yousuf and members of the interim cabinet had many. In addition, most literates in Afghanistan felt that the time had come for a partial, if not complete, break with the past, and hoped that the next cabinet would be filled with new faces, and that a new prime minister not connected with previous governments would be appointed.

Led by Babrak, Dr. Anahita, and other self-proclaimed leftists, and abetted by Khalilullah Khalili, who still claimed to be a King's man though anti-Yousuf, *Wolesi Jirgah* members heaped abuse on the Prime Minister-designate and members of the interim cabinet, particularly the Ministers of Finance, Commerce, Interior, Justice, and Education (see Appendix G). None of the interim cabinet escaped mention. Some of the more vocal *Wolesi Jirgah* members attacked the royal family concept, and, by implication, even the King. Persian, it must be again noted, is a language that easily lends itself to *double-entendre*.

The denunciations increased in volume and vituperative content as students in the eighty-seat spectators' gallery shouted slogans for or against Dr. Yousuf. Some Afghans believe that Dr. Zahir was lax during the first days of the outpourings. Many think he hoped Dr. Yousuf would be forced to resign, so that he himself would be in the running for prime minister. Possibly, however, Dr. Zahir simply thought the vituperation would run its course and did not want to appear suppressive in the opening days of the new parliament.

In a frenzy of parliamentary zeal, the *Wolesi Jirgah* passed a resolution requiring cabinet ministers to make public statements concerning their finanical status, but quickly voted down a motion that *Wolesi Jirgah* members do likewise.

Dr. Yousuf, disturbed, appeared before the *Wolesi Jirgah* on October 21, and dramatically appealed to members to stop making unsubstantiated accusations of bribery, corruption, graft, and nepotism. He asked that any charges against him or his former ministers be lodged formally in courts of law. He then asked the *Wolesi Jirgah* to approve or reject him, his cabinet, and his policies in three days. Amid wild cheers the Prime Minister-designate left. Dr. Yousuf's supporters had packed the spectators' gallery, and a decision that day would probably have given him at least a seventy-five percent majority vote of confidence. Dr. Yousuf's surprise visit, however, displeased many of his followers, some members of the cabinet, and, reportedly, the King. He had made his dramatic appearance without the knowledge or consent of His Majesty.

Babrak and his followers encouraged the students to appear in Paliament on October 24, the day Dr. Yousuf was to present his cabinet for approval. The students had been stirred by catch phrases about "gaining their freedom," "exercising their constitutional rights," "throwing the corrupt ones out of office," and they filled the spectators' gallery and overflowed onto the floor of the *Wolesi Jirgah,* where they sat in the deputies' seats and refused to leave until "our rights have been granted," and "the dishonest rascals have been driven from government." They ignored repeated pleas to leave, and Dr. Zahir had no choice but to adjourn until October 25. The jubilant students cheered, believing their parliamentary sit-in had won some sort of victory. Babrak exhorted them to return the next day, "And to return every day until our rights have been granted." The government-controlled radio and press reported the incident without comment, but a worried, confused, and surprised Afghan government (Dr. Yousuf's interim cabinet still impotently and reluctantly ruled) made preparations for the worst. On the night of October 24 the *Wolesi Jirgah* decided, by an informal straw vote (191 to 6), as it had a right to do under the Constitution, to hold a closed session on the following day.

October 25, 1965 (*sehum-i-aqrab*) will live long in the memory of Afghans as a day of tragedy. Demonstrations began at 7 A.M. and lasted until a little after 5 P.M., when Afghan troops armed with Russian weapons fired on a group of slogan-shouting students near the home of Dr. Yousuf. At least three people died and scores were wounded.[4] The blame for this tragedy must be shared by several factions: by the

---

[4] For two detailed versions of the *sehum-i-aqrab* tragedy, see L. Dupree (1965c) and Reardon (1969).

government, for not recognizing the threat and quelling the trouble before it began, and for then calling out armed troops when police could possibly have controlled the situation; by the *Wolesi Jirgah,* for its two-week orgy of inflammatory denunciations; by Babrak and his followers for using leftist tactics to pervert incipient democratic processes for their own ends; by the Kabul University authorities for not maintaining control of the students and faculty, and for not punishing the ringleaders of the first demonstrations; and by the students for blindly following well-tutored ringleaders.

I talked to many student demonstrators on *sehum-i-aqrab* and they all believed they were doing their bit for *democracy-yi-naw.* It should be noted, however, that the student population of all Kabul's schools exceeds 20,000 and that probably no more than a maximum of 2,000 students actually participated during the day, the number at any one time seldom exceeding 1,000.

The demonstrations never indicated an anti-foreign bias, nor did they indicate pro-Soviet or pro-American attitudes. While marching, the student demonstrators walked past the residence of the American ambassador, and a spontaneous cheer arose from a group of the demonstrators in favor of Afghan-American friendship. A cheer in favor of Soviet-Afghan friendship arose as some of the demonstrators passed near the old Soviet embassy. The concept of *bi-tarafi* was maintained throughout the day. It may have been fortunate, however, that the demonstrators did not pass by the U.S.I.A. compound, because a few months before, U.S.I.A. had installed a huge plate-glass window in order to better display its propaganda. The window makes an excellent target. We can probably say that the Afghan students will not have reached political maturity in the Afro-Asian sense until they have smashed the U.S.I.A. window, still intact as of this writing (May 1972).

About half of Kabul University's 3,000 students come from outside Kabul and live in dormitories. Honored to have been selected to attend the university, they do not wish to risk expulsion and the disgrace it would bring to their families. No matter what their personal feelings, most stayed away from the demonstrations.

A majority of observers feel they recognized an outside hand in the *sehum-i-aqrab* demonstrations. After Mohammad Hashim Maiwandwal emerged as prime minister to succeed Dr. Yousuf on October 29, Russian diplomats chided Americans at the nightly diplomatic cocktail parties: "Well, you Americans should be happy, at last your man got in," referring to Maiwandwal's long and popular tenure as ambassador to Washington. But Maiwandwal, when he was Minister of Press and Information before his appointment as prime minister, could hardly have been accused of pro-Western actions. He was, and he remains, pro-Afghan. Some in the West German embassy claimed to have definite proof that the Tudeh Party (the banned Iranian Communist Party), operating out of East Germany, engineered the demonstrations; but Bonn's representatives, it must be remembered, did anything at that time to discredit East Germany.

The logical question must be asked, however: "Which nation benefits most by internal unrest and political instability in Afghanistan?" Pakistan? Certainly not, for severe internal pressures might tempt Kabul to raise the now relatively quiescent "Pushtunistan" issue. India, one of Afghanistan's most important trading partners? No, because India has too much trouble with its other neighbors (Pakistan, China, Ceylon, Nepal) to risk Afghan antagonism. Iran, a neighboring monarchy? The Iranians feel repercussions when any of the few remaining Muslim monarchies are threatened. The U.S.S.R.? I think not, for the Soviet Union has spent over a decade and millions of rubles to help promote Afghan stability. Soviet-sponsored demonstrations would smudge the Soviet image as economic benefactor without strings attached. The United States? The Americans would like to see Afghanistan maintain its non-aligned position, and an exaggeratedly pro-American government would most certainly invite Soviet counteraction. Under the leadership of Ambassador John M. Steeves, the American embassy staff remained relatively cool during this period of trouble, even though some of the A.I.D. officials and technicians predicted (almost gleefully) a blood-bath.

Some knowledgeable Afghans believe that the perpetrators of the *sehum-i-aqrab* had approached the Soviet embassy for either support or a reading on Soviet reactions. They believe that, although the Soviets may have known that the demonstrations would occur, the Russians preferred to remain in the background, but did not actively discourage the demonstrators. The Soviets, this reasoning goes on, preferred to see how the Afghan government would react to its first demonstrations under the "New Democracy," in order to test the real stability and strength of the current processes.

In my opinion, only the Chinese might possibly benefit. Peking seems to delight in poking its fingers into sensitive areas around its boundaries, without, I believe, any expansionist tendencies. China probably wishes to have its border areas formally stabilized, for it has more than enough internal problems. Not a single bordering nation (including the U.S.S.R.) escapes attention, and Afghanistan bumps into China in the high Pamirs along a boundary some forty kilometers long, in one of the world's more rugged mountain areas. The Chinese maintain a large embassy in Kabul and occasionally Chinese students attend Kabul University to study Persian and Pashto in exchange for Afghan students studying Chinese in Peking. At the time of the demonstrations, six Chinese students attended Kabul University, and I saw several conferring with student leaders during the *sehum-i-aqrab* demonstrations. Naturally, I can no more prove collusion than the Chinese can prove that I had a hand in the demonstrations, for I also talked with these leaders.

My estimate is that the demonstrations were caused largely by home-grown dissatisfaction with the ministerial clique which had played musical chairs during the Daoud regime and the succeeding interim regime, and would now make up a substantial part of Dr. Yousuf's new cabinet.

In the wake of the demonstrations Dr. Yousuf resigned on October 29 because of "ill health," and the King appointed Mohammad Hashim Maiwandwal (a former ambassador to the United Kingdom, the United States, and Pakistan, and Minister of Press and Information in Dr. Yousuf's Interim Cabinet) as prime minister. The *Wolesi Jirgah* approved the new Prime Minister's cabinet and policies on November 2nd in a precedent-setting session broadcast to the nation over Radio Afghanistan, a tactic which held some of the more vitriolic tongues in check.

The schools in Kabul, closed since October 26, reopened on November 1. On November 3, the Kabul University students held a day-long sit-down in front of the Administration Building and presented the Vice-Rector with a petition demanding that the government investigate the tragic deaths of the *sehum-i-aqrab,* punish those responsible (the demonstrators considered themselves blameless), release students and faculty members who had been jailed, and permit the organization of a student union for political debating.

The Vice-Rector took the demands to Prime Minister Maiwandwal, who, in his role as Acting Minister of Education, personally delivered the students' note to the *Wolesi Jirgah,* which appointed a twenty-nine-man committee to take action. The students were released from jail, but the investigation died quickly. One American-educated teacher on the Faculty of Science, Mohammad Osman, served a two-year sentence for his part in instigating the demonstrations.

On November 4, the Kabul University students held a memorial rally for the *shahed* ("martyrs") killed on *sehum-i-aqrab.* University students may feel frustrated for lack of martyrs of their own, however. Of the three persons known dead, two were students from technical institutes and one was a tailor watching the excitement. The rally was dying on its feet when Prime Minister Maiwandwal, again functioning as Minister of Education, dramatically appeared on the campus to speak to the students. He expressed the regrets of the King and himself over the tragic events and promised a prompt investigation. He said that any legitimate student demands would be considered, that the student union would be sanctioned, and that no students now remained in jail.

An effective speaker, Maiwandwal won the day. The students hoisted him onto their shoulders and triumphantly paraded him through the campus. They thought *they* had won the day. Some Afghans criticized Maiwandwal for giving the students an illusion of real political power, but such critics fail to realize that as Kabul University developed, so would political activities among the students. Maiwandwal's gesture, in my opinion, gave the new government a necessary breather, while the new Rector, Tooralay Etemadi, tried to reshape the university.

The students immediately attempted to take advantage of the situation, however. In late November, a general strike occurred at Kabul University. The students put forth ridiculous demands, which, if implemented, would have placed them in total control of university policy. The demands included: that 50% be the passing grade (instead of the existing 65%); that obligatory class attendance be eliminated (75% attendance was required); that students who failed the same examinations for *three* (*sic!*) consecutive years be given a fourth try (a student then had three chances to pass); that a student union be formed immediately; that current examinations be postponed until after *Ramadan* (the Muslim month of fasting).

The university faculty senate did agree to lower the passing mark to 55% and to permit a student union "at the proper time," but rejected the rest of the demands. The students then rejected the rejection; and the senate met once again and rejected this rejection of its initial rejection. The students, under threat of expulsion, capitulated. Another fiasco quickly followed.

The faculty and students in the Faculty of Science went on strike in mid-December 1965, demanding the removal of the German professors. Complaints ranged from the probably justifiable (that the German professors often did not show up for class, occasionally acted arrogantly toward students, spent more time on personal research than on teaching) to the probably fantastic (German professors sold advance copies of examinations, used too rigorous a grading system, stole natural resources by sending specimens away for identification, although scientific specimens could not be properly identified in Kabul).

The science students demonstrated in the streets of Kabul, but were greeted with little sympathy and some amusement by the populace and the rest of the student body. They carried placards in Persian, Pashto and *English* (seldom in German) reading: "We Do Not Want Arrangement with Germany!" and "German Teachers Should Leave from Science Faculty!" The Afghan government seemed to have learned its lesson from the *sehum-i-aqrab* demonstrations, and permitted off-campus marches and speeches only when a cordon of police and soldiers surrounded the students. The university administration stood firm, and the students again capitulated.

Two further incidents occurred in the spring of 1965. A student strike in a technical school protested conditions, particularly the preparation of food, and led to the arrest of several students and the expulsion of others. At the university a mysterious pamphlet appeared, on the theme, "No one will give you your rights—you must seize them!" Rumors of the arrest of students for passing out the pamphlet proved to be false. Several students and faculty members with whom I talked believed that the pamphlets came from, or at least were inspired by, outside sources. No one named the Soviet or Chinese embassies, but the implications were there. An important lesson from all these demonstrations was that the students needed university sponsored, extracurricular activities if Afghanistan hoped to minimize student violence in the guise of political activity on the campus.

The Educational Institution Develops

Education, under the Afghan constitution, is compulsory and free, but currently the nation has neither the financial resources, the teachers, the textbooks, nor the facilities to implement universal education. In spite of giant strides (see Chart 17) made in the past decade, functional literacy is still well under ten percent. Ten years ago, few villagers looked on literacy as a desired ideal, but now many want education for their sons, though generally not for their daughters, whose place is still in the mud hut. An encouraging sign is that all over the country, villagers themselves, prompted by the new breed of young, outward-looking provincial officers, have built schools. Often, however, lack of teachers forces these schools to remain empty or become storehouses. Volunteer foreign teachers (American, British, West German) in Afghanistan helped to fill part of the gap. American Peace Corps volunteers teach in many provincial centers (actually little more than overgrown villages) thus releasing Afghan teachers for schools in smaller towns and selected villages.

Fewer than 1% of Afghan primary and secondary school teachers have any professional college level training (*Survey of Progress*, 1969, 100), but Chart 17 illustrates that Afghan education *below* the university level has gained ground gradually in one very important figure: the average number of students per teacher has dropped from 47 to 1 to 38 to 1 in 4 years.

Kabul University (*Kabul Pohantun*), the goal of all literate young Afghans who cannot afford to go abroad for university training, began in 1932 with a Faculty of Medicine, affiliated with the University of Lyons, France. The college had been a pet project of King Mohammad Nadir Shah.

Subsequent faculties, most with European and American affiliates, were founded:

Faculty and Date of Founding	*Current (1969) Foreign Affiliate*
Law and Political Science (1938)	University of Paris, France
Science (1942)	Bochum and Bonn Universities, West Germany
Letters (1944)	None[5]
Theology (1951)	Al-Azhar, Egypt
Agriculture (1956)	University of Wyoming, U.S.A.
Economics (1957)	Universities of Bochum, Bonn, and Cologne, West Germany
Home Economics (1962)	Now in Faculty of Education
Education (1962)	Teachers College, Columbia University
Engineering (1963)	U.S. Engineering Team[6]
Pharmacy (1963)	Now in Faculty of Medicine
Polytechnic Institute (1967)	U.S.S.R.

In 1947, the Afghan Government formally established Kabul University under a single administrative unit, but the various faculties continued to exist separately, scattered over Kabul. Not until 1964 did all

---

[5] However, since 1966, the Südasien-Institut der Universitat Heidelberg, West Germany, has helped form an Institute of Anthropology section in the Faculty of Letters.

[6] U.S. Engineering Team (U.S.E.T.) is a consortium of American institutions consisting of Carnegie Institute of Technology, University of Cincinnati, Georgia Institute of Technology, Illinois Institute of Technology, Lehigh University, University of Notre Dame, Rice University, North Carolina State University of the State of North Carolina, Purdue University.

the faculties come together in a single physical plant, west of Kabul proper in the Aliabad district, constructed by the West German company, Hocktief, with U.S.A.I.D. money, the usual example of West Germans making friends while making money, a process generally foreign to Americans.

Before 1961, separate Faculties of Letters, Science, and Medicine (all founded in 1957) existed for women, but now all faculties are co-educational.

The language of instruction is primarily Dari, except in advanced language classes. The Faculty of Engineering, incidentally, conducts its classes in English, even those taught by Afghan instructors. But the medieval independent college (*faculté*) system which plagues Kabul University should probably be changed to a departmental system in order to eliminate duplication of courses. Vested interests, however, intrude from two directions, one from inside the Afghan faculties themselves, the other from the varied nations involved in the independent faculties.

A team led by Herman B Wells, Chancellor of Indiana University, visited Kabul University in May 1966, investigated needs, and recommended possible ways of meeting them. Subsequently, in 1967, Indiana University, under an A.I.D. contract, began to assist Kabul University in reorganizing its entire administrative system.

Kabul University today is an educational institution with a student body, faculty, and a curriculum, but few extracurricular goals or activities, a perfect breeding-ground for political discontent. About half of the students from all parts of Afghanistan live in campus dormitories with few university-oriented activities (social clubs, athletics, professional clubs) outside the classroom. Since the university now occupies a single plant, penetration from the outside is easier, but so is internal guidance if officially sanctioned activities can be introduced to provide antidotes for boredom.

The students continue to demand immediate changes in administrative practices, grading systems, and student-faculty relations, but the university, like most educational institutions, remains basically resistant to change, particularly where faculty vested interests are concerned. In 1967, Rector Etemadi resigned, and like the rest of Afghanistan, Kabul University stands still, particularly since the *Shura,* after the student demonstrations, rejected the new Kabul University Constitution (as well as the Basic Education Law) in late 1968. The Kabul University Constitution, as written, prohibited "political activities and political party movements" (Article IV).

Dr. Abdullah Wahedi, formerly Dean of the Ningrahar Medical College (founded in 1965, and now officially a university), became Rector on October 5, 1968. He resigned in the spring of 1969, and was succeeded by Fazl Rabi Pazwak (elected on May 19, 1969), who, in turn, resigned in March 1970. On March 26, 1970, the Senate of Kabul University, composed of thirty-eight members (about half administrators, half elected from the various faculties), chose Dr. Sayed Abdul Qadir Baha, Dean of the College of Medicine, Ningrahar University, as Rector in a secret ballot.

As for the Afghan university students, they will continue to be a political barometer and a prime target for subversive elements, both internal and external. The long, peaceful slide of the Afghan educational system is over (L. Dupree, 1969b).

The Fourth Estate

In principle, the 1964 Constitution of Afghanistan provides for freedom of the press. In practice, the Press Law, promulgated in July 1965, with eight Chapters and fifty-five Articles, attempts to implement this ideal. Many criticize the law as being repressive, but it does establish a code under which a free press might conceivably develop. In a nation which has less than ten percent of its people literate, newspapers have little effect in the countryside, but great impact politically on the increasing literate urban population, particularly on the impressionable students. The Press Law tries to follow a course halfway between complete freedom of the press and close government supervision. At this stage of Afghanistan's political development, total freedom for a press that too often displays a lack of responsible reporting might bring on anarchy and would definitely bring in outside influences.

The Press Law, drafted to safeguard the "fundamentals of Islam, constitutional monarchy, and other values enshrined in the Constitution," gives considerable latitude to any but the most stubborn reactionaries of either the extreme left or right. Article 5 of the law spells out the conditions under which a periodical may operate: a publisher must make application to the Ministry of Information and Culture and offer a security against future government action. The security for a daily newspaper is 15,000 afghanis, for a weekly journal 10,000 afghanis, and for other periodicals a lesser amount. The amount and sources of the periodical's capital must also be listed.

The obstacles to an indigenous free press in Afghanistan appear almost insurmountable. Few Afghan businessmen believe in advertising, for most of their customers cannot read, so newspapers must be financed by interested individuals, and not many appear interested. Then, too, a shortage of competent Afghan journalists exists, even on the staffs of the government-controlled press.

Among other periodicals, the Ministry of Information and Culture sponsors publication of several provincial newspapers.[7] These papers usually parrot the line of the government dailies published in Kabul: *Anis* (*Companion,* mainly Farsi); *Islah* (*Reform,* mainly Pashto); *Heywad* (*Homeland,* Pashto); *The Kabul Times* (English). The role of the government-controlled press remains somewhat obscure. The government proclaims that the press can express its opinions freely, but, although occasional editorials do attack minor points of government policy, radical departures from the government line would be impossible. For a democratic government to develop a healthy atmosphere, however, different paths to democracy must be freely and *responsibly* discussed in opposition press media.

Shortly after the promulgation of the Press Law in July 1965, six private journals sprang into existence (See Chart 23): *Payam-i-Emroz; Khalq; Mardum; Wahdat; Afghan Mellat; Masawat.*

Khalq (*The Masses* or *The People*) was an interesting and instructive experiment. Its liberal publisher (Nur Mohammad Taraki) and editor (Bariq Shafie, a well-known leftist poet) published six issues from April 11 to May 16, 1966, before the government clamped down on May 23. Many Afghans consider the government decision a mistake.

Numbers 1 and 2 of *Khalq,* printed in a single issue, proclaimed under its red-ink title that it was "the publication of the democratic voice of the people." An editorial, printed in both Persian and Pashto, divided Afghanistan's problems into four categories (political, economic, social, and cultural) and set forth the policy of the paper in phrases unlike the usual patterns in modern Afghan literature. An Iranian friend of mine, visiting Kabul at the time, found most of the writing in *Khalq* identical to that of Tudeh Party publications, and an Afghan friend, familiar with Russian propaganda, found parallels to the Tajiki Farsi written in Tajikistan S.S.R.

[7] Among the provincial dailies are: *Tulu-yi-Afghan* (*Afghan Sunrise,* published at Qandahar in Pashto); *'Itefaq-i-Islam* (*Consensus of Islam,* Herat, Farsi/Pashto); *Bidar* (*Vigilance,* Mazar-i-Sharif, Farsi/Pashto); *Etehad-i-Mashriqi* (*Eastern Unity,* Jalalabad, Pashto); *Etehad-i-Baghlan* (*Baghlan Unity,* Baghlan, Farsi/Pashto); *Badakhshan* (Faizabad, Farsi/Pashto); *Sanai* (Ghazni, Farsi/Pashto); *Parwan* (Charikar, Farsi/Pashto); *Wulangah* (*Shining Ray,* Khost (Matun), Pashto). Papers published twice weekly are: *Storeh* (*Star,* Maimana, Farsi/Pashto); *Pamir* (Kabul, Farsi/Pashto); *Sistan* (Farah, Farsi/Pashto); *Hilmand* (Girishk, Farsi/Pashto).

CHART 23
The Free Press in Afghanistan: 1965–72

Newspaper	Publisher	Editor
Wahdat ("Unity") Weekly	Maulana Khasta	Maulana Khasta
Payam-i-Emroz ("Voices of Today") Weekly	Ghulam Nabi Khater	1. Abdul Raouf Turkmani 2. Mohammad Taher Mohsini
*Afghan Mellat[3] ("Afghan Nation") Weekly	Engineer Ghulam Mohammad Farhad	1. Quodrattulah Hadad 2. Habibullah Rafi 3. Quodrattulah Hadad
Khalq ("The Masses") Weekly	Nur Mohammad Taraki	Bariq Shafie
Mardum ("The Masses") Weekly	Sayyid Moqades Negah	Ghulam Mahayuddin Tafwiz
*Masawat[3] ("Equality") Weekly	1. Abdul Shakur Reshad 2. Mohammad Sharif Ayubi	1. Mohammad Rahim El-Ham 2. Abdul Ghani Maiwandi
*Payam-i-Wejdan[3] ("Voice of Conscience") Weekly	Abdul Raouf Turkmani	Abdul Raouf Turkmani
Parcham ("The Flag") Weekly	Sulaiman Laiyek	1. Sulaiman Laiyek 2. Mir Akbar Khyber

(*Still published as of writing March, 1972)

Languages[2]	First Published	Date Closed	Reasons for Closure and Notes
Pashto/Dari	Jan. 31, 1966	June 20, 1966	Financial difficulties. Main supporter, Khalilullah Khalili, appointed Ambassador to Saudi Arabia.
Dari	Feb. 9, 1966	May 25, 1966	Opposition to government. Editor resigned.
Pashto/Dari	April 5, 1966	May 12, 1967	Organ of *Jamiyat-i-Social Demokrat* (Afghan Social Democrats); ultranationalist; pro-"Pushtunistan"; first banned because of article on CIA in government; ban lifted February 20, 1968. Still occasionally banned.
Pashto/Dari	April 11, 1966	May 16, 1966	Organ of leftist (pro-Moscow?) *Jamiyat-i-Demokratiqi-Khalq (Parcham).* Closed on recommendation of Parliament; accused of anti-Islamic, anti-Constitution sentiments.
Dari/Pashto	May 11, 1966	June 15, 1966	Founded to fight *Khalq*; voluntarily folded after *Khalq* banned.
Dari/Pashto	June 24, 1966	Dec. 26, 1966	Organ of *Jamiyat Demokrati-yi-Mottaraqi* (Progressive Democratic Party of former Prime Minister Mohammad Hashim Maiwandwal). Banned for 18 months prior to Oct. 13, 1971. Advocates evolutionary socialism and parliamentary democracy.
Dari/Pashto	July 24, 1966		Champions the rights of non-Pushtun minorities.
Pashto/Dari	March 14, 1968	July 15, 1969	Replaced *Khalq* until banned during 1969 elections. More revolutionary wing of Democratic Peoples Party called *Jamiyat-i-Demokratiqi-Khalq-i-Afghanistan.*

CHART 23 (*continued*)

Newspaper	Publisher	Editor
Seda-yi-Awam ("The Popular Voice") Weekly	Dr. Abdul Karim Ferzan	Mohammad Aref Hanifi
Shu'la-yi-Jawed ("The Eternal Flame") Weekly	Dr. Rahim Mahmudi	Dr. Rahim Mahmudi, assisted by his brother, Dr. Hadi Mahmudi
*Tarjman ("The Interpreter") Weekly	Prof. Dr. Rahim Nevin	Ali Asghar Bashir
*Sabah[3] ("Tomorrow") 1. Weekly 2. Daily 3. Twice a week 4. Sporadic	Ghulam Nabi Khater	Ghulam Nabi Khater
Komak ("Help") Weekly	Mohammad Yaqub Komak	Mohammad Yaqub Komak
*Karwan[3] ("Caravan") Daily	Sabahuddin Kushkaki	Abdul Haq Waleh
*Khyber ("Khyber") Weekly	Mohibur Rahman Hosa	Mohibur Rahman Hosa
*Gahiz[3] ("Morning") Weekly	Menhajuddin Gahiz	1. Menhajuddin Gahiz 2. Abdul Salim Ferghani
Parwanah ("Butterfly") Weekly	Amanullah Parwanah	Amanullah Parwanah
Hadaf ("Goal") Weekly	Ghulam Mohammad Ormul	Mohammad Rahim Mehraban
Jabhai-yi-Melli ("National Front") Weekly	Abdul Rab Akhlaq	Abdul Rab Akhlaq

Languages[2]	First Published	Date Closed	Reasons for Closure and Notes
Dari/Pashto	March 27, 1968	June 20, 1968	Resignation of editor; opposition to government. Organ of *Jamiyat-i-Awam* (Peoples Party), leaned toward Muslim-Gandhian leftism.
Dari/Pashto	April 4, 1968	July 10, 1969	Organ of *Jamiyat-i-Demokrati Nawin* (New Democratic Party; two factions exist). More revolutionary (pro-Peking?) than either branch of Democratic Peoples Party. Like *Parcham,* closed during 1969 elections.
Dari/Pashto	April 18, 1968		An independent satirical paper with political cartoons.
Dari/Pashto	May 8, 1968		Anti-leftist. Replaced *Payam-i-Emroz.* Mild opposition to government. Some Afghans consider opportunistic. Owns private press.
Dari/Pashto	August 1, 1968	August 1, 1968	Banned with first issue; opposition to government.
Dari/Pashto	Sept. 24, 1968		Independent paper; some Afghans say it leans toward Establishment.
Pashto/Dari	Oct. 10, 1968	Oct. 29, 1969	Hosa unsuccessfully ran for Parliament; closed paper voluntarily; began publishing again on Nov. 1, 1971. Pro-"Pushtunistan" and religiously conservative.
Pashto/Dari	Oct. 13, 1968		Anti-leftist; pro-Islamic (conservative). Two conservative religious groups are: *Ikwan-ul-Musulmo 'amin* (Muslim Youth) and *Jamayat-i-Islami* (Muslim or Islamic Party).
Dari/Pashto	Dec. 2, 1968	Jan. 20, 1969	Opposition to government; accused by some of being opportunistic.
Dari/Pashto	Dec. 11, 1968	Aug. 13, 1969	Anti-Maiwandwal; closed after 1969 elections.
Dari/Pashto	Dec. 30, 1968	June 15, 1969	Pro-Establishment; folded because of financial difficulties.

CHART 23 (*continued*)

Newspaper	Publisher	Editor
Paktika (refers to Paktya) Weekly	Shah Zaman Urez Stanizai	Shah Zaman Urez Stanizai
Sepidahdam ("Dawn") Weekly	Sayyid Mohammad Bamdad	1. Abdul Bashir Kabir 2. Mahmud Farani
Afghan Wolus ("The Afghan Nation") Weekly	Senator Qiamuddin Khadem	1. Musafer Sadeq 2. A.Q. Adrimzay
Ittehad-i-Melli ("Unity of the Country") Weekly	Abdul Hakim Muzhda	1. Abdul Hakim Muzhda 2. Abdul Haq Nasiri
Rozgar[3] ("Time") Weekly	Yousuf Farand	Yousuf Farand
Afghan ("Afghan") Weekly	Mohammad Yousuf Wolesmal	Mohammad Yousuf Wolesmal
Nida-yi-Haq ("Voice of Truth") Weekly	Maulavi Abdul Satar Siddiqi	Ghulam Nabi Zormati
Mellat ("The Nation") Weekly	Feda Mohammad Fedayi	Habibullah Rafie
Afkar-i-Nau ("New Ideas") Weekly	Nourullah Nourzad	Zia Haidar
Paikar ("Struggle") Weekly	Ghulam Mohammad Almasak	Ghulam Mohammad Almasak
Shokhak ("Clown") Weekly	Abdul Ghaffar Audaz	Aziz Mukhtar

[1] Compiled with the assistance of Habibur-Rahman Jadir, Adbul Raziq Palwal, and Mohammad Hussain Razi.

[2] Major languages listed first.

[3] Although still published, these papers have occasionally had specific issues banned or been forced to suspend publication for various periods of times.

Languages[2]	First Published	Date Closed	Reasons for Closure and Notes
Pashto/Dari	March 10, 1969		Ideology close to *Afghan Mellat*, but more Establishment-oriented.
Dari/Pashto	March 12, 1969	Sept. 10, 1969	Literary journal; closed because of financial difficulties.
Pashto	July 30, 1969	Sept. 15, 1969	Pro-"Pushtunistan"; closed down for financial reasons.
Dari/Pashto	July 19, 1969		Organ of the National Unity Party (two factions); Establishment oriented.
Dari/Pashto	Oct. 28, 1969		Independent paper; generally supports Constitutional processes.
Pashto/Dari	Sept. 6, 1971		Oriented toward creation of parliamentary democracy; pro-"Pushtunistan."
Dari/Pashto	Sept. 15, 1971	Jan. 18, 1972	Religiously oriented; closed for financial reasons.
Pashto/Dari	Sept. 26, 1971	Jan. 10, 1972	Organ of more leftist group which broke with *Jamiyat-i-Afghan Social Demokrat (Afghan Mellat)*; both *Mellat* and *Afghan Mellat* (Feb. 6, 1972) banned by government for attacks on its "Pushtunistan" policy.
Dari/Pashto	Oct. 30, 1971	Nov. 1, 1971	To support ideals of middle class; create government based on Islam and law and order. Ceased publication after death of publisher Nourzad.
Dari/Pashto	Dec. 15, 1971		Replaced *Afkar-i-Nau* after death of publisher.
Pashto/Dari	Dec. 16, 1971	Jan. 8, 1972	An independent satirical journal; banned by government for lack of decorum.

Roz ("The Day"), published briefly in Kunduz before being banned, was socialist and anti-Spinzar Company (a monopolistic cotton company in north Afghanistan.

Two free press monthlies also exist: *Islam*, a religiously oriented magazine, edited and published by Menhajuddin Gahiz; *Darya* ("The River"), a literary journal published by Miss Spoghmai Raouf and edited by Abdul Satar.

Khalq had announced that its policy would be to alleviate "the boundless agonies of the oppressed peoples of Afghanistan." Another quotation linked the policy to international communism: "The main issue of contemporary times and the center of class struggle on a world-wide basis, which began with the Great October Socialist Revolution, is the struggle between international socialism and international imperialism." Politically, *Khalq* supported the concepts of territorial integrity, political independence, and the concentration of all internal power in the hands of "the people." Economically, *Khalq* favored the public over the private sector, and demanded land reform to release the Afghan peasant from "the feudal system which dominates Afghan society." Socially the paper demanded improvements in labor conditions and "social equality." Culturally, the editor and publisher advocated universal education and social realism in art.

The first double issue, priced at 2 afghanis, sold 20,000 copies; subsequent issues sold about 10,000. The Government Press printed *Khalq* every Monday, and secondary school and university students peddled the papers in the street. Outcries against *Khalq* rose from many quarters, particularly among the conservative religious leaders in the *Meshrano Jirgah,* twenty of whom demanded an investigation of the paper, and on May 4, 1966, the *Wolesi Jirgah* invited the Minister of Information and Culture and the Minister of Justice to discuss the problem. This opposition delighted the staff of *Khalq,* who played a game of semantics with their detractors. Accused of being anti-Islam, anti-monarchy, and anti-constitution, *Khalq* replied in an editorial that its position was not against the principles of Islam or the fundamental rights embodied in the Constitution, and that it recognized the necessity for a monarchy "at this stage of Afghanistan's development." However, *Khalq*'s stand on land reform and public over private ownership was widely held to be anti-Islamic. The Attorney General's office, under Article 1 of the Press Law, banned publication on May 23.[8] The staff of

[8] The following Articles from the Press Law of July 1965 are those under which various papers of the free press have been shut down by the government:

Article 1: Freedom of thought and expression is immune from any encroachment in accordance with Article 31 of the Constitution of Afghanistan.

In order to implement the said article and to take into consideration the other values of the Constitution, the provisions set forth in this law organize the method of using the right of freedom of press for the citizens of Afghanistan. The goals which this law aims to secure consist of:

1. Preparing a proper ground over which all Afghans may express their thought by means of speech, writing, pictures or the like and may print and disseminate various matters.

the paper protested the injustice of the action, for under the Press Law, *Khalq* had no recourse. It had been denied its rights to publish without a day in court, and the staff now became martyrs in the eyes of many literate Afghans.

Two theories, neither of them supported by demonstrable evidence, circulated in Kabul concerning the possible connection between the *sehum-i-aqrab* demonstrations and *Khalq*. One held that both were under Tudeh influence. The other theory stated that the Soviets, tired of being represented as without influence, chose to illustrate graphically through these two incidents that they could, and would, create considerable dissension if the Afghans were to abandon their policy of non-alignment.

Regardless of how these events may have been influenced, the Afghans must prepare for growing legitimate opposition to government as literacy expands and the *khalq* (not the newspaper but the "people") look beyond the Hindu Kush and the Khyber Pass for political, social, and economic inspiration.

Exactly one month after *Khalq* began publication, another weekly, *Mardum,* appeared on May 11, 1966, apparently to take on *Khalq*. *Mardum* (published by Sayyid Moqades Negah and edited by Ghulam

2. Safeguarding public security and order as also the interest and dignity of the State and individuals from harms which they may be subjected to by the misuse of the freedom of Press.

3. Safeguarding the fundamentals of Islam, constitutional monarchy and the other values enshrined in the Constitution.

4. Assisting the healthy development of a press in a way so that this organ of the society may become an effective means for dissemination of knowledge, information and culture among the people of Afghanistan as well as truthfully and usefully reflect public opinion to the society.

.   .   .   .

Article 31: The publication of matter implying defamation of the principles of Islam or defamatory to the King of Afghanistan is not allowed.

Article 32: Incitement through the press to commit actions, the end of which is considered an offence, will also be considered an offence. Such actions may be:

1. Incitement to disobey the country's laws.
2. Incitement to disrupt public security and order.
3. Incitement to seek depravity.

Article 33: Every action which is considered an offence will also be an offence if committed through the press: Such actions may be:

1. Disclosure of state secrets such as:
   (a) Secret government or parliamentary proceeding.
   (b) Secret court proceeding.
   (c) Military secrets.
   (d) Secrets pertaining to Afghanistan's international relations.

Mahayuddin Tafwiz, both respectable, pro-constitution, pro-monarchy liberals) was against corruption, for land reform, for nationalism, and against any outside influence in Afghan governmental affairs. The publisher and editor recognized the social inequalities in Afghanistan, but opposed using the "class struggle" as a political weapon. *Mardum* recommended local, evolutionary solutions to local problems; it opposed the introduction of foreign ideologies, and rejected the international application of the principles of the "October Revolution." As an antidote to *Khalq*, *Mardum* (the title was printed in green, a favorite Muslim color) was well received. Many Afghans hoped that *Mardum* would develop specific proposals along with its general policies, but they were disappointed.

The second paper published under the new Press Law, a Persian-language weekly named *Payam-i-Emroz* (the first issue appeared on February 9, 1966) met a fate similar to that of *Khalq*. The publisher, Ghulam Nabi Khater, edited the early issues but later hired Abdul Raouf Turkmani as editor. *Payam-i-Emroz* attacked corruption, particularly among members of the Yousuf cabinet. Turkmani, a Hazara, also demanded more consideration of the rights of minorities. The government closed the paper on May 25 contending that *Payam-i-*

---

2. Incitement to seek depravity by means of:
   (a) Publication of false or distorted news, in spite of the knowledge that the said news is false or distorted, provided such news causes damage to the interest or dignity of the state or individuals.
   (b) Publication of obscene articles or photos which tend to debase public morals. (Publication of obscene articles or photos prejudicial to good morals.)
   (c) Publication of comments and views the aim of which is to divert the courts from reaching correct decisions on cases under their security.
   (d) Publication of comments and views the aim of which is to divert the public prosecutor, police, witnesses or even public opinion from the correct path over a definite case.
3. Defamation of persons and publication of false statements about them.
4. Attack upon the sanctity of the private life of individuals.

Article 34: If the publication of an item causes direct and actual disruption of the country's social health or economic life, or even deceives public opinion, the editor is required to refrain from publishing it. Such action may be:

1. Publication of items with a view to purposely weakening the state's fiscal credit.
2. Publication of false advertisement of medicines in spite of knowledge about them.

Article 35: Publication of matters with a view to weakening the Afghan Army is not allowed.

. . . .

Article 48: A newspaper will close down if it does not have an editor.

Emroz had no editor as required by the Press Law; but attacks on Prime Minister Maiwandwal's person and policies may be partly responsible for the move. Turkmani had resigned as editor a few days before the closure, but reliable sources reported that certain government officials had told Khater to close down and that he had fired Turkmani to save face.

Many self-professed "modern Afghans" heartily approved the Attorney General's actions, particularly with respect to *Khalq:* "The people in the villages," they said, "will believe anything, and the brand of communism propounded by *Khalq* would have confused them and made them doubt the New Democracy." Such reasons certainly have not held true elsewhere in Asia, for Asian peasant farmers, be they landowners or tenants, constitute a conservative force which tends to resist change, either from the right or the left.

In my opinion, however, the government may have set a bad precedent in the *Khalq* decision. In addition, high officials told me that the Afghan Government knows all the ultra-leftwingers well and has complete dossiers on each of them. If this is true, there would seem to be little advantage in forcing potentially subversive groups underground.

As if to atone for the abrupt closure of the leftwing *Khalq* and the shutdown of *Payam-i-Emroz* on a technicality, the government permitted a proliferation of newspapers, most of which are opposition, all printed by the Government Press. Although most newspapers are anti-government, few are really anti-*Shura.*

Considering the standards of the government papers, it is to be hoped that all the papers of the free press survive; for although they are not newspapers in the sense that they publish news and save editorializing for the editorial page—indeed, they are political tracts from cover to cover—until the time when government-controlled papers can present a full, not a selective, news coverage, they offer an excellent counterbalance to government pap.

Probably the most influential of these new newspapers are *Afghan Mellat*, *Masawat* (*Equality*), *Parcham* (*The Flag*), and—before it was closed on July 20, 1968—*Shu'la-yi-Jawed* (*The Eternal Flame*). *Parcham* is leftist in orientation, but more evolutionary in outlook than revolutionary. Its rival, *Shu'la-yi-Jawed,* was more Maoist and revolutionary.

Afghan Mellat, the oldest of the non-government papers, has been published weekly since April 5, 1966, except for a nine-month forced vacation from May 2, 1967, to February 20, 1968. Its policies can be described as anti-neoimperialist (against capitalist foreign investment, which will "strangle the society"); anti-foreign influence (it attacks the miniskirt, the German and American Peace Corps, all influence of foreign technicians, all British influence, alcoholic beverages, the sale of American and European second-hand clothing in the bazaar, etc.); and pro-"Pushtunistan." *Afghan Mellat* goes farther than any other voice in calling for a "greater Afghanistan," which, as represented on a loosely drawn map printed in the paper, covers most of the eighteenth-century empire of Ahmad Shah Durrani, the last great Afghan imperialist. The paper's slogan boldly proclaims: "We want a united, free, and democratic country. And we want Greater Afghanistan to come into existence."

The publisher and editor refer to "National Democratic Socialism" as their way of life, and to many it appears that Engineer Ghulam Mohammad Farhad (called "Papa Ghulam"), the publisher, is striving to assume the mantle of the aging Pushtun leader, Khan Abdul Ghaffar Khan. *Afghan Mellat* defines National Democratic Socialism as constitutional monarchy, Greater Afghanistan ("water cannot be divided with a stick" is the line), a democratic society, no bribery, land for the landless, the prohibition of luxury imports, no foreign loans that cannot be repaid or are not needed, a progressive income tax, the restoration of Pashto as a popular language, and a free "Pushtunistan" (*Afghan Mellat,* December 27, 1966).

Afghan Mellat accepts advertisements, although blatantly stating that it prefers ads for locally produced products, and it undertakes such causes as attacking Western-produced films that have been dubbed in Iranian Persian. One letter to the editor, on October 11, 1966, succinctly stated the problem: "Why don't they leave the English in? Who in Kabul understands Tehrani Farsi?" (As a matter of fact, Afghan students visiting Tehran sometimes refuse to speak Persian because the Iranians would tease them about their "hillbilly" dialect. Possibly, however, Afghan Dari is the purer Persian. They much prefer to speak English or French in such circumstances.)

Afghan Mellat also undertakes more important causes, however. It does attack government corruption and, much to the discomfort of officialdom, often names names. But it was not until the appearance of the article "How the C.I.A. Turns Foreign Students into Traitors," (which purported to expose the involvement of high-ranking government officials with the C.I.A.) in the April 1967 issue of *Ramparts* magazine that Papa Ghulam really got into serious trouble. The lead article in *Afghan Mellat* for April 25, 1967, was entitled "Are Our Government Officials Spies?" and the result was that the paper was closed down for the next nine months.

Few Americans bothered to read the exposé of Abdul Latif Hotaki in *Ramparts*. Most were too fascinated by the parade of foundations, universities, unions, journals, and individuals, all heretofore assumed to be eminently respectable but now revealed as being intimately and often knowingly involved with the Central Intelligence Agency. In Afghanistan, Prime Minister Maiwandwal's government was shaken, but finally remained firm.

In addition, the disclosures that several foundations (e.g., the Asia Foundation and the American Friends of the Middle East), which have supported the Associated Students of Afghanistan (A.S.A.) in the United States, had received funds from the C.I.A. caused the A.S.A. to break ties with these organizations in letters which are models of decorum under the circumstances (L. Dupree, *AUFS Reports,* LD-6-68,14). Because of this, the A.S.A. has had difficulty meeting its financial obligations. It cut back its operations, but then gradually began to expand again with the combined support of individual Afghans and Americans and the Asia Society, which now assists in the publication of an abbreviated *Afghan Student News.*

Hotaki's accusations met with two reactions in Afghanistan. The official line is typified by an editorial entitled "Latif and His Black Story," which appeared in the government-controlled newspaper, *Anis,* on April 22, 1967:

> . . . the little known magazine *Ramparts* . . . has published reports made by persons for the sake of publicity and are unjustified. . . . They quote a man like Abdul Latif who has a weak conscience and has sacrificed his family for his selfish ends and he has decided to live under an alien flag. . . . Our people will not permit the statements of a defector from his country and server of hidden imperial interests, and the publication of these statements to succeed in causing a spirit of cynicism and creating a lack of trust in our enlightened and progressive circles.

Naturally several different versions of the story developed in the bazaar, and sooner or later practically everyone who had ever visited the United States was named as a C.I.A. agent. The Pakistani press and the B.B.C. (which often parrots the Pakistani line on Afghan–Pakistani relations) reported the rumors, indiscreetly naming names, including those of several cabinet members and other high officials.

Prime Minister Maiwandwal met the threat head on. Along with his cabinet, he faced a barrage of probing questions in the *Wolesi Jirgah,* and he came out with as clean a bill of political health as was possible under the circumstances. His eventual resignation may have had little to do with the C.I.A. episode, however, for he was genuinely ill. But the specter of what *can* happen now hangs over many American-educated leaders in developing nations.

After Maiwandwal's resignation, Papa Ghulam received permission to begin republication of *Afghan Mellat.* The nationalization by Maiwandwal of the *sherkat-i-barq* (the electric company), of which Papa Ghulam was president, at least partly accounts for the anti-Maiwandwal attacks in *Afghan Mellat.* Incorruptible himself, Papa Ghulam had reportedly shown favoritism in granting jobs and, according to many sources, he finally found himself surrounded by ingratiating parasites. Although a public utility, the electric company had never opened its books to either the government or the public until Maiwandwal's nationalism order. Papa Ghulam has never forgiven the former Prime Minister, and he often uses *Afghan Mellat* as his cudgel. For example, the columnist Feda Mohammad Fedayi has attacked Maiwandwal's Progressive Democratic Party (P.D.P.) as "collective dictatorship" (*Afghan Mellat,* February 27, 1967).

Many both in and out of government accuse Maiwandwal of taking unfair advantage of his position as Prime Minister during the formation of the P.D.P. According to many sources, Maiwandwal attempted to create a "cult of personality" around himself, but he has blamed the excessive zeal of his followers for this impression. *Afghan Mellat* has described a session held in the Ministry of Information and Culture, at which all of the invited officials were asked to praise Maiwandwal, rather in the manner of the sessions praising Chairman Mao in China or like American political testimonial dinners. Maiwandwal's detractors say that some officials who refused to participate were subsequently replaced by members of the P.D.P., while his partisans insist that this type of "spoils system" is a common institution in democratic societies, especially in the United States. (Several former ministers in Maiwandwal's and earlier cabinets objected to both the P.D.P. and the "spoils system," and for this reason—or so they say—either left his cabinet or refused to serve when asked.)

In spite of these allegations, many Afghans both inside and outside the government still hold Mr. Maiwandwal in high esteem. His program, which is generally the same as that which he followed while in office, supports the King's dream of a successful constitutional monarchy under the Constitution of 1964 (See *Kabul Times Annual,* 1967, for complete text of the P.D.P platform). To propagate the P.D.P., Maiwandwal and a group of his supporters founded the weekly *Masawat (Equality)* in April 1967. In December 1967, it ceased publication for a few months because of enforced government pressure after Maiwandwal's resignation; but it reopened in April 1968 and continues now as the organ of the party.

Two major leftist opposition papers, which have already been mentioned, also began publication about that time: *Parcham* on March 14, 1968, and *Shu'la-yi-Jawed* on April 4, 1968. The writers for *Parcham* included such well-known socialists as Babrak Karmal and Dr. Anahita, a woman parliamentary deputy from Kabul, serving in the twelfth session—both of whom seem to have quieted down appreciably since the December 1966 *Wolesi Jirgah* fight that put Babrak in the hospital and Dr. Anahita in an embarrassing position. In a cartoon in *Afghan Mellat* on December 26, 1966, she was portrayed upside down and being beaten by other delegates. Her thighs were pointedly exposed (Papa Ghulam often attacks the miniskirt and other "obscene" Western clothing), and the caption read: "This is the condition of the aspirations of the *Wolesi Jirgah*. Here are the deputies we chose. This is the result!" Babrak, on the other hand, reportedly turned the situation to his advantage. He has a great flare for the dramatic, and when his followers demonstrated outside the hospital, he grabbed additional bandages and energetically tied them around his head before appearing to wave feebly to the spirited crowd.

Currently, however, Babrak and *Parcham* appear to be agreed that a milder evolutionary approach to socialism is to be preferred to violent overthrow. *Parcham* believes that all sectors of the Afghan population can contribute to the defeat of "feudalism and imperialism" and promotes the creation of a "United Democratic Front," to work for a change *within* the constitutional system. The editors call for patriotism and "a feeling of humanity" for all the outside world, and the paper constantly uses such slogans as "People Are Awakening!"; "The New Year Begins, a New Year of Our Sacred Struggle!"; and "Long Live the Uplift of the Hardworking Women of Our Beloved Country!"

Parcham's approach drew charges of "revisionism" from *Shu'la-yi-Jawed,* and on May 13, 1968, in the last published issue of the paper, the editor wrote: *"Parcham* is full of false propaganda and buried up to its throat in a muddy mire of revisionism." The Afghans refer to the *Parcham* evolutionists as *chup* (left) and to the *Shu'la-yi-Jawed* revolutionists as *chup-i-chup* (left of left). In fact, the *Shu'la-yi-Jawed* group seems to have taken over the position of "political communists," while the followers of Babrak Karmal and Dr. Anahita and those of Mir Mohammad Siddiq Farhang (a noted liberal) may find themselves uncomfortably occupying the same position near the center—that of the "economic socialists" (in my definition), who wish to work within the existing system to bring about change.

Before it closed down (possibly without adequate justification), *Shu'la-yi-Jawed* attacked not only the semi-racist groups following the "Greater Afghanistan–Pushtunistan" ideas of Papa Ghulam's *Afghan Mellat* and the evolutionary "revisionists," but also the King and his intimate advisers. This, of course, is the real reason why the paper was closed. *Shu'la-yi-Jawed* was published by the brother (Dr. Rahim Mahmudi) and the nephew (Dr. Hadi Mahmudi) of Dr. Abdur Rahman Mahmudi, the well-known Afghan leader of the "Liberal Parliament" movement of 1949–52, who was jailed in May 1952 and died a few months after his release.[9] About a month after the paper was shut down, the government arrested both Mahmudis during the mid-June, 1968, workers' strike at Jangalak.

Many statements in *Shu'la-yi-Jawed,* such as "A ruling class which suppresses its own people can never free another nation" (i.e., "Pushtunistan"), certainly did not endear the already suspect Mahmudi family to the Afghan Establishment. The paper attacked both the "imperialists" (the Americans) and the "reactionaries" (the Russians) and supported national liberation movements throughout the world, implying

---

[9] Another famous leader of the "liberal parliament" who was also imprisoned in 1952 but released in 1963, Mir Ghulam Mohammad Ghubar, recently published a book entitled *Afghanistan's Path Through History (Afghanistan dar Masir-i-Tarikh).* Written under the sponsorship of Prime Minister Maiwandwal's Minister of Information and Culture, Abdul Rauf Benawa (who is still a Maiwandwal supporter and a writer for *Masawat,* as well as a member of Parliament's Lower House), the book, although printed by the Government Press, was immediately suppressed. According to those fortunate enough to have a copy, it contains an excellent socialist interpretation of history, despite the fact that the author discreetly attacks the modern period, including years since 1929 when the present King's father came to power. Many Afghans, including even government supporters, believe that the suppression was unjustified and favor releasing the book so that someone can write a rejoinder. Suppression certainly often adds an aura of respectability and glamour, while exposure sometimes dulls luster.

that it would support one inside Afghanistan. "Peaceful co-existence" was condemned, and even such figures as Nasser of Egypt, Nehru of India, and Ne Win of Burma were described as "bureaucratic capitalists who function under the name of socialism" (*Shu'la-yi-Jawed,* May 9, 1968).

The United States, of course, drew special fire from *Shu'la-yi-Jawed.* Although the war in Vietnam is not supported by every segment of American society and a credibility gap certainly does exist, the following statistics quoted from *Shu'la-yi-Jawed* would not be accepted by the most avid American critic of the war: "In seven years of war the National Liberation Front killed one and a half million of the enemy, including 300,000 Americans—and destroyed 8,560 planes, 15,830 armoured cars, and 463 warships." American and Vietnamese casualties have been high enough without resorting to such exaggeration.

A particularly vicious attack on American imperialism appeared in the June 6, 1968 issue. Its main points were that "capitalistic imperialism" occurs when American companies take over undeveloped countries as private preserves (e.g., the United Fruit Company, the oil companies, and the pre-Castro American sugar combines); that "market and price imperialism" occurs when Americans extract raw materials cheaply and then sell the finished products at a high price in the developing world; and that "aid imperialism" occurs when the United States lends large sums of money to countries and then floods them with agricultural, educational, and Peace Corps types, all drawing enormous salaries. Also, according to *Shu'la-yi-Jawed,* the United States dumps its surplus crops on developing countries—whether they want them or not—in order to keep the American farmer happy. The picture painted may not be a pleasant one for Americans to consider, but it is important to understand that it is certainly believed to be the true one by a sizable and respectable section of the intelligentsia of the present developing world.

One satirical weekly, *Tarjman* (*The Interpreter*), exists. Its cartoons are outrageously barbed, and the entire paper makes extensive use of the *double-entendre* for which the Persian language is famous. *Tarjman* is unlike both the heavy-handed, antagonistic leftist papers and the overly sanitized government publications. One cartoon in *Tarjman* ably expressed the dilemma of the government over the closure of *Shu'la-yi-Jawed.* No one really wanted to take the first step (although the Ministry of Information and Culture finally did), and the cartoon shows the easily identifiable figures of the Ministers of Justice and of Information and Culture in football (soccer) dress, kicking a ball (*Shu'la-yi-Jawed*) back and forth. One says to the other: "You score the goal!" The other replies, "No, *you* score the goal!" The incongruity of such a situation existing within the very aggressive Afghan society proved hilarious to everyone and accurately portrayed the bind in which the government found itself.

The new freedom of the press, therefore, functions as an educational institution while the normal business of government continues. There is much to learn. No adequate libel laws exist, and the free press constantly libels the more important public figures. In open sessions of the *Wolesi Jirgah* and in parliamentary committees face-to face insults flow in a one-way direction. Such attacks often result in government inaction and defeat the real purpose of free speech and a free press, especially as the accusers are not held responsible for their statements and, by their criticisms, whether true or false, can prevent necessary executive action from being taken. Thus the very antithesis of true freedom is created.

Those responsible for censorship in the Ministry of Information and Culture sometimes tend to be too sensitive. Some would like to close down almost all the papers of the free press, but they do not dare to make the first move without support from some higher authority, say, the Minister or the Cabinet. Often demands from the *Wolesi Jirgah* can have an effect on whether or not a newspaper publishes or dies. The censorship of incoming foreign publications sometimes occurs, although it is rare. Exaggeratedly zealous government censors ripped out an article from the *Economist,* July 27–August 2, 1968, which called attention to the current stagnation of the economy and the relatively poor performance of the legislative branch, and which also said that some in Afghanistan predicted the monarchy might not survive much longer.

A group, which by its irresponsible opposition makes certain that no alternatives are possible in government action, can, as easily as an individual, become a "dictator." Thus, an irresponsible press, encouraged by an unprincipled (or foreign-influenced) group in the *Wolesi Jirgah,* can come to seem quite menacing; indeed, it may literally force the King to dissolve Parliament and possibly even to abrogate the Constitution. If this should happen, these "Red Guards" of Afghanistan, dressed in parliamentary immunity, and their companions of the press must be held partly responsible for the King's action. If the present Afghan experiment in democracy should fail, it will probably be because of an absence of the democratic spirit in the opposition, as well as suppressive activities from the right.

Increased education and communications have not brought about that oneness of Afghanistan hoped for by the intelligentsia and the King. The racist policies of *Afghan Mellat* are but one example. Others are surfacing. The non-Pushtun north, some say, may break away to form an autonomous unit, while the south would remain a predominately Pushtun-controlled area.

As literacy increases among non-Pushtun groups, they develop a greater pride and awareness of their own language and cultural patterns, and tend to feel that the Pushtun have been in control too long (an attitude which somewhat parallels the non-Punjabi belief that the Punjabis control everything in Pakistan). Of course, such ethnocentricity or regionalism is widespread among minority groups today in both the developed and developing world—the racial problem in the United States, for instance, is probably part of this worldwide tendency. Enlightenment, it seems, often does not follow literacy.

Worker-Student Demonstrations, 1966–68

On every October 25 (*sehum-i-aqrab* in the Afghan calendar) since 1965, students have held peaceful demonstrations in honor of those killed on that tragic day. Occasional student strikes occurred after 1965, but during the summer of 1968, major disturbances took place (Chart 24). Recent student strikes have usually involved demands for the reform of the curriculum, for graduate programs, and for changes in admission policies. The workers' demands, too, have been rather uniform: for pay raises, better working conditions, annual leave, reduced working hours (e.g, a half-holiday on Thursday to precede the weekly religious holiday, Friday), annual bonuses, cooperative stores, free transportation to and from work, and health and medical insurance.

The occasional student support—even, in some cases, support by grammar-school students—for the workers' strikes has surprised many in Kabul. Indeed, some observers, especially foreigners, have expressed amazement that, given the overall cultural scene, the strikes should have occurred at all. It should not be too surprising, however. In some classrooms, the students often refuse to listen to anti-Marxist views, and an atmosphere has been created in which few academics can favorably discuss anything relating to the West. I do not myself believe that the student population is "pro-communist" (whatever that means today); rather, I believe that their attitudes, and their strikes and demonstrations, are a response to the real inequities in their society as they see

619

CHART 24
A Chronology of Selected Worker and/or Student Strikes and
Demonstrations: 1968

Month	Workers	Students
April	Strike at Kohsar Construction Co., Kabul	Strike of students in Nimroz Province against unfair punishment
May	Strike of Jangalak workers, Kabul (agitation since February)	Strike of 2,000 high school students who had fail Kabul University entrance examinations
	Strike at Government Printing Press, Kabul, on May 26	Strikes at Afghan Institute of Technology (West German sponsored), Technicum, School of
	Strike of government bus and truck drivers, Kabul, on May 28	Nursing, Teachers Training School on May 21; demonstrations, one or two killed in clash,
	Strike at Pul-i-Charkhi textile and bicycle assembly plants near Kabul	students parade with bloody shirts
	Strike at Qandahar Woolen Mill on May 30	Strike of Kabul University Faculties of Theology, Law, and Medicine for graduate programs
	Strike at Ghouri Cement Plant, Pul-i-Khumri, on May 30	
	Strike of Pul-i-Khumri Textile workers	
	Strike of petroleum workers, Shibarghan. March toward Kabul (turned back at Salang Pass)	
	Strike of asphalting unit of Pul-i-Khumri-Shibarghan road project for back pay	
June	Strike at Spinzar Cotton Co., Kunduz, June 2 to 4	Strike at Teachers Training School in support of Kunduz workers
	Strike at Education Press, Kabul	Strike of students to back workers in Gulbahar
	Strike of textile workers at Gulbahar	Strike of students at Jabal us-Seraj in support of
	Strike of workers at Jabal us-Seraj	workers and to demonstrate against principal
	Second strike of Ghouri Cement Plant workers on June 4	Strike of Paktya Teachers Training School and hi school students for library improvement, for a
	Strike of Norabeh gold miners, Takhar	free press, against American testing, and agains
	Strike of Hajeri-Nadjeri workers against German technicians on June 5	colonialists and landlords on June 4 and 5
	Second strike of Pul-i-Khumri textile workers on June 6	Strike at Afghan Institute of Technology continu Strike at Kabul University by Faculty of Educatii
	Strike at Qandahar Fruit Co. when 35 workers were laid off	students (strikes of Faculties of Law and Medicine continue until June 27)
	Strikes at Hazrat Imam and Spinzar Cotton Co. at Kunduz; peasants joined port workers at Sher Khan Bandar on June 6	Students joined workers and peasants in Kunduz strike
	Jangalak strike explodes into violence	

them. They attack those ideologies—primarily religious fanaticism and Western materialistic philosophies—which they believe have created the inequities and which, as they see it, jointly control the country and ultimately their own destinies.

Have all the disturbances by students and workers been part of a united effort? It seems to me that the problems of the nature and inspiration of the strikes can best be considered together. The existing state of communications today encourages, I believe, the rise in worldwide student-worker demonstrations. The news of a "police bust" at Berkeley, of a riot at Columbia, or of students and workers at the barricades in Paris sweeps around the world in hours—and every town and many villages in Afghanistan have their quota of transistor radios. The student disturbances in Afghanistan can be seen as an extension and part of the general student unrest throughout the world; and the involvement of Afghan students and teachers, in turn, becomes a logical development if one remembers that the impassioned student demonstrators of *sehum-i-aqrab* in 1965 have now mostly become teachers and officials in the provinces. Naturally, they maintain contacts with old friends and get together as often as possible. Thus cells are born, ideas proliferate, and action begins. Disgruntled at being away from the intellectual center, Kabul, and nursing a grudge against the "Establishment" which first brought them to the capital and then sent them back to rural areas, these teachers pass on their attitudes, together with their special knowledge, to their students—and sometimes, indeed, to their students' parents, particularly if they work in one of the many factories run by the government or private monopolies. Everything considered, I find it surprising that more coordinated student-worker disturbances have not taken place, and I am sure that they will increase in the future.

A new round of demonstrations and unrest began in the spring of 1969, when the students at Ibn Sina (a teacher-training, boarding high school) protested against the nepotism and favoritism of certain school officials. Police entered the school grounds on May 17 to arrest the ringleaders. A wild melee resulted, which quickly spread to neighboring Dar'ul Mo'alamein (a teacher-training school for high school graduates) and Rahman Baba (a boarding high school for provincial students). The government officially announced no one had been killed, but eyewitness accounts place the dead at between five and fifteen; some sources claim as many as thirty-two. Many of the students involved—or merely trapped—in the fighting took refuge in the resident halls of nearby Kabul University.

621

The students and faculty of the university immediately organized a series of protests against the police action, and the same violent patterns repeated themselves on May 19 when the elite riot squad, the West German trained *Ghundeh Zarabah* (literally *force de frappe*), invaded the university to arrest the leaders of the demonstrations. Things once again got out of hand. The police beat students and faculty unmercifully and indiscriminately and, as before, robbed many victims of watches and other valuables. A dozen professors and about fifty students ended up in the overcrowded hospitals of Kabul.

An intensified mood of militancy spread from the university campus to almost the entire student population of Kabul. A strike was called, and students refused to attend classes. The faculties and student bodies of all Kabul's major schools drew up sets of non-negotiable demands which they presented to the Etemadi regime. Included among the more important demands were: condemn the police actions; punish those responsible; make restitution to the injured and robbed; guarantee independence for university from government interference; permit political activity on the campus; prohibit police from entering the campus and school grounds; release the jailed students.

The government, as it often does, ignored the formal protests and demands, presumably hoping that things would settle down of their own accord. The strike dragged on for forty-eight days. On July 9 the government officially closed Kabul University and sent the boarding students home. At the same time, the Ministry of Education ordered the secondary schools, closed earlier, on June 10, reopened. Most of the ringleaders (those still not in jail) were expelled, and the majority of students returned to classes, encouraged by the seniors who wished to graduate on schedule.

On November 6, the government peacefully reopened Kabul University, and even the most passionate speakers could not lure the students into sustained protests or another strike. Again, the seniors wanted to graduate. The government had won its battle, but the problems remain and the war will continue.

I believe—as I believed after the riots of 1965—that most of the strikes and demonstrations are largely caused by home-grown dissatisfaction. Of course, neither the Americans, the Russians, nor the Chinese will pass up an opportunity to gain friends, influence policy, and—not least—embarrass opponents through growing student-worker unrest; but there are enough inequities at home to bring about the disturbances without importing foreign ideologies. It can only be hoped that Afghan executive and legislative leaders, as well as foreign observers, will be able to distinguish between what is local and what is not; and that the opposition, pressured from all sides, will "keep its cool" and accept only such assistance as will not bring on justifiable charges of external interference in internal Afghan affairs.

Like the more irresponsible actions of the *Wolesi Jirgah* and the free press, the student riots and demonstrations seem to me to be more evolutionary and educational than revolutionary. With expanding education and increasing awareness, however, evolutionary processes might well develop into revolutionary processes if the government does not keep pace with legitimate aspirations.

The Economy, Foreign Assistance, and the Third Five Year Plan, 1967–72[10]

Afghanistan, like most developing countries, dreams of industrialization, but its economy remains fundamentally agricultural. About ninety percent of its people are engaged in agriculture, animal husbandry, or combinations of the two. No matter how one views the present economic patterns in Afghanistan, the outlook, at least at first, seems bleak. With most of the major infrastructure completed (which means a substantial drop in large construction projects), with few real resources capable of earning sizable sums of hard currency, with little or no increase in the area under cultivation or productivity per acre, with little success in fiscal reforms (budgetary deficits totaled over 5 billion afghanis in 1969), with foreign loans coming due, with few industrial or power plants functioning at fifty percent capacity, with the current fear-oriented inertia in the government plus the inflexible *tawildar* (storekeeper accounting) system, Afghanistan gives any economists, socialist or free enterprise, the euphoria of a challenge. In many places outside Kabul (still out of touch with the rest of the country), conservative religious, ethnic, and tribal leaders directly or indirectly resist government attempts at local development, or, conversely, they become avid converts and condemn the government for doing too little within their

---

[10] Those desiring detailed (though not always accurate) data on the economic patterns in Afghanistan since World War II should consult the annual *Survey of Progress*, published by the Department of Statistics, Ministry of Planning, Royal Government of Afghanistan. The U.S.A.I.D. Program Office in Kabul independently tries to keep statistics, as does the United Nations. I shall use the minimum of statistical data necessary to point out trends relating to the total patterns. Also see: Emery and Lee (1967); Palyak (1963); Rheim and Ghausie (1966).

districts. The tendency to demand more increases with each passing year.

Afghan exports revolve about agricultural and animal produce, which account for about 90% of the total (Chart 25).

Fresh and dried fruits are the major export items, but *qarakul* (Persian lamb) skins sold in the West constitute the major source of hard currency. In 1950, the Afghans virtually controlled the *qarakul* markets in New York and London, supplying 80% of the skins, against 15% from South Africa and 5% from the U.S.S.R. In 1965, however, South Africa supplied 54%, Afghanistan 34% and the Soviet Union 12%. The rising popularity of mutated mink partly affected *qarakul* sales in the U.S., but, fundamentally, lack of quality control lost the Afghans the bulk of the market.

To reverse the trend, the Afghans founded the Afghan Qarakul Institute in June 1966, and established uniform standards. In 1968 and 1969, 14.5 million skins were auctioned in the New York–London markets, 4 million more than the 1966–67 figure. More important, the Afghans sold almost 100% of the skins exported in 1968 and 1969, compared to only 50% in 1966 and 1967. In addition to quality control, several other factors contributed to the success of the Afghan Qarakul Institute. The fashion world of the West prefers the gray *qarakul,* on which Afghanistan has a virtual monopoly. The fickleness of fashion may shift at any time, but if this happens, the Afghan Qarakul Institute quality control program should permit the black or golden skins to compete successfully with others on the market. Flock growers are paid higher prices than before—350 afghanis per skin in 1969, compared to 250 afghanis in 1968—which encourages them to increase their flocks. The average price of skins on the market also increased from $6.50 to $8.00 in 1969, with top quality from $10 to $14. The Afghan government, in order to encourage additional exports of skins and to decrease smuggling, established an improved rate of exchange for the industry, and increased the afghani rate from 45 to 65 afghanis to the dollar. The free market in 1969 varied from 75 to 80 afghanis to the dollar; the same was true in 1972.

Now most skins are shipped by air, for the government cut the air freight charges by thirty percent. Previously, most skins were exported over the slow land-routes through the U.S.S.R. A fixed twenty percent of the skins go to the New York market. The success of the Afghan Qarakul Institute may provide a model for other small scale industries in Afghanistan.

CHART 25

Afghanistan's Exports by Commodity: 1966–70

(in millions of $ U.S.)

Commodity	1966-67	1967-68	1968-69	1969-70[1]
Natural gas to USSR[2]	–	2.93	9.03	12.01
Casings (sheep guts)	1.45	1.28	1.11	0.98
Dried fruit and nuts	15.26	18.01	18.96	19.45
Fresh fruit	6.65	8.15	8.01	8.94
Fresh & dried vegetables	0.21	0.04	0.16	0.34
Oilseeds	1.02	0.90	2.80	2.73
Hides and skins	2.18	2.05	2.04	2.71
Qarakul skins	11.71	14.06	8.32	12.46
Other fur skins	0.20	0.33	0.22	0.23
Wool	4.98	4.86	6.99	6.72
Raw cotton	11.90	7.86	5.88	5.65
Medicinal herbs	0.98	0.31	2.85	1.81
Carpets and rugs	8.00	5.17	4.52	6.30
Other commodities	0.23	.46	.91	1.10
Total	64.77	66.41	71.80	81.43

Source: *Survey of Progress: 1969-70,* Department of Statistics, Ministry of Planning, Royal Government of Afghanistan, Kabul, October, 1970, S-14

[1] All estimates.

[2] 1967-68 first year natural gas exported to U.S.S.R. via pipeline under Amu Darya.

In 1966–67, between 35% and 40% of Afghanistan's foreign trade was with the Soviet bloc, 20% with India and Pakistan, and 40% to 45% with the free currency areas (Charts 26 and 27). In order to save hard currency, the Afghans could easily purchase many of their commodities and consumer goods requirements (Chart 28) from India and Pakistan. The rising Afghan middle-class consumer, however, places high prestige value on American and West European products. Another limiting factor is that most foreign assistance commodity loans require that items be purchased from the country of the lender. A scheme now under consideration may loosen up this requirement, particularly when the recipient nation has neighboring countries (Pakistan and India in the case of Afghanistan) with a plethora of counterpart funds from P.L. 480 wheat sales. Under the new plan, the U.S. would lend Afghanistan rupees to purchase commodities in Pakistan, the loan to be repaid in afghanis, which would be used for local costs of American A.I.D. programs in Afghanistan.

Since 1956, Afghanistan's economy has been guided by a series of adjustable Five Year Plans. The First Five Year Plan (1956–57 to 1960–61) proposed an expenditure of 14 billion afghanis. It eventually cost 16.6 billion afghanis, and foreign assistance provided 75% of the total. The second plan (1962–67), like the first, emphasized the development of a transportation and communication infrastructure. Attempting to catch up with the unrealized, unrealistic, and ambitious first Five Year Plan, the Afghans projected a 44.5 billion afghani expenditure for the second plan (including double the amount of foreign assistance under the first plan, or eighty percent of the total.) Neither the Russians nor the Americans came through with the required level of assistance, however, and the Afghans eventually scaled the plan down to 27 billion afghanis. Foreign aid was a major import from 1957 to 1969 (Chart 29).

The United States has been generous with grants, but the recent hardening of the American attitude on aid may bring about major changes. In particular, two amendments to foreign assistance acts could—if implemented—drastically affect American aid to many developing nations. The Symington Amendment to the 1961 act requires that the budgets of all nations receiving U.S. assistance be examined to determine what percentage is being spent on the military establishment. The Conte-Long Amendment to the 1967 act goes further than simple examination of budgets. It requires that American aid to recipient nations be cut in direct proportion to the amount being spent on sophisticated weapons.

CHART 26

Afghanistan's Imports by Country: 1966–69
(in millions of $ U.S.)

Country	1966-67	1967-68	1968-69
U.S.S.R.	22.53	18.65	13.99
U.S.A.	4.07	2.34	2.69
India	6.78	6.33	11.22
Japan	9.56	10.63	11.98
Pakistan	4.56	3.26	3.05
West Germany	4.45	4.73	3.89
United Kingdom	2.20	3.59	3.20
Czechoslovakia	2.89	0.79	0.79
Other barter countries	2.59	2.32	2.48
Other countries	7.03	10.28	12.28
Total	66.66	62.92	65.57
Loan and Grant Imports	84.08	75.43	63.16
Total all imports	150.74	138.35	128.73

Source: *Survey of Progress: 1969-70*, Department of Statistics, Ministry of Planning, Royal Government of Afghanistan, Kabul, October, 1970, S-13.

CHART 27

Afghanistan's Exports by Country: 1966–70
(in millions of $ U.S.)

Country	1966-67	1967-68	1968-69	1969-70
U.S.S.R.	21.51	22.07	26.57	30.75
U.S.A.	5.45	5.56	4.59	2.47
India	8.51	10.80	15.76	15.15
United Kingdom	9.39	10.65	7.42	12.30
West Germany	3.70	0.60	1.33	1.62
Pakistan	5.35	5.51	5.74	6.25
Japan	0.09	0.17	0.11	0.12
Czechoslovakia	2.03	2.26	1.52	1.63
Other barter countries	1.25	0.52	0.11	0.58
Other countries	7.39	8.26	8.67	10.56
Total	64.67	66.40	71.82	81.43

Source: *Survey of Progress:* 1969-70, Department of Statistics, Ministry of Planning Royal Government of Afghanistan, Kabul, October, 1970, S-14.

627

CHART 28
Afghanistan's Imports by Commodity: 1966–69
(in millions of $ U.S.)

Commodity	1966-67	1967-68	1968-69
Wheat	–	5.46	3.46
Sugar	6.42	3.77	0.95
Tea	6.08	4.83	9.48
Other foods	1.73	0.89	1.13
Tobacco	0.37	0.36	0.48
Petroleum products	4.38	3.78	3.09
Medicine, pharmaceutical products	2.29	2.54	2.50
Other chemical products	2.03	2.23	2.47
Rubber, tires, tubes	3.04	3.82	2.84
Cotton fabrics	3.85	3.52	2.77
Fabrics (excluding cotton)	4.91	5.14	6.41
Other non-metalic mineral products	4.06	4.68	6.38
Metals and metal manufactures	2.47	2.30	2.63
Machinery (excluding electrical)	1.37	1.46	1.95
Electrical machinery	2.48	2.02	2.08
Automobiles	1.16	1.23	0.93
Other motor vehicles	1.91	1.29	1.17
Bicycles	0.30	0.31	0.24
Other transport equipment	1.16	1.95	1.70
Plumbing, heating, lighting equipment	0.86	1.06	0.81
Used clothing	1.00	1.00	1.19
Footwear	1.37	1.52	1.73
Misc. manufactured articles	3.46	3.47	4.87
Other commodities	9.97	4.31	4.31
Total commodity imports	66.67	62.94	65.57
Total commodity imports	66.67	62.94	65.57
Non-project loan & grant imports	20.27	13.43	12.96
Project loan & grant imports	63.81	61.99	50.20
Grand total	150.75	138.36	128.73

Source: *Survey of Progress:1969-70,* Department of Statistics, Ministry of Planning, Royal Government of Afghanistan, Kabul, October, 1970, S-13.

One problem with both amendments is the difficulty in obtaining information about the military expenditures of non-aligned countries. The practical application of the Conte-Long Amendment to places like Afghanistan appears doubtful, not only because of the secrecy which surrounds military expenditures, but because of the simple fact that American aid has been decreasing annually to the point where percentages of budgets become irrelevant.

Somewhere in the mythology of foreign aid arose the idea that all foreign assistance constituted give-away programs. Nothing could be farther from the truth. Foreign aid, however, has always been a great boon to American businesses and educational institutions, as well as a benefit to the recipient nations. Most of the money never leaves the U.S.A. For example, the percentage of the annual worldwide aid budgets spent in the United States on commodities from 1961 to 1967 was as follows: 1961, 44%; 1962, 66%; 1963, 79%; 1964, 87%, 1965, 92%; 1966, 90%; 1967, 96%.[11] In addition, the products purchased in the U.S. almost always cost more than similar items purchased elsewhere.

The products (roads, buildings, airports, teaching man-hours, hospitals) end up in the developing countries, but American business and educational interests also gain considerably. In addition, many aided nations now actually repay loans or interest on loans into the U.S. coffers.

Areas of major American and Soviet interests can be seen on Chart 29.

U.S. total assistance (grants, loans, and non-project assistance; e.g., commodity and wheat loans) has averaged about $22 million annually since 1950; the total for 1950 to 1958 was $112.5 million. Recent foreign assistance trends have tended to slacken the pace, as well as the enthusiasm of American technicians, often low as it is. The Americans and Afghans hope to reproduce the Mexi-Pak wheat "miracle" (now having growing pains of its own) of Pakistan; and if the new agricultural plan succeeds, Afghanistan, at least according to the theory, should be self-sufficient in foodcrops by 1972 (that is, by the end of the third Five Year Plan), particularly if the present, officially-estimated 2% annual birthrate can be maintained. With 90% of the population directly concerned with basic food production, and with agriculture accounting

[11] Statistics on A.I.D. Expenditures for Commodities in FY 1966, A.I.D. Office of Program Coordinates, Statistics and Reports Division, October 14, 1966, Washington, D.C. Hearings before the Congressional Subcommittee on Foreign Aid, 1967.

CHART 29
Foreign Assistance to Afghanistan: 1950–71[1]

Country	Total Loans ($ million)	Total Grants[2] ($ million)
Soviet Union[3]	572.0	100.0
United States[4]	81.2	204.8
plus PL 480	18.1	108.7
West Germany[5]	67.3	31.0
China[6]	33.6	
UNDP Special Fund[7]		21.3
Czechoslovakia[8]	12.0	
Yugoslavia[9]	8.0	
World Bank[10]	10.0	
France[11]	10.0	4.1
United Kingdom[12]	1.0	1.0
Japan[13]	3.0	0.3
Asian Development Bank[14]	2.2	
India[15]	5.4	2.0

Sources: *Annual Report on Development Assistance to Afghanistan* by the UNDP Resident Representative, January 1-December 31, 1971; USAID/Kabul; Embassies of France and the U.S.S.R., Economic Sections; IDRB, *Current Economic Position and Prospects, January 12, 1971.*

Other unused credits for the Third Five-Year Plan (1967-72) include: $2.7 million (Denmark); $2.0 million (Bulgaria).

In addition to the above, several nongovernment institutions have permanent missions in Afghanistan, including: Asia Foundation, CARE-MEDICO, NOOR (National Organization of Ophthalamic Rehabilitation), International Afghan Mission (medical).

CHART 29 (*continued*)

1 In 1970, about 1,929 foreign assistance personnel (excluding American Peace Corps and other volunteer workers) lived in Afghanistan: 1,050, U.S.S.R.; 200-220, People's Republic of China; 200, UNO; 152, West Germany; 105, United States; 85, France; 59, India; 32, Czechoslovakia; 31, Bulgaria; 15, Japan. About ten Frenchmen of the total 85 are conscripts on national service; France wisely permits its draftees to serve in Peace Corps type jobs, as well as in the military. Volunteer groups include: US Peace Corps, 140; German Volunteer Service (Deutscher Entwicklungsdienst or DED), 80; British Volunteers, four. Foreign personnel have decreased along with developmant funds. For example, the number of foreign assistance personnel in 1969 was over 2,2000.

2 Most Russian grants have been for highway construction and education. The US pattern is the same, with the addition of food grants. The figures do not include Soviet loans for military assistance, at least $250 million, and probably much more.

3 Russian loans include general economic development, $227.6 million (petrol storage tanks, silo-bakeries, asphalt roads, improved river ports, electrical transmission lines, gas pipeline to U.S.S.R., other infrastructure projects, technician salaries); petroleum-oil-lubricants equipment, $81.1 million (Sher Khan Bandar port, Mazar-i-Sharif fertilizer-thermal power plant, Sardeh irrigation project, Ningrahar Valley Project, Polytechnic Institute, asphalt roads, mineral surveys, technician salaries); Salang Tunnel and Jalalabad canals, $19.5 million; natural gas development, $38.9 million; Begram airport, $3.8 million; petroleum exploration, $13.7 million; Kabul housing project (Nadir Shah Mina), $11.1 million; Naghlu Power and Irrigation Project, $8-9 million; Ningrahar Valley Project, Phase II, $24 million; road maintenance equipment, $3 million; commodities, $33.3 million. Soviet grants have been mainly for technicians to maintain completed projects, and scholarships to Afghans, 650 of whom were undergoing training in the U.S.S.R. in 1970. About 2,000 more received scholarships since 1950.

4 United States project assistance includes: transportation and infrastructure, $109.6 million in grants, $20.8 million, loans; Hilmand Valley Project, $79.2 million grants, $59.3 million loans; education $39.1 million grants; government management and economic planning assistance, $13.2 million grants, $0.4 million loans; agriculture, $10.6 million grants; population/family planning, $0.2 million, current grant, but will grow to $2.1 million by 1972; mining and industry, $3.8 million grants, $0.7 million loans. Non-project assistance includes: fruit airlift (1961-1962, see Louis Dupree, *"Pushtunistan," The Problem and Its Larger Implications,* Parts I, II, and III, [LD-1,2,3-'61], Fieldstaff Reports, South Asia Series, Vol. V, Nos. 2,3, and 4, 1961), $0.8 million grant; commodity assistance loan (wheat, wheat flour), $1.4 million; wheat grant (Sec. 550), $1.2 million; wheat grant (PL 480, Title II), $103.6 million; corn grant (PL 480, Title II), $2.1 million; edible oil grant (PL 480, Title I), $1 million; wheat loan (PL 480, Title IV), $1.6 million; wheat and edible oil loan (PL 480, Title I), $12.6 million; agricultural commodities and fertilizer (loans 010 and 0161), $2.5 million.

About $10.3 million of the technical assistance program (1958-1969) has been used to send 2,142 Afghan students to the United States and other countries for advanced training.

5 West German loans relate mainly to the overall development of Paktya Province, telecommunications, and the Mahipar Power Station (which has been beset with damaging technical problems). Grants are usually in the educational field; German professors to Afghanistan, Afghan students on scholarships to Germany. The Germans assist at the Police Academy, and have an economic advisory group to assist the Ministry of Planning, as do the Russians, the United States (Robert Nathan Associates), and the UNO.

6 The Chinese loans are being spent on the Parwan Province Irrigation Project ($8.4 million), an experimental chicken farm, a carp fishery near Jalalabad, an experimental sericulture project in Kunar Province, an experimental tea plantation in Kunar, the Bagrami textile mill near Kabul, and a lapis lazuli workshop in the Ministry of Mines and Industries.

631

CHART 29 (*continued*)

[7] Main United Nations projects (including World Food Program, UNICEF, UNESCO, etc.) include (of the ca. $25 million): agriculture, 23 per cent; infrastructure, 20 per cent; education, 20 per cent; public health, 17 per cent; other (advisers in public works, meteorology, cartography, small scale industries, etc.), 20 per cent.

[8] Czech assistance has been mainly direct hire contracts between the Royal Government of Afghanistan with Czech technicians. A $10 million loan for the Third Five-Year Plan (1967-1972) remains unused.

[9] Yugoslavia granted Afghanistan an $8 million loan to help develop irrigation on the Hari Rud.

[10] An IDA (International Development Authority, an affiliate of the World Bank) loan of $5 million will be expended on highway maintenance; second loan is public credit to the Agriculture Development Bank. In May 1971, the IDA approved another $5 million loan after this chart was compiled. The new loan will assist the Khanabad Irrigation Project.

[11] France has been active primarily in the field of education, cultural activities, and advice on small scale industries.

[12] The United Kingdom loan went to develop the Hilmand Valley Cotton and Vegetable Oil Factory. The United Kingdom also makes a number of fellowships available for study in Britain.

[13] The Japanese have loaned Afghanistan $2.2 million to develop a pure water supply system for four cities. In 1969, 30 Afghans received scholarships to study in Japan.

[14] ADB has loaned $5.15 million Gawagar and Chahr Darrah Agricultural Development; $44,000 for a feasibility study of the new Kabul Industrial Park; $160,000 for a feasibility study of the Kajakai Floodgate and Flood Control Scheme.

[15] India's grants include a 100-bed children's hospital with attached staff ($1.2 million), teachers in secondary schools ($70,000), agricultural implements ($16,000), restoration and preservation of the Buddhist monuments of Bamiyan.

98. Coal miners at Darra-i-Suf. The mine is a U.S.-assisted project. *Photo: Afghan Films*

99. Qandahar International Airport, a U.S.-assisted project. *Photo: Afghan Films*

for 87% of all commodity exports and 75% of all domestic production, the need for such development is self-evident.

Actually, the government could easily improve productivity by purchasing what it needs from Afghan farmers and releasing all the foreign wheat loans and grants to the open market. Because the price of wheat in the bazaar varies both annually and seasonally, many large Afghan landowners store their wheat until urban prices rise perceptibly and then sell. Smaller, subsistence farmers, of course, must sell if they need money, regardless of the price; but as they seldom need cash, they seldom sell. With the improved infrastructure and communications, however, more and more small farmers annually become involved in a consumer-oriented cash economy.

The joint Afghan-A.I.D. agricultural projects for the remainder of the Third Five Year Plan revolve about six major locations (at Kabul, Jalalabad, Lashkar Gah, Kunduz Mazar-i-Sharif, and Herat), from which varieties of Mexican wheat, fertilizer, and agricultural implements will be distributed. Experimental plots have already shown that an "average" (whatever that may mean) Afghan farmer can increase his present yield of from nineteen to twenty-one bushels per acre to an average of thirty-five to thirty-seven bushels, ranging up to eighty bushels per acre depending on quality of the land and the qualifications of the farmer. Exciting new yields also bring exciting new problems, however. Who will get the excess wheat, landowner or cultivator? And who will control the distribution of the improved seeds, fertilizer, etc., to prevent contamination with local seeds? An additional problem is that the dense stands of the early-ripening Mexican varieties expose the crops to large flocks of seasonally migratory birds and also make excellent breeding grounds for insects and plant diseases.

To encourage wheat production, the Afghan government has virtually abolished the compulsory growing of cotton and sugar beets, but it should also permit free market rates to apply to all agricultural commodities. The various monopolistic companies in northern Afghanistan cannot completely ignore government production orders, although they do maintain control of the farmers, most of whom remain in perpetual debt to company stores, gestating a classic peasant revolutionary situation.

The Hilmand–Arghandab Valley Authority, although still plagued with technical and human problems, has begun to show genuine improvement. In three years wheat acreage increased 51% (1966: 159,522 *jerib;* 1969: 252,151 *jerib;* 2 *jerib* = 1 acre). Yield per *jerib* for the same period jumped from 48.1 *mawn* (1 *mawn* = 10 lbs.) to 69 *mawn*. A sizeable (59%) increase also occurred in corn between 1966 (44,005 *jerib*) and 1968 (69,891 *jerib*), and mung beans (1966: 16,509 *jerib;* 1968: 23,244 *jerib*). Fortunately, the new government policy permitted a reduction in both cotton (1966: 45,554 *jerib;* 1968: 17,375 *jerib*) and barley (1966: 23,575 *jerib;* 1968: 17,472 *jerib*).

By the end of the Fourth Five Year Plan (according to the theory the H.A.V.A. will be self-sufficient in wheat and corn, large quantities of foodstuffs will be exported to the rest of Afghanistan, and a large agro-industrial scene will have come into being (this last accounts for the $12-million proposal for a power plant at the Kajaki Dam site). By 1968, however, over $115 million had been spent (of which $78.4 million in loans and grants was contributed by the U.S.). The planned small-scale industrial development in H.A.V.A. and Qandahar continues to lag. A little-used fruit packing and canning plant (built with Czech assistance) sits in Qandahar near an ancient woolen mill. At Lashkar Gah, capital of the H.A.V.A., a British-constructed cotton gin and seed-pressing mill exists (although there is little cotton), as well as an alabaster factory, a tire-recapping plant, a dairy, and a heavy construction unit (primarily for building and repairing canals, leveling land, and repairing the H.A.V.A. road system).

Human problems still exist. In 1967, the H.A.V.A. moved several hundred farmers from about 2,000 acres at Darweshan and leveled the land with the assistance of the U.S. Bureau of Reclamation. The Americans and the Afghan government (H.A.V.A.) then jointly raised bumper crops of cotton on the acreage, but now the farmers wish to return to their lands and find their efforts blocked. An ugly situation has developed. Under newly advanced plans, the H.A.V.A. now plans to move farmers from 31,000 acres of land in the Shamalan area, level the land, and here too introduce improved seeds, fertilizer, and farming methods. The people in Shamalan, however, have been hesitant about accepting this plan because of what happened to their neighbors in Darweshan. (Actually, the farmers at Darweshan were not physically "moved" from their villages, but only denied the use of their—or, more usually, the landowners'—land during the experiment in leveling and increasing production.) Most of the land is absentee-landlord owned, and the landowners are quite content to have the H.A.V.A. (with American assistance) continue to raise bumper cash crops for their benefit. The individual farmers quickly tired of living on handouts, however, and thus the desire to show a jump in productivity once again overrode the

100. Nadir Shah Mina apartments, a U.S.S.R.-assisted project. *Photo: Afghan Films*

101. Darunta hydroelectric project on the Kabul River near Jalalabad, a U.S.S.R.-assisted project and part of the Ningrahar Valley Project. *Photo: Afghan Films*

more important, long-range problem of integrating the economy with the people in the Hilmand Valley. Plans are underway, however, to return the farmers to the Darweshan fields by the end of 1970.

In the field of transportation, the United States continues to contribute. An Export–Import Bank loan to the Ariana Afghan Airlines permitted the purchase of a Boeing 727, and in May 1968, A.A.A. began to make scheduled jet flights: Kabul–Tehran–Beirut–Istanbul–Frankfurt–London, Kabul–Tashkent–Moscow, and Kabul–New Delhi.[12] With a Canadian loan of $800,000, Bakhtar Airlines purchased two twin-engine Otter aircraft, and "bush pilot" flights connect Kabul with several parts of Afghanistan. Places visited periodically, on a rather loose schedule, are Taliqan, Faizabad, Bamiyan (a great boon to tourists), Lashkar Gah, Maimana, Chakcharan, Herat, Mazar-i-Sharif, Khost, Nimroz, Farah, Aq Chah, Qala-yi-Naw, Kunduz, Khwahan, Khojaghar, Qandahar, Andkhui. Ariana also flies internally from Kabul to Kunduz, Qandahar, Mazar-i-Sharif, and Herat.

Two major American-supported highway links were completed recently. The Kabul–Qandahar highway, begun in August 1961, was completed in July 1966, with a length of 483 kilometers (300 miles). U.S.A.I.D. contributed $44,640,959 and the Afghans spent 163,540,000 afghanis. The Herat–Islam Qala highway was begun in August 1966 and completed in October 1967 at a cost of $10,230,000 (the American contribution was $9,353,290, including a loan of $8,411,000, while the Afghans put up 64 million afghanis, or about $876,712). This 123-kilometer (77 miles) road connects Iran with the Afghan road system, and joins up with the north–south Russian-built road just north of Herat—another example of U.S.–U.S.S.R. "cooperation" in Afghanistan.

The primary difference between Soviet bloc and American loans is that the Afghans pay off many bloc debts in barter goods, whereas Western loans must be repaid in cash. Afghan barter payments include wool, food oils, grains, cotton, goat and sheep skins, and fresh, dried, and canned fruits and nuts. Some Western and Afghan economists continue to worry about the slow—but gradual—increase in exports to the U.S.S.R., many of which, could, with better quality control, be exported to hard-currency areas. But it must be noted that the Afghan

---

[12] Ariana lost its only jet (a Boeing 727) in a crash while approaching Gatwick airport outside London on January 5, 1969. In early February the international flights were resumed with a 727 leased from World Airways, an American company. A new 727 was delivered to Ariana in January 1970.

position in its balance of payments with the Soviet Union continues to improve.

Three important Russian projects have either been completed or nearly completed. The most important of the three is the 201-kilometer (125-mile) pipeline from the Shibarghan natural gas fields to the U.S.S.R., which was opened on April 22, 1968. Over the next fifteen years the Afghans will repay much of their Russian loans (about $375 million of the total) with this gas, which was discovered in 1960. In 1968–69, gas worth approximately $8.4 million was exported; and by 1971, $13.9 million worth will be exported annually to the Soviet Union. As part of the same project, a subsidiary pipeline will feed gas to a fertilizer and thermal-power factory (capacity 36,000 kilowatts) now being constructed at Mazar-i-Sharif. The Afghans may export urea fertilizer to the Soviet Union after 1972, and possibly to other regional markets.

The second project epitomizes much of the stagnation of the Afghan industrial sector today. Russian assistance helped the Afghans to construct seventy-five miles of electrical transmission lines to Baghlan and Kunduz from the 9,000-kilowatt-capacity Ghori hydroelectric plant north of Pul-i-Khumri; but the system was developed without adequate information about annual and seasonal water fluctuation. As a result, at the seasonal peak flow, the plant distributes only about 2,000 kilowatt hours, and in the fall and winter periods of maximum need, minimum flow occurs and the requirements of the Baghlan sugar factory, the Kunduz cotton company, and the Ghori cement plant cannot be met.

The third project, still under construction, is the Nadir Shah Mina (formerly called Zindabanan) housing project in Kabul, a sixty-block housing estate of which forty blocks (containing 11,000 dwelling-units) have been opened. Begun three years ago, this monstrous apartment complex (which looks much like Tashkent, 1964), has a 500-seat cinema, a mosque, a kindergarten, a restaurant, and a shopping center. It is proving very difficult to get Afghans to leave the privacy of even the smallest compound. Another problem is the irregularity of the promised facilities (water, sewage system, electricity, etc.). Acceptance, particularly among younger Afghan couples wishing to break out of the traditional family molds, will probably come with time, however, in spite of high down-payments and total costs. Some Afghans are now actually building small prefab houses inside their own compounds.

The Russians also provided assistance for the construction and development of a Polytechnic Institute, a part of Kabul University. The Insti-

102. Afghan Textile Co. mill at Gulbahar, north of Kabul, a project assisted by the German Federal Republic. *Photo: Afghan Films*

103. Power plant at Naghlu, a U.S.S.R.-assisted project, part of the Ningrahar Valley Project. *Photo: Afghan Films*

tute, completed in 1967, enrolled 240 students and cost 6 million rubles. As the complex increases, 1,500 students will be accommodated, chiefly studying geology and the exploration of mineral deposits, the exploitation of the deposits of useful minerals, the exploitation of oil and gas fields, oil-refining and gas-working technology, the construction of factories and residences, and road and bridge construction. At least for the first few years, the bulk of the staff will be Russian, and this is the first major appearance of the U.S.S.R. on the local educational scene, although many individual Afghans have been trained in the Soviet Union. The Institute will fill a great need as the industrial complex of Afghanistan expands and develops.

Another Russian development scheme, the Ningrahar Valley Project, includes the Naghlu–Darunta dams, which furnish power as well as help control irrigation. As of January 1968, the Ningrahar Valley Project had leveled 22,898 acres, of which 21,186 are ready for production. The eventual total acreage to be under production is about 80,000 acres. In the next four years 45,000 acres will have been leveled, of which 15,000 will be converted into two large mechanized state farms, chiefly manned by the Labor Corps of the Ministry of Public Works, in association with the Ministry of Agriculture and Irrigation. Currently, the Labor Corps cultivates 17,638 acres and will reap 3,000 tons of wheat this year. Many citrus trees will also soon produce bumper crops.

The Ningrahar Valley Project has been plagued with as many problems as the H.A.V.A. First, the dam site at Darunta, selected by the Russians, had unstable strata and had to be grouted. Russian engineers still keep their technológical fingers crossed. Few farmers are being alloted land by the government and Labor Corps conscripts farm the land and care for the orchards. In addition, topsoil has been transported to many areas at great expense, and the rising water table indicates other problems will develop in the future.

How much land should be sold to private farmers and how much kept for large mechanized state farms remains a problem. However, the cost of developing land in the Nangrahar Project is estimated at eight to one over that of the Hilmand–Arghandab Valley Authority. I suspect that, although both may yet become solid regional achievements, neither will live up to the initial optimistic dreams.

Many foreign observers still believe that the Soviets wish to trap the Afghan economy, but I believe that Soviet patience, their liberal terms for loans, and their occasional extension of payments due belie this hardcore Cold War belief. Afghan exports to the U.S.S.R. still account for only about 40% of the total, and imports almost equal exports annually (See Charts 26 and 27). The figures do not seem much out of balance when one considers that about 60% of all foreign assistance comes from the U.S.S.R., and that in the current Third Five Year Plan, Russian aid accounts for 40% of the annual development budget, or about $32 million in 1967–68.

For the 1968–69 Afghan development budget, the following countries led in assistance: U.S.S.R. ($32.04 million); U.S.A. ($16.9 million); West Germany ($6.34 million); People's Republic of China ($5.63 million). The Chinese moved from behind their bamboo curtain to woo the Afghans socially, politically, and, in a lesser degree, economically. In March 1965, during a visit to Kabul by Marshal Chen Yi, the Chinese gave the Afghans a $28-million loan, partly to purchase Chinese commodities, with the remainder to be spent for development assistance projects. Barter trade between the two countries increases annually, and major Afghan exports to China include lapis lazuli, dried fruits and nuts, asafoetida, hides, and skins. In return, the Chinese ship tea, rayon items and thread, paper and paper products, and machines and machine parts to the Afghans.

Chinese economic aid continues to increase. In the 1968–69 Afghan development budget, China ranks fourth, not far behind West Germany. The Afghans have managed to keep the Chinese south of the Hindu Kush, their main project being the Parwan Irrigation Project ($2.74 million in 1968–69), almost 65 kilometers (40 miles) north of Kabul in Parwan Province, originally surveyed by an United Nations feasibility team. The human and technological problems which faced the Americans in the H.A.V.A. and the Russians in the Ningrahar area now confront the Chinese, who are repeating the mistakes of their predecessors. In contradiction to their own Maoist principles, the Chinese assisted Afghan private enterprise in the construction of a textile mill at Begrami just east of Kabul.

Other Chinese projects include developing a carp (karp, Dari) fishery at Darunta, near the Russian-built dam, and testing the feasibility of tea-growing in the Kunar Valley near Jalalabad.

West Germany continues to support primarily the silo projects ($1.5 million), the Kabul Power and Electric projects ($1.06 million), the Paktya Development Authority ($1 million; probably the most successful regional development in Afghanistan, although many tribal elements still oppose the project, and Paktya is administered by the military), and education ($750,000; particularly the Faculty of Science at Kabul

641

University and Nejat, one of the four major foreign-language high schools in Kabul).

The French are a strong presence, and continue their half-century of involvement with Istiqlal (now in the process of reconstruction; cost $750,000), which is generally accepted as the best high school in Kabul. They also support the Faculty of Medicine ($8,000) and have now moved into cotton development ($70,000) and the Balkh Textile Company ($2 million), both in association with the monopolistic Spinzar Company of north Afghanistan. The total French aid for 1968–69 is $2.98 million.

In order to maintain some economic flexibility, Afghanistan has actively encouraged Eastern European countries to assist in its development programs. Czechoslovakia has been active for several years, and in July 1968 Yugoslavia loaned the Afghans $8 million for the Hari Rud Irrigation Project east of Herat. Approximately 250,000 acres will ultimately be affected, whereas at present only 130,000 are under cultivation.[13]

Afghanistan joined the United Nations in 1946, and is the westernmost Asian member of E.C.A.F.E. (Economic Commission for Asia and the Far East). It belongs to the following international organizations and specialized agencies of the United Nations, most of which have assisted Afghanistan at one time or another: Asian Development Bank; International Bank for Reconstruction and Development; International Development Association; International Monetary Fund; International Finance Cooperation; World Health Organization; World Meterological Organization; Food and Agriculture Organization; International Atomic Energy Agency; International Civil Aviation Organization; United Nations Educational, Scientific, and Cultural Organization; Universal Postal Union; International Telecommunications Union; and International Labor Organization.

Afghanistan takes great national pride in the fact that the head of its U.N. delegation, A. R. Pazhwak, was elected President of the General Assembly in 1966.

Afghanistan also has received assistance from C.A.R.E.-M.E.D.I.C.O. (food for school children; M.E.D.I.C.O. doctors and nurses work in Afghan hospitals), the Asia Foundation (which has established varied cultural contacts with the Afghans and assisted students in obtaining foreign educations), and the Medical Assistance Program (an U.S.-

[13] Those interested in exploring the bilateral assistance programs in detail may see the mimeographed *Semi-Annual Reports* of the U.N. office in Kabul.

sponsored mobile health unit),[14] and the National Organization for Ophthalmic Rehabilitation (N.O.O.R.) of the United Kingdom. The Kabul Rotary Club, founded in late 1967, also undertakes projects in the usual Rotary manner, and various diplomatic women's organizations hold charity balls and other functions.

To date, the American Peace Corps has met with remarkable success, on the whole, in Afghanistan.[15] The increase from 6 to 200 volunteers occurred rapidly and with great enthusiasm from the Afghan side. At times, though, individual volunteers leave the country feeling they have accomplished nothing after two years of work. The cultural environment appears less strange the longer they remain. Often, familiarity makes the volunteer less tolerant of Afghan shortcomings—or what the volunteer identifies as shortcomings, using his cultural bias. Doctors and nurses never quite become accustomed to substandard (by Western definition) sanitary conditions; teachers feel they fight a losing battle against the rote system of teaching and open cheating; those working in offices grow depressed at the *tawildar* system; accountants and statisticians feel no progress can be made in their fields for a hundred years. Part of the frustration arises from the desire of each volunteer to "make an impact," "to introduce change," "to see something tangible" from his or her two years of effort, usually most unrealistic goals given the patterns of modern Afghan society. In addition, most volunteers feel they exist in limbo, because their standard of living lies somewhere between that of their Afghan counterparts and that of A.I.D. personnel. Even Afghans cannot understand why the volunteer must live without refrigerators.

Understandable though the frustrations may be, the Peace Corps volunteer often fails to realize the significance of his contribution to the attitudes of those working with him. A.I.D. and other foreign development officials usually operate at the higher levels of the Afghan government, where decisions are made. Highly-paid foreign technicians often implement decisions and leave large, completed projects on the land-

[14] The Royal Government of Afghanistan permits no active proselytizing of any faith but Islam. In spite of this, "cells" of Christian missionaries penetrated various A.I.D. contract teams in the 1950s. The Afghans were very tolerant of their underground proselytizing activities, and pretended to ignore their existence. Although most of these missionary-types have left Afghanistan, some few still remain (still ignored by the Afghan Government), and have been unsuccessful in their attempts to save souls for Christ.

[15] For a short history of the Peace Corps in Afghanistan, see L. Dupree, 1965b.

scape without regard to their cultural impact. Peace Corps volunteers, however, work with the middle- and lower-level government officials and technicians, and unless new attitudes develop along with the new technology the upper-level decisions simply founder in a welter of signatures. (I have sometimes referred to Afghanistan as functioning as a government by signature.)

By working with the lower-range officials, the volunteers accomplish more in the attitudinal sense than is immediately apparent. They succeed in stimulating implementation of policy decisions at that level. In years to come, the rising middle-class official will remember and talk about the accomplishments jointly made with the volunteer. But replacement Peace Corps members and their attendant set of attitudes must continue over a long period of time in the same work positions. Consistency and continuity are the two best ways to encourage involvement in change processes.

Other nations have sent volunteers to participate in the same types of projects. Among the nations represented have been West Germany (Deutsche Entwicklung Dienst, with about one hundred now active, probably to be doubled by 1971); the United Kingdom (under British Council auspices, about ten); France (National Service volunteers, about a dozen). The French permit conscripts for National Service to select either the military or some sort of overseas service, similar to Peace Corps work.

The Third Five Year Plan for Economic and Social Development (1967–72) appeared more than one year late because of the shifting cabinet situation, intransigence in the *Shura,* the difficulty of pinning down the Americans to foreign assistance commitments in an election year, and the difficulty in pinning down the Russians before the Americans had been pinned down.

The first two plans had emphasized the creation of a transportation and telecommunications infrastructure, which simply means the destruction of the zones of relative inaccessibility, so necessary if a country is to involve its population in the development of a nation-state. Because of the emphasis on infrastructure, the Afghans now have one of the better road systems in Asia. The following asphalt (with one exception) roads have been completed: Kabul–Torkham (224 km., or 140 mi., American assistance); Kabul–Jabal us-Seraj (77 km., or 48 mi., Russian assistance); Doshi-Sher Khan Bandar (214 km., or 133.5 mi., Russian aid); Kabul–Qandahar–Spin Baldak (558 km., or 367.5 mi., American aid); Qandahar–Herat–Torghundi (680 km., or 425 mi., all concrete, Russian assistance); Herat–Islam Qala (123 km., or 76.5 mi., American aid).

Probably the most spectacular infrastructure achievement was the Doshi–Jabal us-Seraj road (107 km., or 66.5 mi., Russian aid), which included the magnificent engineering feat of the 2.7-kilometer (1.7 mi.) tunnel, with 5.4 kilometers (3.4 mi.) of galleries. The tunnel (5.2 meters, or 17 feet, high; 7.6 meters, or 25 feet, wide) cost $638 million and took 6 years to complete. Cutting through the Hindu Kush, it eliminates 202 kilometers (126 mi.) and several miles of the previous roundabout route from Kabul to the Russian border. A passenger car can now reach the Russian border of Afghanistan from the Pakistani border in a long day's drive.

Since the Salang Tunnel (possibly the world's highest, at 11,100 feet, or 3,363 meters, above sea level) opened in August 1964, about 600 overloaded trucks per day have strained over the pass. The road is maintained by thousands of members of the conscripted Afghan Labor Corps, and, with few exceptions, has been kept open year-round. Blizzards and snowstorms can occur at any time of the year, however, and one of the worst blizzards I have ever seen in Afghanistan occurred at Salang in May 1965.

The tunnel may still cause the Afghans major headaches, for many engineers, Afghan and foreign, believe it should have been constructed several thousand feet lower. The effects of the severe Afghan winters have already begun to deteriorate the tunnel and galleries, and the seasonal melting and freezing has produced many cracks in the concrete. The climb up and down, particularly on the northern side, taxes the habitually overloaded trucks to the extreme. The favorite truck of the Afghan *motorwan* is a large International Harvester (the diesel-powered British Bedford is gaining in popularity, however), which they constantly overload, often dangerously threatening the efficient operation of the vehicles in mountainous terrain. Not uncommonly, the *motorwan* drive their lorries downhill in low-low gear and with brakes practically full on.

As a result of its road network Afghanistan, a great commercial and in-transit center when the Silk Route plied between Cathay and the ancient classical world, may find itself in the process of repeating history. Today, many in-transit goods pass through the Soviet Union and Afghanistan on their way to Pakistan and India, and vice-versa.

The Third Five Year Plan, although it certainly does not ignore the infrastructure (particularly in creating a farm-to-market road system)

CHART 30

Third Five-Year Plan for Economic and Social Development: 1967–72

Non-Development	Amount (billions of afghanis)
Government operating expenses	17
Payments of foreign loans[1]	5.3
Subscriptions to development banks	1
Reserve for public employee salary increase	1
Total	24.3
Development	
From budgets	12.9
Foreign loans and grants	19
Private sector investments	2
Total	33.9
Total Expenditures	58.2

Source: Ministry of Planning, Kabul

[1] A great increase over Second Plan (1.7 billion afghanis) when the Soviets gave a voluntary moratorium on bulk of payments due.

emphasizes agriculture and irrigation, largely neglected or inadequately handled in the past. The goal of self-sufficiency in foodstuffs by 1972 is not impossible, but highly improbable, given all the cultural, economic, and psychological factors involved. During the second plan the agricultural sector changed little in either total average under production or productivity per acre.

Total expenditures of the plan should be about 58.2 billion afghanis; about 33–34 billion afghanis would be for development and two-thirds of this would come from foreign aid. (Chart 30). The second most important sector of public investment will be mining and industrial development; third, education and social services.

Other generalized goals include expansion of the private sector in agriculture and industry; improved methods of national savings; strengthening the balance of payments by increasing export potential; increased social justice and social welfare; increased per capita income and better distribution of wealth; developed educational system; expansion of health facilities; regional economic development.

The problem of declining foreign assistance is minor as compared to the Afghan budgetary deficit (now something less than 500 million afghanis annually), which directly involves the collection—or non-collection—of taxes. If Afghanistan would levy and collect adequate land and livestock taxes, abolish export tax on major hard-currency earners, and try to control their imports by increasing duties, the economy would benefit. But in this period of transition, few ministers wish to take the steps to reform the present fiscal situation. It can get much more serious unless active steps are taken within the next few years. For example, although the same amount of taxes appears to be collected each year and has been for many years now, government expenditures rise tremendously each year. With the completion of the Land Inventory project, being undertaken with U.S. assistance, the tax situation may improve and become more equitable.

As long as Afghanistan can depend on economic assistance from both East and West, it is not likely to take a hard look at its financial position. In fact, if the Cold War evaporated over night, most developing nations would be forced to reappraise their chances to survive in the harsh world of economics, and meaningful regional groupings such as the Regional Cooperation for Development (R.C.D.) of Iran, Pakistan, and Turkey might actually come into being.

Afghanistan's major economic contribution to the R.C.D. might, incidentally, come from its large iron ore deposits at Hajigak near Bamiyan.

647

Foreign advisers (Russian, American, West German) all estimate the existence of about 2 billion tons of high grade ore in the area.

Private investment continues to move ahead slowly. In human terms, the process of urbanization still outstrips industrialization, as farm surplus labor comes to towns and cities following rumors—or more often relatives—to seek out fortunes, and then, almost inevitably, returns to the farm.

A liberal investment law has been in existence since 1967,[16] but the Afghan bureaucratic system often places unnecessary stumbling blocks before both foreign and local investors. As of December 31, 1969, however, the government, under the 1967 law, had received about 170 investment applications and approved 113, including 18 projects with foreign investors. Forty-three of the approved projects were at least partially implemented. If—and this is a big if—all 113 eventually function at full operational capability, about 18,000 jobs (including 1,500 skilled positions) will be created. Total value of the approved applications amount to $41.5 million, of which $6.3 million comes from foreign investors. Among those functioning in various stages of implementation are: Da Nabatat Sherkat, a rose-oil factory just outside Kabul, financed by Italian and Afghan funding; a frozen-meat plant at Girishk, completely Afghan; Shahabuddin Yasaury Sherkat, an Afghan cloth-weaving company in Kabul; Sherkat Sahami Pashtun, an Afghan cold-storage plant for fruit in Qandahar; Maqsudi Rayon Company, a textiles firm in Kabul; Afredi Auto Maintenance Service in Kabul, wholly Afghan; and the 100% Pakistani-financed Century Steel Re-rolling Mill in Kabul (which produces steel reinforcing rods, window grills, etc.). A Coca Cola plant began operations in 1971; later, ice cream and concentrated fruit essence manufacturing elements will be added.

The External Crisis Over, the Internal Crisis Begins (or Vice-Versa?)

From October 1966 to January 1970, several interrelated factors began to test the strength of the *democracy-yi-naw:* the *Shura* (Twenty Parliament) refused to be a rubber-stamp institution and had taken its investigative prerogatives much more seriously than its legislative obligations; many free-press papers plagued both the conscience and the patience of the government; student and worker strikes and demonstrations in-

---

[16] The Foreign and Domestic Private Investment Law, passed February 20, 1967.

tensified and spread to the provinces; fiscal and budgetary problems escalated; development programs lagged or sagged; the 1969 elections brought in the Thirteenth Parliament; the King reappointed the old prime minister, who brought in a new cabinet.

On June 11, 1968, Prime Minister Nur Ahmad Etemadi (who replaced Mohammad Hashim Maiwandwal in November, 1967) delivered a long speech in the *Wolesi Jirgah*. The Prime Minister and his cabinet appeared in response to a demand made by the *Wolesi Jirgah* on May 13, 1968, that he answer questions, primarily relating to widespread internal corruption, inaction in some local development programs, and certain apparent inconsistencies in Afghanistan's foreign policy, e.g., the lip-service given to the "Pushtunistan" issue without real follow-up action.

Prime Minister Etemadi gave a measured statement of his government's policies on all issues, and he answered questions for several hours after completing his speech. Even so, before the session ended, he and his cabinet had to sit through a barrage of invective that would have infuriated the mildest member of any Western cabinet. As no political parties exist in Afghanistan to back up a minister or the government as a whole, each cabinet member had to sit as an individual before the 216 hostile—indeed, often insulting—faces. The session proved to be an excellent exercise in freedom of speech, but it certainly did nothing to add brilliance to the generally lackluster performance of the *Wolesi Jirgah*.

This was not the first unpleasant confrontation of the Etemadi cabinet with the people's representatives. In November 1967, three days of debate, all broadcast over Radio Afghanistan, during which 163 of the 186 members present spoke, preceded the final vote of acceptance (163 for, 7 against, and 6 not voting) of the Etemadi cabinet and policies. The seven negative voters (all leftists) had also voted against the Maiwandwal cabinet exactly two years earlier.

Political parties could function as disciplinary organs for parliamentary members, as well as serve as protective shields for members of the cabinet. Unless checked by the formation of active, functioning political parties and a strong executive, parliamentary individualism, such as exists today, may possibly lead to anarchy. Although both the *Wolesi Jirgah* and the *Meshrano Jirgah* have passed the Political Parties Bill,[17] the King has yet to sign it, so officially no parties exist.

[17] The Political Parties Bill has had a checkered life. The designers of the bill (with the approval of the King) established 25 as the minimum voting

Some around the King have advised him against opening the Pandora's box of political parties, but others have pointed out that the promise was made, the Constitution legalized the issue, and the *Shura* has spoken. And, as is true in all major decisions concerning the future of Afghanistan, His Majesty King Mohammad Zahir Shah must make the final gesture. In him rests the ultimate power.

The *Wolesi Jirgah* first began to feel its oats in 1965 when investigations by its committees interfered with government operations. As a result, many Afghans outside government and some in government accused the *Wolesi Jirgah* of using such issues as corruption and "Pushtunistan" (which had been relatively quiescent since the resignation of Daoud Khan as prime minister in 1963) to cover up inadequacies in the legislative process. Slowly, however, the *Wolesi Jirgah* emerged as a genuine popular force, and an attendant loss in executive influence followed.

Because no political parties exist, few genuine coalitions can be formed in the *Wolesi Jirgah,* and this at least partly accounts for its failure to pass legislation. Certainly, the legislative record to date is not impressive.[18] Aside from the four annual operating and development budgets, Parliament passed little meaningful legislation, although it did pass thirteen bills having force of law, exclusive of budgetary, loan, and cultural items. Forty-eight bills remained unacted upon at the end of the final session.

The three most important items passed, the Political Parties Bill, the Municipalities Bill, and the Provincial Councils Bill, lie unsigned by the King and therefore moribund. Other bills passed included cultural agreements with France and the United Kingdom; foreign loans from the United States (9 for $19 milion, plus 110,000 tons of wheat and 46,000

---

age. The Lower House passed the bill in July 1966; the Upper House followed suit in May 1967. The King held the bill while student unrest grew. The Lower House then reconsidered the bill, and in April 1969 passed an amended version which lowered the age to 20, recognizing the growing power of student elements. The more conservative Upper House rejected the amended bill. The Twelfth Parliament ended with no action's having been taken. A joint committee (15 members from each House) of the parliament unsuccessfully tried to find an acceptable compromise durin the 1970 legislative session.

An interesting final comment: several members of the 1964 Constitutional Committee have informed me that it was generally agreed in the Committee that it would be better if no political parties should function during the elections for the Twelfth and Thirteenth Parliaments.

[18] A list of proposed legislation can be found in *The Kabul Times Annual,* 1967, 20–22.

tons of edible oil), U.S.S.R. (2 for 120 million rubles), Yugoslavia (1 for $8 million), West Germany (1 for DM 10 million), Japan (1 for ¥720 million), I.D.A. (1 for $3.5 million), United Kingdom (1 for £200,000); an exchange commodities agreement with the People's Republic of China; a trade agreement with Czechoslovakia; and air agreements with Iraq, Sweden, Norway, and Denmark.[19]

An example of fiscal irresponsibility and the growing fear of the executive branch of the *Wolesi Jirgah* occurred in November 1967, when the government agreed to the abolition of the lucrative livestock tax rather than face a showdown on the issue with Parliament, a miscue which increased the budgetary deficit and increased the power of the legislature to coerce the administration.

An example of the social irresponsibility of some deputies took place on July 22, 1968, when, even while the *Wolesi Jirgah* discussed the Kabul University Constitution, several conservative members proposed that Afghan girls be prohibited from studying abroad. Immediate demonstrations outside the *Shura,* however, by hundreds of women students quickly reminded Parliament that the new constitution guarantees equal rights (even if the government does not enforce them) for men and women. The do-nothing parliament passed into history when it adjourned in August 1969 (*Wolesi Jirgah,* August 12; *Meshrano Jirgah,* August 13).

With the exception of the Seventh ("liberal") Parliament (1949–52), the preceding eleven *Shura* had been largely "rubber-stamp" institutions. Members came largely from the second line of power, sent to Kabul by the local power elites to maintain the façade of constitutional parliamentarianism. The 1965 elections, however, began a new era in Afghan politics, a genuine attempt to create a constitutional monarchy with at least a theoretical emphasis on parliamentary procedures. Many in the rural areas were at first skeptical of the *democracy-yi-naw,* but eventually many new faces appeared for election. Some younger, educated types returned to their village homes and successfully challenged incumbents. In Kabul and other larger urban centers many newcomers appeared and were elected. Most proved to be liberal, leftist, or religiously conservative and became the chief architects of the investigative activities of the *Wolesi Jirgah.*

The key feature of the Twelfth Parliament, however, was the rapid

[19] Most of the information on the legislative record of the Twelfth Parliament is taken from *Legislative Record of the Twelfth Afghan Parliament: October 1965–August 1969,* (Unclassified), U.S. Embassy, Kabul, 1969.

realization by its members that it did have power—legitimate constitutional power—and, because the executive remained relatively inactive (and unprotected, because of the lack of responsible political parties), Parliament seized more and more power but did little constructive with it.

By the time King Mohammad Zahir Shah officially announced the opening of the 1969 election campaign on April 21, it also became obvious to the local khans that the accretionary collecting of power at the center by the *wakil* or *vakil* (members of the *Wolesi Jirgah*) would tend eventually to erode their power, particularly as government control and development programs creeped into the countryside. Actually, some of the local khans had anticipated this development and successfully ran for the Twelfth Parliament, thereby early establishing themselves in the central as well as the local power arena.

In the north, Pushtun immigrants had controlled the political scene since the early twentieth century, but in the 1969 campaign were challenged (often successfully) by the numerically dominant non-Pushtun elements. The Uzbak, Tajik, Turkoman, and other regional power elites had at last been convinced that the elections would be free.

Elections for the Thirteenth Parliament were held in late August and early September, and when the government announced the official results on October 6, it became apparent that the new parliament (particularly the *Wolesi Jirgah*) had a representation closely coinciding with the true political picture in Afghanistan. Officially, 2.5 million Afghans registered to vote, but the actual number voting was probably close to two million. Only 7 incumbents returned to the *Meshrano Jirgah*, out of a total of 28; in the *Wolesi Jirgah*, only 60 of 216 returned, and most belonged to the real power elite and had already served in several prior parliaments. In addition, many of the old Eleventh Parliament once again emerged from behind the "mud curtain," convinced that the government was serious in its attempts to create a parliamentary system. The true conservative power of the countryside, including many more non-Pushtun than had served in previous national assemblies, came to Kabul for the next session, opened by the King on October 14.

Subtle and not so subtle government pressures and tactics helped defeat some of the more able candidates, however. Missing were most of the urban liberals (Mir Mohammad Siddiq Farhang of Kabul, for example) and others (i.e., ex-Prime Minister Mohammad Hashim Maiwandwal, who stood for Moqor), who will be sorely missed as "devil's advocates" by the Thirteenth Parliament. Also missing from the

Wolesi Jirgah are the four women (Dr. Anahita, Roqia Abubakr, Khadija Ahrari, Ma'suma 'Esmati Wardak) from the Twelfth; only the last named chose to run again and she was defeated.

However, with the conservative cast of characters now in parliament, legislation may be passed much more rapidly, particularly if the King judiciously wields the influence and respect he possesses in order to undo the previous legislative logjams, and if a meaningful Political Parties Bill is finally promulgated. Informal political parties continue to flourish, however, usually connected with free-press newspapers, e.g., *Afghan Mellat, Parcham,* and the banned *Shu'la-yi-Jawed.* A new group, *Etehad-i-Melli* ("Unity of the Country" or National Party; also see above, p. 590), came into existence on July 20, 1969, formed by reformist (mainly economic) conservatives, such as 'Ishaq Osman (who defeated Farhang in the election) and Sardar Jai Singh of Kabul, the only non-Muslim in the Thirteenth Parliament.

The new *Shura* met for a two-month session before January 1, 1970, from October 14 to December 13, during which time it accredited its members, elected its officers (Dr. Mohammad Omar Wardak, elected president of the *Wolesi Jirgah,* had resigned as Minister of the Interior to stand successfully for parliament; the King reappointed Abdul Hadi Dawi as president of the *Meshrano Jirgah*), and approved of Nur Ahmad Etemadi, his cabinet, and his policy statement. The vote of confidence session lasted from November 13 to December 2, and continued the tradition of broadcasting the entire proceedings to the nation over the radio. Of the 216 members of the *Wolesi Jirgah,* 204 spoke.

The King surprised many when he reappointed Etemadi as prime minister, for most observers agreed Etemadi desired to step down. Once again, however, King Mohammad Zahir Shah showed his political astuteness. In reappointing Etemadi, he gave the parliamentarians an opportunity to express their displeasure at an old recognizable symbol of their discontent. If His Majesty had appointed a new prime minister, the *wakil* would not have been able to express their true feelings about the ineffective (in their view) performance of the former government. And when troubles arise again, it will be easier to replace Etemadi and bring in a new prime minister. As things developed, the legislators, one after the other, ticked off the inequities of the previous Etemadi regime, aiming most of the slings and arrows at Etemadi himself, as he and his new cabinet sat patiently through the sixteen-day (excluding holidays) ordeal. In the end, however, as everyone predicted, because, after all, the King had reappointed Etemadi, the Etemadi government received an overwhelming vote of confidence, 186 to 16 (204 members present and voting). Etemadi's 17-man cabinet (1 woman) included 13 new faces, all of whom are under 50 years old (9 of these under 45) and have advanced Western academic training (Appendix G). With a young, vigorous cabinet stabilized by four older experienced members (Abdullah Yaftali, First Deputy Prime Minister; Dr. Abdul Kayeum, Second Deputy Prime Minister and Minister of Education; General Khan Mohammad Khan, Minister of Defense; Engineer Mohammad Azim Gran, Minister of Communications—plus the President of the Tribal Affairs Department, also a cabinet post, Sayyid Masud Pohanyar), a new conservative *Shura,* with schools open and seniors trying to keep them open in order to graduate in the spring of 1970, Afghanistan continues to move toward its announced goal of *democracy-yi-naw.*

Even if the Thirteenth Parliament begins to pass meaningful legislation, the administrative apparatus in the various ministries may continue to interfere with implementation. Cabinet ministers and their advisers have openly declared their surprise at the knowledge parliamentary deputies have about the inner workings of their respective ministries. Two interrelated factors account for this: many deputies have relatives in the lower-to-middle range brackets of the civil service and kinship ties still outweigh government loyalties; and many middle-range civil servants, jealous of the power of the foreign-educated ministers and deputy ministers, do not hesitate to pass on information detrimental to the ministry for which they work.

Below the level of the ministers and deputy ministers, the ministries are a veritable bureaucratic jungle. Although ministers, deputy ministers, and their immediate advisers generally have a liberal, action-oriented outlook and do attempt to get things moving, the system under which their underlings function precludes the rapid completion of any given approved project. Few bureaucracies in the world equal—although many approach—Afghanistan in its built-in slowdown mechanisms.

In a developing nation like Afghanistan, two major indicators of freedom are the presence or absence of a free press and the rate of change in the bureaucratic process, where implementation should speedily follow any given approved application for action and the time-gap between the two should narrow until a minimum time-lag is achieved. This means, in other words, the creation of a relatively honest, rapidly efficient government bureaucracy which serves the interests of both government and governed as impartially as time, custom, law, and individual deviations permit.

In some areas, it might seem that there has been a small improvement. For example, although current tourists might not believe it, a foreign visitor to Afghanistan today will find it much simpler and quicker to pass through immigration and customs than his counterpart did in 1966. Incidentally, tourism could well become one of the major foreign-exchange earners for Afghanistan. In 1969, over 63,000 tourists visited the country, spending many hard-currency dollars, pounds sterling, and Deutsche marks. Over 26,000 of them were free-spending Pakistanis, who look on *laissez-faire*, import-minded Afghanistan as a shopper's paradise; the next in order of numbers were the British, Americans, French, West Germans, and Australians (Chart 31). The tourists also included many hippies from the United States and Western Europe, either on their way to, or returning from, Nepal or Goa. Marijuana, called *chars*, is very cheap in Afghanistan and many of these itinerants purchase large quantities to be smuggled back to Europe or America. Several have been picked up and jailed in the Soviet Union, which is very strict about the import of drugs into Russian territory. Many new hotels, definitely not first class but comfortable enough, have sprung up to take care of this influx of tourists, and a new luxury hotel, built with joint Afghan–British funds by a British construction company, sits near Bagh-i-Bala overlooking Kabul.

The tourists may have it easier today, but deep within the bowels of most Afghan government offices any simple application for action must still make a long insecure trip through the workings of the system. At any point in its progress a signature may not be forthcoming and the entire procedure can be blocked. If one begins near the bottom, the trip can be particularly hazardous, unless one is willing to *bakhshish* (tip or bribe) all the way up until someone finally takes the responsibility for signing his name to a petition. Then the approved application begins its way down the track for implementation.

Most of the present ministers do try to delegate authority and encourage subordinates to make decisions within their jurisdiction, but the increase in the numbers of those who exercise actual decision-making powers remains small. Some attempts have been made at administrative reform.[20] Usually, however, documents ready for an ultimate decision

[20] For example, in March 1969, the Government Monopolies died by executive order but gave birth to a hydra-headed enterprise. There are now *three* offices: (1) sugar monopoly; (2) petroleum-oil-lubricants monopoly; (3) a litigation department whose function is to settle all outstanding cases on file. The new scheme should, in theory, speed up operations.

CHART 31
Tourists by Country: 1969–71[1]
(in 000)

Country	1969[2]	1970	1971[3]
Pakistan	26.2	51.2	51.8
U.S.A.	7.6	9.6	11.9
United Kingdom	8.2	9.3	10.1
France	4.7	6.5	8.1
West Germany	4.0	5.5	7.5
Australia	1.9	2.0	2.7
Canada	1.0	1.5	2.3
Switzerland	1.0	1.8	2.2
Italy	.6	1.2	1.8
Japan	.7	1.1	1.7
Iran	—	1.2	1.6
India	.7	.8	1.3
Denmark	.6	nd	nd
Austria	.4	nd	nd
Sweden	.4	nd	nd
U.S.S.R.	.3	nd	nd
Other (48 countries)	4.8	8.5	10.1
Total	63.1	100.2	113.1

Source: R.A. Sultani, Afghan Tourist Organization, Afghan Air Authority

[1] As compared to raw totals of 44,539 in 1967-68; 23,413 in 1965-66; 6,862 in 1963-4.
[2] 1969: by air, 10,383; land, 52,706.
[3] 1971: by air, 18,174; by land, 94,935.

and final signature continue to flow upstream and then back down again—wasting time and money, and creating psychological fears in petitioners and Napoleonic complexes in many minor officials, who, unless properly kowtowed to and handsomely *bakhshished,* can block any legitimate petition by simply refusing to sign and pass it on. Often, however, the officials fall back on the general concept of *usulnamakhormoqar'rarat* ("according to the regulations"), a term frequently written on an application or petition, which is not a demand for action but a passing of responsibility to a lower official, who usually refuses to try to follow the "regulations" unless they are spelled out in detail by a more senior official. Again, inconsistency in interpretation and implementation plagues the entire system, for no one seems to know what the "regulations" say. Many literate Afghans with advanced degrees from European or American universities admit that they fear to approach a ministry with a petition.

An important figure in any transaction is the *tawildar,* thousands of whom exist for the sole purpose, it would appear, of frustrating the desires of all Afghans from peasant to prime minister. The *tawildar* holds the keys to all storerooms and supply rooms, and is held personally responsible for everything contained therein. Periodically, often daily, he will count the items under his charge, and he fiercely resists any attempt to remove them from his custody, even if one has the proper papers.

Many observers, Afghan as well as foreign, tend to underestimate the strength and importance of the middle-range bureaucrat and his attitudes. The dominant inward-looking, self-perpetuating society tends to breed and perpetuate its own unpleasant environment. The great mass of civil servants remain perpetuators, not innovators.

There is another new pattern that contributes to this bureaucratic malaise. Young men with post-World War II foreign educations rose rapidly to the highest ranks within the government, some with particular speed after the 1963 resignation of Prime Minister Mohammad Daoud Khan. The locally trained middle-range bureaucrats, passed over many times, have naturally resented this favoritism, and many slowdowns in ministries can be directly attributed to their resentment. Today young Afghans returning home with foreign degrees find no room at the top and often little enough in the middle, so many receive lower-rank appointments in the various ministries. They, in turn, channel their resentment into growing political activity, primarily leftist in orientation.

Favoritsm and nepotism, corollaries of a tribal system superimposed on a government and long rampant in Afghanistan, remain widespread. Some collateral members of the royal family have never completely accepted the *democracy-yi-naw* and look on its structure as simply a personal inconvenience. They ask official favors of cabinet ministers and other high-ranking officials, and, if rebuffed, they usually manage to have their requests approved somewhere in the middle-range bureaucratic levels, in return for reciprocities, present or anticipated. Many tribal leaders go to members of the royal family with petitions, which are then transmitted to acquiescent middle-range bureaucrats in the ministries concerned. (The pattern resembles that of the multiple courts, or durbar, held during the Abdur Rahman–Habibullah periods, with the various ministries now replacing the durbar.) Of course, such motives and actions exist in varying degrees in all states, democratic and non-democratic alike.

Afghanistan still has the opportunity to succeed in its experiment in democracy, and the key figure remains King Mohammad Zahir Shah. The King genuinely wants to construct a full modern constitutional democracy, but he must contend with powerful anti-government forces and vested-interest groups. Unless he acts to strengthen the executive (i.e., the cabinet), and if the Thirteenth *Shura* moves, as did its predecessor, in an anarchistic direction, the Afghan military may well step in, possibly led by a member of the royal family.

What is actually needed is a vision of the future, not blinders to the inequities of the present, a positive strength, not negative suppression. At the present time, the legislative branch holds too much power but does too little with it; and the executive, with the King's backing, must successfully contend with Parliament. This does not mean suppression of the opposition, and the Prime Minister and his cabinet must be able to differentiate between opposition to policy and intent to overthrow. Being for democratic reform is one thing—making it work, another. But better a slowed-down democracy than a rapidly growing totalitarianism.

CHAPTER 25

Problems and Prospects

IN ESSENCE, Afghanistan, like the rest of the Afro–Asian world (and parts of Latin America), is attempting to create a nation-state out of a hodgepodge of ethnic and linguistic groups. A nation-state, in the Western sense, is not simply a piece of real estate enclosed by boundaries, but more a pattern of attitudes, a reciprocal, functioning set of rights and obligations between the government and the governed—with emphasis on the individual rather than the group. In non-literate societies, however, kinship replaces government and guarantees men and women born into a specific unit or functioning set of social, economic, and political rights and obligations.

Possibly, a nation-state in the non-literate sense should be defined in forms of special relationships between a central government and any collection of tribal, ethnic, or linguistic (or other identifying criteria) groups within a set of boundaries. Need "tribalism" (however it is defined) necessarily be bad? A desire to retain group identity and, more important, sets of rights and obligations within the group are not in themselves a threat to the creation of a nation-state. Unfortunately, many of the national leaders in the non-Western world have been educated in the West and have the individualistic conceptions of nation-state. These leaders look on attempts to perpetuate tribal prerogatives as anarchistic, archaic, and anti-unity. But how many central governments can *replace* the delicate network of rights and obligations which make group survival possible?

And literacy is certainly not the answer, for literacy is simply a cultural tool to be used by man. Literacy can be used to create and perpetuate a totalitarian state as well as a system of representative government. Germans under the Nazis were certainly a most literate people. Literacy is an important tool for use in the creation of a nation-state;[1] initially, however, it intensifies ethnocentrism. Once members of a minority group learn to read and write and come in sustained contact

---

[1] A colonial power usually educates a small segment of the population (often from a minority group) to serve as the bookkeepers of empire. This clerk-class apes its colonial masters, but commonly finds its aspirations blocked, and the era of the cooperating "Uncle Tom" ends.

with the world outside an "inward-looking" tribal milieu, they begin to realize how much they have been taken advantage of by others. Rather than work (and at times the Establishment refuses to give them the opportunity) with a central government, they often return to their own group and help keep it regionally intact and regionally oriented. Usually, central governments look on these attempts to perpetuate group identity as threats to the nation-state, and, if rapprochements cannot be reached, demands for independence and civil war may ultimately result.

Western and Western-oriented administrators often tend to equate ethnic pride, a positive attitude, with racial discrimination, a negative attitude, related primarily to massive urbanization in the Western world, particularly the ultra-specialized United States. Negative discrimination grows out of ethnic pride as urbanization develops and a government finds it impossible to implement a reciprocal set of rights and obligations with the governed.

Since the Tower of Babel is here to stay, regional autonomy for various ethnic groups (however defined) may actually assist in the development of a functioning nation-state. Group identity and pride will probably push regional economic and political development as the tool of literacy reaches the minds of the bulk of the population. Horizontal links can be forged simultaneously among the regional leaders at the central government level and periodic meetings of a body of elected representatives.

In the post-World War II era, both the Americans and the Soviets were convinced they had *the* answers for social, economic, and political development. Having the answers made both countries almost tribally oriented (see above, Chapter 12). Overkill in literacy had lulled the world's most technologically oriented nations into seeking technological answers for human problems with little or no understanding of the cultures involved. Neither had *the* answers, and now the entire literate world questions many of the basic concepts put forward, while the dehumanized Western urban situation with its breakdown of the patterns of individual rights and obligations is at least partly responsible for the attempts by certain minority elements to seek once again meaningful identity within easily recognizable ethnic groups.[2]

The developed world[3] has introduced many changes, technological

---

[2] For a more detailed discussion, see L. Dupree, 1968d.

[3] A loose relative term at best, for, with any hope, *all* nations continue to develop.

and ideological, to the developing world and unsuccessfully tried to predict what would happen on the basis of what had occurred in the developed world. A culture takes all induced change elements, be they educational, social, military, political, or economic, and shapes them to its own needs and within its own patterns.

In summation, Afghanistan in the late sixties and early seventies presents several faces to the world and to its own people. The keystone of its foreign policy, *bi-tarafi,* remains the same, and in spite of the "Pushtunistan" dispute with Pakistan and the unsettled problems of the distribution of the Hilmand River waters with Iran, Afghanistan's relations with its neighbors have never been better. Educational opportunities increase annually, but literacy embraces a woefully low 5 to 10 percent of the population. The private business sector continues to grow, but the government does not fully trust businessmen, and vice versa. Foreign investors usually think more than twice before sinking money into Afghanistan.

Government economic planners continue to stay ahead of reality and, often, preoccupied with visions of the future, forget the facts of the present. Recurring deficits, caused by unrealistic fiscal policies, plague the budgeteers and foreign advisers in the Ministry of Planning and elsewhere. Foreign loans are coming due, and both internal revenue and exports must be increased considerably or the Afghans will find themselves in a financial quagmire. Balance of payments with the Soviet bloc improves annually, but some Western observers still fear the Soviet gamble to trap the Afghan economy may pay off. However, the Soviets continue to give the Afghans favorable credit terms, and appear to realize they have nothing to gain, at this time, by promoting a collapse of the Afghan economy.

On the contrary, and to the delight of the Russians (who accuse the West of unfair economic practices), the gap in the balance of payments with the hard currency area widens almost annually, partly because of the unrealistic, too-liberal Afghan import regulations, which permit luxury consumer goods to flow into the country to satisfy the desires of the small, wealthy upper class and a growing, Western-trained middle class. Ironically, many of the luxury items never reach the Afghan bazaars, but are smuggled across the border into Pakistan.

A shortage of trained administrators, technocrats, and technicians compounds the country's problems. But enlightened Afghan officials do tackle them and realize that internal efforts must be intensified to continue internal development. Meanwhile, a shortage of competent Afghan personnel forces a continued dependence on foreign administrators and technicians, with the necessary attendant foreign loans and grants.

In the political sphere, Afghanistan's government must pay attention to its students who, having tasted their first political blood, can be counted on to be heard from again—and again. The government must, in addition, be able to cope with growing influence from the left. I prefer to divide the Afghan left into two simple groupings: the political communists (revolutionists who wish to overthrow the constitutional monarchy and substitute an undefined government of their own) and the economic socialists (evolutionists who wish to evolve a state-controlled economy within the already functioning system but with free enterprise recognized in commerce). Outsiders should not assume that either group will come under the direct control of Moscow or Peking, a mistake frequently made in the past concerning indigenous leftwing elements in Afro–Asia and Latin America.

The bulk of Afghanistan's adult population must become actively involved if constitutional government is to succeed. To Afghan villagers and nomads (ninety percent of the population), involvement in the social, economic, and political sense means nuclear and extended family units. In the creation of democratic states, modern Asian governments feel that they cannot wait the two or three generations necessary to create a qualitatively literate middle class whose aims and ties are naturally toward the nation rather than toward a smaller group.

Involvement is an up-and-down-the-line proposition. Not only must the intellectuals and government officials interact among themselves, but they must also have contact with the non-literate masses. Most of the literate middle and upper classes can best be described as comfortable stagnates, a term applicable to most middle classes around the world.

Involvement, however, might have a dangerous backlash. Many intellectuals, usually Western-trained, often liberal, bleed mightily for the plight of the villagers, urban workers, and nomads. These three groups, well-versed in the ways of deception, are the avaricious, grasping products of an avaricious grasping system, and they are well able to play on literate "bleeding hearts." An articulate liberal group could sway the non-literates, who could become a breeding ground for revolution if convinced they were not getting a fair share of the national wealth, a not very difficult conviction to come by in the present situation of haves and have-nots.

Once the masses have their heads and hearts turned away from their village and tribal matrix of kinship and geographically localized rights and obligations, the struggle for their votes—or weapons—will intensify. If the groups involved keep up with the aspirations of both the literate population (more participation in decision-making processes) and the non-literate masses (improved economic well-being), revolution can probably be avoided, or at least delayed. But once begun, the processes cannot be reversed. Suppression will cause revolution; permissiveness encourages evolution but still may not prevent eventual revolution.

Afghanistan must complete at least ten years (to about 1975) under its constitutional patterns before a first assessment can be made of the processes in action. Theoretically, the Afghans are off to a fine start, even with their massive non-literacy problem and general public apathy toward government.

Problems the Afghans may have, efficient middle-range administrative talent they may lack, and increased qualitative literacy they may need, but they do have visions of a democratic future. Some of the visions appear hazy and ill-defined, others too rigidly ordered step by step—but the visions persist, and, hopefully for all concerned, the vigor for imple-mentation will be found. The Constitution has become a cultural docu-ment, expressing the ideals of the society and establishing the mechanics for achieving these ideals. In addition, the fate of the Constitution relates to the fate and fortunes of King Mohammad Zahir Shah. If anything should happen to him, the whole course of political development could be drastically changed. The King serves as a symbol to his people until constitutional ideals can be transformed into realities—until the nation-state ceases to be an abstraction.

Afghanistan's problems and prospects are not unique in the Afro–Asian world, but, so far, its actions toward problem solving have been more sensible and less bloody than most. On whatever social, eco-nomic, political, or cultural scale one wishes to use, the Afghans have made as much, if not more, progress (however defined) as any other developing nation. The problems remain, however, and the solutions are for the future.

* * *

Unforeseen and unavoidable circumstances have delayed publication of this book for a year or so, but in general nothing has happened to disturb the patterns described in this final Chapter. Certain specifics, however, deserve mention.[4]

---

[4] Since I completed this book in early 1970, several important events have occurred, all, however, well within the patterns described in the book. For example, a new cabinet, led by Dr. Abdul Zahir, was approved by the *Wolesi*

In 1970–71, politics achieved so convoluted a state as to boggle the minds of even veteran observers. One is tempted to complete the charade by tackling the problem in language more appropriate to describe a Hollywood-type thriller: *Afghanistan's Experiment in Parliamentary Politics: Will the Façade Become a Reality?* or *From Dictatorship to Oligarchy to Constitutional Experiment to Oligarchy to ?*. In a serious vein, Afghanistan may have turned another corner with the fall of the Etemadi government on May 16, 1971, over a constitutional question: In the conduct of the parliamentary "question hour," should the minister involved answer each question as asked, or should the government answer collectively at the end of the session? The question remains unanswered.

On June 8, 1971, King Mohammad Zahir Shah asked Dr. Abdul Zahir to form a government, and on July 26, after 17 days of debate, the Lower House approved his cabinet of 18, which includes one woman (Appendix G). Although Afghanistan has a new prime minister and cabinet, it still has the same old, conservative *Wolesi Jirgah,* which seldom meets in plenary session because of lack of quorum. Parliamentary "benign neglect" may be what Afghanistan needs (up to a point), for even the laws on the books are seldom promulgated equitably. The seeds of parliamentarianism have begun to sprout, however, and it is to be hoped that the communication and credibility gaps between the executive and legislative branches will narrow.

Officially, the free press continues to flourish and, unofficially, incipient political parties evolve about ideologies, primarily at the polar ends of religious conservatism and various leftist spectra (Chart 23). The comfortable stagnates of the urban middle class remain so, waiting, as do most Afghans, for the King to promulgate the Political Parties Bill, the Provincial Councils Law, and the Municipal Elections Act before they become actively involved.

Political activity, as predicted, has intensified at Kabul University, both among students and faculty. Student strikes, often over inconsequential administrative issues (e.g., grades necessary for passing courses and required classroom attendance) have effectively kept the university from functioning for almost four months as of March 1, 1972. Neither

---

Jirgah on July 26, 1971, but legislative action still remains relatively moribund. Those interested in reading about the specifics of the 1970 to mid-1971 period should consult: "A Note on Afghanistan: 1971," Louis Dupree, *Fieldstaff Reports,* American Universities Field Staff, South Asia Series, Vol. XV, no. 2, July 1971.

the government nor the university (in consultation with student leaders) has been able to devise acceptable guidelines for student participation in political activities which do not disrupt classroom work and normal school administration. The police, with few exceptions, have shown remarkable restraint since the bloody restrictive actions of 1969.

In Kabul, women and school girls took to the streets in April and October, 1970, protesting the violent actions of certain religious elements to the emancipation of women. Several women had been shot in the legs (or elsewhere), others burned by acid.

Outside Kabul, political demonstrations spread to the provinces. Clashes between various groups (usually religious *vs.* leftist, or so-called pro-Moscow *vs.* pro-Peking leftists) resulted in bloodshed and at least one death.

A serious two-year drought appears to have ended with heavy snows and rains (including several disastrous floods, however) in late fall 1971. The wheat shortfall has been largely met by grants and loans from the U.S.A., and U.S.S.R., the People's Republic of China, West Germany, and other nations. Much livestock (some estimate as many as 40% of the herds) died during the drought, the most serious in modern Afghan history. A new "Wheat for Work" program, under which (among other things) canals and wells were dug and farm-to-market roads constructed, was implemented in several provinces, and the Afghan government hopes to institutionalize the effort permanently.

Externally, the Bangladesh situation has affected Afghanistan both economically and politically. In June, 1971, Pakistan, economically pinched in the middle of a growing civil war, withdrew all 500- and 100-rupee notes from circulation, leaving many in Afghan economic circles holding millions of illegal rupees, for, legally, rupees cannot be brought outside Pakistan. With the independence of Bangladesh assured by the December Bangladesh War, the issue of "Pushtunistan" once again surfaced, but not so much in official government circles as in the free press. Iran's announced intention to expand its authority in the Persian Gulf caused some Afghans to worry least Iran also look to the east.

As the final quarter of the twentieth century draws near, most nations find themselves facing ever increasing crises, both in number and intensity. Pollution, population growth, senseless wars (including foreign adventures inconsistent with the times), internal civil strife and revolution plague the scene. Man has already begun to clutter up the moon, space, and other planets with scientific garbage. Even Afghanistan, landlocked and non-aligned, rapidly approaches a crisis in political and economic direction. Although few will be involved in the final decisions, the entire nation will be affected, and the results may demonstrate whether Afghanistan can peacefully continue to move forward toward some sort of democratic system consistent with its cultural and historical patterns or, as have many developing nations, degenerate into a round robin of successive military coups and abortive leftist and rightist revolutions.[5]

L. D.

May, 1972

[5] As the book goes to press, King Mohammad Zahir Shah accepted the resignation of Dr. Abdul Zahir on December 6, 1972. The next day, he appointed Mohammad Moosa Shafiq, Foreign Minister, as Prime Minister. Members of the new cabinet (approved by Parliament on December 12) are: National Defense, General Khan Mohammad (same post in Zahir cabinet); Interior, Dr. Nehmatullah Pazhwak (former Governor of Kabul Province); Finance, Mohammad Khan Jalalar (former Deputy Minister of Finance); Public Works, Khwazak Zalmai (same post); Information and Culture, Sabahuddin Kushkaki (publisher of the free press newspaper, *Karwan*); Communications, Nasratullah Malekyar (same post); Mines and Industries, Ghulam Dastagir Azizi (same post); Agriculture and Irrigation, Dr. Abdul Wakil (former Minister Without Portfolio); Planning, Dr. Abdul Wahid Sorabi (same post). Prime Minister Shafiq continued as Foreign Minister. Presumably, he will later appoint Ministers of Education, Justice, and Commerce, and probably Deputy Ministers and Ministers Without Portfolio, as well as a President of Tribal Affairs. For the first time since 1965, the cabinet (as of this writing) contained no women.

Under Dr. Zahir, the patterns remained the same, only the *dramatis personae* changed. Whether the new cabinet will save Afghanistan's experiment in democracy remains for the future to tell.

APPENDICES

APPENDIX A

DOMESTICATED PLANTS IN AFGHANISTAN

Cf. Humlum, 1959, 188-89.

CEREALS

Hordeum (barley)
Triticum[1] (wheat)
Secale cereale (spring and winter rye)
Panicum miliaceum and *P. italium* (millet)
Zea mays var. *indurata* (maize)
Oryza sativa (rice)
Ricinus sp. (castor oil plant)

FRUITS AND NUTS

Prunus armeniaca (apricot)
Pirus communis (pear)
Pirus malus (apple)
Juglans regia (walnut)
Prunus persica (peach)
Morus alba (mulberry)
Amygdalus communis (almond)
Cydonia oblonga (quince)
Prunus domestica (plum)
Vitis vinifera (grape)
Punica granatum (pomegranate)
Citrus sinensis (orange)
Ficus carica (fig)
Phoenix dactylifera (date)
Musa paradisiaca (banana)

VEGETABLES, ETC.

Pisum sativum (garden peas)
Vicia faba (broad bean)

Vicia ervilia (vetch)
Raphanus sativus (radish)
Linum usitalissimum (flax)
Brassica campestris (rape)
Lathyrus sativus (vetch)
Eruca sativa (a salad)
Medicago sativa (alfalfa)
Papaver somniferum (opium poppy)
Ervum lens (lentil)
Trifolium respupinatum (clover)
Daucus carota (carrot)
Cucumis sativus (cucumber)
Brassica sp. (mustard)
Nicotiana rustica (tobacco)
Solanum tuberosum (potato)
Cicer arietinum (chick pea)
Cucurbita moschata (pumpkin)
Cucumis melo (melon)
Anethum graveolens (fennel)
Helianthus annuus (sunflower)
Phaseolus mungo (Zanzibar pea)
Elaeagnus hortensis (oleaster)
Gossypium herbaceum (cotton)
Allium cepa (onions)
Citrullus vulgaris (watermelon)
Helianthus tuberosus (Jerusalem artichoke)
Sesamum indicum (sesame)
Saccharum officinarum (sugarcane)

Plus: beets, spinach, salad greens, cabbage, garlic, leek, tomatoes, cherries, pine nuts, strawberries, asparagus, turnips, jubejube, brussels sprouts, eggplant, cauliflower, squash.

Although not domesticated, various species of pistachio trees (*Pistacia khinjuk, P. vera,* et al.) are important in the economy of north Afghanistan. The government regulates the harvest, and in the late summer whole villages go to the mountains to pick the ripe nuts.

[1] Two types of *lalmi* (highland, non-irrigated) wheat exist: *lalmi termai,* planted in the autumn; *lalmi bahrami,* planted in the spring. *Abi* (irrigated) wheat is planted in September–October.

FAUNA IN AFGHANISTAN

Sources: author's notes; Ellerman and Morrison-Scott (1951); Perkins (1968); *Science*[1] (1965); Walker (1968).

CARNIVORA, ARTIODACTYLA, PRIMATES

Felis pardus (leopard)
Felis unica (Snow leopard)
Felis chaus (Jungle cat)
Felis caraeal (caracal)
Lynx lynx (lynx)
Canis lupus (wolf)
Canis aureus (jackal)
Vulpes vulpes (fox)
Vulpes corsac (corsax)
Hyaena hyaena (hyaena)
Herpestes auropunctatus (mongoose)
Vormela peregusna (Marbled polecat)
Vormela sp. (ferret)
Mustela nivalis (weasel)
Lutra lutra (otter)
Martes foina (marten)
Meles meles (badger)
Ursus arctos (Brown bear)
Gazella subgutturosa (gazelle)
Capra ibex (ibex)
Capra falconeri (markhor)
Ovis ammon (Argali)
Ovis ammon polii (Marco Polo sheep)
Ovis orientalis (Mouflon)
Ovis urueli (Urial)
Cervus elephas (Red deer)
Sus scrofa (Wild pig)
Macaca mulatta (Rhesus monkey)

INSECTIVORA, LAGOMORPHA, RODENTIA

Hemiechinus auritus (Long-eared desert hedgehog)
Hemiechinus megalotis (Long-eared desert hedgehog)
Paraechinus hyomelas (Desert hedgehog)
Suncus murinus (Thick-tailed shrew)
Crocidura russula (House shrew)
Lepus capensis (Cape hare)

Ochotona rufescens (Pika)
Hylopetes fimbriatus (Flying squirrel)
Spermophilopis leptodactylus (Long-clawed ground squirrel)
Citellus fulvus (suslik or gopher)
Marmota caudata (marmot or groundhog)
Hystrix indica (Indian crested procupine)
Allactaga elater (Five-toed jerboa)
Allactaga williamsi (William's five-toed jerboa)
Salpingotus thomasi (Thomas' three-toed dwarf jerboa)
Dryomys nitedula (dormouse)
Apodemus sylvaticus (field mouse)
Rattus rattoides (Common rat)
Mus musculus (Common mouse)
Nesokia indica (Pest rat)
Calomyscus bailwardi (Mouse-like hamster)
Cricetulus migratorius (Rat-like hamster)
Gerbillus nanus (Pygmy gerbil)
Tatera indica (Large naked-soled gerbil)
Meriones persicus (Tamarisk gerbil)
Meriones meridianus (gerbil sp.)
Meriones libycus (gerbil sp.)
Meriones crassus (gerbil sp.)
Rhombomys opimus (Sand rat or Great gerbil)
Ellobius talpinus (Mole vole)
Ellobius fuscocapillus (Mole vole)
Alticola roylei (High mountain vole)
Blanfordimys afghanus (Afghan vole)
Microtus arvalis (Meadow mouse)

CHIROPTERA

Tadarida teniotis (Free-tailed bat)
Tadarida aegyptiaca (Free-tailed bat)

[1] Kullmann, in *Science*, 1965; 1–17; Meyer-Oehme, in *Science*, 1965: 42–56; Niethammer, in *Science*, 1965; 18–41.

Nyctalus (?) *leisleri montanus* (Noctule bat)

Myotis formosus (Mouse-eared bat, *Myotis* most common genus)

Myotis longipes (Mouse-eared bat)

Pipistrellus mimus glaucillus (Pipistrelle)

Pistrellus babu (Pipistrelle)

Scotophilus heathi (House bat)

Otonycteris hemprichi (Desert long-eared bat)

Barbastella leucomelas (Barbastelle)

671

MEDICINAL PLANTS IN AFGHANISTAN

Sources: author's notes; Pelt, Hayton, and Younos (1965); L. Fischer (1966); Miner Associates (1968).

LOCAL *hakim* (doctors) use many local plants and herbs for medicinal purposes. Some, particularly artemesia and asafoetida, are collected for export. In every bazaar, several shops specialize in medicaments. Many of these old medicines serve as fever-reducing agents or purgatives for diarrhea, to relieve headaches and cold discomfort, or as poultices to combat infection. Generations of hit-and-miss experimentation have produced many nostrums of definite therapeutic value. The *hakim* call the use of medicinal plants *dawa-yunani,* "Greek medicine," and claim to be the followers of the physicians who traveled with Alexander the Great.

PLANT	MEDICINAL USAGE
Anise Seed (*Pimpinella anisum, Pimpinella illicum*)	Oil used to flavor medicines.
Asafoetida (*Ferula asafoetida*)	An antispasmodic, used as a poultice on wounds; to prevent colds; to aid digestion.
Caraway (*Carum carvi*)	To improve digestion, blood circulation; to mask unpleasant-tasting medicine.
Common Jujube (*Ziziphus jujuba*)	For dysentery; to calm fevers; as a stimulant.
Common Olive (*Olea europaea*)	Oil for constipation.
Common Wormwood (*Artemisia absinthium*)	Powder used for malaria.
Coriander (*Coriandrum satium*)	To improve digestion.
Cilician Tulip (*Tulipa montana*)	Bulbs eaten for strength
Cumin (*Cuminum cyminum*)	To improve digestion.
Fleatwort (*Plantago psyllium*)	A laxative.
Garlic (*Allium sativum*)	For malaria; scorpion stings; skin infection.
Great Burdock (*Arctium lappa*)	Root used for venereal diseases.
Hairy Onosma (*Onosma echiodes*)	To color medicines red.
Henbane (*Hyoscyamus reticulatus*)	Leaves used as a poultice for syphilitic ulcers.
Holarrhena (*Holarrhena antidysenterica*)	Oil taken to combat dysentery and diarrhea; also used as an aphrodisiac.
Leopardbane (*Doronicum pardalianches*)	A depressant; used for snakebite and scorpion sting.
Licorice Root (*Flycyrrhiza glabra*)	A laxative and masking agent.

672

PLANT	MEDICINAL USAGE
Marihuana (*Cannabis sativa*)	Narcotic used as painkiller and time-killer.
Madwort (*Asperugo procumbens*)	Asthma and nervous disorders.
Morning Glory (*Ipomoea turpethum*)	Used for lumbago and as a purgative.
Opium Poppy (*Papaver somniferum*)	A narcotic; a pastime and painkiller.
Oriental Sesame (*Sesamum indicum*)	Used as food oil; made into soap; mixed with opium it is used for rheumatism.
Red Pepper (*Capsicum frutescens*)	Used to aid digestion.
Rice (*Oryza sativa*)	Rice water used for diarrhea and chest troubles.
Rippleseed Plantain (*Plantago major*)	Used for diarrhea and dysentery; mucilage is also made from plant.
Safflower (*Carthamus tinctorius*)	Oil used for rheumatism.
Saffron (*Crocus sativus*)	To cool a fever, and as an antispasmodic and aphrodisiac.
Sage (*Salvia hydrangea*)	Used to stop excessive menstrual bleeding.
Santolin Yarrow (*Achillea santolinoides*)	Used for headache, toothache.
Sweetflag (*Acorus calamus*)	A stimulant.
Yellowbark Cinchona (*Cinchona clisaya*)	Powder used for malaria.

673

APPENDIX D

CALENDARS (*JANTARI*) USED
IN AFGHANISTAN[1]

MOST calendars printed in Afghanistan have three systems delineated: *Shamsi* (solar); *Qamari* (lunar); Gregorian.[2] The *Shamsi* (secular) calendar resembles the Gregorian in that the months always occur in sequence at the same time of the year. The impact of the West and its emphasis on regular time-systems forced Muslim countries to adopt their current secular calendars. Afghanistan adopted a *Shamsi* calendar during the reign of King Amanullah (1919–29); Iran chose one in 1925, at the time of Reza Shah Pahlavi. *Qamari* months occur 11 days *earlier* each year. For example, *Ramazan,* the month of fasting from sunup to sundown and other religious holidays fall 11 days earlier each year, rotating around the seasons, completing a full cycle every 32.5 to 33 years. The Muslim world uses modified variants of Arabic names for *Qamari* months, but the names of the secular months may vary by nation and at times by ethnic groups within the country.[3] Rarely do Muslims have separate, local names for the *Qamari* months, but the Pushtun of Afghanistan and West Pakistan represent one such exception.

Both *Shamsi* and *Qamari* calendars date from the *Hijra,* the migration of the Prophet Mohammad and his followers from hostile Mecca to friendly Yathrib (now Medina). Therefore, the year 1 in the Muslim dating-system equates with A.D. 622, according to some traditions on September 20 (approximate date of the Prophet's arrival in Medina), but probably a few days earlier (Gibb and Kramers, 1953, 139). Other traditions place the beginning date on July 15 or 16, A.D. 622, the day the Prophet departed Mecca (Gaudefroy–Demombynes, 1968, 184;

[1] For an excellent general discussion of Christian and Muslim calendars and conversion tables to the year A.D. 2000, see Freeman-Grenville (1963). Those interested in learning how to convert A.D. to A.H. and vice versa should also consult Gibb and Kramers (1953, 578–79) and Yusufi (1963).

[2] The Christian calendar ordained by Pope Gregory XIII in 1582 replaced the unwieldy Julian Calendar. The Pope decreed that October 15 of that year be October 25, and that leap years occur every fourth year. Most Catholic countries (Italy, Spain, Portugal, France, the Low Countries, etc) adopted the Gregorian Calendar in 1582. Others (both Catholic and Protestant) followed: Austria, Catholic Germany, Catholic Switzerland (1584); Poland (1586); Hungary (1587); Prussia (1610); Protestant Germany, Protestant Low Countries, Denmark, Norway (1700); England, Sweden (1752); Protestant Switzerland (1753); Japan (1873); China (1911); Bulgaria (1917); Yugoslavia, Rumania (1919); U.S.S.R., Greece (1923); Turkey (1926).

[3] For example, see Ferdinand (1959b, 40–46) for a discussion of the calendars of the Hazarajat.

Freeman–Grenville, 1963, 1). Because the *Qamari* year annually loses 11 days, the lunar year A.D. 1968–69 read 1386 A.H (After Hijra), while the solar year was 1347 A.H.

The following comparative tables should clarify the different systems. (I have also included the Iranian Farsi *Shamsi* terms for comparative purposes):

SHAMSI (SOLAR) CALENDAR FOR A.D. 1347 (A.D. 1968–69)

Afghan Terms (Arabic variations)	Iranian Farsi	Pashto	Astrological Symbols[4]	No. of days	Gregorian Equivalent of First Day of Month
Hamal	Farvardin	Wray	Aries the Ram	31	March 21
Saur	Ordibehest	Ghway	Taurus the Bull	31	April 21
Jawza	Khordad	Ghargholy	Gemini the Twins	31	May 22
Saratan	Tir	Chungash	Cancer the Crab	31	June 22
Asad	Mordad	Zmaray	Leo the Lion	31	July 23
Sunbulah	Shahrivar	Wazhay	Virgo the Virgin	31	August 23
Mizan	Mehr	Talah	Libra the Scales	30	September 23
Aqrab	Aban	Larun	Scorpio the Scorpion	30	October 23
Qaus	Azar	Lindah	Sagittarius the Archer	30	November 22
Jadi	Dey	Merghumay	Capricornus the Goat	30	December 22
Dalwa	Bahman	Salwagah	Aquarius the Water Carrier	30	January 21, 1969
Hut	Esfand	Kab	Pisces the Fish	29[5]	February 20

[4] Persian-Pashto terms usually conform in translation.
[5] *Hut* has 30 days in leap year. Next leap year is 1349 A.H. (A.D. 1970–71).

QAMARI (LUNAR) CALENDAR FOR A.H. 1368 (A.D. 1968–69)

Arabic: used in all Muslim Countries	Pashto Terms (No separate Persian terms)	No. of days	Gregorian and Shamsi equivalents of 1st day of month
Muharram	Hasan-Husain (refers to martyrdom of two grandsons of Mohammad in this month)	29	Mar. 30, 1968; Hamal 10, 1347
Safar	Safar (Same as Arabic)	30	April 28; Saur 8
Rabi' ul-Awwal	Lamrai Khor (First Sister)	29	May 28; Jawza 7
Rabi' ul-Akhir (or Sani)	Dwohamma Khor (Second Sister)	30	June 26; Saratan 5
Jumadi ul-Aula	Drayyemeh Khor (Third Sister)	29	July 26; Asad 4
Jumadi ul-Ukhra (or Sani)	Tsalarama Khor (Fourth Sister)	30	Aug. 24; Sunbulah 2
Rajab	Da Khalai Ta'Allah Myast (Month of God)	29	Sept. 23; Mizan 1
Sha'ban	Barat	30	Oct. 22; Mizan 30
Ramadan (called Ramazan in Afghanistan)	Ragha (fast)	29	Nov. 21; Aqrab 30
Shawwal	Kuchnai Akhtar (on first day of the month breaking of fast, called 'Id-al-Fitr, "Little 'Id."	30	Dec. 20; Qaus 29
Dhu'l Qa'deh	Myani (Month between two 'Ids; "myani" means "between.")	29	Jan. 19, 1969; Jadi 29
Dhu'l Hijra	Loy Akhtar ('Id-al-Adha, "Big 'Id" celebrated on 10th; called 'Id-i-Qurban in Afghanistan.)	30	Feb. 17; Dalwa 28
Muharram (occurs 11 days earlier)	Hasan-Husain	29	Mar. 19; Hut 27

FOLK MUSIC AND INSTRUMENTS

Notes by Peter Gold
Photography by David Schalliol

THE instruments described were collected by me for the Archives of Traditional Music, Indiana University. In addition, I have taped folk music and folklore in most regions in Afghanistan. The tapes are also in the Archives. Although not an ethnomusicologist, I have been struck by several similarities and contrasts of Afghan music and other folk music. Like other aspects of Afghan cultural patterns, folk music and instruments contain elements of Central Asia, Iran, and the Indian subcontinent. Some cultural continuity appears to exist among the mountaineers of Eurasia from the Carpathians and the Balkans to the Hindu Kush, and possibly the western end of the Himalayas. Many poems, written and unwritten, have been set to music, but vary with region and performer, who improvises, adds or subtracts, as the muse strikes.

For an excellent review of recorded Afghan folk music (with pertinent comments on the field as a whole), see Archer, 1964. Recent (1967–68) research by ethnomusicologist Mark Slobin expands our knowledge of Afghan music, particularly in the north. For example, see the record: *The Music of the Uzbeks,* AST 4001 (Library of Congress No. 70-750847) Stereo-Anthropology Record and Tape Corp. L.D.

I: *Dhol:* a two-headed membranophone. The heads are made of animal (goat) skin and are retained and tightened in a direct manner by means of continuous loops of a single twisted cord passing through both heads at several points on their circumferences. The cord passes through the head and around a wooden collar which is wrapped in the skin. Every two strands of the cord pass through a brass ring (movable) which serves to regulate the tension of the heads. Two *dhol* are in the colection at Indiana University. Photo I is brown in color; dimensions: 39 cm. in length, heads are 22 and 23 cm. in diameter. The other is chocolate brown with the dimensions: 42 cm. long, both heads 22 cm. in diameter. Both are made of *tut* (mulberry) wood and contain small kernels of seeds or stones which strike the sides and heads during performance and add to the percussive effect. The *dhol* is suspended from the neck of the musician and played with the hands or sticks. Designs are carved in concentric circles. *Dhol* are used primarily by the Pushtun tribesmen. The illustrated specimen was purchased in Gardez. Analogs are found in India and Pakistan.

II: *Doholak:* a pair of single-headed kettle drums from Gardez. They are made from *jeldis* wood and the heads are of goatskin. A black circle, approximately 8 cm. in diameter, is painted in the center of each head. The heads are secured by segments of twisted cord passing directly through the circumference of the skin and meeting at the base of the drum. There they pass around a purple, cloth-covered ring. The drums are played with drumsticks—*chub-i-doholak*—which are made from *charmass* (walnut) wood. They resemble the Central Asian drum pair or trio: *Naqqara*. Large drum: 21 cm. diam., 10 cm. depth. Small drum: 19 cm. diam., 9 cm. depth. Drumsticks: 24 cm. long, 1.5 cm. thick.

III: *Daira:* single-headed membranophone found throughout the Circum-Polar region, Central Asia, and the Middle East. A translucent skin head is attached to a bent rim (wooden) and the glued bond is covered by a green and white woven piece of cloth. The Persians have an analogous instrument also called the *daira,* and the Turkish version is known as the *def.* Both versions often have brass rings or bells attached to the inside of the rim for an added percussive effect. It is commonly played in a vertical position with the rim resting on the extended palm of one hand while it is beaten with the extended fingers of the other. Fine shades of tone are produced when it is beaten on different places of the head. Dimensions: 26 cm. diameter, 6 cm. depth. From Paktya Province.

IV: *Zerbagali:* single-headed membranophone. The shape is that of the "hour-glass" drum of the Middle East. Analogs are found among surrounding peoples, such as the Darbuka of Turkey and the Dumbek of the Persians. The body is made of baked clay and has several concentric designs in its surface created during the beginning stages of its manufacture on the potter's wheel. The clay is painted yellow with designs in silver. The head is of goatskin with a black circle, approximately 8 cm. in diameter, painted in its center. A piece of red and white woven cloth with a few strands of gold sewn in covers the perimeter of the skin. There is also a type of "eye" added to the clay body before firing. Height, 40 cm.; diameter of the head, 20 cm.

Chordophones

V: *Tambur:* Two in the collection, similar in construction but of different sizes. Metal strings pass over an ivory bridge which rests on the wooden face of the resonating chamber (made of gourd). This instrument is almost identical with the Indian instrument of the same name but has gut (in the case of the larger) and nylon (in the smaller) frets tied around the hollow wooden neck. The larger of the two has 18 strings and corresponding tuning pegs on

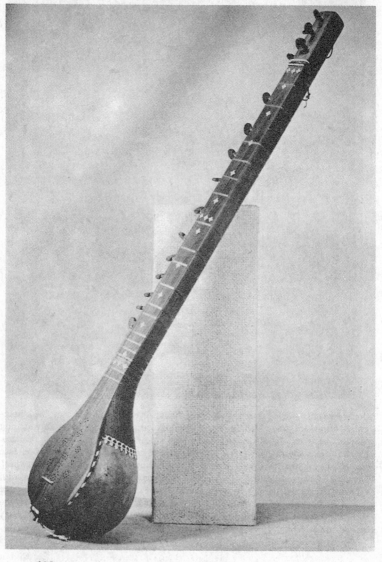

the end (6 pegs with 1 missing) of the neck and 12 pegs on the side of the neck. The smaller version has 17 strings with 6 from the end and 11 from the side of the neck. In both cases the only strings fretted are the two making up the first course (pair) farthest from the player. The other strings are used as drones. The *tambur* may be used as a solo instrument or, as in the case of its Indian counterpart, as a drone to accompany singers. The topnuts, tailpieces, bridges and inlays are ivory; the wood is *tut*. From Kabul. Large tambur: length, 137 cm.; width of face, 25 cm. Small tambur: length, 115 cm.; width of face, 17 cm.

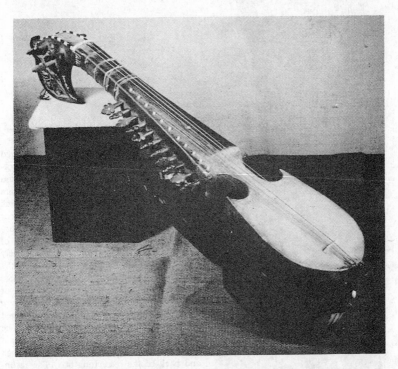

VI: *Rebab:* Two in collection. Both are constructed of *tut* wood and closely resemble the north Indian classical lute, the *sarod*. The face is made of goatskin and frets are made of gut. The wooden body is decorated by means of carving (relief) and mother of pearl inlays. The larger of the two is profusely inlaid on the fingerboard while the smaller is sparsely inlaid. Tuning pegs are made of *tut* wood. Both have a carved open-design peghead. The topnut and bridge are made of ivory. Both are played with a small wooden plectrum approximately 3 cm. long. Smaller *Rebab:* 74 cm. long, 3 plucked and fretter strings, 3 drone strings, 11 sympathetic (i.e., vibrate in sympathy with plucked strings) strings which are unfretted; these originate from pegs on right side of fingerboard. Larger *Rebab:* 80 cm. long, 3 plucked and fretted strings, 3 drone and 12 sympathetic strings originating from pegs on right side of fingerboard. From Kabul.

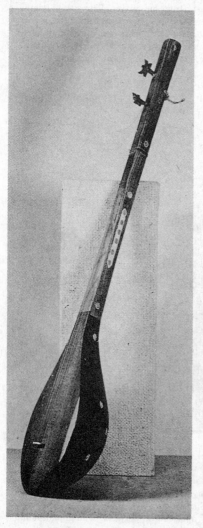

VII: *Dhamboura:* most common stringed instrument in Afghanistan. Two in collection. Both have two strings made from one strand of nylon doubled over. Both are unfretted of two-part construction: neck and resonating box. The smaller is made of *tut* wood with a bone bridge and ivory topnut. Tuning pegs of both are made of wood. The smaller *dhamboura* is profusely engraved on the back of the neck of the resonating box and on the fingerboard. There are 8 sound holes on the wooden face of the resonating box of the small *dhamboura* and 15 on the large *dhamboura,* arranged in triangular groups and individually. The large *dhamboura* is decorated with inlaid ivory with red circular intaglio on the neck and back of the resonating box. The resonating box is of *tut,* and the neck of a light-colored wood (*chenar*). The bridge is of ivory. Large *dhamboura,* 99 cm. long. Small *dhamboura,* 70 cm. long. Both are from Qataghan and are played with a plectrum or stemmed with the finger(s).

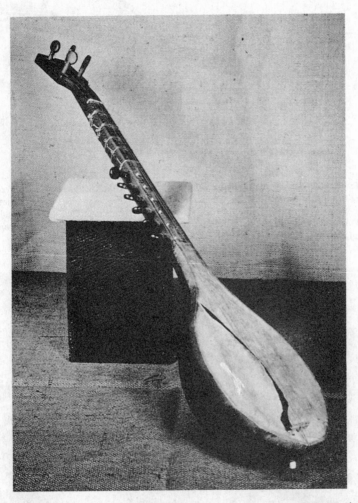

VIII: *Shashtar:* 10-stringed chordophone with 4 plucked and fretted strings and 6 sympathetic strings. The 5 tied frets are made of gut; bone topnut; wooden bridge. It is profusely engraved on the fingerboard, back of neck and back of resonating box. Two-piece construction: resonating box (*tut*) and neck (*chenar*). The head of the resonating box is made of skin (skin is slit, however). Played with plectrum. 75 cm. long. From Aibak

IX: *Richak:* bowed chordophone. The two strings, cylindrical neck, and carved peg-head are similar to the Persian equivalent, the *kemencha.* The resonating box is a round frame of *tut,* covered with goatskin. The neck is made of *chenar.* It is played in a vertical position with a bow. 87 cm. long. From Badakhshan.

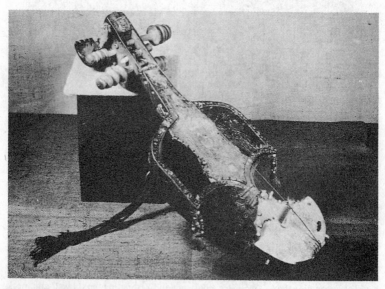

X: *Smaller Sarinda:* bowed lute. From the Baluch people of south Afghanistan, where it is known as *Sarud* or *Sarang;* it is also encountered in Pakistan. It is played with a finger-tension horsehair bow. Its strings are made of catgut (1) and steel wire of varying thicknesses (6). Some strings are used for melody, others are unstopped and produce a drone. The sound is transmitted into a resonating chamber by means of a wooden bridge and goatskin head at the base of the chamber. 58 cm. long.

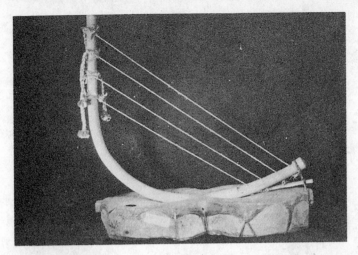

XI: *Waj* or *Wunz*. Like the vocal polyphony of the Nuristanis, which it often accompanies, this instrument is an anomaly to Central Asia. It consists of four strings of. twisted fiber tuned in a tritone, i.e., in intervals of a major second. A cross between a harp and a musical bow, it is closer to the latter. The wooden figure-eight-shaped resonating chamber is covered with a goatskin head which serves to transmit the sound from the strings into the chamber. The four twisted gut strings are secured across the span of a curved piece of hard, dark, brown wood which passes through the center of the head at two points and is secured at either end by strips of hide lashing. For the *waj*, a common tuning would be that of a tritone: c d e f (acording to Dupree tapes: ATL 3266–3267). Length; 47 cm.; height 35 cm. Attached by a piece of twisted gut is a plectrum made of similar wood.

XII: *Sarani:* bowed chordophone. Also from Wama, Nuristan. The resonating box is identical in construction to that of the harp. The wood and goatskin head are tained dark brown; the holes in the head are in single and triangular patterns. The neck and peghead are both extensions of the same piece of wood from which the hollow resonating box is carved. The two twisted gut string segments are retained at the peghead by means of two roughly hewn friction pegs. The strings, which are actually one longer string doubled into two segments, pass over a bridge 1.5 cm. in height. It appears to be a bowed chordophone with the center area of the sounding box the most likely place for the bow to be employed. The strings may then be fretted from below by means of the top of the fingernails of the left hand, while the instrument is held in a vertical position. 59 cm. long; 10 cm. high.

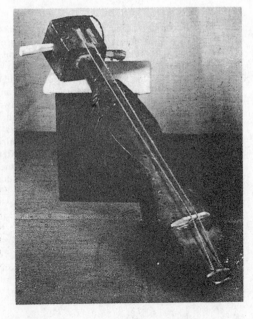

Aerophones

XIII. *Tula:* fipple-mouthed whistle flute. Wooden, painted red, green, and yellow, it has six fingerholes on the frontal plane and a single thumbhole on the dorsal plane. Stained dark brown. From Qandahar. Scale A c d e# a b c.

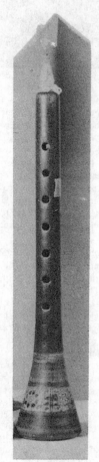

XIV: *Surnai:* Made of a dark wood, possibly *tut,* it has a conical bore with the bell painted brown, yellow, and orange. There are seven fingerholes on the frontal plane and one thumbhole on the dorsal plane. The double reed, which is made from a single stalk of natural reed, is attached to the bore by means of a brass tube protuding from the bore. This shawm is found throughout central-south Asia, the Middle East, and Southern Europe, where it is known as the *shanai* (India), *surnai* (Afghanistan), *zurna* (Central Asia and Turkey), and *zurla* (Macedonia). It is often played in conjunction with another *surnai* and either a single-headed drum (such as the *daira*) or a double-headed drum (such as the *dhol*). In this case one plays a drone while the other plays the melody, and they usually accompany the dance. From Logar Valley. 40 cm. long.

Miscellaneous

Chang (no photo). a jew's harp played with the mouth, but plucked toward the mouth instead of away from it.

688

MÉMOIRES DE LA DÉLÉGATION ARCHÉOLOGIQUE FRANÇAISE EN AFGHANISTAN (D.A.F.A.)

(All but XII and XIII published in Paris)

I   *La vieille route de l'Inde, de Bactres à Taxila*. A. Foucher, in collaboration with Mme. E. Bazin-Foucher (2 vol., 1942–47).

II   *Les antiquités bouddhiques de Bamiyan*. A. and Y. Godard and J. Hackin (1928).

III   *Nouvelles recherches archéologiques à Bamiyan*. J. Hackin in collaboration with J. Carl (1933).

IV   *Les fouilles de Hadda. Stupas et sites, texte et dessins*. J. Barthoux (1933).

V   Not published.

VI   *Les fouilles de Haddà. Figures et figurines, album photographique*. J. Barthoux (1930).

VII   `` *Recherches archéologiques au col de Khair Khaneh près de Kâbul*. J. Hackin in collaboration with J. Carl (1936).

VIII   *Diverses recherches archéologiques en Afghanistan (1933–1940)*. J. Hackin, J. Carl, and J. Menuié, with studies by R. Ghirshman and J.-C. Gardin (1959).

IX   *Recherches archéologiques à Begram*. J. Hackin in collaboration with Mme. J.-R. Hackin (2 vol., 1939).

X   *Shotorak*. J. Menuié (1942).

XI   *Nouvelles recherches archéologiques à Begram (1939–1940)*. J. Hackin in collaboration with J.-R. Hackin, J. Carl, and P. Hamelin. Comparative studies by J. Auboyer, V. Elisséeff, O. Kurz, and Ph. Stern (2 vol., 1954).

XII   *Begram. Recherches archéologiques et historiques sur les Kouchans*. R. Ghirshman (Cairo, 1946).

XIII   *Les Chionites-Hephtalites*. R. Ghirshman (Cairo, 1948).

XIV   *Trésors monétaires d'Afghanistan*. R. Curiel and D. Schlumberger (1953).

XV   *Céramiques de Bactres*. J.-C. Gardin (1957).

XVI   *Le minaret de Djam. La découverte de la capitale des sultans Ghorides (XII–XIII siecles)*. Andre Maricq and Gaston Wiet (1959).

XVII   *Fouilles de Mundigak*. J.-M. Casal (2 vol., 1961).

XVIII   *Lashkari Bazar, une résidence royale ghaznévide; 2) Les trouvailles: Ceramiques et monnaies de Lashkari Bazar et de Bust*. J.-C. Gardin (1963).

XIX   *Monuments préislamiques d'Afghanistan*. B. Dagens, M. Le Berre and D. Schlumberger (1964).

XX   *Le trésor monétaire de Qunduz*. R. Curiel and G. Fussman (1965).

AFGHAN CABINETS: 1963–71

Interim Cabinet: March 14, 1963–October 25, 1965

MINISTRY

Ministry	
Prime Minister	Dr. Mohammad Yousuf[1]
1st Deputy Prime Minister	Abdullah Malikyar[1, 3]
2nd Deputy Prime Minister	Dr. Ali Ahmad Popal[1, 5]
Deputy Prime Minister	Dr. Abdul Zahir (Sept. 30, 1964)
Court	Ali Mohammad[1, 2]
Foreign Affairs	The Prime Minister
National Defense	Gen. Khan Mohammad Khan[1]
Interior	Sayyid Abdullah; Dr. Abdul Kayeum (appointed May 23, 1963)
Finance	1st Deputy Prime Minister; Said Qassim Rishtya[1] (Jul. 7, 1964)
Justice	Sayyid Shamsuddin Majrooh[1]
Mines and Industry	The Prime Minister; Mohammad Husain Messa (Nov. 12, 1963)
Agriculture	Dr. Mohammad Nasir Keshawarz
Public Works	Brig. Gen. Mohammad Azim[1]
Education	2nd Deputy Prime Minister; Dr. Mohammad Anas (Jul. 7, 1964)
Press and Information	Said Qassim Rishtya; Mohammad Hashim Maiwandwal (Dec. 19, 1964)
Commerce	Mohammad Sawar Omar (Oct. 20, 1963)
Planning	Abdul Hai Aziz; Abdullah Yaftali (Oct. 20, 1963)
Public Health	Dr. Abdur Rahim; Dr. Abdul Zahir (Sept. 30, 1964)
Communications	Dr. Abdul Kayeum; Dr. Mohammad Haider (Nov. 12, 1963)
Tribal Affairs[4]	Sayyid Shamsuddin Majrooh[1]; Gul Pacha Ulfat (Apr. 25, 1963)

Yousuf's Cabinet: October 25, 1965
(Never actually served but approved by the Wolesi Jirgah)

Ministry	
Prime Minister	Dr. Mohammad Yousuf
Deputy Prime Minister	Sayyid Shamsuddin Majrooh
Foreign Affairs	Dr. Mohammad Yousuf
National Defense	General Khan Mohammad Khan
Interior	Mohammad Husain Messa
Finance	Abdullah Yaftali
Justice	None appointed
Mines and Industries	None appointed

Agriculture	Mir Mohammad Akbar Reza
Public Works	Ghulam Dastagir Azizi
Education	Dr. Mohammad Anas
Press and Information	Mohammad Hashim Maiwandwal
Commerce	Dr. Nour Ali
Planning	Dr. Abdul Samad Hamed
Public Health	Dr. Abdul Majid[1, 8]
Communications	Dr. Mohammad Haider
Tribal Affairs[4]	None appointed

Maiwandwal Cabinet: November 2, 1965–October 12, 1967[9]

Prime Minister	Mohammad Hashim Maiwandwal
1st Deputy Prime Minister	Nur Ahmad Etemadi (Jun. 20, 1966)
2nd Deputy Prime Minister	Abdul Satar Shalizi (Jun. 20, 1966)
Foreign Affairs	Nur Ahmad Etemadi
National Defence	General Khan Mohammad Khan[7]
Interior	Abdul Satar Shalizi; Engineer Ahmadullah (Jan. 26, 1967)
Finance	Abdullah Yaftali; Abdul Karim Hakimi (Jan. 26, 1967)
Justice	Dr. Abdul Hakim Tabibi; Dr. Mohammad Haider (Aug. 17, 1966); Mohammad Ehsan Taraki (Jul. 27, 1967)
Mines and Industries	Engineer Abdul Samad Salim
Agriculture	Engineer Mir Mohd. Akbar Reza
Public Works	Engineer Ahmadullah; Mohammad Husain Messa (Jan. 26, 1967)
Education	Mohammad Hashim Maiwandwal; Dr. Mohd. Osman Anwari (Dec. 1, 1965)
Press and Information (renamed Information and Culture)	Mohd. Osman Sidqi (Dec. 1, 1965); Abdul Rauf Benawa (June 13, 1967)
Commerce	Dr. Nour Ali
Planning	Dr. Abdul Hakim Ziayee (Dec. 1, 1965); Abdullah Yaftali (Jul. 27, 1967)
Public Health	Dr. Mohammad Osman Anwari; Miss Kubra Nurzai (first woman minister; Dec. 1, 1965)
Communications	Dr. Mohammad Haider; Abdul Karim Hakimi (Aug. 17, 1966); Engineer Mohd. Azim Gran (Deputy Minister, acted as Minister from Jan. 26, 1967)
Minister Without Portfolio	Dr. Mohammad Anas (Jul. 27, 1967)
Minister Without Portfolio	Abdullah Yaftali (Jan. 26, 1967)
Tribal Affairs	Mohammad Khalid Roashan (Dec. 1, 1965)
Secretary of the Council of Ministers	Dr. Abdul Ghafoor Ravan Farhadi[10]

691

Etemadi's First Cabinet: November 15, 1967–December 2, 1969[11]

Prime Minister	Nur Ahmad Etemadi
1st Deputy Prime Minister	Dr. Ali Ahmad Popal[12]
2nd Deputy Prime Minister	Abdullah Yaftali
Foreign Affairs	The Prime Minister
National Defense	General Khan Mohammad Khan[7]
Interior	Dr. Mohammad Omar Wardak[13]; Engineer Mohd. Bashir Ludin (Deputy Minister, acted as Minister from June 23, 1969)
Finance	Dr. Mohammad Anwar Ziayee
Justice	Dr. Mohammad Asghar
Mines and Industries	Engineer Abdul Samad Salim[14]; Mohammad Husain Messa[15]
Agriculture and Irrigation	Engineer Mir Mohd. Akbar Reza
Public Works	Mohammad Husain Messa
Education	Dr. Ali Ahmad Popal[16]; Dr. Mohd. Akram (Mar. 3, 1969)
Information and Culture	Dr. Mohammad Anas
Commerce	Dr. Nour Ali
Planning	Dr. Abdul Samad Hamed
Public Health	Miss Kubra Nurzai
Communications	Engineer Mohammad Azim Gran
Minister Without Portfolio	Dr. Abdul Wahid Sorabi
Tribal Affairs	Sayyid Masood Pohanyar

Etemadi's Second Cabinet: December 2, 1969–May 16, 1971

Prime Minister	Nur Ahmad Etemadi
1st Deputy Prime Minister	Abdullah Yaftali
2nd Deputy Prime Minister	Dr. Abdul Kayeum[17]
Foreign Affairs	Nur Ahmad Etemadi
National Defense	General Khan Mohammad Khan[7]
Interior	Engineer Mohd. Bashir Ludin[18]
Finance	Dr. Mohammad Aman
Justice	Abdul Satar Seerat
Mines and Industries	Amanullah Mansoori
Agriculture and Irrigation	Abdul Hakim
Public Works	Engineer Mohd. Yaqub Lali
Education	Dr. Abdul Kayeum
Information and Culture	Dr. Mahmud Habibi
Commerce	Dr. Mohd. Akbar Omar
Planning	Dr. Abdul Wahid Sorabi
Public Health	Professor Ibrahim Majid Seraj
Communications	Engineer Mohd. Azim Gran
Minister Without Portfolio	Mrs. Shafiqa Ziayee
Minister Without Portfolio	Ghulam Ali Ayeen
Tribal Affairs	Sayyid Masood Pohanyar

Cabinet of Dr. Abdul Zahir: July 26, 1971–?

Prime Minister	Dr. Abdul Zahir[6]
Deputy Prime Minister	Dr. Abdul Samad Hamed[17, 21]
National Defense	General Khan Mohammad Khan[7]
Foreign Affairs	Mohammad Musa Shafiq[19]
Interior	Amanullah Mansoori[20]
Commerce	Mohammad Asef Ghausi[22]
Finance	Ghulam Haider Dawar[23]
Planning	Dr. Abdul Wahid Sorabi[24]
Justice	Mohammad Anwar Arghandiwal[25]
Information and Culture	Mohammad Ibrahim Abbasi[26]
Education	Hamidullah Enayat Seraj[27]
Public Health	Prof. Mohammad Ibrahim Seraj[28]
Public Works	General Khwazak Khan[29]
Mines and Industries	Mohammad Yaqub Lali[30]
Agriculture	Abdul Hakim[28]
Communcations	Nasratullah Malikyar[31]
Tribal Affairs	Dr. Abdul Samad Hamed (temporary)
Without Portfolio	Mrs. Shafiqa Ziayee[28]
Without Portfolio	Dr. Abdul Wakil[32]
Without Portfolio	Abdul Satar Seerat[33]

[1] At one time or another served in a Daoud Cabinet (1953–63).

[2] Appointed by royal *farman*. Technically a protocol post, but Ali Mohammad is a close confidant of the King. No longer considered a cabinet post after 1965.

[3] Malikyar appointed Ambassador to the U.K. July 7, 1964. On February 12, 1967, exchanged embassies with Dr. Majid (note 8, below).

[4] Administered by a "President" (not a Minister), who holds cabinet rank.

[5] Dr. Ali Ahmad Popal appointed Ambassador to West Germany on July 7, 1964.

[6] Dr. Abdul Zahir as *the Single* Deputy Prime Minister, replacing both Malikyar and Popal. Dr. Zahir served as President of the *Wolesi Jirgah* (Lower House of Parliament), 1965–69; Ambassador to Italy fom 1969 to 1971.

[7] The resiliency of the Defense Minister illustrates the power of the army, and its relatively non-political outlook.

[8] At the time of his appointment, Ambassador to the U.S.A.; appointed Ambassador to the U.K. on February 12, 1967.

[9] Dr. Yousuf resigned on October 29; Maiwandwal's cabinet approved on November 2 by *Wolesi Jirgah*.

[10] Dr. Farhadi held this important post until the resignation of the Second Etemadi Cabinet. As this is written, he is Deputy Foreign Minister.

[11] Maiwandwal resigned on October 12, 1967; Abdullah Yaftali served as Acting Prime Minister until Etemadi's cabinet was approved on November 15, 1967.

[12] Dr. Popal was appointed Ambassador to Pakistan in June 1969.

[13] Dr. Wardak resigned on June 23, 1969 to stand for the *Wolesi Jirgah*, to which he was elected. He now serves as President of the Lower House.

[14] Resigned because of scandal in his ministry in summer 1968, although Engineer Salim apparently not involved.

[15] Messa held both ministries, Mines and Industries and Public Works, after Salim's resignation.

[16] Dr. Popal resigned as Minister of Education on November 19, 1968.

[17] Served in prior cabinet of Dr. Yousuf.

[18] Served as Acting Minister after Dr. Wardak's resignation.

[19] Ex-Ambassador to Cairo, and a "father" of the 1964 Constitution.

[20] Minister of Mines and Industries in Second Etemadi Cabinet.

[21] Minister of Planning in First Etemadi Cabinet.

[22] Ex-Deputy Minister of Planning.

[23] Ex-President of Customs, Ministry of Finance.

[24] Same post in Second Etemadi Cabinet; Minister w/o Portfolio in First Etemadi Cabinet.

[25] Ex-President of Civil Service Department, Prime Ministry.

[26] Ex-Governor of Herat; resigned April 12, 1972.

[27] Ex-Deputy Minister of Foreign Affairs (Administration).

[28] Same post in Second Etemadi Cabinet.

[29] Ex-Commandant of Labor Corps, Ministry of Public Works.

[30] Minister of Public Works in Second Etemadi Cabinet.

[31] Ex-Governor of Kapisa.

[32] Ex-President, Hilmand-Arghandab Valley Authority; businessman and farmer.

[33] Minister of Justice in Second Etemadi Cabinet.

AMERICAN UNIVERSITIES FIELD STAFF REPORTS ON AFGHANISTAN BY LOUIS DUPREE: 1959–71

"The *burqa* comes off." Vol. III, #2, Sept. 1959. 4 pp. (LD-2-59).

"An informal talk with Prime Minister Daud." Vol. III, #3, Sept. 1959. 4 pp. (LD-3-59).

"Afghanistan's 'Big Gamble,' Part I: Historical background of Afghan–Russian relations." Vol. IV, #3, April 1960. 20 pp. (LD-3-60); Part II: "The economic and strategic aspects of Soviet aid." Vol. IV, #4, May 1960. 20 pp. (LD-4-60); Part III: "Economic competition in Afghanistan." Vol. IV, #5, May 1960. 10 pp. (LD-5-60).

"The mountains go to Mohammad Zahir—observations on Afghanistan's reactions to visits by Nixon, Bulganin–Khrushchev, Eisenhower, and Khrushchev." Vol. IV, #6, May 1960. 40 pp. (LD-6-60).

"The Bamboo Curtain in Kabul—an American finds communications with the Chinese Embassy closed to him." Vol. IV, #7, Jul. 1960. 7 pp. (LD-7-60).

"A note on Afghanistan." Vol. IV, #8, Aug. 1960. 32 pp. (LD-8-60).

"American private enterprise in Afghanistan: the investment climate, particularly as it relates to one company." Vol. IV, #9, Dec. 1960. 12 pp. (LD-9-60).

" 'Pushtunistan': The problem and its larger implications. Part I: The complex interrelationships of regional disputes." Vol. V, #2, Nov. 1961. 11 pp. (LD-2-61); Part II: "The effects of the Afghan–Pakistan border closure." Vol. V, #3, Nov. 1961. 16 pp. (LD-3-61); Part III: "The big gamble continues." Vol. V, #4, Dec. 1961. 7 pp. (LD-4-61).

"India's stake in Afghan–Pakistan relations." Vol. VI, #1, Feb. 1962. 5 pp. (LD-1-62).

"The Indian merchants in Kabul." Vol. VI, #3, Feb. 1962. 9 pp. (LD-3-62).

"Landlocked Images." Vol. VI, #5, Jun. 1962. 25 pp. (LD-5-62).

"Afghanistan's slow march to democracy." Vol. VII, #1, Jan. 1963. 14 pp. (LD-1-63).

"The Afghans honor a Muslim saint." Vol. VII, #2, Jan. 1963. 26 pp. (LD-63).

"A suggested Pakistan–Afghanistan–Iran federation. Part I: The empty triangle." Vol. VII, #3, Feb. 1963. 18 pp. (LD-3-63).

"A suggested Pakistan–Afghanistan–Iran federation. Part II: Political and economic considerations." Vol. VII, #4, Feb. 1963. 14 pp. (LD-4-63).

"The green and the black: Social and economic aspects of a coal mine in Afghanistan." Vol. VII, #5, Apr. 1963. 30 pp. (LD-5-63).

"The decade of Daoud ends: Implications of Afghanistan's change of government." Vol. VII, #7, May 1963. 29 pp. (LD-7-63).

"An informal talk with King Mohammad Zahir of Afghanistan." Vol. VII, #9, Jul. 1963. 8 pp. (LD-9-63).

"Mahmud Tarzi: Forgotten nationalist." Vol. VIII, #1, Jan. 1964. 22 pp. (LD-1-64).

"The Peace Corps in Afghanistan: The impact of the volunteers on the country and of the country on the volunteers." Vol. VIII, #4, Oct. 1964. 18 pp. (LD-4-64).

"Constitutional development and cultural change. Part I: Social implications of constitution making." Vol. IX, #1, May 1965. 5 pp. (LD-1-65); Part II: "Pre-1964 Afghan constitutional development." Vol. IX, #2, May 1965. 18 pp. (LD-2-65); Part III: "The 1964 Afghan constitution (Articles 1–56)." Vol. IX, #3, Sept 1965. 29 pp. (LD-3-65); Part IV: "The 1964 Afghan constitution (Articles 57–128)." Vol. IX, #4, Sept. 1965. 34 pp. (LD-4-65); Part V: "The background of constitutional development on the subcontinent." Vol. IX, #7, Dec. 1965, 15 pp. (LD-7-65); Part VI: "The first Pakistani constitution of 1956." Vol. IX, #8. Dec. 1965. 22 pp. (LD-8-65); Part VII: "The 1962 constitution of Pakistan." Vol. IX, #9, Dec. 1965. 17 pp. (LD-9-65); Part VIII: "The future of constitutional law in Afghanistan and Pakistan." Vol. IX, #10, Dec. 1965. 24 pp. (LD-10-65).

"An ethnographic 'puzzle': Three similar wooden objects from Norway, Iran, and Afghanistan." Vol. X, #1, Feb. 1966. 11 pp. (LD-1-66).

"Kabul gets a supermarket: The birth and growth of an Afghan enterprise." Vol. X, #2, Feb. 1966. 14 pp. (LD-2-66).

"Afghanistan: 1966, Comments on a comparatively calm state of affairs with reference to the turbulence of late 1965." Vol. X, #4, Jul. 1966. 32 pp. (LD-4-66).

"Aq Kupruk: A town in north Afghanistan. Part I: The people and their cultural patterns." Vol. X, #9, Nov. 1966. 29 pp. (LD-9-66); Part II: "The political structure and commercial patterns." Vol. X, #10, Dec. 1966. 24 pp. (LD-10-66).

"The Chinese touch base and strike out." Vol. X, #11, Dec. 1966. 30 pp. (LD-11-66).

"A Kabul supermarket revisited: A successful Afghan entrepreneur views the future." Vol. XII, #2, Aug. 1968. 7 pp. (LD-2-68).

"Afghanistan: 1968. Part I: Government and bureaucracy." Vol. XII, #4, Aug. 1968. 8 pp. (LD-4-68); Part II: "Economy and Development." Vol. XII, #5, Aug. 1968. 19 pp. (LD-5-68); Part III: "Problems of a Free Press." Vol. XII, #6, Aug. 1968. 14 pp. (LD-6-68); Part IV: "Strikes and Demonstrations." Vol. XII, #7, Aug. 1968. 6 pp. (LD-7-68).

"Sports and games in Afghanistan." Vol. XIV, #1, Jan. 1970. 20 pp.

"Free enterprise in Afghanistan: Part I: The private sector and the new Investment Law." Vol. XIV, #3, Jan. 1970. 20 pp.

"Free enterprise in Afghanistan: Part II: Peter Baldwin and Indamer Afghan Industries, Inc." Vol. XIV, #4, Feb. 1970. 12 pp.

"The 1969 student demonstrations in Kabul." Vol. XIV, #5, May 1970. 13 pp.

"Free enterprise in Afghanistan: Part III: Programs, problems and prospects." Vol. XIV, #6, May 1970. 19 pp.

"Population dynamics in Afghanistan." Vol. XIV, #7, Apr. 1970. 11 pp.

"Population review 1970: Afghanistan." Vol. XV, #1, Dec. 1970. 20 pp.

"A note on Afghanistan: 1971." Vol. XV, #2, Jul. 1971. 35 pp.

"Afghanistan continues its experiment in democracy: The Thirteenth Parliament is elected." Vol. XV, #3, Jul. 1971. 15 pp.

"Comparative profiles of recent parliaments in Afghanistan." Vol. XV, No. 4, Jul. 1971. 18 pp.

"Parliament versus the executive in Afghanistan: 1969–1971." Vol. XV, #5, Sept. 1971. 17 pp.

"Nuristan: 'The Land of Light' seen darkly." Vol. XV, #6, Dec. 1971. 24 pp.

BIBLIOGRAPHY

SOURCES CITED AND BIBLIOGRAPHIC NOTES

THE following bibliography is not meant to be exhaustive, but merely lists the references cited. Those desiring detailed bibliographic materials are referred first to the work of Donald N. Wilber, *An Annotated Bibliography of Afghanistan,* 3rd. ed., New Haven, 1968. Others are: Dr. Mohammad Akram, *Bibliographie analytique de l'Afghanistan,* Paris, 1947; Serge de Laugier de Beaurecueil, Les Publications de la Société d'Histoire d'Afghanistan, *Mélanges, Institut Dominicain d'Études Orientales du Cairo* 7:236–40, 1962–63; *Bibliography of Recent Soviet Source Material on Soviet Central Asia and the Borderlands,* Central Asian Research Centre, London, 1957–62; *Bibliography of Russian Work on Afghanistan,* Central Asian Research Centre, London, 1956; A. Fairid, *Bibliyugrafi,* Kabul, 1965; M. Heravi, *Fihrist-i-Kutub-i-Matbut-i-Afghanistan az sal-i-1330 ila 1344,* Kabul, 1965; T. Kukhtina, *Bibliografiya Afganistana,* Moscow, 1965; D. Sinor, *Introduction à l'étude de l'Eurasie Centrale,* Wiesbaden, 1963.

An excellent recent two-volume bibliography has been published jointly by the Dokumentationsleitstelle für den Modernen Orient beim Deutschen Orient-Institut (Hamburg) and the Institut für Entwicklungsforschung und Entwicklungspolitik der Ruhr-Universität (Bochum): *Bibliographie der Afghanistan-Literatur, 1945–1967:* Teil I, *Literatur in Europäischen Sprachen,* 1968; Teil II, *Literatur Orientalischen Sprachen und Ergänzungen in Europäischen Sprachen,* 1969, Hamburg.

Several commentaries on bibliographies about Afghanistan are also worthwhile: M. Schinasi, Bibliography, *The Kabul Times Annual,* 156–58, 1967; A. Habibi, "A glance at historiography and the beginning of the Historical Society of Afghanistan," *Afghanistan* 21(2):1–19, 1968; M. Ahang, Cumulative index of *Afghanistan,* vols. 1–20, *Afghanistan* 21(2):20–40, 1968; C. Kieffer, (Bibliographie, *Afghanistan* 15(3):48–52, 1960, 16(2):52–56, 1961, and "Les problemes d'une bibliographie exhaustive de l'Afghanistan," *Afghanistan* 13(2):1–15, 13(3):12–40, 1958.

For additional comments on available sources, see Gregorian, 1969, 409–11, 503–05.

Additional valuable commentaries on bibliographies and other source materials are found in M. Kakar, 1968, 271–82, and Grassmuck, et al., 1969, 339–405.

Several periodicals published in Afghanistan also offer good source material: *The Kabul Times,* a government-controlled, English daily which began publication in 1962, can be purchased in bound volumes; *The Kabul Times Annual,* first published in 1967 in English, with a new edition published in 1970; *Afghanistan,* a cultural quarterly published in western languages (mainly English) by the *Anjuman-i-Tarikh* (Historical Society) since 1946; *Ariana,* a monthly published in Dari and Pashto by the *Anjuman-i-Tarikh* since 1942; *Da Kabul Kalani* or *Da Afghanistan Kalani*—after 1952—(*The Kabul Yearbook,* called *Sal-nameh-yi-Kabul* until 1940), published in Dari and Pashto (with occasional summaries in French and English) by the Ministry of Information and Culture (formerly Press) since 1933; *Ariana da 'iratu 'l ma'arif* (*Ariana Encyclopedia*), still incomplete Dari edition begun in 1949, Pashto in 1951, published by the Ministry of Information and Culture; *Rasmi Jarideh,* official gazette of the Afghan government, first published on March 8, 1964, by the Ministry of Justice; *Wolesi Jirgah,* the proceedings of the Lower House of Parliament.

The various ministries, faculties of Kabul University, and other institutions (e.g., banks) also publish monthly or quarterly informational periodicals in Dari, Pashto, and occasionally Western languages, as well as reports on specific topics (e.g., the five year plans and related development projects).

SOURCES CITED

Abdur Rahman Khan. *The Life of Abdur Rahman, Amir of Afghanistan* (ed. by Sultan Mahomed Khan), 2 vols., London, 1900. Also see *Taj-ul-tawarikh,* Persian edition, Bombary, ca. 1904.

Abridged Official Account of the Second Anglo–Afghan War, London, 1908.

Adamec, L. *Afghanistan, 1900–1923,* Berkeley, 1967.

Adamec, L. "Germany, Third Power in Afghanistan's Foreign Relations," in Grassmuck, et al., 1969, 204–59.

Afghanistan: British Intelligence Survey. J.I.B. 2/3, London, 1948.

Afghanistan: Field Notes of General Staff, India. 2nd ed., Calcutta, 1915.

Afghanistan: Preliminary NIS Gazetteer. Div. of Geog., Dept. of the Int., Washington, July, 1952.

Afghanistan dar dowreh-i hukumat-i entaqali, hut 1341-mizan 1344 (*Afghanistan Under the Interim Government: March, 1963–October, 1965*), Kabul, 1965.

Agricultural Development in Afghanistan with Special Emphasis on Wheat. Kabul, July, 1967.

Ahang, M. "The background and beginning of the Afghan press system," *Afghanistan* 21(1):70–76, (2):41–48, (3):43–47, (4):37–47, 22(1):28–31, (2):73–80, 1968abcd–1969ab, (3–4):52–73, 1969–70.

————. *A Short History of Journalism in Afghanistan* (in Dari), Kabul, 1970.

Ahmad, A. "Afghani's Indian contacts," *Journal of the American Oriental Society* 89(3):476–504, 1969.

Ahmad, N. "The patterns of rural settlement in East Pakistan," *Geographical Review* 46(3):388–98, 1956.

Aitchison, C. *Treaties, Engagements, and Sanads Relating to India and Neighboring Countries,* vol. 13, Delhi, 1933.

Akhramovich, R. *Outline History of Afghanistan After the Second World War* (in English), Moscow, 1966.

Akhramovich, R. *Concerning the Recent Stages in Afghanistan's Social History* (in English), Moscow, 1967.

Alberts, R., and L. Dupree. Unpublished manuscript on Irano–Afghan subculture area of the greater Middle East.

Alekseyev, L. *Sovetskiy Soyuz I Iran,* Moscow, 1963.

Ali, Chaudri Mohd. . . . *And Then the Pathan Murders,* Peshawar, 1966.

Ali, M. *A Manual of Hadith,* Lahore, n.d.

Ali, Mohd. *Aryana or Ancient Afghanistan,* Historical Society of Afghanistan, #47, Kabul, 1957.

————. *Afghanistan: An Historical Sketch,* Kabul, 1958a.

————. *Afghanistan: The National Awakening,* Lahore, 1958b.

————, *Manners and Customs of the Afghans,* Lahore, 1958c.

————. *Afghanistan (the Mohammadzai Period),* Kabul, 1959.

————. "The story of Koh-i-Nur," *Afghanistan* 16(4):1–7, 1961.

————. *The Afghans,* Lahore, 1965.

Altheim, F., et al., *Geschischte der Hunnen,* 2 vols., Berlin, 1959, 1960.

Amoss, H., "Dari-zul: Village in transition," in *Am. Historical Anthropology: Essays in Honor of Leslie Spier,* ed. W. Taylor, C. Riley, Carbondale, 1967.

Anderson, M. *Eleven Verse Plays,* New York, n.d.

Andreev, M. *On the ethnography of Afghanistan (Po ethnografii Afghanistan),* Tashkent, 1927.

————. *On the ethnology of Afghanistan (Po etnologii Afghanistan),* Tashkent, 1932.

Angel, L. Personal communication, 1968.

Arberry, A. *Introduction to the History of Sufism,* London, 1942.

————. *Sufism,* London, 1950.

————. (ed.) *The Legacy of Persia,* Oxford, 1953.

————. *Classical Persian Literature,* London, 1958.

————. *Discourses of Rumi,* London, 1961.

Archer, W. "The music of Afghanistan and Iran," *The Society for Asian Music Quarterly Letter,* 1–9, New York, 1964.

Arez, G. *Eqlim Afghanistan (The Climate of Afghanistan),* Kabul, 1969.

————. "Geography of Afghanistan," *Kabul Times Annual:* 19–93, 1970.

The Atlas of Ancient and Classical History, New York, 1914.

Avery, P. *Modern Iran,* London, 1967a.

————. Personal communication, 1967b.

————, and J. Heath-Stubbs. *Hafiz of Shiraz,* London, 1952.

Azad, A. *India Wins Freedom,* New York, 1960.

Bacon, E. "An inquiry into the history of the Hazara Mongols of Afghanistan," *Southwestern Journal of Anthropology* 7:230–47, 1951.

————. *OBOK,* Wenner-Gren No. 25, New York, 1958.

————. *Central Asians Under Russian Rule,* Ithaca, 1966.

Baghban, H. "An overview of Herat folk literature," *Afghanistan* 21(1):81–90, 1968a; *Afghanistan* 21(2):51–62, 1968b.

Bailey, H. "Gandhari," *Bulletin of the School of Oriental and African Studies* 11:764–97, 1943–46.

Barth, F. *Indus and Swat Kohistan: An Ethnographic Study,* Oslo, 1956.

———. *Political Leadership Among Swat Pathans,* London, 1959.

Barthold, W. *Turkestan Down to the Mongol Invasion,* London, 1928.

Barton, W. *India's North-West Frontier,* London, 1939.

Basham, A. *Papers on the Date of Kaniska,* Leiden, 1968.

Baynes, N. *The Byzantine Empire,* London, 1952.

Beaurecueil, S. de. *Abdullah Ansari,* Kabul, 1957. (translated into Persian by A. R. Farhadi, 1962).

Beazley, E. "The pigeon towers of Isfahan," *Iran* IV:105–09, 1966.

Bell, M., ed. *An American Engineer in Afghanistan,* Minneapolis, 1948.

Benawa, A. *The Hotakis* (in Persian), Kabul, 1956.

———. *Landai,* Kabul, 1958.

———. *Awsani Likwal* (in Pashto: *Current Writers*), 3 vols., Kabul, 1961–62, 1967–68.

Benveniste, E., and A. Dupont-Sommer, "Une inscription indo-araméenne d'asoka provenant de Kandahar (Afghanistan)," *Journal Asiatique* CCLIV (3–4):437–66, 1966.

Bennigsen, A., and C. Lemercier-Quelquejay. *Islam in the Soviet Union,* London, 1967.

Berg, L. *Freshwater Fishes of the U.S.S.R. and Adjacent Countries,* Smithsonian, 1948.

Bernard, P. Personal communications, 1966, 1970.

———. "La première campagne de fouilles à Aï Khanoum," *Comptes rendus d'Académie des Inscriptions et Belles-Lettres:* 604–57, 1966.

———. "Deuxième campagne de fouilles d'Aï Khanoum en Bactriane," ibid, 306–24, 1967.

———. "Aï Khanoum," *Proceedings of the British Academy* LIII: 71–95, 1968a.

———. "Aï Khanoum, Troisième campagne de fouilles à Aï Khanoum," *Comptes rendus d'Académie des Inscriptions et Belles-Lettres:* 263–79, 1968b.

———. "Ai Khanoum," *L'Enciclopedia dell'arte,* in print.

Biddulph, C. *Afghan Poetry of the 17th Century: Being Selections from the Poems of Kushhal Khan Khatak,* London, 1890.

Biddulph, H. "Shah Shujah's Force," *Journal of the Society for Army Historical Research* (20):65–71, 1941.

Bivar, A. "The Bactrian treasure of Qunduz," *Numismatic Society of India,* Bombay, 1955.

Blake, R., and R. Frye. "History of the Nation of the Archers (the Mongols)," *Harvard Journal of Asiatic Studies* 12(3–4):269–399, 1949.

Bombaci, A. "Summary report of the Italian archaelogical mission in Afghanistan, I: Introduction to the excavations at Ghazni," *East and West* n.s. 10(1–2): 3–22, 1959.

———. "The kufic inscriptions in Persian verses in the court of the royal palace of Mas'ud III at Ghazni," *ISMEO Reports and Memos* vol. V, Rome 1966.

Bosworth, C. *The Ghaznavids,* Edinburgh, 1963.

———. *The Islamic Dynasties, Islamic Survey #5,* Edinburgh, 1967.

Boulnois, L. *The Silk Route,* London, 1966.

Bowen, J. *The Golden Pomegranate,* London, 1966.

Bowie, T. et al. *East-West in Art,* Bloomington, 1966.

Braidwood, R., and B. Howe. *Prehistoric Investigations in Iraqi Kurdistan,* Chicago, 1960.

Brockelmann, C. *History of the Islamic Peoples*, New York, 1947.

Bruno, A. "Notes on the discovery of Hebrew inscriptions in the vicinity of the minaret of Jam," *East and West* n.s., 14(3–4):206–08, 1963.

Buddruss, G. "Zur mythologie der Prasun (Cafiren)," *Paidemus* 7(4/6):200–09, Wiesbaden, 1960.

Burn, A. *Alexander the Great and the Hellenistic World*, N.Y., 1962.

Burnes, A. *Voyages de l'Embouchure de l'Indus à Lahor, Caboul, Balkh, et à Boukhara et Retour par le Perse, Pendant les Annees 1831, 1832, et 1833*, 4 vols., Paris, 1835.

————. *Cabool*, London, 1843.

Caillat, C., "La séquence SHYTY dans les inscriptions indo-araméennes d'ashoka," *Journal Asiatique* CCLIV(3–4):467–70, 1966.

Cammann, S., "Ancient symbols in modern Afghanistan," *Ars Orientalis* 11:5–34, 1957.

Caroe, O., *Soviet Empire*, London, 1953.

————. *The Pathans*, London, 1965.

Carratelli, G., and G. Garbini. Foreword by G. Tucci. Introduction by U. Scerratio. "A bilingual Graeco–Aramaic Edict of Asoka: the first Greek inscription discovered in Afghanistan," *Serie Orientale Roma* XXIX, Rome, 1964.

Centlivres, M. and P., "Calottes, Mitres et Toques," *Bull. Annuel du Musée et Institut d'Ethnographie de la Ville de Genève* 11: 11–46, 1968.

Chavarria–Aguilar, O. *Pashto Instructor's Handbook*, Ann Arbor, 1962.

Childe, V. *What Happened in History?*, New York, 1946.

Chowdhury, K. "Plant remains from Deh Morasi Ghundai, Afghanistan," in Dupree 1963a, 126–131.

Churchill, W. *The Story of the Malakand Field Force*, London, 1916.

Civil and Military Gazette. Lahore, January 1, 1960.

Concise History of Islam, A. Amsterdam, 1957.

Constitution of Afghanistan. Franklin Book Programs (Education Press), Kabul, 1964.

Coon, C. *Cave Exploration in Iran*, Philadelphia, 1951a.

————. *Caravan*, New York, 1951b.

————. *The Seven Caves*, New York, 1957.

————, and E. Ralph, Radiocarbon dates for Kara Kamar, Afghanistan, *Science* 122(3176):921–922, 1955.

Coulson, N. *A History of Islamic Law*, Edinburgh, 1964.

Cunningham, A. "Coins of the Indo–Scythians," *Numismatic Chronicle* 3 series, vols. 8–10, 12, 1888–92.

Dada, H., and L. Pickett. *1968 Supplement to the Bibliography of Material Dealing with Agriculture in Afghanistan*, Kabul, 1969.

Dales, G. "A suggested chronology for Afghanistan, Baluchistan, and the Indus Valley," in *Chronologies in Old World Archaeology*, R. Ehrich (ed.), Chicago, 1966.

Dani, A. *Gandhara Art in Pakistan*, Peshawar, 1968.

Davies, C. *The North-West Frontier, 1890–1908*, Cambridge, 1932.

————. *An Historical Atlas of the Indian Peninsula*, New Delhi, 1949.

Davis, R. "Prehistoric investigation in north Afghanistan 1969," *Afghanistan* 22(3–4):75–90, 1970.

Davydov, A. "O sel'skoy obshchine i yeye Khozyaystvennom znachenii v Afghanistane," *Voprosy Ekononiiki Afganistana*:57–124, 1963.

————. *Afganskaya derevnya*, Moscow, 1969.

Debets, G. *Antropologicheskie issledovaniia Afganistane,* Moscow, ı(1965), ıı(1966a), ııı(1966b), ıv(1966c).

———. *Physical Anthropology of Afghanistan: I–IV,* Illustrations and Notes by L. Dupree. Translated by E. Prostov. Edited by H. Field. Russian Translation Series of the Peabody Museum of Archaeology and Ethnology, Vol. V, No. 1, 1970.

de Cardi, B. "Bampur," *Archaeologia Viva* 1:151–55, 1968.

Demont, M., and P. Centlivres. "Poteries et potiers d'Afghanistan," *Bull. Annuel du Musée et Institut d'Ethnographie de la Ville de Genève* 10:23–67, 1967.

Dianous, H. de. "La littérature Afghane de langue persane," *Orient* 31:138–44, Paris, 1964.

Dichter, D. *The North–West Frontier of West Pakistan: A Study in Regional Geography,* Oxford, 1967.

Dilks, D. *Curzon in India,* London, 1969, 1970.

Diskalkar, D. "Some letters about the First Afghan War, 1838–42," *Journal of Indian History* xıı(II):251–68; xıı(III):405–22, 1933.

Diver, M. *The Hero of Herat,* London, 1912.

———. *The Judgment of the Sword,* London, 1924.

Doyle, A. *The Complete Sherlock Holmes,* 2 vols., New York, 1930.

Duchesne-Guillemin, J. *Zoroastre,* Paris, 1966.

Dunsterville, L. *The Adventures of Dunsterforce,* London, 1920.

Dupaigne, B. "Aperçus sur quelques techniques afghanes," *Objets et Mondes* 7(1):84, 1968.

Dupree, L., *Cultural Study of Afghanistan,* Air Force Contract 01(600)-472, RSI 53-5, ADTIC, Air University, Maxwell AFB, Alabama, 1953.

———. "The disintegration of the clan village in Badwan, a Pathan farming village in southwest Afghanistan," *Journal of the Alabama Academy of Science* 29:98, 1954.

———. "The artificial small group study and archaeological excavations," *American Antiquity* 20(3):271, 1955.

———. "The changing character of south–central Afghanistan villages," *Human Organization* 14(4):26–29, 1956.

———. "Medieval European feudalism and the contemporary Middle East," *Report on Current Research, Spring, 1957,* 47–55, Middle East Institute, Washington, 1957.

———. *Shamshir Ghar: Historic Cave Site in Kandahar Province, Afghanistan,* New York, 1958a.

———. "The Arabs of modern Libya," *The Muslim World* 48(2):113–24, 1958b.

———. "Religion, technology and Islam," in *Aspects of Religion in Indian Society,* L. Vidyarthi (ed.), Meerut, 1961a.

———. "The Durand line of 1893," in *Current Problems in Afghanistan,* T. Cuyler Young, Sr. (ed.), Princeton, 1961b.

———. "The 'good dictator,'" *American Universities Field Staff Reports Service South Asian Series* 6(4), 1962.

———. *Deh Morasi Ghundai,* New York, 1963a.

———. "Tribalism, regionalism and national oligarchy," in *Expectant Peoples: Nationalism and Development,* K. H. Silvert (ed.), New York, 1963b.

———. "Afghanistan: the canny neutral," *The Nation* 199(7):134–37, 1964a.

———. "Prehistoric surveys and excavations in Afghanistan, 1959–1960 and 1961–1963," *Science* 146(3644):638–40, 1964b.

———. "Tribal traditions and modern nationhood: Afghanistan," *Asia: A Selection of papers delivered before the Asia Society,* 1:1–12, New York, 1964c.

————. *Changing patterns of social structure in Afghanistan* (unpublished monograph), UNESCO Research Centre on Social and Economic Development in Southern Asia, contract R/2/3/Afghanistan/1590, Delhi, 1965a.

————. "Moving mountains in Afghanistan," in *Cultural Frontiers of the Peace Corps*, R. B. Textor (ed.), pp. 107–24, Cambridge, Mass., 1965b.

————. "Democratic trouble in Kabul," *Foreign Report, The Economist*, Nov. 25, 4–7, London, 1965c.

————. "Islam in Politics: Afghanistan," *The Muslim World* LVI-4:269–76, 1966.

————. "The political uses of religion: Afghanistan," in *Churches and States*, K. H. Silver, (ed.), New York, 1967a.

————. "The prehistoric period of Afghanistan," *Afghanistan* 20(3):8–27, 1967b.

————. "The retreat of the British Army from Kabul to Jalalabad in 1842: History and folklore," *Journal of the Folklore Institute* 4(1):50–74, 1967c.

————. "Prehistoric excavations in Afghanistan," *The American Philosophical Society Yearbook: 1967*, 504–08, 1968a.

————. "The oldest sculptured head?" *Natural History* 77(5):26–27, 1968b.

————. "Aq Kupruk: A town in north Afghanistan," 2 chapters in *City and Nation in the Developing World*, Associates of A.U.F.S., pp. 9–61, New York, 1968c.

————. "Democracy and the military base of power," *Middle East Journal* 22(1):29–44, 1968d.

————. "Archaeology: Recent research in Afghanistan," *Explorers Journal* 47(2):84–93, 1969a.

————. "Afghanistan and the unpaved road to democracy," *Royal Central Asian Society Journal* 56(3):272–278, 1969b.

————, and N. "Dr. Brydon's report on the British retreat from Kabul in January 1842: an important historical document," *Afghanistan* 20(3):55–65, 1967.

————, and B. Howe. "Results of an archaeological survey for stone age sites in north Afghanistan," *Afghanistan* 18(2):1–15, 1963.

————, L. Lattman, and R. Davis. "Ghar-i-Mordeh Gusfand ("Cave of the Dead Sheep"). A new Mousterian locality in north Afghanistan," *Science* 167(3925):1610–12, 1970.

Dupree, N. *The Road to Balkh*, Kabul, 1967a.

————. *Bamiyan* (2nd ed.), Kabul, 1967b.

————. *Kabul* (2nd ed.), Kabul, 1972.

Dvoryankov, N. *Yahzyk Pushtu*, Moscow, 1960.

————. "Pashto dialects and the literary languages in Afghanistan," (in English) XXVI International Congress of Orientalists, Moscow, 1963.

————. (ed.), et al. *Sovremennyy Afghanistan*, Moscow, 1960.

Eastern World, London, October, 1961.

East Indian (Military) Report on the Air Operations in Afghanistan Between December 12, 1928, and February 25, 1929, London, 1929.

Edelberg, L. "Status de bois rapportées du Kafiristan á Kabul aprés la conquête de cette province par l'Émir Abdur Rahman en 1895/96," *Arts Asiatiques* VII:243–86, 1960.

————. "Nuristanske solupokaler [Silver cups of Nuristan]," *Kuml*, 153–201, Copenhagen, 1965.

————. and K. Ferdinand. "Henning Haslund-Christensens Minde-Ekspedition 1953–55 til Afghanistan," *Statens almindelige Videns Kabsfond*, 1955–56.

————. and K. Ferdinand. "Arselan," *Naturens Verden*, 257–88, September, 1958.

Edmonds, P. Personal communication, 1968.

Educational Statistics, Afghanistan, 1968/1347, Dept. of Planning, Directorate of Statistics, Ministry of Education, Kabul, 1969.

Educational Statistics, Afghanistan, 1969, Dept. of Planning, Directorate of Statistics, Ministry of Education, Kabul, 1970.

Education in Afghanistan during the Last Fifty Years, 2 vols., Kabul, 1968.

Egerton, J. "TVA: the halo slips," *The Nation* 11–15, July 3, 1967.

Ellerman, J., and T. Morrison-Scott. *A Checklist of Palaearctic and Indian Mammals,* London, 1951.

Elliot, H., and J. Dowson (ed.). *History of Ghazni,* 2 vols., (first published 1869), Calcutta, 1953.

Elliott, J. *The Frontier: 1839–1947,* London, 1968.

Elphinstone, M. *An Account of the Kingdom of Caubul and Its Dependencies in Persia, Tartary and India, Comprising a View of the Afghaun Nation and a History of the Dooraunee Monarchy,* London, 1815.

Elwell–Sutton, L. "The Omar Khayyam puzzle," *Royal Central Asian Society Journal* LV(2):167–79, 1968.

Emery, R., and H. F. Lee. *Economic Trends in Asia in 1966,* Asia, Africa and Latin America Section, Division of International Finance, Board of Governors of the Federal Reserve System, July 17, 1967, Mimeo.

Encyclopedia of Islam, continuing series, Leiden.

Engert, C. *A Report on Afghanistan,* Department of State, Division of Publications, Series C, #53, Afghanistan #1, Washington, 1924.

Evans–Pritchard, E. *The Sanusi of Cyrenaica,* Oxford, 1949.

Eyre, V. *The Military Operations at Cabul,* 4th ed., London, 1843.

———. *The Kabul Insurrection of 1841–42,* London, 1879.

Fairservis, W. "Archaeological research in Afghanistan," *Transactions of the New York Academy of Science* series 2, 12(5):172–74, 1950a.

———. "Exploring the desert of death," *Natural History,* 59(6):246–53, 1950b.

———. *Excavations in the Quetta Valley, West Pakistan,* New York, 1956.

———. *Archaeological Surveys in the Zhob and Loralai Districts, West Pakistan,* New York, 1959.

———. *Archaeological Studies in the Seistan Basin of Southwestern Afghanistan and Eastern Iran,* New York, 1961.

Farhadi, A. R. *Le persan parlé en Afghanistan. Grammaire du Kâboli,* Paris, 1955.

———. "Die Sprachen von Afghanistan," *Zentralasiatische Studien* 3:409–16, 1969.

———. *Zendigi-yi-Khwaja 'Abdullah Ansari,* Kabul, 1962.

———. "Language," in *Kabul Times Annual,* 83–85, Kabul, 1967.

———. Personal communication, 1970.

Ferdinand, K. "Afghanistan nomade," *Fra Nationalmusetts Arbejdmsark* 61–72, 1956.

———. "Nomadestudier I Afghanistan," *Menneskets Mangfoldighed E. Wangels Forlag AIS* 1–16, 1957.

———. "Ris," *KUML,* 195–232, 1959a.

———. "Preliminary notes on Hazara cultures," *Hist. Filos Dan.vid. Selsk.* 37(5):1–51, 1959b.

———. "The Baluchistan barrel-vaulted tent and its affinities," *Folk* 1:27–50. 1959c.

———. "Les Nomades," 1959d, in Humlum, 1959.

———. "The Baluchistan barrel-vaulted tent: supplement material from Iranian Baluchistan and Sistan," *Folk* 2:33–50, 1960a.

706

————. "Nomadism and studies in Pushtun nomadism," *Wazma*, Mizan–Aqrab, 1–20, 1960b.

————. "Nomad expansion and commerce in central Afghanistan," *Folk* 4:123–159, 1962.

————. "Nomadisme," *KUML*, 108–47, 1963a.

————. "The horizontal windmills of western Afghanistan," *Folk* 5:71–89, 1963b.

————. "Ethnographical notes on the Chahar Aimaq, Hazara and Moghuls," *Acta Orientalia* 28(1–2):175–203, 1964.

————. "The horizontal windmills of western Afghanistan: An additional note," *Folk* 8–9:83–88, 1966–67.

Ferrier, J. *Caravan Journeys and Wanderings in Persia, Afghanistan, Turkistan, and Baluchistan*, London, 1857.

————. *History of the Afghans*, London, 1858.

Fieldhouse, D. *The Colonial Empires*, London, 1966.

Fischer, K. "Neue Funde und Forschunger zur indischen Kunst in Arachosien, Baktrien, und Gandhara," *Archäologischer Anzeiger* 72:416–35, 1957.

————. *Schöpfungen indischer Kunst*, Köln, 1959.

————. "Zur Lage von Kandahar an Landverbindungen zwischen Iran und Indien," *Bonner Jahrbücher*, 167:129–232, 1967.

————. Preliminary remarks on archaeological survey in Afghanistan, *Zentralasiatische Studien* 3:327–408, 1969.

————. Personal communication, 1969.

Fischer, L., *Afghanistan: Eine geographisch-medizinische Landeskunde, A Geomedical Monograph* (English section translated by J. and I. Hellen), Heidelberg and New York, 1968.

Fisher, M., L. Rose, and R. Huttenback. *Himalayan Battleground: Sino–Indian Rivalry in Ladakh*, New York, 1963.

Fletcher, A. *Afghanistan: Highway of Conquest*, Cornell, 1966.

Forbes, A. *The Afghan Wars, 1839–1842 and 1878–1880*, London, 1892.

Foucher, A. *L'art Gréco-bouddhique de Gandhara*, Paris: I, 1905; II-1, 1918; II-2, 1922; II-3, 1951.

————. "Bustes provenant de Hadda (Afghanistan) en Musée Guimet," *Extrait des Monuments et Mémoirs publiés par l'Acádémie des Inscriptions et Belles-Lettres* 30:101–10, 1930.

Fox, E. *Travels in Afghanistan, 1932–1938*, New York, 1943.

Franck, D. "Pushtunistan—disputed disposition of a tribal land," *Middle East Journal* 6(1):49–68, 1952.

Franck, P. *Afghanistan Between East and West*, Washington, 1960.

Fraser–Tytler, W. *Afghanistan* (3rd. ed., revised by M. Gillett), London, 1967.

Freeman–Grenville, G. *The Muslim and Christian Calendars*, Oxford, 1963.

Frye, R. *The Heritage of Persia*, Mentor MQ 662, New York, 1966.

Fuller, Major-General J. F. C. *The Generalship of Alexander the Great*, London, 1958.

Furse, P. "Iran and Afghanistan, 1964," *Journal of the Royal Horticultural Society* XC(11):462–75, 1965a; XC(12):504–09, 1965b; XCI(1):18–26, 1966.

———— and P., "Afghanistan 1966," *Journal of the Royal Horticultural Society* XCIII(1):20–30; XCIII(2):92–97; XCIII(3):114–24, 1968abc.

Fussman, G. "Notes sur la topographie de l'anciénne Kandahar," *Arts Asiatiques* 13:32–57, 1966.

Gabelentz, H. von der. "Uehe die Sprache der Hazâra und Aimak," *Zeitschrift der Deutschen Morgenländischen Gesellschaft* 20:326–35, 612–613, 1966.

Gafferberg, E. *Khazareisikaia (Afganista) i urta khanaikhyrga: kvoprosu ob istorii kochevogo zhilishcha,* Moscow, 1953.

Gansser, A. *Geology of the Himalayas,* New York, 1964.

Gardin, J.-C. "Poteries de Bamiyan," *Ars Orientalis* 227–45, 1957.

Gaudefroy–Demombynes, M. *Muslim Institutions,* London, 1968.

Gazetteer of Afghanistan, Part I, Badakhshan (1914); Part II, Afghan Turkistan (1907); Part III, Herat (1910); Part IV, Kabul (1910); Part V, Kandahar (1908), Calcutta.

Ghani Khan. *The Pathans,* Bombay, 1947.

Ghazanfar, M. Personal communications, 1968.

Ghirshman, R. "Fouilles de Nadi Ali, dans le Seistan Afghan," *Revue Arts Asiatiques* 13(1):10–22, 1939 (also published in *DAFA:* VIII:39–48, 1959).

———. *Iran,* Harmondsworth, Middlesex, 1954.

———. "Le problème de la chronologie des Kouchans," *Cahier d'Histoire Mondiale* III:689–722, 1957.

———. *Persian Art: 249 B.C.–A.D. 651,* New York, 1962.

Ghose, D. *England and Afghanistan: A Phase in Their Relations,* Calcutta, 1960.

Ghubar, G. *Ahmad Shah baba-yi-Afghan,* Kabul, 1943.

Ghubar, G., *Afghanistan dar Masir-i-Tarikh (Afghanistan's Path Through History),* Kabul, 1968.

Gibb, H. A. R. *Mohammedanism,* London, 1949.

——— (S. Shaw and W. Polk, eds.). *Studies on the Civilization of Islam,* Boston, 1962.

——— and H. Bowen. *Islamic Society and the West. Vol. 1: Islamic Society in the Eighteenth Century,* Pt. 1, London, 1951.

——— and J. H. Kramers (eds.). *Shorter Encyclopedia of Islam,* Leiden, 1953.

Gleig, G. *Sale's Brigade in Afghanistan,* London, 1861.

Glubb, J. *The Story of the Arab Legion,* London, 1948.

Gnoli, G., "Jewish inscriptions in Afghanistan," *East and West,* n.s. 13(4):311–312, 1962.

Goldman, M. *Soviet Foreign Aid,* New York, 1967.

Grassmuck, G., L. Adamec and F. Irwin (eds.). *Afghanistan: Some New Approaches,* Ann Arbor, 1969.

Gray, J. *At the Court of the Amir,* London, 1895.

Greenwood, Lt. *Narrative of the Late Victorious Campaign in Afghanistan Under General Pollock,* London, 1844.

Gregorian, V. "Mahmud Tarzi and the Saraj-al-Akhbar," *Middle East Journal* 21(3):345–68, 1967.

———. *The Emergence of Modern Afghanistan,* Stanford, 1969.

Grey, C., and H. Garrett. *European Adventurers of Northern India: 1785–1849,* Lahore, 1929.

Griesbach, C. Field-notes #5: to accompany a geologic sketch map of Afghanistan and north-eastern Khorissan, *Records of the Geological Survey of India,* no. 20, 93, 1887.

Griffin, L. *Ranjit Singh,* Oxford, 1890.

Griffith, G. (ed.). *Alexander the Great, the Main Problems,* Cambridge, 1966.

Groetzbach, E. "Economic Processes and their Regional Differentiation in the Hindu Kush, Afghanistan," *The Geographical Review of Afghanistan* 7(2):1–7, 1969.

———. "Kulturgeographische im Farkhar-Tal (afghanischer Hindukusch)," *Die Erde* 96(4):279–300, 1965.

——. "Berucht über eine Reise nach Nordost-Afghanistan 1965," *Die Erde* 97(2):145–48, 1966.

Grousset, R. *L'Empire des Steppes,* Paris, 1939.

——. *L'Empire Mongol,* Paris, 1941.

Grunebaum, G. von. *Muhammadan Festivals,* New York, 1951.

Guevara, C. *Reminiscences of the Cuban Revolutionary War,* New York, 1968a.

——. "Bolivia Campaign diary," *Evergreen Review* 57:32–40, 82–86, 1968b.

Guillaume, A. *The Life of Muhammed* (a trans. of Ibn Ishaq's *Sirat Rasul Allah*), Oxford, London, 1955.

Gurevich, N. *Gosudarstvennyy sektor v ekonomike Afganistana,* Moscow, 1962.

——. *Voprosy ekonomike afganistana,* Moscow, 1963.

Habberton, W. *Anglo-Russian Relations Concerning Afghanistan: 1837–1907,* Urbana, 1937.

Habib, M. *Sultan Mahmud Ghazvin,* Bombay, 1951.

Habibi, A. *The History of Afghanistan after Islam,* Kabul 1967a.

——. "Paxto literature at a glance," *Afghanistan* 20(3):45–54, 1967b; *Afghanistan* 20(4):51–64, 1968a; *Afghanistan* 21(1):53–57, 1968b.

——. "A glance at historiography and the beginning of the Historical Society of Afghanistan," *Afghanistan* 21(2):1–19, 1968c.

——. "Afghan and Afghanistan," *Afghanistan* 22(2):1–6, 1969.

Habibi, K. "A glance at literature: a box of jewels," *The Kabul Times* III(75):3, 1967.

Habibullah, Amir. *My Life: from Brigand to King,* London, n.d.

Hackin, J., "Les fouilles de la Délégation Archéologique Française à Hadda (Afghanistan)," *Arts Asiatiques* 5(2):66–67, 1928.

Hackin, R., and A. A. Kohzad. *Légendes et Coutumes Afghans,* Paris, 1953.

Hahn, H. "Die Stadt Kabul (Afghanistan) und ihr Umland" *Bonner Geographische Abhandlung* 34/35, 1964, 1965.

Haim, S. *The Larger English–Persian Dictionary,* 2 vols., 1934–6.

Haim, Sylvia G. *Arab Nationalism: An Anthology,* Berkeley, 1962.

Hamilton, A. *Afghanistan,* London, 1906.

Hanafi, M. *A Short History of Muslim Rule in Indo–Pakistan,* Dacca, 1964.

Hanna, H. *The Second Afghan War 1878–79–80. Its Causes, its Conduct, and its Consequences,* London, 1899.

Hatt, G. Review of C. Feilberg, *La Tente Noire,* in *Geografisk Tidsskrift* 47:257–61, 1945.

Haughton, J. *Char-ee-kar and Service there with the 4th Goorkha Regiment (Shah Shooja's Force) in 1841: An Episode of the First Afghan War,* London, 1879.

Havelock, H. *Narrative of the War in Affghanistan in 1838–39,* London, 1840.

Hazard, H. *Atlas of Islamic History,* Princeton, 1951.

Hedin, S. *The Silk Route,* 1938.

Heissig, W. "Der Moghol-Dichter 'Abd al-Qadir," *Zentralasiatische Studien* 3:431–38, 1969.

Henning, W. "The Aramaic inscription of Ashoka in Lampaka," *Bulletin of the School of Oriental and African Studies* 13:80–88, 1949–50.

——. "The Bactrian inscription," *Bulletin of the School of Oriental and African Studies* 23(1):47–55, 1960.

——. Appendix in Zaehner (1961), 349–59.

Hentig, W. von. *Mein Leben eine Dienstreise,* Göttingen, 1963.

Herzfeld, E. "A new Aśoka inscription from Taxila," *Epigraphia Indica* XIX:251, 1928.

————. *Kushano-Sasanian Coins,* Memoirs of the Archaeological Survey of India, #38, Calcutta, 1930.

Higgs, E. "Search for Greece of the Stone Age," *Natural History* LXXIV(9):18–25, 1965.

Hitti, P. *History of the Arabs,* 4th ed., New York, 1949.

Holdich, T. *The Indian Borderland: 1880–1900,* London, 1901.

————. *The Gates of India,* London, 1910.

Hough, W. *A Narrative of the March and Operations of the Army of the Indus in the Expedition to Affghanistan in the Years 1838–1839,* London, 1841.

Howell, E., and O. Caroe. *The Poems of Khushal Khan Khatak,* Peshawar, 1963.

Huckreide, R. "Jung–Quartär und End-Mesolithikum in der Provinz Kerman (Iran)," *Eiszeitalter und Gegenwart* 12:25–42, 1961.

Hughes, D. "Finger dematoglyphics from Nuristan, Afghanistan," *Man* 2(1):119–25, 1967.

Hughes, T. *Dictionary of Islam,* London, 1885.

Humlum, J. *La Géographie de l'Afghanistan,* Copenhagen, 1959.

Humphreys, C. *Buddhism,* 3rd ed., Harmondsworth, Middlesex, 1962.

Hutchinson, H. *The Campaign in Tirah: 1897–1898,* London, 1898.

Istoriya Tadzhikskogo Naroda, Tom. 1: *Sdrevneyshikh vremen do V.v.n.e.* (*The History of the Tadzhik People.* Vol. 1: *From Ancient Times to the Fifth Century A.D.*), Moscow, 1963.

Iwamura, S., and H. Schurmann. "Notes on the Mongolian groups in Afghanistan," *Silver Jubilee Volume of the Zibun–Kagaku–Kenkyusyo,* 480–515, Kyoto, 1954.

Al-Jadaan, K. *Caste Among the Yazidis, an ethnic group in Iraq,* Master's thesis in Rural Sociology, Pennsylvania State University, 1960.

Janata, A. "Verlobung und Hochzeit in Kabul," *Archiv für Völkerkunde* 17/18: 59–72, 1962/63a.

————. "Die Bevölkerung von Ghor. Beitrag zur Ethnographie der der Chahar Aimaq," ibid., 73–156, 1962/63b.

————. "Die landwirtschaftliche Struktur Afghanistans," *Bustan* 4(3):36–48, 1963.

————. *Elphinstone: Kingdom of Cabul: Bio-Bibliographical Notes,* Vienna, 1969.

Jarring, G. "On the distribution of Turk tribes in Afghanistan: an attempt at a preliminary classification," *Lunds Universitets Arsskritt,* N.F., Ard. 1, 35, #44, Lund, 1939.

Jeanneret, A. "Contribution à l'etude des boulangers de Kaboul (Afghanistan)," *Bull. Annuel du Musée et Institut d'Ethnographie de la Ville de Genève,* no. 7, 35–48, 1964.

Jeffery, A. (ed.). *Islam: Muhammad and His Religion,* Indianapolis, 1958.

Jettmar, K. *Art of the Steppes,* New York, 1967.

Jones, S. *An Annotated Bibliography of Nuristan (Kafiristan) and the Kalash Kafirs of Chitral,* Hist. Filos. Medd. Dan. Vid Selsk, 41, Copenhagen, 1966; Part II, 1969.

————. *The Political Organization of the Kam Kafirs,* Copenhagen, 1967.

Kabul Times Annual, 1967 (N. Rahimi, editor), *1970* (S. Khalil and S. Rahel, editors).

Kakar, M. *The Consolidation of the Central Authority in Afghanistan under Amir 'Abd Al-Rahman 1880–1896,* M. Phil. thesis, School of Oriental and African Studies, University of London, 1968.

Kapur, H. *Soviet Russia and Asia: 1917–1927,* Geneva, 1966.

Kardas, K. Personal communication, 1959.

Katrak, S. *Through Amanullah's Afghanistan*, Karachi, 1929.

Kaye, J. *History of the War in Afghanistan*, 3rd. ed., 3 vols., London, 1874.

Keddie, N. "Religion and irreligion in early Iranian nationalism," *Comparative Studies in Society and History* 4(3):265–95, 1962.

――――. "Afghani in Afghanistan," *Middle Eastern Studies* 1(4):322–49, 1965.

――――. *An Islamic Response to Imperialism: Political and Religious Writings of Sayyid Jamal ad-Din 'al-Afghani*, Berkeley, 1968.

Kedourie, E. *Afghani and 'Abduh*, London, 1966.

Kennedy, R. *Narrative of the Campaign of the Army of the Indus in Sind and Kaubool in 1838–1839*, 2 vols., London, 1840.

Kenny, L. "Al-Afghani on types of despotic government," *Journal of the American Oriental Society* 81(1):19–27, 1966.

Kessel, J. *The Horsemen*, New York, 1968.

Kessler, M. "Ivan Viktorovich Vitevich (1806–39): A Tsarist Agent in Central Asia," *Central Asian Collectanea*, #4, Washington, 1960.

Khafi, M. *Padshahan-i-Muta'khir-i-Afghanistan* (*The Recent Kings of Afghanistan*), Afghan Historical Society #40, 2 vols., Kabul, 1957.

Khalili, K. *Saltanat-i-Ghazaviyum* (*The Ghaznavid Empire*), Kabul, 1954.

Khan, F. A. "Before Mohenjo-daro: New light on the beginnings of the Indus Valley civilization from recent excavations at Kot Diji," *Illustrated London News* LIV:866–67, May 24, 1958.

Kharuzin, N. *Istorija razvitija zilishca u Kocevykh i polukorevykh Tjurkskikhi mongols khelich narodvoster*, Moscow, 1896.

Khrushchev, N. "On peaceful coexistence," *Foreign Affairs*, October, 1959.

Kieffer, C. "A propos de la circoncision à Caboul et dans le Logar," *Festschrift für Wilhelm Eilers*, 191–201, Wiesbaden, 1967.

Klass, R. *Land of the High Flags*, New York, 1964.

Klimburg, M. *Afghanistan: Das Land in historische spannungsfeld Mittelasiens*, Vienna, 1966.

Kohzad, A. A. "Cultural relations between Afghanistan and India," *Afghanistan* 1(2):12–30, 1946.

――――. "The tour of the archaeological mission of the American Museum of Natural History in Seistan," *Afghanistan* 5(1):28–32, 1950a.

――――. "Two coronations," *Afghanistan* 5(3):38–40, 1950b.

――――. *In the Highlights of Modern Afghanistan*, Kabul, n.d. (originally published in 1952).

――――. "L'Afghanistan au point de vue de la religion," *Afghanistan* 8(3):1–17. 1953a.

――――. *Lashkargah* (in Persian), Kabul, 1953b.

――――. "Indo–Afghan cultural relations," *Afghanistan* 9(1):1–10, 1954.

Kökten, I. "Die stellung von Karain Immerhalb der Türkischen vorgeschichte," *Anatolia* VII:59–86, 1963.

Kolars, J. "Locational aspects of cultural ecology: the case of the goat in non-western agriculture," *Geographical Review* 5(4):577–84, 1966.

Kukhtina, I. *Bibliografiya Afganistana*, Moscow, 1965.

Kullmann, E. See *Science*, 1965.

Kumorek, M. *A Cross Cultural Handbook for Peace Corps/Afghanistan* (mimeographed), Kabul, 1970.

Kussmaul, F. "Badaxšan und Seine Tağiken," *Tribus* 14:711–99, 1965.

Lal, B. "A picture emerges—an assessment of the Carbon-14 datings of the protohistoric cultures of the Indo–Pakistan subcontinent," *Ancient India* 18–19:208–21, 1962–63.

————. *Indian Archaeology since Independence*, New Delhi, 1964.

Lal, M. *Life of the Ameer Dost Muhammed Khan of Kabul*, 2 vols., London, 1846.

Lamberg–Karlovsky, C. "Archeology and metallurgical technology in prehistoric Afghanistan, India, and Pakistan," *American Anthropologist* 69(2):145–62, 1967.

————. "Tepe Yahya," *Iran* 7:184–86, 1969.

Lambton, A. *Key to Persian Grammar*, Cambridge, 1967.

Leech, R. "A vocabulary of the language of the Moghol Aimak," *Journal of the Royal Asiatic Society of Bengal* 7:785–87, 1838.

Legislative Record of the Twelfth Afghan Parliament (unclassified), U.S. Embassy, Kabul, 1969.

Lentz, W. "Über einigen Fragen der materiellen Kultur von Nuristan," *Zeitschrift für Ethnologie* 69(6):277–306, 1937.

Leshnik, L. "Kushano-Sassanian ceramics from Central Afghanistan: a preliminary note," *Berliner Jahrbuch für Vor-und Frühgeschichte* 7:311–34, 1967.

————. "Ghor, Firuzkoh and the Minar-i-Jam," *Central Asiatic Journal* XII(1):36–49, 1968.

Le Strange, G. *The Lands of the Eastern Caliphate*, Cambridge, 1930.

Levine, B. Review of Carratelli, et al., 1964, in *Journal of the American Oriental Society* 87(2):185–87, 1967.

Levy, R. *Persian Literature*, London, 1923.

Ligeti, L. "O mongolskikh i tjurkskikh jazikakh Afganistana," *Acta Orientalia* 4:93–119, 1955.

Lissant, Sergeant–Major. "The retreat from Kabul (a survivor's story)," *Army Quarterly* XVII:143–50, London, 1928.

Litvinski, B. Chapters V–VI (pp. 236–89) in *Istoriya Tadzhikskogo Naroda*, vol. 1, Moscow, 1963.

————. "Archaeology in Tadzikistan," *East and West*, n.s. 18(1–2):125–46, 1968.

Lobanov–Rotovsky, A. *Russia and Asia*, Ann Arbor, 1951.

Lockhart, L. *Nadir Shah: A critical study based upon contemporary sources*, London, 1938.

————. *The Fall of the Safavi Dynasty and the Afghan Occupation of Persia*, Cambridge, 1958.

Lunt, J. (ed.). *From Sepoy to Subedar: Being the Life and Adventures of Subedar Sita Ram, A Native Officer of the Bengal Army, Written and Related by Himself*, Delhi, 1970.

McChesney, R. "The economic reforms of Amir Abdur Rahman Khan," *Afghanistan* 21(3):11–34, 1968.

McGovern, W. *The Early Empires of Central Asia*, Chapel Hill, 1939.

Mackenzie, A. Personal communication, 1955.

Mackenzie, D. "A standard Pashto," *Bulletin of the School of Oriental and African Studies* 22:229–35, 1959.

————. *Poems from the Divan of Khushal Khan Khattak*, London, 1965.

Maclean, F. *A Person from England and other Travellers to Turkestan*, London, 1958.

MacMunn, G. *Afghanistan from Darius to Amanullah*, London, 1929.

Macrory, P. *Signal Catastrophe*, London, 1966 (published as *The Fierce Pawns*, Philadelphia, 1966).

Mahler, J. "The art of the Silk Route," in *East–West in Art*, Theodore Bowie (ed.), Bloomington, 1966.

Majumdar, R., H. Raychaudhuri, and K. Datta. *An Advanced History of India*, 2nd ed., London, 1961.

Malinowski, B. *Magic, Science and Religion*, New York, 1954.

Malleson, W. "The British Military Mission to Turkestan, 1918–1920," *Journal of Central Asia Studies*, 9:pt. 1, January 24, 1922.

Maranjian, G. "The Distribution of ABO Blood Groups in Afghanistan," *Am. Journ. Physical Anthrop.* 10:263, 1958.

Marshall, J. *Taxila*, 3 vols, Cambridge, 1951.

Masson, C. *Narrative of Various Journeys in Baluchistan, Afghanistan and the Punjab*, 3 vols., London, 1842. (4 vol ed., 1844).

———. The Masson Papers, Nos. 631–657, unpublished, Eur. Mss., Vol. II, Part II, India Office Library, London.

Masson, V., and V. Sarianidy. "Afghanistan in the ancient east," *Afghanistan* 22(2):7–19, 1969.

Masters, J. *Bugles and a Tiger*, New York, 1956.

Maxwell, N. *India's China War*, London, 1970.

Meyer-Oehme. See *Science*, 1965.

Michel, A. *The Kabul, Kunduz, and Helmand Valleys and the National Economy of Afghanistan*, Washington, 1959.

———. "On writing the geography of strange lands and faraway places— Afghanistan, for example," *Economic Geography* 36(4):355–68, 1960.

———. Personal communication, 1968.

Miller, J. *The Spice Trade of the Roman Empire: 29 B.C.–A.D. 641*, London, 1969.

Miner, Thomas, H., and Associates, Inc. *Developing the Herb Industry in Afghanistan*, Prepared for Ministry of Commerce, U.S.A.I.D./Afghanistan Project 306-11-990-087, Kabul, June, 1968.

Mirsky, J. (ed.). *The Great Chinese Travelers*, New York, 1964.

Mitsukuni, Y. and K. Kihei. *Western Asia at Work* (in Japanese), Kyoto, 1966.

Mizuno, S. *Haibak and Kashmir-smast, Buddhist Cave Temples in Afghanistan and Pakistan Surveyed in 1960* (in Japanese, with English summary) Kyoto, 1962.

Mizuno, S., et al. *Ancient Art in Afghanistan*, Tokyo, 1964.

Mohammad, Faiz. (full title and name, Mullah Faiz Mohammad Katib Hazara, see *Seraj-uttawarikh*)

Molesworth, G. *Afghanistan 1919*, New York, 1962.

Morgenstierne, G. *An Etymological Vocabulary of Pashto*, Oslo, 1927.

———. *Indo–Iranian Frontier Languages. I. Parachi and Ormuri*, Oslo, 1929a.

———. "The languages of the Ashkun Kafirs," *Norsk Tidsskrift for Sprogvidenskap* 2:192–289, 1929b.

———. *Report on a Linguistic Mission to North–Western India*, Oslo, 1932.

———. "Additional notes on Ashkun," *Norsk Tidsskrift for Sprogvidenskap* 7:56–115, 1934.

———. *Indo–Iranian Frontier Languages. II. Iranian Pamir Languages (Yidgha-Munji, Sanglechi-Ishkashmi, and Wakhi)*, Oslo, 1938.

———. *The Archaisms and Innovations in the Pashto Morphology*, Oslo, 1940.

———. *Indo–Iranian Frontier Languages. III. The Pashai Languages. 2. Tests and Translations*, with comparative notes on Pashai folktales by Reidar Th. Christiansen, Oslo, 1944.

———. "The language of the Prasun Kafirs," *Norsk Tidsskrift for Sprogvidenskap* 15:188–334, 1949.

――――. *Indo–Iranian Frontier Languages,* III: *The Pashai Language. 3. Vocabulary,* Oslo, 1956.

Mostamindi, M. and S. "Nouvelles fouilles à Hadda (1966–1967) par l'institut Afghan d'archaeologie," *Arts Asiatiques* xix:15–36, 1969.

Moustamindy, S. "La fouille de Hadda," *Comptes Rendus d'Académie des Inscriptions et Belles Lettres,* 119–30, 1969.

Movius, H. "The Mousterian cave of Teshik-Tash, southeastern Uzbekistan, Central Asia," *American School of Prehistoric Research,* Bull. 17:11–71, 1953a.

――――. "Paleolithic and mesolithic sites in Soviet Central Asia," *Proceedings of the American Philosophical Society* 97(4):383–421, 1953b.

―――― and S. Judson. "The Rock-shelter of La Colombière," *American School of Prehistoric Research,* Bull. #19, 1956.

Murdock, G. *Social Structure,* New York, 1949.

Mustamandi, S. "A preliminary report on the excavations of Tapa-i-Shotur in Hadda," *Afghanistan* 21(1):58–69, 1968a.

――――. "The fish porch," *Afghanistan* 21(2):68–80, 1968b.

―――― and M. "The excavation of the Afghan Archaeological Mission in Kapisa," *Afghanistan* 20(4):67–79, 1968.

Najibullah (see Ullah, Najib)

Narain, A. "The coin types of the Indo–Greek kings," *Numismatic Notes and Monographs,* #1, Bombay, 1955.

――――. *The Indo–Greeks,* Oxford, 1962.

Neamat Ullah, Khwaja. *History of the Afghans* (trans. by B. Dorn from the Persian), 2nd ed., London, 1965.

New Republic, Washington, October 30, 1961.

Nicholson, R. *The Mystics of Islam,* London, 1914.

――――. *Studies in Islamic Mysticism,* Cambridge, 1921.

――――. *The Idea of Personality in Sufism,* Cambridge, 1923.

Niedermayer, O. von. *Im Weltkrieg von Indiens Toren,* Hamburg, 1942.

Niethammer. See *Science,* 1965.

Nizami, *The Story of Layla and Majnun,* translated from the Persian into German by R. Gelpke; English version in collaboration with E. Mattin and G. Hill, London, 1965.

Norris, J. *The First Afghan War: 1838–1842,* Cambridge, 1967.

Nove, A., and J. Newth. *The Soviet Middle East,* London, 1967.

Nutting, A. *Lawrence of Arabia,* New York, 1962.

O'Dwyer, M. *India as I Knew It,* London, 1925.

O'Kearney, J. *Red Mirage,* London, 1958.

Olmstead, A. *History of the Persian Empire,* 3rd. impression, Chicago, 1960.

Paludan, K. *On the Birds of Afghanistan,* Copenhagen, 1959.

Palwal, A., History of former Kafiristan, *Afghanistan* 21(3):48–66; 21(4):61–88; 22(1):6–27; 22(2):20–43, 1968, 1969abc.

Pares, B. *Russia: Past and Present,* Mentor Books M37 15–32, New York, 1949.

Parliamentary Papers: East India (copy of the Treaty with Runjeet Singh and Shah Shujah-ool-Moolk, concluded at Lahore 26 June 1838, etc.), London, 1839.

Parliamentary Papers: East India (Cabul and Affghanistan), London, 1859.

Patai, R. "The Middle East as a culture area," *Middle East Journal* 6(1):1–22, 1952.

Pazhwak, A. *Paktunistan: The Khyber Pass as the Focus of the New State of Pakhtunistan,* London, 1953.

Pehrson, R. (compiled and analyzed from his notes by F. Barth). *The Social Organization of the Marri Baluch,* Chicago, 1966.

Pelt, J., J. Hayon, and C. Younos. "Plantes médicinales et drogues de l'Afghanistan," *Bull. Soc. Pharm. Nancy* 66:16–78, 1965.

Penzer, N. *The Harem,* London, 1936.

Penzl, H. *A Grammar of Pashto: A Descriptive Study of the Dialect of Kandahar, Afghanistan,* Washington, 1955.

———. Review of Wilber (1962) in *Journal of the American Oriental Society* 83(2):263–65, 1963.

Perkins, D., Jr. Personal communication, 1968.

Pettigrew, H. *Frontier Scouts,* Sussex, n.d.

Pfannmuller, G. *Handbuch der Islam–Litteratur,* Leipzig, 1923.

Phillips, E. *The Royal Hordes: Nomad Peoples of the Steppe,* London, 1965.

Pickthall, Mohammad Marmaduke. *The Meaning of the Glorious Koran,* New York, 1954.

Piggott, S. *Prehistoric India,* Harmondsworth, Middlesex, 1960.

Pikulin, M. *Razvitiye natzional'noy ekonomiki i kul'tury Afganistana, 1955–1960,* Tashkent, 1961.

Pipes, R. "The Muslims of Soviet Central Asia: Trends and prospects," *Middle East Journal* 9(2,3):147–62, 295–308, 1955.

Polyak, A. *Ekonomicheskiy stroy afghanistana: orcherki,* Moscow, 1964.

Pope, A. (ed.). *Survey of Persian Art,* 4 vol., New York, 1938–39.

Population and Agricultural Survey of 500 Villages, Department of Statistics, Ministry of Planning, Kabul, 1963.

Porada, E. *Ancient Iran,* London, 1965.

Poullada, L. "Some international legal aspects of Pushtunistan dispute," *Afghanistan* 21(4):10–36, 1969a.

———. "Political modernization in Afghanistan: The Amanullah Reforms," in Grassmuck, et al. (1969), 99–148, 1969b.

———. *Reform and Rebellion in Afghanistan 1919–1929: King Amanullah's Failure to Transform a Tribal Society,* in press.

Pradel, L. "Transition from Mousterian to Perigordian: Skeletal and industrial," *Current Anthropology* 7(1):33–50, 1966.

Pratap, M. "My German Mission to High Asia," *Asia* 25:382–455, 1925.

Prinsep, J. "New types of Bactrian and Indo–Scythic coins," *Journal of the Asiatic Society of Bengal* 702 ff., 1836.

Pugachenkova, G. "The architecture of Central Asia at the time of the Timurids," *Afghanistan* 22(3–4):15–27, 1969–70.

Puglisi, S. Personal communication, 1962.

———. "Preliminary report on the researches at Hazar Sum (Samangan)," *East and West,* n.s. 14(1–2):1–8, 1963.

The "Pukhtunistan" Stunt, Karachi, 1956.

Qor'an (see Pickthall, 1954).

Radiocarbon 9:360, 1967.

Rahim, M. *History of the Afghans in India: A.D. 1545–1631,* Karachi, 1961.

Ramazani, R. *The Northern Tier: Afghanistan, Iran, and Turkey,* Princeton, 1966.

Ramstedt, G. "Mogholica Beiträge zur kenntnis der mogholsprache in Afghanistan," *Journal de la Sociéte Finno-Ougrienne* 23(4):1–60, 1906.

Ranov, V. "Dva Novykh Pamiatnika Kamennogo Veka v Iozhnom Tadzhikistane," *Arkheologicheskie Raboty v Tadzhikistane* 8:130–39, Dushambe, 1962.

———. *Kamennyi Vek Tadzhikistane,* Dushambe, 1963.

BIBLIOGRAPHY

——. "Itogi Razvedok Ramiatnikov Kamennogo Veka na Vostochncm Pamire (1956–1958)," *Materialy i Issledovaniia po Arkheologii S.S.R. 124 Trudy Tadzhikskoi Arkheologicheskoi Ekspeditsii,* Vol. IV, 7–50, 1954–59, Moscow–Leningrad, 1964a.

——. *On the Relations Between the Paleolithic Cultures of Central Asia and Some Oriental Countries* (in English), Moscow, 1964b.

——. *Arkheologia na Kryshche Mira,* Dushambe, 1967.

Rapp, E. "On the Jewish inscriptions from Afghanistan," *East and West* n.s., 15(3–4):194–99, 1965.

Rapson, E. "Indian coins," *Grundriss der Indo–Arischen Pailologie und Altertumskunde,* 11 Band, 3, Heft B., Strassburg, 1897.

Rawlinson, H. *Bactria,* London, 1912.

Reardon, P. "Modernization and reform: the contemporary endeavors," in Grassmuck, et al., 149–203, 1969.

Rehatsek, E. *The Gulistan or Rose Garden of Sa'di,* New York, 1966.

Reisner, R. *Razvitie feodalizma i obrazovanie gosudarstva u Afgantsev,* Moscow, 1954.

Rhein, E., and A. Ghaussy. *Die wirtschaftliche Entwicklungen Afghanistans 1880–1965,* Köln/Opladen, 1966.

Rice, C. *The Persian Sufis,* London, 1964.

Rice, T. *Ancient Arts of Central Asia,* New York, 1965.

Rishtya, Said Qassim. *Afghanistan dar nozdah-quran (Afghanistan in the Nineteenth Century),* Kabul, 1958.

Robert, L. "De Delphes à l'Oxus, Inscriptions Grecques nouvelles de la Bactriane," *Comptes Rendus d'Académie des Inscriptions et Belle Lettres,* 416–58, 1968.

Roberts, Field-Marshal Earl. *Forty-One Years in India.* London, 1911.

Robertson, G. *Chitral,* London, 1898.

——. *The Kafirs of the Hindu Kush,* London, 1900.

Robertson, W. *Official Account of the Chitral Expedition,* London, 1898.

Robson, E. *Arrian: The History of Alexander and Indica,* 2 vols., London and Cambridge, Mass., 1961.

Rodenbough, T. *Afghanistan and the Anglo–Russian Dispute,* New York, 1885.

Roos–Keppel, G. et al. *A Manual of Pushtu,* London, 1901.

Rosenfield, J. *The Dynastic Arts of the Kushans,* Berkeley and Los Angeles 1967.

Rosenthal, E. *Political Thought in Medieval Islam,* Cambridge, 1962.

Roskoschny, H. *Afghanistan und seine Nachbarländer,* Leipzig, 1885.

Ross, F. (ed.). *Personal Narrative of General Josiah Harlan, 1823–1841,* London, 1939.

Rostovtzeff, M. *Iranians and Greeks in South Russian,* London, 1922.

——. *The Social and Economic History of the Hellenistic World,* 3 vols., Oxford, 1941.

——, et al. *The Excavations at Dura–Europos,* 4 pts., New Haven, 1943–49.

Rowland, B. *The Wall-Paintings of India, Central Asia and Ceylon,* Boston, 1938.

——. "The dating of the Sassanian paintings at Bamiyan and Dukhtari-Nushirvan," *Bulletin of the Iranian Institute* 6–7:35–42, 1946.

——. *The Evolution of the Buddha Image,* The Asia Society, New York, 1963.

——. *The Art and Architecture of India,* Harmondsworth, Middlesex, 1966a.

——. *Ancient Art in Afghanistan,* The Asia Society, New York, 1966b.

Rymalov, V. "Soviet assistance to underdeveloped countries," *International Affairs* 5-9:23-31, Moscow, 1959.

Sale, Lady Florentia. *A Journal of the Disasters in Affghanistan, 1841-2*, London, 1843.

Saunders, J. *A History of Medieval Islam*, London, 1965.

Scerrato, U. "The first two excavation campaigns at Ghazni, 1957-58 (Survey Report)," *East and West*, n.s., 10(2):23-55, 1959.

———. "Islamic glazed titles in moulded decoration from Ghazni," *East and West*, n.s., 13(4):265-72, 1962.

Scheibe, A. (ed. and contributor). *Deutsche im Hindukusch, Bericht der deutschen Hindukusch expedition 1935 der deutschen Forschungsgemeinschaft*, Berlin, 1937.

Schlumberger, D. "Les fouilles de Lashkari Bazar: recherches archéologiques de l'époque ghaznévide," *Afghanistan* 4(2):34-44, Kabul, 1949.

———. "Les fouilles de Lashkari Bazar: les résultats de la deuxième et de la troisième campagne," *Afghanistan* 5(4):46-56, 1950.

———. "Le grande mosquée de Lashkari Bazar," *Afghanistan* 7(1):1-4, 1952a.

———. "Les palais Ghaznavides de Lashkari Bazar," *Syria* 252 ff., 1952b.

———. "Surkh Kotal," *Archaeology* VI:232-37, 1953.

———. "Surkh Kotal," *Archaeology* VIII:82-87, 1955.

———. "Surkh Kotal," *Antiquity* XXXIII:81-86, 1959.

———. "Déscendents non-Méditeranéens de l'art grec," *Syria* XXXVII:131-66, 252-318, 1960.

———. "The excavations at Surkh Kotal and the problems of Hellenism in Bactria," *Proceedings of the British Academy* XLVII:77-95, 1961.

———. "Une nouvelle inscription grecque d'Açoka," *Comptes Rendus d'Académie des Inscriptions et Belles-Lettres*, 126-40, 1964.

———. "Aï Khanoum, une ville hellenistique en Afghanistan," *Comptes Rendus d'Académie des Inscriptions et Belles-Lettres*, 36-46, 1965.

———, and P. Bernard, "Aï Khanoum," *Bulletin de Correspondance Hellénique* LXXXIX(ii):590-657, 1965.

———, L. Robert, A. Dupont-Sommer, and É. Benveniste, "Une bilingue greco-araméenne d'Asoka," *Journal Asiatique* CCXLVI(1):1-48, 1958.

Schulze-Holthus. *Daybreak in Iran*, London, 1954.

Schurmann, H. *The Mongols of Afghanistan*, The Hague, 1962.

Schwarz, F. von. *Alexander des Grossen Feldzüge in Turkestan*, Munich, 1893.

Science: Quarterly journal published by the Faculty of Science, Kabul University, August, 1965; several articles on fauna of Afghanistan by E. Kullmann, D. Meyer-Oehme, et al.

Selincourt, A. de (trans.). *Arrian's Life of Alexander the Great (Anabasis)*, Penguin Classics, 1962.

Seljuki, F. *Gazaghah* (in Persian), Kabul, 1962.

Sellman, R. *An Outline Atlas of Eastern History*, London, 1954.

Seraj-uttawarikh, Kabul, ca. 1912 (also see Mohammad, Faiz).

Shah, I. A. *Afghanistan of the Afghans*, London, 1928.

Shah, Idries. *The Exploits of the Incomparable Mulla Nasrudin*, London, 1967.

Shakur, B. *A Dash Through the Heart of Afghanistan*, Peshawar, 1947.

Shepherd, D. "Iran between East and West," in *East-West in Art*, T. Bowie (ed.), Bloomington, 1966.

Shpoon, S. "Paxto folklore and the *landey*," *Afghanistan* 20(4):40-50, 1968.

———. Personal communication, *landey* collected from Pushtun nomads, 1969.

Siddiqi, A. *A Path for Pakistan*, Karachi, 1964.

717

BIBLIOGRAPHY

Siiger, H. "Shamanism among the Kalash Kafirs of Chitral," *Folk* 5:295–303, 1963.

Singh, G. *Ahmad Shah Durrani: Father of Modern Afghanistan*, New Delhi, 1959.

Singh, J. *The Persian Mystics, the Invocation of Sheikh 'Abdullah Ansari of Herat, A.D. 1005–1090*, London, 1939.

Singh, K. *Ranjit Singh, Maharajah of the Punjab: 1780–1839*, London, 1962.

Singhal, D. *India and Afghanistan: 1876–1907*, Queensland, 1963.

Sinha, S. *The Chinese Aggression*, New Delhi, 1961.

Sicar, D. "Gujarra inscription of Aśhoka," *Epigraphica Indica* 31:204–10, 1956.

Skeen, A. *Passing It On*, Aldershot, 1943.

Skrine, C. *World War in Iran*, London, 1962.

Smith, W. C. *Islam in the Modern World*, New York, 1959.

Snoy, P. *Die Kafieren: Formen der Wirtschaft und geistigen Kultur*, Phil. Diss. Mainz, 1962.

———. "Nuristan and Mungan," *Tribus* 14:101–49, 1965.

Solecki, R. "Prehistory in Shanidar Valley, Northern Iraq," in *New Roads to Yesterday*, J. Caldwell (ed.), New York, 1966.

Southern, R. *Western Views of Islam in the Middle Ages*, Cambridge, Mass., 1962.

Spain, J. *The Way of the Pathans*, London, 1962.

———. *The Pathan Borderland*, The Hague, 1963.

Spear, P. *India, Pakistan and the West*, 4th ed., London, 1967.

Stein, M. *Serindia* (Central Asia and westernmost China), 5 vol., London, 1921.

———. *Innermost Asia*, 4 vol., Oxford, 1928.

Steingass, F. *A Comprehensive Persian–English Dictionary*, London, 1930.

Stevens, I., and K. Tarzi. *Economics of Agricultural Production in the Helmand Valley*, Denver, 1965.

Stewart, T. "The skull of Shanidar II," *Smithsonian Report for 1961*, 521–33, 1962.

Survey of Progress: 1968–1969, Department of Statistics, Ministry of Planning, Kabul, 1969.

Swinson, A. *North–West Frontier Peoples and Events: 1839–1947*, London, 1967.

Sykes, P. *The Rt. Honourable Sir Mortimer Durand*, London, 1926.

———. *History of Afghanistan*, 2 vols., London, 1940.

Symonds, R. *The Making of Pakistan*, London, 1954.

Taddei, M. "Tapa Sardar: First Preliminary Report," *East and West*, n.s., 18(1–2):109–24, 1968.

Tarn, W. *The Greeks in Bactria and India*, 2nd. ed., Cambridge, 1951.

———. *Alexander the Great*, Boston, 1962.

Technical Research Reports: 3. Aspects of the Nationality Problems in the U.S.S.R., 1952; 4. Social Change in the U.S.S.R., 1952; Air University Manual, Air Force Base, Alabama, 1952.

Temple, R. "Rough notes on the distribution of the Afghan tribes about Kandahar," *Journal of the Asiatic Society of Bengal* XLVIII, 1(3):181–85, 1879.

The Third Five Year Economic and Social Plan of Afghanistan, Ministry of Planning, Kabul, April, 1967.

Tendulkar, D. *Abdul Ghaffar Khan: Faith is a Battle*, Bombay, 1967.

The Times Atlas of the World: Vol. II. South–West Asia and Russia, London, 1959.

Times of India, Delhi, October 1, 1961.

Tolstov, S. Personal communication, 1962.

Tolstova, S., et al. *Narody Srednej Azii Kazakhstana*, 2 vols., Moscow, 1962–63.

Toynbee, A. *Between Oxus and Jumna*, London, 1961.

Tosi, M. "Excavations at Shahr-i-Sakhta," *East and West*, n.s., 18(1–2):9–66, 1968.

———. Preliminary report on the second campaign. Ibid., n.s. 19(3–4):283–386, 1969.

Trousdale, W. "The minaret of Jam: a Ghōrid monument in Afghanistan," *Archaeology* 18(2):102–08, 1965.

Tucci, G. "Oriental Notes IV: The syncretistic image of Mazar-i-Sharif," *East and West*, n.s., 18(3–4):293–94, 1968.

Tudor Engineering Company, Inc. *Report on Development of Heimand Valley, Afghanistan*, Washington, 1956.

Ullah, Najib. "Afghanistan in historical perspective," in *Current Problems in Afghanistan*, T. C. Young, Sr. (ed.), Princeton, 1961.

———. *Islamic Literature*, New York, 1963.

Vavilov, N., and D. Bukinich. *Zemiedel'cheskiy Afghanistan* (with long English summary), Supplement 33 to the *Bulletin of Applied Botany, of Genetics, and Plant Breeding*, Leningrad, 1929.

Vigne, G. *A Personal Narrative of a Visit to Ghuzni, Kabul, and Afghanistan and of a Residence at the Court of Dost Mohamed*, London, 1840.

Vladimirtsov, B. *The Life of Chingis Khan*, London, 1930.

———. *Le Régime Social des Mongols: Le Féodalisme nomade*, Paris, 1948.

Volk, O. "Landwirtschaftliche Probleme des Landes," *Mitteilungen des Institut für Auslandsbeziehungen* 4(9–10):233–36, 1954.

Vorobevya, M. Chapter VII in *Istoriya Tadzhikskogo Naroda* (1963).

Walker, E., et al. *Mammals of the World*, vols. I, II, Baltimore, 1968.

Warriner, D. *Land Reform and Economic Development*, Cairo, 1955.

Weiers, M. "Vorlaufiger Bericht über sprachwissenschaftliche Aufnamen bei den Moghol von Afghanistan 1969," *Zentralasiatische Studien* 3:417:30, 1969.

Wheeler, G. *The Peoples of Soviet Central Asia*, London, 1966.

Wheeler, R. E. M. "Romano–Buddhist art: an old problem restated," *Antiquity* XXIII:4–19, 1949.

———. *5000 Years of Pakistan*, London, 1950.

———. *Rome Beyond the Imperial Frontiers*, Harmondsworth, Middlesex, 1955.

———. *Early India and Pakistan*, New York, 1959.

———. *Charsada*, Oxford, 1962.

———. *The Indus Civilization*, 3rd. ed., Cambridge, 1968a.

———. *Flames Over Persepolis*, London, 1968b.

———, A. Ghosh, and Krishna Deva. "Arikamedu: An Indo–Roman Trading station on the east coast of India," *Ancient India* 2:7–124, 1946.

Wickens, G. "Religion," in Arberry, 1953.

Wilber, Donald N. "The structure of Islam in Afghanistan," *Middle East Journal* 6(1):41–48, 1952.

———. *Iran*, Princeton, 1958a.

———. "Prospects for federation in the Northern Tier," *Middle East Journal* 12(4):385–94, 1958b.

———. *Afghanistan*, 2nd ed., New Haven, 1962.

———. "Constitution of Afghanistan," *Middle East Journal* 19(2):215–29, 1965.

———. "Language and Society: The Case of Iran," *Behavior Science Notes* 2(1):22–30, 1967.

Wilcox, W. *Pakistan: The Consolidation of a Nation*, New York, 1963.

Wilson, A. *North From Kabul*, London, 1961.

Wilson, D. "Afghan Literature: A Perspective," in Grassmuck et al., 1969.

Wilson, E. *Sacred Books of the East*, New York, 1945.

Winsinck, A. *La Pensée de Ghazzali*, Paris, 1940.

Wirtz, D., et al. "Zur Geologie von Nordost-und Zentral-Afghanistan," *Bull. of the Afghan Geological and Mineral Survey*, No. 1, Kabul, 1964.

Wise, D., and T. Ross. *The Invisible Government*, New York, 1965.

Wittfogel, K. *Oriental Despotism*, New Haven, 1957.

Wolfe, N. *Herat*, Kabul, 1966.

Wolski, K. "Les Karez: Installations d'irrigation de terrains semi-désertiques, Afghanistan–Béloutchistan," *Folia Orientalia* 6:179–204, 1965.

Wood, J. *A Journey to the Source of the River Oxus*, 2nd. ed., London, 1872.

Woodcock, G. *The Greeks in India*, London, 1966.

Woodd–Walker, R., H. Smith, and V. Clarke. "The blood groups of the Timuri and related tribes in Afghanistan," *American Journal of Physical Anthropology* 27(2):195–204, 1967.

Wright, G. *The Writing of Arabic Numerals*, London, 1952.

Wulff, H. *The Traditional Crafts of Persia, their Development, Technology and Influence on Eastern and Western Civilizations*, Cambridge, Mass., 1966.

Yapp, M. "Disturbances in eastern Afghanistan, 1839–42," *Bulletin of the School of Oriental and African Studies* 25(3):499–523, 1962.

———. "Disturbances in western Afghanistan, 1839–41," ibid., 26(2):288–313, 1963.

———. "The revolution of 1841–2 in Afghanistan," 27(2):333–381, ibid., 1964.

Yate, A. *England and Russia Face to Face in Asia: Travels with the Afghan Boundary Commission*, London, 1887.

Young, R. "The south wall of Balkh, Bactria," *American Journal of Archaeology* 59(4):267–76, 1955.

Young, T. C., Sr. (ed.). *Current Problems in Afghanistan*, Princeton, 1961.

Younghusband, F. *The Relief of Chitral*, London, 1895.

Yusufi, M. *Tatbiq-i-sanavat (Comparative Years)*, Kabul, 1963.

Zaehner, R. *The Dawn and Twilight of Zoroastrianism*, London, 1961.

Zeigler, J. "Geological study of Shamshir Ghar cave, southern Afghanistan, and report of terraces along Panjshir Valley near Kabul," *Journal of Geology* 66(1):16–27, 1958.

INDEX

Abbasid Dynasty, 312–15
Abbas Mirza Qajar, 364
Abduh, Mohammad, 82
Abdul Aziz, 324, 326
Abdul Ghaffar Khan, Khan, 90, 487, 612
Abdul Ghani Khan, 334
Abdul Hai Aziz, 495
Abdul Hamid, Sultan, 434, 438
Abdul Hussain Aziz, 478
Abdul Karim, 449
Abdul Khaliq, 475, 477
Abdullah, see Mullah-i-Lang
Abdullah Jan, 404, 407–408
Abdullah Khan, the Georgian, 322
Abdullah Khan Saddozai, 323–24
Abdul Majid, 441
Abdul Quddus Khan, see Quddus Khan, Sardar Abdul
Abdul Rashid, Mullah, 449
Abdul Wahid, 435
Abdur Rahman Khan, Amir, 204, 403, 415–30, 458, 474, 485, 556; administration, 461–62; forced migrations, 166, 174, 187, 577; "internal imperialism," xix, 343, 437; Pamir boundary, 5; Russian exile and return, 410, 413; tomb, 222; treatment of religious leaders, 108, 464; Yaghistan defined, xvii
abi wheat, 43
Ab-i-Istada, Lake (32°32' N, 67°57' E), 39, 52
Ab-i-Pamir (37°00' N, 72°40' E), 35
Ab-i-Panja (37°01' N, 72°41' E), 6, 8, 35
Ab-i-Qaisar (36°13' N, 64°42' E), 36
Ab-i-Safed (36°44' N, 65°38' E), 36
Ab-i-Safed Tangi, gorge (34°58' N, 61°36' E), 36
Ab-i-Wakhan (37°00' N, 72°40' E), 35

Abu Bakr, 101, 110
Abubakr, Roqia, 186, 653
Abdul-Faiz Hazrat, of Badakhshan, 81
Abu Shukur, of Balkh, 76
Achaemenid Dynasty, 98, 266, 272ff, 286
Achakzai, Abdullah Khan, 384
Adam aw Durkhani, 123
Adam Kheleh Afridei, of Khushal Khan Khattak, 83–86
Adina Beg Khan, 337–38
Aegean, 263
Afghan Academy, 93n
Afghan-American Trading Cooperation of New York, 479
Afghan Construction Unit (A.C.U.), 506
Afghan hound (tazi), 50, 117–18, 215, 217
Afghan Institute of Archaeology, 306
Afrhan Mellat, 601, 611ff, 653
Afghan Olympic Federation, 218, 221
Afghan Qarakul Institute, 624
Afghan Student News, 613
Afsharid Dynasty, 340. See also Nadir Shah Afshari
Afzal Khan, Amir Mohammad, 181, 403, 417
Agha Khan III, 102
Agha Khan IV, 102
Agra, 337
Agathocles, 285
Agency for International Development (A.I.D.), 516, 537, 549ff, 599, 634. See also Hilmand Valley Authority
Ahmad, H., 83
Ahmad Khan, 332
Ahmad Shah Durrani (Abdali), Amir, 322, 612; elected paramount chief, 333–34; empire builder, xix, 334–40; poetry, 81; service with Nadir Shah

* Most geographic coordinates in the index are courtesy of Professor Ludwig W. Adamec and taken from his forthcoming Historical and Political Gazetteer of Afghanistan: Vol. 1, Badakhshan; Vol. 2, Farah; Vol. 3, Herat; Vol. 4, Kandahar; Vol. 5, Northern Provinces; Vol. 6, Kabul. The six volumes are being published by Akademische Druk-u. Verlagsanstalt, Graz, Austria.

Afshari, 332; taxes, 536.
Ahmad Shah Bahadur, 335–37
Ahmad Shah, Musahiban, 437
Ahmadiya of Egypt, 103
Ahrari, Khadija, 653
Aibak (36°14′ N, 68°03′ E), 256, 311
Ai Khanoum (37°09′ N, 69°25′ E), 286, 289, 291–92
Aimaq, 57, 161, 170, 172, 174, 180, 238–39, 244, 569
airports, 637
'A'isha, 101
'Ajuzak, 98–99
Ak Sakat Pass (34°25′ N, 66°30′ E; 10,200 ft, 3,100 mt), 10
Akbar Khan, Wazir Mohammad, 403; after british retreat, 396; British retreat, 391; death, 401; defeats Shahpur, 398; defeats Sikhs, 369; at Jalalabad, 394–95; in Kabul, First Anglo-Afghan War, 384, 386–88; treatment of British prisoners, 397
Akbar, Moghul Emperor, 321
Akbar-Namah of Hamid of Kashmir, 82
Akhramovich, R., 512
Akram Khan, 397, 404
Aktur Khan, 397
al-Afghani, Jamal ad-Din, 82, 438
Ala Mohammad Khan, 365
Alamgir II, Moghul Emperor, 337
Alaska, 363
al-Biruni, 314
Alexander the Great, *xviii,* 5, 10, 223, 274ff, 276n, 281n, 295
Alexander II, King, 283
Alexandria-ad-Caucasum, 278, 282
Alexandria-Eschate, Alexandria at the end of the world, 280
Alexandria in Arachosia, 278
Alexandria-of-the-Arians, 276
Alexandria-on-the-Oxus, 292
Alexandria-on-the Tarnak, 278
al-Ghazzali, 79n
Ali Ahmad Khan, 443
'Ali ibn-abi-Talib, son-in-law of Prophet Mohammad, 101–102, 105–106, 115
Ali Masjid, 381, 408
al-Jilani, Abdul Qadir, 103
Alikhanoff, Colonel, 422
al-Mansur, 312

al-Mushasibi, 79n
Alingar River (34°39′ N, 70°14′ E), 14, 42
al-Qadir, 314
Alishang River (34°38′ N, 70°14′ E), 14, 42
Alishar Huyuk, 291
Allah Yar Khan, Abdali, 329–30
Alpamysh, 119
Alptigin, 313
al-Utbi, 314
Aman-i-Afghan, 440
Amanullah Khan Logari, 384, 396
Amanullah, King, 120, 429–54, 457, 475; constitution, 463ff; flight, 474; modernization, 458, 531; people believe still alive, 554; seizes power, 435, 437
Ambala, India, 381; Conference (1869), 404
American Friends of the Middle East, 613
American Museum of Natural History, 255
American Universities Field Staff, *xxiii,* 695–96
Amir Khan, 335
Ampthil, Lord, 432
Amritsar, India, 337–39
Amu Darya, classical Oxus River, 1, 8, 25, 33–36; Alexander the Great, 279, 281; Amir of Bokhara, 339, 343; fish, 52; Hepthalites, 302; nomads, 174; Saka, 298; Sher Ali, 409; Soviet Union, 520; Subuktigin, 314–15; *thalweg,* 424; Tsarist Russia, 404–405, 423; Turkestan Plains, 43; Turks, 303; valleys, 243
Anahita, Dr., 591, 615, 653
Anatolia, 263, 285
Anbia Khan Taimani, 418
Andarab River, Valley (35°47′ N, 68°49′ E), 21, 35, 279
Andarabi, 70, 183.
Anderson, Mary, 391
Andkhui (36°56′ N, 65°08′ E), 21, 406
Angar, 495
Angar, Faiz Mohammad, 495
Angel, J. L., 260
Anglo-Afghan Pact (1905), 492, 485
Anglo-Afghan Treaty (1921), 486, 492

Anglo-Russian Agreement (1872), 405; (1873), 405, 423–24; Boundary Commission (1895–96), 5; competition, 380, 408ff, 422ff, 430; Convention (1907), 433

animal fights, 217

Anis, 440n, 564, 601, 613

Anjuman Pass (35°57′ N, 70°24′ E), 42; River, (36°01′ N, 70°40′ E), 35

Anoshah, *see* Dorah An

Anquetil, Brigadier T., 384

Ansari, Dr. Mir Najmuddin, 566

Ansari, of Kabul, 79, 81, 103, 318–19

Ansari, Pir of Herat, Khwaja Abdullah, 79, 103, 105, 318–19

Antioch, 291, 301

Aornos, 279

Apama, 281

Apollo, 296

Apollodotus, 285

Aq Chah (36°56′ N, 66°11′ E), 35, 66

Aq Kupruk (36°05′ N, 66°51′ E), 256, 301, 590; I (Snake Cave), 262–63, 269, 271; II (Horse Cave), 261, 269, 271; III (open-air site), 261; IV, 269, 271

Aq Ribat, Aq Robat Pass (34°57′ N, 67°39′ E; 10, 255 ft, 3,125 mt), 21

"Arab," 503–504

Arabian Sea, 283, 285, 302, 334

Arabic, 66, 74

Arabic numerals, 103

'Arabi, Ibn, 79n

Arachosia, Qandahar, 274, 278, 299

Aral Sea, U.S.S.R., 33, 299

Aramaic, 286–87

Arandu, *see* Arnawai

Ardashir Í, 301

Arghandab Dam, 484

Arghandab River, Valley (31°27′ N, 64°23′ E), 33, 37, 39, 43, 214–15, 278, 484

Arghastan River (31°23′ N, 64°45′ E), 39

Aria, 274

Ariana Afghan Airlines, 98, 532, 547, 552, 563, 637

Ariaspians, 278

Arikamedu, 300

Aristotle, 291

Armenians, 327

Army of the Indus, 373, 377–78

Arnawai, Pakistan (35°19′ N, 71°35′ E), 42

Arpatch, 363

Arrian, 278

Artaxerxes, King, 276. *See also* Bessus

Asadabad, *see* Chiga Serai

Asadullah, Saddozai, 325

Asghar, Professor Mohammad, 571

Ashab al-Kahf, Sura, *Qor'an,* 116–118

Ashoka, Rock and Pillar Edicts, 285–88, 296

Ashraf, 325–29

Ashukan and Arafan, Shrine, 105

Ashuni, 72

Asia Foundation, 613, 642

Aslanduz, 364

Asmar, 419

Aspasii, Bajauri, 283

Assaceni, Swati, 283

Associated Students of Afghanistan (A.S.A.), 613

Asterabad, 336

Ata Mohammad Khan, 407

atan, see dance

Atatürk, Mustafa Kemal, 435, 451–52

Atta, 79n

Attock (33°53′ N, 72°15′ E), 33, 335, 425

Auckland, Lord, 369, 373–74, 376, 379–83, 399–400

"Aurignacian" of Kara Kamar, 261

Aurangzeb, Moghul, 321, 338, 361

Australoid, 57

Avar Mongolian Empire, 302

Avesta, 272

Ayub Khan, Mohammad, 405, 410, 413, 418

Ayub Khan, Mohammad, ex-President of Pakistan, 490, 510, 541, 554

Azad, Maulana Abdul Kalam, 489

Azam Khan, Amir, 403

Aziz Khan, Mohammad, 449

Babur, Moghul Emperor, 10, 226, 319

Baba Darwesh, 256; Black Ware, 264. *See also* Chenar-i-Baba Darwesh

Babrak Karmal, 591–92, 615ff

Babylon, 278, 282–83

Bacha Saqqao, *see* Habibullah Ghazi

Bactra, 279, 289, 301, 309. *See also* Balkh

Bactria, 285, 296, 298, 302

Bactrian art, 292, 295

Bactrian camel, 6, 48

"Bactrian" language, 292

Bactriana, 274, 282

Badakhsban (35°26′ N to 38°29′ N, 69°53′ E to 74°52′ E), 5, 8; Abdur Rahman Khan, 418–19; Ahmad Shah Durrani, 336; archaeology, 256, 260; Bactrian camel, 48; birds, 52; boundary with Russia, 405; Dost Mohammad Khan, 401; flora, 243; horses, 47; hunting, 215; independent khanate, 343; Moghol, 74; Moghuls, 321; nomads, 12; semi-sedentary farmers, 164; *sherbashi,* 213; Silk Route, 306; villages, 148

bad-i-sad-o-bist roz, 28

Baghdad, 103, 313, 329

Bagh-i-Bala, 204, 500

Bagh-i-Umumi, 341

Baghlan (36°13′ N, 68°46′ E), 161, 638

Baha, Dr. Sayed Abdul Qadir, 600

Bahram Shah, 315

Baisunghur, 318

Bajaur, 425, 539

Bajaur Scouts, 539

Bajauri, Aspasii, 283

Bajgah, 503

Bakhtar Airlines, 637

Bala Murghab (35°35′ N, 63°20′ E), 37

Balkh (36°46′ N, 66°53′ E), "Arabs," 66; Amir of Bokhara, 369; archaeology, 303–307, 309; Bactriana, 274; Dost Mohammad, 402; literature, 77; Moghuls, 321; "Mother of Towns," 289; resettlement program, 502; Sher Ali, 409; Silk Route, 301, 513; Timur Shah, 340; Tsarist Russia, 406; Uzbak, 336; Zoroaster, 272

Balkh Ab (35°30′ N, 66°30′ E), 35

Balkh Textile Company, 642

Balkhash, Lake, U.S.S.R., 301

Baltic, 301

Baluch, 57; Constitutional *Loya Jirgah,* 569; dwellings, 170, 180; folktale, 127–28; language, 72; nomads, villagers, 164, 174; physical type, 65; raiders, 48; Safavids, 322–23

Baluchi, 57, 72

Baluchistan, 28; archaeology, 269; Baluch-Brahui confederation, 376; Dost Mohammad, 369; First Anglo-Afghan War, 378; Great Britain, 380; independence, 343; "Pushtunistan," 491; tribal territory, 431

Baluch-Brahui Confederation, 376

Bamiyan Pass, Valley (34°50′ N, 67°50′ E 8,900 ft, 2,710 mt), 12, 21; Ahmad Shah Durrani, 336; Alexander the Great, 279, 282; archaeology, 303–306; First Anglo-Afghan War, 379, 381, 385, 397; Genghis Khan, 316; nomads, 174; Silk Route, 301–306

Bamiyan Rud (34°54′ N, 68°02′ E), 35

Band-i-Amir (35°12′ N, 66°30′ E), 36

Band-i-Turkestan Mountains (35°30′ N, 64°00′ E), 21, 37

Bandar Abbas, 283

Bangladesh, 523, 538, 660

Bank-i-Melli, 472, 479, 590

Barak, Baharak (36°55′ N, 70°50′ E), 35

Barakatullah, Maulana, 435, 444

Barakzai Sardars, *see* Qandahari Sardars, Peshawari Sardars

Barakzai, Abdul Aziz, 453

Baraq, 116

Barbari, Berberi, 57

Bari, Nuristan, 142, 244

Bariq Shafie, 601

Baroghil Pass (36°65′ N, 73°21′ E; 12, 460 ft, 3,800 mt), 6

Barqi Rajan (33°56′ N, 68°55′ E), 36

barter agreement (1936), 478

Barton, W., 426

Barsaentes, 276, 278

Bashgal River (35°20′ N, 71°32′ E), 14, 42

Bashgali, 72

basmachi, 448, 460, 472, 562, 514, 528

Basra, Iraq, 363

bast, 536

bazaars, 153–54, 245

Beaconsfield, Earl (Disraeli), 406

Beas River, 283

Bedford lorries, 645
Begram (34°58′ N, 69°17′ E), 19, 279, 303, 306–307, 309, 508, 523. *See also* Kapisa
Begrami, 390, 641
Behzad, 317
Beidel, 80
Benares, 300
Benawa, A., 91–92
Bengal, 321, 339
Bentinck, Governor-General, *see* Cavendish-Bentinck, Lord
Berberi, Barbari, 57
Bernard, P., 291, 291–92
Berowski, 370
Bessus, 274, 276, 279–81
Besudi, Malang Jan, 112
Bibi Halima, 430
Bidar-bakht, 338
Biddulph, C., 83, 88, 408
Bijan Sultan, 324
birth and childhood, 192ff
Bisitun, Iran, 260
bi-tarafi, 511, 524, 557, 593, 661
black magic, 106
Boghra, 482, 484
Bokhara, Abdur Rahman Khan, 403; Akbar Khan, 385; Alexander the Great, 281; Amirs of, 343, 369, 423; Dost Mohammad Khan, 378, 381; Londoni, 471; Mangit Dynasty, 341; Nadir Shah Afshari, 332; Samanids, 313; Soviet Union, 448; Stoddart, 374; Tsarist Russia, 380, 404
Bolsheviks, 443
Bombaci, A., 315
Bootkhak, 391
Bordj-i-Abdullah, 278, 306
borqʻa, chadri, 246–47, 460, 531
Bost (31°35′ N, 64°21′ E), 39, 227, 313, 503. *See also* Lashkar Gah.
Bosworth, C., 319
Bowen, J., 86–87, 91
Brahmanism, 296
Brahui, 57, 65, 72, 174, 335
Brahui-Baluch Confederation, 338
Bravin, K., *see* Bravin, Michael
Bravin, Michael, 443
British Broadcasting Corporation (B.B.C.), 613
British Retreat (1842), 388ff

Broadfoot, Major George, 384, 394
Bronze Age, 255, 266, 268–69
Browne, General Sir Sam, 408
Brydon, Dr. W., 285n, 388ff
Buddhism, Buddhist art, xviii, 297, 305ff
Budeabad, 397
bukhari, 138
Bulganin, Premier, 508
Bulola (34°53′ N, 68°05′ E), 12, 21, 35
Bullard, Sir Reader, 481
Burma, 296
Burnes, Sir Alexander, 370–72, 375–78, 383, 385, 388, 398, 423
Burrows, Brigadier G.R.S., 410
Butler, Lady, 389
Buwayhid Dynasty, 314
buzkashi, 194, 213, 218–21
Byroade, Ambassador Henry, 506, 549, 564
Byzantine Empire, 302

cabinets, post-World War II, 690–94
calendars, 674–76; of the Hazarajat, 674n
California, 363
Caliph, *Khalifa,* 101
Cambodia, 296
Campbell, William, 417
Canja, 364
C.A.R.E., 551, 642
Caroe, O., 79, 427
Carmania, 278
carp fishery, 641
Carpathian Mountains, 244
Carratelli, G., 287
Casal, J.-M., 255, 266
Caspian fauna, 51
Caspian Sea, 276, 299, 316, 364
Caucasoid, 57, 65
Caucasus, 364
Cavagnari, Sir Louis, 408–409
Cavendish-Bentinck, Lord William, 377
Central Asia, Ahmad Shah Durrani, 334; Alexander the Great, 276, 279–80; archaeology, 307; *buzkashi,* 218; clothing, 241; food, 224; Genghis Khan, 315; "goat cult," 264; Indo-Greeks, 285; Kushans, 289ff; Moghuls, 319; Silk Route, 301;

Timurids, 317, 319; Tsarist Russian-British confrontations in, 370, 372, 380, 404; Turks, 303; Zaman Shah, 365; Zoroaster, 272

Central Asian khanates, 404; nomads, 296

Central Forces Kabul, 498

Central Intelligence Agency (C.I.A.), 559, 612–14

Central Treaty Organization (C.E.N.T.O.), 510

Ceylon, 296

chadri, borq'a, 246–47, 460, 531

Chagai Hills, Pakistan (29°30′ N, 64°-15′ E), 31

Chagatai Turkic, 92

Chagatai Turks, 319

Chahar Darra (36°42 N, 68°47 E), 8, 35

Chahardeh-i-Ghorband (35°29′ N, 68°52′ E), 105, 172

Chahbahar, Iran, 507, 551

Chakansur (31°10′ N, 62°04′ E), 40

Chakari (34°20′ N, 69°26′ E), 48

Chalcolithic, 255

chaman, Kabul, 122, 222

Chaman, Pakistan (30°55′ N, 66°27′ E), 31, 425

Chamberlain, Sir Neville, 408

Charikar (35°01′ N, 69°11′ E), 12, 19; Abdur Rahman Khan, 410; archaeology, 306; First Anglo-Afghan War, 384, 386, 388, 398; Habibullah Ghazi, 121; house types, 138; Islamic shrine, 105

Charkhi family, 474–75

Charkhi, Ghulam Ghilani, 474–75

Charkhi, Ghulam Haider Khan, 418, 458, 474

Charkhi, Ghulam Nabi, 453, 458, 474ff

Charkhi, Ghulam Sadiq, 453, 474ff, 476

Charsada, 300

Chashmah-yi-'Ayub, 115

Chehel Zina, 286–87

Chenar-i-Baba Darwesh (36°48′ N, 70°00′ E), 256. *See also* Baba Darwesh.

Chicago Tribune, 454

Chiga Serai, now Asadabad (34°52′ N, 71°09′ E), 42

child socialization, 192ff

Ch'in Dynasty China, 298

China, 224, 296, 298, 300–301, 317, 424; People's Republic of, 8, 52n, 433n, 510, 530, 587–88, 594–95, 597, 622, 641

China Sea, 316

Chinese Sinkiang, 109

Chinggis Khan, *see* Genghis Khan

Chitral, Pakistan (36°15′ N, 72°15′ E), 6, 42, 57, 240, 244, 425, 431

chol, 21

Chorienes, Rock of, 282

Chowdhury, K., 268

Christianity, 95, 113; compared to Judaism and Islam, 99–101

Civil and Military Gazette, 534

"Clactonian," 256

Clearchos, 291

Clerk, G. R., 387

Clive, Sir Robert, 338, 363

Coca-Cola, 235, 648

Colombe, Philippe, 325

Colvin, John, 375

Congress of Berlin (1878), 407

Conolly, Captain A., 374n

Conolly, Lt. John, 386

Constitutional Advisory Commission, 566

constitutional development to 1931, 461ff

Constitution of 1964, 68, 159, 183, 565ff, 572n, 573ff, 663

Coon, C. S., 100, 180, 256

cosmetics, 246

cotton development, 642

Cotton, Sir Willoughby, 379, 383

cotton gins, 635

court system, 582. *See also* Supreme Court.

"covered wagon complex," 528

Craig, Sir J., 365

Craigie, Captain J. H., 395

Crimean War, 401

Curzon, Lord, 370, 430–31, 446

cyrillic, 74

Cyropolis, 280

Cyrus the Great, 274

Czechoslovakia, 243, 520, 523, 529, 635, 642

Da Afghanistan Bank, 479

Dahla (31°50′ N, 65°50′ E), 28

Dakka (34°13′ N, 71°03′ E) 42, 442
Daldal, 115
dams, 640
dance, 238
Danda, 309
Dane Mission, 432
Dane, Sir Lewis, 432
Danish Expedition to Central Asia, Third, 54n
Daoud Khan, Prime Minister Mohammad, 70, 474–75, 478, 499ff, 559; administration, 588, 657; cabinet, 595; Constitutional *Loya Jirgah,* 577; "Pushtunistan," 538ff, 650; removal of the veil, 530ff; resigns, 554; seizes power, 485; treatment of religious leaders, 108, 536–38
Daqiqi of Balkh, 76–77
Darband-i-Kilrekhta (35°18′ N, 63°27′ E), 36
Dardenelles, 363
Dardic, 72
Dargai, 431
Dari, *xxiii,* 66, 70, 599, 612
Darius the Great, 274
Darius III, 276, 276, 278, 283
Darra Chakhmakh, 260
Darra Dadil, 260
Darra-i-Kur, 256, 260, 264. *See also* Baba Darwesh.
Darra, Kohat, Pakistan, 214
Darra-yi-Nur (34°45′ N, 70°36′ E), 14
Darra-yi-Suf (35°55′ N, 67°20′ E), 174, 180–81, 191, 529
Darra Yusuf (33°43′ N, 68°15′ E), 36
Dar'ul Aman, 452
Dar'ul Mo'alamein, 622
Darunta (34°28′ N, 70°22′ E), 42, 641
Darweshan, 505, 635
Darya-yi-Panj (37°06′ N, 68°20′ E), 289
Darya-yi-Siah, Ab-i-Siah (34°21′ N, 67°01′ E), 36
Dasht-i-Kash (31°50′ N, 62°30′ E), 31
Dasht-i-Margo (30°45′ N, 63°10′ E), 28, 31
Dasht-i-Narmung (31°55′ N, 61°30′ E), 39
Dasht-i-Rewat (35°29′ N, 69°49′ E), 42
Daulatabad (36°59′ N, 66°50′ E), 36, 66

Dawi, Abdul Hadi, 440, 653
death and inheritance, 206ff
Debets, G., 65
Deghani, 72
Délégation Archéologique Française en Afghanistan (DAFA), 288–89; 307, 309, 446, 689
Delhi, 321, 328, 331, 334–37
Delhi Sultans, 319n
Demetrius, 285
Denmark, 362
Dennie, Brigadier William, 384
Dera Dun, 445
Dera Ghazi Khan, 335
Dera Ismail Khan, 335
Derbent, 281
diet and food, 224ff
Dilaram (32°11′ N, 63°25′ E), 40, 324
Diodotus, 285
Dionysius, 283, 307
Dir State, 425
Diskalkar, D., 381n
Disraeli, Benjamin, *see* Beaconsfield
Diugamel, A. O., 374
divorce, 205
Doab, Doab-i-Mekh-i-Zarin (35°16′ N, 67°58′ E), 21, 35
Dobandi Pass, 459
Dobbs Mission, 445
Dobbs, Sir Henry, 445–46
domesticated animals, 47–50
domesticated plants, 669
Dorah An Pass, Anoshah, Kach in Pakistan (36°07′ N, 71°15′ E; 22,418 ft, 6,800 mt), 6
Dori River (31°29′ N, 65°12′ E), 39
Doshi (35°37′ N, 68°41′ E), 21, 35
Dost Mohammad Khan, Amir, 430; early power struggles, 368–72; First Anglo-Afghan War, 375–76, 378, 381–82, 384, 387, 394, 396; poetry, 81; returns from exile in India, 399; second reign, 401ff, 406
Drangiana, 274, 278
Drapsaka, 279
Dravidian, 57, 66, 72
dress and ornaments, 238
Dufferin, Lord, 423
Dukhtar-i-Nushirwan, 311
Dunsterforce, 443
Dupree, L., 255–56
Dupree Reports, 695–96

Dura Europos, 289, 291
Durand Agreement (1893), 492
Durand Line of 1893 ; Abdur Rahman Khan, 425–28; Amanullah, 444–45; 1955 border closure, 538–39; 1961–63 border closures, 169, 538ff; foreign reactions to closures, 553ff; Frontier Scouts, 442; Habibullah, 438; literature, 90; 1959 Mangal revolt, 534–35; Partition, 488–89; "Pushtunistan," 492; Saqqaoist War, 458; 1919 Treaty of Rawalpindi, 485–86
Duran, Lt. Henry, 379
Durand Mission, 426
Durand, Sir Mortimer, 426
Durga, 311
Durrani Dynasty, 334ff, 342, 379
Durrani-Ghilzai rivalry, 419
Dvoryankov, N., 72
Dzungarian Gates, Kazakhstan S.S.R. ca. 48°00′ N, 85°00′ E), *viii*, 298, 301

East Africa, 272
East and West, 315
East India Committee Report, First Anglo-Afghan War, 400
East India Company, 361, 377, 383, 388, 400
Eastern World, 553
Ecbatana, ancient Hamadan, Iran, 279, 301
Economic Commission for Asia and the Far East (E.C.A.F.E.), 642
"economic Korea," *xx*, 514ff, 519
Economist, 618
economy, 623, 661
education, 516, 597ff, 640. *See also* Kabul University.
Edwardes, Herbert, 402
Egypt, 301, 307, 450
Eisenhower Doctrine, 511
Eisenhower, President Dwight D., 549
Elbruz Mountains, Iran, 2, 28
elections, *see* parliamentary elections
Elgin, Lord, 430
Ellenborough, Lord, 393, 397–99
Elphinstone, Major General William, 383, 388, 392, 395, 397
Elphinstone, Mountstuart, 363, 365, 387

Engert, Cornelius, H. van, 478
Engineering Team (U.S.E.T.), 598n
Enver Pasha, 434, 448
Ephthalites, *see* Hephthalites
Erigyiues, 279
Etehad-i-Melli, 648
Etemadi, Prime Minister Nur Ahmad, 649, 653, 692
Etemadi, Tooralay, 596, 599
Eucratides, 285
Europe, 227
Euthydemus, 285
Export-Import Bank, 484, 507, 513, 637
exports, 624

Fairservis, Jr., W., 255, 268
Faiz Hotel, 237
Faiz Mohammad Khan, Major, 408
Faizabad (37°06′ N, 70°34′ E), 282
Faizullah Khan, 341
Fakir of Ipi, Hajji Mirza Ali Khan, 480, 487, 491–92
Faoghan, *see* Qala Shahar
Farah (31°48′ N to 33°52′ N, 60°37′ E to 64°43′ E), 5, 26, 49, 323–24, 329–30, 350, 403
Farah Rud (31°27′ N, 61°25′ E), 39
Faranj, 278
Farhad aw Shirin, 123
Farhadi, Dr. R., 66
Farhad, Ghulam Mohammad, 591, 612
Farhang, Mir Mohammad Siddiq, 186, 495, 531, 566, 591, 616, 652
farmers, sedentary and semi-sedentary defined, 164
Farsiwan, Parsiwan, Parsiban, 57, 70, 240, 503–504
Fateh-i-Kabul, see Shah Wali Khan, Field Marshal
Fateh Khan aw Rabia, 123
Fateh Khan Barakzai, 365, 368
Fath Ali Khan Qajar, 328, 363, 368
Fath Jang, Saddozai, 395, 398
Fatima, 109
fauna, 51–54, 670–71
Fazl Akbar, *see* Pacha Gul
Feda Mohammad Fedayi, 614
Ferdinand, K., 74, 170
Ferghana, 268, 301, 319
Ferozepore, 373, 378, 398

Ferrier, J., 74
Finland, 450
Firdausi, 75, 314
Firozkoh Mountains (35°30' N, 63°30' E), 21
First Anglo-Afghan War, 82, 369ff, 409
First Punjab Regiment, 540
fish, 51–52
Five Year Plans, First, 509, 557, 626; Second, 626; Third, 634, 644ff; Fourth, 635
folklore, music, 112ff
folk music, 677–88
folksongs, 90n
Fondukistan, 303, 307
food and diet, 224ff
foreign assistance, 630–34, 641, 644ff, 661
foreign relations, 661. See also *bi-tarafi*.
foreign subjects, 469
Forty-Fourth Foot, 393
Forward Policy, 404, 406, 408, 425, 430
Foucher, A., 289, 292, 307
Fourth Gurkha Regiment, 386
France, 361, 363, 446, 638, 640
Frazer-Tytler, Sir W., 369–70, 474
French mercenaries of Mahrattas, 338
Frontier Congress, 487
Frontier Corps or Scouts, 442, 490, 539
Frontier Inquiry Committee (1922), 487
Frye, R. N., *xxiv*

Gabelentz, von der, 74
gambling, 213
game birds, 52–53
Gandamak (34°18' N, 70°02' E), 331, 393, 409, 425–26
Gandhara, 274, 292, 296, 299, 305
Gandharan art, 292, 296
Ganges River, 285
Gardez (33°37' N, 69°07' E), 311, 459
Gardin, J.-C., 309
Garm Ab (32°14' N, 65°01' E), 39
gastro-intestinal diseases, 238
"Gates of Somnath," 397, 399
Gaud-i-Zirreh, salt swamp (30°05' N, 61°35' E), 28, 37
Gaugamela, Battle of, 274, 276

Gawhar Shad, 318
Gazargah, 318
Gedrosia, 278
Genghis Khan, 8, 10, 161, 316, 319
George III, King, 363
George V, King, 435, 446
Georgia, 363
Georgians, 322–23, 331
Germany, pre-World War I and World War I, 213, 433–35, 439, 445, 449–52, 473–76, 478–82
Germany, East, 523; West, 42, 236–37, 439, 596–99, 612, 622, 641–42, 644
Geser, 119
Ghaffar Khan, Khan Abdul, *see* Abdul Ghaffar Khan, Khan
Ghani Khan, 90
Ghar-i-Mordeh Gusfand, 260
Ghausuddin Khan, General, 422
Ghazan, 317
ghazi, 395
Ghazi College, 447
Ghazi Stadium, Kabul, 222
Ghazipur, 300
Ghazi-ud-Din, Wazir, 337
Ghaznavid Dynasty, *xviii,* 313, 361, 397
Ghazni (33°33' N, 68°26' E), 21, 155; Ahmad Shah Durrani, 334; Alexander the Great, 278; Amanullah, 453; culture climax, 77; dam, 223; Dost mohammad, 369; First Anglo-Afghan War, 378ff; "Gates of Somnath," 397; Ghaznavids, 313ff; house types, 138; independent, 343; "National Party," 410; Sir John Keane's victory, 378; surrender of Lt. Col. Palmer, 395; Waziri horses, 47
Ghazni Rud (32°35' N, 67°58' E), 39
Ghirshman, R., 255, 266, 278, 307
Ghiyasuddin Ghuri, Ghori, 318
Ghor, 74, 313–14
Ghorband River, Valley (35°02' N, 69°17' E), 10, 12, 14, 282, 306–307
Ghori cement plant, 638
Ghubar, Mir Ghulam Mohammad, 495, 497, 566, 616n
Ghulam Rasul, 435
Ghundeh-Zarabah, 622
Ghurid Dynasty, 314–15
Gibb, Sir H., 100

Gilgit, Pakistan (35°30′ N, 74°30′ E), 8

Giorgi XI, 322–23

Girishk (31°48′ N, 64°34′ E), 37, 343, 403, 418, 484

Gladstone, 413

Glubb Pasha, 480–81

"Goat Cult," 215

"Goat Cult" Neolithic, 264–65

Gobi, 298

Golden Horde, 119

Goldsmid Award (1872), 406, 432

Goldsmid Boundary Commission (1872), 432

Goldsmid, Sir Frederic, 432

Gorchakov, Prince, 404

Gordon, General Charles "Chinese," 413

Government of India Act (1935), 487

Graeco-Bactrians, 292

Graeco-Buddhist, 295–96

Gran, Engineer Mohammad Azim, 654

Grant, Sir Hamilton, 443

Great Britain, Abdur Rahman, 318, 404–407, 417; aid and trade, 236, 478, 624, 635, 643, 650–51; Amanullah, 442ff; Baluch, relations with, 48; boundary commissions, 423–28, 432; Dost mohammad, 369, 401–402; First Anglo-Afghan War, 369ff; Forward Policy, 404; Habibullah, 430ff; Nadir Shah, 461ff, 475; Panjdeh incident, 422–23; Peace Corps, 644; Second Anglo-Afghan War, 408ff; Shah Shuja, 368; Sher Ali, 405ff; Third Anglo-Afghan War, 442–43; World War II, 480ff

Great Wall of China, 298

Guevara, Che, 385n

Gujar, Gujur, Guji, gypsies, 57, 180, 337

Gulbahar (35°09′ N, 69°17′ E), 42, 121

Guldara stupa, 311

Gulnabad, Iran, 325

Gulran, 423

Gupta Dynasty, 110, 296, 302, 305

Guriz, 430

Gurziwan, 260

gypsies, 57, 180, 337

Habib, Said, 186

Habibi, K., 78

Habibiya College, 447

Habibullah, Amir, 223, 430ff, 485; assassination, 435–441, 456; modernization, 438ff; treatment of religious leaders, 462, 464; villagers believe still alive, 555; World War I, 434–35

Habibullah Ghazi, Bacha Saqqao, 120–24, 441, 452–54, 458ff, 534

Habibullah, Mangal, 534

Hackin, R., 306

Hadda, 289, 303, 306

Haider, Ghulam, 401, 403

Haider Khan, Ghulam, 378

Hajigak iron, 647

Hajji Mirza Ali Khan, *see* Fakir of Ipi

Hajji Turangzai, 435, 487

"Hajji Wilhelm," 434

Hamadan, Iran, 279, 312, 328

Hamid of Kashmir, 82

Hamidullah, Professor, 566

Hamun-i-Sabari (31°30′ N, 61°20′ E), 39, 52

Hamun-i-Hilmand (31°00′ N, 61°15′ E), 28, 37, 52

Han Dynasty China, 298, 306

Hanzala of Badghis, 75

Harappa, 266

Hari Rud (37°24′ N, 60°38′ E), 10, 26, 33, 36, 43, 51, 170, 423; Irrigation Project, 642

Hari Singh, 369

Harlan, Dr. Josiah, 378–79

Harut Rud (31°35′ N, 61°18′ E), 39

Hashim, Mir Mohammad, 186

Hashim Khan, Prime Minister Mohammad, 449, 458–59, 466, 476–77, 481, 494, 498

Hassanabad, 66

Haughton, Lt., 386

Havelock, Captain Henry, 394

Hayatullah Khan, 335, 441

Hazara, 57; Abdur Rahman, 419; Ahmad Shah Durrani, 336; clothing, 239, 244; Constitutional *Loya Jirgah*, 569; discrimination against, 161; dwellings, 172; hair style, 238–39; Hilmand Valley Project, 503; religion, 102; rural-urban migrants, 227; villages, 159, 180

Hazara, Besud, 161

Hazara, Jaghori, 161

Hazaragi, 70

Hazarajat (33°45′ N, 66°00′ E), 14, 37, 39–40, 42, 47, 74, 102, 114n, 255, 343, 418

Hazar Sum, 256, 261

Hazrat Sahib of Shor Bazaar, 109, 453, 460

Heissig, W., 74

Heliocles, 285

Hellenism, 283, 289, 291, 296, 307

Henning, W. B., 292

Hentig, Lt. Werner Otto von, 434, 480

Hephthalites, Ephthalites, "White Huns," 301–303, 307

Heracles, Hercules, 291, 307

Herat (32°20′ N, 62°12′ E), 1, 5, 26, 28, 39, 155; Abdali-Ghilzai rivalry, 329–32, 365, 368; Abdur Rahman, 418; Ahmad Shah Durrani, 332, 335–36; aid and trade, 451, 508, 642; Alexander the Great, 276, 279; Amanullah, 451, 454; Dost Mohammad, 401–402; 1964 elections, 587, 590; First Anglo-Afghan War, 380; Habibullah Ghazi, 461; independent, 344, 401; literature, 79; Moghol, 74; Mohammad Ayub Khan Durrani, 405, 413, 418; Nadir Shah Afshari, 329ff; Persians occupy and evacuate, 418; Qajar seige of, 370–75, 377; Safavids, 322ff; Sher Ali, 406; Timur Shah Durrani, 340; Timurids, 317–19; Tsarist Russia threatens, 421–24; windmills, 140, 142

Herawi, Khwaja Abdullah Ansari, *see* Ansari, Khwaja Abdullah

Hermaeus, 285, 299

Hermes, 291

Heywad, 553, 601

Hijrat Movement, 447

Hilmand, Helmand, Hirman* River, Valley (31°12′ N, 61°34′ E), 2, 5, 10, 19, 26, 28, 31, 33, 37–40, 43; Alexander the Great, 278, 283; development, 482–85, 496ff, 629ff, 640; dispute with Iran, 432, 661; fauna, 51–52; Goldsmid Award, 432; hunting birds, 214; Śakas, 298; Sayyad hunter-fishermen, 51

Hilmand Valley Authority, 482ff, 497, 499ff, 550

Hilmand-Arghandab Valley Authority (H.A.V.A.), 634–35, 641

Himalayas (28°00′ N, 84°00′ E), 1, 6, 10, 51

Hindu Kush Mountains (35°00′ N, 71°00′ E), 1–3, 5–6, 43; archaeology, 256, 263; clothing, 238, 243–44; diet, 235; fauna, 51–52; fish, 51; house types, 138, 174; Indo-Greeks, 285; languages, 72; Second Anglo-Afghan War, 409

Hindu Shahi Dynasty, 110, 303, 312–13

Hindus, Hindi, 66, 110, 206, 227, 243, 303, 464

Hitti, P., 316

Hitum, 299

Holdich, T., 426

Holland, 362

Holmes, Sherlock, 411n

homosexuality, 198

Horse Cave (Aq Kupruk II), 261

Hotaki, Abdul Latif, 613

house types, 133ff

Howell, E., 89

Hughes, T., 100

Huingnu, Hsiung Nu, 298

Hulagu, 317

Humayun, Moghul Emperor, 286, 319

Humi, 299

Hulum, J., 3

Humphrys, Sir Frances, 444

Hungary, 523

hunting, 214–15

Hunza, Pakistan (36°30′ N, 75°30′ E), 6

Husain Baiqara, *see* Sultan Husain Baiqara

Husain Sultan, Ghilzai, 327, 329–30

Hutaosa, Queen, 272, 274

Havishka, 292, 300

Hyrcania, 274

Hystaspes, King, 274

Ibn Sina, Avicenna, 621

Ibrahim Beg, 460

Ibrahim II, Lodi Sultan, 319

ijtihad, 579

Ilek, Ilaq, Khan Turks, 313

* Medieval name, now in popular usage.

Il-Khanid Dynasty, 317
Illustrated London News, The, 388
"Illustrious Garrison," 389, 394, 398
Imam Sahib, 35, 508. *See also Qizil* Qala; Sher Khan Bandar.
Imami Shi'a, 102
Inayatullah, King, 441, 453, 456
India, 388; Ahmad Shah Durrani, 334ff; Alexander the Great, 276, 282–83; archaeology, 262, 307; cattle, 49; fauna, 51; food, 224, 227; Ghaznavids, 314ff; Gupta, 296; Indo-Greeks, 285; Kushans, 299–302; Mauryans, 285ff; Moghuls, 319ff, 362; "Pushtunistan" support, 491; Partition, 491; Silk Route, 300; trade, 242–43, 547, 552, 626; War for Independence, 402
Indian Ocean, 301–302, 363
Indian Mutiny (1857–58), *see* War for Indian Independence
Indiana University, 596
Indus, Army of the, 373, 377–78
Indus River, Valley, *xviii,* 40, 266, 287, 299, 302, 335, 370
industrial development, 647–48
Information and Culture, Ministry of, 601, 614, 617
inheritance, 209
Inland Exploration Company of New York, 479
insects, 53–54
Intercontinental Hotel, 237
International Airport, Kabul, 523; Qandahar, 516
International Cooperation Administration (I.C.A.), 505, 516
International Harvester, 645
International Monetary Fund, 563
international organizations, membership in, 642
Interim Government, 565, 595, 686–87
investment law, 648
"inward-looking society" defined, 248ff
Iran, 26, 588; Ahmad Shah Durrani, 335–36; Alexander the Great, 276, 279, 283; archaeology, 262, 268; dispute over Hilmand water, 661; food, 224, 227; intermediates 1961–63 border closure, 565; nomads, 179; Qajars, 363–64; religion, 101; Saf-

avids, 319ff; Silk Route, 300; trade, 236, 507, 551; Turks, 315; World War II, 433n, 480–81
Iranian Plateau, 266
Iraq, 262
iron deposits, Hajigak, 647
irrigation projects, 642
Isfahan, Iran, 322ff
'Ishaq Khan, Mohammad, 418
'Ishaq Osman, 653
Ishkabad Canal System (36°53′ N, 66°14′ E), 36
Ishkamishi, 102
Ishkashim (36°42′ N, 71°34′ E), 6, 8
Iskander, *see* Alexander the Great
Iskander, Saddozai, 341
'Iskarzar (36°01′ N, 70°41′ E), 35
Islah, 459, 476, 601
Islam, in Afghanistan, 95ff, 579–80; compared with Christianity and Judaism, 99–100; in rural Afghanistan. 104ff; shrines, 104ff; in Soviet Central Asia, 103
Islamia College, 487
Islam Qala (34°40′ N, 61°04′ E), 36, 329
Islamic Literature, 83
Islamic rituals, 95ff
Isma'iliya Shi'a, 102
'Ismatullah Allah, 410
Issik-Kul, Lake, now Lake Balkhash, 298
Istalif, 245, 398
Istiqlal Lycée, 447, 642
Istituto Italiano per il Medio ed Estremo Oriente (Is.M.E.O.), 315
Italy, 213, 445–46, 478–79
Ithna 'Ashariya Shi'a, Imami, 101–102
Iwamura, S., 74

Jalalabad (34°26′ N, 70°28′ E), 2, 42, 155, 161, 223, Alexander the Great, 282; British retreat, 389ff; development, 511, 522, 529; fauna, 51; First Anglo-Afghan War, 379ff; food, 227, 229, 231; "Illustrious Garrison," 394–95; independent, 343; Muslim shrine, 105, 125, 495; Nadir Shah Afshari, 331; Ningrahar Valley Project, 640; nomads, 12; religious leaders, 460; Śaka, 299; Second

Anglo-Afghan War, 408–409; Silk Route, 301
Jalaogir (36°25′ N, 68°55′ E), 36
Jamal Khan, Hajji, 332–33
Jam'iyat ul-'ulama (1931), 108
Jam (ca. 34°30′ N, 64°30′ E), 315
Jami, 75, 317
Jamrud, 369, 431
Jangalak, 508
Japan, 163, 242–43, 297, 450, 478ff
Jarxartes River, 280
Jat, 180
Jat, India, 337
Jaubert, M., 363
Jehangir, Moghul Emperor, 321
jeshn, 218, 451, 530, 532, 543
Jewett, A. C., 439
Jews, 66, 95, 111, 464
Jhelum, Battle of, 283
Jilga River (33°15′ N, 68°20′ E), 39
Joint Boundary Commission (1886), 423–24
Judaism, 95; compared with Christianity and Islam, 99–100
Jugdulluk, Jagdalak, Jugdalak (34°27′ N, 69°45′ E), 395, 396
Jullundur Doab, 337
Jabal us-Seraj (35°07′ N, 69°14′ E), 42, 439
Jahan Khan, General, 337

Kabul (34°31′ N, 69°12′ E), 3, 12, 14, 43, 49, 159; Abdur Rahman, 418ff; Ahmad Shah Durrani, 334; Amir of Bokhara, 448; archaeology, 305, 309; 'askari bazaar, 222; bazaars, 155, 245, 549; British occupation, resistance to, 386ff, 410; central government, 163; clothing, 243; development, 507–509, 513, 520, 526ff, 638; Dost Mohammad, 402; Durranis, 365; 1965 elections, 587–90; 1969 elections, 651ff; First Anglo-Afghan War, 369–73, 376, 378ff, 394ff; food, 227, 335ff; games, 213; Hindu Shahi, 303; hunting, 214; International Club, 528; Kushans, 300; migrant labor, 161; Moghuls, 319, 322; pedestrian problems, 223; Śaka, 299; Saqqaoist War, 452ff; Second Anglo-Afghan War, 408–10; Sher Ali, 403ff; student demonstrations, 619ff, 664–65; Third Anglo-Afghan War, 442ff; Timur Shah Durrani, 343; villages near, 138, 140; wedding customs, 203–204
Kabul China Factory, 532
Kabul Hotel, 204
Kabul Museum, 256
Kabul Power and Electric, 641
Kabul-Qandahar Field Force, 411
Kabul River (33°55′ N, 72°14′ E), 10, 12, 14, 19, 33, 40, 42, 282, 331, 395
Kabul Rotary Club, 643
Kabul Times, The, 601
Kabul University, 82, 247, 496, 550, 563, 581ff, 621ff, 638, 641ff; Constitution, 599, 651; faculties, 598; Senate, 600
Kaccha, modern Kutch, 299
Kach, *see* Dorah An
Kadanai River (31°02′ N, 66°09′ E), 39
Kafir, Kafiri, 72, 208, 222, 236, 283
Kafiristan, 12, 343, 418–19. *See also* Nuristan.
Kahi of Kabul, 81
Kai Khusrau, 323
Kajakai (37°16′ N, 65°03′ E), 28, 37; Dam, 484, 505, 635
Kajao River (34°05′ N, 68°32′ E), 42
Kai Rud (32°55′ N, 65°30′ E), 37
Kakar, Mohammad Hasan, 426
Kakrak, 305
Kalat-i-Ghilzai (33°29′ N, 60°53′ E), 39, 343, 376ff, 395, 397, 403
Kalat State, 57, 338, 376, 491
Kali, 269
Kalinga, 286, 288
Kamard River, village (35°20′ N, 67°30′ E), 35
Kamdeshi, 72
Kami, 72
Kamran, Prince, 368ff
Kanishka, 292, 299–300
Kantiwa (35°13′ N, 70°50′ E), 14
Kao Rud, Kulam Darra (35°06′ N, 70°18′ E), 14, 36
Kapisa, 300. *See also* Begram.
Karakorum (34°00′ N, 78°00′ E), 1, 6

Kara Kamar, 256, 261–62
Kara Kalpak, 512
Karawal Khana River, town (35°43′ N, 63°14′ E), 37
Kardas, Dr. Korkut, 148
karez, see qanat
Karez-i-Atta, 418
Karnal, India, 331
Karrack, Iran, *see* Kharg
Kart Dynasty, 317
Kashan River (35°55′ N, 62°52′ E), 37
Kashgar, 300–301
Kashmir, 231, 300–301, 334ff, 365ff, 380
Kashmir War (1965), 510
Kassandros, 283
Kataghan, *see* Qataghan
Katawaz (32°00′ N, 69°00′ E), 47, 155
Kati, 72
Kaufmann, General, 401ff
Kaye, J., 370, 375
Kayeum, Dr. Abdul, 506, 654
Kayyum Khan, Nawwab Sahibzada Abdul, 445
Kazakh, 243, 512
Kazakhstan S.S.R., 168, 363
Kazim Bey, 434
Keane, General Sir John, 378–79
Keddie, N., 82
Kedourie, E., 82
Kelift, 279
Kennedy, President John F., 541
Kenny, L., 83
Kerman, Iran, 272, 283, 324ff
Khaireah, Queen, 453
Khair Khaneh, 305, 309
khakbad, 28
Khalifa, Caliph, 101
Khalifate, 447n
Khalifate Party, 447
Khalili, Khalilullah, 590
Khanabad (36°41′ N, 69°07′ E), 35, 336
Khanabad River (36°52′ N, 68°37′ E), 35
Khan Mohammad Khan, General, 537, 654
Khan of Jandol, 539
Khan of Kalat, 335
Khan of Khar, 539
Khan Sahib, Dr. 487

Kharg, Iran, 373
Khash Rud (31°11′ N, 62°05′ E), 26, 33, 40
khassadars, 492
Khater, Ghulam Nabi, 610
Khawak Pass, *see* Kotal-i-Khawak
Khawat Rud (34°05′ N, 68°45′ E), 42
Khalq, 601ff, 611
Khist Tepe (36°57′ N, 68°05′ E), 25
Khiva, 332, 380, 408
Khoja, 110
Khoja Saleh, 405, 423
Khost, 72, 449, 459, 479, 537
Khotan, 300–301
Khrushchev, N., 508, 514–15
Khuda-yi-Khidmatgaran, "Red Shirts," 487–89
Khulm, Tashkurghan (36°42′ N, 67°41′ E), 25, 35, 279, 381, 401
Khurasan, Iran (34°00′ N, 56°00′ E), 26, 70, 77, 313, 330ff, 335–36, 340
Khushalabad, 68
Khushal Khan Khattak, 83ff, 127, 321
Khushk Rud (31°49′ N, 61°16′ E), 39
Khusrau II, 307
Khurd Kabul (34°23′ N, 69°23′ E), 91
Khwarazm Shahs, 315
Khyber Agency, 486
Khyber Pass, Pakistan (34°07′ N, 71°10′ E), 42, 331, 381, 395, 408–409, 431, 442
Khyber Restaurant, 237, 500
Kiang, 298
Kidara, 302
Kieffer, C., 72
Kilik Darwan Pass, Kashmir, *see* Wakhjir Darwan
Kineas, 291
kinship patterns, 181ff
Kirghiz, 5–6, 47; boundary in northeast, 424; Constitutional *Loya Jirgah,* 569; dress, 238ff; Khiva disaster, 380; language, 72; *Manas,* 120; yak, 49; yurts, 172
Kishm (36°55′ N, 69°84′ E), 8
kite fighting, 212
Koblandy, 119
Koh Daman (34°17′ N, 67°35′ E), 12, 208
Kohat, Pakistan, 214
Kohendil Khan, 369, 401

Koh-i-Baba (34°30′ N, 67°30′ E), 1, 10, 12, 37

Koh-i-Changar (35°37′ N, 67°58′ E), 21

Koh-i-Duzdan, "Mountain of Thieves," 122

Koh-i-Foladi, *see* Shah Foladi

Koh-i-Khwaja Mohammad (36°22′ N, 70°17′ E), 8

Koh-i-Mor, 283

Koh-i-Mori, 307

Koh-i-Nur diamond, 331–32, 365, 368

Kohistan (35°05′ N, 69°35′ E), 12, 14, 118, 138, 309, 382, 386, 452, 460

Kohistani, 57

Kojend, 280

Kokand, 408, 421

Kokcha River (37°10′ N, 69°24′ E), 8, 33, 35, 289

Köppen-Trewartha system, 3

Korea, 296

Koruto, 299

Kotal-i-Anjuman (35°57′ N, 70°24′ E; 13,860 ft, 4,350 mt), 8

Kotal-i-Khawak (35°40′ N, 69°47′ E), 138, 278, 461

Kotal-i-Shibar, *see* Shibar Pass, 279

Kot-i-Ashro, Maidanshan (34°27′ N, 68°47′ E), 159

Kufa, Iraq, 115

Kujula Kadphises, Kadphises I, 299

Kulam Darra, Kao Rud (35°09′ N, 70°14′ E), 14

Kullmann, E., 51

Kumrak (33°12′ N, 63°43′ E), 39

Kunar River, Valley (34°34′ N to 36°03′ N, 70°26′ E to 71°20′ E), 2, 14, 33, 42, 282–83, 418, 641

Kunduz (36°45′ N, 68°30′ E), 8, 35, 135; administration, 159; Ahmad Shah Durrani, 336; Alexander the Great, 279; "Arabs," 66; archaeology, 311; development, 472ff, 502, 634, 637–38; Dost Mohammad, 401; 1965 elections, 587; food, 227; migrations, 188; water buffalo, 49

Kunduz Cotton Company, 473–74, 494, 638

Kunduz River (37°00′ N, 68°16′ E), 21, 33, 35

Kunlum, Kashmir (36°00′ N, 84°00′ E), 6

Kuprukian, Upper Palaeolithic, 261–62

Kurds, 340

Kurram, Pakistan (33°49′ N, 70°18′ E), 14, 403, 408–409, 486, 534–35

Kushan, 256, 289ff, 299–302, 309, 312–14

Kushano-Buddhist periods, 256

Kushano-Sasanian, 301–302, 305, 309

Kushk-i-Nakhud (31°30′ N, 64°58′ E), 39

Kushk River (36°03′ N, 62°47′ E), 357

Labor Corps, 640, 645

Ladakh, 542

Laghman (34°34′ N to 35°23′ N, 70°26′ E to 71°20′ E), 8; Abdur Rahman, 418; Alexander the Great, 282; archaeology, 311; 1965 elections, 589–90; folktale, 130–31; food, 227; nomads, 12

Laghman River, 33, 42

Lahnda, 66

Lahore, 314, 331, 335ff, 365, 368, 418

lalmi wheat, 43

Lal, Mohan, 383, 386

Landai Sin (35°20′ N, 71°32′ E), 14

landay, 90

Land Inventory Project, 647

Landsdowne, Lord, 425

land tenure, 148–53

lapis lazuli, 245, 318

Lashkar Gah (31°28′ N, 64°20′ E), 503, 506, 635. *See also* Bost.

Lashkari Bazaar, 314. *See also* Qala Bist.

Lataband Pass (34°30′ N, 69°34′ E), 42

Latvia, 450

Lawrence, Captain George, 387

Lawrence, Col. T. E., *xxiv*, 458n

Lawrence, Henry, later Lord Lawrence, 368n, 387, 404–405, 413

Lawrence, Sir John, 401–402

League of Nations, 477

LeBerre, M., 309

Leech, R., 74

Leila and Majnun, 123

Le Matin, 448

Leshnich, L., 315

Liaquat Ali Khan, Prime Minister of Pakistan, 493

"Liberal Parliament" (1949–52), 494ff, 616

Liberia, 450

Ligeti, L., 74

Lissant, Sgt.-Major, 389n

literacy, 654

literature, 74ff; modern, 92–94

Lockhart, L., 323, 325–27

Lodi Sultans, 319

Logar River, Valley (34°33′ N, 69°17′ E), 33, 42, 48, 138

Londoni, Abdul Aziz, 471ff

Lora I River (31°33′ N, 66°33′ E), 39

Lora II River (29°09′ N, 64°55′ E), 39

Loralai, Pakistan, 425

Lower House of Parliament, *see Wolesi Jirgah*

Loya Jirgah, 421, 469; 1924, 462; 1930, 460, 463; 1941, 482; 1949, 492; 1955, 539; 1964, 566ff

Lufthansa, 478

Ludhiana, India, 365, 368

Luqman Khan, 335

Lumsden, Major H. B., 402

Lumsden, Sir Peter, 422

Lyismachos, 283

Lytton, Lord, 406–407, 413

Mackenzie, A., 74

Mackenzie, Captain Colin, 384, 387

Mackenzie, D., 74, 84–89

Mackeson, Captain Frederick, 387

Macgregor, Captain, 386

Macnaghten, Sir William, 375–76, 379–84, 386–88, 398

MacNeill, John, 375

Majlis-i-Shura-yi-Melli, 467

Majrooh, Sayyid Shamsuddin, 566

Maharashtra, 338

Mahayana Buddhism, *xviii,* 296, 305

Mahipar (34°39′ N, 69°42′ E), 42

Mahisasura, 311

Mahrattas, 337–38

Mahmud, Sultan Mir, Ghilzai, 324ff

Mahmud, Yamini ad-Dawlah, of Ghazni, 77, 314–15, 397

Mahmudi, Dr. Abdur Rahman, 497, 616

Mahmudi, Dr. Hadi, 616

Mahmudi, Dr. Rahim, 616

Maidanshahr, Kot-i-Ashro, 159

Maidan, 138. *See also* Wardak-Maidan.

Maimana (35°55′ N, 64°47′ E), 21, 161; Abdur Rahman, 419; Ahmad Shah Durrani, 336; "Arabs," 66; independent khanate, 410; nomads, 174

Maimana River (36°32′ N, 64°54′ E), 36

Maiwand, Battle of (1880), 410–11, 418

Maiwandwal, Prime Minister Mohammad Hashim, 593, 595–96, 611, 613ff, 649, 652; cabinet, 691

Majlis-i-A'yan, 467

Makran, Pakistan and Iran, 283, 314, 491

Malakand, 486, 539–40

Malalai, 411

malaria, 148

maldar, 245

Malik, General Abdul, 507

Malik Mohammad, 328

Maliki Sunni, 103

Malleson Force, 443

Malman River (32°52′ N, 63°16′ E), 39

Malsowski, Colonel, 513

mana, 245

Manas, 120

Manchuria, 302

Mangal revolt (1959), 556

Mangit Dynasty, 340

manna, 31

Mansoor Qadir, 542

Manupur, 335

Marcanda, Samarkand, 280

Marco Polo, 8

Marco Polo sheep (*ovis polii*), 6, 51, 215

Mardum, 601, 610

Margiana, Merv, 274

Mariq, A., 74, 315

Marja (34°20′ N, 61°59′ E), 504

Marri Baluch, 492

marriage, 188ff, 197ff

Maruchak (35°48′ N, 63°09′ E), 37, 423

Masawat, 501, 611, 615

Masjid-i-Jami-Kherqa Mobarak, 536

Mashhad, Iran (36°18′ N, 59°36′ E), 2, 328–29, 332, 335, 339–40
Mashriqi, Mehrdel Khan, 81–82
mashruta, 437
Massaga, Battle of, 283
Masson, C., 383
Mastung, 338
Masud III, 315
Masum, Amir of Bokhara, 341
Mathura, modern Muttra, India, 299–300
Matun (33°22′ N, 69°57′ E), 459, 479
Mauryan Dynasty, 110, 285, 292, 296
Mawlawiya Sufi Order of Rumi, 80, 103
Mayar, Mohammad Ismail, 571
Mayo, Lord, 404, 406
Mazanderan, Iran, 332
Mazar-i-Sharif (36°42′ N, 67°06′ E), 155; Abdur Rahman, 403; Achaemenids, 274; archaeology, 311; development, 523, 630–34; dost Mohammad, 401; 1965 elections, 587; *nawruz* festivals, 105–106, 218; nomads, 174; Sher Ali, 409
McGovern, W., 299–300
McMahon, Colonel A. H., 432
Mecca, 206, 208, 323
Media, 272
Medical Assistance Program, 642
M.E.D.I.C.O., 506, 551
medicinal plants, 672–73
Mémoires de la Délégation Archéologique Française en Afghanistan (DAFA), 689
Menander, 285
Merchant, Livingston T., 550
Merchant Mission, 550
Merovingians, 307
Merv, classical Margiana; Achaemenid, 274; Alexander the Great, 282; Silk Route, 301; Tsarist Russian encroachments and annexation, 408, 421–22, 444
"Mervousness," 421
Meshrano Jirgah, 467–68, 587, 589, 608, 649, 652–53
"Mesolithic," 261–62
Mesozoic, 10, 14, 26
Metcalfe, Sir Charles, 377, 399
Mexi-Pak wheat, 629

Michel, A., 3, 37, 503
Michni Pass, 409
Middle East, 268, 303
migrations, forced, 187–88, 191
Miletopolis, 291
Minto, Lord, 432–33
Minto-Morley Reforms, 432
mirab, watermaster, 501-502
Mirabad Canal system (36°28′ N, 64°54′ E), 36
Mir Alam, General, 335
Mir Bacha Khan, 410
Mir Hajji, 396
Mir Mahmud Ghilzai, *see* Mahmud, Sultan Mir, Ghilzai
Mir Mannu, 335–36
Mir Moman Khan, 337
Mir Samander, 322
Mir Wais Khan, 322–24
Mir Wali, 381
Mirza Ahmad, 318
Mirza Shah Rukh, 318
Mithra, 309
Mithradites II, 299
Moghol people, 74
Moghul Dynasty, *xviii,* 80, 319ff, 331, 335–38, 361–63
Moghulgai, 492
Mohammad Ali, 403
Mohammad Ali Khan, Musahiban, 437, 449–50
Mohammad Amin (Sher Ali family), 403
Mohammad Amin (Amanullah family), 501
Mohammad Azim, 475
Mohammad Aziz Khan, Musahiban, 449, 474–75, 497
Mohammad Hashim Khan, Musahiban, *see* Hashim Khan, Prime Minister
Mohammad 'Ishaq Khan, 419
Mohammad Jan of Wardak, 410
Mohammad Khan, 341
Mohammad Nadir Khan, Musahiban, *see* Nadir Shah, King
Mohammad Sabir Khan, 333
Mohammad Saddiq, *see* Hazrat Sahib of Shor Bazaar
Mohammad Shah Khan, 397
Mohammad Shah, Moghul, 331, 335
Mohammad Shah, Qajar, 370–71, 374

Mohammad Sharif, 403

Mohammad Yusuf, 402

Mohammad Wali Khan, Tajik, 443–46, 475

Mohammad Zaman Khan, Abdali, 329, 332

Mohenjo-daro, 266

Momem Khan aw Shirini, 123

Mongolia, 218, 241, 296, 315

Mongolian, 66, 74

Mongoloid, 57, 65

Mongols, *xviii,* 19, 119, 317

Mongol-Uzbak, 319

monopolies, 655n

Montagu-Chelmsford Reforms, 486

Moosa Shafiq Kamawi, Mohammad, 531, 566, 571–72, 666

Moqor, ·391

Morasi Ghundai, Deh, 136, 138, 255–56, 266, 268–69, 271

Morrison-Knudsen Afghanistan, Inc. (M.K.A.), 483ff, 499ff

Mountbatten, Lord Louis, 488

Mousterian, 258, 260

Mudki, Battle of, 389

Mughlani Begum, 336–37

Mujadidi family, 109, 590

Mujadidi, Fazl Omar, 460

Mujadidi, Mohammad Ibrahim, 571

Mullah-i-Lang, 449

Multan, Pakistan, 330

Mundigak, 255–56, 266, 268–69, 271

municipal councils, 469

Municipalities Bill, 645

Munjan (36°09′ N, 71°06′ E), 35

Munji, 102

Murad Beg, Amir of Bokhara, 339

Murad, Moghul, 321

Murchakur, Iran, 329

Murdock, G. P., 188

Murghab River (38°18′ N, 61°12′ E), 21, 36, 422

Murray, James, 223

Musahiban, 437, 449, 458, 471

Musahiban-Charkhi feud, 474ff

Musali, gypsies, 180

Mushk-i-Alam Akundzadah, 409–10

musical instruments, 677–88

Muslim ritual in Afghanistan, 95ff

Mussooree, 443

Mustamandi, Dr. Shahibye, 306

Nad-i-Ali, Hilmand Valley (ca. 31°70′ N, 64°20′ E), 502–505

Nad-i-Ali, Sistan (31°00′ N, 61°51′ E), 255, 278, 503, 504–505

Nadir Shah Afshari, 328–32, 334

Nadir Shah, King Mohammad, 458ff, 477, 497; assassinated, 475; 1931 Constitution, 463–71; Habibullah's death, 437, 441; Minister to Paris, 450; observes *basmachi,* 448; opposed Amanullah, 449; proclaimed king, 460; Pushtun tribes, 486, 535; Saqqaoist War, 120–22, 453, 458–59; Shibar Pass road, 10, 461; Third Anglo-Afghan War, 442, 445; treatment of religious leaders, 581

Nadir Shah Mina, 638

Naghlu (34°37′ N, 69°44′ E), 42, 508–509, 522, 526, 640

Naib Sultan, 374

Naim Khan, Mohammad, 478, 498, 530, 545, 555

Najaf, Iraq, 115

Najib Ullah Khan, 70, 83, 488

Namin-i-Sahar, 440n

Napier, Lord, 413

Napoleon, 362, 363

Narain, A., 285

Naranjan Das, Diwan, 445

Narbada River, 57

Nashir, Loe Sher Khan, 471, 473

Nasir Khan, 334

Nasir Khan, Brahui, 338

Nasruddin, Mullah, 128–30

Nasrullah Khan, 430, 435, 437, 441

Nasrullah Khan, Amir of Bokhara, 378

Nasrullah Mirza, 340

National Democratic Party, 495

National Organization for Ophthalmic Rehabilitation (N.O.O.R.), 643

nation-state defined, 659

natural gas, 638

Nautaka, 281

Nawai, Ali Sher, 92, 318

nawruz, 98ff, 105–106, 218, 236, 432n

Nawwab of Dir, 539

Neanderthal Man, 260

Nearchus, Admiral, 283

Negah, Sayyid Moqades, 609

Nehru, J., 542

Nejat College, 447, 475, 644

Neogene, 12, 28, 43

Neolithic, *xvii;* Ceramic, 263–64; Kashmir, 264; Middle East, 266; Non-Ceramic, 262; South Russian, 266; South Siberian, 256, 264, 266

Nesselrode, Count, 374

New Republic, 553

Nicolls, General Sir Jasper, 383

Nida'-yi-Khalq, 495

Niedermeyer, Captain Oskar von, 434

nightingale (*bulbul*), 53

Nihawand, Iran, 312

Nijrao (34°58′ N, 69°22′ E), 12, 121

Nile Valley, 266

Nil Kotal (34°48′ N, 67°22′ E; 11,610 ft, 3,540 mt), 21

nimroz, 313

Ningrahar (33°37′ N to 34°49′ N, 69°28′ E to 71°10′ E), 2, 138, 159, 163; irrigation project, 522, 526, 636–37; Medical College, 600

Ningraharian, 72

Nishapur, 75, 313, 336

Niya, 301

Nizami, 123

Nizamnameh, 463

Nizaris, Wakhi, 102

Nochak, Naochak, highest mountain in Afghanistan, (36°25′ N, 71°50′ E; 24,500 ft, 7,470 mt), 1

nomads, 166ff, 560

Nomadic Iron Ages, 256, 269, 271

nomad-village symbiosis, 174, 177, 179–80

Norris, J., 370

North Africa, 303

Northbrook, Lord, 406

Northern Tier, 510

North-West Frontier Province, 373; annexed by British, 380; kinship, 188; language, 72; Nadir Khan raises an army, 458; One Unit problems, 490; Pakistan take over, 490; Pushtun tribes, 57; Settled Districts, 431, 486; Tribal Agencies, 486; warfare, 480

Nott, Major General William, 383, 393, 396–98

Nuristan, Nuristani, formerly Kafiristan (35°30′ N, 70°45′ E), 12, 14, 19, 42, 161; Alexander the Great, 283; burials, 208; dress, 238, 240–41, 244, 246; fauna, 51; food, 236; games, 213, 222–23; German Mission, 478; house types, 142; Kafiristan War, 419; language, 72; physical type, 57, 65

Nur Mohammad Khan, Sayyid, 407

Nushki, 426

Nysa, 283

Obeh (34°22′ N, 63°10′ E), 36

Olbia, 291

Oldfield, Captain C., 394

Olynthus, 291

Omar Jan, Mohammad, 430

One Unit (1955), Pakistan, 490, 538

ornaments, 244ff

Ormuri, 72

Osman, Mohammad, 595

Ottoman Dynasty, 328, 330, 361, 408, 431

Oudh, 365

ovis polii, see Marco Polo sheep

Oxus River, *see* Amu Darya

Oxyartes, 279, 282

Pacha Gul, 540

Pacific Ocean, 363

Paghman Mountains (34°44′ N, 68°54′ E), 12

Pahlavi, Reza Shah, 168, 454, 504

Pahlavi, Mohammad Reza, Shah of Iran, 561, 565

Paiminar, 105

Paitava, 307

Pakistan, American aid, 514; archaeology, 292; Bajaur fighting, 539–40; clothing, 243; Darra weapons, 214; ethnic groups, 57; food, 224, 227, 229, 231; kinship, 188; Mangal problem, 534–35; One Unit, 490, 538; "Pushtunistan," 493ff, 507, 541ff; Second Kashmir War, 510; Turks, 315; trade, 236, 240, 544ff; Zoroastrians, 272

Pakistan Air Force, 539

Paktya (33°30′ N, 69°30′ E), 2, 14, 19, 21; administration, 155, 159; clothing, 242–43; house types, 142; kinship, 190; puberty, 194; urban migration, 163; warfare, 119, 534

Paktya Development Authority, 641

Paktyan, 72
Palaearctic fauna, 51
Palaeolithic, *xvii;* Middle, 256, 260–61, 264; Upper, 256, 260–62
Palaeozoic, 12, 26
Palmer, Ely E., 478
Palmer, Lt. Colonel T., 395
Palmerston, Lord, 370
Palmyra, 301
Paludan, K., 53
Pamir (38°00′ N, 73°00′ E), 1; boundaries, 5, 424; clothing, 240, 243–44; fauna, 51–52; Kanishka, 300; Kirghiz nomads, 164; yak, 49; yurts, 172
Pamiri, 49, 102
Pan American, 547
Panipat, Battle of, 319, 328, 338
Panjdeh Incident (1885), 421–22, 424, 443–44
Panjsher River, Valley (34°38′ N, 69°42′ E), 12, 33, 42; Alexander the Great, 278; archaeology, 306; development, 522; house types, 138; pre-Islamic forests, 19; "ward" specialization, 159
Panjsheri, 70, 183, 214
Panjwai (31°32′ N, 65°28′ E), 39
Pantaleon, 285
"Papa Ghulam," *see* Farhad, Ghulam Mohammad
Parachinar, Pakistan (33°54′ N, 70°06′ E), 14, 72, 534, 543
Parcham, 611, 615ff, 653
Parian Dara (35°43′ N, 70°02′ E), 42
Parliament, *see Wolesi Jirgah*
parliamentary elections (1965), 587 ff, 651ff; 1969, 652ff
Parliamentary Papers, 371–73, 375
Paropamisus Mountains (35°00′ N, 71°00′ E), 21, 39
Parsees, 279
Parsiwan, *see* Farsiwan
Parthia, Parthian, 274, 285, 298–299, 310, 307
Partition Agreement (1947), 488ff
Parun River (71°00′ N, 35°30′ E), 14
Parwan Irrigation Project, 641
Pashai, 72
Pashto, 66, 70, 72, 83
Pashto Academy, Afghanistan, 93
Pashto Academy, Peshawar University, 90

Patai, R., 244
Patao Canal System (31°40′ N, 65°50′ E), 39
Patna, India, 285
Payam-i-Emroz, 601, 610ff
pay-yi-luch, 537
Payinda Khan Mohammadzai, 365, 368
Pa-zand, 272
Pazhwak, A. R., 642
Pazwak, Fazl Rabi, 600
Peace Corps, 597, 612, 643ff, 644
Peacock Throne, 331
Pech River (34°52′ N, 71°09′ E), 14
Peiwar Kotal (33°58′ N, 69°51′ E), 409
Pelly, Sir Lewis, 407
Pergamon, 291
Perkins, Dexter, Jr., 262–64, 271
Persepolis, 276
Persia, *see* Iran
Persian Gulf, 298, 202, 363, 373
Peshawar (34°01′ N, 71°39′ E), 12, 42; Ahmad Shah Durrani, 335; consulates attacked, 543; Dost Mohammad, 371–72, 401; First Anglo-Afghan War, 386; food, 229; Gandhara, 299–300; language, 72; Lawrence, Sir John, 402; Musahiban brothers, 459; Nadir Shah Afshari, 331; Sher Ali, 407; Silk Route, 306; Timur Shah Durrani, 341
Peshawar Conference (1877), 407
Peshawari Sardars, 376
Peter the Great, 363
Petra, 301
Pharnuches, 280
Phoenicia, 307
Phrada, 278
pigeons, 142, 212
Pilger, Hans, 480–81
Pingala, 309
Piodasses, Piyadassi, *see* Ashoka
Pir-Hadjat of Herat, *see* Ansari, Pir of Herat
Pir-i-Lang, see Mullah-i-Lang
Pishin, 409, 425
plants, domesticated, 669; medicinal, 672–73
Pleistocene, 8, 10, 12, 28
Pohanyar, Sayyid Masud, 654
Poincaré, Raymond, 447
Point IV, 485

Poland, 450, 516–20, 523

political parties, 584–85, 590

Political Parties Act, 590, 649–50

Pollock, Major General George, 384, 389, 395, 397–98

Polytechnic Institute, 638, 640

Population and Agricultural Survey of 500 Villages (1963), 142, 148

Poros, 283

portable dwellings, 170, 172, 174

Portugal, 362, 363

Pottinger, Eldred, 370, 384, 386, 388, 395

powindah, 169–70

Pradel, L., 260

Prakrit, 286

Prasun, Vermir, 72

Pratap, Raja Mahendra, 435, 444

prehistory, 255ff

Press Law (1965), 600, 608ff

"Prester John," 315

Priene, 291

Progressive Democratic Party (P.D.P.), 614

prostitution, 198

provincial administration, 469

Provincial Advisory Committee, 468

Provincial Councils Act, 650

provincial system, 155, 159

Ptolemy, 283

Puglisi, S., 256

Pul-i-Darunta, 287n

Pul-i-Khumri (35°56′ N, 68°43′ E), 155; archaeology, 292; development, 161, 472–73, 507–509, 529, 634; mines, 191

Punjab, Ahmad Shah Durrani, 335–38; Alexander the Great, 274; British annex, 380, 401; Durranis lose control, 343, 365; Hijrat movement, 447; Kushans, 301–302; Mahmud of Ghazni, 314; Moghuls, 331; mules, 48; Nadir Shah Afshari, 331; North-West Frontier formed, 431

Punjabi, 66, 111

purdah, 460, 463, 531–33, 554

Purdel, Tajik, 460

Purushapura, ancient Peshawar, 301

Pushtun, Pushtun tribes, 49, 57, 65, 161, 163–64, 170, 180, 191, 194, 208, 222, 238–39, 246, 321, 459–60, 479, 485, 499, 512, 552, 569, 652; *Afridi,* 240, 341, 492, Matai, 504; *Daftani,* 504; *Durrani,* formerly Abdali, 170, 190, 211, 322–24, 328, 330–34, 340, 343, 365, 397, 561, Achakzai, 333, 504, Alikozai, 333, Barakzai, 333, 350, 396, 504, Mohammadzai, 332–33, 343, Popalzai, 333, 365, 396, Saddozai, 332–33, 340, 343; *Ghilzai,* 170, 187–88, 190, 211, 322, 324, 326, 329–30, 334, 385, 388, 394–97, 419, 460, Ahmadzai, 460, Andar, 40, 132, 410, Andar, Ut Khel, 130–31, Hotaki, 322, 504, Jabar Khel, 410, Mandozai, 174, Suleiman Khel, 479, 504, Taraki, 418; *Kakar,* 323, 504; *Khugiani,* 504; *Jadran, Zâdran,* 190, 211, 475, 534; *Jaji,* 459; *Mahmund,* 241; *Mangal,* 190, 211, 240, 449, 459, 534; *Mohmand,* 240, 341, 490, 492; *Mushwani,* 246; *Safi,* 419, 504, 537; *Shinwari,* 188, 419, 452, 460; *Wardak,* 504; *Waziri,* 479, Darwesh Khel, 459, Tota Khel, 459; *Yusufzai,* 72, 322; *Zirak* (Barakzai and Popalzai), 333

"Pushtunistan," 485ff, 492, 538ff; Afghan press support, 612; border closures, 538–54, 485ff; Constitutional *Loya Jirgah,* 585–86; Daoud Khan's support, 557; 1965 election issue, 589; 1949 *Loya Jirgah,* 492; 1955 *Loya Jirgah,* 538; Mangal problem, 534; *powindah,* 169; problem lessens after 1963 border reopening, 565, 594, 649, 661; Soviet support, 508, 519

Pushtunwali, 104, 126–27

Puteh-Khazaneh, 83

Pyandzh, U.S.S.R. (37°59′ N, 66°55′ E), 35

Qadisiya, Battle of, 312

qadiya, 579

Qajar Dynasty, 328n, 363–64, 368, 370–72

Qala Bist, *see* Lashkari Bazaar

Qala Panja (37°00′ N, 72°34′ E), 6, 49

Qala Shahar, Faoghan (35°33′ N, 65°34′ E), 36

Qamari calendar, 674–75

qanat, 40, 42, 132

Qandahar, Kandahar (31°35′ N, 65°45′ E), *xviii*, 2n, 21, 31, 39, 155; Ahmad Shah Durrani, 330ff; Alexander the Great, 278; Amanullah, 442, 453; Arab raids, 312; archaeology, 255, 266ff, 286ff, 319; Ashraf, 326ff; clothing, 240–41; development, 520, 635, 637; Dost Mohammad, 401ff; early Islamic dynasties, 313; 1965 elections, 587, 590; First Anglo-Afghan War, 378ff, 393, 395–96; folktale, 122–23; grapes, 140; independent, 369; language, 72; land reforms, 152–53; marriage customs, 203; Mir Wais, 322ff; Moghul-Safavid rivalry, 321ff; Mohammad Ayub Khan Durrani, 410; Nadir Shah Afshari, 329ff; 1959 riots, 536–38, 556; Second Anglo-Afghan War, 408ff; Sultan Mahmud Ghilzai, 324ff; Shah Shuja, 368, 373; Tarzi, Mahmud Beg, 437; water buffalo, 49

Qandaharian, 72

Qandahar International Airport, 513

Qandahari Sardars, 365, 371, 376, 378

Qarakhanids, Toquz-Oglu Turks, 313–14

qarakul, Persian Lamb, 48, 240, 471–72, 482, 624

Qargha Lake (34°31′ N, 69°02′ E), 51, 558

Oataghan, Kataghan (37°00′ N, 69°00′ E), 47, 49, 148, 401, 418

qazi, 109, 204, 580–81

Qavam-ud-Din, 318

Qazvin, Iran, 326, 329

Qizilbash, 172, 465; Ahmad Shah Durrani, 334; First Anglo-Afghan War, 398; merchants, 547; Safavid mercenaries, 323, 331–32; Timur Shah Durrani, 340–41

Qizil Qala, 35, 508–509. *See also* Sher Khan Bandar.

qiyas'aqli, 579

qiyas shar'i, 579

Quchan, Iran, 332

Quddus Khan, Abdul, 418, 442

Queen Elizabeth I, 362

Queen Soraya, *see* Soraya, Queen

Queen's 16th Lancers, 384

Quetta, Ahmad Shah Durrani, 338; First Anglo-Afghan War, 381, 395; Foward Policy, 404, 406; language, 72; mines, 170; nomad, 170; "Pushtunistan," 543; railroad, 425

Quhandiz, Herat, 79

Qum, Iran, 327

Quraish tribe, 101

Qutb Minar, India, 315

Rabi' a Balkhi, 77

Radio Afghanistan, 532, 554, 564, 595, 649, 653

Radio Free Afghanistan, 491

Raghunath Rao, 337–38

Rahimi, Professor Ghulam Sarwar, 571

Rahman Baba, 83, 89–90, 211

Ramparts, 612

Ram, Sita, 389n

Ramstedt, G., 74

Ranjit Singh, 368, 370, 373, 378

Rasa, Sayyid Mian Rasul, 90

Rashid Ali el-Gilani, 480

Rawalpindi, Pakistan (33°27′ N, 73°15′ E), 48, 423, 425; Treaty of 1919, 443, 530n

Rawlinson, Major Henry, 395, 404, 413

Ray, Iran, 314

Raza Quli, 332

Razmak, 492

Redard, G., 74

"Red Shirts," *see Khuda-yi-Khidmatgaran*

Regional Cooperation for Development (R.C.D.), 479, 642

Registan (31°00′ N, 65°00′ E), 2, 31

Reg-i-Rawan, Dasht-i-Rawan (33°01′ N, 64°29′ E), 19

religion, folk, 104ff

reptiles, 53

Resht, Iran, 328

Rhineland, 301

Richard Mission, 511

Ridgeway Line (1887), 424

Ridgeway, Sir West, 424

Rig Veda, 272

religious hierarchy, 108–10

Ripon, Lord, 413

Rishtin, S., 93

Rishtya, Said Qassim, 186, 532, 564, 566

ritual, Muslim, 95ff
road system, 644ff
Roashan, 419
Robert Nathan Associates, 530
Roberts, General Sir A., 384n
Roberts, Lord, 408–409, 411, 413
Robertson, T. C., 387
Rodaki of Samarkand, 76
"Romance of Alexander," 276
Rome, Roman Empire, 285, 295–96, 300–302, 307
Roos-Keppel, Sir George, 486–87
Rostovtzeff, M., 253
Roland, B., 292, 305
Roxane, 282–83
Royal Air Force, 442
Rud-i-Band-i-Amir (35°12′ N, 66°30′ E), 33, 36
Rud-i-Gaz (33°37′ N, 62°15′ E), 39
Rud-i-Ghor (33°13′ N, 63°40′ E), 39
Rud-i-Musa Qala (32°22′ N, 64°46′ E), 37
Rue, Larry, 546
Ruka (35°17′ N, 69°29′ E), 159
Rumi, 75, 79n
rural-urban migration, 162, 163, 166
Russia, Tsarist, in Central Asia, 318, 328, 363–64, 370, 372, 404, 433
Russo-Afghan barter agreement (1936), 478
Russo-Japanese War (1904–05), 431, 433, 439
Russo-Afghan Treaty of Friendship (1921), 445
Rustam Muhammad Sa'dlu, 324
Rymalov, V., 516

Sabzawar, *see* Shindand
Sacae, variants of, 296
Saddo, 333
Sa'di, 79n
Safavid Dynasty, *viii,* 319ff, 324, 328–29, 361
Safed Koh Mountains (34°30′ N, 63°30′ E), 12
Saffarid Dynasty, 313
Safi, Mohammad Ghulam Hassan, 495, 589
Safi revolt, 537
Saghir, Mustafa, 435
Saiful Maluk aw Bandri Jamaleh, 123

Saighan River (35°14′ N, 67°58′E), 35
Saiyidabad (38°59′ N, 68°43′ E), 36
Śaka, 291, 296, 298–99
Sakae, 280
Śakastan, modern Sistan, 298–99
Salang Pass (35°22′ N, 69°04′ E; 13,350 ft. 4,075 mt), 3, 10; Tunnel, 461, 508, 645
Sale, Sir Robert, 384, 389, 393
Sale, Lady Florentia, 384, 397
Saleh Mohammad, 398
Saleh Mohammad Khan, General, 442
Salisbury, Lord, 406
Samad Hamed, Dr. Abdul, 566
Samangan, *see* Aibak
Samanid Dynasty, 76, 313
Samaria, 291
Samarkand, 281, 313, 317, 332, 408, 410
Sampson, General, 370
Sana'i, 79n
sandali, 138
Sanglechi, 102
Saozma-Kala, 311
Sar Cheshma (34°10′ N, 67°40′ E), 40
Sar-i-Köl, Lake Victoria (37°24–26′ N, 73°34–46′ E), 6
Sar-i-Pul (35°32′ N, 66°43′ E), 36
Sar-i-Pul Ab (35°55′ N, 66°04′ E), 36
Sar Koshak, 316
Sarmatians, 307
Sarobi (34°36′ N, 69°43′ E), 42
Sarwar, Q., 90
Sasanian Dynassy, *xvii,* 301–303, 307, 309, 311–12
Sasanian-Gupta elements, 305
Satibarzanes, 276, 279
Sattagydia, 274
Saudi Arabia, 544
Sayyad hunter-fishermen, 51, 53, 214–15
Sayyid 'Alim Khan of Bokhara, 448
Sayyid-i-Kayan, 109
Sayyid Kemal, 475
Sayyid Mohammad Sa'adi, 479
Sayyid Nur Mohammad Shah, 406
Sazai, River, village (36°06′ N, 66°17′ E), 36
Scerrato, U., 315

Schlumberger, D., 288, 291–92, 309, 314

Schurmann, H., 74

Scythians, 280–81

Se, 298

Second Anglo-Afghan War, 370, 405, 408

Second Anglo-Sikh War, 401

second-hand clothes, 241–42

sehum-i-aqrab, 592ff, 597, 608, 620

Se-jung, 298

Seleucia on the Tigris, 291, 301

Seleucid Dynasty, 283, 285

Seleucus, 281, 283

Seljuk Dynasty, 314–15

Seljuki, Fikri, 318

Seljuki, Professor Salahuddin, 566

semi-nomads defined, 164

Semitic, 66

Senusiya of Libya, 103

Seraj-ul-Akhbar, 437, 439–40, 456

Seraj ul-Atfal, 440

Seraj-ul-Mellat-wa-ad-din, 438

Serapis-Hercules, 307

Settled Districts, N.-W.F.P., 487, 490, 539

Sewang, 298

Sewangi, 299

Shafi 'i Sunni, 103

Shah Abbas II, 321–22, 333

Shah Abbas III, 330

Shah Alam, 322

Shah Alam II, 338

Shah Ali Reza Khan, Colonel, 435

Shah, Dr. S. W., 482

Shah Foladi, Kop-i-Foladi (34°38′ N, 67°32′ E; 16,874 ft, 5,140 mt). 1, 10

Shah Jahan, Moghul Emperor, 321–32

Shah Jahan II, 338

Shah Jahan III, 338

Shah Khan, Mohammad, 384

Shah Mahmud, Prime Minister, 477, 482, 494, 497–99; Amanullah period, 449; army commander, 476; Ibrahim Beg fight, 461; Saqqaoist War, 121, 459

Shah Mahmud, Saddozai, 365, 368, 403

Shah-Namah by Firdausi, 77

Shahr-i-Gholghola, 316

Shahr-i-Kona, Qandahar, 288

Shahr-i-Naw, Kabul, 204

Shahr-i-Zohak, 316

Shahrud, Iran, 276

Shah Rukh, 317

Shah Rukh, Afshari, 335–36, 340

Shah Shuja, 81, 363, 365, 368, 373, 375ff, 394–95, 398, 403

Shah Nawaz Khan, *see* Hayatullah Khan

Shah Wali Khan, Field Marshal, 120–21, 437, 441, 445, 449, 458, 471, 497

Shah Wali Khan, Saddozai, 340

Shaikh Mohammadi, 180

Shaker, N., 74

Shakespear, Captain Richmond, 398

Shanhdi Khan aw Bibu, 123

Shanidar, Iraq, 260

Shamalan, 505, 635

Shamshir Ghar, 269, 303, 309, 311

Shami Pir, 479

Shamsi calendar, 674–76

Shams-i-Nahar, 405

Shamsuddin, 384, 397

Shapur I., 307

Shahpur, Saddozai, 398

Sharif Khan aw Mabaie, 123

Shaybani, Mohammad, Uzbak, 319

Sheikh Mohammad Ali Hazin, 327

Shelton, Brigadier John, 383, 388, 390, 392

Sher Agha Naguib, 460

Sher Ali Khan, Amir, 403–404, 407–10, 419, 425

sher-bacha, 537

Sher Darwaza, Kabul, 97

Sherkat-i-Sahami-i-Afghan, see Bank-i-Melli

Sher Khan Bandar (37°11′ N, 68°36′ E), 35, 508. *See also* Imam Sahib; Qizil Qala.

Sher Khan Nashir, *see* Nashir, Loe Sher Khan

sherkat, 472–73, 507

Sherpur, 384, 410

Shewa, Lake (37°21–25′ N, 71°16–23′ E), 8

Shibar Pass (34°54′ N, 68°14′ E; 10,700 ft, 3,260 mt), 10, 12, 21, 279, 461

Shibarghan (36°41′ N, 65°45′ E), 36, 66, 174

Shighnan (37°30′ N, 71°28′ E), 419

Shigni, 102

Shih Huang-ti, 298

Shindand, Sabzawar (33°18′ N, 62°08′ E), 39, 523

Shiniz Rud (34°03′ N, 68°46′ E), 42

Shiraz, Iran, 340

Shirin Tagao (36°26′ N, 64°55′ E), 36

Shooja-ool-Moolk, *see* Shah Shuja

Shotorak, 307

Shpoon, S., 75–77, 81–82, 91

Shuja Dawla, 437

Shuja Mirza, *see* Shah Shuja

Shu'la-yi-Jawed, 611, 615ff, 653

Siberia, 52, 301

Siberian Tiger, 51, 215

"Siberia of the Persian Empire," 274

Sibi, Pakistan, 409

Sidon, 307

Siemens Company, 478–79

Sikhs, 110–11; empire, 368–69, 371–74; language, 66; wars with British, 389, 401

Silk Route, *xviii,* 292, 296, 300–301

Simla Manifesto (1873), 375–76, 379, 406

Simon Commission, Royal Stationary Commission (1928–30), 487

Simonich, Count Simoultch, 371–72, 374

Sind, 337, 340, 350, 365, 369, 378, 380

Singh, G., 340

Singh, J., 79

Sing, Jai, 653

Singhal, D., 421

Sinkiang, Chinese (40°00′ N, 85°00′ E), 8, 299–300, 302, 306

Sino-Siberian art, 296

Sirhind, 337

Sistan, Seistan (30°57′ N, 59°30′ E), 5, 26, 28, 31, 37; archaeology, 255, 268; Alexander the Great, 283; birds, 52–53; early Islamic period, 312–13; Goldsmid Award, 406, 432; Hilmand Valley project, 482; MacMahon Commission, 432–33; Sayyad hunter-fishermen, 51, 53, 214–15; Sultan Mahmud Ghilzai, 326; Timur Shah Durrani, 340; "wind of 120 days," 140

Śiva, 311

skiing, 213

Skull Cave (Aq Kupruk IV), 269, 271

Smithsonian Institution, 260

Snake Cave (Aq Kupruk I), 262–63

socialization, child, 191ff

Sogdiana, Sogdians, 279–81, 285, 301–302

Sogdian Rock, Battle of, 281

Sohail, Dr. Mohammad Asif, 567

Somerset Light Infantry, 13th Foot, 395

Soraya, Queen, 438, 450, 479

Southeast Asia Treaty Organization (S.E.A.T.O.), 510

South Siberian bronze mirror, 271

Soviet-Afghan Treat of Neutrality and Non-Aggression (1931), 508

Soviet-American "cooperation," 526ff

Soviet Central Asia, 262, 517ff

Soviet Union, aid to Amanullah, 451; Amanullah's visit, 478; arms aid, 179, 522–26; *basmachi,* 448, 460–61, 472, 512, 514, 528; boundary with, 33, 42, 166, 425; Central Asian republics, 57, 517ff; "cooperation" with United States, 526ff; grape air lift, 552; Marxist students, 587–89, 594, 597, 660; post-World War II aid and trade, 236, 242–43, 493ff, 507ff, 542–43, 626ff, 637ff, 640ff, 660–62, 665; pre-World War II political relations, 443–44; pre-World War II economic relations, 471–72

Spain, 362

Spin Baldak (31°01′ N, 66°24′ E), 39

Spin Baldak-Qandahar highway, 550

Spinzar Company, 642

Spinzar Hotel, 237

Spitamenes, 279–81

sports and games, 209ff

Stalin, 451

State Bank of Afghanistan, *see* Da Afghanistan Bank

Stateira, 286

Steeves, Ambassador John M., 561, 594

Stevens and Tarzi, 502ff

Stewart, General Donald, 408, 413

Stoddart, Colonel Charles, 374, 408
St. Petersburg, 407, 409; Convention (1907), 433
Strabo, 285
student demonstrations, 590ff, 619ff, 651, 662. *See also sehum-i-aqrab.*
Sturt, Captain J., 384, 391
Subuktigin, Nasir ad-Dawla, 314
Südasien Institut der Universität Heidelberg. 598n
Sufi, Sufism. 78ff, 79n, 103
Sulaiman Mirza, 340
Sulaiman Mountains, 340
Sultan Abdul Hamid, *see* Abdul Hamid, Sultan
Sultan Aregh, 66
Sultan Husain Baiqara, 317–18
Sultan Husain I, Shah, Safavid, 322–28
Sultan Jan, 397
Sultan Mahomed Khan, 417n
Sultan Mohammad Khan, Barakzai, 369
Sung Dynasty of China, 313
Supreme Court, 567, 585. *See also* court system.
Surashthia, modern Kathiawar, 299–300
Surkh Ab, north (37°00′ N, 68°16′ E), 10, 21, 33, 35; south, (34°27′ N, 70°23′ E), 42
Surkh Kotal, 286, 292, 295, 311n
Suri Afghan Dynasty of Delhi, 319
Surya, 309
Sutherland, Colonel, 400
Swat, Pakistan, 322, 425
Swatis, Assaceni, 283
Switzerland, 450
Syria, 301

Tabriz, Iran, 326
Tadmor, Syria, 301
Tafwiz, Ghulam Mahayuddin, 610
Tagao (34°55′ N, 69°35′ E), 12, 311
Tahirid Dynasty, 75, 313
Tahmasp I, Safavid, 321
Tahmasp Quli Khan, *see* Nadir Shah Afshari
Tahmasp II, Safavid, 326–30
tahwildar, 623, 643, 656
Tajik, 57, 161, 183; Abdur Rahman, 419; Ahmad Shah Durrani, 336; clothing, 238–41, 244, 246; 1964

Constitutional *Loya Jirgah,* 569; dwelling types, 172; 1969 elections, 652; First Anglo-Afghan, War, 410; Habibullah Ghazi, 452–53; Karts, 317; language, 70; merchants, 547; physical type, 65; Nadir Shah, revolt against, 460; religion, 465; villagers, 180, 187–88
Tajiki, 70
Tajikistan S.S.R., 35, 70
Takht-i-Pul, 403
Takht-i-Rustam, 313
Takht-i-Sulaiman (36°30′ N, 70°20′ E), 8
Tamerlane, 10, 317, 319
Tamtama, Iran, 260
T'ang Dynasty China, 312
Tang-i-Gharu (34°34′ N, 69°30′ E), 12, 40
Tang-i-Tashkurghan (37°19′ N, 66°14′ E), 35, 279
Tapa Maranjan, 311
Tapa Sardar, 311
Tapa Shotor, 306
taqiya, 465
Taraki, Nur Mohammad, 601
tarika, Sufism, 103
Tarim Oasis, 301
Tarjman, 617
Tarmita, 282
Tarn, W., 276, 282
Tarnak River (31°26′ N, 65°31′ E), 39
Tarsus, 289
Tarzi, Ghulam Mohammad, 82, 437
Tarzi, Mahmud Beg, 430, 437ff, 442–47, 450–51, 453–54, 456–57
Tarzi, Rahmdel, 82
Tasawwuf, 78
Tashkent, U.S.S.R., 410, 435, 448, 471–72
Tashkurghan, *see* Khulm
Tashkurghan River (35°50′ N, 67°30′ E), 35
tatooing, 246
taxes, 647
Taxila, 287n, 301, 305–307
tazi, see Afghan hound
tea, 641
Technical Cooperation Administration (T.C.A.), 485

Tedzhen River, U.S.S.R. (37°24′ N, 60°38′ E), 36
Tehran, Iran, 272, 364, 374–75, 454
tent-pegging, 221
tents, 170, 172
Termez, U.S.S.R. (37°14′ N, 67°16′ E), 25, 282
Tertiary, 10
Teshik-Tash, U.S.S.R., 260
Tethys Sea, 10
textile mills, 641–42
Tezeen, 396
Thailand, 297
Thal, Pakistan (33°22′ N, 70°32′ E), 14, 431, 442, 534
thalweg, 33, 424
Theravada Buddhism, 297
Third Anglo-Afghan War, *x*, 442ff, 444, 456, 459, 485
Tibet, 224, 300, 431, 433
Tibetans, 233
Tigiri, 435
Tigris-Euphrates, 266
Timur-i-Lang, *see* Tamerlane
Timur Shah, 81, 337, 340, 363, 365
Timurid Dynasty, 256, 317ff, 362
Tirah Bagh, 492
Tirin River (32°38′ N, 65°26′ E), 37
Tiwa, China, 8
Toquz-Oghlu Turks, 313
Torrens, Henry, 375
tourism, 655
"Towers of Victory," Ghazni, 315
towns, 153ff
Transoxiana, 313, 315, 319
transportation, 134
treaties, Anglo-Afghan (1905), 479; Anglo-Afghan (1921), 446, 486; Fars (1807), 363; Gandamah (1879), 409, 425–26; Gulistan (1813), 364; Neutrality and Non-Aggression (1931), 460; Non-Aggression and Friendship (1937), 479; Non-Aggression and Neutrality (1926), 448; Paris (1763), 363; Peshawar (1855), 401, 405, 1857 Supplement, 402, 405; Rawalpindi (1919), 443, 485, 492; Turkmanchai (1828), 364; U.S. Friendship (1936), 478
Trevor, Captain, 387

Tribal Agencies, 57, 214, 480, 486–87, 538–39, 553
"tribalism," 659
tribal warfare, 118ff
Tripartite Agreement of 1838, 373, 375
Trousdale, W., 315
Tucci, G., 311, 315
Tudeh Party, 601
Tudor Engineering Company, 505
Tudor Report (1956), 506
Tukhi, General Ata Mohammad, 571
Tun Huang, 300
Turco-German Mission (1915), 434
Turco-Mongols, *xviii*, 37, 317
Turdalai aw Shahi, 123
Turfan, 301
Turkabad, 74
Turkestan, 47, 51, 296, 306
Turkestan Plains, 1, 5, 8, 21, 25–26, 28, 35, 43, 174, 179
Turkey, 315, 317, 446, 439, 507, 538
Turkmani, Abdul Raouf, 610
Turkoman, 57, 161; Abdur Rahman, 418–19; Ahmad Shah Durrani, 336; Amanullah, 453; bride capture, 205; *buzkashi*, 218; Central Asian, 512; clothing, 238, 241; 1964 Constitutional *Loya Jirgah*, 569; 1969 elections, 652; jewelry, 245: language, 72; Mawri rugs, 245; Nadir Shah Mohammadzi, 461; Tsarist Russian conquests, 421–22; yurts, 172
Turks, 303, 312–13, 315, 328
Tus, 77
Twenty-Fourth International Congress of Orientalists (1957), 74
Tyre, 307

Ulugh Beg, 317
'Umar, 101, 109
Umayyid Caliphate, 312, 361
Unai Pass, Kotal-i-Unai (34°27′ N, 68°22′ E; 11,000 ft, 3,350 mt), 14
United Arab Republic, 544
United Nations, 491, 551, 641ff
United States, 1919 Afghan Mission, 445; aid and traide, 236–37, 484ff, 499ff, 507, 509ff, 549, 560, 624, 626, 629ff, 647, 665; arms aid, 510ff, 522–24; Central Intelligence Agency, 559, 612–14; "covered wagon" com-

plex, 528; first exchange of ambas-
sadors, 478; offers to mediate "Push-
tunistan," 493; oil exploration, 479;
Peace Corps, 643–44; Qandahar riots,
537; road assistance, 644–45; 1936
Treaty of Friendship, 478
United States Bureau of Reclamation,
506
University of Peshawar, 487
Uralic-Altaic, 66, 72
Urgun, 155
Urta Tagail, Yangi Qala (37°28′ N,
69°36′ E), 448
Urumchi, China (43°43′ N, 87°38′ E),
8, 301
usulnamakhor moqar'rarat, 657
Uthman, 101, 109
Ut Khel, 130–31
U-2 flights, 529
Uzbekista̅n S.S.R., 92, 260
Uzbak, 1, 161; Abdur Rahman, 418–19;
Ahmad Durrani, 336; *basmachi,*
448, 460–61, 512; *buzkashi,* 218;
clothing and ornaments, 238–41,
243, 245–46; 1964 Constitutional
Loya Jirgah, 569; Dost Mohammad,
378; dwelling types, 172; 1969 elec-
tions, 652; epic legends, 119; First
Anglo-Afghan War, 381; food, 233;
Hilmand Valley project, 503; independent khanates, 343; kinship,
183; language, 72, 74; Magits, 340;
merchants, 547; Moghul-Uzbak confrontations, 321; Shaybanis, 319;
Timurids, 317–18; villagers, 180,
187–88

Vakhsh River (37°10′ N, 68°20′ E),
35, 282
Vasudeva, 300
Vermir, Prasun, 72
Victor Emmanuel, King, 454
Victoria, Lake, *see* Sar-i-Köl
Vigne, G., 181
viliages, 132ff
Vima Kadphises, Kadphises II, 299
"Virgin Lands," Kazakhstan S.S.R., 168
Vishtaspa, Hystaspes, King, 274
Vitkevich, Captain Ivan, 371–72, 374
Volga Tartars, 517
von Hentig, Lt. Werner Otto, 434, 480

von Niedermeyer, Captain Oskar, 434
voodoo, 106

Wade, Captain H., 389
Wafadar Khan, 365
Wahdat, 601
Wahdat-i-Melli, 590
Wahedi, Dr. Abdullah, 590
Waigal (34°59′ N, 70°59′ E), 14
Waigali, 72, 244
Wakhan Corridor (36°51′ N to 37°29′
N, 72°45′ E to 73°30′ E) 2, 5–6,
8, 48–49, 74, 405, 424
Wakhi, Nizaris, 102
Wakhi-Pamiri groups, 57, 70
Wakhjir, Kilik Darwan (37°06′ N,
74°29′ E; 16,150 ft, 4,900 mt), 8
Wakil, Dr. Abdul, 506
Wali Khan Afridi, 492
Wamai, 72
waqf, 108, 110
Warburton, Sir R., 390n
Wardak, 397–98, 410
Wardak, Abdul Ahad, 453
Wardak, Dr. A. R., 256
Wardak, · Dr. Mohammad Omar, 653
Wardak hydroelectric station, 579
Wardak-Maidan, 159
Wardak, Ma'suma 'Esmati, 653
Warduj River (36°09′ N to 37°01′ N,
70°47′ E to 71°35′ E), 35
warfare, 118ff
War for Indian Independence, 402
Warraq, Mahmud, 75
Warsak Dam, 492
Watan, 495
Waterloo, Battle of, 363
Watson, Dr. John H., 411n
Waziristan, 490; North, 486; South, 486
Weiers, M., 74
Wellington, Duke of, 377
Wells, Chancellor Herman B., 599
Wellsley, Lord, 377
Wheeler, R. E. M., 288, 292
Wickens, G., 80
Wiet, G., 315
Wikh-i-Zalmaiyan, 496–97
Wilber, D., 98, 274
Wild's Brigade, 395
Wilson, J. C., Jr., 59
windmills, 140, 142

witches, 105–106
Wolesi Jirgah, 587, 589–91, 595, 608, 615, 618, 623, 649ff, 651ff, 653
Wolseley, Lord, 413
women, position of, 466, 531–32, 578, 590, 651ff
Woodcock, G., 274
worker-student demonstrations (1966–68), 619ff, 622
World Health Organization (W.H.O.), 291, 551
World War II, 480
wrestling, *pahlwani,* 211–12
Wusun, 298

Yaghistan, *xvii*
Yaftali, Abdullah, 654
yakhdan, 66
Yamini Dynasty, *see* Ghaznavid Dynasty
Yangi Qala, Urta Tagail, (37°28′ N, 69°36′ E), 448
Yaqub Khan, 404–405, 409, 425, 449
Yarkand, China, 300–301
Yar Mohammad Khan, Wazir, 368, 370–71
Yazd, Iran, 272, 324
Yazidi "Devil Worshipers," 102
Yedigy, 119
Yemen, 102
Yer-Targyn, 119
"Young Afghan" revolt, 497
Young, R., 289
Young Turks, 438
Yousuf, Dr. Mohammad, 554, 561, 565, 570, 572, 586–87, 591, 690–91
Yeuh-chih, 298–99
Yugoslavia, 642

yurts, 172
Yusuf aw Zulaika, 123–24

Zabuli, Abdul Majid, 471ff, 484, 590
Zagros Mountains, Iran, 168, 301
Zahir, Dr. Abdul, 186, 567, 571–72, 585, 589–90, 664
Zahir Shah, King Mohammad, 477ff; accedes to throne, 476; 1964 Constitutional monarchy, 658, 663; 1965 elections, 589; 1969 elections, 652ff; Interim Government, 591; New Democracy, introduction, 161; oligarchy, 498, 554; Political Parties Bill, 650; resignation of Daoud Khan, 554
Zaidiya Shi'a, 102
Zakaria Khan, 331
Zaman Khan, Nawab Mohammad, 386, 388, 390, 394, 396
Zaman Shah, 364, 368, 402
Zamindawar (32°00′ N, 64°30′ E), 313
Zand, 272
zann, 579
Zaranj, 278
Zards, 340
Zard Sang, Sang-i-Zard Mountains (34°39′ N, 67°19′ E), 35
Zarnegar Park, Kabul, 222
Zhob Valley, 268, 425
ziarat, 104ff
Zindabanan, 638
Zoroaster, Zarathustra, 272
Zoroastrians, 95, 111, 272, 279, 292, 301, 324
Zulfiqar (35°35′ N, 61°15′ E), 423
Zulfiqar Khan, Abdali, 329–30, 332

EPILOGUE

ON 17 JULY 1973, just as this book was going to press, Afghanistan came face to face with its "crisis in political and economic direction" (see p. 666). King Mohammad Zahir's experiment to create a constitutional monarchy, with a theoretical ultimate emphasis on constitutional power, had failed. Sardar Mohammad Daoud Khan, first cousin and brother-in-law of the king and prime minister from 1953 to 1963 (Chapter 23), declared Afghanistan a republic and on 18 July his Central Committee named him founder, president, and prime minister of the Republic of Afghanistan.

Many accumulative factors led to the coup. They have been mentioned in the final chapter and include both internal and external elements. The internal failures embrace all three branches of government as defined in the 1964 Constitution, as well as the failure of the king to promulgate the Political Parties Law, the Provincial Councils Law, and the Municipal Councils Act, all passed by Parliament. Implementation of these important pieces of legislation would have made possible the formation of incipient political parties to link up on a regional basis. Many Afghans, however, including some of the king's closest advisers in the royal family, argued that if parties became legal the left would become stronger and threaten the monarchy. But de facto, if not de jure, political parties already existed on the left and right and, at the very least, promulgation of the Political Parties Law may have drawn moderate activists from both extremes, and forced the comfortable stagnates of the growing urban middle class to join responsible groups. Then party discipline and an acceptable spoils system (essential to democracy, if kept within culturally allowable bounds of deviance) could have helped political parties define their positions vis-à-vis any existing government. The government, for its part, could have become integrated with the party system and formed its own platform for action.

Implementation of the Provincial Councils Law would have given more substance to the Constitution, which required that each Provincial Council (of which there would have been twenty-eight, one for each province) elect one of its members to serve in the *Meshrano Jirgah* for three years. Before the coup, the Upper House consisted of twenty-eight senators, one elected from each province to serve for four years, and another twenty-eight appointed by the king for five-year terms. Because the *Meshrano Jirgah* had existed with one-third of its required membership missing, a number of Afghan legal experts questioned its constitutionality.

The post-Constitution Municipal Elections Act called for more liberalized procedures for the elections of mayors and city councils. Until the coup, government-appointed "caretaker" (or "undertaker," according to certain Afghan commentators) mayors administered the cities.

The judicial never was, and the Parliament (particularly the *Wolesi Jirgah*, or Lower House) spent most of its time investigating rather than legislating.

The *Wolesi Jirgah* seldom had a quorum, but always an argument. From mid-March to early June 1973, the *Wolesi Jirgah* failed to have quorums for eighty-two sessions, forty in a row until 2 July! With no political parties to ensure unity on issues or enforce discipline on absentees, each *wakil* virtually acted as an independent party.

The intention of an initial partyless democracy originally was that the *wakil* from all parts of Afghanistan, constituting elements of most ethno-linguistic power groups, would meet for sustained periods twice a year in Kabul, in order to get them acquainted. It was hoped that political parties would grow from such contact, as would the recognition for united attacks on regional and national problems. Some critics, however, always insisted Afghan ethnocentrism precluded success, and that those in power planned it that way. Whatever the intent, the attempt to create an active parliamentary system without political parties failed.

Few doubted the basic sincerity of the post-Constitution prime ministers (Dr. Yousuf, Maiwandwal, Etemadi, Dr. Zahir, Moosa Shafiq), but given the absence of a parliamentary base of power rooted in a political party system, the relationships between the executive and the legislative seldom evolved beyond mutual wariness or encroachments into each other's prerogatives, and often erupted into mutual, acrimonious antagonism.

Unfortunately for the monarchy, the king, the nexus and center of power, sat out most of the squabbles, hoping the system would shake itself down and function of its own accord. He received contrary advice from family and close intimates, and anti-parliamentary elements within the royal family, reportedly led by Major-General Abdul Wali Khan (Commander of the Central Forces, which constitute all military units from Kabul to the Durand Line), first cousin and son-in-law of the king, convinced His Majesty that anti-Royalist, communist-dominated parties would gain control in a party system. But the absence of legal sanctions has seldom—if ever—discouraged the formation of extremist parties, left or right, and both extremes of the spectrum functioned openly in Afghanistan, proclaiming ideological (albeit muted) programs via the free press. Neither subtle pressure nor actual suppression totally inhibited these elements.

Student power movements, usually directly related to the nascent political parties and providing some of their leadership, continued a long series of strikes that were often without substance, one period lasting almost six months in 1971, and issued manifestos, many of them without relevance. Possibly, genuinely free debating-societies at the university would have brought out the quality that does exist, but that largely remained silent.

Another growing student problem had little to do with ideology: too many graduates began to compete for too few jobs. Each year, between fourteen and eighteen thousand students (depending on which set of statistics one prefers) graduate from high schools, and Kabul University can accommodate only about two thousand. In the past, government absorbed almost all high school and university graduates, as various ministries and development project organizations expanded to meet needs of the force-fed foreign assistance programs. An apparent (if not real) withering-away of the Cold War led to development interruptus, and resulted in severe cuts in foreign loans and grants.

In his initial statement over Radio Afghanistan, the new president emphasized that he wanted to bring the Afghan government back to the principles of Islam and save the nation from economic disaster. The leading Traditionalist religious leaders may not whole-heartedly support the new president, but they respect his power and the way he previously introduced various social reforms, particularly the voluntary removal of the veil from women in 1959. Daoud Khan tolerated little opposition to his programs, but used Modernist interpretations of Islam to justify his actions.

In addition, President Daoud Khan will probably feel little sympathy for the five to six thousand hippies residing in Kabul. These foreigners have intensified the drug problem in Afghanistan manyfold, and brought the country into international smuggling networks. Many Modernist and all Traditionalist religious leaders condemn the massive influx of such foreign influences, and the numerous bars and clubs now flourishing in Kabul may come under more stringent controls—or be completely shut down. Puritanism is fine for a dedicated elite, but those who bear the brunt of decision-implementing need convivial outlets. Government-sponsored Parks of Culture and Rest have long offered such opiates to the masses in the Soviet Union.

Afghanistan's economic problems are nothing new, but have been growing since the advent of overkill in foreign aid, which reached its peak during the 1953-63 decade of Daoud Khan's previous tenure. No matter how one viewed Afghanistan's economic problems, the outlook at first glance certainly appeared bleak. With most major infrastructure projects completed, with few real resources capable of earning vast sums of hard currency, with smuggling and corruption steadily eroding income from customs (a major source of government revenue), with little statistical data for intelligent planning, with minimal overall increases in agricultural production (and two years of drought, disastrous to men, livestock, and crops), with small success in attempted fiscal reforms, with debt repayment on foreign loans coming due, with annual budget deficits of about 500 million afghanis, with few of the country's limited industrial and power plants operating at 50 percent capacity, with a bureaucracy oriented toward perpetuation rather than innovation, Afghanistan offered any economist—free enterprise, socialist, or mixed—extreme challenges.

In many areas outside Kabul—and the capital remained largely out of touch with the rest of the country—conservative tribal, regional ethnolinguistic, and religious leaders either resisted government attempts at development, or (and the tendency increased annually) demanded more money for local projects. Many urban, Western-educated Afghans (as well as Westerners) tended to underestimate the strength of regional leadership in Afghanistan.

In spite of the problems listed above, genuine *movement* had been achieved during the short, seven-month tenure (12 December 1972-17 July 1973) of Prime Minister Mohammad Moosa Shafiq and his cabinet.

Possibly, the king hoped that ten years would bring the young parliament and young Moosa Shafiq to joint maturity. Shafiq spent the ten years as an adviser to the Foreign Ministry, as Ambassador to Egypt, among other places, and Foreign Minister in the Dr. Zahir cabinet. But a decade of parliamentary "benign neglect" and executive inaction proved fatal.

Shafiq, however, did begin to break the executive-legislative impasse, and, although plagued by frequent lacks of quorum, the Lower House considered and passed several important pieces of legislation. Among them were the 1972-73 regular and development budgets, several foreign loan agreements, and the Hilmand River Water Treaty with Iran; and a new Civil Service Law was considered. The prime minister moved his Office of Parliamentary Relations to the parliament building, and held weekly meetings with various *wakil.*

Prime Minister Shafiq tried—and at least partly succeeded—to establish better relations with the free press. He and other cabinet members gave periodic interviews, and results of the weekly cabinet meetings were disseminated immediately by the Minister of Information and Culture, Sabahuddin Khushkaki, former publisher of the free press newspaper, *Karwan*. In December 1972, shortly after his appointment, Shafiq announced that government advertising to free press papers would meet 30 percent of the total publishing cost of weeklies, 20 percent of the dailies. By this move, the government also had the means to exert pressure on free press policies.

Until the end, Shafiq continued to move ahead imaginatively on all fronts. Recognizing the increasing importance of mollifying various tribal and regional units, he raised the Department of Tribal Affairs to ministry status on June 5. Back taxes were being collected in Kabul, and plans were under way to revalue property, overdue for several decades. The prime minister held talks with the speakers of the two houses of parliament and key members of the judiciary in attempts to bring about closer coordination between the three branches of government.

Plans for the August-September 1973 elections for the fourteenth Parliament ran into snags, and postponement appeared inevitable, unless the judiciary and the executive could agree on the role of the Supreme Court in the elections. Although it served as election watchdog in the 1965 and 1969 elections, in April 1973 the Court declared this role unconstitutional. Many Afghan legal authorities disagreed, and since May a joint judiciary-executive committee had considered, without success, ways of breaking the impasse. As summer approached, however, most observers doubted that the king would give Prime Minister Shafiq the tools he needed to make the elections a success: promulgation of the Political Parties Law, the Provincial Councils Law, and the Municipal Councils Act.

Economically, the Shafiq regime saw Afghanistan's exports rise over $100 million ($117.37 m.) for the first time in its history. Also, by May 1973 the government had received about two hundred applications to establish plants, approved eighty-two, out of which about twenty-five functioned with varying degrees of efficiency. In addition, the Indian-assisted Kabul Industrial Park was inaugurated on 13 June 1973.

The fate of the Western-sponsored Industrial Development Bank of Afghanistan (60 percent Afghan investment; 40 percent Chase Manhattan Bank, First National City Bank of New York, Industrial Bank of Japan, National Westminster Bank, and Credit Lyonnais), established 3 March 1973, will depend on the economic policies of the new republic. Just before the July coup, both houses of Parliament voted to permit the Shafiq government to seek foreign loans for forty-seven approved development projects, particularly in agriculture and related fields. The previous government of Dr. Zahir, after much early vacillation and some bungling, minimized the effects of the potentially disastrous two years of drought, and the Shafiq government planned measures to prevent such horrors in the future. The 1973 bumper crop was a tribute to the skill of the Afghan farmer under adverse conditions, the timely distribution of fertilizer by the government, and the weather.

An increase in foreign loans meant a jump in total indebtedness, but if it were to move ahead the Shafiq government had little choice. What really disturbed some critics of the IDBA was the spectre of "neocolonialism" or "economic imperialism": a rise in internal investments without a solid knowledge of finance or government protection for those small-scale industries competing with cheap imports, combined with the need for external advisers, few equipped with knowledge and understanding of, or sympathy with, local cultural patterns.

At least superficially, the educational policies of the Shafiq government calmed down all but the more radical right and left, especially at Kabul University, rapidly being redirected by Chancellor Ahmad Jawaid.

The positive achievements of the Shafiq Cabinet in so short a time did not satisfy many rapid reformists, both military and civilian, particularly after postponement of the elections became generally conceded. Members of the intelligentsia cheered the departure of Daoud Khan in 1963, but increasingly, over the past few years, yearned for the dynamic socio-economic direction provided from 1953 to 1963, minus the suppressive aspects on the political scene.

Ironically, the issue of "Pushtunistan," mainly responsible for the resignation of Daoud Khan in 1963, played a major role in his return to power in 1973. Daoud Khan recognized the instability of Pakistan, although he did not refer to it in this manner in his first message over Radio Afghanistan. Significantly, the new president delivered his 17 July announcement in Pashto, not the Dari preferred by most members of the royal family. Pakistan's instability had been brought on by the independence of Bangladesh (recognized by Afghanistan 18 February 1973), and the subsequent unrequited demands of the Pushtun of the North-West Frontier Province and the Baluch and Brahui of Baluchistan Province for regional autonomy within a federation of Pakistan. The problem weighs heavily on Pakistan's charismatic president, Zulfikar Ali Bhutto, who, as of this writing, has not yet found a satisfactory compromise acceptable to all parties.

Coupled with worries about Pakistani instability is the fear of Iranian expansionism, as expressed by the transboundary chauvinism of Iran's celebration of its twenty-five hundredth pseudo-birthday in 1972, and Shah Mohammad Reza Pahlavi's blunt statements that Iran would not stand by and watch Pakistan collapse without taking steps to safeguard her interests in the area: i.e., Iran would occupy Baluchistan, with implications that more might be bitten off.

Several recent Irano-Afghan agreements have been under attack by the free press and many anti-Iranian Afghans. On 13 March 1973 Prime Ministers Shafiq and Abbas Hoveida signed an agreement that should have ended the long-standing problems concerning the distribution of the waters of the lower Hilmand River between Afghanistan and Iran. Both houses of Parliament approved the treaty: *Wolesi Jirgah*, 22 May; *Meshrano Jirgah*, 30 May. Critics claimed the Iranian outsnookered the Shafiq government. In early July, Afghan and Iranian negotiators agreed to expand links and air facilities for Iranair and Ariana Afghan Airlines. The export (and smuggling) of sheep to Iran just after drought depleted Afghanistan's herds has also come under fire. Finally, the presumed close friendship between the Shah of Iran and the King of Afghanistan caused concern.

None of the nations bordering Afghanistan, however, wants to see "Pushtunistan" or the Baluchistan Province of Pakistan become tribal, ethno-linguistic battlegrounds, for all (the USSR, Iran, and the People's Republic of China, as well as Pakistan) have similar regional problems. So does India, which neither wants to embarrass Pakistan nor see it disintegrate at this delicate point in both their histories.

A perceptive Afghan recently pointed out an almost macabre (but far from impossible) chain of events should Mr. Bhutto permit unrest in the North-West Frontier Province, Baluchistan, and Sind to develop into full-scale rebellion: "The Iranians would occupy Baluchistan, the Afghans the North-West Frontier Province, India could move into Sind, and the Punjab would become the Lichtenstein of Asia." Probably (and one hopes) an overstatement, but some sort of major realignments may occur in the near future; witness Bangladesh farther east.

Many authorities believe that the Cold War (which falsely assumed a monolithic communist bloc against an equally monolithic capitalist bloc) has diminished, if not disappeared. But confrontations between the great powers (USA, USSR, China) continue, with the Indian Ocean shaping up as the next arena. For several years, the Soviet Union has maintained a naval squadron of ten to twelve ships in the Indian Ocean. In December 1971, during the Bangladesh War, the United States attempted to pressure the Indians by dispatching Task Force 74 to the Bay of Bengal from "Yankee Station" off Vietnam. The competition for refueling, supply, and rest and rehabilitation centers will probably intensify in the late 1970s.

The problem, then, is not whether Afghanistan will remain non-aligned under the new regime but whether all the Indian Ocean nations can remain relatively non-aligned as the Warm Water War heats up.

None of the great powers, however, stands to benefit politically in Afghanistan at the expense of the other two. All three may increase economic assistance to help ensure that Afghanistan remains *bi-tarafi*. All post-1964

Constitution prime ministers have practiced *bi-tarafi*, but some have been more non-aligned than others. Daoud Khan was largely responsible for bringing in massive Soviet assistance, in particular military aid, and the Western press cited this fact after the July coup as evidence of his being pro-Russian. I feel this is both an oversimplification and an overstatement: Daoud Khan is neither pro-Russian, pro-Chinese, or pro-American: he is vigorously pro-Afghan.

Among the reasons for his seizure of power in 1953 was the fear that the Afghan government, to its detriment, had become too pro-American. This may also be ultimately listed as a reason for the July coup.

What can be expected of the new Daoud regime—if it survives? The patterns of the old 1953-63 Daoud Khan give us a number of hints. His considerable achievements are discussed in Chapter 23 (see especially pp. 554-558).

When the 1961 border closure with Pakistan occurred, Daoud Khan was already considering a new constitution, chiefly advised by Mohammad Moosa Shafiq, the man who ultimately played a key role in writing the king's 1964 Constitution, and whom Daoud Khan replaced as prime minister in July 1973. The 1964 Constitution incorporated many features envisioned by Daoud Khan.

One article, however, surprised and shocked Daoud Khan. Article 24 precluded him (and other members of a tightly defined royal family, p. 576), from participating in political activities and denied them certain government positions. Probably Daoud Khan stepped down voluntarily in 1963 because he believed the new constitution would enable him to return to power through legitimate means. For ten years after, he waited patiently, and obviously at some point decided that the democratic experiment, as constituted, was doomed.

On 25 June 1973 King Mohammad Zahir left for England and Italy for eye treatment. Major-General Abdul Wali preceded the king to England, but returned to Kabul on 5 July. With the king, an important symbolic rallying point, safely out of the country, Sardar Daoud and his army supporters struck at 0230, 17 July, declared Afghanistan a republic, pronounced Daoud Khan president and prime minister, and proclaimed martial law in an almost bloodless coup. Sardar Abdul Wali, after initial resistance in his home, was taken prisoner.

President Daoud Khan appointed a Central Committee, mainly army officers, to assist him temporarily in governing the country. Probably in the near future, the army will step down and leave the day-to-day decision-making and implementing to President Daoud and a civilian cabinet. The loyalty of the army, however, remains essential, to assist, if necessary, in the implementation of reform schemes and to prevent coup succeeding coup.

King Mohammad Zahir, for the good of his people and to prevent unnecessary bloodshed, decided not to precipitate violence and accepted exile with those of his family who, for one reason or another, preferred him to Daoud. The monarch with the longest tenure in modern times (1933-1973) joined the list of kings deposed since World War II.

Some months will pass before the policies of the second Daoud regime become clear, but if the new president follows his initial statements with acts Afghanistan should soon have a new constitution, followed by elections with some sort .of political party system. President Daoud Khan may also establish an extra-ministry organization to remove development processes from the grip of the old bureaucracy.

Daoud Khan always favored order, and if he now couples order with law, Afghanistan will not necessarily lose ground in its own peculiar march toward a democratic government consistent with its past history and its current cultural patterns. Probably no major change in Afghanistan's non-alignment vis-à-vis the great powers will occur, even though the Soviet Union may appear superficially to have gained. This, however, will be only a logical reaction to the apparent pro-Western "tilt" of the past few years, but the new regime will probably continue its *bi-tarafi* policy in regard to great power confrontations.

In addition, meaningful confrontations (hopefully, though not necessarily, peaceful) with Pakistan and Iran, as these two allies attempt to come to an accommodation with a revitalized and less acquiescent Afghanistan, may convince President Bhutto of the value of provincial autonomy and curb the nascent expansionism of Shah Mohammad Reza Pahlavi. Both Pakistan and Iran (prompted by the Americans *and* the Chinese) will be prone to believe that the Russian bear is lumbering toward the Indian Ocean. Peter the Great would be pleased.

Under the leadership of a mature Daoud Khan, Afghanistan may become a catalytic agent to bring about closer regional cooperation between these three nations, which nature and culture—if not politics—have closely aligned. If regional cooperation proves impossible, chaos for all three may not be far behind.

King's College, Cambridge
21 July 1973

EPILOGUE TO THE SECOND PRINTING

WHEN THE FIRST PRINTING was published in 1973, the Afghan monarchy had just been overthrown and a Republic established.[1] Slowly, but continuously, Afghanistan moved toward a system of representative government consistent with its cultural and historical patterns. Whether the successive steps were planned or, like Topsy, "just grew," remains a question. Several patterns will be briefly examined.

The Search for Security

The coup had been textbook perfect—almost too perfect—and encouraged others to plot against the new regime. One group, led by military officers disaffected with the monarchy, had been preparing a coup at the time Daoud successfully struck. The 45 ringleaders, including former Prime Minister Mohammad Hashim Maiwandwal, were arrested, questioned, and received sentences varying from death (5) to acquittal (2).[2]

Before the official sentences were announced in December 1973, a great tragedy occurred. Sometime between midnight and dawn on 20 October, Maiwandwal met his fate. Officially, he committed suicide, but in all probability he was murdered by overenthusiastic police guards. President Daoud, shocked, tightened up his own security, and got rid of unreliable leftists in his entourage. Many believe that Maiwandwal's death was leftist-inspired, because elimination of potential rivals has long been a communist tactic. Maiwandwal, one of the few Afghan politicians with an international reputation, would probably have been a leader in any subsequent democratic processes, and, therefore, a prime target for elimination.

President Daoud dismissed unwanted cabinet members one by one, and the survivors, hoping to hold on to their newly-won positions of power, did not demur. None of the dismissed ministers were executed or imprisoned, and the president appointed several as ambassadors.

At another level, *Parcham* (*The Flag*), a moderate leftist party with a sizeable government civil service following, initially supported the coup and the Republic. Almost immediately after·the coup, Daoud sent about 160 of these enthusiastic, reform-minded young men (including many in the police) to man district and subdistrict administrative positions and spread the message of the Republic. These young men, either Kabul born or ultra-

---

[1] For details see L. Dupree: "A new decade of Daoud?", *American Universities Field Staff Reports, South Asia Series*, Vol. 17, No. 4, 1973; "A note on Afghanistan 1974," *ibid.*, Vol. 18, No. 8, 1974; *The New Republic of Afghanistan: The First Twenty-One Months*, Special Paper, Afghanistan Council of the Asia Society (N.Y.), 1976.

[2] A list of conspirators and their sentences can be found in *Anis, Heywad, Jamhouriat, The Kabul Times* (English), and the quarterly *Aryana* (English).

urban oriented, ran headlong into the rural power elites, who, although they outwardly accepted rapid change, effectively isolated the administrators from the people. Frustrated, the new cadre took one of two opposing paths: accepted the fact that change would be slow, and decided to work within the existing patterns; or, cynically turned as corrupt (or more so) than their predecessors. Still others, totally disillusioned, returned to Kabul and resigned, or were dismissed for leaving their posts without permission.

By March 1975, some *Parchamis* sat quietly at home, while others cooperated with the Republic. But in July 1977, a new development occurred. The leadership of *Parcham* and a more revolutionary offshoot, *Shu'la-yi-Jawed* (*The Eternal Flame*), agreed to reunite (they had split in 1968), and once again present a common front.

To forestall possible countercoups from the royalist right, the government, on the day of the coup (17 July 1973), arrested Major-General Abdul Wali, commander of the Central Forces, which includes all units from Kabul to the Pakistani frontier. Abdul Wali, first cousin to both ex-king Mohammad Zahir and President Daoud, and married to a daughter of Zahir (Bilqis), had great influence in the conservative ranks of the royal family. His ambitions might ultimately have led him to the throne. In September 1975, after more than two years under arrest, Abdul Wali was tried by a military tribunal for alleged crimes against the state (never tightly defined), unanimously acquitted, restored to full rank and privileges—but requested to leave the country. He now lives in Rome with most of the exiled royal family.[3] Always a good soldier, Abdul Wali now exercises to stay in shape, and keeps a close political eye on Kabul.

During the 1975 *jeshn* (national independence holidays), an event occurred which shook the complacency of many in the power elite. The Panjsher Insurgency erupted.[4] Led by religious leaders, right wing elements (mainly students, some possibly trained in Pakistan, a charge denied by the Pakistani government) struck at several points during the night and early morning of 21–22 July. In addition to Panjsher, the insurgents hit Paktya, Laghman, Jalalabad, and Badakhshan, among other places. A general uprising did not take place, for the people refused to believe the announcement by the insurgents that a "godless, communist dominated regime" ruled in Kabul. The local populations also resented the intrusions into their areas by outsiders, and, as usual, preferred to remain aloof from national political problems. Government forces, aided by helicopters, quickly killed or captured the hapless insurgents. Of the 93 brought to trial, 3 were executed and 16 acquitted. The rest received sentences ranging from life imprisonment to one year in jail.[5]

Two other plots (September 1975, December 1976) by dissident military officers resulted in arrests.

[3] Abdul Wali's father, Marshal Shah Wali Khan, the famous "Conqueror of Kabul" during the 1929 civil war, died in Rome in March 1977, still bitter against the current regime.

[4] The Panjsher Valley is a Tajik area north of Kabul (see Panjsher in index).

[5] Complete list in *The Kabul Times*, 5 July 1977.

Elections by Selections and the New Constitution[6]

In January 1977, the Republic of Afghanistan held elections "in the traditional manner," and the partly-elected, partly-appointed *Loya Jirgah* (Great National Assembly) passed a constitution in sessions which lasted from 31 January to 13 February. The government capitalized on the *jirgah* (village council) system to elect the majority of the *wakil* (delegates). The *jirgah* functions as a conflict-solving, decision-making body, with decisions reached through popular acclamation, not the secret ballot. Most Afghan villagers are non-literate and believe the secret ballot to be rather sneaky. A man can talk one way in public and vote another in private.

A total 219 *wakil* (including four women) were elected from the rural administrative districts and urban wards. To give the *Loya Jirgah* more balance, President Daoud (on the advice of his cabinet) appointed an additional 130 *wakil*, including military officers, factory workers, tribal and religious leaders, small farmers, urban intellectuals, professionals, university students, and women. Naturally, the government investigated and approved all the delegates. Few leftists participated, although encouraged to do so by the president. However, several well-known opponents of the regime were elected to the *Loya Jirgah*.

The lively debates in the *Loya Jirgah* indicated that the *wakil* did not simply rubber stamp the constitution. They amended 34 of the original 131 articles and wrote six new articles, mainly defining and enhancing the role of the judiciary, and transferring the investigative powers of the police to the Attorney General's Office.

Chapter 6 of the constitution perpetuates the *Loya Jirgah* as the "paramount power of the will of the people." The *Loya Jirgah* will be convened only to perform specific functions, and the *Meli Jirgah* (a unicameral National Assembly), elected every four years in universal, secret balloting, will be responsible for ordinary legislation.

The *Loya Jirgah*, when called to session, will consist of the elected *Meli Jirgah*, the president, his cabinet, the Central Council (*shura markazi*) of the *Hezbeh Enqelab-i-Meli* (National Revolutionary Party[7]), the High Military Council,[8] the Supreme Court, and an additional five to eight representatives from each province, depending on relative populations. Also, the president will appoint 30 members-at-large to insure that all shades of opinion will be heard—as well as to reward people for services rendered.

A few other features of the constitution include the following: a mixed, guided (regulated, not controlled) economy is envisioned (Articles 17, 18), but most natural resources and basic industries are nationalized (Article 13).

[6] The complete constitution was published in *The Middle East Journal*, with comments by L. Dupree, in 1978.

[7] The constitution permits only one party initially, but allows for others when political "maturity" (undefined) is reached. The appointment of a four-man Central Council on 7 November 1977 brought on a cabinet crisis, when six cabinet ministers resigned in protest but withdrew their resignations at the request of the president. The internal struggle for post-Daoud power may have begun.

[8] Appointed in September 1977. The military is still the ultimate base of power.

Although Islam is referred to as "the religion of Afghanistan," no mention was made of state ritual being Hanafi, as prescribed in the 1964 constitution (Article 22, which further guarantees freedom of worship to non-Muslims). Article 26 called for a strong central government, but hints at possible administrative reforms, which may revolutionize the current provincial system.[9] Men and women have equal rights (Article 27). The constitution provides for an Interim Period until 22 November 1979, when the first elected *Meli Jirgah* must meet.

At the end of the Constitutional *Loya Jirgah*, Mohammad Daoud, to the surprise of no one, was elected first president of the Republic of Afghanistan for six years.

A meaningful constitution had been written, but implementation will be more difficult than the writing.

New Laws and Old Problems

Continuously and contrapuntally, the Republican regime promulgated laws designed to implement its ideals. The publication of each new law caused the literati to pause and mull over its contents and discuss its implications.[10]

Among the more important recent laws are the Land Reform Law and the Graduated Land Tax Law.[11] The Civil Service Law of June 1977 nobly attempted to cope with the perpetuative government bureaucracy. An adequate pay scale might also help motivate civil servants to do their jobs without the *bakhsheesh* complex. Not that all civil servants are corrupt, but traditionally the *bakhsheesh* paid to lower and middle range civil servants simply supplements their meager salaries.

The new Civil Service Law attempted to raise the level of excellence in the bureaucracy by requiring high school educations for new appointees. Promotions based on superior work can occur every three years instead of the current four. If implemented fairly and without the usual nepotism, the Civil Service Law will represent a giant step forward toward administrative reform.

The Penal Code (*Qanun-i-Jaza*, September 1976) represents the first major attempt since the time of King Amanullah (1919–1929) to cope with the elements of secular law. The Code defines crimes, criminality, and punishments in such a way that the *qazi* (judge) can no longer (in theory, at least) impose arbitrary punishments on individuals accused of crimes.

Another important move was the promulgation of the four-volume Civil Law (*Qanun-i-Madani*, December 1976), based on (but superseding) the Islamic *Shari'a* (code of law) and certain customary laws. The Civil Law

[9] For one such scheme, see L. Dupree, "Imperialism in South Asia," *AUFS Reports, South Asia Series*, Vol. 20, No. 3, 1976.

[10] About 20 new laws have been promulgated since the publication of L. Dupree, "A note on Afghanistan 1974," *ibid.*, Vol. 18, No. 8, 1974. For English translations of many of the new laws, see the *Afghanistan Council Newsletter*, published periodically by the Asia Society, N.Y.

[11] For a discussion of these laws by Christopher Brunner, see L. Dupree, "USAID and social scientists discuss Afghanistan's development prospects," *AUFS Reports, South Asia Series*, Vol. 21, No. 2, 1977.

covers the entire field of social justice, including marriage, divorce, inheritance, contracts, real estate transactions, mortgages, movable and non-mov-
able property, etc. Afghan interpretations of the Hanafi *Shari'a* tend to be
quite liberal. For example, under the Civil Law, women have equal rights
with men in instituting divorce cases. Naturally, the more conservative religious leaders still resist these interpretations.

But the four and one-half year old Republic was not without problems
or critics, and, although no freedom of the press existed, freedom of the
mouth did. In addition, *Shab Nameh* (Evening History[12]) appeared periodically. These clandestine broadsides usually represented the views of the
extreme right and left.

The lack of a free press, however, did hamper effective two-way communications between the concerned literati and the government. Rumors
dominated the scene, and a free press could have helped counter the rumors
and given the intelligentsia platforms from which it could have argued for
or against various programs and means of implementation. The government
controlled media (newspapers, journals, radio, and TV as of the early
1970s) inspired no one.

Increased urbanization brought on increased crime, which, to the surprise
of many, the media reported, at least partly. Two significant murders occurred. The chief pilot of Ariana Afghan Airlines, Capt. I. Gran, who led
a successful strike in August 1977 of the cockpit and cabin crews for better
working conditions, was gunned down by unknown assailants. On 16 November 1977, a man armed with a pistol forced the Minister of Planning, Ali
Ahmad Khuram, to march from his office to "Pushtunistan" Square in the
center of Kabul city. Shot in the head, Khuram died on the spot. Whether
or not these killings were politically motivated remains undetermined as of
this writing.

The campaign to play down the existence of the several ethnolinguistic
groups continued (though not with official sanction),[13] although these non-
Pushtun groups constituted about one-half of the population.

Trade, Aid and the Seven Year Plan[14]

Afghanistan's favorable balance of payments and amount of foreign reserves grew phenomenally after 1973. Its $2.2 million surplus balance of
payments in 1972–73 jumped to about $65 million in 1976–77; convertible
foreign exchange (hard currency) increased from $18.09 million to $128.47
in the same four year period. The balance in its barter trade (nonconvertible
currencies), mainly with the USSR and the Eastern Bloc, improved from a
deficit of $3.52 million in 1972–73 to a surplus of $17.22 in 1976–77.

This remarkable improvement in Afghanistan's economic situation was

[12] A play on the 11th century A.D. *Shah Nameh* (History of the Kings), by
Firdausi.

[13] L. Dupree, "A note on Afghanistan 1974," *AUFS Reports, South Asia Series*,
Vol. 18, No. 8, 1974.

[14] For more details, see L. Dupree, "Afghanistan 1977: Does trade plus aid
guarantee development?", *ibid.*, Vol. 21, No. 3, 1977.

due to a number of factors. Among the more important were a rise in the quantity and quality of exportable items, less demand for expensive imports (partly because of the insecurity of the commercial sector in its relations with the present regime), debt-servicing relief from the USSR until 1980, the financing of the bulk of Afghanistan's external development costs through foreign assistance programs, and increased hard currency earnings by Afghan migrant labor in Iran and the Persian Gulf States.

The Soviet Union remained Afghanistan's most important trading and aiding partner, and, along with the Eastern Bloc countries, accounted for 40% of Afghanistan's import-export transactions. But Afghanistan remained eminently flexible, especially because of increased economic interactions with India, Iran, Saudi Arabia, and the Persian Gulf States. For example, Iranian aid commitments to Afghanistan during the 10 years from 1974 to 1984 could conceivably reach $2 billion, more than the *total* foreign assistance to Afghanistan from *all* donors for the past 30 years. About $1.7 billion was earmarked for a rail line to extend from the Iranian border opposite Herat to Kabul through Kandahar. Recent drops in oil income, combined with worldwide inflation (among other factors) forced the Iranians to take a second look at its grandiose commitments to Afghanistan and other developing countries.

The continued reliance of Afghanistan on foreign assistance for development is less than healthy for the economy, and debt-servicing repayments increase annually. The new Seven Year Plan[15] projected a continued high level of foreign involvement. At the same time, the government had a larger surplus of afghanis in its coffers than ever before in history. Back taxes were energetically collected and new taxes imposed. One suspects that the peasant mentality of hoarding currency (and other valuables) extends to the highest planning circles. The idea of spending money to make money does not appear to have fully penetrated the thinking of some Afghan economic planners.

The Seven Year Plan as a whole is a relatively feasible, reasonably realistic document, particularly when compared to the results of the previous four Five Year Plans. The new plan envisions an annual GNP growth of 6.3% and projects an annual increase of 3.75% in per capita income.

The Plan probably errs in its reluctance to allow a larger role for the private sector, limited to small- and medium-sized industries that are import-saving (plastics, textiles) and export-promoting (food processing, drugs, qarakul, rugs and carpets). Total private investment estimates do not exceed $188 million for the entire seven years, an annual increase of no more than 10%, modest by any yardstick.

The absence of any mention of agribusiness in the Seven Year Plan was an especially significant oversight, for encouraging this segment of the private sector could help Afghanistan not only gain self-sufficiency in foodstuffs but expand its export potential. Independent, mid-range farmers have purchased

[15] *First Seven Year Economic and Social Development Plan* (1355–1361) (March 1976–March 1983), 2 vols., Ministry of Planning, Kabul, 1355 (1976). Available in Pashto, Dari (Afghan Persian), and English.

over 2,000 tractors over the past 12 years, and with a little government encouragement a takeoff in agriculture could occur.

Probably the main constraints to the success of the Plan are a lack of qualified administrators, technicians, and skilled manpower, and the improper utilization of available Afghan technocrats, who are often bogged down in mountains of paperwork. The export of labor to Iran and the Persian Gulf may also complicate the task of finding adequate manpower. In addition, the Central Statistical Office announced in May 1977 that of the 3,890,000 people in the Afghan labor force, 343,000 were unemployed. The Seven Year Plan predicts the creation of an additional 830,000 jobs, but the labor force may increase by 1.5 million during the same period.

Defusing the "Pushtunistan" Problem

As predicted in the Epilogue to the first printing, President Daoud took a major role in bringing about a rapprochement with Pakistan over the "Pushtunistan" issue. On their part, the Pakistanis came to realize that the British did not consider the Durand Line to be an international boundary until just before Partition in 1947. Many official British sources attest to this fact. The following quote is typical (italics mine): "The Line was not described [in the 1893 Treaty] as the boundary of India, but as the eastern and southern frontiers of the Amir's [Abdur Rahman] dominions, and the limits of the respective spheres of influence of the two governments, *the object being the extension of British authority, and not that of the Indian frontier*."[16]

Prime Minister Zulfikar Ali Bhutto of Pakistan and President Mohammad Daoud of Afghanistan exchanged visits in 1976. From 7 to 11 June, Bhutto visited Afghanistan; Daoud visited Pakistan from 21 to 24 August, on his way home from the Fifth Summit Conference of the Heads of States and Governments of Non-aligned Countries, held in Colombo, Sri Lanka.

A relatively harmless sounding communiqué resulted from the first meetings,[17] but, for the first time, Pakistan admitted that "a political difference" existed between the two nations. Because of this, the Afghans agreed to solve the "political difference" within the spirit of the *Panch Sheela* (Five Principles) of the 1955 Bandung Conference. The two most important principles are respect for the boundaries of neighbors and non-interference in the internal affairs of others.

Therefore, Afghanistan will probably accept the Durand Line (with minor adjustments) as an international boundary, *if* Pakistan effectively implements the regional autonomy guarantees in its 1973 Constitution (Part IV). In theory, all that remained after the first Daoud-Bhutto moot was to complete the drawn-out choreography required by diplomacy, those time-consuming steps which international law (if not reason and justice) demand.

The August meeting in Pakistan added little substance to the beginning rapprochement, although Prime Minister Bhutto wanted an agreement signed as soon as possible. If, however, the Afghans had signed such an agreement,

---

[16] *Military Report on Afghanistan* (Classified), General Staff, India, Government of India Press, 1925, p. 69.

[17] *The Kabul Times*, 12 June 1976.

they would have indicated their support of Bhutto's anti-autonomy policies. Therefore, President Daoud wisely (which future events justified) decided to wait until after the Pakistani elections in March 1977 before signing a final agreement. He still waits, for the March elections in Pakistan proved to be a massively-rigged disaster, resulting in bloody demonstrations, the promulgation of Martial Law (for the fourth time in Pakistan's short history), and the arrest and trial of Mr. Bhutto for alleged complicity in political murders.

The Pakistani Chief Martial Law Administrator, General Zia ul-Haq, continued the dialogue when he visited Kabul in October 1977, but the Afghans want to conclude negotiations after a stable Pakistani government comes into being.

Paucis Verbis[18]

Just as the success or failure of the 1963-73 attempt to create a constitutional monarchy depended largely on what the former king did or did not do, so the success (or failure) and survival of the new Republic depends largely on what President Mohammad Daoud (and his closest advisers) does or does not do. The future is still far from clear, but the directions have been charted with reasonable assurance. Given time, non-interference by its neighbors, and sympathetic understanding from aid donors and loaners, Afghanistan can move toward the achievement of its modest Seven Year Plan. The major constraint to Afghanistan's development, however, is its current bureaucratic system, but if its leadership can intensify the involvement of the competent (and partly idle) Afghan technocratic class, Afghanistan just might pull off its gamble to develop through evolutionary processes.

If not, comes the revolution.

Hanover, New Hampshire
December 1977

[18] Much important research has been undertaken and published since the first printing in 1973. Most of it is discussed in *American Universities Field Staff Reports, South Asia Series*, Vol. 20, Nos. 4 and 5, 1976: "Afghan Studies" and "Anthropology in Afghanistan."

EPILOGUE 1980

WHY DID THE RUSSIANS choose to invade Afghanistan and establish a puppet regime? We are still too close to the question to have an answer, but it is interesting to consider what Russia stands to lose or gain by its naked act of aggression. One fact is clear: the Russians have established an important and potentially dangerous precedent. In addition, the growing rapprochement with the Third World (particularly Muslim countries) has been damaged, possibly irreparably. Also, the Central Asian Muslim Soviet Socialist Republics do not appreciate being the springboard for the invasion and occupation of a brother Muslim state. The Russians will have to face a growing Islamic cultural revival in Central Asia in the next few years, as well as problems of a rapidly increasing non-Russian population in all minority republics. By the year 2000 fifty-three percent of the population in the USSR will be non-Russians and one-third will be Muslims.[1]

The fate of Afghanistan is not pleasant to contemplate, unless, to the surprise of all, the Russians withdraw and leave their puppet, Babrak Karmal, to his fate. First, the Russians will probably seal off the country and attempt to pacify the countryside. This will lead to a bloodbath, amounting to genocide. The peoples of northern Afghanistan (Uzbak, Turkoman, Tajik), traditionally anti-Russian, are either *basmachi* or sons and grandsons of *basmachi*, who fled to Afghanistan in the 1920s and 1930s to escape Soviet tyranny.[2] They will revolt. In fact, the entire country will revolt. Up to December 1979 only a relatively small number of freedom-fighters fought against the Afghan army and their Russian advisers. Now, what is left of the army will join the freedom-fighters.

I am among those who thought the Russians would not invade Afghanistan. As predicted, however, they did not support Hafizullah Amin, but, instead, established Amin's arch rival, Babrak Karmal as Prime Minister, President of the Revolutionary Council, Secretary-General of the leftist party, *Jamiyat-i-Demokratiki-yi, Khalq-i-Afghanistan* (People's Democratic Party of Afghanistan, PDPA, or *Khalq*), and Supreme Commander of the Armed Forces. Most of the missing (and surviving) leadership of *Parcham* (The Flag) have returned to serve in the new Central Committee, Politbureau, or Cabinet, including General Qader, Dr. Anahita, Nur Ahmad Nur, Lt.-Colonel Mohammed Rafi, and Sultan Ali Keshtmand.

[1] C. d'Encausse, *L'Empire Éclaté*, Paris, 1978.
[2] About 1,300 of the Kirghiz remaining in the Pamir fled to Gilgit in Pakistan in the fall of 1978.

THE DEMOCRATIC REPUBLIC OF AFGHANISTAN
(APRIL 1978—DECEMBER 1979)[3]

Opposition to Daoud and the Accidental Coup

The turnaround began in March 1977. The Republic of Afghanistan, after four and a half years of on-again, off-again, mostly ineffectual reforms, waited for President Mohammad Daoud to appoint a new Cabinet.[4] Most observers hoped the Cabinet would include moderate leftists. Instead, at this crucial point, Daoud reverted to the behavior of an old-style tribal khan and appointed friends, sons of friends, sycophants, and even collateral members of the deposed royal family.

More ominously, President Daoud began to depend increasingly on an "inner Cabinet," consisting of Sayyid Abdulillah (Vice-President and Minister of Finance), General Ghulam Haider Rasuli (Minister of National Defense), Abdul Qadir Nuristani (Minister of Interior) and Mohammad Naim (Daoud's brother and close adviser, although not formally a Cabinet member). By November 1977, this drift to the right precipitated a Cabinet crisis. Reinforcing the conservatives in the Cabinet, Daoud appointed a Central Committee (*Shura Markazi*) for the *Hezb-i-Inqelab-i-Meli* (National Revolutionary Party), the one party initially permitted under the new Constitution to supervise preparations for the proposed elections. The Central Committee consisted of Dr. Abdul Majid (Minister of State), Sayyid Abdulillah, General Rasuli, and Professor Dr. Abdul Kayoum (Minister of Frontier Affairs). Six Cabinet members sent in letters of resignation but withdrew them at the personal request of the President.[5] Even Mohammad Naim broke with Daoud over the continued favoritism to rightists in the Cabinet.

President Daoud finally seemed to recognize the seriousness of the opposition by early April 1978, and family members were able to effect a reconciliation between Daoud and Naim. On 17 April the President told his family that he planned to announce new administrative reforms, broaden the base of power in the Central Committee, and establish a new Cabinet of technocrats that would include leftists. Ten days later the concept of reforms became academic, and 150 years of Mohammadzai domination (with few exceptions) of Afghan politics met a bloody end in a military coup d'état.

Initial Western press reports erroneously portrayed the leaders of the coup as members of an illegal, underground Communist Party. This was not so,

---

[3] For more details, see L. Dupree, "The Democratic Republic of Afghanistan, 1979," *AUFS Reports, Asia*, No. 32, 1979; and L. Dupree, "Afghanistan under the *Khalq*," *Problems of Communism* 28:34-50, Washington, 1979.

[4] L. Dupree, "Toward representative government in Afghanistan," Parts I and II, *AUFS Reports, Asia*, Nos. 1 + 14, 1978.

[5] The six: Waheed Abdullah (Minister of State for Foreign Affairs); Prof. Wafiullah Samayee (Justice); Ghausuddin Faeq (Public Works); Azizullah Wasifi (Agriculture and Irrigation); Eng. Abdul Karim Attayee (Communications); Prof. Dr. Abdullah Omar (Public Health).

as a brief summary of leftist history and review of the events leading to the coup reveal.[6] In 1967, a split had occurred in Taraki's PDPA, the major post-World War II leftist party, and consequently Babrak Karmal formed the PDPA-*Parcham* Group. Three reasons precipitated the original split: personality conflicts between Babrak and the *Khalq* leadership; Babrak's desire to form a united front of all anti-government elements, in opposition to the *Khalq* rejection of all coalitions; and Babrak's soft stand on the "Pushtunistan" issue (see p. 767).

Babrak and *Parcham* chose to support Daoud in the 1973 coup, a move which gave Daoud the opportunity to downgrade *Parcham* politically (see pp. 761-762). *Khalq*, meanwhile, had not been idle. The official *Khalq* history[7] claims the party began to recruit among the military after the 1973 Daoud coup, but I believe that both *Khalq* and *Parcham* initiated recruitment as early as the late 1960s.

Continually frustrated in their attempts to participate legally in the political mainstream, *Khalq* and *Parcham* joined forces in July 1977 after a ten-year separation.[8] Their objective was obviously to oppose the Daoud

A series of accidents led to the 27 April 1978 coup, and additional accidents determined the outcome. On 17 April Mir Akbar Khyber, well-known *Parcham* ideologue, was murdered.[9] Alarmed by massive anti-government demonstrations at graveside, and anti-American later when marching past the U.S. Embassy, the government began arresting the leftist leadership. Hafizullah Amin, however, was able to contact party members within the armed forces and devised a makeshift plan. The twenty-four hour coup was launched as the Daoud Cabinet met on the morning of 27 April to consider the fate of jailed *Khalq* and *Parcham* leaders.

President Daoud and about thirty men, women, and children of his family (including Mohammad Naim) were killed. Less than 1,000, it seems, died in the fighting.

The DRA Leadership

In their first public statements, the leaders of the newly proclaimed Democratic Republic of Afghanistan (DRA) insisted they were not Communists.[10] Their policies, they announced, would be based on Afghan nationalism,

[6] For example, see pp. 494-497; 600-623. For an excellent, measured, leftist interpretation of modern historical processes, see Fred Halliday, "Revolution in Afghanistan," *New Left Review* 112:3-44, 1978.

[7] *A Short Biography of Noor Mohammad Taraki*, published by the Political Department of the People's Democratic Party of Afghanistan in the Armed Forces of Afghanistan, Kabul, 1979.

[8] I was wrong in stating that *Parcham* united with *Shu'la-yi-Jawed*, see p. 762. regime.

[9] L. Dupree, "Inside Afghanistan yesterday and today: A Strategic Appraisal," *Strategic Studies* 2(3):64-83, 1979, Islamabad.

[10] I define Communists as those who come directly under Moscow's control. The term communist (lower case) refers to nonaligned Marxists.

respect for Islam, social and economic justice, nonalignment in foreign affairs, and respect for all foreign agreements signed by previous Afghan governments. Few could object to these noble goals, but, as often happens after a bloody coup, the regime's primary interests became *legitimacy* and *security*, at the expense of human rights and a disrupted economy.

Once in power the *Khalq-Parcham* regime issued a number of decrees to establish its legitimacy. *Decree Number 1* (30 April 1978), issued by the thirty-five person Revolutionary Council (RC), announced the "election" of Nur Mohammad Taraki ("the great national and revolutionary figure of Afghanistan") as its Chairman and as Prime Minister of the Democratic Republic of Afghanistan. Taraki continued to hold the post of Secretary-General of the PDPA, a position he had held since the foundation of the party on 1 January 1965.

Decree Number 2 (1 May 1978) announced the names of the twenty-one Cabinet members elected by the Revolutionary Council. Thirteen had been regular or alternate members of the original 1965 Central Committee of the PDPA. At least ten of the civilians participated in the 1965 and 1969 elections, and none ever denied leftist political leanings. None ever expressed loyalty to any country other than Afghanistan. None, to the best of my knowledge, attended, or was invited to attend, international Communist meetings.

Only Taraki and Babrak were even remotely connected with the liberal movements of the late 1940s and early 1950s. Most of the others cut their political teeth during the 1963-1973 decade of the constitutional "new democracy." Six had spent time in jail for political activities: Babrak Karmal (Deputy Prime Minister); Hafizullah Amin (Deputy Prime Minister and Minister of Foreign Affairs); Abdul Hakim Sharayi Jozjani (Minister of Justice and Attorney General); Dastigir Panjsheri (Minister of Education); Sulaiman Layek (Minister of Radio and TV); Dr. Saleh Mohammad Zeri (Minister of Agriculture and Land Reform).[11]

Eleven of those named to Cabinet posts had held government jobs at the

[11] In terms of party affiliations, eleven of the twenty-one Cabinet members were *Khalqi*, of which two had previously considered themselves independents. Ten were *Parcham*. Only one civilian, Engineer Mohammad Ismail Danesh (Minister, Mines and Industries), and the three military men received training in the USSR, and they considered themselves nationalists, not pro-Russian. (Apparently, as a Kabul wit remarked, the U.S.A. trains Communists, the Soviets produce anti-Communists.)

Almost all spoke English. Only four (including the three military men) spoke Russian. Nine Cabinet members were Pushtun, the dominant (about 50 percent) ethnolinguistic group in Afghanistan. Eight were Persian-speaking Tajik, two were Persian-speaking Hazara, and two were Turkic-speaking Uzbak. All spoke Pashto and Persian, the two major languages in Afghanistan. For biographical sketches, see: *Democratic Republic of Afghanistan Annual*, Saur 7, 1358 (April 1979), published by *Kabul Times* Publishing Agency in English, Kabul. For a discussion of linguistic groups, see L. Dupree, "Language and Politics in Afghanistan," in *Contributions to Asian Studies*, XI:131-141, Leiden, 1978. Edited by C. Maloney.

time of the coup: three were in the military; two were on the faculty of Kabul University; one was a staff member of Radio Afghanistan; and five were civil servants in various ministries (two as physicians). There were three unemployed poets and journalists, two unemployed physicians, two lawyers, two educators, and one person described as a landlord.

As I wrote earlier, "All should examine the words of the new leaders carefully, for governments, like persons, should be considered innocent until proven guilty."[12] Not published, but submitted, was this final observation: "Their (the leadership's) actions will speak louder than their innuendos." They have.

The Coalition Splits

The coup successful, the regime picked up some pieces—and smashed others. The jails quickly filled with important surviving members of the royal family and collateral relatives[13] and with large numbers of able administrators whose only crimes had been to hold responsible positions in previous regimes. The DRA replaced these invaluable officials with often unqualified *Khalq* party members.

Another pattern emerged. When coalitions of the left or right topple a regime, fission occurs almost immediately. The *Khalq-Parcham* graft proved no exception. The Mohammadzai eliminated, the dominant *Khalq* leadership decided to remove *Parcham*'s ambitious leader, Deputy Prime Minister Babrak Karmal, and his followers.

Babrak anticipated this behind-the-scenes power struggle and, during the first hectic months of consolidation after the coup, tried unsuccessfully to elicit support from prominent nationalist leaders such as Major-General Abdul Qader. Also, the *Parcham* leaders found their Soviet friends pragmatic and unhelpful. The important military units in Kabul favored Nur Mohammad Taraki and Hafizullah Amin.

The Revolutionary Council was therefore able to exile the *Parcham* leadership, including Babrak, to ambassadorships,[14] a pattern earlier established by Daoud to immobilize the opposition, freeing itself to move against a more formidable group, the nationalist-Muslim factions in and out of the Cabinet.

In late August, the regime charged and arrested Major-General Qader, Lt.-General Shapur Ahmadzai (Army Chief-of-Staff), and Dr. Mir Ali Akbar, President of Jamhuriat Hospital, for plotting to overthrow the

---

[12] *New York Times*, May 20, 1978, editorial page.

[13] Seventy-three women and children were eventually released. Most joined relatives outside Afghanistan. For list, see *Kabul Times*, October 26, 1978.

[14] In July 1978, Babrak was posted to Prague; Nur Mohammad Nur to Washington; Abdul Wakil, London; Mahmud Baryalai (Babrak's brother), Islamabad. Dr. Anahita, Minister of Social Affairs and Tourism, went to Belgrade. She was the only woman in Taraki's first Cabinet, but not the first woman to serve in Afghan cabinets. With Dr. Anahita's departure, her important ministry was abolished. Tourism reverted to the Afghan Air Authority.

773

regime. The government also collected evidence which led to the arrest of two other Cabinet members: Lt.-Colonel Mohammad Rafi (Minister of Çommunications, and a key figure in the coup), and Sultan Ali Keshtmand (Minister of Planning). All those arrested had *Parcham* connections.

The confessions—extorted by means usually employed in Afghanistan regardless of the regime in power (physical and mental torture, threats to family members)—were broadcast over Radio Afghanistan. The government-controlled press published facsimiles in the handwriting of the accused persons, a familiar Afghan gimmick to "legitimize" confessions. Although the confessions implicated Babrak as instigator and ringleader, most of those involved appeared to have been more nationalist-Muslim than *Parcham* in orientation and favored a genuinely nonaligned Afghanistan.

The Revolutionary Council expelled Babrak, Qader, Nur Ahmad Nur, Keshtmand, Rafi, and Dr. Anahita from the coalition party and in October ordered all the *Parcham* ambassadors home. Under the circumstances, they refused to comply, reportedly circulated throughout eastern Europe, but ultimately ended up in Moscow.

As the *Khalq* regime pre-empted or eliminated the leftist and nationalist-Muslim opposition, it decreed a number of administrative procedures and far-reaching reforms. The decrees announced a new flag (Decree No. 4), withdrew citizenship from members of the royal family (Decree No. 5), eliminated usury (Decree No. 6), confirmed equal rights for women (Decree No. 7), and introduced land reforms (Decree No. 8).[15] Few would argue with the ideals expressed in the decrees, several of which resembled the reform programs of former President Daoud.

Throughout, the regime denied being Communist, but whereas Daoud used basic Persian and Pashto to announce his reform programs, the rhetoric of the *Khalqis* was pure Marxist-Leninist. The Afghans listened to the government's pronouncements over Radio Afghanistan and drew their own conclusions. They had heard the rhetoric before over Radio Tashkent and other Communist radio stations in Soviet Central Asia. They concluded the *Khalqis* were Communist, dominated by the Russians, and anti-Islamic, although the regime constantly tried to put forward an Islamic image.

As unrest spread throughout the countryside, several changes occurred at the top. On 28 March 1979, Hafizullah Amin was appointed Prime Minister (or First Minister) and retained the foreign affairs portfolio in the "new" eighteen-man Cabinet announced by Nur Mohammad Taraki, who retained his own positions as President of the Revolutionary Council, Secretary-General of the PDPA, and Supreme Commander of the Armed Forces.[16] All cabinet ministers were *Khalq*, or *Parcham* converted to *Khalq*, and only two new faces appeared in the "new" cabinet. The other departed

---

[15] For texts, see reference in fn. 11.

[16] Amin's academic background includes Teachers' College, Columbia University, and the University of Wisconsin. Taraki was Cultural Officer, Embassy of the Royal Government of Afghanistan, Washington, D.C., 1952 to 1953. He worked for USAID in Kabul from 1955 to 1958 and was U.S. Embassy Translator in Kabul from May 1962 to September 1963.

Parcham and nationalist-Muslim members had already been replaced by *Khalq* stalwarts: Abdul Rashid Jalili (Education); Lt.-Colonel Sher Jan Mazdooryar (Interior); Sahib Jan Shahrayee (Frontier Affairs); and Sayyid Mohammad Gulabzoi (Communications). The two new faces were Engineer Mohammad Sadiq Alamyar (Planning) and Khayal Mohammad Katawazi (Information and Culture).

The "new" cabinet merely legitimized Amin as number one in the power elite, with Taraki continuing to play the role of "the Great Leader of the Afghan People." *Khalq* had tightened its control at all levels of government in Kabul.

To implement reforms, however, any regime needs both *expertise* and *stability*—the Afghan expertise existed, trained during thirty-five years of abortive development, but much of it sat at home or lay in prison. Stability eluded the Taraki-Amin government almost from the beginning.

The Opposition Takes the Field

For several reasons, it took some time for the opposition to surface. Initially, most people were stunned by the coup. Afterward, many wanted to give the regime a chance to succeed. Finally, spring and summer are months of major economic activity (farming and herding) in the countryside. Beginning in late summer and fall (the off-agricultural season), however, unrest exploded in the rural areas. Also, periodic explosions rocked Kabul, and opposition groups began to publish a plethora of *Shab Namah* (Evening News), reminding the regime that opposition did exist. To meet the challenge, the government intensified its rhetoric and repression.

When the April 1978 coup occurred, the Americans adopted a sensible policy of wait-and-see. This all changed on 14 February 1979. Four armed terrorists seized the U.S. Ambassador, Adolph (Spike) Dubs, and held him hostage in a room in the Kabul Hotel. The kidnappers, apparently from the ultra-left *Setem-i-Meli*,[17] planned to hold the Ambassador hostage to obtain the release of recently arrested comrades. The Afghan authorities ignored repeated requests from the U.S. Government that no actions be taken which might jeopardize the life of Ambassador Dubs. Afghan police, presumably under the orders of Colonel Daoud Taroon, then Commandant of Afghan Security Forces,[18] assaulted the room where two terrorists held Ambassador Dubs at gunpoint. The ambassador and the terrorists died in the shootout, but the American Embassy in Kabul has not yet been able to learn the identity of the terrorists. Neither have the Americans received a satisfactory answer concerning the role of several Russians consulting with the Afghan police at the Kabul Hotel at the time of the incident.

[17] The *Setem-i-Meli* (Against National Oppression) is a small, far-leftist party advocating revolution. Its ideology is a unique mixture of Maoism and Shia Islam. The group's strength is centered in Badakhshan.

[18] Taroon, an Amin man, was killed in the 14 September shootout. Amin obligingly renamed Jalalabad, Taroon Shahr, in memory of his friend. With Amin's execution, Jalalabad regained its old name.

The first major uprisings occurred in Nuristan, eastern Afghanistan, north of Jalalabad. By March 1979, Nuristani rebels controlled most of the upper Kunar Valley and had actually declared an *Azad* (Free) Nuristan.

Revolts, largely uncoordinated, spread to all Afghanistan's twenty-nine provinces. Major uprisings occurred in Paktya, Paktika, Ningrahar, Kapisa, Uruzgan, Parwan, Badghis, Balkh, Ghazni, Farah (where rebels temporarily controlled a major air base at Shindand), and in Herat rebels killed an undetermined number of Russian technicians, their wives, and children before loyal army units restored order.

About a dozen separate rebel groups came into being, ranging from the secular left (*Parcham* survivors) to the monarchical right, which had a minuscule following. The more important elements were regionally (Nuristani, Hazara, Badakhshi) or religiously-oriented. Three main groups functioned among the Pushtun along the Afghan-Pakistan frontier: *Mahaz-i-Meli-Inqelab-i-Islami Afghanistan* (National Front for the Islamic Revolution of Afghanistan), led by Sayyid Ahmad Gailani Effendi, an Islamic moderate; *Jabhai-yi-Nejat-i-Meli* (National Liberation Front), several loosely organized groups led by Hazrat Sebratullah Mojadidi; and *Hezb-i-Islam* (Islamic Party), a small, well-organized, conservative group functioning in Pakistan since Daoud's 1973 coup and led by Engineer Gulbuddin Hekmatyar. Both the Gailanis and Mojadidis are families of well-known religious leaders.[19]

This guerrilla war has driven over 400,000 refugees into Pakistan and about 60,000 into Iran. (The official figure is obviously lower than the actual number, for many refugees have moved in with kinsmen.) The status and fate of these refugees directly and immediately affects Afghan-Pakistani relations, for both Radio Afghanistan and *Pravda* have accused Pakistan of aiding the Muslim rebels.

The real problem is the Durand Line of 1893, which separates Afghanistan from Pakistan (see p. 169). The border has always been a sieve. During the Baluch Insurrection of 1973-1977, thousands of Baluch fled to Afghanistan, and guerrillas drifted back and forth with impunity. Certainly Afghans can do the same today.

The Military Phases of the Insurrection

Until late December 1979, four separate struggles dominated the Afghan scene: 1) the uncoordinated, generalized guerrilla war against the regime; 2) the competition (mainly in Peshawar) between conservative and moderate religious leaders in the Pushtun area to monopolize funds from

---

[19] Other Pushtun groups included a breakaway group of the *Hezb-i-Islam* led by Maulvi Mohammad Yunus Khalis, *Harakat-i-Inqelab-i-Islami* (Islamic Revolutionary Movement) of Maulvi Mohammad Nabi Mohammadi, *Jama'at Islami Afghanistan* (Islamic Society of Afghanistan) of Professor Burhanuddin Rabani, and *Itehad-i-Inqelab-i-Islam-wa-Meli Afghan* (Afghanistan Islamic and Nationalistic Revolution Council) of Zia Khan Nassry, an Afghan-born American citizen.

friendly Arabs; 3) the attempts by *mujahidin* (freedom-fighters) to establish local bases of power (Nuristan, Hazarajat, Badakhshan) so that any new regime in Kabul would have to grant regional autonomy to the various ethnolinguistic groups; and 4) the internal struggle for power within the *Khalq* leadership.

On 2 September, Nur Mohammad Taraki stopped in Moscow on his way to the Havana conference of non-aligned heads of state and then met with Brezhnev on his way home. No one knows exactly what happened during those September meetings, but immediately after Taraki returned to Kabul, the Amin-Taraki split errupted. Most observers assume that the Russians encouraged Taraki to oust Amin and try to calm down the countryside. Under Amin, a two-phase military operation to contain and control the *mujahidin* had failed miserably.

Phase I involved unsuccessful attempts by the conscript Afghan army to put down the ever-spreading revolts. About one-half of this 92,000-man army had either deserted to the freedom-fighters, crossed into Pakistan or Iran as refugees, or simply gone home. *Phase II* began when the *Khalq* regime requested increased Soviet military aid in the form of advisers and better technological equipment, such as the much vaunted Mi-24 helicopter gunships. This phase was also faltering when Taraki returned from Moscow.

Taraki summoned Amin to his office. There was a shootout, and Taraki was either killed or mortally wounded. (Rumors suggest that the Soviet Ambassador, Aleksander M. Puzanov, was with Taraki when the shooting began.) Taraki's supporters in the Cabinet, primarily the military men, fled, presumably to the Soviet Embassy in Kabul.

From 14 September to 24 December, Amin frantically tried to broaden his base of support. He appointed a constitutional commission, pushed the Islamic side of the *Khalqi* "revolution" (never a revolution, only a coup, however), launched new slogans (Security! Legality! Justice!), ordered tribal leaders to Kabul and begged for their support, unsuccessfully launched two new offenses (Paktya and Badakhshan) against the freedom-fighters, encouraged his tame *ulema* (religious leaders) to declare a holy war against *mujahidin*, and released a number of political prisoners.

All this was to no avail. On 24 December 1979, the Russians invaded Afghanistan.

The Soviet Invasion

Most nations of the world have condemned the Russian intervention. Several reasons for the Soviet action come to mind. The Soviets are obviously disturbed at the instability along their southern rim. The emergence of Islam as a worldwide political factor may have caused the Russians to act strongly in order to forestall any potential Muslim movements in Central Asia. Also, the Soviets now outflank Iran and squat poised over the Arabian Sea. Perhaps the Soviets reason that now is the time to strike, not just for influence, but for domination.

But did the Russians actually *need* the warm water ports to the south? They have access through the Dardanelles into the Mediterranean, and through the Suez Canal to the Arabian Sea and Indian Ocean. A Russian naval squadron of about twenty-five vessels operates constantly in the warm waters, partly in response to the U.S. air and naval facilities at Diego Garcia (or is it vice versa?) and the American flotilla of about ten ships. Each nation has an aircraft carrier on patrol.

Also, the Soviets have naval facilities in East Africa and the southern end of the Arabian Peninsula. Finally, the Russian Asiatic Fleet easily can move additional task forces into the Indian Ocean waters.

Where does all this leave the United States, détente, and SALT-II? Obviously, the Russians must have considered these questions in their calculations. The arguments may have gone something like this: "The Americans are weaker now than ever before, in will more so than military capability. They, and the rest of the world, will do nothing but talk while we consolidate. They may even re-arm Pakistan, but in eighteen-months' time or less the world will have adjusted to us and our actions. The Americans never act; they only react." Is it possible that the younger hawks have won in the Kremlin and that Brezhnev and the older leaders, who appeared to want peace, have been shoved aside? I think so.

The hawks will pick the bones of the Afghan nation until nothing is left, but many Russian soldiers will pay the price. The lessons of Vietnam and the nineteenth-century Anglo-Afghan Wars have been lost.

As I write, the gauntlet has been thrown down, over 50,000 Russian troops fan out over Afghanistan, and the Warm Water War continues to heat up. If Afghanistan is the Rhineland of the early 1980s, will Pakistan and Iran be its Austria and Sudetenland?

Lahore, Pakistan
6 January 1980